A

GENERAL HISTORY

OF THE

BAPTIST DENOMINATION

IN

AMERICA

VOL. I.

A GENERAL HISTORY

OF THE

BAPTIST DENOMINATION

IN

AMERICA,

AND OTHER PARTS OF THE WORLD.

BY DAVID BENEDICT

And he said unto them, Go ye into all the world, and preach the gospel to every creature. HE THAT BELIEVETH AND IS BAPTIZED, shall be saved; but he that believeth not, shall be damned......................Mark xvi. 15, 16.

And the eunuch said, See, here is water, what doth hinder me to be baptized?...... If thou believest with all thine heart, thou mayest..........I believe that Jesus Christ is the Son of God......AND THEY WENT DOWN BOTH INTO THE WATER, both Philip and the eunuch, and he baptized him........AND WHEN THEY WERE COME UP OUT OF THE WATER, &c.................................Acts viii. 36—39.

IN TWO VOLUMES.

VOL. I.

BOOKS FOR LIBRARIES PRESS
FREEPORT, NEW YORK

BX 6231
B4
V. 1

First Published 1813
Reprinted 1971

DISTRICT OF MASSACHUSETTS, to wit :

District Clerk's Office.

BE IT REMEMBERED, that on the twenty second day of April, A. D. 1813, and in the thirty seventh year of the Independence of the United States of America, DAVID BENEDICT, of the said District, has deposited in this Office the title of a Book, the right whereof he claims as Author in the words following, to wit : " A GENERAL HISTORY OF THE BAPTIST DENOMINATION IN AMERICA, AND OTHER PARTS OF THE WORLD. By David Benedict A. M. Pastor of the Baptist Church in Pawtucket, R. I. And he said unto them, go ye into all the world, and preach the gospel to every creature. He that believeth and is baptized, shall be saved ; but he that believeth not, shall be damned............Mark xvi. 15, 16. And the eunuch said, See, here is water, what doth hinder me to be baptized ?.....If thou believest with all thine heart, thou mayest....I believe that Jesus Christ is the Son of God... And they went down both into the water, both Philip and the eunuch, and he baptized him......And when they were come up out of the water, &c......Acts viii. 36—39."
In conformity to the Act of the Congress of the United States, intitled, " An Act for the Encouragement of Learning, by securing the Copies of Maps, Charts and Books, to the Authors and Proprietors of such Copies, during the Times therein mentioned ;" and also to an Act intitled, " An Act supplementary to an Act, intitled, An Act for the Encouragement of Learning, by securing the Copies of Maps, Charts and Books, to the Authors and Proprietors of such Copies during the times therein mentioned ; and extending the Benefits thereof to the Arts of Designing, Engraving and Etching Historical, and other Prints."

WILLIAM S. SHAW, { *Clerk of the District of Massachusetts.*

INTERNATIONAL STANDARD BOOK NUMBER:
0-8369-5726-1

LIBRARY OF CONGRESS CATALOG CARD NUMBER:
73-152974

PRINTED IN THE UNITED STATES OF AMERICA

PREFACE.

I CAN hardly inform the reader how I came to engage in this work. According to the best of my recollection, I first conceived the design of the laborious task I have since pursued, in the summer of 1802, and in a short time I found myself travelling in Kentucky, Georgia, and the other States, asking questions, searching records, and collecting materials. From this time, the history of the Baptists, both at home and abroad, became the subject of my interested attention. For between seven and eight years from this period, I was so much engaged in classical and professional studies, that I did but little more towards perfecting my plan, than read what books I could find, which, in any manner related to it, collect pamphlets, minutes of Associations, &c. and inquire of all, who, I thought, could give me any of the information I wanted. I soon became convinced, that if ever I pursued the undertaking to any considerable extent, I must travel for it; and accordingly in the autumn of 1809, I set out on a journey, in which I was gone almost nine months. I went into Ohio, Kentucky, and Tennessee, and then crossed over into the southern States, and explored the Carolinas and Georgia, first in the back regions, and then along the sea coast, and returned through Virginia, Maryland, and so on. I next went eastward beyond the Penobscot river in the District of Maine. After that I went into the northern parts of the State of New-York, and in the course of about thirteen months, travelled about five thousand miles. Since then I have travelled between one and two thousand miles in different parts of New-England on the business of this history. Most of these journies have been performed on horse back and alone. And I consider it a peculiar favour of Divine Providence, that amidst all my excursions in some of the most rugged and dreary parts of the country, I have been preserved from every kind of accident and harm.

Notwithstanding I was often lodged and refreshed by hospitable brethren and friends, yet my journies were unavoidably attended with expenses, which I was not well able to bear; and, indeed, I know not what I should have done, had it not been, that a number of churches and individuals made me very liberal contributions, for the purpose of aiding my undertaking.

PREFACE.

In these journies, besides collecting many materials, I formed a very extensive acquaintance, and engaged correspondents in every part of the country, many of whom have contributed largely towards the accomplishment of this work. Still there were many parts of this extensive continent, which I had not visited, and many materials yet remained to be collected. In the close of the year 1810, I printed a Circular Address, &c. stating the progress I had made, and the materials I yet wanted, and distributed three hundred of them in places I had not visited. And besides these, I have written between five and six hundred letters to solicit information of various kinds.

In the summer of 1811, I was brought low by debility and disease; for about four months, my studies were almost wholly suspended; but a gracious God was pleased to renew my strength, and I have since enjoyed, for me, an unusual portion of health.

Soon after I began to arrange my materials, I found the need of some one to copy after me for the press, and to lend other assistances, which a second person might perform. And I soon had the happiness to obtain Mr. George H. Hough, of New-Hampshire, a young ministering brother, acquainted with printing, whose assistance has facilitated my work, and taken off my hands the whole laborious task of transcribing it for the press, which, on account of my numerous quotations, I found absolutely necessary to be done.

I did not, at first contemplate any thing more at present, than the history of the American Baptists. I had, however, designed, at some future period, to compose a General History of the Baptists in other countries; but learning that Mr. Ivimey, a Baptist minister in London, was engaged in writing the History of the English Baptists, and concluding that his work would, in a great measure, if not wholly, supersede the necessity of any further exertions of mine, I resolved to throw together in one view, with as much precision as possible, a general account of all who have maintained the peculiar sentiments of the Baptists, in foreign countries and ancient times. And as I must, in order to do this, travel an extensive round of ecclesiastical affairs, and refer to many characters and events, which might not be fully understood by all my readers, I concluded, at a late period, to give, in the first place, *A Summary view of Ecclesiastical History*, and then *A Miniature History of Baptism, from the Apostolic age to the present time.*

This work, scanty and imperfect as it may appear, has been collected from many hundred sources; the field of inquiry has been wide, and I have endeavoured to explore it with faithfulness and care.

The history of the American Baptists abounds with incidents of a common kind, but it furnishes very few of those events which give pomp and splendour to the historick page. I therefore found it necessary to descend into minute details, to write much journal-wise, and, indeed, in any form, by which I might preserve from oblivion facts, which I thought worthy of being transmitted to posterity, and which might at the same time be edifying to the present generation.

Many of the events described are of the most familiar kind; an attempt to elevate them by the flowers of diction, would be preposterous in itself, and disgusting to the reader. I expect most of my readers will be a plain people, unaccustomed to the trappings of art, and to the labour of decyphering learned figures and distant similitudes. But while I have dispensed with the decorations of style, I have endeavoured to regard an observation, which Cowper has made in some of his prose writings : " Perspicuity is half the battle ; for if the sense is not so plain as to stare you in the face, but few people will take the pains to poke for it."

I have found it somewhat difficult to determine how to manage the business to my own satisfaction, respecting the histories of individual churches. There are now in all the Associations upwards of two thousand ; to have given a detailed account of the origin, progress, and present circumstances of every one, would have made the work too voluminous and costly, and the narratives would have been so similar, that there would have been too great a sameness in them, to make them generally interesting. To have given the histories of no churches, in their individual capacities, would have made the work too general, and many interesting narratives and anecdotes must have been omitted. There remained, therefore, no alternative, but to give the particular history of some churches, and to omit that of many others. I suggested something on this subject in my Proposals, and there stated, that my intention was to take particular notice of those churches which are the most distinguished for age, for numbers, for prosperity, or adversity, for being mother establishments, or for their local situation. Upon these principles I have proceeded in my selection of churches for particular notice. But after all my care, it is possible I may have been partial and injudicious. And as every one is fond of reading something about himself and his own people, it is also possible I may be blamed where I ought not to be. I should have been glad to have said more of some churches and neighbourhoods than I have done ; I have written a multitude of letters which have not been answered, and therefore shall acquit myself of blame in these cases.

When I began this work, I had not determined what plan to pursue respecting biographical accounts. But I soon found that it would be impracticable, and in the judgment of my most enlightened brethren, improper to say much of the living. I took many accounts while travelling, and many have been communicated by others, which must be omitted ; but they shall be preserved with care, and will be of use to some future historian. Some of my fathers and brethren have rested from their labours since this work was begun, and others may, and all of us must soon follow them.

I observed at first, that I hardly knew how I came to engage in this undertaking, and I now can say, I hardly know how, with my feeble health and scanty resources, I have carried it through. The cordial approbation, which my brethren have so generally manifested towards my design, has been a powerful stimulus to perseverance : and I have had the happiness of believing that I have been employed in the path of duty, and that God, in his providence, has prospered my labours. And if no other person should receive any advantage from this publication, my labour will not be lost ; for the pleasure and profit, which it has afforded me, are more than sufficient to compensate all the labour and anxiety it has cost. But I cannot but flatter myself, that the accounts of the wonderful displays of the grace of God, which are here imperfectly related, will be read with pleasure by many, in the present and in future generations.

My desire has been, to record on the page of history, important events, which were fast sinking into oblivion ; to arrange in one view those which were already recorded, and to place the history of the American Baptists on such a foundation, that it may easily be continued by the future historian.

I have found it difficult in many cases, to fix the date of events, which have been taken from the enfeebled memories of the aged, or from documents in part obliterated, and throughout indefinite and obscure. Cases have not unfrequently occurred, where aged people could not perfectly agree among themselves respecting things which transpired in their youth. Correspondents have communicated accounts, which did not always agree with each other. Young men have stated things according to tradition, and old men according to their remembrance. In these ways difficulties have arisen, which I have laboured hard to solve, by writing many letters, and by every other means within my reach. And I cannot but feel a degree of confidence, that no great mistakes will be found in my statements. But as this history will be exposed to the observation of thousands, who have been eye-witnesses of the scenes it describes, if any essential errors should be discovered, I shall esteem it a favour to be informed of them, and they shall be corrected with cheerfulness and care.

DAVID BENEDICT.

Pawtucket, near Providence, R. I.
April 16, 1813.

A GENERAL HISTORY, &c.

CHAP. I.

A SUMMARY VIEW OF ECCLESIASTICAL HISTORY.

THE introduction of the gospel system was a most glorious and important event. At the time the Sun of Righteousness arose upon the world, it was in a state of profound ignorance, and the deepest moral misery.

The Jews, the ancient people of God, had generally departed from the piety of their ancestors, and were sunk into formality and hypocrisy. The Gentile nations, whether barbarous or civilized, were involved in the grossest idolatry; their deities were multiplied to an extravagant degree, almost every thing in creation was worshipped, and the enlightened city of Rome contained, at one time, thirty thousand different deities, which had been collected from the conquered nations. A magnificent temple, called the Pantheon, that is, the temple of all the gods, had been erected, in which this mighty host of divinities was assembled.

Towards the conclusion of the reign of Herod the Great, the Son of God, who had long been foretold by the ancient prophets, descended upon earth. Although the world was involved in darkness at this time, yet the nations were generally in a state of tranquillity and repose. The vast Roman empire, in which Palestine was then included, was less agitated with wars and tumults at the birth of Christ, than it had been for many years before. And, indeed, some historians have maintained that the temple of Janus* was then shut, and that wars and discords absolutely ceased throughout the world.

The manner in which the Messiah appeared, his ministry and death, and all the affairs of his kingdom and people, for many years after he ascended on high, are recorded in the New Testament. His disciples began to congregate into churches, soon after he left the earth. The church at Jerusalem was formed the evening of the glorious day of his ascension, in an upper room, and consisted of about a hundred and twenty believing men and women. The persecution, which arose about the time of Stephen's death, caused all the disciples of Jesus, except the apostles, to leave Jerusalem. They proceeded out every way like the radii of a circle from the centre, and formed churches in many places, first in Palestine, then in other parts of Asia, next in the Asiatic islands, and lastly in Europe.

Mr. Robinson has shown that the apostles and primitive preachers gathered churches in between sixty and seventy different cities, towns, and provinces, and in many instances a number were gathered in each. These churches were all composed of reputed believers, who had been baptized by immersion on the profession of their faith. Their bishops and elders were merely overseers of their spiritual flocks; they claimed no right to lord it over God's heritage; every church was an independent body, and no one claimed a right to regulate the affairs of another. If they met in council, as they did at Jerusalem, it was to advise, not to give law.

The church of Christ has always been taught by the conduct of the people of this world, that this is not her home. She was persecuted at first by the Jews, then by the pagans, and next by monsters under the christian name.

---

* Janus, according to heathen fable, was the most ancient king, who reigned in Italy. Some authors make him son of Apollo, some of Cœlus and Hecate, and others, a native of Athens. Janus is represented with two faces, because he was acquainted with the past and the future; or, according to others, because he was taken for the sun, who opens the day at his rising, and shuts it at his setting. He was chiefly worshipped among the Romans. His temple, which was always open in times of war, was shut only three times, for the space of seven hundred years, for during that long period of time the Romans were continually employed in war. *Classical Dictionary.*

Christianity prospered greatly under the ministry of the apostles and primitive preachers, and in a short time was carried to most parts of the Roman empire, which extended in length above three thousand miles, from the river Euphrates in the east, to the western ocean; in breadth it was more than two thousand miles, and the whole consisted of above sixteen hundred thousand square miles. This vast empire was an assemblage of conquered kingdoms and provinces, and comprehended, at the commencement of christianity, most of the civilized world. And at this period, it is said to have contained, one hundred and twenty millions of souls.*

Providence seems to have chosen this vast dominion, for the scene of the first gospel labourers. The multitude of languages amongst its inhabitants was no obstruction to them, for they were inspired to speak with other tongues. Opposition they frequently met with, but this fell out to the furtherance of the gospel; for when persecuted in one city they fled to another, and carried with them the light of truth. The Lord gave the word to his servants, and great was the company, who published it abroad.

It would be difficult to form any probable conjecture of the number of converts to christianity in the early ages of the church, but it must have been immensely great, for it is supposed that three millions were sacrificed in the three first centuries, to the rage of pagan persecutors. In these three centuries there were ten general persecutions, fomented by so many cruel pagan emperours. They did not reign, however, in regular succession, and in the intervening spaces between their reigns, the empire was governed by princes, who entertained a great variety of opinions respecting christianity. Some turned it into ridicule, others shewed some degree of clemency towards the christians; some repealed the persecuting laws of their predecessors, while others left them to their destructive operation. But the pagan priests continually employed their malicious eloquence to defame the disciples of Christ, and to rouse the persecuting sword against them. They laid to their charge the earthquakes, famines, pestilences, and conflagrations, and all the national calamities which happened where they resided. And they persuaded the magistrates that the

* Robinson's Ecclesiastical Researches, p. 13, 14.

gods sent down these judgments to avenge their lenity towards the christians.

The first of these ten persecutions was begun by the abandoned Nero. He was the first emperour who shed the blood of christians, and it is said that Peter and Paul were of the number. The city of Rome took fire, and a considerable part of it was consumed. The perfidious Nero was thought to have kindled the fire, but that cruel prince accused the innocent christians of the horrid crime, and avenged it upon them in a most barbarous manner. He caused some to be wrapped up in combustible garments, which were set on fire; others were fastened to crosses, others were torn to pieces by wild beasts, and thousands suffered death in the most horrid and cruel forms.

The persecutions under all the ten emperours, were similar in many respects; some of them were but short, and others of longer duration. The christians suffered every privation, and were put to death by all the excruciating tortures, which infernal ingenuity could invent. Multitudes were confined in theatres, where wild beasts were let loose upon them, and they were worried and devoured, for the diversion of thousands of barbarous spectators, who sat elevated above the reach of harm.

The third persecution was under Trajan, a prince renowned for many excellent qualities, but who was, nevertheless, a dreadful scourge to the disciples of Christ. The letters which passed between him and Pliny, the governor of Bythinia, I shall here transcribe.

C. Pliny to Trajan Emperour, health.

"It is my usual custom, Sir, to refer all things, of which I harbour any doubts, to you. For who can better direct my judgment in its hesitation, or instruct my understanding in its ignorance? I never had the fortune to be present at any examination of christians, before I came into this province. I am therefore at a loss to determine, what is the usual object, either of inquiry or punishment, and to what length either of them is to be carried. It has also been with me a question very problematical, whether any distinction should be made between the young and the old, the tender and the robust; whether any room should be given for repentance, or the guilt of christianity once incurred is not to be expiated by the most unequivocal retraction; whether the name itself, abstracted from any flagitiousness of conduct, or the crimes connected with the name, be the object of punishment. In the mean time this has been my method, with respect to those who were brought before me as christians. I asked them whether they were christians? If they pleaded guilty, I interrogated them twice afresh, with a menace of capital punishment. In case of obstinate perseverance, I ordered them to be executed. For of this I had no doubt, whatever was the nature of their religion, that a sullen and obstinate inflexibility called for the vengeance of the magistrate. Some there were infected with the same madness, whom, on account of their privilege of citizenship, I reserved to be sent to Rome, to be referred to your tribunal. In the course of this business, informations pouring in, as is usual when they are encouraged, more cases occurred. An anonymous libel was exhibited, with a catalogue of names of persons, who yet declared, that they were not christians then, or ever had been, and repeated after me an invocation of the gods and of your image, which, for this purpose, I had ordered to be brought with the images of the deities, performed sacred rites with wine and frankincense, and execrated Christ, none of which things, I am told, a real christian can ever be impelled to do. On this account I dismissed them. Others, named by an informer, first affirmed and then denied the charge of christianity, declaring that they had been christians, but had desisted, some three years ago, others still longer, some even twenty years ago. All of them worshipped your image, and the statues of the gods, and also execrated Christ. And this was the account which they gave me of the nature of the religion they once had professed, whether it deserves the name of crime or error, that they were accustomed on a stated day to meet before day-light, and to repeat among themselves an hymn to Christ as to a God, and to bind themselves by an oath with an obligation of not committing any wickedness, but on the contrary, of, abstaining from thefts, robberies, and adulteries, also of not violating their promise, or denying a pledge, after which, it was their custom to separate, and to meet again at a promiscuous, harmless meal, from which last they yet desisted, after the publication of my edict in which, agreeably to your orders, I forbade any societies. On which account, I judged it the more necessary, to inquire by torture from two females, who were said to be deaconesses, what is the real truth. But nothing could I collect, except a depraved and excessive superstition. Deferring, therefore, any further investigation, I determined to consult you. For the number of culprits is so great, as to call for serious consultation. For many are informed against of every age and of both sexes, and more still will be in the same situation. For the contagion of the superstition hath spread not only through cities, but even villages and the country. Not that I think it impossible to check and correct it: The success of my endeavours hitherto forbids such desponding thoughts; for the temples once almost desolate, begin to be frequented, and the sacred solemnities, which had long been intermitted, are now attended afresh; and the sacrificial victims are now sold every where, which once could scarce find a purchaser. Whence I conclude, that many might be reclaimed, were the hope of impunity on repentance absolutely confirmed."

Trajan to Pliny.

" You have done perfectly right, my dear Pliny, in the inquiry which you have made concerning christians. For truly, no one general rule can be laid down, which will apply itself to all cases. They must not be sought after. If they are brought before you and convicted, let them be capitally punished, yet with this restriction, that if any renounce christianity, and evidence his sincerity by supplicating our gods, however suspected he may be for the past, he shall obtain pardon for the future, on his repentance. But anonymous libels in no case ought to be attended to; for the precedent would be of the worst sort, and perfectly incongruous to the maxims of my government."

This letter of Pliny's was written about 106 or 107. It suggests many remarks, which have been judiciously made by the late Rev. John Newton. They are found in the sixth volume of his works, New-York edition.

Notwithstanding the violence with which persecution raged in the three first centuries, yet christianity never prospered more than in these trying times. The constan-

Constantine the Great embraces Christianity. 13

cy of the christian sufferers emboldened their brethren to persevere, and led many to examine into the nature of that religion, which exposed its professors to such calamities, and which, at the same time, inspired them with such holy fortitude, amidst the torturing agonies of death. And their enemies soon found that *the blood of the martyrs was the seed of the church.*

We are now about to take a view of the christian cause, under circumstances very different from those which have been related.

A little more than three hundred years after the birth of Christ, the Roman Emperour, Constantine the Great, embraced the christian faith, and not only abolished all the persecuting edicts of his predecessors, but established religion by law. And under legal establishments of different kinds, the great mass of christian professors have been included from that inauspicious period to the present time. The conversion of this emperour was effected by the miraculous appearance of a cross in the heavens, while he was marching at the head of his armies. This story has, however, been considered, and not without just grounds, a fabulous invention of after-times. And, indeed, the sincerity of this royal convert has never been fully established. But so it was, that either from motives of civil policy, or from a genuine conviction of its truth, he espoused the christian cause, and established it as the religion of his empire. This was hailed by most as an auspicious and promising measure ; but it proved in the end to be a dangerous favour, big with calamity and harm. It was indeed a desirable thing to be freed from the rage of a persecuting power ; it was also a pleasant sight, to the worshippers of the true God, to see the whole system of paganism, which had been the pride of ages, gradually dissolved and sinking into insignificance and contempt. And had Constantine repealed all persecuting laws, and left religion to stand upon its own foundation, he would have done essential service to the church of Christ, and every christian would have reason to respect his memory. But when princes undertake in religion, they either do too much for it, or against it. "This zealous prince, (says Mosheim) employed all the resources of his genius, all the authority of his laws, and all the engaging charms of his munificence and liberality, to efface by degrees the superstitions of paganism, and propagate christianity in every corner of the Roman empire."* "Nothing (says Milner) can be more splendid than the external appearance of christianity at this time. An emperour, full of zeal for the propagation of the only divine religion, by edicts, restores every thing to the church of which it had been deprived, indemnifies those who had suffered, honours the pastors exceedingly, recommends to governors of provinces to promote the gospel—he also erects churches exceedingly sumptuous and ornamental, with distinctions of parts, corresponding in some measure to those in Solomon's temple ; his mother Helena also fills the whole Roman world with her munificent acts in support of religion, and so on."†

Many were elated beyond measure at this external prosperity and magnificence: but the old veterans in the christian cause, foresaw the evils which were brooding over them. They judged rightly when they suspected that these splendid benefits were purchased at too dear a rate, for the emperour, who had taken the church into his princely favour, claimed the privilege of regulating its affairs.

Now religion assumed a prosperous appearance, but very little of the spirit of godliness was to be seen. Now the bishops and pastors, especially those in populous cities and towns, were exalted to a pitch of worldly grandeur, in consequence of the princely endowments which their churches had received. Now multitudes came swarming into the church, in pursuit of the emoluments which it offered them. Now blasting errors, augmented superstitions, and pompous and unmeaning forms of piety, which had long been gaining ground, ripened apace, and soon arrived to a dreadful maturity. In a word, every thing in faith and practice, that was opposite to the pure religion of Jesus, came pouring in like a flood, and this heavenly system was disrobed of its primeval beauty, and sunk beneath an oppressive load, from which it has never yet fully recovered.

The Bishop of Rome soon rose to preeminence among his brethren, on account of his local situation, and the foundation for the magnificent papacy was laid. The bishops of Antioch, Alexandria, and of Constantinople, were

* Vol. I. p. 318.   † Vol. II. p. 57.

soon exalted to superior dignity. Next came Archbishops, Patriarchs, Exarchs, Metropolitans, Suffragans, Popes, Cardinals, Monks, Nuns, Synods, Councils, Anathemas, Dungeons, Gibbets, Flames, and Death, all for the glory of a God of mercy, and the honour of his holy name.

We have now opened to a wide field, and a mighty mass of materials presents itself, which, however, we can but just glance upon without extending this article farther than would comport with its design.

In farther pursuing this subject, I shall relate, under separate heads, accounts of some of the most distinguished bodies of professed christians, and also of the most striking events which have occurred in the christian world.

The Church of Rome.

"The Church of Rome is now a phrase of magnitude and splendour, yet at first it stood for no more than an assembly of converted Jews, dwelling at Rome, who met for worship in the hired house of Paul of Tarsus then a prisoner."*

The early history of this church is covered with obscurity, but the deficiency of historical facts has been supplied by Papist writers with a multitude of fabulous tales. But it is sufficiently evident, that the church of Rome remained for a long time a small body of christians, who were but little known to the rest of the people of this great city. The bishop of Rome preached in a private house, and merely superintended the care of his little flock, and doubtless never expected his successors would arise to the highest summit of blasphemous eminence, and hurl their anathemas to distant nations, dethrone kings and emperours, and make them bow at their feet.

Sylvester was bishop of Rome in the reign of Constantine, and Catholics pretend that he was the thirty-fourth in succession. In the days of Sylvester, it is believed, that the people, who were afterwards called Waldenses, began to separate from the church, which had become a tool of state, and was fast plunging into error and superstition.

The bishop of Rome arose by gradual steps to eminence and authority, until he acquired the title of Universal

* Robinson's Ecclesiastical Researches, p. 117.

Bishop.* This title was conferred upon Boniface III. by the emperour Phocas, in 606 ; and from this period writers generally date the rise of Antichrist. If this be correct, his reign will end, or the 1260 years will expire about fifty years hence.

From the time of Boniface III. to that of Gregory VII. a period of a little less than five hundred years, there were no less than a hundred and fourteen pontiffs elevated to the Papal chair,† and from the outrageous reign of the last mentioned pope, to the present time, the number of these antichristian bishops has been peculiarly great, but I am not able now to state it.

* The manner in which the pope obtained the title of Universal Bishop, is very ingeniously described by Mr. M'Gowan in his Dialogues of Devils. Fastosus, that is, the proud or haughty devil, is represented as speaking. This devil was the author of all the ambitious projects of aspiring ecclesiastics. He had set up a work shop near the throne of St. Peter, and had already furnished many bishops with medals, inscribed with FATHER, PATRIARCH, and so on. " Long (says Fastosus) and very successfully had I followed this medalian trade, when a famous and worthy prelate of Rome, who was a great admirer of my productions, came into my office. After doing obeisance to me, and turning over my pretty devises, he asked me, " If I thought, with all my ingenuity, I could produce a genuine medal with this inscription, PAPAS SUPREMUS; or EPISCOPUS UNIVERSALIS." I told him that if all the artists in hell were to unite their wisdom in one mechanical head, it would be utterly impossible ; for, said I, the whole creation doth not furnish sufficient materials. But if it please your holiness, I can make you a sham medal of that sort, which may, perhaps, answer all the ends you have in view, as well as if it were real. " Oh! (said he) I care not, for my part, whether it is real or counterfeit, if I can only, by your assistance, my worthy Fastosus, impose upon the credulity of mankind, and make the world believe that I am supreme pope and universal bishop ; then I should reign, with despotic power, over the estates and consciences of all christians. My good friend, please you to make me the medal, and I will cause the world to believe that I had it from the Almighty, with letters patent under the broad seal of heaven, for the sole use of it to me and my successors forever." I well know, returned I, that your holiness means no more, than in a pious manner to impose the cheat upon the world, the better to fill your coffers, and aggrandize your name ; in which laudable undertaking, your adored Festosus shall be ever ready to direct and assist. To work I went, having called in the assistance of several of our friends, and made a counterfeit medal, in the likeness of a treble crown, with certain inscriptions of the cabalistick kind upon it. They were short but pithy sentences, as you shall hear. On the one side of the first crown was inscribed, " He that is honoured as the wearer of this medal, is possest of infallible knowledge." Opposite to that was carved in fine Italian, " He is supreme over all laws, divine and human." On the right side of the second crown were these words in large capitals, " This is the Head of the Church." On the left were these, " This is the vicar of Christ, and successor of Peter." On the third and uppermost crown were the following, " The keys of Heaven, Hell, and Purgatory, are in his possession, and used only at his pleasure." Round the edge was this writing, " He reigneth supreme over all the kings of the earth, putteth down one, and exalteth another at his pleasure." *Dialogues of Devils*, p. 217—219.

† Trial of Antichrist, p. 14.

The Pope becomes a temporal Prince. 17

The history of the Roman pontiffs is replete with every thing shocking to the feelings of piety and humanity. Notwithstanding their high pretensions to sanctity, many of them were the most flagitious monsters that ever walked the earth; their scandalous amours were notorious throughout their dominions, and many of their illegitimate children have cut distinguished figures in the world. Their ambitious projects set the world in commotion; their avarice drained the coffers of their blind devotees, and Sixtus V. left behind him at his death, above five millions of gold.*

Some of those spiritual potentates were respectable as earthly princes, but others were the most violent and perfidious wretches that ever swayed a sceptre. And in their quarrels with surrounding sovereigns, they had the advantage of adding to their military forces, their thundering anathemas, by which princes were deposed from their thrones, their subjects absolved from their allegiance, and promised with pardons for rebellion, and heaven for success.

Although the popes had arisen to the highest summit of splendour and magnificence, and had, according to their pretensions, the spiritual destinies of all at their disposal, yet the first who became a temporal prince was Zachary I. The manner in which earthly dominions were attached to the papacy, is described by Mosheim in the following manner.

" The honours and privileges, which the western nations had voluntarily conferred upon the bishops, and other doctors of the church, were now (eighth century) augmented with new and immense accessions of opulence and authority. The endowments of the church and monasteries, and the revenues of the bishops, were hitherto considerable; but in this century a new and ingenious method was found out of acquiring much greater riches to the church, and of increasing its wealth through succeeding ages. An opinion prevailed universally at this time, though its authors are not known, that the punishment, which the righteous Judge of the world has reserved for the transgressions of the wicked, was to be prevented and annulled, by liberal donations to God, to the saints, to the

---

* Millot's History, Vol. IV. p. 279.

churches and clergy. This new and commodious method of making atonement for iniquity, was the principal source of those immense treasures, which from this period began to flow in upon the clergy, the churches, and monasteries, and continued to enrich them through succeeding ages down to the present time.

"But here it is highly worthy of observation, that the donations, which princes and persons of the first rank presented, in order to make expiation for their sins, and to satisfy the justice of God, and the demands of the clergy, did not only consist in those *private* possessions, which every citizen may enjoy, and with which the churches and convents were already abundantly enriched; no: these donations were carried to a much more extravagant length, and the church was endowed with several of those *public* grants, which are peculiar to princes and sovereign states, and which are commonly called *regalia* or royal domains. Emperours, kings, and princes, signalized their superstitious veneration for the clergy, by investing bishops, churches, and monasteries, in the possession of whole provinces, cities, castles, and fortresses, with all the rights and prerogatives of sovereignty that were annexed to them under the dominion of their former masters. Hence it came to pass that they, who, by their holy profession, were appointed to proclaim to the world the vanity of human grandeur, and to inspire into the minds of men, by their instructions and their example, a noble contempt of sublunary things, became themselves scandalous spectacles of worldly pomp, ambition, and splendour; were created *dukes*, *counts*, and *marquises*, judges, legislators, and sovereigns; and not only gave laws to nations, but, also, upon many occasions, gave battle to their enemies at the head of numerous armies of their own raising. It is here that we are to look for the source of those dreadful tumults and calamities, that spread desolation through Europe in after-times, particularly of those bloody wars concerning *investitures*, and those obstinate contentions and disputes about the *regalia*."*

The domains which were bequeathed by princes to the Holy See, were afterwards claimed by their successors, and by this means a foundation was laid for perpetual quarrels between the popes and many of the European sovereigns.

* Mosheim, vol. II. p. 216.

The pontificate was elevated to its highest pitch of worldly grandeur in the eleventh century, and the Man of Sin appeared to have attained the summit of arrogance and blasphemy in the person of Gregory VII. This pope was a monk before he was elevated to the papal chair. His name was Hildebrand; *Firebrand*, he might more properly be called. He assumed not only the appellation of Universal Bishop, but also those of Sovereign Pontiff, Christ's Vicar, Prince of the Apostles, God on earth, Lord God the Pope, His Holiness, King of kings and Lord of lords, Prince over all nations and kingdoms, The Most Holy and Most Blessed, Master of the Universal World, Father of Kings, Light of the World, Most High and Sovereign Bishop, &c. &c.*

Gregory VII. was undoubtedly the most audacious pope that ever sat on St. Peter's throne, and his whole pontificate was a continual scene of tumult and bloodshed. He impiously attempted to submit to his jurisdiction the emperours, kings, and princes of the earth, and to render their dominions tributary to the See of Rome. He dethroned the emperour Henry IV. and then excommunicated him from the church, and obliged him to stand three days barefoot before the gates of Canosa on the Appinees, where he was regaling himself with his mistress Matilda, before he would grant him absolution.

This was the first instance of a prince being deposed by the pope; but this served as a precedent for many others, which the limits of this sketch will not permit us to name.

It may seem altogether incredible now, to those who have not studied the history of ancient times, that emperours, kings, and princes, should be hurled from their thrones, and disrobed of the functions of royalty, by the anathemas of the pretended vicar of Christ. What regard would the sovereigns of Europe now pay to the denunciations of Pius VII.? But the case was far different when Antichrist was reigning in the meridian of his strength. Then all the world were wondering after the beast, and the voice of St. Peter, by his pretended vicegerent on earth, was regarded as the voice of God. Sovereigns might spurn at the thunders of the Vatican, but their sub-

* Trial of Antichrist, p. 41.

jects regarded them as the mandates of Heaven; kingdoms were soon filled with rebellion; the lives of princes were in danger from those about them; for the bulls of his Holiness must be obeyed; kingdoms were laid under interdicts; every thing was thrown into confusion, and in these dreadful circumstances, the proud, imperious princes of the earth, were reduced to the humbling necessity of bowing to the feet of St. Peter's successor, and becoming reconciled in the best manner they could to their spiritual master. And having gained the friendship of his Holiness, their subjects returned to their allegiance, and their kingdoms were restored to order. It was, however, certainly unfair for the popes to interpose the charms of their spiritual influence, in their quarrels with princes about worldly things.

The pope was surrounded by ten thousand satellites, all receiving their light, or rather their darkness from him. But above them all, were seventy-two cardinals, by whom he was elected. Armies of monks and ministers stood ready to obey his summons, and were dispersed in every country to execute his high commands. These emissaries were constantly employed in the affairs of princes, in the intrigues of courts, and many of them were elevated to the highest summit of worldly grandeur.

"Cardinal Ruixoga, archbishop of Toledo, in Spain, had, under his command in 1764, the chapters of an hundred and eight cathedrals, the members of three hundred and twelve colleges, the governors and officers of two thousand and eight hospitals, the parish priests of more than twenty one thousand cities, towns and villages, the officers of all the courts of inquisition, and of the chancery of Castile, &c. But this great man was nothing but a tool of the pope.*

It would make too many heads to consider separately every article which it may be proper to notice. We shall, therefore, throw together, in as much order as can be done, some of the most striking events which have occurred in this astonishing body of professing christians.

The church of Rome for many centuries prevailed generally throughout most of the European kingdoms, and

* Robinson's Ecclesiastical Researches, p. 262.

its emissaries also made large conquests in many remoter regions; and this corrupt and idolatrous communion is now thought to embrace not far from a hundred million of souls. The religious orders of priests, monks, nuns, friars, and so on, form an innumerable company of lazy, ambitious, and unprofitable beings.

The history of the monastick orders would, of itself, make a voluminous work; but it is sufficient to observe that they began in early times, in a mistaken manner of weaning the mind from sublunary things. The first monks were merely religious hermits, who, in the third century retired to the solitary deserts of Egypt, both to avoid persecution, and to enjoy religious repose. In the persecution under Decius, one Paul fled to the deserts of Thebais, where he spent ninety years in religious solitude. This kind of hermitage becoming popular, thousands fled to the wilderness when they might have remained in society. At first they lived a vagrant life, and were scattered throughout the deserts; but in the fourth century one Anthony began to form them into societies, and from hence-forward they erected habitations, which were called monasteries, and every thing was regulated by laws punctilious and absurd. From the east the monks came swarming into the west, and finally overspread the christian world. From the monastick orders were elected most of the cardinals, popes, legates, and other dignified ecclesiasticks in the church of Rome.

As so many of the brethren had taken it upon them to live a single life, a corresponding number of sisters, finding they must live alone, took upon them the vows of chastity, were called nuns, and were collected in habitations called nunneries. And so great was the rage for retirement, that in many countries, a large portion of the inhabitants were associated in these irrational and sanctimonious communities. But the monks and nuns, although under vows of perpetual chastity, did not always keep apart, and many shocking things are related of the horrid measures which they took to conceal their iniquity, and dispose of the fruits of their infamous commerce.

The celibacy of the clergy was a practice early introduced in the church of Rome. " Marriage was at first permitted to all the various ranks and orders of the clergy, high and low. Those, however, who continued in a state of celibacy, obtained by this abstinence a higher reputation of sanctity and virtue than others."* But Paul foretold that in the reign of Antichrist marriage would be forbidden, and accordingly, in due time, the celibacy of the clergy was enjoined by law. This law was, however, never carried into general effect. Some took wives in a lawful manner and lived like other men, and the answer which some of the clergy in France made to the legate of Gregory VII. is full of humour and spirit. Gregory forbid the people to hear mass from the married priests, and gave orders that celibacy should be religiously observed. The priests utterly refused to obey this command, and "*if the pope persists in it,*" added they, "*we will rather renounce our priesthood than our wives, and he may find angels to govern his churches.*"†

This clerical celibacy was no friend to virtue, but it was, on the other hand, the means of a torrent of lasciviousness, debaucheries, and crimes. Uncleanness prevailed, not among all, but among every order of these holy men, who pretended to live like angels upon earth. Many of the popes were the illegitimate children of popes who had gone before them. Henry, bishop of Leige, in the eleventh century, boasted in publick, that he had been the parent of fourteen children, within two and twenty months. Pope Gregory VII. reproved this bishop for squandering the revenues of the church on his bastard children, but he did not depose him from his holy office. It is not strange that Gregory was so indulgent to this amorous bishop, as he was himself then carrying on a scandalous amour with Matilda, the countess of Tuscany, by which he obtained a vast estate for the Holy See. "Illiterate prelates habited in purple robes, converted nunneries into stews, and had parks for seraglios. Some few pacified their scruples by private marriage, but by far the greater part either committed fornication and adultery promiscuously, or kept mistresses whom they called vice-wives. It must not be understood that all were sunk to this deplorable state of wretchedness and vice. There were sober bishops, who looked with grief and shame, on the infamous conduct of their clergy, and tried to resist

* Mosheim, vol. 1. p. 262. † Millot's History, vol. III. p. 171.

the torrent of concupiscence, with which their diocesses were overwhelmed. But their headstrong clergy paid no attention to their remonstrances. Incontinence was a tide which could not be stopped, and the first council of Toledo, to their shame, rather than permit the clergy to marry, made a law to allow them concubines.* So blind and invincible is superstition, when established by custom and laws.

COUNCILS.

THE custom of holding councils, according to Mosheim, commenced in Greece in the second century. They were, by the Greeks, called synods. Councils were, at first, mere provincial assemblies, collected together for the purpose of regulating the affairs of particular districts; but they soon arose to the most august and powerful assemblies, and assumed the supreme command of the whole catholick world.

The popes frequently attended councils in person, and at other times, they were represented by their legates and nuncios. Some of them were called by the pontiffs, at other times, they were afraid of their power, and tried to hinder their meeting, or dissolved them when assembled.

The first general council was held at Nice, in Bythinia, in 325, wherein the deputies of the church universal were summoned by the emperour Constantine, to put an end to the Arian controversy, which then began to rage extensively. At this council upwards of three hundred bishops were assembled; it held about a year. Some of the catholick councils sat many years, and assembled a standing army of bishops and ecclesiasticks, who stood ready to suppress every heretical whisper.

The council of Placentia, was the most numerous of any that had been hitherto assembled, and was, on that account, held in the open fields. There were present at it, two hundred bishops, four thousand ecclesiasticks, and three hundred thousand laymen.†

The council of Constance was begun in 1414, and was held four years. It was opened by pope John XXIII. and was ended by Martin V. At this council were assembled, (says Millot) a prodigious number of cardinals,

* Robinson's History of Baptism, p. 311.   † Mosheim, vol. II. p. 429.

prelates, and doctors; above a hundred sovereign princes of Germany, with the emperour at their head; twenty-seven ambassadours, and innumerable deputies from all the different states and communities of Europe, and among the rest a crowd of minstrels, courtesans, &c. All Europe was in commotion about this council; it was summoned at the instance of the emperour Sigismond, for the purpose of reforming the church, and checking the ambition of the pontiffs.

The papal chair, at this time, was deputed by three ambitious rivals, who had assumed the names of John XXIII. Gregory XII. and Benedict XIII. But during the sitting of the Council, all the rival popes were deposed, and a new one was elected by the name of Martin V. John had been a corsair, that is a pirate, in his youth; a profession, says Millot, more suited to his temper, than the functions of an ecclesiastick; in the habit of a postillion, he escaped from Constance, to avoid the vengeance of an enraged populace.*

The famous council of Trent was held eighteen years, and during the lives of five popes. It commenced in 1545, some time after the reformation was begun by Luther.†

The resolutions of a general council, as well as the decisions of a pope, are, by the Catholicks, considered equal to scripture commands; but it is an unlucky circumstance that both popes and councils have passed decrees, not only different from, but in direct opposition to each other.

The Romans borrowed councils from the Greeks, and Protestants borrowed them from the Romans; and Presbyterian Synods and Congregational conventions, are considered by some as vestiges of the august and imposing councils we have thus briefly described. And, indeed, the meetings, called councils, among the Baptists, are thought by some to be branches of the same corrupt tree. I know not what Baptist councils may arrive to, but at present they are certainly very harmless things. A church calls a number of neighbouring elders and brethren, to give them their advice in matters of difficulty. This ad-

---

* Millot's History, vol. IV. p. 22. This account is given by a zealous Catholick, who does not, however, hesitate to censure, in the severest terms, the vices and enormities of his own community.

† Trent was the rendezvous for prostitutes from every quarter, during the sitting of the council. *Trial of Antichrist, p.* 139.

vice is often received and proves highly beneficial; but it may be neglected, as it often is, and still no breach of fellowship, no interruption of communion between the advisers and the advised is occasioned thereby. But it must be acknowledged that churches founded on congregational and independent principles, cannot consistently have much business for councils, and I think the fewer there are among the Baptists the better. Our churches do undoubtedly sometimes refer difficulties to councils, which they might easy enough settle themselves.

CRUSADES OR HOLY WARS.

In the eleventh century an attempt was made by the church of Rome, to recover the holy land from the possession of the Mahometans, and incredible numbers volunteered their services in these holy expeditions. But almost every thing under the name of religion, was at this time profligate and vile. The popes of Rome, from the time of Sylvester II. had contemplated the holy wars, but the troubles of Europe long prevented the execution of their arduous designs. Gregory VII. boasted that upwards of fifty thousand men were mustered to follow him in a holy war, which he intended to conduct in person, but was prevented by his quarrel with the emperour Henry IV. At length the long premeditated war was undertaken. A monk of Picardy, commonly called Peter the Hermit, at his return from Jerusalem where he had been on pilgrimage, represented the oppression of the holy city, and the cruel treatment which the christians suffered, in such striking colours, that Urban II. thought proper to set both kings and people in motion to recover it. This hermit of a hideous figure, covered with rags, walking barefoot, speaking as a prophet, and hearkened to as such, inspired the people every where, with an enthusiasm similar to his own. He went through all the countries of *Europe* sounding the alarm of the holy war against the infidel nations, and with a view to engage the superstitious and ignorant multitude in his cause, he carried with him a letter which he said was written in heaven, and addressed to all true christians, &c. Success every where attended the declamations of this ragged orator, and innumerable multitudes of all ranks and orders offered themselves as volunteers in the sacred expedition. They all received from the pope or bishops a cross of red stuff, which they wore upon their shoulders, and hence they were called crusaders, or cross-bearers, and the expedition was also from this circumstance denominated a crusade. The red cross procured a dispensation from all penance; but, when once taken, the wearers were obliged to set out under pain of excommunication. But few, however, were inclined to draw back, for they never doubted that the riches of Asia would recompense them a hundred fold; and if they died in the attempt, they were sure of heaven as the reward for their meritorious services. Cotemporary writers make the number of the first crusaders to exceed six millions; but the best authors make it only about one million and a quarter. This army, says Mosheim, consisted of a motley assemblage of monks, prostitutes, artists, labourers, lazy tradesmen, merchants, boys, girls, slaves, malefactors, and profligate debauchees, who were animated solely by the prospect of spoil and plunder, and hoped to make their fortunes by this holy campaign. Eighty thousand of this miserable rabble set out under the command of Peter the Hermit, and Walter the Needy. The rest followed under different leaders. They committed dreadful ravages in passing through Europe, and multitudes perished before they arrived in Asia. We cannot here give a history of the progress of this mighty army of pilgrims, but it is sufficient to observe that but a handful of them lived to return.

A second crusade was preached up by St. Barnard, the Abbot of Clairval, whom Mr. Milner has tried to make out, a humble and holy man. He is represented by historians as running from town to town, performing numberless miracles to promote the cause of the holy war. The *miracle of miracles*, according to him, was his prevailing on the emperour Conrad III. to take upon him the cross, which he was not inclined to do. The second army of cross-bearers was not numbered, but it was immensely great. It was led on by the emperour Conrad, and most of them perished in the expedition.

Notwithstanding these unsuccessful campaigns, a blind infatuation prevailed, and a third crusade was undertaken by the emperour Frederick Barbarossa. Richard I. king of England was engaged in this crusade.

A fourth crusade was undertaken by Baldwin, count of Flanders; in this expedition Constantinople was taken, which was then inhabited by christians.

After this, a holy war was proclaimed in France against the poor innocent Albigenses; and thousands of them were slain by a band of bloody cross-bearers, for the glory of God, and the good of the church. Multitudes of Baptists perished in this bloody scene, as we shall show more fully when we come to their history.

These wars, impiously called holy, were carried on in the twelfth and thirteenth centuries; they set all Europe in commotion; they drained kingdoms of their inhabitants, and filled the east with wretches, rapine, and blood. But we can pursue their history no farther. From the crusades a number of the orders of knighthood arose.

INDULGENCIES.

The sale of indulgencies was one of the most impious and infamous kinds of traffick, practised by the church of Rome. The bishops had long made a trade of the vices of mankind; that is, they compounded with transgressors, and for certain sums remitted the severe penances, which they had been sentenced to endure; and sinners, especially rich ones, finding it less troublesome to pay their money than to repent of their crimes, the bishops soon established a gainful trade. Every order of ecclesiasticks had their peculiar modes of fleecing the people. The monks could not sell pardons, but they carried about the country the relicks of the saints, and permitted the deluded multitude to see, touch, and embrace them, at certain fixed prices. And thus the monastick orders gained as much by this rare-show, as the bishops did by their indulgencies.*

But at length the popes engrossed this profitable traffick to themselves; and Leo X. who afterwards hurled his thunderbolts against Martin Luther, for the purpose of replenishing his exhausted coffers, employed certain monks to travel abroad, to promote the sale of indulgencies.

* Mosheim, vol. III. p. 81.

Supererogation.

Among these detestable characters none acted a more conspicuous part, than a Dominican friar, named John Tetzel. He travelled through Germany, proclaiming the pardons of the pope, promising to sinners of every description, for fixed prices, a full remission of all sins past, present, and future. In describing the efficacy of indulgencies, he, among other horrid expressions, declared that, *if any one had defloured the mother of God, he had power from the pope to efface his guilt.* He further boasted that he had saved more souls from hell by these Indulgencies, than St. Peter had converted to christianity by his preaching.*

SUPEREROGATION.

Cardinal Cajetan declared that *one drop of Christ's blood was sufficient to redeem the whole world, and that the remaining quantity, that was shed in the garden and on the cross, was left as a legacy to the church, to be disposed of by his vice-gerent on earth.*†

The doctrine of supererogation had been invented long before this time. This doctrine was founded upon the false supposition, that the superabundant good deeds of the saints, had procured a boundless treasure of merit, which might, by the pope, be applied to the benefit of others.

The preaching of Indulgencies in Germany, opened the eyes of many, roused the zeal of Luther, and the reformation in the sixteenth century immediately succeeded.‡

---

* The pardon-mongers collected immense sums from every nation they were sent to, as appears by one friar Samson, who collected 120,000 crowns among the Swiss only.   *Trial of Antichrist, p.* 138.

† Trial of Antichrist, p. 21.

‡ In the second volume of Saurin's sermons, Mr. Robinson, the translator, has inserted an extract from the tax-book of the Roman Chancery. There we meet with such articles as these :

"Absolution for killing one's father or mother, 1 ducat, 5 carlins.

Ditto for all the acts of lewdness committed by a clerk, with a dispensation to be capable of taking orders, and to hold ecclesiastical benefits, &c. 36 tournois, 3 ducats.

Ditto for one who shall keep a concubine, with a dispensation to take orders, &c. 21 tournois, 5 ducats, 9 carlins.

As if this traffick were not scandalous enough of itself, it is added, *Take notice particularly*, that such graces and dispensations are not granted to the *poor ;* for not having wherewith to pay, they cannot be *comforted.*

The zeal of the reformers against the church of Rome ceaseth to appear intemperate in my eye, when I consider these detestable enormities."

Some Account of the Persecutions which have been carried on by the Church of Rome.

THIS church, among other enormities, is covered with the blood of saints, which is crying for vengeance on its polluted head. The murders and cruelties of which this bloody community has been guilty, can be but briefly touched upon here; but it is supposed, if I mistake not, that three millions of lives have been sacrificed to the persecuting rage of the papal power. Among these, upwards of a million were of the people called Waldenses or Albigenses.

On the fatal night of St. Bartholomews, August 24, 1572, about seventy thousand persons were murdered in Paris, in the most barbarous manner, by the influence of the pope, and by the instrumentality of the bloodthirsty Charles IX. Within thirty years, there were murdered in France 39 princes, 148 counts, 234 barons, 147,518 gentlemen, and 760,000 persons of inferiour rank in life, but whose blood equally called for justice. Three hundred thousand of these were murdered in a few years, by that furious catholick, Charles IX.*

The massacre of St. Bartholomews happened in the following manner; a match was concluded between Henry, (afterwards Henry IV.) the young king of Navarre, a protestant, and the French King's sister. The heads of the protestants were invited to celebrate the nuptials at Paris, with the infernal view of butchering them all, if possible, in one night. This horrid scene is thus described by the author of the Trial of Antichrist : "Exactly at midnight on the eve of St. Bartholomews, (so called) 1572, the alarm bell was rung in the Palais Royale, as the signal of death. About five hundred protestant barons, knights and gentlemen, who had come from all parts to honour the wedding, were, among the rest, barbarously butchered in their beds. The gentlemen, officers of the chamber, governours, tutors, and household servants of the king of Navarre, and prince of Conde, were driven out of the chambers where they slept in the Louvre, and being in the court, were massacred in the king's presence.

* Many of the Waldenses and Albigenses are included in this number.

The slaughter was now general throughout the city, and as Thuanus writes, "that the very channels ran down with blood into the river." This was, however, magnified as a glorious action, and the king, who was one of the most active murderers, boasted that he had put 70,000 *hereticks* to death. I might quote the words of a French author, who wrote the history of France, from the reign of Henry II. to Henry IV. and say, " How strange and horrible a thing it was, in a great town, to see at least 60,000 men with pistols, pikes, cutlasses, poniards, knives, and other bloody instruments, run, swearing and blaspheming the sacred Majesty of God, through the streets and into houses, where most cruelly they massacred all, whomsoever they met, without regard of estate, condition, sex, or age. The streets paved with bodies cut and hewed to pieces; the gates and entries of houses, palaces, and public places, dyed with blood. Shouting and hallooings of the murderers, mixed with continual noise of pistols and calivers discharged; the pitiful cries and shrieks of those that were murdering. Slain bodies cast out of the windows upon the stones, and drawn through the dirt. Strange noise of whistlings, breaking of doors and windows with bills and stones. The spoiling and sacking of houses. Carts, some carrying away the spoils, and others the dead bodies, which were thrown into the river Seine, all now red with blood, which ran out of the town and from the king's palace." While the horrid scene was transacting, many priests ran about the city, with crucifixes in one hand and daggers in the other, to encourage the slaughter."*

In the short reign of the ever to be execrated popish Mary, queen of England, there were burnt in that kingdom, one archbishop, four bishops, twenty-one preachers, eight gentlemen, eighty-four artificers, a hundred husbandmen and labourers, twenty-six wives, twenty widows, nine unmarried women, two boys and two infants.

Forty thousand perished in the Irish massacre, in 1641.

In a very short time, there were hanged, burned, buried alive, and beheaded, 50,000 persons in the Netherlands.

* Trial of Antichrist, p. 134-5.

The Greek Church.

The single order of Jesuits alone are computed, in the space of thirty or forty years, to have put to death 900,000 christians, who deserted from popery. And the Inquisition, the bloody instrument of papal vengeance, in the space of about thirty years, destroyed, by various torture, 150,000.*

We shall now take leave of this corrupt and bloody church. It has evidently been declining between two and three hundred years. The pope, its once furious and powerful head, is now reduced to a state of humiliation and dependence. But the instrument of his reduction has become so unpopular, that christians generally do not appear to regard with much interest, the astonishing change of circumstances in this troubler of nations, and bloodthirsty enemy of the church of God.†

THE GREEK CHURCH.

This name is given to a very large body of christians, who reside in the east. The Greek church is said to be as large or larger than the Roman, and is probably as much loaded with unnecessary ceremonies; but it is not sunk so deep in absurdity and blood.

The history of the Greek church is covered with obscurity, and but a very brief view of it can be given here. Multitudes of the first converts to christianity resided where were once the ancient republicks of Greece, and spake the Greek language, in which the New-Testament was written.

* Trial of Antichrist throughout.

† Notwithstanding the cruelties and abominations of the church of Rome, it is charitably hoped that amongst the millions of this community, there always have been many humble and pious souls; but I cannot gain the least evidence, that any one of the popes was acquainted with the power of godliness, and many wonder that any real christian should remain in a church so superstitious and vile. But we can have but a faint view now of the darkness in which all were involved, and of the danger to which dissenters were exposed. All who dissented from popery were denounced hereticks, and the thunder of excommunication followed them, and they were immediately excluded from all civil rights. Hereticks could make no wills, nor acquire any thing by the testaments of others. They could not be admitted to any dignities, offices, or communities. They could not avail themselves of any courts, or derive any benefits from laws. Their friends could not obtain decent burial for them. They were exposed to popular contempt and hatred; in some cases to banishment, in others to imprisonment, confiscation of property and ignominious deaths. *Robinson's Ecclesiastical Researches, p.* 144.

Separation of the Greek and Latin Churches.

Constantine, the Roman emperour, soon after he had embraced christianity, removed the seat of empire from Rome, in Italy, to Byzantium, in Thrace, and having enlarged, enriched, and adorned it, solemnly conferred on it his own name, and called it Constantinople, that is, Constantine's city. It still remains one of the most magnificent cities of the east, and is now the seat of the Turkish emperour.

Eusebius was the bishop of Constantinople in the time of Constantine, while Sylvester was bishop of Rome. As the new metropolis arose in grandeur, its bishop experienced a proportionable increase of dignity and opulence, and the bishop of Rome soon found in him an ambitious and powerful rival. These two imperial bishops struggled hard for dominion ; each claimed the whole, secured what they could gain, and in the end divided the command of all the churches in christendom, or at least of those who would submit to their authority.

The bishop of Rome took the name of Pope, from the Greek word *papas*, which signifies *father ;* the bishop of Constantinople assumed the Old-Testament title of Patriarch, and by this appellation he is yet distinguished. The struggles between the Roman pontiff and the Grecian patriarch, for preeminence and power, were long and obstinate ; both claimed the title of Universal Bishop, which was finally conferred on the pope, in 606, by the emperour Phocas, and thenceforward the bishop of Rome arose superiour to his rival in dignity and crimes.

Constantinople and a considerable part of the ancient dominions of the Greek church, has, for a number of centuries, been in possession of the Mahometans, and the patriarch himself exercises the high functions of his office, merely by the toleration of the disciples of the prophet of Mecca.

The bishops of Rome and Constantinople continued their rivalship, and reciprocal accusations, without coming to an open rupture, until the eleventh century. Then a war of anathemas commenced ; they hurled their thunderbolts at each other, and a total separation took place between the Greek and Latin churches, which, notwithstanding the soothing artifices of the popes and Jesuits, has never been healed.

Russia, a Branch of the Greek Church.

Besides the patriarch already mentioned, there are three other Grecian bishops, distinguished by this high appellation. They reside at Jerusalem, Antioch, and Alexandria. But the patriarch of Constantinople is the head of the Greek church; all the other patriarchs, and all the Episcopal dignitaries are nominated by him.

The government of the Greek church is reputed a mild aristocracy. The patriarch of Constantinople is elected by twelve bishops, who reside nearest that famous capital; but the right of confirming his election, as well as of the other patriarchs, belongs only to the Turkish emperour. After the patriarch is elected, he is presented to the Sultan with a handsome fee. The Sultan's approbation runs in some such style as this; "I command such an one to go and reside as bishop, &c. according to the ancient custom and idle ceremonies of those people." The patriarchs of Alexandria have always avoided this submission to the Mahometan Sovereign. The rest yield to it; and on these terms more than two hundred thousand christian Greeks reside unmolested in Constantinople.

One of the largest branches of the Greek church is in Russia; the millions of that empire are included in this extensive community, and are under the superintendence of the powerful patriarch of Constantinople.

Some further account of the Greek church, of its boundaries, &c. and also of the Oriental churches, will be given in the succeeding chapter.

The Greek church has never carried persecution to any great extent; this may be owing to the mildness of its spirit, but probably more to its external circumstances, for it has, for many ages, been hemmed in, and restrained by the Mahometan powers.

Thus we see that the Greek and Roman churches have always embraced by far the greatest part of what is called the christian world. In these two great establishments, there are probably contained one fifth, and perhaps one fourth of the inhabitants of the globe. In these extensive communities we find popes, patriarchs, bishops, archbishops, rites and ceremonies in abundance; but the humble followers of Jesus have generally been found in every age, among those who have dissented from them.

The dissenting sects, both in the Greek and Latin churches, have been numerous; some were doubtless wild and fantastick, others were humble and devout; but they have all been branded with the odious name of hereticks, thrown by historians into one common mass of refuse, and devoted to infamy here and misery hereafter. This vast pile of heretical lumber has been rummaged over by every protestant sect, in search of their sentimental relatives and friends. All have succeeded in their own estimation, and the success which the Baptists have had will be related when we come to speak of our brethren in foreign countries and ancient times.

Before we leave this subject, it may be proper just to observe, that there was a large body of dissenters among the Greeks, called by the general name of Massalians and Euchites, the one a Hebrew and the other a Greek name, both signifying a people that pray, because they placed religion not in speculation, but in devotion and piety.

The Euchites among the Greeks were similar to the Waldenses or Waldensians among the Romans. The terms, Waldenses, Valenses or Vadois (all of the same import) signify the people of the vallies, and were applied in early times to those, who, tired of tyranny, pomp, and oppression, retired to obscure retreats where they might enjoy gospel purity and religious freedom. And in the end, all of their sentiments, and many who were not, were called Waldenses, whether they dwelt in vallies or on mountains, in cities or in caves: Just as a sect of christians are called Moravians, whether they dwell in Moravia, in England, in Greenland, or the West-India Islands. And the terms Euchites and Waldenses answered to that of Non-conformist in England, which every reader will understand. Among the English non-conformists, are comprehended Presbyterians, Independents, Baptists, Methodists, Quakers, and so on. And so among the Greek Euchites and the Roman Waldenses, were a great variety of sects, who maintained a great diversity of opinions and practices, and among them were many who would be called Baptists, as we shall attempt to show in the next chapter but one.

PROTESTANTS.

Long before the time of Luther many had attempted to shake off the papal yoke, and revive the spirit of godliness among the multitudes, who were groaning beneath an oppressive load of absurdities and superstitions. Among the principal men of this character we may reckon Claude of Turin in Piedmont, Peter de Bruys and Henry his disciple, Peter Waldo of Lyons in France; Wickliff, the morning of the Reformation; John Huss, and Jerome of Prague; either of these men, had the time arrived for the pillars of Babylon to be shaken, and had Providence seconded their views, might have done as much as was performed by Luther. They successively made noble stands against the man of sin, and sometimes struck terrour even to the seat of the beast; and by their evangelical exertions, multitudes of their fellowmen were enlightened, and led into the paths of salvation. But the Dragon was permitted to make successful war against them, and most of them fell victims to his rage. Their followers were either destroyed or dispersed, and their names and principles were covered with infamy and disgrace. Wickliff was hunted with violence at first, but he outlived the persecuting storm, which had been raised against him, and died in peace at the parish of Lutterworth in England in 1387. But forty years after, his bones were dug up by order of the council of Constance, and publickly burnt. Wickliff's followers were called Lollards, and among them were many Baptists, as we shall show when we come to treat of their history.

But while the Roman pontiff slumbered in security at the head of the church, and saw nothing throughout the vast extent of his dominion but tranquillity and submission; and while the worthy and pious professors of genuine christianity almost despaired of seeing that reformation on which their most ardent desires and expectations were bent; an obscure and inconsiderable person arose, on a sudden, in 1517, and laid the foundation of this long expected change, by opposing, with undaunted resolution, his single force to the torrent of papal ambition and despotism. This extraordinary man was Martin Luther, a native of Aisleben in Saxony, where he was born in

1483. Luther was a man of a bold and fearless spirit, and well qualified to hear undaunted the terrifick thunders of the pope, and to execute the work, which, we cannot hesitate to believe, he was raised up by Divine Providence to perform. But although his virtues were many, his failings were great; and his temptations to think more highly of himself than any fallible man ought to think, were many. Soon after he began his successful career, he drew the attention of most of the European world, not because of his own personal greatness, but on account of the glorious work in which he took the lead. Pope Leo X. and all his creatures, both ecclesiastical and civil, fixed their jealous eyes on this threatening innovator, and levelled their vengeance against his devoted head. On the other hand, all the pious, who groaned in bondage, looked up to him with the most lively hopes and expectations. The powerful Elector of Saxony, soon took him under his patronage; other princes of Germany became his admirers and defenders, and the sovereigns of other kingdoms invited him and his associates, into their dominions. With all these stimulations to pride, with all these attentions from enemies and friends, it is not altogether strange, that Luther became conceited and dogmatical, and discovered a portion of that intolerance towards others, which had been exercised towards him. Had Luther possessed the mild and yielding spirit of Melancthon, his cotemporary and successor, he might not have withstood, with such heroick fortitude, the vehemence of the papal power, but he doubtless would have treated with more condescension, those who importuned him to carry the reformation farther than he did, and especially the German Baptists, who vainly hoped to see a reformation in the article of baptism.

But it is not my intention or desire, to detract one particle of merit from this distinguished reformer; nor will the limits of this review permit me to make any further strictures on his character. He was educated an Augustine monk, and in the monastick habit, under the vows of celibacy, he began that mighty career, which elevated him to the pinnacle of fame, and terminated in essential and abundant good to mankind.

The traffick of indulgencies, which was carried to a most scandalous and impious height, by the famous, or rather infamous Tetzel, provoked his resentment and aroused his zeal. At Wittemberg, in 1517, he began by declaiming against the sale of popish pardons; his censures were at first levelled against Tetzel in particular; next against the whole band of infamous taxgatherers, who were fleecing the multitude by the most iniquitous and detestable means, ever devised by ecclesiastical avarice; and finally he proceeded to attack the authority and supremacy of the pope. And thus by gradual steps proceeded forward that memorable revolution in Europe, called the Reformation.

Luther does not appear at first to have had any thing more in view than to oppose the abominable traffick of indulgencies, and to reform some of the superstitions and errours of popery; but he was carried forward by the ardour of his own zeal much beyond the bounds he had contemplated; and in the end was driven, by the thundering vehemence of the Roman pontiff, and his insolent emissaries, to a total separation from a church, so full of vengeance and corruption.

About three years after Luther had began his new course of writing and preaching, he was solemnly excommunicated by the pope; but this terrible sentence he treated with the utmost derision and contempt, and " on the 10th of December, 1520, he had a pile of wood erected without the walls of the city Wittemberg, and there, in the presence of a prodigious multitude of people of all ranks and orders, committed to the flames both the bull which had been published against him, and the canons and decretals relating to the pope's supreme jurisdiction." From this period Luther formed the project of founding a church in opposition to that of Rome; his bold and successful attempts flew on the wings of fame to distant regions, multitudes were encouraged by his example to throw off the popish yoke, and rally round the standard of the Saxon Reformer, and the principles of the reformation were henceforward propagated with an amazing rapidity through all the countries of Europe. But still Luther was in imminent danger from the emissaries of Rome; he was conducted by his patron the Elector of Saxony, to the Castle of Wartenberg, where he resided in safety ten months, and employed his time in writing and translating the scriptures. From this retreat, which he called his Patmos, he again repaired to the city of Wittemberg, and in a short time, he, with the assistance of other learned men, completed the translation of the Bible in the German language. This being spread abroad among the people produced sudden and almost incredible effects, and a prodigious number of persons in different regions received the light of truth.

Hitherto the principles and progress of the reformation appear pleasant and commendable. But we must now leave, for a while, the humble promoters of evangelical piety, and listen to the din of arms, and behold with grief and sorrow the sanguinary conflicts of contending religious parties.

The reformation soon became a thing of political consequence, and was prostituted to purposes altogether foreign to the genuine spirit of christianity. Many of the German princes seconded Luther's exertions from motives of civil policy; they were glad to free themselves from the power of the pope, which they had long found troublesome and oppressive: they therefore declared in favour of the new religion; their subjects followed their example, and whole provinces and kingdoms were at once in arms against popery, and enlisted on the side of the great Reformer. These princes formed a confederacy, and in connexion with Luther and his associates, in 1529, entered a solemn *Protest* against the oppressive measures of the papal power, and hence arose the denomination of Protestants, which from this period was given to all who espoused the principles of the reformation, whether they did it from evangelical motives or from worldly policy. Soon protestants and papists became two powerful contending parties; many reasoned and debated, but princes and all who would follow them, decided their controversies in the field of battle. But we cannot pursue, any farther, an account of the religious commotions, which now began to agitate the kingdoms of Europe. It is sufficient to observe, that under Luther, a church arose, which was called after his name, and which has, for almost three hundred years, been the established religion of a considerable part of Europe. But the Lutheran church is acknowledged to be the least removed from popery of any of the protestant churches; the church of England not excepted. Luther did much, but he left much to be done. He opposed and rejected some of the superstitions and absurdities of popery; but he still retained many of them in his creed. The pope's supremacy, and all the prerogatives of the papacy he renounced, together with the doctrines of purgatory, transubstantiation, and so on. But he established, or took the lead in establishing a national hierarchy to be fenced round and protected by the civil power. He seemed to have no notion of founding churches of visible believers only, but all who were comprehended within certain bounds, and who assented to his creed, were admitted to communion. Luther rejected *transubstantiation*, but he substituted in its room what he called *consubstantiation*, a word almost as long, and which conveyed ideas just as unscriptural and absurd.*

The Lutheran church has its Augsburg confession, its liturgies, its holy days, its bishops, superintendents, and so on. It has but one archbishop, and he is the primate of Sweden. But Luther's exertions were, notwithstanding, of essential service to mankind; for in opposing the doctrines of popery, he warmly advocated the sufficiency of revelation to instruct mankind in all the duties of religion. This main principle of all reformations, Luther maintained more clearly in theory than practice, and multitudes by following his maxims up to their legitimate consequences, carried forward the reformation, much farther than he had done.

Out of the Lutheran church arose another, which was called the reformed, and which was founded by Ulrich Zuinglius, a native of Switzerland. Zuinglius began a successful opposition to indulgencies, and to the whole fabrick of papacy in Switzerland, about the time that Luther

* According to the papists, the bread and wine employed in the sacrament of the supper, are, by a miraculous operation, changed into the real body and blood of Christ. This is called the doctrine of transubstantiation. This doctrine Luther rejected, but still he would not admit, that the elements of bread and wine were merely symbols, but maintained that the body and blood of Christ were really present in the sacrament, the same as two elements are united in *red hot iron*. This he called consubstantiation. This nonsensical doctrine was strenuously maintained by this famous reformer, and occasioned violent disputes between him and Carolostadt, Zuinglius, Bucer and others.

began in Saxony. The Swiss reformer differed widely from Luther in many articles, and was much more evangelical and consistent in his views of the eucharist, and of other matters both of faith and practice. But he fell in the battle that was fought in Urich, in 1530, between the protestants and catholicks.*

Calvin began his course a little after Luther and Zuinglius. He was born at Noyon, in Picardy, in France, in 1509. Luther, Zuinglius, and Calvin, became the heads of three distinguished parties, which were called after their names. They acted at first in concert, in the great business of the Reformation, but soon they clashed most violently with each other both in their sentiments and measures.

Besides these three reformers, there were a number of others who engaged with much zeal and success in the protestant cause, and were distinguished in their day for various qualities and performances, and for a common principle of opposition to the church of Rome. Among these we may reckon Melancthon, Carolostadt, Bucer, Erasmus, Menno, Oecolampadius, and others. Luther and Calvin, however, have shared most of the glory of the great and important change which was effected in the religious world in the beginning of the sixteenth century. But Calvin surpassed not only Luther, but all his cotemporaries in learning and parts, as he did most of them in obstinacy, asperity, and turbulence. Luther fixed his stand at Wittemberg in Saxony, and was succeeded in the general care of the great hierarchy, which he established, by the soft and complying Melancthon. Calvin made his stand at Geneva, on the confines of Switzerland. Calvin is famous for his defence of predestination and absolute decrees, and also for his opposition to the Anabaptists. From Calvin's followers originated the Presbyterians ; and many other sects, who have adopted either in full or in part, his notions of

* It was not indeed to perform the sanguinary office of a soldier that Zuinglius was present at this engagement, but with a view to encourage and animate by his counsels and exhortations, the valiant defenders of the protestant cause: A lame cause that needs the defence of the sanguinary soldier. In a note, Dr. Moshiem has given a much more satisfactory apology for Zuinglius, than the above, which is found in the body of his work. " At this time the Swiss were universally obliged to take the field. Neither the ministers of the gospel nor the professors of theology were exempted from military service." Vol. iv. p. 353.

predestination and grace, have consented to be called by his name.*

The Church of England assumes the name of *Protestant*, although multitudes have *protested* against her on various accounts. This church arose about the time of the terrible tumults of Munster, which have been so uniformly and exultingly, but falsely ascribed to the German Anabaptists. It was founded by the amorous Henry VIII. a prince, who, in vices and abilities, was surpassed by none who swayed the sceptre in his age. Henry at first opposed with the utmost vehemence, both the doctrines and views of Luther ; but because the pope would not grant him a divorce according to his mind, he renounced his jurisdiction and supremacy, and was declared by the parliament and people, *Supreme Head, on earth, of the Church of England*. Henry put down one thousand, four hundred and forty eight popish religious houses, and seized on their lands, amounting to one hundred and eighty three thousand, seven hundred and seven pounds per annum ; he gave his subjects an English translation of the Bible, but ordered all such books to be destroyed as might help to explain it to them. The same monarch, who renounced the dominion of Rome, yet superstitiously retained the

---

* The denomination *Reformed* was given to those protestant churches, which did not embrace the doctrine and discipline of Luther. The title was first assumed by the French protestants, who were often called Hugonots, and afterwards became the common denomination of all the Calvinistical churches on the continent This great body of dissenters from Lutheranism, Mosheim describes under the general denomination of the Reformed Church. But this church was at first composed of many parts, which preserved a nominal union for a time, and then split into a multitude of sects and parties. Out of the Reformed Church arose, among other sects, the Arminians and Quakers. The Arminians were so called from James Arminius, who died at Leyden in Holland, in 1609, just a hundred years after Calvin was born. Arminius warmly opposed Calvin's notions, respecting predestination and absolute decrees, but he did not carry his system so far as many of his followers have done. The doctrine of falling from grace he left doubtful, but his followers soon determined it in the affirmative. Arminius met with severe treatment from his reformed brethren. His party flourished for a time, and then dwindled away. But his peculiar sentiments have prevailed extensively, and are now imbibed by multitudes in every sect of protestants.

The Church of England, since the time of the intolerant Laud, has generally embraced the doctrines of Arminius. The Lutherans are also more inclined to Arminianism than Calvinism. Episcopalians and Lutherans subscribe their Augsburg confession and thirty-nine articles, and immediately preach and write directly against them. Calvin and Arminius have their partisans in every country, and thousands spend much time, in disputing about these favourite chiefs, (of whom they know but little) which they might devote to a much better purpose.

greatest part of its errours along with its imperious and persecuting spirit. Henry, in a word, renounced the dominion of the pope, that he might become a pope himself, and the Church of England, as established by law at this time, was not *a new church*, but an *old one fitted up in a new fashion*. It underwent some improvements in the reign of the young and amiable prince Edward VI. the son and successor of Henry. But still there is, in the opinion of many, great room for improvement in this ecclesiastical body. Whoever sways the British sceptre, whether male or female, is of course the head of the English church, and the hopeful Prince of Wales will, probably, according to the course of nature and law, soon succeed to this important station.

In the reign of Edward VI. but more especially in that of his sister Elizabeth, the successor of the furious and implacable Mary, many were desirous of a purer church than had hitherto been established. These persons were called Puritans, and under this denomination was, for a long time, comprehended a large body of English dissenters and non-conformists, among whom there existed a great variety of opinions and practices. From the Puritans originated the Independents, and many of the Baptists in England, the Congregationalists of America, and a multitude of other sects and parties, whom the limits of this work will not permit us even to name.

To close these brief sketches, it may be proper to observe, that the great body of christians who protested against the church of Rome, and who, for that reason, received the general name of Protestants, preserved a common bond of union, so long as they were oppressed and endangered by the church of Rome. But when they arrived beyond its power, they filed off into a multitude of parties. Some stood by their Augsburg confession, their Helvetic and Genevan creeds, their English liturgy, and so on, and resolved to remain by the standards their leaders had set up. Others went in pursuit of farther light, and those, who took the Scriptures for their guide, actually found it, while those who followed their mistaken impulses, and capricious fancies, ran wild into the mazes of errour and deception, and exhibited to the view of astonished beholders, the most fantastick reveries and delusions. The stronger sects of Protestants forged chains for the weaker, and prepared dungeons and flames for all, who would not wear them.

It could not be expected that a people lately come out of Babylon, should, all at once, understand the principles of religious freedom. The old popish idol of uniformity was set up in Protestant countries, and all were commanded, under penalties of different kinds, but always severe, to bow down and worship it. But a milder policy has succeeded, and we trust the period will arrive, when not only the righteous principles of religious freedom, but the glorious system which contains them, shall prevail from the rising to the setting sun, and the knowledge of the glory of God, cover the earth as the waters do the sea.

MISSIONS.

THE apostles and early preachers were almost all Missionaries, and their evangelical journies were performed on missionary ground. They had no regard to parish lines, nor ecclesiastical districts; they asked not for licences, they waited not for appointments, they sought no emoluments, but by the call of God they went forth, dependent on the treasury of heaven they journied, and aided by the common succours and miraculous influences of the Holy Spirit, they went every where preaching the word and performing wonders in the name of the Lord Jesus.

The church of Rome has done much in the missionary cause. Multitudes have been sent forth in every age by that august community. Some of them were doubtless better than their masters, and rendered essential service to mankind, while others were artful and ambitious men, full of every thing vile and detestable, and destitute of every thing good; and having imbibed the spirit of their masters, laboured more for the glory of the See of Rome, than for the everlasting benefit of the heathen.

The priests at Rome, in many instances, drew geographical lines of parishes and bishopricks among the pagan nations, and sent forth booted apostles with military fame, to dragoon the perishing heathen into a belief of christianity, and nations were baptized at the point of the sword.

In 1622, there was founded at Rome by pope Gregory XV. an institution called *The Congregation for propagating the faith*. It was enriched with ample revenues by Urban VIII. and an incredible number of donors, who were emulous to excel each other in munificent acts. By this Congregation a vast number of missionaries were sent forth into the remotest parts of the world ; and multitudes of persons, in the fiercest and most barbarous nations, were converted to the profession of the Catholick faith. In India and the inaccessible regions of China and Japan, many thousands were won over by the artful and industrious Jesuits and monks. But these insidious men temporized and dissembled, and it is more proper to say that they were converted to paganism, than that the pagans were converted to christianity. But their boasted career was of short duration. By interfering in political affairs, they fell under the suspicions of the jealous emperours, were furiously expelled from their dominions, and many thousands of their converts perished by the sword, and the rest returned to paganism, if returning it might be called.

But leaving the church of Rome, we will take a short view of the Protestant communities which have made laudable exertions for the promotion of missions. And among these the Moravians deserve first to be mentioned. It is said by Dr. Haweis, that no denomination of Protestants has displayed an equal degree of zeal, or met with equal success in their missionary labours. To a number of the different tribes of the American Indians ; to many of the West India Islands ; to the frozen regions of Greenland ; to the coast of Coromandel ; and to the ignorant and brutish Hottentots, the zealous Moravians have carried the word of life, and many thousands have, by their means, been converted to the Lord.

The Danish nation began in the missionary cause, about a hundred years ago. Their labours have been directed to Greenland and the Malabar coast, and multitudes have been converted to the profession of christianity at least.

The Church of England possesses ample revenues for missionary purposes, but she has hitherto done but little.

But within a few years past a remarkable missionary spirit has prevailed on both sides of the Atlantic. The

Evangelical Missionary Society of London has done much and promises to do much more. The Baptist Missionary Society of England is a most important establishment, and will be noticed in its proper place. Many noble exertions have been made in the Missionary cause by the American Pedo-baptists; and the American Baptists have not been idle in this important cause, as will be shown towards the close of this work.

The present is an eventful period. The nations of the earth are convulsed, and are dashing against each other with furious rage. On the one hand we hear nothing but the clangour of arms and the rage of battle. The devoted fields of Europe are drenched with human gore, and covered with the carcases of the slain. The god of war is driving his crimson car amidst carnage and blood. But the God of armies is riding in his chariot of salvation, and gathering his elect from the four winds of heaven, and increasing exceedingly the number of redeemed souls. May the time soon come, when he whose right it is to reign shall come, and when all nations shall bow to his sceptre.

I have extended this article to a much greater length than I at first intended, but still it is but a very brief view of the extensive subject of which it professes to treat. It has been selected mostly from Mosheim, Milner, Robinson, and Millot. I have not referred to all the parts of these works from which I have made quotations. This would have made an abundance of references, and was, I conceived, altogether unnecessary, as I have stated no facts, nor advanced any sentiments which can be disputed.

This Compendium is intended to be introductory to the chapters, which will immediately follow, and may serve as a key to many events and circumstances, which will there be referred to.

CHAP. II.

A MINIATURE HISTORY OF BAPTISM.

BAPTISM, as it was instituted by the great Christian Lawgiver, was a plain and significant rite. And for a long time, after corruptions in doctrine had crept into the church, baptism was maintained in its original simplicity and purity, and was free from that pompous round of ceremonies, with which it was afterwards encumbered.

Nothing is more evident, than that in the primitive ages of the church, professed believers were the only subjects of this sacred rite, and immersion or dipping was the only mode. But in process of time, baptism passed from visible believers, to catechumen minors, and from them to unconscious babes. And from immersion it was reduced to pouring, then to sprinkling, and now to any mode, which the inventive fancies of capricious candidates may devise, provided always, that some part of them be *wet*.

The limits of this review will not permit me to do any thing more than merely to glance at the most prominent parts of this extensive subject, and relate some of the most remarkable circumstances which have attended the progress of baptism from its introduction to the present time.

The New-Testament account of baptism demands our first attention; and there we find, that the first performer of this sacred rite, and who administered it to the great Messiah and to multitudes of repenting Jews, was John the Baptist.

This singular person is supposed to have been born in Hebron; he began preaching the doctrine of repentance in the wilderness of Judea, and soon multitudes, from all the region round about, flocked to the harbinger of the Messiah, and confessing their sins were baptized by him in Jordan and Enon.

But John's ministry was of short duration. By some means he was introduced to king Herod, whom he reproved for living in adultery with his brother Philip's wife. For this honest freedom John was cast into prison, where he was assassinated by the means of the guilty and enraged Herodias.*

For the purpose of performing his great work, John selected a number of baptismal stations. The first appears to have been at the river Jordan. Mr. Robinson supposes it was on its eastern bank, about four or five miles from its mouth, where it discharges itself into the lake Asphaltites, or the Dead Sea, and near the place where it was miraculously parted for the Israelites to pass over it, when they entered into the promised land. "About half a mile from the river, the remains of a convent, dedicated to John the Baptist, are yet to be seen : for the Syrian monks availed themselves of the zeal of early pilgrims, who aspired to the honour of being baptized, where they supposed John baptized Jesus."

As much has been said to prove that John could no where in Judea find water of sufficient depth for immersion, it may be proper to give a brief description of the river Jordan, and also of Enon near to Salim.

* The Catholicks have paid the most extravagant veneration to the memory of John the Baptist; and the most ridiculous fables are told respecting him. John himself lies all over the Catholick world. His head is in the city of Amiens, in France. That finger, with which he pointed to Christ, when he said, " Behold the Lamb of God," is at Florence : his others are at different places. The knights of St. John have his right hand, with which he baptized Jesus, enclosed in one of the richest and most elegant shrines ; it is made of solid gold, and adorned with a profusion of jewels. A piece of the stone, on which Jesus stood when he was baptized, is at Chiusi, in Sienna. And there is another at the Lateran at Rome. It is a fact, that of all the saints in paradise, St. John the Baptist bore the bell in the middle ages of the Catholick church. When no new baptisteries were wanted, old ones were enlarged with vestries, chapels, oratories, and adjoining houses. Then they were adorned with inscriptions, pictures, mosaick work, statues, bells, altars, plates, cups, vases, and all manner of utensils ; John being depicted on every one. Next they were endowed with houses, lands, farms, and revenues of various kinds. Blessed John the Baptist was engraved on seals, publick and private, cut in precious stones of all descriptions for rings and ornaments, exhibited on the crowns of princes, the altar cloths and other ornaments of churches, and chosen by towns, cities, and whole kingdoms as their patron. The multitude imbibed the delicious frenzy, and when the priest inquired at baptism, What is his name ? not Jove : but John was the popular cry, and the baptismal hall resounded with John—John—John !

To protestant gentlemen, who have not turned their attention to the history of this old-fashioned saint, it may, at first, appear improbable, but on examination it will be found very credible, that if a thesaurus of what relates to this subject were collected and published in one work, it would swell to the size of the Acta Sanctorum, which amount to sixty or seventy volumes in folio.

Robinson's History of Baptism, p. 4, 93, 358, 359.

It is presumed that no Baptist will be proud of the superstitious honours, which have been paid to their ancient brother, since it is evident, that all have overlooked that which made him the greatest born among women.

Jordan is a considerable river in the ancient land of Israel, and ran from north to south, through almost the whole of that once delightful country. It rises from the lake Phiala, in the mountain called Anti-Libanus, and after running fifteen miles under ground, breaks out at Peneum. A little below *Dan*, the stream forms the lake Samachonites, anciently called Menon, which is about four miles over and seven miles long. Two miles after its leaving the lake, is a stone bridge of three arches, called " Jacob's Bridge," supposed to have been built before the days of Jacob. After leaving the lake Samachonites, it runs fifteen miles further, and forms the lake, or as it is sometimes called, the *sea*, of Tiberias, which is, in its broadest part, five miles in width, and in length eighteen ; thence at its opposite end, it proceeds forward again, and after a course of sixty-five miles, some part of the way through a vast and horrid desert, the rest through a fertile region, it falls into the lake Asphaltites or the Dead Sea, where it is lost.*

Thus we see this little stream, this trifling brook, rises out of one lake, forms or passes through two others, and falls into a fourth. Morse and Parish say it is generally four or five rods wide, and nine feet deep.

Robinson says that this river, so far from wanting water, was subject to two sorts of floods, one periodical at harvest time, in which it resembled the Nile in Egypt, with which some suppose it had a subterranean communication. When this flood came down, the river rose many feet, and overflowed the lower banks, so that the lions, that lay in the thickets there, were roused up and fled. To this Jeremiah alludes : *Behold, the king of Babylon shall come up like a lion from the swelling of Jordan.* The other *swellings* of Jordan were casual, and resembled those of all other rivers in uneven countries.†

On the banks of this noble river, John the Baptist fixed one of his baptismal stations, not merely for the purpose of supplying the company, and the horses, and camels, and mules, and asses, on which they rode, with drink, as is supposed by a late Pedo-baptist writer,‡ but for the conveniency of immersing the repenting candidates.

---

* Morse's and Parish's Gazetteer.—Robinson's History of Baptism.

† Robinson's History of Baptism, p. 11, 12.   ‡ Dr. Reed.

Description of Enon.

Another of John's baptismal stations was at Enon near to Salim. " This was at least fifty miles north of the river Jordan, from the place where John had begun to baptize. One of the apostles was said to be a native of Salim, and some think this was the city of which Melchisedec was king." It is not so easy to describe Enon as Jordan, for historians and geographers are not agreed respecting it. Some suppose that Enon was a deep spring, called the *dove-spring*, or, in the figurative language of the east, the *dove's-eye ;* others think it signified the fountain of the sun ; while others are of an opinion that it was either a natural spring, an artificial reservoir, or a cavernous temple of the sun, prepared by the Canaanites, the ancient idolatrous inhabitants of the land. Such are the variety of opinions about the meaning of the word Enon. But although some things are doubtful, yet one thing is certain, it was a place where there was much water. This was sufficient for John the Baptist, and it was immaterial to him, as it is to every other Baptist, whether water be found in an artificial reservoir, or in a receptacle formed by nature, provided that it be of sufficient depth for immersion, which, for most administrators, is about three feet, and from six to nine inches. The Greek, for *much water*, is *polla udata ;* and these two little words have furnished matter for much learned criticism and many futile quibbles. " Since sprinkling came in fashion," says Mr. Robinson, " criticism, unheard of in all former ages, hath endeavoured to derive evidence for scarcity of water, from the Greek text of the Evangelist John, and to render *polla udata* not *much water*, but *many waters*, and then by an ingenious supposition, to infer that many waters signify not many waters collected into one, but waters parted into many little rills, which might all serve for sprinkling, but could not, any one of them, be used for dipping : as if one man could possibly want many brooks for the purpose of sprinkling one person at a time. It is observable, that the rivers Euphrates at Babylon, Tiber at Rome, and Jordan in Palestine, are all described by *polla udata*. The thunder which agitates clouds, charged with floods, is called the voice of the Lord upon *many waters ;* and the attachment, that no mortifications can annihilate, is a love, which *many waters* cannot quench, neither can the *floods* drown. How it comes to pass that a mode of speaking, which on every other occasion signifies *much*, should in the case of baptism signify *little*, is a question easy to answer."*

The scripture account of the baptism, which John administered, must impress the mind of every unprejudiced person, that professed believers were the subjects of his baptism, and that immersion was the only mode adopted by this ancient Baptist.

But notwithstanding the scripture account of John and his ministry is so plain, yet to serve the purposes of infant baptism, all has been thrown into confusion, covered with mystery, and reduced to insignificance. Some have pretended to find infants among John's disciples; but this is an opinion so extravagant and absurd, that but few Pedobaptist writers have advanced it.

Dr. Guyse supposed that John administered baptism by sprinkling. This opinion he expressed in the following manner: "It seems to me that the people stood in ranks, near to, or just within, the edge of the river; and John, passing along before them, threw water upon their heads or faces, with his hands or with some proper *instrument*."

The name of this divine ought always to be mentioned with respect; but this exposition is truly ridiculous, and is sarcastically, but yet ingeniously, paraphrased in a poem attributed to the late Benjamin Francis.

"The Jews in Jordan were baptiz'd,
Therefore ingenious John devis'd
A scoop or squirt, or some such thing,
With which some water he might fling
Upon the long extended rank
Of candidates, that lin'd the bank.
Be careful, John, some drops may fall
From your rare instrument on all;
But point your engine, ne'ertheless,
To those who do their sins confess.
Let no revilers in the crowd,
The holy sprinkling be allow'd."

We have seen, not long since, that John the Baptist has been most extravagantly extolled by the Roman Catholicks; but it appears that many modern Pedo-baptists very lightly esteem both John and his ministry. They would fain make us believe that the baptism which he administered, was not gospel baptism, but was merely a con-

* Robinson's History of Baptism, p. 14.

tinuation of Jewish ablutions, and that the gospel dispensation did not commence until after his death. By this supposition, John is left in a forlorn condition, for he is neither a Jew nor christian, he is neither an Old-Testament priest, nor a New-Testament minister, but stands like the young ass-colt, where two ways met, and is not permitted to go in either.

The Jews sent priests and Levites to ask of him, Who art thou ? And at another time they acknowledged they knew not whether his baptism was from heaven or of men. But notwithstanding all this the Pedo-baptists of the present day turn him over to the Jewish side. Such attempts are worthy the cause which requires their aid. Mark calls John's ministry, *The beginning of the gospel of Jesus Christ, the Son of God.* The Pedo-baptists are at liberty to make their own expositions ; but the Baptists are willing to believe that Mark's statement is correct. This novel notion of placing John under the law, leads to another absurdity respecting the baptism of the Saviour. A few years since a pamphlet was published with this very singular title, " The Baptism of Jesus Christ not to be imitated by Christians !!" The title of this piece is shocking to an obedient mind, and its contents are altogether frivolous and absurd. They go to make John a Jewish priest, and that when he baptized the Saviour, he did it with a view to introduce him into his priestly office. This singular work was published by two Pedo-baptist ministers, whose names were Fish and Crane. I know not why two learned divines should unite to publish a pamphlet, unless it were that its contents were so novel and strange, that neither was willing to take the responsibility of it alone. But they had no occasion for fear ; any thing that can afford the least relief to the tottering cause of infant baptism, will be sure to gain credit with its fearful advocates. *The baptism of Jesus Christ not to be imitated by christians,* and John consecrating Christ into the priestly office, were great discoveries ; they were handed from one to another, and have gone an extensive round of Essayists and Pamphleteers.

These groundless propositions have been amply refuted by many Baptist writers, and particularly by Dr. Baldwin, in his late work on baptism. The substance of his arguments is as follows: Had Christ been about to be consecrated into the priestly office, John, with his garment of camel's hair, and a girdle of skin about his loins, was not the person to officiate on such an occasion; but it belonged to the sons of Aaron, with their priestly vestments—And again, the consecration was to be at the door of the tabernacle, and not on the banks of Jordan—And again, none but the tribe of Levi and the house of Aaron could be admitted to the Jewish priesthood. But it is evident our Lord sprang out of Judah, of which tribe Moses spake nothing concerning priesthood*—And, finally, Christ was a priest after the order of Melchisedec, and not after the order of Aaron.†

These passages need no comment; they carry with them their own invincible testimony, that our Saviour was not consecrated a Jewish priest, and that his baptism was not a Jewish ceremony, but a christian rite. The Baptists have derived peculiar consolation from being buried with their Lord in obedience to his command, and in imitation of his example. And they have never felt conscious of any great impiety or presumption in so doing, all that Messrs. Fish, and Crane, and Worcester, and others, have said notwithstanding.‡

I have been longer on the history of John's baptism, than I should have been, were it not that so many are attempting to reason out of countenance this ancient and eminent character, and set at nought, or at least Judaize all his important ministrations. Had his name been John the Pedo-baptist, and had it been said that he sprinkled men, women, and *children*, in the synagogue and in the temple, from a bowl or bason, it is highly probable that thousands who are now seeking to invalidate his im-

---

* Heb. vii. 14.   † Baldwin on Baptism, p. 300—303.

‡ Dr. Worcester, of Salem, in a late piece upon baptism, has the following interrogation: "Does not the idea, then, of following Christ into the water, which has unhappily so powerful an effect upon many minds, partake very much of the nature of *delusion* and *superstition* ?"
"Christ's baptism," saith he, "was designed regularly to introduce him into his priestly office, according to the law of Moses, under which he commenced his ministry, and which it behoved him to fulfil."
"There is no evidence that Christ was buried in the water; and even if he were, his baptism was of an import very different from that of the baptism, which he afterwards instituted for his followers. Are we to go into the water under the idea of following Christ—into his priestly office ? Ought we to call this *delusion* and *superstition*, or ought we to call it the *height of impiety* ?"

portant offices, would have found him a place in the gospel dispensation, and considered him a very important character.

The whole account of baptism in the New-Testament is plain and intelligible, and the state of this ordinance, during the lives of the apostles, is to be gathered mostly from the book of Acts, written by Luke, the first ecclesiastical historian. It extends from the ascension of Christ to the residence of Paul at Rome, a space of more than thirty years.

"In this book there are frequent narrations of the baptism of believers, as of Cornelius, the Ethiopian eunuch, and others, but not one infant appears in the whole history; yet, no doubt, some christians had married, and had young families within the thirty years between the ascension of Jesus and the settlement of Paul at Rome. There is no mention of any of the ceremonies, which modern christians have affixed to baptism : no consecration of water, no sprinkling, no use of oils and unguents, no sponsors, no kneeling in the water, no catechumen-state, no giving a name, no renunciation of any demon, none of the innumerable additions, which, under pretence of adorning, have obscured the glory of this heavenly institute. It belongs to those who practise such additions, to say how they came by them, and under what master they serve."

From writers of unquestionable authority, it is evident, that the primitive christians continued to baptize in rivers, pools, and baths, until about the middle of the 3d century. Justin Martyr says, that they went with the catechumens to a place where there was water, and Tertullian adds, that the candidates for baptism made a profession of faith twice, once in the church, and then again when they came to the water, and it was quite indifferent whether it were the sea, or a pool, a lake, or a river, or a bath. Such are the accounts given by Justin Martyr in his Apology, and by Tertullian on baptism as quoted by Robinson.

The sacrament of baptism, says Mosheim, was administered in the first century, without the public assemblies, in places appointed and prepared for that purpose, and was performed by immersion of the whole body in the baptismal fount.*

* Ecclesiastical History, Philadelphia edition, vol. I. p. 126.

Had the professed disciples of Jesus Christ always maintained this plain and significant rite, according to its primitive form, the history of baptism would have been short, and an account of persons baptized, and the reasons and circumstances of their baptism would have composed it. But now the case is far different. The fancies, the passions, and interests of mankind, have so perverted this heavenly institute, that its history has become difficult and voluminous; and so greatly has it been varied, abused, and prostituted, that in different parts of its progress, you see no resemblance of its original form, except that some portion of the element of water is applied to animal beings in human shape. And since so large a portion of the christian world has received by inheritance a counterfeit baptism, which they will not give up, he, who would plead for that, which is apostolical and pure, must work his way against ten thousand opponents, all armed with different weapons of defence, some *forcible* and some futile, but none of them capable of producing the least conviction upon an enlightened and conscientious mind.

We must now leave the apostolical and primitive ages, for a wide wilderness of obscurity and errour; and in going over it, we shall but just glance at the most remarkable occurrences, which present themselves to our view.

The history of baptism naturally divides itself into two branches; the one regards the subjects, and the other the mode. These two branches, we shall, for the most part, treat separately; but, in some cases, it will be proper to speak of them in connexion.

The limits of this sketch are so short, and the incidents to be thrown together so numerous and varied, that the transitions must of necessity be frequent, and they may not always be the most easy; but I trust, that in the end, every unprejudiced reader will be convinced, that believers' baptism is an institution of Jesus Christ, and that infant sprinkling is an invention of men.

The subjects of baptism deserve first to be considered. We have already seen that believing men and women were the only persons baptized by John and the apostles of our Lord. From the Acts of the Apostles, from the Epistles, and from the book of Revelation, it appears that upwards of sixty churches were gathered by the apostles and primitive preachers. These churches were constituted of Jews, Proselytes, and Pagans; we have an account of many of their names, characters, and baptisms, but no mention is made of the baptism of infants, and on no occasion do infants appear.

A Roman Catholick does not hesitate to acknowledge, that infant baptism is a human tradition; but he can prove that it has been established by law—that is sufficient for his purpose, and there is an end of the business with him. But most protestants are unwilling to make this honest confession. They persist that it is found in the Bible, and their attempts to prove it have cost them an almost infinite deal of labour, which, after all, is to no purpose.

Irenæus is represented as saying, *The church received a tradition from the apostles to administer baptism to little children or infants.* Irenæus lived in the second century; he is said to have been a disciple of Polycarp, and Polycarp was a disciple of John the Evangelist. This would seem to be getting within between one and two hundred years of the point. But Dr. John Gill challenged the whole literary world to produce such a passage from the writings of Irenæus. It was afterwards acknowledged that Origen, of the third century, and not Irenæus of the second, was the writer intended.*

But it is generally supposed that Tertullian of Africa, in the third century, is the first writer who makes any mention of infant baptism, and he, (says Dr. Gill) opposed it. But his opposition is considered by Pedo-baptists as evidence in the case. If, say they, infant baptism was not then practised, why did this father oppose it? But others make very different reflections on the subject. The catechumen state had arisen to some degree of maturity in the third century. Catechumens were those who were put into a class to be catechised and instructed into the first rudiments of christianity, and when they had acquired a certain degree of knowledge, or had been in a catechumen state a certain time, they were baptized. This method of making christians is supposed to have originated at Alexandria in Egypt, and from thence in process of time, spread over the christian world. Nothing of this catechumen state is found in the New-Testament, and at what

* Backus' History, vol. II. p. 238.

time it commenced, I have not been able to learn; but it was probably towards the close of the second, or in the beginning of the third century. It gained maturity in its progress, and continued a popular and prevalent establishment, so long as it was needful. Catechumens were generally persons in a state of minority; sometimes, however, those of mature age were enrolled among the children, and when christianity became a political engine, princes were added to the lists, and were catechised awhile before they were baptized. The catechumen state continued as long as minors were the subjects of baptism, but when it was found out by the skilful priests, that infants came into the world *crying for baptism*, and that they would be doomed to eternal perdition if they should die without it, the business of catechising became not only useless, but impracticable; godfathers and godmothers stood forward to answer all the questions which children used to answer for themselves; they took the whole responsibility of their faithfulness upon themselves, and promised what was never or seldom performed, either by the children or sponsors. The catechumen state being thus superseded by a more expeditious method of making christians, it dwindled away and fell into disuse.

It is easy to conceive, that among catechised children, some would be more forward than the rest, and of course would be prepared for baptism at an earlier age. A French Catholick writer observes, that he saw a little child in the country, who, at seven years of age, would promiscuously open the Greek Testament, and read and explain it with facility. " I heard," says he, " of two other *infants*, brother and sister, the one nine years of age, the other eleven or twelve, speak Greek and Latin perfectly well." A little superstition, of which there are numberless curious instances, added to such cases, handed baptism downwards from minors to babes.

A monumental inscription in Italy informs the reader, that Joanna Baptista de Peruschis, daughter of Alexander de Peruschis, and Beatrix Gorzei, when she was only six months old, mostly, sweetly, and freely pronounced the name of Jesus every day before she sucked the breast, and mostly, devoutly *adored the images of the saints.**

* Robinson's Hist. Baptism, p. 157, 158.

It seems pretty clear, that forward children laid the foundation for infant baptism, but other and more powerful motives hastened its progress, as we shall presently show.

But to return: In Tertullian's time some had begun, or were about beginning to baptize infants, that is, minors, who could ask for baptism. When Tertullian was informed of this business, he wrote a book to oppose it, in which we find the following passage. " The condescension of God may confer his favours as he pleases ; but our wishes may mislead ourselves and others. It is, therefore, most expedient to defer baptism, and to regulate the administration of it, according to the condition, the disposition, and the age of the person to be baptized ; and especially in the case of little ones.* What necessity is there to expose sponsors to danger ? Death may incapacitate them for fulfilling their engagements ; or bad dispositions may defeat all their endeavours. Indeed, the Lord saith, forbid them not to come unto me ; and let them come while they are growing up, let them come and learn, and let them be instructed when they come, and when they understand christianity, let them profess themselves christians."

In the year 1700, Dr. Mather, one of the Massachusetts divines, complained that there were reports, that some of the Congregational churches received members on the strength of written relations of their religious experience, which had been dictated by their ministers. This was a strange thing in his day, and it would doubtless have shocked and grieved this good old man, if he could have foreseen that the churches of his order, would, in a short time after, get to receiving members, without any relations either written or verbal, and that some would hold that a minister who knew himself destitute of saving grace, might preach the gospel and administer its ordinances.†

So Tertullian had but just heard the report of the innovations which were about to be introduced in the Church of Christ. He had but some faint intimations of that flood of errour, in regard to baptism, which, in a few succeeding centuries, deluged the christian world.

---

* The word, here translated *little ones*, is, in the original *parvulos*, which, we shall show presently, was used then for minors, who might be of every age under twenty-one.

† Backus' History, vol. II. p. 26—33.

But before we proceed, it may be proper to subjoin the testimony of two following Pedo-baptist writers. The first is a learned divine of Geneva, who succeeded the famous Episcopius in the professorship at Amsterdam, in the seventeenth century. This learned writer thus frankly acknowledges : " Pedo-baptism was unknown in the two first ages after Christ ; in the third and fourth it was approved by a few ; at length, in the fifth and following, it began to obtain in divers places ; and therefore this rite is indeed observed by us as an *ancient custom*, but not as an *apostolick tradition*." The other is Bishop *Taylor*, who calls infant baptism " a *pretended* apostolical tradition ;" but further says, " that the tradition cannot be *proved* to be *apostolical*, we have *very good evidence from antiquity*."* These are honest and fair concessions, and if all Pedo-baptists would make the same, their cause would stand on as good a foundation as it now does, and they would save themselves much labour and care.

The account of Tertullian's opposing the baptism of little ones, who were capable of asking for it, but who, in his opinion, were not sufficiently enlightened to be admitted to the sacred rite, was in the beginning of the third century. About the middle of this century, that is, about forty years after the account of Tertullian, the people in Africa had got baptism down from catechised minors to new-born babes, and Fidus, a country bishop, wrote to Cyprian of Carthage, to know whether children might be baptized before they were eight days old, for by his Bible he could not tell ; nor could Cyprian tell, without first consulting a council or association of bishops, which was about to be assembled. When the council met, which consisted of between sixty or seventy bishops, after some other business had been transacted, Fidus' question was brought before them. Fidus thought that infants ought to be baptized at eight days old, because the law of circumcision prescribed this time. " No," replied the council, " God denies grace to none ; Jesus came not to destroy men's lives, but to save them, and we ought to do all we can to save our fellow creatures. Besides," added they, " God would be a respecter of persons if he denied to infants what he grants to adults. Did not the prophet Elisha lay upon a child,

---

* Baldwin's Letters to Worcester, p. 167, 168.

and put his mouth upon his mouth, and his eyes upon his eyes, and his hands upon his hands? Now the spiritual sense of this is, that infants are equal to men; but if you refuse to baptize them, you destroy this equality, and are partial."*

Some other questions were agitated respecting new-born infants, which might do well enough for African bishops to discuss, but which might be somewhat offensive to a modern ear.

The reader may here see, what kind of arguments were used at first to support infant baptism, and it must be acknowledged that they are about as good as ever have been discovered since.

We hear but little more about infant baptism, until the fifth century, that is, until the year 416, when it was decreed in the council of Mela, of which St. Austin was the principal director, " That whosoever denieth that infants newly born of their mothers are to be baptized, let him be accursed."*

This council is generally supposed to have been held at Mela, in Numidia, now in the kingdom of Algiers. According to others it was held in the island of Malta. Thirteen years after this council, this part of Africa was overrun by the Vandals, and the Catholicks here were dispersed, and some of them fled into Europe, and carried with them infant-baptism, superstition, and intolerance.

As Africa has been frequently mentioned in the preceding narrative, it may be proper to observe what part of that dark quarter of the globe is intended. A person, acquainted with ecclesiastical history, will need no explanation, but others, into whose hands this work may fall, may desire one.

Africa, which is now generally in a deplorable state of ignorance, once contained a number of civilized kingdoms, famous for commerce and the liberal arts. Among these Carthage was probably the most distinguished. It

* Robinson's History of Baptism, p. 197.

† " An honest indignation," says Robinson, " rises at the sound of this tyranny, and if a man were driven to the necessity of choosing one saint out of two candidates, it would not be Saint Austin, it would be Saint Balaam, the son of Bosor, who, indeed, loved the wages of unrighteousness, as many other saints have done, but with all his madness, had respect enough for the Deity to say, *How shall I curse whom God hath not cursed?*"

was situated on the north of Africa, along the southern shore of the Mediterranean sea, where are now the Barbary States of Tunis, Algiers, and so on. Carthage once vied with Rome in power; but it was finally subdued by her, and reduced to a province. It was overrun by the Vandals in the fifth century, and by the Saracens in the seventh; and from that period, Mahometanism has been the established religion of the country. In this part of Africa, christianity was planted in early times, and here too it was early corrupted. Here, and not in Judea, infant baptism originated, as is evident to every candid investigator of historical facts.

The limits of this sketch will not permit us to give a circumstantial account of the progress of the baptism of babes; but it is sufficient to observe, that it gained ground, at first, by slow degrees, so strongly did scripture and reason operate against it; but having enlisted on its side, the interested views of priests and princes, and the tender feelings of anxious mothers, who were taught to believe, that their babes would be doomed to the gulf of ruin, if they died without this renovating rite, then called the laver of regeneration; under these circumstances, infant-baptism began most rapidly to prevail, and in a few centuries overrun the whole catholick church.

We have seen that infant baptism arose in Africa, that the baptism of minors began to be practised in the beginning of the third century, and that the baptism of new-born babes was determined under awful anathemas, by Saint Austin's council at Mela, in the fifth century. But its entrance into Europe is of a later date. The first ecclesiastical canon in Europe, for infant baptism, was framed at Girona in Spain in the sixth century, and the first imperial law to establish the practice, was made in the eighth century, by the Emperour Charlemagne. The council at Girona consisted of only seven obscure bishops, who met without authority, but who legislated with some effect, for people began to be concerned about the salvation of their children. This council framed ten rules of discipline. One was, " that catechumens should be baptized only at Easter and Pentecost, except in case of sickness; and another was, that in case infants were ill and would not suck their mother's milk, if they were offered,

Infant Baptism hastened forward. 61

to baptize them, even though it were the day they were born." Charlemagne's law to establish infant baptism was almost three hundred years after this council. The practice was then generally prevalent, and this Emperour, for political purposes, obliged the Saxons, on pain of death, to be baptized themselves, and laid heavy fines on those who should neglect to have their children baptized within the year of their birth.*

Now priests had no further trouble to vindicate the cause of infant baptism, popes and princes had undertaken to manage the cause; it was established by laws civil and ecclesiastical, and if any dared to oppose it, fire and sword ended the dispute.

It is now proper that we should go back to the time when infant baptism began to gain some ground, and consider the causes which hastened its progress.

About the time that catechumen minors began to be baptized, the words of Christ, " *Except a man be born of water and of the Spirit, he cannot enter the kingdom of God*, were misapplied to baptism. This erroneous exposition led to an undue reliance on this sacred rite, and many began to extol its efficacy, in the most absurd and extravagant manner; and represented it as a sure and sovereign antidote to all the moral maladies of depraved nature. It could wash away original sin, and place in a state of certain and everlasting salvation, all to whom it was applied; and more than all this, all who died without it, whether infants or adults, were sure of eternal misery. These errours were not all introduced at once; it took some time to bring them to perfection. But while they were gaining ground, there was another errour considerably prevalent, which produced an inconvenient collision with the former. Some held to a doctrine similar to the Arminian notion of falling from grace, and many were afraid that they should relapse into sin after their baptism, and thereby lose all its salutary benefits. This led Constantine and many others to defer their baptism till near the close of life. And this again led into the practice of pouring and sprinkling in baptism, instead of immersion, the then universally prevalent mode. These people who had deferred their baptism, were often suddenly alarmed

* Robinson's History of Baptism, p. 269—282.

with the prospect of death. Sickness disabled them from going to the baptismal font, and misery was their portion if they died unbaptized, and in this painful dilemma, they made the best shift they could, and were sprinkled if they could not be immersed. But this inconvenience was of no long duration, for as soon as parents were made to believe that baptism was the laver of regeneration, they were careful that all their children should be washed in it, as soon as they were born, and their relapsing or rather continuing in sin was another affair.

We have now arrived at the period in which baptism was exalted to a most astonishing pre-eminence. Its efficacy was the constant theme of pulpit declaimers, and its praises were chanted by all who could sing. Laws were enacted, canons were made, and the most vigilant precautions were taken by popes and princes, and every order of ecclesiasticks, by nurses and midwives, and every benevolent creature in christendom, that no human being, whether adult or infant, whether born or unborn, should depart to the world of spirits without this heavenly passport. Baptism, indeed, suffered violence, and the violent took it by force.

As this may seem a mere fanciful reverie, to those who have not studied this subject, I shall here quote verbatim, Mr. Robinson's account of the matter. The passage may be found in his History of Baptism, under the article Aspersion, where the authorities are quoted.

"The absolute necessity of dipping in order to a valid baptism; and the indispensable necessity of baptism, in order to salvation, were two doctrines which clashed, and the collision kindled up a sort of war, between the warm bosoms of parents who had children, and the cold reasonings of monks, who had few sympathies. The doctrine was cruel, and the feelings of humanity revolted against it. Power may give law; but it is more than power can do to make unnatural laws sit easy in the minds of men.

"The clergy felt the inconvenience of this state of things, for they were obliged to attend any woman in labour at a moment's warning, night or day, in any season, at the most remote parts of their parishes, without the power of demanding any fee, whenever a case of necessity required, and if they neglected their duty, they were severely punished.

"A great number of expedients were tried to remedy this evil; but for a long season nothing succeeded. There was a regular train of trials. At first, infants were baptized along with catechumens in publick, by trine immersion, at two times in the year; when it was observed, that some died before the season for baptizing came, priests were empowered to baptize at any time, and in any place in case of sickness. When it was remarked that a priest was not always at hand, new canons empowered him to depute others to perform the ceremony, and midwives were licensed. It happened sometimes, while the midwife was baptizing a child not like to live many minutes, the mother was neglected and died. To prevent such accidents in future, it was decreed, that any body, licensed or unlicensed, a Jew, or a degraded priest, a scullion or felon, might baptize. It fell out, sometimes, that a vessel large enough, or a quantity of water sufficient to dip an infant, could not be procured on a sudden; and while in the dead of the night, and perhaps in a severe frost, the assistants were running to borrow utensils, or to procure water, the ill-fated infant expired. In vain were laws made expressly to require pregnant women, to have every thing ready prepared, the laws of nature defied human controul, the evil was incurable, and the anguish intolerable. Some infants died the moment they were born, others before, both unbaptized, and all for the comfort of the miserable mother, doomed like fiends to descend instantly to a place of torment."

In the year 1751, a humane doctor of laws of Palermo, published at Milan, in the Italian tongue, a book of three hundred and twenty pages in quarto, dedicated to all the guardian angels, to direct priests and physicians how to secure the eternal salvation of infants by baptizing them when they could not be born. The surgical instrument and the process cannot be mentioned here, and the reader is come to a point in infant sprinkling, where English modesty compels him to retreat and retire, so that it is impossible to say any thing more on lustrating infants by way of baptizing them.*

* Robinson's History of Baptism, p. 435.

The baptism of abortives was a very common practice, but this also is a subject too indelicate to be discussed.

It may be well for Dr. Osgood to read these accounts of infant baptism, before he again declaims against our "indecorous" mode of baptizing.

We have now traced the baptism of babes to its highest pitch of frenzy, and also to its lowest point of corruption and debasement. In most protestant churches, and in many parts of the catholick church, it has been practised in a more rational and becoming manner. But in every form it is an absurd and useless thing, and at its best estate it is altogether vanity. The baptism of a believer is an interesting thing, but the sprinkling of a new-born child, is an unanimated, insignificant affair.

It was customary in the early ages, as it is now with the Baptists, for ministers, previous to baptism, to preach on the subject, and address the candidates on the important business, in which they were about to engage; but where infant baptism prevails, this custom, for good reasons, is generally laid aside, for they who are the most interested in the matter, are, from their incapacity, precluded from participating in the transaction. It would be a curious sight for a Reverend Divine, to address infants in their mothers' or nurses' arms, on the subject of baptism; but such a thing, ludicrous as it might seem, would be just as rational, and scriptural, and useful, as it is to baptize them.

THE MODE OF BAPTISM.

BAPTISM, as to the manner of its administration, has been subject to a great variety of changes, of which we shall now give a brief account. Baptism, beyond all doubt, was administered, in the apostolick age, by immersion. A cloud of witnesses bear testimony to this point, and place it beyond a doubt in the mind of every candid and unprejudiced man.

Ordinary baptism was universally performed by single or trine immersion for thirteen hundred years; from thence till after the reformation, it was generally performed by trine immersion.

Baptism was administered by pouring or sprinkling in cases of necessity all along from the third century to Calvin's time.

The first appearance of sprinkling for baptism was in the third century, in Africa, in favour of clinicks or bedridden people. Baptism was now considered essential to salvation; the poor sick people, who could not go to the baptistery, but were in danger of destruction if they died unbaptized, made the best shift they could, and were sprinkled as they lay upon their beds. But the African Catholicks reputed this no baptism, or at least a very imperfect one.

The first appearance of baptizing by pouring, was in the eighth century, when Pope Stephen III. allowed the validity of such a baptism of infants in danger of death. His Infallible Holiness had been driven from Rome by Astulphus, king of the Lombards; he fled to France to implore the assistance of Pepin, who had lately been proclaimed king. During his residence in the monastery of St. Denis, some monks consulted his opinion on nineteen questions; one of which was, whether *in case of necessity*, occasioned by the illness of an infant, it were lawful to baptize by pouring water out of the hand or a cup on the infant. Stephen answered, if such a baptism were performed in such a case of necessity, in the name of the holy Trinity, it should be held valid. The learned James Basanage makes several very proper remarks on this canon: as that "although it is accounted the first law for sprinkling, yet it doth not forbid dipping; that it allows sprinkling only in case of imminent danger: that the authenticity of it is denied by some Catholicks: that many laws were made after this time in Germany, France, and England, to compel dipping, and without any provision for cases of necessity: therefore that this law did not alter the mode of dipping in public baptisms: and that it was not till five hundred and fifty years after, that the Legislature, in a council at Ravenna, in the year thirteen hundred and eleven, declared dipping or sprinkling indifferent." The answer of Stephen is the true origin of private baptism and of sprinkling.*

---

* Robinson, p. 429, 430.

Modern Pedo-baptist writers have picked up historical scraps of these clinical and necessitous baptisms, and have endeavoured to derive evidence from them of the universality of infant sprinkling. I say modern Pedo-baptists, for Dr. Wall, who was a strenuous advocate for infant *baptism*, also warmly contended for *immersion*. He published his elaborate History of Infant Baptism in 1705. This work was answered by Dr. John Gale, a famous General Baptist, in a very learned work, entitled, Reflections, &c. Dr. Wall published a Defence of his History in 1720. He appears to have been half right and half wrong, and he was as strenuous for the wrong half as for the right. He warmly contends that infant *baptism* is of divine appointment, and he as warmly contends that infant *sprinkling* is a " scandalous thing." " Calvin, (saith he) was I think the first in the world, that drew up a liturgy that prescribed pouring water on the infant, absolutely, without saying any thing of dipping. It was (as Mr. Walker has shewn) his admirers in England, who, in queen Elizabeth's time, brought pouring into ordinary use, which before was used only to weak children. But the succeeding Presbyterians in England, about 1644, when their reign began, went farther yet from the ancient way; and instead of *pouring*, brought into use, in many places, *sprinkling;* declaring, at the same time, against all use of fonts, baptisteries," &c.

" There has (saith he again) no novelty or alteration, that I know of, in the point of baptism, been brought into the church, but in the way and manner of administering it. The way that is now ordinarily used we cannot deny to have been a novelty, brought into this church (of England) by those that had learned it in Germany, or at Geneva. And they were not contented with following the example of pouring a quantity of water, which had there been introduced instead of immersion, but improved it, (if I may so abuse that word) from pouring to sprinkling, that it might have as little resemblance of the ancient way of baptizing as possible."

I cannot leave this ingenious author, before I select another passage. " Another struggle (says he, whether the child shall be dipped or sprinkled) will be with the midwives and nurses, &c. These will use all the interest they have with the mothers, which is very great, to dissuade them from agreeing to the dipping of the child. I know no particular reason, unless it be this: A thing, which they value themselves and their skill much upon, is, the neat dressing of the child on the christening-day; the setting all the trimming, the pins, and the laces, in their right order. And if the child be brought in loose clothes, which may presently be taken off for the baptism, and put on again, this pride is lost: And this makes a reason. So little is the solemnity of the sacrament regarded by many, who mind nothing but the dress, and the eating and drinking."*

Christians at first baptized in rivers and fords, and wherever water of sufficient depth could be found. About the middle of the third century baptisteries began to be built. They at first, like the manners and conditions of the people, were very simple, and were merely for use; but in the end they arose to as high degree of elegant superstition, as enthusiasm could invent.

By a baptistery, which must not be confounded with a modern font, is to be understood an octagon building, with a cupola roof, resembling a dome of a cathedral; adjacent to a church, but no part of it. All the middle part of this building was one large hall, capable of containing a great multitude of people; the sides were parted off, and divided into rooms, and, in some, rooms were added without-side, in the fashion of cloisters. In the middle of the great hall was an octagon bath, which, strictly speaking, was the baptistery, and from which the whole building was denominated. This was called the pool, the pond, the place to swim in, besides a great number of other names of a figurative nature, taken from the religious benefits, which were supposed to be connected with baptism; such as the laver of regeneration, the luminary, and many more of the same parentage. Some had been natural rivulets before the buildings were erected over them, and the pool was contrived to retain water, sufficient for dipping, and to discharge the rest. Others were supplied by pipes, and the water was conveyed into one or more of the side rooms. Some of the surrounding rooms were vestries, others school rooms, both for the instruction of youth, and

* Dr. Wall's Defence, p. 146, 147, 403.

for transacting the affairs of the church; and councils have been held in the great halls of these buildings. It was necessary they should be capacious; for as baptism was administered only twice a year, the candidates were numerous, and the spectators more numerous than they.*

It may be proper here to give a brief description of a few of those splendid buildings which were erected for the purpose of performing baptism by immersion.

We will begin with the one attached to the splendid church of St. Sophia, of Constantinople, which church is now converted into a Mahometan mosque. The church of St. Sophia was built by Constantine, the first christian emperour.

Succeeding emperours amplified and adorned it. Justinian at an immense cost rebuilt it, and his artists, with elegance and magnificence, distributed variegated marbles of exquisite beauty, gold, silver, ivory, mosaick work, and endless ornaments, so as to produce the most agreeable and lasting effects on all beholders.

The baptistery was one of the appendages of this spacious palace, something in the style of a convocation-room in a cathedral. It was very large, and councils have been held in it, and it was called the great Illuminatory. In the middle was the bath, in which baptism was administered; it was supplied by pipes, and there were outer rooms for all concerned in the baptism of immersion, the only baptism of the place.

Every thing in the church of St. Sophia goes to prove, that baptism was administered by trine immersion, and only to instructed persons; the canon laws, the officers, the established rituals, the Lent sermons of the prelates, and the baptism of the archbishops themselves.†

To the account of this baptistery, I will subjoin the following extracts from the discourses of Basil, archbishop of Cæsarea, which may serve to show both how and for what purpose they baptized in the Greek established church, in the fourth century.

" It is necessary for the perfection of a christian life, that we should imitate Christ; not only such holy actions and dispositions, as lenity, modesty, and patience, which he exemplified in his life, but also his death, as Paul

* Robinson's Hist. of Baptism, p. 59. † Robinson, p. 63.

saith, *I am a follower of Christ, I am conformable to his death, if by any means I might attain unto the resurrection of the dead.* How can we be placed in a condition of likeness to his death? By being *buried with him in baptism.* What is the form of this burial, and what benefits flow from an imitation of it? First, the course of former life is stopped. No man can do this, unless he be *born again,* as the Lord hath said. Regeneration, as the word itself imports, is the beginning of a new life; therefore, he that begins a new life must put an end to his former life. Such a person resembles a man got to the end of a race, who, before he sets off again, turns about, pauses, and rests a little; so in a change of life it seems necessary that a sort of death should intervene, putting a period to the past, and giving a beginning to the future. How are we to go down with him into the grave? By imitating the *burial* of Christ in baptism; for the bodies of the saints are, in a sense, buried in water. For this reason the Apostle speaks figuratively of baptism, as a *laying aside the works of the flesh; ye are circumcised with the circumcision made without hands, in putting off the body of the sins of the flesh by the circumcision of Christ, buried with him in baptism.*—Two things are proposed in baptism; to put an end to a life of sin, lest it should issue in eternal death; and to animate the soul to a life of future sanctification. The water exhibits an image of death, receiving the body as into a sepulchre; the spirit renews the soul, and we rise from a death of sin into a newness of life. This is to be *born from above of water and the Spirit;* as if by the water we were put to death, and by the operation of the Spirit brought to life.—If there be any benefit in the water, it is not from the water, but from the presence of the Spirit; for baptism doth not *save us by putting away the filth of the flesh, but by the answer of a good conscience toward God."*——It seems clear that the homilies of archbishop Basil were addressed, not to pagans old or young, but to the children of christians, whom he calls the church. That the Greek church of those times did not force a profession of christianity upon their children, but conducted them to baptism by instruction and argument—that baptism was administered by trine immersion—and that, as the sermons of their bishops were intended to persuade, so the lessons for the day, read openly in the church, were intended to explain and enforce the subject of baptism. Nothing like this is to be found in the Lent sermons of modern times; and a translation of the Lent homilies of the ancient Greek bishops could not be read to any congregation of modern christians, without great absurdity, except to Baptist assemblies, and there they would be heard in raptures, for their singular propriety and beauty.*

The baptistery pertaining to the church of St. John Lateran, at Rome, is thus described by Mr. Robinson: " A traveller, entering Rome by the gate *Del Popolo*, must go up the street *Strada Felice*, till he arrive at the church St. John Lateran. Turning in and passing along through the church, he must go out at the door behind the great choir, which lets him into a court surrounded with walls and buildings. On the left hand is a porch supported by two marble pillars, which leads into the octagon edifice, called the baptistery. On entering, he will observe that eight large polygonal pillars of porphyry support the roof, and there is a spacious walk all round between them and the wall. In the centre of the floor under the cupola, is the baptistery, properly so called, lined with marble, with three steps down into it, and about five Roman palms, that is thirty-seven inches and a half deep; for the Roman palm is seven inches and a half English measure. Some antiquaries are of opinion that this baptistery was deeper formerly. Perhaps it might be, before the baptism of youths was practised; but this, all things considered, is the most desirable of all depths for baptizing persons of a middle size; and in a bath, kept full as this was, by a constant supply of fresh water, the gauge was just, and any number might be baptized with ease and speed."†

Mr. Robinson has given similar descriptions of the baptisteries of Revenna, Venice, Florence, Novara, and Milan; but those which have been mentioned will give the reader an idea of the form and design of these baptismal structures, which were erected in the front of christian temples, to show that baptism was the entrance into the church.

* Robinson's Hist. Baptism, p. 65, 66, 67.   † Robinson, p. 72, 73.

Baptism administered by the Pope.

I shall here insert an account of a baptism performed by the pope in the baptistery of St. John Lateran, about the eighth or ninth century.——"At nine in the morning the pontiff, attended by a great number of prelates and clergy, went to the sacristy, and after they had put on the proper habits, proceeded in silent order into the church. Then the lessons for the day were read, and several benedictions performed. When this part was finished, his holiness, with his attendants, proceeded to the baptistery, the choir singing all the way the forty-second psalm: *As the hart panteth after the water-brooks, so panteth my soul after thee, O God,* and so on. This ended at the porch of the first chapel, where his holiness sat down. Then the cardinals presented themselves before him, and one, in the name of the rest, prayed for his benediction, which was bestowed. This was repeated thrice, and immediately after the last, the pontiff added, *Go ye and baptize all nations in the name of the Father, and of the Son, and of the Holy Ghost.* The cardinals having received their mission, withdrew immediately, and, mounting their horses, proceeded each to his own station to baptize. The pope went on to the baptismal hall, and after various lessons and psalms consecrated the baptismal water. Then while all were adjusting themselves in their proper places, his holiness retired into the adjoining chapel of St. John the Evangelist, attended by some acolothists, who took off his habits, put on him a pair of waxed drawers, and a surplice, and then returned to the baptistery. There three children were waiting, which was the number usually baptized by the pontiff. Silence was ordered. When the first was presented, he asked, What is his name? The attendant answered John. Then he proceeded thus: John, dost thou believe in God the Father Almighty, the Creator of heaven and earth? I do believe. Dost thou believe in Jesus Christ, his only Son our Lord, who was born and suffered death? I do believe. Dost thou believe in the Holy Ghost, the holy catholick church, the communion of saints, the remission of sins, the resurrection of the body and life eternal? I do believe. John, do you desire to be baptized? I desire it. I baptize thee in the name of the Father, dipping him once, and of the Son, dipping him a second time, and of the Holy Ghost, dipping him a third time. The pontiff added, May you obtain eternal life! John answered, Amen. The same was then repeated to Peter and Mary, the other two. Attendants with napkins received the children, and retired to dress them. The attendants of his holiness threw a mantle over his surplice, and he retired. The rest of the catechumens were baptized by deacons, who in clean habits, and without shoes, went down into the water, and performed the ceremony as the pontiff had set them an example. After all was over and the children dressed, they waited on the pope in an adjacent room, where he confirmed them, and delivered to each crism and a white garment. The part, relative to the habits of the pope, is taken from the twelfth ordinal in the collection of Father Mabillon, and it was written by a cardinal in the latter end of the twelfth century.

" That these ordinals were originally composed for the baptism of those of riper years, seems not to admit of a doubt, and that baptism was performed by immersion cannot be questioned, nor can any one hesitate to determine, that the candidates were the children of christians. The scrutiny ; the service in part in the night ; the command of silence ; the change of deacons' habits ; the wax or oil-skin drawers, breeches, or trousers for the pontiff; the interrogations and answers ; the kneeling and praying of the candidates ; the proper lessons for the days ; the services for susceptors, parents, patrini, and matrini, who were uncles, aunts, relations, or assistants, and not modern god-fathers performing sponsion ; the addresses to the young folks ; the total omission of charges to sponsors ; all go to prove the point."*

When the baptism of infants became an established custom, it was unnecessary for the administrators to go into the water, and they contrived cisterns which they called fonts, in which they dipped children without going into the water themselves. In the first baptisteries, both administrators and candidates, went down steps into the bath. In after ages the administrators went up steps to a platform, on which stood a small bath which they called a font, into which they plunged children without going into the water themselves. In modern practice the font remains, but a bason of water set into the font serves the purpose, because

Robinson's History of Baptism, p. 78, 79, 80.

it is not now supposed necessary either that the administrator should go into the water, or that the candidate should be immersed.

Fonts were made of different materials, some of wood, some of stone, and at Canterbury, in England, there was one of silver, in which many of the English nobility were baptized. In these fonts infants were baptized naked, and accidents frequently happened while they were in the font, which were painful to the feelings of parents and spectators, and which a good Doctor of Massachusetts would doubtless consider altogether "indecorous." But the poor babes ought not to be blamed.*

But baptisteries and fonts are all become useless, since it has been found out, that for a priest to moisten his hand in a bason, and lay it gently on the child's face, or to scatter a few drops from his flexible fingers, will answer all the purposes of baptism.

To recapitulate what has been said on this subject, every thing tends to prove, that baptism means dipping or immersion, and that it has been so understood and practised in most ages of the christian church. Baptisteries, baptismal fonts, going down into the baptistery, coming up out of it, dressing, undressing, napkins, vestments, and so on, all agree with this mode; and we may add collections of pictures, inscriptions, medals, coins, festivals, and histories of all kinds of the middle ages, have some connexion, near or remote, with baptism by immersion. Even punsters and writers of jest-books, have dipping in baptism for the object of their wit. In the history of the Byzantine theatre, it is said that in the year two hundred and ninety seven, the players on a theatre in a city in Asia, diverted the pagan spectators with a mock baptism. For this purpose they provided a large bathing-tub, filled it with water, and plunged Gelasinus into it, to the no small diversion of the company.

The evidences in favour of immersion are so numerous that it is difficult, in this short sketch, to ascertain which are the most proper to select. We will, however,

* In consequence of an accident of this kind, the Emperour Constantine, in the eighth century, received from his enemies the nick-name of *Copronimus*, which signifies that he did that in the sacred font, which he ought not to have done. Many others received nick-names on the same account.

Mosheim—Robinson.

proceed next to the concessions which Pedo-baptists have made on the subject, and begin with the Roman Catholicks.

Learned men of that community differ, as may naturally be supposed, concerning the time when infant sprinkling was introduced; but none of their accurate writers pretend to say, the first christians did not baptize by dipping. On the contrary they laugh at such as affect either to render the word baptism sprinkling, or to give a high antiquity to the practice. It would be easy to adduce a great number of examples; but four shall suffice.

The first is that learned and elegant antiquary, Paul Maria Paciandi. This great man published by authority at Rome, in the year 1755, dedicated to pope Benedict XIV. a beautiful volume of christian antiquities. His holiness, being fond of antiquities, admitted him to his presence, and took pleasure in examining his compilations. In the fourth chapter of the second dissertation, he speaks of the two baptisteries at Ravenna, and finds fault with the artists for representing John the Baptist pouring water on the head of Jesus. "Nothing (exclaims he) can be more monstrous than these emblems! Was our Lord Christ baptized by aspersion? This is so far from being true, that nothing can be more opposite to truth, and it is to be attributed to the ignorance and rashness of workmen." The officers of the apostolical palace, and the other examiners of this work speak of it in terms of the highest approbation.

The second is that excellent judge, Dr. Joseph De Vicecomes, of Milan, whose book on the mass was examined and approved by the head of the college of St. Ambrose, by one officer of the inquisition, another of the Cardinal Archbishop, and a third of the Senate of Milan. In the sixth chapter of the fourth book, on the ceremonies of baptism, he says, "I will never cease to profess and teach, that only immersion in water, except in cases of necessity, is lawful baptism in the church. I will refute the false notion, that baptism was administered in the primitive church by pouring or sprinkling." He proceeds through the whole chapter to prove, and particularly refutes the objection, taken from the baptism of three thousand in one day by the apostles, by observing that it was a long summer day; that the words pronounced in baptism were as long in the mode of sprinkling, as in that of dipping; that dipping might be performed as quick as sprinkling; that many ceremonies now in use were not practised then; and that even since several ceremonies had been added, many fathers at Easter and Whitsuntide had been known to baptize great numbers in a day by dipping. He remarks in another place, that some men were highly fitted for this service, as, for example, Ambrose, bishop of Milan, who, Paulinus affirms, (and he knew him well) had such spirits and strength, that he baptized as many persons in a day by immersion, as five ordinary men could do after his decease.*

The third is Father Mabillon. He says, that although there is mention made in the life of S. Lindger of baptizing a little infant by pouring on holy water, yet it was contrary to an express canon of the ninth century; contrary to the canon given by Stephen, which allowed pouring only in cases of necessity; contrary to the general practice in France, where trine immersion was used; contrary to the practice of the Spaniards, who used single

* A man always dreaming of sprinkling, concludes that the apostles could no where in Jerusalem, find places for immersion. He can imagine there was an abundance of pitchers and basons; but to think of dipping places in this great city, is altogether improbable and absurd. But Dr. Gill has shown that Jerusalem was not so destitute of this refreshing element as many Pedobaptists suppose. " In the city of Jerusalem, (says he) in private houses, they had their baths for purifications, by immersion, as in the case of menstruas, gonorrhœas, and other defilements, by touching unclean persons and things, which were very frequent; so that a digger of cisterns, for such uses, and others, was a business in Jerusalem. And in the temple there was an apartment, called the *dipping-place* or *room*, where the high-priest dipped himself on the day of atonement. And besides these were ten lavers of brass, made by Solomon; and every laver held forty baths of water, and each was four cubits broad and long, sufficient for immersion of the whole body of a man. Add to this that there was the molten sea also for the priests to wash in, 2 Chron. iv. 6, which was done by immersion; on which one of the Jewish commentators has these words: " The sea was *for the dipping* of the priests; "for in the midst of it they dipped themselves from their uncleanness; but " in the Jerusalem Talmud, there is an objection, is it not a vessel? as if it "was said how can they *dip* in it, for is it not a vessel? and there is no *dip*-"*ping* in vessels: R. Joshua ben Levi replied, a pipe of water was laid to "it from the fountain of Etam, and the feet of the oxen, which were under "the molten sea, were open at the pomegranates; so that it was as if it was "from under the earth, and the waters came to it, and entered, and ascend-"ed, by the way of the feet of the oxen, which were open beneath them and " bored."—And it may be observed, that there was also in Jerusalem the pool of Bethesda, into which persons went down at certain times, John v. 1, and the pool of Siloam, where persons bathed and dipped themselves, on certain occasions. So that there were conveniences enough for baptism by immersion in this place.

immersion; contrary to the opinion of Alwin, who contended for trine immersion; and contrary to the practice of many, who continued to dip till the fifteenth century. For all this he quotes his authorities.

The fourth is the celebrated Lewis Anthony Muratori.— This perfect master of the subject, in the fourth volume of his antiquities of the middle ages of Italy, in the fifty-seventh dissertation, treats of the rites of the church of Milan, called the Ambrosian, from St. Ambrose, the first compiler of the ritual of that church. As usual, he confirms every word, by original, authentick papers. Speaking of baptism by trine immersion, which was the Ambrosian method, he says: "Observe the Ambrosian manner of baptizing. Now-a-days, the priests preserve a shadow of the *ancient* Ambrosian form of baptizing, for they do not baptize by pouring as the Romans do; but taking the infant in their hands, they dip the hinder part of his head three times in the baptismal water, in the form of a cross, which is a vestige yet remaining of the most ancient and universal practice of immersion."*

A Catholick is not unwilling to acknowledge, that infant sprinkling is a human tradition; "he is not shocked to find that a ceremony is neither scriptural nor ancient, because an order of the council of Trent is as valid with him as an apostolical command."

All the authors, just quoted, believed in infant sprinkling, not because it was found in scripture, but because it had been established by law in the church of Rome. And when Protestant Pedo-baptists rail against their superstitious rites, they often retort upon them their own arguments, and expose the sandy foundation of infant baptism. A curious anecdote of this kind is related of a Roman Catholick priest, who was called by king Charles II. to dispute with a Baptist minister by the name of Jeremiah Ives, whom the Catholick supposed to have been a church priest. The affair will be related at large in the History of the English Baptists.

A short time since, a pamphlet was published in Baltimore by the Roman Catholick College of St. Mary, against an attack from the Presbyterians on them, (for their unwritten traditions) to which the Catholicks reply

---

* Robinson's History of Baptism, p. 433, 434, 435.

" Presbyterians with Catholicks admit the baptism of infants. *Baptism by sprinkling, by effusion, &c.* let them find for all this, and for many other practices, any foundation in scripture." Again, " It is then an unquestionable *fact,* that *even* for Presbyterians, *tradition* has preserved many unwritten dogmas and religious institutions."*

A Catholick, by thus acknowledging that infant baptism is an unwritten tradition, saves himself an infinite deal of labour; but a Protestant, who will not give to such traditions, however solemnly established, the force of a scripture command, finds himself in an awkward situation, and is obliged to go in search of proof, which none ever did and never can find, until two or three more words are added to the Bible.

While Catholicks and Presbyterians are contending about unwritten traditions, the Baptists look on as calm spectators, and rejoice, that for their practice, they have a " *thus saith the Lord.*"

We will not, however, confine our attention to the concessions of Catholicks. A host of Protestants might be produced, who have all conceded that the primary meaning of baptizo, is to dip, to immerse, and so on ; and that in this manner baptism was administered in the primitive church.

Calvin, in his commentary on the passage in Acts viii. 38, *they went down into the water,* thus remarks : " Here wee see the rite used among the men of old time in baptisme; for they put all the bodie into the water ; now, the use is this, that the minister doth only sprinkle the bodie or the head." After several remarks upon the use of the ordinance, he adds, " It is certain that wee want nothing which maketh to the substance of baptisme. Wherefore the churche did graunt libertie to herselfe *since the beginning,* to change the rites somewhat excepting this substance. Some dipped them thrice, some but once; wherefore there is no cause why wee should bee so strait-laced in matters which are of no suche weight; so that that externall pompe doe no whit pollute the simple institution of Christe."†

* Massachusetts Baptist Missionary Magazine, vol. iii. p. 207.
† Baldwin's Letters to Dr. Worcester, p. 201.

Dr. Campbell, a late learned Scotch writer, in his Preliminary Discourses to the Translation of the Four Gospels, observes, that " in several modern languages we have, in what regards Jewish and Christian rites, generally followed the usage of the old Latin version, though the authors of that version have not been entirely uniform in their method. Some words they have *transferred* from the original into their language; others they have *translated*. But it would not always be easy to find their reason for making this difference. Thus the word *peritome* they have translated *circumcisio*, which exactly corresponds in etymology; but the word *baptisma* they have retained, changing only the letters from Greek to Roman. Yet the latter was just as susceptible into Latin as the former. *Immersio, tinctio*, answers as exactly in the one case as *circumcisio* in the other." He further adds, " We have deserted the Greek names where the Latins have deserted them. Hence we say *circumcision*, and not *peritomy*, and we do not say *immersion*, but *baptism*. Yet when the language furnishes us with materials for a version so exact and analogical, such a version conveys the sense more perspicuously than a foreign name. *For this reason*, I should think the word *immersion* (which though of Latin origin, is an English noun, regularly formed from the verb *to immerse*) a better name than baptism, were we now at liberty to make a choice." The same writer thus translates the passage in Luke xii. 50: " I have an IMMERSION to undergo, and how am I pained till it be accomplished."

Mr. Booth, in his Pedo-baptism examined, has quoted eighty Pedo-baptist writers, who concede that the original meaning of the Greek verb *baptizo*, is to dip, to immerse, and so on.

The Baptists do not rely on these concessions, to establish their opinion of baptism; they have other reasons for believing that immersion is an apostolical rite; but they are produced to show, that Pedo-baptists were more candid and consistent in former times, than they are in general at the present day. One would think that these concessions must have some effect upon the minds of those, who, in any measure, lay themselves open to conviction. Sure I am, that if one respectable Baptist writer should concede half so much in favour of pouring or sprinkling, as Calvin has in favour of immersion, it would be instantly taken for proof, and trumpeted from Dan to Beersheba against them.

But it is an indisputable fact that no Baptist writer, and their number is considerably great, and some of them have been very learned, their enemies being judges, has ever had the least misgiving on the subject, or in any way conceded, that any thing short of a total dipping, plunging, or immersion of the body in water, can be valid baptism.

But few of the Baptists pretend to understand Greek; some, however, do undoubtedly understand it, as well as do their adversaries, and have gone laboriously into the investigation of the meaning of the terms *bapto, baptizo, baptisma,* and so on, not so much to establish their own opinions, as to refute the skeptical evasions and unsound criticisms of their opponents.* " The meaning of doubtful words is best fixed by ascertaining the facts which they are intended to represent;" and when we read that they were *baptized in Jordan, buried in baptism, went down into the water before baptism, and came up out of it after ;* I say, when the Baptists read these and many similar passages, no man, woman, or child, among them, has, or can have, any doubt of the meaning of the word baptize. And if Pedo-baptists will still spend their time in hammering Abraham's covenant and the Greek prepositions, *eis* and *en,* and *ek,* and *apo,* to prove that *baptizo* may mean *to sprinkle* or *pour,* they are welcome to all the pleasure and fruits of their labour.

The Greeks have always understood baptism to mean immersion. The Greek christians according to Dr. Wall, are more numerous than Roman Catholicks,† which, if I

* That learned Baptist, Dr. John Gale, has taken much pains in this matter. He hath traced the original word in profane writers, and hath proved by a great variety of examples, that with the Greeks, *bapto* signified *to dip, baptai dyers, baphia* a dye-house, *bapsis* dying by dipping, *bammata* dying drugs, *baphi kee* the art of dying, *dibaphos* double-dyed, *baptisterion* a dying-vat, &c. In these senses were *bapto* and its derivatives understood before they were selected to describe a christian institute.—*Gale's Reflections upon Wall's History of Infant Baptism, Letter III.*

Mohammed, in the Alcoran, calls baptism *sebgatallah,* that is, *divine dying,* or the tinging of God, from *sebgah* dying and *dallah* God. A celebrated orientalist says, Mohammed made use of this compound term for baptism, because, in his time, christians administered baptism as dyers tinge, by immersion, and not as now (in the west) by aspersion.

Robinson's Hist. of Baptism, p. 7.

† Defence, &c. p. 148.

mistake not, are estimated at a hundred millions or more. The Greek religion, according to Robinson, is professed through a considerable part of Greece, the Grecian isles, Wallachia, Moldavia, Egypt, Nubia, Lybia, Arabia, Mesopotamia, Lyria, Cilicia, and Palestine, the Russian empire in Europe, greater part of Siberia in Asia, Astracan, Casan, Georgia, and White Russia in Poland.* Besides the established Greek church, which is governed by the four patriarchs of Constantinople, Alexandria, Antioch, and Jerusalem, there are many communities of Greek christians, called oriental churches, which never were of any hierarchy, but have always retained their original freedom. These churches are dispersed all over Syria, Arabia, Egypt, Persia, Nubia, Ethiopia, India, Tartary, and other eastern countries. The most considerable of them are the Nestorians, the Armeneans, the Georgians, and so on.

Now it is an indisputable fact, acknowledged by all historians, that all these millions of Greeks, ever have, and now do, administer baptism by immersion. They generally baptize infants, but they do it by dipping not only in the warm climes of Arabia and Lybia, but in the frozen regions of Russia and Siberia.† This circumstance outweighs ten thousand criticisms upon Abraham's covenant, Greek prepositions, the little sprinkling brooks of Palestine, and the baptism of the three thousand.

Mr. Robinson has made a very good use of this circumstance in his Ecclesiastical Researches, under the head Greek Church, pages 91 and 92, which I will here transcribe in his own forcible words. " The state of baptism in the Greek church is an article of more consequence than it may at first appear. If pity for the wretched be a generous passion, who can help indulging it when he sees

* Ecclesiastical Researches, p. 93.

† It is said by an English historian, that at Petersburg, they sometimes baptize their children in a river or canal, by cutting a hole through the ice, upon which he observes, " I have heard that a priest, in immersing a child, (for baptism is performed by the immersion of the whole body) let it slip, through inattention, into the water. The child was drowned; but the holy man suffered no consternation. " *Give me another*," said he, with the utmost composure, "*for the Lord hath taken that to himself.*" The Empress, however, having other uses for her subjects, and not desiring that the Lord should have any more in that way, at least, gave orders, that all children, to be baptized in a hole in the river, should henceforth be let down in a basket."
Baldwin's Baptism of Believers, 2d edit. p. 100.

an illiterate Baptist hang his head daunted and dismayed by the unfair criticism of a learned teacher, who tells him the word baptize is Greek, and signifies pouring as well as dipping? Great men love sometimes to trifle. The inference which these translators draw from their own version, is not exactly logical; for I prove, says a Vossius, going to baptize an infant, that the word baptize signifies to pour as well as to dip. In virtue of this, what does he? He takes the infant and neither pours nor dips, but sprinkles, and then lifts up his voice and says to a congregation of English peasants, the Greek will bear me out. Verily, this is not fair!

"Suppose an honest Baptist peasant should stand up and say to such a man, "Sir, I have understood that Jesus "lived and died in the east; that four of his disciples "wrote his history in the Greek language; that his apos- "tles preached in Greek to the inhabitants of Greece, and "that the Greeks heard, believed and were baptized; eve- "ry nation understands its own language best, and no "doubt the Greeks understand Greek better than we do; "now I have been informed, set me right if I be wrong, "that from the first preaching of the apostles to this day, "the Greeks have always understood, that to baptize was "to dip; and, so far are they from thinking that to baptize "is to pour or to sprinkle, I have been told they baptize "by dipping three times. I do not understand Greek, "but I think the Greeks themselves do. If, therefore, I "were not to dip for other reasons; and if I were obliged "to determine my practice, by the sense of the single "word baptism; and if I were driven to the necessity of "trusting somebody, my reason would command me to "take that sense from the natives of Greece, rather than "from you a foreigner." That this honest man would suppose a true fact is beyond all contradiction.—In determining the precise meaning of a Greek word, used to signify a Greek ceremony, what possible chance hath a session of lexicographers against whole empires of native Greeks? Let the illiterate then enjoy themselves, and recollect when they baptize by dipping, they understand Greek exactly as the Greeks themselves understand it.

"Greatly as the Greeks were divided in speculative opinions, and numerous as the congregations were, which dissented from the church, it is remarkable, and may serve to confirm the meaning of the word baptize, that there is not the shadow of a dispute, in all their history, in favour of sprinkling. Because they were Greeks, they all thought that to baptize was to baptize, that is, to dip was to dip. They all baptized, and rebaptized; the established church, as was observed before, by order of council, for speculative reasons, and the dissenters for moral reasons."*

Nothing of the kind staggers the charity of the Baptists so much, as for a learned man, with all these historical evidences before his eyes, to tell his hearers, and publish to the world, that nothing definite can be determined respecting the meaning of the Greek word *baptizo*. And many are tempted to think that they do but half believe their own assertions, but that they make them merely to gain time, or to bewilder the minds of inquirers.

" If, (says Robinson) there be a word in the New-Testament, of a determinate meaning, it is the word *baptism*. Yet by a course of sophistry, it shall be first made synonimous with *washing*, and then *washing* shall be proved synonimous with *sprinkling*, and then *sprinkling* shall be called *baptism*. Thus the book, intended to instruct, shall be taught to perplex; the book in the world the most determinate shall be rendered the most vague; the book, the credit of which is absolutely ruined if it admit of double meanings, shall of all others be rendered the most mysterious book in the world, saying every thing, and of course narrating and proving nothing."

Miscellaneous Articles nearly or remotely connected with Baptism.

BAPTISM is one of the most curious and complicated subjects of ecclesiastical history. Among men who stepped off the ground of scripture, and laid another foundation, it was variable as the wind, and in every province practised for a different reason. At Alexandria, inserted into rules of academical education; at Jerusalem, administered to promiscuous catechumens; in the deserts of

---

* " Since my arrival in this country, I was once in the company of a gentleman, whose vernacular tongue was the Greek. One of the company asked him the meaning of the word *baptizo*. He said it meant *baptizo*, what else could it mean? After asking more particularly, he signified that it meant immersion." *Dr. Staughton's account of the India Mission, p.* 209.

Catholicks have twenty Ceremonies at Baptism.

Egypt, united to monastical tuition; in Cappadocia, applied as an amulet to entitle the dying to heaven; at Constantinople, accommodated to the intrigues of the court; in all places, given to children extraordinarily inspired; and in the end it was employed by an African monk, to wash away original sin.

According to Cardinal Bellarmine, the Roman Catholicks have no less than two and twenty ceremonies at baptism. Twelve are preparatory to it, five are at the administration of it, and the remaining are after it. Others, it is said, make many more. These twenty-two are all stated in their order by Mr. Robinson, but we have not room to do it here. The principal ones, however, are the Scrutiny, Exsufflation, by which devils are expelled, Insufflation, by which the Spirit of God is communicated, Consecration of the water, the Chrismal Unction, the Lighted Taper, and the Milk and Honey.*

* Every thing pertaining to baptism was marked with pomp and extravagance, and the preparations for a christening day, among the nobility, were as great as they are now for a public dinner in a populous town. The following is a bill of fare of a dinner at Tynningham, the house of the Right Hon. the Earl of Haddington, on Thursday the 21st of August, 1679, when his Lordship's son was baptized:

Fresh beef	6 pieces.
Mutton,	16 do.
Veal,	4 do.
Legs of Venison,	3
Geese,	6
Pigs,	4
Old Turkeys,	2
Young do.	8
Salmon,	4
Tongues and Udders,	12
Ducks,	14
Roasted fowls,	6
Boiled fowls	9
Chickens roasted,	30
do. stewed,	12
do. frickaseed,	8
do. in pottage,	10
Lamb,	2 sides
Wild Fowl,	22
Pigeons baked, roasted, and stewed,	182
Hares roasted	10
do. frickaseed,	6
Hams,	3

A puncheon of Claret, &c.

No one will think it strange, after reading this account, that Dr. Wall accused many in his day, of regarding nothing at a christening but the dress, and the eating and drinking.

In Venice, the meanest plebeian hath at least three god-fathers, the wealthy have twenty, and sometimes a hundred.

Many of these ceremonies, which now appear altogether absurd and unmeaning, may be traced to a rational origin. We will mention only two, the lighted taper, and the milk and honey. What use is a lighted taper to an infant eight days old? Yet President Brisson hath proved by undeniable evidence, from ancient and allowed authorities, that in the middle ages, when baptism was administered by dipping only at Easter and Whitsuntide, the number of catechumens being very great, the administrators began to baptize in the night, or at least long before break of day, and so many flambeaus were lighted up for public convenience, that the darkness was turned into day. Could any thing be more natural than for some of the attendants to give a taper to a person coming up out of the water, or to walk before him and light him? It served at once to distinguish him in the crowd for freedom of passage, and to light him from the baptistery to the dressing room.

After these baptized persons had retired from the baptistery to the dressing room, it was very common to refresh themselves with milk and honey. Many other of these ceremonies may be explained in a similar manner, but some originated in the capricious fancies of superstitious people, and others go to show the invisible and salutary benefits of the baptismal rite, which Catholicks have magnified to a most extravagant degree. What can be more shocking and irrational, than to suppose that in a world inhabited by eight or nine hundred millions of rational beings, the eternal destiny of any should depend on the precarious application of a few drops of water to their faces, soon after they were born? Yet thousands and millions have professed to believe this monstrous doctrine, and if an ill-fated infant was likely to expire, before water could be obtained, the priest or midwife would baptize it with *wine*.*

---

* Some in Upper Saxony, a little before the Reformation, practised baptism upon sickly new-born infants with only using the baptismal form of words, without the application of water in any form whatever. There is an account of a Jew, who suddenly turned christian where there was no water, and at the point of death, was baptized with sand. Some of the Irish, in the twelfth century, baptized their children by plunging them into *milk*, and were superstitious enough to imagine, that every part so plunged became invulnerable. *Robinson—Baldwin.*

How long must the Baptists be accused of holding, that baptism is a saving ordinance and essential to salvation, when they expressly and uniformly declare, that none but christians are entitled to it, and that it is not the putting away the filth of the flesh, but is the answer of a good conscience towards God ?

We will not accuse the Protestants of holding an opinion so shockingly absurd, but still, all Pedo-baptists, however evangelical, do attach to the baptism of a child, certain *invisible* benefits, which, as may well be supposed, no person yet could ever discover; and some, even of the Independents, have accused the hard-hearted Baptists of holding " *an infant damning doctrine*—and of maintaining with an audacious cruelty, a principle, which evidently excluded dear infants from the kingdom of God—and would send them by swarms into hell—and strike darts of anguish into the hearts of both parents and children."*

The liturgy of the Church of England defines baptism to be *regeneration*, and the funeral service is refused to such infants as die unbaptized.†

The meaning of the term Infant has been a matter of much dispute, in baptismal controversies. Pedo-baptist writers have generally gone upon the supposition, that it always means a babe. But Mr. Robinson has produced numerous and undeniable proofs, that in ancient ecclesiastical history, the words *pais, brephos, brephullion, puer, puerulus, infans, infantulus*, and so on, were used indiscriminately for minors. Out of the multitude of examples, which that ingenious author has produced, I shall select the following:

" *The last Will and Testament of Adald, a little infant of Lucca.*

"IN the name of God—in the twenty-first year of the reign of our Lord Charles, by the grace of God, king of the Franks and Lombards—I, Adald, the *little infant* son of Waltper, being sick and in danger of death, considering in myself the mercy of Almighty God, for the redemption of my soul, and according to a statute of king Liutprand,

* Robinson's History of Baptism, p. 476.

† The following anecdote is related by Dr. Baldwin, in his Letters to Rev. Samuel Worcester, in a note, p. 183: " A few years since, I was called to attend the funeral of an infant in this town, in a family, which, I was informed, belonged to the Episcopal church. I asked where the Rev. Dr. ———— was? and was answered he was out of town. Where is the Rev. Mr. ————? It was said, he was engaged. At length the gentleman of the house told me plainly, " The child was not baptized!" To this I replied, that I had the happiness to believe the child was gone equally as safe, as though it had been baptized."

of holy memory, offer to God, and to the church of blessed St. Martin—my house—out houses—gardens—lands—vineyards—olive yards—woods—underwoods—meadows—pastures, cultivated and uncultivated—and all my effects, moveable and immoveable—and also my house at—— and also my house at——and also all other rights, whatsoever and wheresoever—I offer as aforesaid, and confirm by this deed, which Ghislebert wrote at my request. Done at Lucca, in the year of Christ, seven hundred and ninety four."

This Will was witnessed by five *infants*, viz. Gumpert, Asprand, Pascal, Ghisprand, Erminari, four of whom were then presbyters.*

In the year three hundred and seventy-four, the church of Milan assembled to elect a bishop instead of Auxentius, lately deceased. They were divided into two violent parties, the one Arian, the other Trinitarian. Disputes ran so high that the city was in an uproar, and Ambrose the Governor, who was only a catechumen, and therefore had no vote, went thither to keep the peace. No sooner had he, by a conciliatory address, quieted the tumult, than to his great surprise, the whole assembly shouted, " Let Ambrose be bishop ! Let Ambrose be bishop !" and he soon found himself unanimously elected. And the first person who exclaimed, " Let Ambrose be bishop !" was an *infant*, that is, a church member who was under age.

Origen is quoted to prove infant baptism ; but Origen's infants were capable of repentance and martyrdom ; and infants are said to have nominated kings, erected churches, composed hymns, and so on.†

The truth of the case, says Mr. Robinson, is, circumstances must determine the ages of those, who were anciently called infants. The various words, translated infant, taken singly, crumble away in the hands of an investigator : they may signify a new-born babe, or a little boy of seven, or a great boy of fourteen years, or a young man turned of twenty ; and in support of this proposition, he has produced evidences in abundance from manuscripts, books, inscriptions, and laws.

* It was very customary, at this time, to introduce boys into holy orders for the purpose of securing them a future living, and of laying an early foundation for promotion.
† Robinson's History of Baptism, p. 157.

The passage in Acts, "*the promise is unto you and your children,*" has been much disputed. On this passage, many Pedo-baptists build half their superstructure. But it is evident the term children there is applied to posterity, without any regard to their age. We read of the children of Israel—the children of Benjamin—the children of promise—the children of God—the children of light—and so on. Infant baptism may as well be proved from either of these passages, as from the one in Acts.

A zealous Pedo-baptist lately asserted, that he could prove infant baptism from this passage, "*Ephraim is a cake unturned.*" And cardinal Bellarmine contended that he could prove the pope's supremacy from the first chapter of Genesis. And truly one may be done as easily as the other.

Dr. Wall observes that all national churches practise infant baptism. "Very true, (says Mr. Robinson) infant baptism, as it was intended, created national churches, and gives them continuance, as it gave them being. Let what will be said in praise of such churches, it can never be affirmed that they were either formed or continued by the free consent of their members. It was for this reason the learned Dr. Gill called infant baptism the main ground and pillar of popery, and a great number of Baptists are of the same opinion.

Time only can discover what the fate of this singular ceremony will be. If a judgment of the future may be formed by the past, infant baptism, like infant monachism, will fall into total disuse, and for the same reasons. It was formerly a practice, both in France and England, but most in England, to make monks and nuns of infants of seven, five, two, and even one year old; but this is now every where disused."

"Baptism (says this same writer in another place) arose pure in the east: it rolled westward, diminished in lustre, often beclouded with mists, and sometimes under a total eclipse; at length it escaped the eye, and was lost among attenuated particles, shades, non-entities, and monsters; then it took a contrary direction, and probably in time it will emerge from every depression, and shine in its original simplicity and excellence."

Proselyte Baptism demands a few words of attention. Many Pedo-baptist writers have depended much upon it to help them to evidence, which the Bible does not furnish; and Dr. Wall founds his main argument in favour of infant baptism on the practice. But after all that has been said about proselyte baptism, it remains a very doubtful affair, and Pedo-baptist writers are much divided among themselves respecting it. Dr. John Owen calls the opinion, that christian baptism came from the Jews, an opinion destitute of all probability.

That the Jews had frequent ablutions or washings, no one ever denied, but the washing of proselytes, which is improperly called baptism, is not found in the law of Moses, nor in the writings of Philo, or Josephus, but was evidently introduced after the destruction of the temple at Jerusalem.

" It is remarkable (says Robinson) of this controversy, that they, who most earnestly take the affirmative, are of all men the least interested; for could a christian rite be taken off the ground of immediate divine appointment, and placed on that of human traditions, christianity would lose much of its glory; least of all are they interested in it, who intend to establish a law to sprinkle the infants of christians, upon proving, that the Jews had a custom of dipping men and women when they renounced Paganism. In this hopeless affair, could the fact be demonstrated, no advance would be made in the argument; for it would be easy to prove, that if it were by tradition, Jewish traditions neither have, nor ought to have, any force with christians: and that if it were even an institute of Moses, the ceremonies of Moses were abolished in form by an authority, which no christian will oppose."

I have now gone through with narrating all the incidents, which the limits of this sketch will permit me to insert, and shall recapitulate the whole in the words of the the author I have so often named. Protestants have discovered great genius in inventing arguments for the support of infant baptism, and to some Baptists they seem to reason in this manner: It is written, God made a covenant with Abraham and his family: therefore, though it is not written, we ought to believe he makes a covenant with every christian and his family. God settled on Abraham and his family a large landed estate : therefore, he gives every christian and his family the benefits of the christian religion. God commanded Abraham and his family to circumcise their children: therefore, all professors of christianity ought, without a command, not to circumcise but to baptize their children. Jesus said, " suffer little children to come unto me :" therefore, infants who cannot come ought to be carried, not to Jesus, but to a minister, not to be healed, but to be baptized. Paul advised married believers at Corinth not to divorce their unbelieving yoke-fellows, lest they should stain the reputation of their children, with the scandal of illegitimacy: therefore, children, legitimate and illegitimate, ought to be baptized. A man of thirty years of age says he believes the gospel : therefore, his neighbour's infant of eight days ought to be baptized, as if he believed the gospel. And finally, the scripture does not mention infant baptism ; but it is, notwithstanding, full of proof that infants were and ought to be baptized.

Really, the Baptists ought to be forgiven for not having a taste for this kind of logic ; yea, they ought to be applauded for preferring argument before sophistry.

St. Austin and his company were the first who attacked believer's baptism at law ; but Zuinglius and Calvin are said to be the first, who invented the method of proving infant baptism from Abraham's covenant. The dispute between Baptists and Pedo-baptists has long been maintained, and still it remains unsettled. Every thing which slander could utter has been cast upon the Baptists, and every cruelty, which malicious ingenuity could devise, has been practised against them. Thousands of them have been slain, and thousands more have been dispersed into obscure corners and caves of the earth. But still they remain, and are rapidly advancing in numbers and strength. As a body, like others, they have been much divided on many other points, but in the article of baptism they have been uniform and unshakingly fixed. They have never persecuted, although they have had it in their power to do so. But they have reasoned and remonstrated, and against infant baptism they have urged the following objections :

First. It is not in our Lord's commission ; and what is not in a commission, must, of necessity, be out of it.

Second. It is no where found in the Bible ; and, therefore, it cannot be a Bible institution.

Third. They deny that infants derive any benefit from baptism, and thousands of them have had the opportunity of knowing ; but on the contrary affirm, that a great injury is done them by it, because they grow up in a prejudice, that they are christians, and, therefore, never examine what christianity is.

Fourth. Every person ought to be left free to choose his own religion ; but infant baptism imposes a religion upon its subjects, before they know it, and they often have much trouble to get rid of it, when they become capable of refusing the evil and choosing the good.

For these and many other reasons, the Baptists without the least misgiving, reject infant baptism ; and if saint Austin, and a thousand other saints beside, have said that it was an apostolical tradition, it does not in the least affect their belief, so long as they find that saint Luke, saint Paul, and saint Peter, have no where mentioned it, but have laid down principles, which go entirely to exclude it. They do not wonder that many saints have asserted what none ever proved, but they wonder that some of them have not interpolated scripture to serve their hypothesis.

The Baptists are accused by their opponents of having an assurance peculiar to themselves. This accusation they are not unwilling to admit. Their peculiar assurance arises from the clear and peculiar evidence with which their sentiments are supported. This assurance has been called presumption, and those who persisted in it, in former days, were denounced obstinate hereticks, and doomed to suffer fire and sword in this world, and eternal perdition in the world to come. But a gracious Providence has now delivered us from the force of these terrible arguments.

While Pedo-baptists send inquirers to their pamphlets and doctors, the Baptists send them to the Bible, and they cannot but exult that their sentiments are there so plainly expressed. And what emboldens them, and disgusts their opponents is, that every man, woman, and child has the leading passages by heart, on which their sentiments are founded, and can, at once, produce arguments, which the greatest doctors cannot answer without *much time*, nor then without *much sophistry*.

It is a very unlucky circumstance, that infant baptism is no where mentioned in the Bible, and I pity the person, who, with a tender conscience, sets out to find it there; for, sure I am, he will have a hard and fruitless task, and if he finally succeeds, it must be by subverting his own understanding.

The study of infant baptism is the most perplexing study in the world, as many, who are now Baptists, know by experience. And the reason is, it perverts the order of scripture. But in the study of believer's baptism every thing is plain and easy.

Infant baptism is supported by a long string of texts from the Old Testament and New, none of which mention the thing, and none of which refer to such a practice, any more than Hagar's going out into the wilderness of Beersheba, leading her sulky son Ishmael, and carrying with her a loaf of bread and a bottle of water. In this passage we find a *child* and *water*, and these are not found in many of the passages brought to support infant baptism.

As to all the shocking consequences which follow from Baptist principles, we have only to say, they are drawn by Pedo-baptists, and not by us.

And since three-fourths of the terraqueous globe is covered with water, we never expect to find any difficulty in procuring a full supply of this element.

The substance of this sketch has been selected from Robinson's incomparable history of baptism, to which I have often referred; and many sentiments and sentences, for which no formal credit has been given, have been taken from that laborious and invaluable work. There are but few copies of it in this country. It is a quarto volume of between six and seven hundred pages, with very copious Latin notes. This work will bear to be abridged; and by omitting the notes and some other articles, it might be reduced to an octavo volume of four or five hundred pages, without leaving out any of the important matter which relates to baptism. In making out the above sketch, which has been selected from every part of it, I have been obliged to study it with considerable attention, and have conceived the design of undertaking to abridge it, after I have had a little respite from my present labour.*

CHAP. III.

A GENERAL ACCOUNT OF THE BAPTISTS IN FOREIGN COUNTRIES AND ANCIENT TIMES.

THIS chapter will extend from the introduction of christianity to about the time of the reformation under Luther and his associates.

All sects trace their origin to the Apostles, or at least to the early ages of christianity. But many, and especially the powerful ones, have laboured hard to cut off the Baptists from this common retreat. They have often asserted and taken much pains to prove that the people now called Baptists originated with the mad men of Munster, about 1522. We have only to say to this statement, that it is not true. And notwithstanding all that has been said to the contrary, we still date the origin of our sentiments, and the beginning of our denomination, about the year of our Lord twenty-nine or thirty ; for at that period John the Baptist began to immerse professed believers in Jordan and Enon, and to prepare the way for the coming of the Lord's Anointed, and for the setting up of his kingdom.

But before we proceed any farther, it is proper that the terms Baptist and Anabaptist should be defined.

A Baptist is one, who holds that a profession of faith, and an immersion in water are essential to baptism. An Anabaptist is one who is rebaptized. The name of Baptist we admit is significant and proper ; but that of Anabaptist we reject as slanderous, and no ways descriptive of our sentiments and practice ; and when our opponents accuse us of Anabaptism, we always understand the charge

---

* Many articles which are largely and learnedly discussed by Mr. Robinson, have not been referred to in the preceding sketch ; as baptism connected with Monachism—with social obligations—with Human Creeds—with Judaism—with Chivalry—with Sacerdotal Habits—and with Witchcraft ; The baptism of Bells, Tropical Baptism, the Christening of Fleets, and so on.

as the language either of ignorance or malice. In one sense there were never any Anabaptists in christendom, and yet according to historians there have been multitudes in different ages and countries. All, who ever administered baptism a second time, did it upon the supposition that the first baptism was imperfect. No party of christians ever held to two baptisms, or presumed to repeat the baptismal rite, after it had been, in their opinion, once properly administered. In this sense there never have been any Anabaptists, although multitudes have rebaptized, or, in other words, performed in a right manner, what, upon their principles, had been improperly done. According to Robinson there have been six sorts of christians, who have been called Anabaptists, as different from one another, as can well be imagined. The first placed the essence of baptism in the virtue of the person baptized ; the second placed it in the form of words pronounced in the administration ; the third in the virtue of the administrator ; the fourth in the consent of the person baptized ; the fifth in dipping ; and the sixth in both a profession of faith and an immersion.

By all of these classes multitudes were rebaptized, and yet no party acknowledged themselves Anabaptists ; for they all thought that there was one Lord, one faith, and one baptism, and that their own. The Catholicks most eagerly contend that pope Sylvester baptized Constance the Great into the faith of the Trinity at Rome, and the evidence seems respectable. It is however certain that he was baptized at Nicomedia just before his death, and it is supposed by Eusebius, into the Arian faith. Both affirm they baptized him ; neither says he was rebaptized, because neither accounted the other a valid baptism. Probably, some Catholic writers express the matter exactly as it was. Sylvester baptized the emperour, and Eusebius rebaptized him. They affirm the same of the emperour Valens, and denominate both these emperours Anabaptists.

Dionysius and his followers in Egypt, the Acephali, Novatus of Rome, Novatian of Carthage, all the Novatian churches, Donatus and his numberless followers, called after him Donatists, of whom there were four hundred congregations at one time in Africa, all rejected the baptism administered by those, who have since been called Catholicks, whom they reputed hereticks, and whose churches they called habitations of impurity, and all such as came from those churches to them they rebaptized.

In the year 325, the council of Nice decreed, that all who came over to the established church, from the Paulianists, both men and women, should be rebaptized, while proselytes from the Novatians or Puritans were admitted by the laying on of hands. The reason for this difference was, that the Novatians baptized in the name of the Father, Son, and Holy Ghost, while the Paulianists, who denied the Trinity, omitted this form. For a long time the Catholics rejected the baptism of the Arians, and the Arians in return rejected theirs. Both parties rebaptized their proselytes, and all practised dipping.

These are a few of the many facts, which might be adduced to show that Anabaptism, as it is improperly called, is not peculiar to the Baptists. According to the common acceptation of the term, her imperial majesty Catherine III. late empress of all the Russias, was an Anabaptist. " For it is strictly true," as an elegant and accurate historian observes, "that in the year 1745, Peter, afterwards Czar Peter III. espoused Sophia Augusta, princess of Anhalt Zerbst, who, upon being rebaptized, according to the rites of the Greek church, was called Catherine Alexiefna, and so on."*

Thus much for the general subject of rebaptization. Whatever notions of impiety people may now attach to the practice, it is certain that all parties have been more or less guilty of it.

We shall now turn our attention to that class of Anabaptists, with whom we claim relation, and who would now be considered Baptists, by whatever name they were formerly called. This is the sixth class in Mr. Robinson's list of rebaptizers. They have ever held, that a personal profession of faith, and an immersion in water are essential to baptism. Christians of these sentiments have existed in every age, and their number has been larger than their friends generally imagine, or than their opposers are ever willing to acknowledge. The first christians were undoubtedly all Baptists, and we believe they will all be Baptists again, when they are all brought to keep the ordinances of Christ as they were first delivered to the saints.

* Robinson's History of Baptism, p. 459, 460.

For almost three centuries baptism was in the main rightly administered by all parties, for they all required a profession of faith, and all immersed.

We do not pretend that the primitive saints were called Baptists ; all went under the general denomination of Christians, and when they began to file off into parties, they took the names of the men by whom they were led. It is not the history of a name, but the prevalence of a principle, of which we are in search. No denomination of Protestants can trace the origin of its name farther back than about the time of the reformation, and most of them have originated since that period. And I suppose it was about this time that our brethren began to be called Baptists. And I am inclined to think that they assumed the name in opposition to that of Anabaptists, with which their enemies were continually reproaching them. But that all the primitive christians would have been called Baptists, if sentimental names had then been in use, and that there always has been a people on earth, from the introduction of Christianity, who have held the leading sentiments by which they now are, and always have been peculiarly distinguished, is a point which I most firmly believe, and which I shall now attempt to prove.

I know that all denominations take this ground, and attempt to prove that their sentiments have existed from the Apostles through every age. The Catholick pretends that his church is of Apostolic origin, and was founded by St. Peter, and he can easily prove that a very large portion of the christian world, has, for many centuries, been and now is of his belief. The Churchman pleads that all the first christians were Episcopalians, and that Bishops Paul, Peter, Timothy, and Titus, governed the churches ; and he moreover supposes that Paul's parchment, which he left at Troas, contained his episcopal authority. The Presbyterians, Independents, Congregationalists, Quakers, Methodists, and all contend that their churches are built after the Apostolic model. And even the Shaking Quaker, although he can make no good pretension to Apostolical succession, yet claims relation to the hundred and forty and four thousand who have not defiled themselves with women. I am not about to dispute the pretensions or proofs of any one sect in christendom. It is not my object to show what is not true respecting them, but what is true respecting ourselves. The Episcopalian can find Bishops, and the Presbyterian Elders or Presbyters among the primitive christians, and the Congregationalist and Independent, have good grounds for saying that the Apostolic churches were of their belief respecting church government. The Baptists believe in Episcopacy and Presbyterianism or eldership, when explained according to their sense of the terms. They hold to the zeal of the Methodists, and the inward light of the Quakers, when regulated and explained according to their sense of propriety and correctness. With most denominations they find something with which they agree. But in the article of baptism they differ from all. While their brethren all around admit infants to baptism, they have always confined the rite to professed believers, and a baptism without an immersion is, in their opinion, "like a guinea without gold."

The Baptists have been distinguished from other sects, not only in their views of the subjects and mode of baptism, but they have always held to other sentiments peculiar to themselves, and which they consider essential important truths, but which their opponents have branded with the name of dangerous errors or damnable heresies.

The supporters of believer's baptism have, under every form of government, been the advocates for liberty ; and for this reason, they have never flourished much except in those governments where some degree of freedom has been maintained. Arbitrary states have always oppressed them, and driven them for refuge to milder regions. "They cannot live in tyrannical states, and free countries are the only places to seek for them, for their whole publick religion is impracticable without freedom." In political changes they have always been friendly to the cause of liberty, and their passion for it has at different times led some into acts of indiscretion, and scenes of danger. But with a few exceptions, we may say in truth, that the Baptists have always adhered to their leading maxim, to be *subject to the powers that be ;* and all the favour they as christians have asked of civil governments has been, *to give them their Bibles, and let them alone.* The interference of the magistrate in the affairs of conscience, they

Leading Maxims of the Baptists.

have never courted, but have always protested against. Classical authority and priestly domination, they have ever opposed and abhorred, and the equality of christians as such, and the absolute independency of churches, they have most scrupulously maintained. Learning they have esteemed in its proper place; but they have also uniformly maintained, that the servants of God may preach his gospel without it. The distinction between their ministers and brethren is less than in almost any other denomination of christians; whatever abilities their ministers possess, they reduce them to the capacity of mere teachers; and they consider all not only at liberty, but moreover bound to exercise, under proper regulations, the gifts they may possess, for the edification of their brethren.

We have thus endeavoured to define the term Anabaptist, and have shown that it never has been admitted by any party as a significant term, but has always been considered slanderous and improper. We shall frequently make use of it in the following sketches, but it must be understood, that we use it as a word, which custom has made necessary.

We have also attempted to give a brief definition of the term Baptist, and have at the same time exhibited some of the leading principles and features of the people to whom it is applied. We shall endeavour to give some few sketches of the history of that class of christians, whom we consider Baptists, or who have maintained the ordinances of Christ as they were first delivered to the saints. This chapter embraces a period of about fifteen hundred years; most of which time the church was in the wilderness, and for that reason we cannot expect to learn much respecting her. No human pen has recorded her history with any degree of correctness, but it is registered on high, and will be exhibited in the great day of accounts. In travelling down the records of a worldly sanctuary we get a glimpse now and then of the friends of godliness, and we generally behold them destitute, afflicted, and tormented. Some of the saints mistook the time of their Lord's coming, and ventured out from their obscure retreats, in hopes to meet him in his providential dealings, but they generally met with disaster and death. Antichrist sent his archers into the wilderness to hunt the disciples of Jesus, and by them some reports have been communicated of their character and situation. But after all, we know but very little of the real church of Christ, for the long lapse of many hundred years. We have very ample accounts of the antichristian church through all her movements; and the affairs of some of the saints in Babylon are very minutely detailed. But the history of the uncorrupted church, which maintained the worship and ordinances of Christ, while all the world was wondering after the beast, is covered with obscurity, and probably lost in oblivion.

From the New-Testament account of the primitive christians, we are led to think they were Baptists. But we will quote the accounts given of them by two authors, and then the reader may judge for himself. Mosheim was no friend to the Baptists, and yet he has made many important concessions in their favour; and in relating the history of the primitive church, he has given a description, which will not certainly apply to his own church, the Lutheran, nor to any sect in christendom except the Baptists. " Baptism," he observes, " was administered in the first century without the public assemblies, in places appointed for that purpose, and was performed by immersion of the whole body in water." By this account it appears that the first christians went " streaming away (as Dr. Osgood would say) to some pond or river" to be baptized. Respecting church discipline, the same writer observes : " The churches in those early times were entirely independent, none of them subject to any foreign jurisdiction, but each one governed by its own rulers and laws. For though the churches, founded by the Apostles, had this particular deference shewn them, that they were consulted in difficult and doubtful cases, yet they had no juridical authority, no sort of supremacy over the others, nor the least right to enact laws for them. Nothing on the contrary is more evident than the perfect equality that reigned among the primitive churches,"* and so on. " A bish-

* Respecting the council at Jerusalem, Mosheim has the following note, vol. I. p. 105. " The meeting of the church at Jerusalem, mentioned in the xv. chapter of the Acts, is commonly considered as the *first christian council*. But this notion arises from the manifest abuse of the word *council*. That meeting was only of one church; and if such a meeting be called a *council*, it will follow that there were innumerable councils in the primitive times. But every one knows, that a *council* is an assembly of deputies or commissioners sent from several churches associated by certain bonds in a general

op, during the first and second century, was a person who had the care of one christian assembly, which at that time was, generally speaking, small enough to be contained in a private house. In this assembly he acted not so much with the authority of a *master*, as with the zeal and diligence of a faithful *servant*,"* and so on.

" There was," says Robinson, "among primitive christians, an uniform belief that Jesus was the Christ, and a perfect harmony of affection. When congregations multiplied, so that they became too numerous to assemble in one place, they parted into separate companies, and so again and again, but there was no schism; on the contrary all held a common union, and a member of one company was a member of all. If any person removed from one place to reside at another, he received a letter of attestation, which was given and taken as proof; and this custom very prudently precluded the intrusion of impostors. In this manner was framed a catholick or universal church. One company never pretended to inspect the affairs of another, nor was there any dominion, or any shadow of dominion, over the consciences of any individuals. Overt acts were the only objects of censure, and censure was nothing but voting a man out of the community."

Let any candid man compare the different denominations of christians of the present day with these descriptions of the primitive church, and he will, we think, be at no loss to determine which comes the nearest to it. But Mr. Robinson goes farther, and determines the matter just as a Baptist believes. " During the three first centuries, christian congregations all over the east subsisted in sepa-

body, and therefore the supposition above mentioned falls to the ground." Mosheim appears to understand the word council in a high ecclesiastical sense, and in this point of view his observations are doubtless correct; but according to the ideas which a Baptist would affix to the term *council*, I see no impropriety in applying it to this assembly. But I find our brethren differ in their opinions respecting the nature of this council, whether it was advisory or authoritative. Dr. Gill gives the decisions of this assembly no higher name than *advice*, sentiments, determinations, &c. and in this point of view, I think it proper to consider them. But it ought to be observed at the same time, that the advice of so respectable a body as the apostolic mother church at Jerusalem, assisted in its deliberations, by the apostles and elders, and all acting under the influence of the Holy Ghost, became a law or a rule of action to the church at Antioch, and to other christians in the primitive ages. " This advice," says Dr. Gill, "was regarded as a law," &c.

* Mosheim, vol. i. p. 103, 104, 105, 126.

rate, independent bodies, unsupported by government, and consequently without any secular power over one another. All this time they were Baptist churches, and though all the fathers of the four first ages down to Jerome were of Greece, Syria, and Africa, and though they gave great numbers of histories of the baptism of adults, yet there is not one record of the baptism of a child till the year 370, when Galates, the dying son of the emperour Valens, was baptized by order of a monarch, who swore he would not be contradicted. The age of the prince is uncertain, and the assigning of his illness as the cause of his baptism indicates clearly enough that infant baptism was not in practice."

But the primitive Baptist churches, in process of time, became corrupted with many errours, and with infant baptism among the rest. And when Constantine established christianity as the religion of his empire, errours, which before had taken root, soon grew up to maturity, the christian church as established by law became a worldly sanctuary, and those who would maintain the gospel in its purity were obliged to separate from the great mass of professors, and retire to the best refuges they could find. We have shown in the Review of Ecclesiastical History, that the church of Rome and the Greek church have ever comprehended the great majority of those, who have borne the christian name. But from these two extensive establishments multitudes have dissented. The dissenters have been of every possible description and character, and it may be truly said of every religious absurdity and fantastical opinion, that there is nothing new under the sun, for they have all been broached and maintained in former times. All dissenters were denounced hereticks, and in many cases the name was not misapplied; but on the other hand it is certain, that for many centuries we must search among reputed hereticks, for what little of godliness remained on the earth.

Mr. Robinson, in his Ecclesiastical Researches, under the head *Greek Church*, has entered largely into the history of dissenters from that wide spread community, and the following sketches collected from different parts of the article, contain the substance of what he has said respecting them.

"The first founders of the dissenting sects were primitive christians, who would not conform. They had, as an ancient writer says, neither head nor tail, neither princes nor legislators, and consequently no slaves; they had no beginning nor no end, and in this respect they answered one of their nick names, which was Melchisedecians, for like Melchisedec they were without father, without mother, without beginning of days or end of life. The church thought them enthusiasts and blasphemers. The truth is, they followed no one, but acted as their own understandings ordered them, as good men in all ages have always done."

"This large body of dissenters was resident in the empire from the first establishment of the church in the fourth century to the destruction of it in the thirteenth. They were named Massalians and Euchites, the one a Hebrew, the other a Greek name, and both signifying a people that pray, for they placed religion, not in speculation, but in devotion and piety. Euchite among the Greeks was a general name for a dissenter, as Waldensian was in the Latin church, and as Nonconformist is in England."*

"Some of these dissenters dogmatized as the established clergy did, and they became Manichean, Arian, and Athanasian Euchites. Others were named after the countries where they most abounded, as Bulgarians, Macedonians, Armenians, Phrygians, Cataphrygians, Galatians, Philippopolitans, or, as it was corruptly sounded in the west, Popolicans, Poblicans, Publicans. Others were named after some eminent teacher, as Paulicians, and Paulianists from Paul of Samosata, or, says the princess Comnena, from Paul and John the sons of Callinices, Novatians, Donatists, Artemonites, and many more were of this class."

The first council of Nice took notice of two sorts of dissenters, the Cathari or Puritans, and the Paulianists. "The first held the doctrine of the Trinity, as the Athanasians in the church did; but thinking the church a worldly community, they baptized all that joined their assem-

---

* Mosheim has given a similar account of the Massalians or Euchites and the Waldenses, and Dr. Maclaine has explained the matter more fully in a note, vol. III. pp. 105—6.

blies by trine immersion, in the name of the Father, Son, and Holy-Ghost, on their own personal profession of faith, and if they had been baptized before, they rebaptized them. The latter baptized by dipping once in the name of Christ, and though they varied from the Arians, yet they all thought Christ only a man."

The Cathari or Puritans would, according to this author's account, now be called Predestinarians or Calvinists; and the Paulianists would be entitled to the appellation of Arminians and Socinians.

Dr. Mosheim, in speaking of the Greek dissenters, says truly, "that the accounts, which have been given of them, are not in all respects to be depended upon ; and there are several circumstances, which render it extremely probable, that many persons of eminent piety and zeal for genuine christianity, were confounded by the Greeks with these enthusiasts, and ranked in the list of hereticks, merely on account of their opposing the vicious practices and the insolent tyranny of the priesthood, and their treating with derision that motley spectacle of superstition that was supported by public authority. In short, the righteous and the profligate, the wise and the foolish, were equally comprehended under the name of Massalians, whenever they opposed the reigning superstition of the times, or looked upon true and genuine piety, as the essence of the christian character."*

The sum of the matter seems to be, that the established Greek church held both the subject and the mode of baptism as the first institution prescribed for four or five hundred years, losing the subject by degrees, but retaining the mode to this day : and that the bulk of the dissenters, perhaps all, retained both the subject and the mode, always dipping, and never dipping any but on their own personal profession of faith."

Much the same may be said respecting the number and character of dissenters from the church of Rome. Some separated, because the leading party had become corrupt, and others to follow reveries of enthusiastic zeal. The Novatians appear to have been among the earliest dissenters of the former kind. In the third century, when the primitive simplicity of the gospel was fast going into de-

* Moshiem, Vol. III. pp. 105—6.

cay, a great separation took place at Rome, and multitudes bore a noble testimony against the prevailing corruption of the times. At Rome, these dissenters were called Novatians, from Novatus, one of the chief managers of the affair. They called themselves Puritans, or, as the Greeks translated the word, Cathari; and they intended by the name to signify the fact, that they separated from the rest, because their morals were impure.*

As yet, all baptized by immersion; and the Novatians or Puritans rebaptized all, who came over from the prevailing party. They were of course Baptists.

Milner acknowledges that the Novatians were the most respectable of all the dissenting churches; notwithstanding he complains much of their narrow bigotry in things of no moment.†

Mosheim, always disposed to be the advocate of the great body which he calls *the church*, has, amidst his severe strictures on the Novatians, given them a character, which all evangelical christians cannot but in the main approve. "This sect," says he, "cannot be charged with having corrupted the doctrine of christianity by their opinions; their crime was that by the unreasonable severity of their discipline, they gave occasion to the most deplorable divisions, and made an unhappy rent in the church. They considered the christian church as a society where virtue and innocence reigned universally, and none of whose members, from their entrance into it, had defiled themselves with any enormous crime; and, of consequence, they looked upon every society, which readmitted heinous offenders to its communion, as unworthy of the title of a true christian church. It was from hence also, that they assumed the title of *Cathari*, i. e. the *pure;* and what shewed still a more extravagant degree of vanity and arrogance," (this language is perfectly understood by all the advocates for believer's baptism) "they obliged such as came over to them from the general body of Christians, to submit to be baptized a second time, as a necessary preparation for entering into their society."‡

* Robinson's Ecclesiastical Researches, pp. 124—5.
† Milner's Church History, Vol. II. p. 240.
‡ Mosheim, vol. i. p. 299, 301.

The church, whose tranquillity the Novatians disturbed, was, according to Mosheim's own account, in a most deplorable condition. " Her rulers were sunk in luxury and voluptuousness, puffed up with vanity, arrogance, and ambition, possessed with a spirit of contention and discord, and addicted to many other vices." All nonconformists know what is meant by the crime of disturbing the church.

It is generally admitted by all who have written their history, that the Novatians laid it down as a fundamental principle, that no apostate or heinous offender, should be readmitted into their communion, however genuine his repentance might appear. This maxim unquestionably deserves the name of " unreasonable severity." It was probably suggested by the corruptions of the times, and we cannot suppose it was long maintained.*

The Catholick party tax Novatian with being the parent of an innumerable multitude of congregations of Puritans all over the empire. And it is probable that the people, who were afterwards called Waldenses, were his descendants. " Great numbers," says Robinson, " followed the example of Novatian, and all over the empire, Puritan churches were constituted and flourished through the succeeding two hundred years. Afterward, when penal laws obliged them to meet in corners and worship God in private, they were distinguished by a variety of names, and a succession of them continued till the reformation."†

" It is impossible to prove that the nonconformists of early times baptized their children ; on the contrary, it is certain some of them did not."

In other countries, within the jurisdiction of the church of Rome, we meet with many dissenters, who appear to have maintained the peculiar sentiments of the Baptists.

---

* Mr. Robinson supposes that a church of the Novatians would address a candidate for admission in the following manner : " If you be a virtuous believer, and will accede to our confederacy against sin, you may be admitted among us by baptism, or if any Catholick has baptized you before, by rebaptism ; but, mark this, if you violate the contract by lapsing into idolatry or vice, we shall separate you from our community, and do what you will, we shall never readmit you. God forbid we should injure either your person, your property or your character, or even judge of the truth of your repentance, and your future state ; but you can never be readmitted to our community, without our giving up the best and only coercive guardian we have of the purity of our morals."

† Ecclesiastical Researches, p. 126—7

Anabaptists in Spain....Paterines in Italy.

Spain, which was long one of the main pillars of the papal power, and in which the bloody inquisition has displayed all the terrors of its sanguinary spirit, was once a land of piety, where a good degree of freedom was enjoyed. As the established church sunk into corruption, the pious dissented from it, and for a time were permitted, without much molestation, to enjoy their peculiar opinions. But in process of time, the inquisition, with its solemn horrors, like death, put all under its feet, and dissenters were either terrified into conformity, or dispersed into other countries.

While dissenters were permitted to reside in Spain, they were called, in general, Anabaptists. They baptized converts from pagans and Jews, and rebaptized all Catholicks, who came over to their communion, and they baptized none without a personal confession of faith.*

The Paterines of Italy were, for a time, a numerous and flourishing sect. Different accounts are given of their doctrinal sentiments. They were charged by their enemies with being Manicheans; this charge, however, was often brought against the most pious and orthodox. Mr. Robinson thinks they were Unitarians, but it is not probable they all rejected the doctrine of the Trinity. They were sometimes called Gazari, which is a corruption of Cathari or Puritans. But Patrini or Paterines, was the name by which they were generally distinguished. In Milan, where this name was first used, it answered to the English words vulgar, illiterate, low-bred; intimating what was a fact, that these despised christians were of the lower order of people. It is remarkable of the Paterines, that in their examinations, they were not accused of any immoralities, but were condemned for speculations, or rather for virtuous rules of action, which all the world counted heresies. They said—a christian church ought to consist of only good people—that it was unlawful to kill mankind—that the church ought not to persecute any, even the wicked—that there was no need of priests, especially wicked ones. In these and other reasons and rules they all agreed, but in doctrinal speculations they widely differed.

* Robinson's Ecclesiastical Researches, p. 246.

As the Catholicks of those times baptized by immersion, the Paterines, by what name soever they were called, as Manicheans, Gazari, Josephists, Arnoldists, Passagines, Bulgarians or Bougares, made no complaint of the mode of baptizing : but, when they were examined, they objected vehemently against the baptism of infants, and condemned it as an error. They said, among other things, that a child knew nothing of the matter, that he had no desire to be baptized, and was incapable of making any confession of faith, and that the willing and professing of another, could be of no service to him.*

The great Waldensian body demands our next attention, and in giving their history we shall comprehend that of most of the other Baptist dissenters in the dark ages of popery, for they all appear to have been in some measure connected with it.

The Waldenses are, by all parties of Protestants, considered to have been witnessess for the truth, through all the dark reign of superstition and error. And the Waldensian heresy, was by the Catholicks counted the oldest in the world and the most formidable to the church of Rome. These people, for a number of centuries, had their chief residence in the vallies of Piedmont, and from thence, in process of time, they spread over most of the countries of Europe.

Piedmont is a principality of Italy 175 miles long and 40 broad, bounded north by Vallais, east by Milan and Montferrat, south by Nice and Genoa, west by France and Savoy. This country was formerly a part of Lombardy, afterwards it was subject to the king of Sardinia, but in 1800 it was conquered by France. Piedmont lies at the foot of the Alps, and contains many high mountains, among which are rich and fruitful vallies, as populous as any part of Italy. Turin is the capital. But we must distinguish between the principality of Piedmont and the vallies which were famous for the Waldenses, between the common inhabitants and the established religion of the country, and the faithful witnesses for the truth, which resided here from time immemorial.

The church of Rome is the established religion of the principality of Piedmont, and has been from early times ;

* Researches p. 408.

but several causes contributed to render the establishment, for many centuries, more mild and less troublesome to dissenters here, than in other parts of the papal dominions. The bishop of Turin, the capital of Piedmont, was not a Metropolitan, till 1515. No bishops before were subject to him. At present, there are in the principality of Piedmont, eight bishopricks. Of these only three are suffragan to the archbishoprick of Turin. One of them was not erected into an episcopal see till the year 1388, nor another till 1592, and one hath only seven parishes in it. Three of the remaining five are subject to the archbishop of Milan; one is an exempt, and subject only to the pope, and the other is united to another province. This is the modern arrangement; but in the middle ages, what few bishops there were, considered themselves in the province of Milan, and subject to the archbishop; but as their bishopricks were in different states, none of which suffered the incumbents to exercise temporal dominion, except in particular cases on their own lordships, and generally not there, it is easy to infer that episcopacy in Piedmont was not materially injurious to the liberties of the people.

Under these circumstances the Waldenses enjoyed a degree of repose, and maintained the pure worship of God, in the remote ages of idolatry and superstition.

It is supposed by President Edwards that the ancient Waldenses dwelt mostly in five vallies on the southern side of the Alps, which were begirt around with high and almost impassable hills, and if any local residence is intended in the twelfth chapter of Revelation, this mountainous retreat promises most of all others to be the one.

But it is evident these people dwelt in many other vallies, on both sides of the Alps, in France and Italy, and were dispersed in many places in all the surrounding country. But the cruel inquisitors at length found their way to the happy asylums of these faithful witnesses, multitudes were slain, and others were dispersed in almost all the European kingdoms.

It will be proper, before we proceed any further, to give some account of the beginning of the Waldenses, and of the manner in which they received their name. And respecting the origin of this body of christians, two leading sentiments have prevailed. The papists date their origin in the twelfth century, under the famous reformer Peter Waldo. With this account Moshiem and some others seem to agree. The papists are interested in disputing the antiquity of the Waldensian sect, and dating its origin as late as possible ; for if they can prove that they had no existence until the twelfth century, they thence infer that the church of Rome prevailed universally from the early ages up to that time. But Protestants generally of all classes contend that the Waldenses are of much higher antiquity than the time of Peter Waldo of Lyons; but they are not all agreed respecting the time and circumstances of their origin.

Robinson and Milner consider Claude, bishop of Turin, the founder of the sect of the Waldenses. The former calls him the Wickliff of Turin, and the latter the christian hero of the ninth century. This famous reformer was a native of Spain. He was chaplain to the emperor Lewis the Meek, who preferred him to the bishoprick of Turin, where he distinguished himself by his zeal against images, relicks, pilgrimages, and crosses, all of which abounded in his diocess. Three or four French monks wrote against him as a blasphemer and a heretick ; and his own people were so refractory that he went in fear of his life. He bore a noble testimony against the prevailing errors of his time, and was undoubtedly a most respectable character. He was alive in the year 839. He denied the supremacy of the bishop of Rome ; but it is also said that he expressed a great respect for catholicism, and opposed schism and heresy with all his might.* Thus far the history of Claude of Turin appears plain ; but respecting the effects of his ministry in Turin and other parts of Piedmont different opinions are entertained. But it appears evident he was a man of evangelical zeal ; that he was the means of promoting the cause of the dissenters in Piedmont, while he himself remained in the establishment ; that he laid down principles in his preaching, which he did not carry through in his practice, a thing very common for reformers of his character ; that his disciples reasoned consequentially on the principles of their master, and after his death, if not before, renounced the communion of the church of Rome, together with all the pompous and superstitious appendages

* Robinson's Ecc. Res. p. 447—8.

Origin of the Name Waldenses. 109

with which it was surrounded. But I cannot think that Claude of Turin was the founder of the sect of the Waldenses. They doubtless profited by his ministry, and received great accessions from his converts; but from the suggestions of both enemies and friends, I must believe that there was a body of christians in the vallies of Piedmont and in the recesses of the Alps, of the same character of the Waldenses, long before the time of Claude.

Dr. Allix, in his history of the churches of Piedmont, gives this account of the origin of the Waldenses: That for three hundred years or more, the bishop of Rome attempted to subjugate the church of Milan under his jurisdiction; and at last the interest of Rome grew too potent for the church of Milan, planted by one of the disciples; insomuch, that the bishop and the people, rather than own their jurisdiction, retired to the vallies of Lucern and Angrogne; and thence were called Vallenses, Wallenses, or the People of the Vallies.*

President Edwards, as quoted by Mr. Merrill in his Miniature History of the Baptists, has the following observations respecting these ancient witnesses for the truth: "It is supposed that these people first betook themselves to this desert, secret place among the mountains, to hide themselves from the severity of the heathen persecutions, which were before Constantine the great, and thus the woman fled into the wilderness from the face of the serpent, as related in Revelation." &c.

Cranz, in his history of the United Brethren, as quoted by Ivimey, has the following statement respecting the origin of the Waldenses. "These ancient christians, (who, besides the several names of reproach given them, were at length denominated Waldenses, from one of the most eminent teachers, Peter Waldus, who is said to have emigrated with the rest from France into Bohemia, and there to have died) date their origin from the beginning of the fourth century; when one Leo, at the great revolution in religion under Constantine the great, opposed the innovations of Sylvester, bishop of Rome," &c.†

* See Alix's History of the churches in Piedmont, and Perrin's History of the Waldenses, as quoted by Hannah Adams, in her View of Religion, p. 304.

† Ivimey, p. 57.

The cruel Reinerus, who spent much time in examining these people, observes, that "some aver their existence from the days of Sylvester,* and others from the very time of the Apostles." This account the inquisitor seems to have taken from the Waldenses themselves, and it appears highly probable, that it is in substance correct. Their doctrine had existed from the time of the Apostles, and they, as a body, had probably existed from the time of Sylvester, when the church sunk into superstition and formality, and the pious retired from the pompous parade of a worldly minded throng.

I might quote concurring testimonies of the high antiquity of the Waldensian christians. Some popish writers own that they never submitted to the church of Rome, and all acknowledge, that all her cruel laws and persecuting measures, could never extirpate them.

The beforementioned inquisitor pretends, that there had been more than seventy sects of hereticks, of which, through the grace of God, all were extinct, except four, Manicheans, Arians, Runcarians, and Leonists, or the poor men of Lyons, another name of the Waldenses.

From all we can learn it appears, that the recesses of the Alps and the Pyrenees, together with the adjoining hills and vallies in France, Spain, and Italy, were distinguished retreats of the faithful friends of God, in the darkest ages of the christian world. Mr. Robinson with his usual singularity, observes "that Greece was the parent, Spain and Navarre the nurses, France the step-mother, and Savoy the jailer of this class of christians called Waldenses."†

The Waldenses received their name either from the vallies which they inhabited, or from Peter Waldo or Valdus of Lyons, in France. From the Latin *vallis*, came the English *valley*, the French and Spanish *valle*, the Italian *valdesi*, and the low Dutch *valleye*. The word for *valley* in the language of Piedmont is *vaux*, and the inhabitants of vallies were hence called *vaudois*, the name, which

---

* The Sylvester, whose name thus frequently occurs, was the bishop of Rome in the time of Constantine, and the one, who, the Catholicks contend, baptized the emperor.

† Robinson's Res. p. 320.—Piedmont was, for a long time, subject to the dukes of Savoy.

the people now in question gave themselves. But English and Latin writers used the term *Vallenses* instead of *vaudois*, which was, in process of time, changed into *Valdenses* and then into *Waldenses*, which last term, all at present agree to use. This account of the origin of the name Waldenses is highly probable, and would seem to admit of no dispute, were it not for Peter Waldo, a famous reformer of the twelth century. This eminent man was a wealthy merchant of Lyons, in France, who, upon his embracing the truth, quitted his mercantile employment, distributed his wealth among the poor, procured a translation of the Scriptures in the French language, became a zealous and successful preacher of the gospel, had many disciples and followers, who formed religious assemblies first in France and afterwards in Lombardy, and in a short time throughout the other provinces of Europe. His followers were sometimes called Leonists, or the poor men of Lyons, but generally they were denominated Waldenses. And Mosheim asserts that the whole sect of the Waldenses received their name from Waldo. But Dr. Maclaine, his translator, asserts the contrary, and contends that Waldo derived his name from the true Valdenses or Waldenses of Piedmont.*

* " Certain writers, says Mosheim, give different accounts of the origin of the *Waldenses*, and suppose that they were so called from the vallies in which they had resided for many ages before the birth of Peter Waldus. But these writers have no authority to support this assertion, and beside this, they are refuted amply by the best historians. I do not mean to deny, that there were in the *vallies of Piedmont* long before this period, a set of men, who differed widely from the opinions adopted and inculcated by the church of Rome, and whose doctrine resembled, in many respects, that of the Waldenses ; all that I maintain is that these inhabitants of the vallies abovementioned are to be carefully distinguished from the Waldenses, who according to the unanimous voice of history, were originally inhabitants of Lyons, and derived their name from Peter Waldus, their founder and chief."

☞ " We may, says Maclaine, venture to affirm the contrary with the learned Beza and other writers of note ; for it seems evident from the best records, that Valdus derived his name from the true *valdenses* of Piedmont, whose doctrine he adopted, and who were known by the names of *vaudois* and *valdenses*, before he or his immediate followers existed. If the *valdenses* or *waldenses* had derived their name from any eminent teacher, it would probably have been from Valdo, who was remarkable for the purity of his doctrine in the ninth century, and was the contemporary and chief counsellor of Berengarius. But the truth is, that they derive their name from their vallies in Piedmont, which in their language are called Vaux, hence Voidois, their true name ; hence Peter, or as others call him, John of Lyons, was called in Latin, *Valdus*, because he had adopted their doctrine ; and hence the term *valdenses* and *waldenses* used by those, who write in English or Latin, in the place of *vaudois*. The bloody inquisitor Reinerus Sacco, who exerted such a furious zeal for the destruction of the *waldenses*, lived but about eighty years after Valdus of Ly-

But leaving the dispute about the manner in which the Waldenses received their name, it is certain that they had existed as a distinct and peculiar people, many ages before Waldo, that his numerous followers united with them in promoting the cause of godliness, that they all, together with all others of their character, were henceforward denominated Waldenses; and that besides the name of Waldenses, they had many more which were taken from their peculiar sentiments, their habitations, their circumstances, their connections, their teachers, their own infirmities, or the inventive malice of their enemies.*

Bruno and Berengarius, Peter de Bruis and Henry his disciple, Arnold of Briscia, Peter Waldo, and Walter Lollard, seem to have been among the principal leaders of the Waldenses in ancient times. They all had numerous followers, who, according to the custom of the times, were called after the names of their leaders. We have the testimony of Mosheim, Robinson, and others, that the papists comprehended all the adversaries of the pope and the superstitions of Rome, under the general name of Waldenses. The Albigenses or Albienses, a large branch of this sect, were so denominated from the town of Albi, in France, where the Waldenses flourished.† The term Cathari or Puritans, was also frequently applied to the Waldensian christians, as it was to evangelical dissenters in other countries. Whenever, therefore, in the following sketches, the terms Berengarians, Petrobrusians, Henricians, Arnoldists, Waldenses, Albigenses, Leonists, or the poor men of Lyons, Lollards, Cathari, &c. occur, it

ons, and must therefore be supposed to know whether or not he was the real founder of the *valdenses* or *leonists ;* and yet it is remarkable that he speaks of the *leonists,* mentioned by Dr. Mosheim in the preceding page as synonymous with Waldenses, as a sect that had flourished above five hundred years ; nay, mentions authors of note, who make their antiquity remount to the apostolic age. See the account given of Sacco's book by the jesuit Gretser, in the *Bibliotheca Patrum.* I know not upon what principle Dr. Mòsheim maintains, that the inhabitants of the *vallies of Piedmont* are to be carefully distinguished from the *waldenses ;* and I am persuaded, that whoever will be at the pains to read attentively the 2d, 25th, 26th, and 27th, chapters of the first book of Leger's *Histoire Generale des Eglises Vaudoises,* will find this distinction entirely groundless. When the papists ask us *where our religion was before* Luther ; we generally answer, *in the Bible ;* and we answer well. But to gratify their taste for *tradition* and *human authority,* we may add to this answer, *and in the vallies of Piedmont.*"
Mosheim, vol. III. p. 118, 119.

* Robinson's Researches, p. 307.

† Milner's Church History, vol. III. p. 455.

must be understood that they intend a people, who agreed in certain leading principles, however they might differ in some smaller matters, and that all of them were by the Catholicks comprehended under the general name of Waldenses.

Most of our information respecting the character of the Waldenses must be taken from the accounts of their enemies, and therefore every favourable hint concerning them will be the more likely to be true. I have not been able to obtain Moreland's and Allix's histories of the Waldenses; I must therefore avail myself of the labours of those who have consulted them, and shall, for the present, quote mostly from the third volume of Milner's Church History, and Ivimey's History of the English Baptists. These writers appear to have consulted with much attention all the records which shed any light on the history of this ancient people of God.

Evervinus of Steinfield, in the diocess of Cologne, wrote to Bernard, a little before the year 1140, a letter preserved by Mabillon, concerning certain hereticks in his neighbourhood. He was perplexed in his mind concerning them, and wrote for a resolution of his doubts to the renowned abbot, whose word was a law at that time in christendom. Some extracts of this letter are as follows. " There have been some hereticks discovered among us near Cologne, though several of them have, with satisfaction, returned again to the church. One of their bishops and his companions openly opposed us in the assembly of the clergy and laity, in the presence of the archbishop of Cologne, and of many of the nobility, defending their heresies by the words of Christ and the apostles. Finding that they made no impression, they desired that a day might be appointed for them, in which they might bring their teachers to a conference, promising to return to the church, provided they found their masters unable to answer the arguments of their opponents, but that otherwise they would rather die, than depart from their judgment. Upon this declaration, having been admonished to repent for three days, they were seized by the people in the excess of zeal and burnt to death; and what is very amazing, they came to the stake, and bare the pain, not only with patience, but even with joy. Were I with you, Father, I should be glad to ask you, how these members of Satan could persist in their heresy with such courage and constancy, as is scarce to be found in the most religious believers of christianity. Their heresy is this : they say, that the church is only among themselves, because they alone of all men follow the steps of Christ, and imitate the apostles, not seeking secular gains, possessing no property, following the pattern of Christ, who was himself perfectly poor, and did not allow his disciples to possess any thing. Ye (say they to us) join house to house and field to field, seeking the things of this world ; so that even those who are looked on as most perfect among you, namely, those of the monastick orders, though they have no private property, but have a community of possessions, do yet possess these things. Of themselves they say, we, the poor of Christ, who have no certain abode, fleeing from one city to another, like sheep in the midst of wolves, do endure persecution with the apostles and martyrs ; though our lives are strict, abstemious, laborious, devout, and holy, and though we seek only what is necessary for the support of the body, and live as men who are not of the world. They do not believe infant baptism to be a duty, alleging that passage of the gospel, *whosoever shall believe, and be baptized, shall be saved.* They put no confidence in the intercession of saints, and all things observed in the church, which have not been established by Christ himself or his apostles, they call superstitious. They do not admit of any purgatory after death ; but affirm, that as soon as the souls depart out of the bodies, they enter into rest or punishment, proving their assertion from that passage of Solomon, which way soever the tree falls, whether to the south or to the north, there it lies, whence they make void all the prayers and oblations of believers for the deceased. Those of them, who have returned to our church, told us, that great numbers of their persuasion was scattered almost every where, and that among them were many of our clergy and monks."

St. Bernard, the furious adversary of the Waldenses, amidst all his railing accusations against them, has given them a character much better than christians in general have given him. He condemns their scrupulous refusal to swear at all, which, according to him, was one of their peculiarities. He upbraids them with the observance of secrecy in their religious rites, not considering the necessity which persecution laid upon them. He finds fault with a practice among them of dwelling with women in the same house without being married to them ; though it must be owned, he expresses himself as one, who knew very little of the manners of the sect. From the strength of prejudice, and from the numberless rumours propagated against them, he suspects them of hypocrisy ; yet his testimony in favour of their general conduct seems to overbalance all his invectives. " If, (says he) you ask them of their faith, nothing can be more christian ; if you observe their conversation, nothing can be more blameless ; and what they speak they prove by deeds. You may see a man for the testimony of his faith, frequent the church, honour the elders, offer his gift, make his confession, receive the sacrament ; what more like a christian ? As to life and manners, he circumvents no man, overreaches no man, and does no violence to any. He fasts much, he eats not the bread of idleness, he works with his hands for his support. The whole body, indeed, are rustick and illiterate ; and all whom I have known of this sect are very ignorant."

Egbert, a monk, and afterwards abbot of Schonauge, tells us, that he had often disputed with these hereticks, and says, " These are they who are commonly called Cathari or Puritans. They are armed with all those passages of holy scripture, which in any degree seem to favour their views ; with these they know how to defend themselves, and to oppose the catholick truth, though they mistake entirely the true sense of scripture, which cannot be discovered without great judgment. They are increased to great multitudes throughout all countries, their words spread like a cancer. In Germany we call them Cathari ; in Flanders, they call them Piphles; in France, Tisserands,* because many of them are of that occupation."

" It appears," says Milner, " that their numbers were very considerable in this century (the twelfth;) but Cologne, Flanders, the South of France, Savoy, and Milan were their principal places of residence."

This people, says the same writer, continued in a state of extreme persecution throughout this century. Galdinus, bishop of Milan, who had inveighed against them

* That is, *weavers*.

during the eight or nine years of his episcopacy, died in the year 1173, by an illness contracted through the excess of his vehemence in preaching against them.

Reinerus, an apostate and persecutor of the Waldenses in the thirteenth century, writes, that amongst all sects none is more pernicious than that of the *Poor of Lyons*, for three reasons: 1st. Because it is the most ancient. Some aver their existence from the days of Sylvester; others from the very time of the apostles. 2d. Because it is so universal; for there is scarcely a country into which this sect has not crept. 3d. Because all others render themselves detestable by their blasphemies; but this has a great appearance of godliness, they living a righteous life before men, believing right concerning God, confessing all the articles of the creed, only hating the pope of Rome, &c.

The same inquisitor owns that the Waldenses frequently read the Holy Scriptures, and in their preaching cited the words of Christ and his apostles concerning love, humility and other virtues; insomuch that the women who heard them were enraptured with the sound. He further says, that they taught men to live by the words of the gospel and the apostles; that they led religious lives; that their manners were seasoned with grace and their words prudent; that they freely discoursed of divine things, that they might be esteemed good men. He observes, likewise, that they taught their children and families the epistles and gospels.

Jacob de Riberia says, that he had seen peasants among them, who could recite the book of Job by heart; and several others, who could perfectly repeat the whole New-Testament.

The bishop of Cavaillon once obliged a preaching monk to enter into conference with them, that they might be convinced of their errors, and the effusion of blood be prevented. This happened during a great persecution in 1540, in Merindal and Provence. But the monk returned in confusion, owning that he had never known in his whole life so much of the Scriptures as he had learned during those few days in which he had held conferences with the hereticks. The bishop, however, sent among them a number of doctors, young men, who had lately come from the Sorbonne, which was at that time the very centre of theological subtilty at Paris. One of them openly owned, that he had understood more of the doctrine of salvation from the answers of the little children in their catechism, than by all the disputations, which he had ever heard.

Hereticks, an ancient inquisitor observes, are known by their manners and words; for they are orderly and modest in their manners and behaviour. They avoid all appearance of pride in their dress, they neither wear rich clothes, nor are they too mean and ragged in their attire. They avoid commerce, that they may be free from falsehood and deceit. They live by manual industry, as day-labourers or mechanicks, and their preachers are weavers and tailors. They seek not to amass wealth, but are content with the necessaries of life. They are chaste, temperate, and sober. They abstain from anger. They hypocritically go to the church, confess, communicate, and hear sermons, to catch the preacher in his words. Their women are modest, avoid slander, foolish jesting, and levity of words, especially falsehood and oaths.

But notwithstanding the enemies of these ancient saints made so many reluctant acknowledgments of their worth; yet they looked upon them as vile hereticks, fit objects for ecclesiastical vengeance, and the more pious and devout they were, the more dangerous they became to the church of Rome, whose abominations they opposed.

The Waldenses rejected the whole economy of the priesthood, and laughed at the distinctions between the clergy and laity; yet they had pastors whom they called Barbs, which is a contraction of Barbanus, and signifies first, an uncle, and then it was used figuratively for father, guardian, tutor, &c.

The Waldenses were often accused of worshipping their pastors or barbs; a charge which they easy refuted. They were at the same time complained of for obliging them to follow some trade. Both these charges put together prove, that these people made gods of their pastors, and then obliged them to work for their living. " We do not think it necessary, (said they) that our pastors should work for bread. They might be better qualified to instruct us, if we could maintain them without their own labour; but our poverty has no remedy." So they speak in letters published in 1508.*

Nothing, says Milner, can exceed the calumnies which were cast on these innocent people. Poor men of Lyons, and dogs, were the usual terms of derision. In Provence they were called cut-purses; in Italy, because they observed not the appointed festivals, and rested from their ordiary occupations only on Sundays, they were called insabathas, that is, regardless of sabbaths. In Germany, they were called gazares, a term expressive of every thing flagitiously wicked. In Flanders they were denominated turlupius, that is, inhabitants with wolves, because they were often obliged to dwell in woods and deserts. And because they denied the consecrated host to be God, they were accused of Arianism, as if they had denied the divinity of Jesus Christ.

Rapin, in relating the transactions of the councils of Henry II. gives the following account of these people: " Henry ordered a council to meet at Oxford in 1166, to examine the tenets of certain hereticks, called Publicani. Very probably they were disciples of the Waldenses, who began then to appear. When they were asked in council, who they were? they answered they were christians, and followers of the apostles. After that, being questioned upon the creed, their replies were very orthodox as to the trinity and incarnation. But (adds Rapin) they rejected baptism, the eucharist, marriage, and the communion of saints. They shewed a great deal of modesty and meekness in their whole behaviour. When they were threatened with death, in order to oblige them to renounce their tenets, they only said, *Blessed are they that suffer for righteousness' sake.*"

There is no difficulty, Mr. Ivimey judiciously observes, in understanding what were their sentiments on these heretical points. When a monk says, they rejected the eucharist, it is to be understood that they rejected the absurd doctrine of transubstantiation; when he says, that they rejected marriage, he means, that they denied it to be a sacrament, and maintained it to be a civil institution; when he says, that they rejected the communion of saints, nothing more is to be understood, than that they refused to hold communion with the corrupt church of Rome; and when

* Milner, vol. iii. p. 428.

Raineus' Commendation of the Waldenses. 119

he says, that they rejected baptism, what are we to understand but that they rejected the baptism of infants? These were the errors for which they were branded with a hot iron in their foreheads, by those who had " the mark of the beast, both in their foreheads and in their hands."*

We can give but a very brief account of the persecutions which the Waldenses suffered and of the success which attended their exertions. They underwent the most dreadful persecutions; and every means which malice and cruelty could invent, was used to exterminate them and their principles from the earth. The crusade against them consisted of five.hundred thousand men. More than three hundred gentlemen's seats were razed, and many walled towns destroyed.†

The subjects of Raymond, earl of Toulouse, and of some other great personages in his neighbourhood, so generally professed the Waldensian doctrines, that they became the peculiar objects of papal vengeance. The inhabitants of Toulouse, Carcassone, Beziers, Narbonne, Avignon, and many other cities, who were commonly called the Albigenses, were exposed to a persecution as cruel and atrocious as any recorded in history. Rainerus indeed owns, that the Waldenses were the most formidable enemies of the church of Rome, " because," saith he, " they have a great appearance of godliness; because they live righteously before men, believe rightly of God in all things, and hold all the articles of the creed; yet they hate and revile the church of Rome; and in their accusations they are easily believed by the people."

It was reserved to Innocent III. than whom no pope ever possessed more ambition, to institute the inquisition, and the Waldenses were the first objects of its cruelty. He authorised certain monks to frame the process of that court, and to deliver the supposed hereticks to the secular power. The beginning of the thirteenth century saw thousands of persons burned or hanged by these diabolical devices, whose sole crime was, that they trusted only in Jesus Christ for salvation, and renounced all the vain hopes of self-righteous idolatry and superstition.

About the year 1400, the persecutors attacked the Waldenses of ᛫the valley of Pragela. The poor people

* Ivimey, p. 56—7.   Ibid, p. 55.

seeing their caves possessed by their enemies, who assaulted them during the severity of the winter, retreated to one of the highest mountains of the Alps, the mothers carrying cradles, and leading by the hand those little children, who were able to walk. Many of them were murdered, others were starved to death, a hundred and eighty children were found dead in their cradles, and the greatest part of their mothers died soon after them. In the valley of Loyse, four hundred little children were found suffocated in their cradles, or in the arms of their deceased mothers, in consequence of a great quantity of wood being placed at the entrance of the caves and set on fire. On the whole, above three thousand persons belonging to the valley were destroyed, and this righteous people were in that place exterminated. The Waldenses of Pragela and Fraissiniere, alarmed by these sanguinary proceedings, made provision for their own safety, and expected the enemy at the passage and narrow straits of their vallies, and were in fact so well prepared to receive them, that the invaders were obliged to retreat. Some attempts were made afterwards by the Waldenses of Fraissiniere to regain their property, which had been unjustly seized by their persecutors. The favour of Lewis XII. of France was exerted towards them; yet they could never obtain any remedy.

The princes of Piedmont, who were the dukes of Savoy, were very unwilling to disturb their subjects, of whose loyalty, peaceableness, industry, and probity they received such uniform testimony. A fact, which seemed peculiarly to demonstrate their general innocence, must be noticed. Their neighbours particularly prized a Piedmontese servant, and preferred the women of the vallies above all others, to nurse their children. Calumny, however, prevailed at length, and such a number of accusations against them appeared, charging them with crimes of the most monstrous nature, that the civil power permitted the papal to indulge its thirst for blood. Dreadful cruelties were inflicted on the people of God; and these, by their constancy, revived the memory of the primitive martyrs. Among them Catelin Girard was distinguished, who, standing on the block, on which he was to be burned at Revel, in the marquisate of Saluces, requested his executioners to give him two stones; which request being with difficulty obtained, the martyr holding them in his hands, said, "when I have eaten these stones, then you shall see an end of that religion for which ye put me to death," and then he cast the stones on the ground.

But our limits forbid our pursuing any farther an account of the sufferings of these people. It is sufficient to observe, that their enemies were far from accomplishing their designs. Archbishop Asher observes, that as the persecution about Stephen proved for the furtherance of the gospel in other parts of the world, so was it here. Insomuch that Æneas Sylvius, afterwards pope Pius II. confessed, that neither the decrees of popes, nor armies of christians could extirpate the Waldensian sect.

Various accounts mention their dispersion abroad, and the papists complain much of their infesting most parts of their dominions and disturbing the peace of the church.

We learn from Fox, on the authority of Robert Guisborne, that in the time of Henry II. about the year 1158, two eminent Waldensian preachers or barbs, Gerhardus and Dulcinus, came into England to propagate the gospel ; and archbishop Usher, from Thomas Walden, says, that "several Waldenses, that came out of France, were apprehended, and by the king's command were marked in the forehead with a key or hot iron." "Which sect (says William of Newbury, in his history of England) were called the Publicani, whose original was from Gascoyne ; and who, being as numerous as the sand of the sea, did sorely infest both France, Italy, Spain, and England."

Archbishop Usher informs us on the authority of Matthew Paris of Westminster, that "the Berengarian or Waldensian heresy had, about the year 1180, generally infected all France, Italy, and England." Guitmond, a popish writer of that time, also says, that "not only the weaker sort in the country villages, but the nobility and gentry in the chief towns and cities, were infected therewith ; and therefore Lanfranc, archbishop of Canterbury, who held this see both in the reigns of William the Conqueror and of his son William Rufus, wrote against them in the year 1087." The archbishop adds from Poplinus' history of France, that " the Waldenses of Aquitain did, about the year 1100, during the reigns of Henry I, and

Stephen, kings of England, spread themselves and their doctrines all over Europe," and mentions England in particular.*

From the recesses of the Alps and Pyrenees and the adjoining vallies, these people were driven out by heretick hunters, and were obliged to seek refuge in other countries. Wherever they went, light increased and persecution raged. The word of God, says Milner, grew and multiplied, in the places were Waldo planted churches, and even in still more distant regions. In Alsace and along the Rhine, the gospel was preached with a powerful effusion of the Holy Spirit ; persecutions ensued, and thirty-five citizens of Mentz were burned at one fire in the city of Bingen, and at Mentz eighteen. The bishop of Mentz was very active in these persecutions, and the bishop of Strasburg was not inferior to him in vindictive zeal ; for, through his means, eighty persons were burned at Strasburg. Every thing relating to the Waldenses resembled the scenes of the primitive church. Numbers died praising God, and in confident assurance of a blessed resurrection ; whence the blood of the martyrs again became the seed of the church ; and in Bulgaria, Croatia, Dalmatia, and Hungary, churches were planted, which flourished in the thirteenth century, governed by Bartholomew, a native of Carcassone, a city not far distant from Toulouse, which might be called in those days the metropolis of the Waldenses, on account of the numbers who there professed evangelical truth. In Bohemia in the country of Passaw, the churches were reckoned to have contained eighty thousand professors in the former part of the fourteenth century. Almost throughout Europe Waldenses were to be found ; and yet they were treated as the offscouring of the earth, and as people against whom all the power and wisdom of the world were united. But " the witnesses continued to prophesy in sackcloth," and souls were built up in the faith, the hope, and the charity of the gospel.

" From the borders of Spain, (says the same writer) throughout the south of France, for the most part among and below the Alps, along the Rhine, on both sides of its course, and even to Bohemia, thousands of godly souls were seen patiently to bear persecution for the sake of

* Ivimey, p. 55, 56.

Christ, against whom malice could say no evil, but what admits the most satisfactory refutation; men distinguished for every virtue, and only hated because of godliness itself. Persecutors with a sigh owned, that, because of their virtue, they were the most dangerous enemies of the church."

One quotation more from Mr. Milner, shall close this part of the narration. From the year 1206, when the inquisition was first established, to the year 1228, the havock made among helpless christians was so great, that certain French bishops, in the last mentioned year, desired the monks of the inquisition to defer a little their work of imprisonment, till the pope was advertised of the great numbers apprehended; numbers so great, that it was impossible to defray the charge of their subsistence, and even to provide stone and mortar to build prisons for them. Yet so true is it that the blood of the martyrs is the seed of the church, that in the year 1530, there were in Europe above eight hundred thousand who professed the religion of the Waldenses.

It is proper that we should now take notice of some of the evidences on which we ground our opinion, that many, if not most of the Waldenses, were Baptists. We have already seen that one of the grievous sins, which their enemies laid to their charge, was denying *infant baptism*. We shall exhibit in one view, the substance of what can be gathered from different historians on this subject.

Chessanion, in his history of the Albigenses, has given the following very candid account of this matter. " Some writers (he says) affirm, that the Albigenses approved not the baptism of infants; others, that they entirely slighted this holy sacrament, as if it were of no use either to great or small. The same may be said of the Waldenses, though some affirm that they have always baptized their children. This difference of authors kept me sometime in suspense before I could come to be resolved on which side the truth lay. At last considering what St. Bernard saith of this matter in his sixty-sixth homily, on the 2d chapter of the Song of Songs, and the reasons he brings to refute this error and also what he wrote *ad Hildefonsum Comitem sancti Ægidii*, I cannot deny but the Albigenses, for the greatest part, were of this opinion. And that which confirms me yet more in this belief is, that in the history of the city of Treves, there were some, who denied that the sacrament of baptism was available to the salvation of infants; and one Catherine Sauhe, who was burnt at Montpelier, in the year 1417, for being of the mind of the Albigenses in not believing the traditions of the Romish church, was of the same mind respecting infant baptism; as it is recorded in the register of the town-house of the said city of Montpelier. The truth is, (continues Chessanion) they did not reject the sacrament and say it was useless, but only counted it unnecessary to infants, because they are not of age to believe, nor capable of giving evidence of their faith. That which induced them, as I suppose, to entertain this opinion is, what our Lord says, *He that believeth and is baptized shall be saved; but he that believeth not shall be damned.*"

This statement is in part at least corroborated by Dr. Wall in his History of Infant Baptism; and as he was desirous of establishing the contrary opinion, his concessions in our favour are certainly of weight. Speaking of the Petrobrussians, whom he calls a sect of the Waldenses, he says, " withdrawing themselves about the year 1100, from the communion of the church of Rome, which was then very corrupt, they did reckon infant baptism as one of the corruptions, and accordingly renounced it, and practised only adult baptism." Part II. Chap. vii. Section 5, 6, 7.

Mosheim, in his Ecclesiastical History, speaking of Peter de Bruis, who was a celebrated itinerant preacher, and who was burnt to death by an enraged populace at St. Giles, in the year 1130, says, " It is certain that one of his tenets was, *that no persons whatever were to be baptized before they were come to the full use of reason.*"

The testimony of Mr. Brandt, respecting the antiquity of these churches and of their sentiments respecting baptism is of importance to our argument. He says, that " the errors and crafty inventions of popery had never been able to find a passage to these people; since being shut up in their vallies, separate from the rest of the world, and conversing chiefly among themselves, they had retained a great deal of the simplicity and purity of the *Apostolic Doctrine:* That this antiquity of the doctrine of the Waldenses, is acknowledged even by their greatest enemies.—Some of them likewise rejected infant baptism."

To corroborate this last clause many things are produced by Dr. Allix in his remarks on the ancient churches of Piedmont. " The followers of Gundulphus in Italy were many of them examined by Gerhard bishop of Cambray and Arras upon several heads in the year 1025. It seems as if these people were surfeited with the vicious and debauched lives of the Romish clergy, and did rather choose to go without any baptism, rather than have it administered by such lewd hands, or that they had agreed to have it performed privately in their own way. Let things have been as it would, it is plain they were utterly against infant baptism."

In a little time after this, lived the noted Arnold of Brescia, a follower of Berengarius, who eminently opposed the Romish corruptions. And amongst some notions imputed to him, it is observed, " there was yet a more heinous thing laid to his charge, which was this ; that he was unsound in his judgment about the sacrament of the altar and infant baptism." This excellent man was condemned, hanged, and his body burnt at Rome, and the ashes cast into the Tiber. But there is a letter of Everinus to St. Bernard, a little before the year 1146, wherein he speaks clearly of a sect which approved of *adult baptism upon believing* and strenuously opposed *infant baptism*. The words of the letter are, " They make void the priesthood of the church and condemn the sacraments besides *baptism* only, and this only in those who were come to *age*, who, they say, are baptized by Christ himself, whosoever be the ministers of the sacraments. They do not believe *infant baptism*, alleging that place of the gospel, *whosoever shall believe and be baptized, shall be saved.*"

The same learned gentleman gives us an extract taken by Claudius Caissord in the year 1548, out of an old manuscript of Rainerus a friar, wrote by him 296 years before, against the Waldenses, wherein he has these words, " They say, that when first a man is baptized, then he is received into this *sect*. Some of them hold, that baptism is of no advantage to infants, because they cannot actually believe."*

Dr. Wall allows, that the Lateran council under Innocent II. 1139, condemned Peter Bruis and Arnold of

* Ivimey, pp. 60, 61, 62, 63, 64.

Brescia, who seems to have been a follower of Bruis, for rejecting infant Baptism.*

Bishop Bossuet, a Catholick, complaining of Calvin's party, for claiming apostolical succession through the Waldenses, observes, "You adopt Henry and Peter Bruis among your predecessors, but both of these, every body knows, were Anabaptists."

"The Waldenses," says Francowitz, "scent a little of Anabaptism; but they were nothing like the Anabaptists of our times." "Yes," replies Limborch, "to say honestly what I think, of all the modern sects of christians, the Dutch Baptists most resemble both the Albigenses and the Waldenses, but particularly the latter."†

The following passage from Robinson, though somewhat lengthy, I will take the liberty to transcribe, as it must be gratifying to the reader, to hear what an account a sulky enemy could give of one of these ancient christians: Reinerus thus describes the manner in which the Waldenses insinuated their principles into the gentry: "Sir, will you please to buy any rings, or seals, or trinkets? Madam, will you look at any handkerchiefs, or pieces of needle-work for veils? I can afford them cheap." If, after a purchase, the company ask, "Have you any thing more?" The sale's-man would reply, "O yes, I have commodities far more valuable than these, and I will make you a present of them, if you will protect me from the clergy." Security being promised, on he would go: "The inestimable jewel I spoke of is the word of God, by which he communicates his mind to men, and which inflames their hearts with love to him. In the sixth month the angel Gabriel was sent from God into a city of Galilee named Nazareth;" and so he would proceed to repeat the remaining part of the first chapter of Luke. Or he would begin with the thirteenth of John, and repeat the last discourse of Jesus to his disciples. If the company should seem pleased, he would proceed to repeat the twenty-third of Matthew, "The scribes and Pharisees sit in Moses' seat....Wo unto you, ye shut up the kingdom of heaven against men; for ye neither go in yourselves, neither suffer ye them that are entering to go in.... Wo unto you, ye devour widows' houses"...." And pray,"

* Ivimey, p. 25. † Robinson's Researches, p. 476. Ibid. p. 311.

should one of the company say, "against whom are these woes denounced think you?" he would reply, "Against the clergy and the monks. The doctors of the Roman church are pompous both in their habits and their manners, they love the uppermost rooms, and the chief seats in the synagogues, and to be called Rabbi, Rabbi. For our parts, we desire no such Rabbies. They are incontinent; we live each in chastity with his own wife. They are the rich and avaricious, of whom the Lord says, "Wo unto you rich, for ye have received your consolation;" but we "having food and raiment are therewith content." They are voluptuous and devour widows' houses; we only eat to be refreshed and supported. They fight and encourage war, and command the poor to be killed and burnt, in defiance of the saying, "he that taketh the sword shall perish by the sword." For our parts, they persecute us for righteousness' sake. They do nothing, they eat the bread of idleness; we work with our hands. They monopolize the giving of instruction, and "wo be to them that take away the key of knowledge;" but among us women teach as well as men, and one disciple as soon as he is informed himself teaches another. Among them you can hardly find a doctor, who can repeat three chapters of the New-Testament by heart; but of us there is hardly man or woman, who doth not retain the whole. And because we are sincere believers in Christ, and all teach and enforce a holy life and conversation, these scribes and Pharisees persecute us to death, as their predecessors did Jesus Christ." Father Gretzer, the first editor of the complete book of Reinerus, has put in the margin against the above, these words: "This is a true picture of the hereticks of our age, particularly Anabaptists." Happy for the Anabaptists, indeed, (says Robinson) if they can affirm all that with truth of themselves, which the old Waldensian preaching pedlar affirmed of himself and his company."

To recapitulate the sum of the preceding extracts, we find that the Waldenses, by whatever name they were called, were constantly, for the space of many centuries, charged with the heinous crime of denying infant-baptism, and that the reasons which they gave for so doing, as taken from the mouths of their enemies, were many of them verbatim, and all of them in substance, just such as the Baptists now give. Have not then the Baptists good reasons for believing that the Waldenses were generally of their sentiments?

I admire the piety of Mr. Milner, and every evangelical christian has reason to respect his memory; and to his laborious researches, I am indebted for many of the preceding sketches respecting these ancient witnesses for the truth; but in his account of their baptism, his prepossessions in favour of the rites of his own church, lead him to state the matter in a manner peculiarly vague and unfair. He seems much at a loss to know how to support his own theory, and satisfy his own mind. But he at length concludes, " I cannot find any satisfactory proofs that the Waldenses were, in judgment, Antipedobaptists strictly!" But soon after, as if dissatisfied with this statement, he observes, " I lay no great stress on the subject, for the Waldenses might have been a faithful, humble, and spiritual people, as I believe they were, if they had *differed* from the general body of christians on *this article*."* Thus he at last reluctantly gives up the matter in favour of the Baptists.

But Dr. Mosheim, notwithstanding all the hard names which he has bestowed on the Baptists, has, in the following passages, put this matter beyond all doubt or disputation. " The true origin," says he, " of that sect which acquired the denomination of the *Anabaptists*, by their administering anew the rite of baptism to those who came over to their communion, and derived the name of Mennonists from the famous man, to whom they owe the greatest part of their present felicity, is *hid* in the *remote depths* of *antiquity*, and is, of consequence, difficult to be ascertained."†

This we look upon as a most important concession by one of our most powerful adversaries. This account utterly refutes the long repeated, slanderous story, that the Baptists originated with the madmen of Munster in 1522. " This uncertainty," continues the doctor, " will not appear surprising, when it is considered, that this sect started up, all of a sudden, in several countries, at the same point of time, under leaders of different talents and differ-

---

* Ch. Hist. vol. iii. pp. 426—7.   † Mosheim vol. iv. p. 424

erent intentions, and at the very period when the first contests of the reformers with the Roman pontiffs drew the attention of the world, and employed the pens of the learned, in such a manner, as to render all other objects and incidents almost matters of indifference. The modern *Mennonites* not only consider themselves as the descendants of the Waldenses, who were so grievously oppressed and persecuted by the despotic heads of the Roman church, but pretend, moreover, to be the purest offspring of these respectable sufferers, being equally averse to all principles of rebellion, on the one hand, and all suggestions of fanaticism on the other."

In the above quotation it is acknowledged that the origin of the Baptists is *hid* in the *remote depths* of *antiquity*; in the following passage the same subject is amplified and more fully explained. " It may be observed that the Mennonites (that is, the Baptists of Germany) are not entirely mistaken, when they boast of their descent from the Waldenses, Petrobrussians and other ancient sects, who are usually considered as *witnesses of the truth*, in the times of universal darkness and superstition. Before the rise of Luther and Calvin, there lay concealed in almost all the countries of Europe, particularly in Bohemia, Moravia, Switzerland, and Germany, many persons, who adhered tenaciously to the following doctrine, which the Waldenses, Wickliffites, and Hussites had maintained, some in a more disguised, and others in a more open and public manner, viz. *That the kingdom of Christ or the visible church he had established upon earth, was an assembly of true and real saints, and ought therefore to be inaccessible to the wicked and unrighteous, and also exempt from all those institutions, which human prudence suggests, to oppose the progress of iniquity, or to correct and reform transgressors.* This maxim is the true source of all the peculiarities that are to be found in the religious doctrine and discipline of the Mennonites; and it is most certain that the greatest part of these peculiarities were approved of by many of those, who, before the dawn of the reformation, entertained the notion already mentioned, relating to the visible church of Christ."*

---

* Mosheim Vol. IV. p. 424—429.

130   *The Peculiar Maxims of the Anabaptists.*

This grand *maxim*, which is thus acknowledged to be the true source of all the peculiarities of the Mennonites, and of all the ancient Waldenses, is most fairly stated, and when stripped of the verbose attire, with which the learned doctor has arrayed it, is, by every Baptist, most heartily adopted. This *maxim* goes to exclude all the inventions and traditions of men, and infant baptism among the rest. With this *maxim* in his heart, and his Bible in his hand, a Baptist marches forward in his religious course, and leaves the world and worldly christians, to dispute among themselves about the traditions of the fathers, and rites, which God has never commanded.

But strange to tell, this *maxim* the great Mosheim calls a fanatical principle, productive of errors, chimeras, tumults, seditions, &c. Well might Robinson say, that a Baptist day-labourer understands liberty better than this learned historian and divine. It seems evident enough from the tenor of Mosheim's writings, that he could not comprehend how a man could be a good citizen, and yet hold, that magistrates, as such, have nothing to do with the kingdom of Christ. It is this grand *maxim* with its appendages, and not rebaptizing, that hath occasioned most of the persecutions, which our brethren have endured in ancient or modern times.

A few general observations shall close this chapter, which has already been extended to a greater length than was at first intended.

The Waldenses, like the scriptures, have been resorted to by all parties of protestants in defence of their peculiar sentiments. The papists accused the protestants of being a new sect, whose principles had no existence till the days of Luther. This charge they all denied, and each party went to rumaging to find predecessors, and trace a line of succession down to the apostles. The corruptions of popery stood as a mountain in the way, and there was no alternative but to find a by-path through the land of the Waldenses. This circumstance induced many learned men of different communities, to investigate the history of this people with more care and attention, than it is any ways likely they would otherwise have done. They doubtless had no thought of helping the cause of the Baptists, who were, at the time of these altercations, universally despised and trodden under foot. But it has so happened, that these researches have furnished us with important evidence, which was not intended for our use ; and it now appears plain, that of all parties the Baptists have the best claim to the ancient Waldenses as their predecessors.

But the same researches which have assisted the Baptists in their inquiries into the character of the Waldenses, have caused them much perplexity and trouble. For the researchers having each one a different standard set up, went in quest of a people who would conform to it. The natural consequence was, that they were all tempted to mould the character of the Waldenses to suit their views. The pious Milner is a notable example of this kind. But a number of older writers, who do not seem to have thought of the Baptists, nor in the least suspected that they would derive any advantage from their statements, have told without reserve all that the accusers of these people said of their rejecting infant baptism, and they have also stated their arguments in favour of the baptism of *believers* and of them *only.*

" Little," says Robinson, " did the old Waldenses think, when they were held in universal abhorrence, and committed every where to the flames, that a time would come, when the honour of a connexion with them, would be disputed by different parties of the highest reputation. So it happened, however, at the reformation, and every reformed church put in its claim."*

Uninterrupted succession was the cause of these different claims, but all attempts to prove such a succession have proved ineffectual.

" Protestants by the most substantial arguments have blasted the doctrine of papal succession ; and yet these very protestants have undertaken to make proof of an unbroken series of persons of their own sentiments, following one another in due order from the apostles to themselves. The papal succession is a catalogue of names of real and imaginary men, of christians and atheists, blasphemers and saints. The Lutheran succession runs in the papal channel till the reformation, and then in a small stream changes

---

* Robinson's Researches, p. 310.

its course. The Calvinist succession, which includes the Presbyterians and all sects which originated from Geneva, is a zig-zag, and it is made up of men of all principles and all communities, and, what is very surprising, of popes, arians, and anabaptists, exactly such men as Calvin and his associates committed to the flames for heresy.

" The doctrine of uninterrupted succession is necessary only to such churches as regulate their faith and practice by tradition, and for their use it was first invented."*

But a Baptist has not the least trouble about what is called a lineal or apostolical succession. His line of succession is in faithful men, and it is a matter of indifference with them, when or where they lived, by what name they were called, or by whom they were baptized or ordained. But one thing is certain, that if any thing has been omitted or done wrong, they are sure to correct it according to their views of the apostolical model.

One observation farther, respecting the Waldenses, ought not to be omitted. Some have attempted to prove that they were all Pedobaptists, and others, that they were all Baptists. Both, in my opinion, attempt to prove too much. That many and probably most of them were Baptists, or would now be esteemed such, I think has been clearly proved; but it is evident that others baptized their children, and some of them fell in with Calvin's party at Geneva, soon after the commencement of the reformation. Some of them appear to have been like the Quakers, and rejected baptism altogether. Some were Arians, Unitarians, &c. Some are represented as a turbulent faction in the church, while others had wholly separated from it. Some, we find, engaged in political struggles and in scenes of war, while others would not swear at all, nor bear arms in any case, nor shed human blood. This circumstance seems to cast a gloom over the character of the Waldenses, but it admits of an easy and satisfactory explanation.

We have shown that the terms Waldenses and Albigenses were, by the papists, generally applied to all the adversaries of the pope and the tyranny and superstitions of Rome.

* Robinson's Researches, p. 476.

The term Waldenses was most generally used and answered very nearly to that of Nonconformist in England, which every one knows comprehends a multitude of sects, among whom there exists a great variety of opinions and practices. Considering then the term Waldenses as a general name for a dissenter, it is easy to conceive that it would comprehend a great variety of characters ; and it is a well known fact that this term was applied without any distinction, to the righteous and profligate, to the wise and foolish, to the orthodox and heterodox, to the sober christian and the turbulent incendiary. The adversaries of Rome dissented for different reasons, some for conscience' sake, and others from political motives, some were christians and others were not ; but it is always found that an infidel is as anxious for liberty of conscience as a christian. These things make it necessary to distinguish between the evangelical Waldenses, who are usually considered as the *ancient witnesses for the truth*, and that promiscuous assemblage of dissenters, to whom the papists misapplied the name.

The people properly called Waldenses were remarkable for the purity of their morals and the simplicity of their faith, their enemies themselves being judges ; and so far from engaging in any political struggles, many of them would not in any case bear arms nor shed human blood. Others seem to have believed in defensive war, and when their enemies came to molest them in their vallies and obscure retreats, they assembled at the defiles of the mountains, and with bows and arrows disputed their passage, and often repelled them.

It has often been the lot of christians to be charged with tumults and seditions in which they had no hand, but which they heartily abhorred. It has also often happened, that they have had officious patrons and defenders, who have done them more hurt than good. There is a remarkable example of this kind in the history of the Waldenses. In the beginning of the twelfth century, these people were very numerous in the southern parts of France, and particularly in the dominions of Raymond, count of Toulouse. They appear to have emigrated hither from the other side of the Alps. Raymond strongly protected his Waldensian subjects, though there seems no evidence that he under-stood or felt the vital influence of their doctrine. At this time the horrid inquisition was just established, and its cruel instruments were dispersed in different countries. But this bloody engine met with violent opposition, and in many cases the inquisitors were apprehended and confined, and some were murdered either by an enraged populace, or by the secret contrivances of princes. Two inquisitors were sent into the dominions of Raymond, who met with rough treatment, and one of them was murdered, and Raymond was considered the author of his death. This circumstance furnished pope Innocent with a specious pretence for executing his bloody purposes; a holy war was undertaken against Raymond and his subjects, and multitudes of the innocent Waldenses were slain and dispersed, in revenge for one rash act of their patron, which was committed without their knowledge or desire.

Among the people properly called Waldenses, there was doubtless some diversity of opinion as it respects matters both of faith and practice. But it is certain from the testimony of both friends and enemies, that many of them rejected infant baptism, and held, that professed believers were the only subjects of the baptismal rite. It is, on the other hand, evident, that some of them baptized their children, but all were obnoxious to the Church of Rome, and sorely felt the weight of her revengeful hand. But "as thunder storms drive timorous animals together for shelter," so the storms of persecution induced these christians to associate together for their common safety and mutual edification in the things of God.

Some further information respecting the Waldenses will be given in the accounts which will follow in the next chapter. And it will be found that wherever they prevailed infant baptism was opposed, and the baptism of believers was maintained.

CHAP. IV.

ALL the scenes described in the preceding chapter transpired before the reformation in the sixteenth century. We have seen that the Waldenses were first found in the vallies of Piedmont, in Italy ; that they were thence dispersed into France, Spain, Germany, England, and other European kingdoms. We have hitherto considered them as a collective body, without any regard to the kingdoms or countries which they inhabited. In this chapter we shall treat of them and their descendants, and of all who maintained their principles, under the heads of the governments in which they were found, and in some cases we shall find it necessary to go back beyond the period, to which in the last chapter we arrived.

GERMANY.

The German empire, properly so called, before the late revolutions in Europe, contained twenty-eight millions of inhabitants. It was six hundred miles in length, and five hundred and twenty in breadth. It was divided into ten circles or great districts, which were called Franconia, Bavaria, Suabia, Upper Rhine, Westphalia, Lower Saxony, Austria, Burgundy, Lower Rhine, and Upper Saxony. This great empire was singular for being a combination of upwards of three hundred sovereignties, independent of each other, but composing one political body under an elective head, called the emperor of Germany. Eight princes of the empire, called the electors, had the right of electing the emperor. The seventeen provinces known by the name of the Netherlands, in which are the seven United Provinces of Holland, were not included in the great Germanic body. Great changes have taken place in the civil divisions and government of this country since the revolution.

Our information respecting the Baptists in Germany in ancient times is extremely limited. But Mosheim assures us that they were in this empire long before the rise of Luther and Calvin. They were the descendants of the Waldenses, Petrobrussians, and other eminent sects,

Anabaptists in Germany.

They were called by their ancient names, until about the time of the reformation; then they began to be denominated Anabaptists, and according to Robinson, this name was given to them by a Swiss pedant, who could not be easy without letting the world know that he understood Greek. In this chapter we shall treat of the Baptists under three different names. They were first called *German Anabaptists*, which term is familiar to all who have studied the history of the Baptists as related by their adversaries. After Menno they were generally called Mennonites. But the Mennonites in process of time settled mostly in Holland, and here they received the common name of the inhabitants of the country, and were called Dutch Baptists. These few explanatory remarks the reader ought to bear in mind while perusing the following sketches.

It is said the Dutch Baptists have published voluminous histories of themselves, but I do not find that any of their works have been translated into English, or that the Baptists in England or America have had much acquaintance with them. I find Crosby and other writers often make mention of a folio volume, called the martyrology of the foreign Anabaptists. I have taken much pains to learn something about this book, but have hitherto been unsuccessful. It is said however to contain a numerous list of ancient Baptist martyrs.

Most of the information I can find respecting the old German Anabaptists, is contained in Mosheim's Ecclesiastical History, and his accounts are taken from slanderous reports, and the writings of Lutherans, who, like himself, were all intent on covering the Baptists with shame, and exalting on their ruins, their own august Pedobaptist establishment.

"Mr. Arnoldi and Dr. Schyn, two Dutch Baptist writers, have proved by irrefragable evidence from state papers, public confessions of faith, and authentic books, that Ezechiel and Frederic Spanheim, Heidegger, Hoffman, and others have given a fabulous account of the history of the Dutch Baptists, and that the younger Spanheim, had taxed them with holding thirteen heresies, of all which, not a single society of them believed one word; yet later historians quote these writers as devoutly, as if all they had affirmed were undisputed and allowed to be true."

Frightful Accounts of the Anabaptists. 137

No Pedobaptist writer has made more important concessions in favour of the advocates of believer's baptism than Mosheim, and yet no writer has treated them with more roughness and asperity, or loaded them with a greater number of reproachful terms. Whenever he has referred to their history, he has given full scope to his stupendous verbosity, and poured upon them a tremendous shower of invective and reproach. The German Anabaptists, according this writer, were a *wrongheaded*, a *hotheaded*, *dangerous*, *deluded*, *fanatical*, *chimerical*, *tumultuous*, *seditious*, *furious*, *ferocious*, *pestilential*, *heretical*, *rebellious*, *turbulent*, *odious*, *pernicious*, *wild*, *savage*, *detestable*, *flagitious*, *mad*, *insane*, *delirious*, *miserable rabble of wretches*, *a motly tribe of enthusiasts*, *mad-men and monsters*, whom all sober people abhorred, and whom the magistrates found it necessary to put to the most miserable deaths, for the safety of the church and the peace of the land. These and many other expressions of a similar nature are found in Mosheim's account of the Anabaptists of Germany; indeed, he seems to have almost exhausted the vocabulary of slander, in describing this despised and unfortunate people. But in the midst of this thunder-storm of defamation, there are some intervals of candour and correctness; and some of the statements of this majestic writer every Baptist most heartily approves. And after all the frightful stories about Nicholas Stork and the mad-men of Munster, he, like other writers on the same subject, " concludes with a compliment to the modern Baptists, for having seen into the *errors* of their ancestors, and behaved with propriety for several years past, like a very good sort of men."

But after all these reproachful invectives, it is found, upon strict examination, that the tumults in Germany were first commenced by Catholicks, that all parties helped to carry them on, and that the affair at Munster was begun, not by the Anabaptists, but by Bernard Rotman, a Pedobaptist minister of the Lutheran persuasion, as will be shown in its proper place.

That there were tumultuous scenes in Germany, in the beginning of the sixteenth century, no person can deny. That some real and many reputed Baptists had a hand in them, every understanding Baptist will allow; but that the Baptists were the principal promoters of these scenes, that their Baptistical sentiments led them to engage in political struggles, and that their denomination originated at this time, are statements which they now do, and always have contended, are slanderous and false. But leaving this subject for the present, we will attempt to give some brief sketches of the history of the Baptists in Germany, and some of the neighbouring states.

Before the rise of Luther and Calvin, there lay concealed in almost all the countries of Europe, particularly in Bohemia, Moravia, Switzerland and Germany, many persons who adhered tenaciously to the doctrine which the Waldenses, Wickliffites, and Hussites had maintained.

These concealed christians we have good reasons for believing were mostly Baptists; and by Mosheim's concessions, and a number of concurring testimonies, they were the remains of the ancient Waldenses, who had been driven hither by papal persecutions. This hint of Mosheim's, is the first account we have of them; and from this period we must begin to trace their progress. "The drooping spirits of these people, who had been dispersed through many countries, and persecuted every where with the greatest severity, were revived when they were informed that Luther, seconded by several persons of eminent piety, had successfully attempted the reformation of the church. They now started up, all on a sudden, under different leaders in Germany, Switzerland, and the Netherlands," and fondly hoped that the happy and long expected period had arrived, in which God was about to visit his people, and restore his church to her primitive purity and simplicity. They looked up to Luther and his associates, with the most lively hopes and expectations; they commenced their labours in an open and zealous manner, great success attended their exertions, and great numbers fell in with their views. Their progress was rapid and extensive, and soon, in a great part of Europe, they had a prodigious multitude of followers. They were pleased to find the pillars of Babylon shaken, by means of Luther and his companions; but they soon became dissatisfied with the plan of reformation proposed by the Saxon reformer. "They looked upon it as much beneath the sublimity of their views," and therefore under-

Some Reformers inclined to reject Infant Baptism. 139

took to carry it forward to greater perfection. Luther built his church after the old popish model, or rather he christened the old church with a new name, and called it *reformed*. Luther *repaired* the old house, but the Baptists thought it should be taken down, the rotten timbers left out, and be built anew of what good materials remained. Luther's churches were not made up of good people only, but they embraced all within the parish bounds, and all, whether righteous or wicked, were admitted to communion. This mode of building, which makes all church and no world, was contrived in Babylon, but it is still followed by many, who profess to have come out of her. The Baptists held then, as they have done in every age, *that the church of Christ was an assembly of true and real saints, and ought, therefore, to be inaccessible to the wicked and unrighteous*. It is not strange, therefore, that Luther's plan of reformation was much beneath the sublimity of their views.

The Baptists were also dissatisfied with Luther, and much disappointed when they found he had determined on retaining the old popish custom of admitting infants to baptism. They vainly hoped to see a reformation in this matter, and it is asserted on respectable authority, that "infant baptism was agitated among the reformers themselves, and that some of them were for rejecting it."

Arnoldus Meshovius, a historian of those times, says, "that the business of Anabaptism began at Wittemburg in 1522. Luther then lurking in the castle of Wartpurg in Thuringia, and that he had companions at first, Carolostadt, Philip Melancthon, and others; and that Luther, returning from his Patmos, as he called it, banished Carolostadt and the rest, and only received Philip Melancthon into favour again."*

Carolostadt, one of Luther's associates, was almost constantly charged, even by his own party, of being a favourer of the Anabaptists; and John Gerhard, a Lutheran minister says, that he was called the father of the Anabaptists, by Erasmus Alberus.† Zuinglius the famous Swiss reformer, who flourished about the year 1520, was, according to his own confession, for a time inclined to reject in-

---

* Crosby's Hist. of the English Baptists, vol. I. p. 20.   † Ibid p. 19.

fant baptism ; but he, like many other Pedobaptist ministers, at length gained a victory over his scruples, and afterwards became a bitter persecutor of the despised Anabaptists, whose snare he had so mercifully escaped.* And even the great Luther himself at first suggested some Baptistical opinions. In a conference with some of the Vaudois, who practised infant baptism, he contended that faith and baptism ought always to be connected together ; and to support his opinion, brought the passage, *He that believeth and is baptized shall be saved.* This reasoning of the reformer appears strange ; however, he retained infants, and found out a very convenient and ingenious way of getting rid of the charge of inconsistency.†

The mode of baptism Luther at first clearly defined to be dipping. " The term," says he, " is Greek, and may be rendered dipping, as when we dip any thing in water, so that it is covered all over. And although the custom be now abolished among many, (for they do not dip children, but only pour on a little water) yet they ought to be wholly immersed, and immediately taken out. The etymology of the word seems to require this. The Germans call baptism tauff, from tieff, depth, signifying, that to baptize, is to plunge into the depth.‡ " The Catholicks tax Luther with being the father of the German dippers, some of the first expressly declare, they received their first

* Crosby's Hist. p. 20.   † Robinson's Researches, p. 541.

‡ Johannes Bugerchagius Pomeranius, who was a companion of Luther, and succeeded him in the ministry at Wittemburg, a very pious and learned divine, tells us in a book he published in the German tongue in 1542, "that he was desired to be a witness of a baptism at Hamburg, in the year 1529. That when he had seen the minister only sprinkle the infant wrapped in swathling-clothes on the top of the head, he was amazed ; because he neither heard nor saw any such thing, nor yet read in any history, except in case of necessity, in bed-rid persons. In a general assembly, therefore, of all the ministers of the word, that was convened, he did ask a certain minister, John Fritz by name, who was some time minister of Lubec, how the sacrament of baptism was administered at Lubec ? Who, for his piety and candour did answer gravely, that infants were baptized naked at Lubec, after the same fashion altogether as in Germany. But from whence and how that peculiar manner of baptizing hath crept into Hamburg, he was ignorant. At length they did agree among themselves, that the judgment of Luther, and of the divines of Wittemburg, should be demanded about this point. Which, being done, Luther did write back to Hamburg, that this sprinkling was an abuse, which they ought to remove. Thus plunging was restored at Hamburg.
Crosby, vol. 1. p. 22, 23.

ideas of it from him,* and the fact seems undeniable, but the article of reforming without him he could not bear."

Luther fell out with Carolostadt, for breaking down popish images without his consent, with Zuinglius and others, for holding that the bread and wine were mere symbols, and with Munzer, Stork, and the Baptists generally, for refusing to admit whole parishes to their communion, and for endeavouring to restore the ordinance of baptism, to its original purity.

Luther was undoubtedly an instrument of great good to the church of God, but his rough and dogmatizing spirit caused dissensions among the reformers, and they soon filed off into separate parties. The advocates for Pedobaptism had great patrons, but the Baptists had none. They had always been persecuted by the papists, and soon the protestants engaged in the same cruel business.

I find no accounts by which we can form an estimate of the probable number of those, who embraced the sentiments of the Baptists in these times. According to Mosheim there was a prodigious multitude, but we are informed at the same time that they were an ignorant miserable rabble. There is every reason for believing that the number of real Baptists was great, but it is also evident that the number of those, who were falsely so called, was much greater. Formerly all who opposed the corruptions of Rome, were, by the papists, called Waldenses; and now by the protestants, all who opposed infant baptism, sighed for liberty, or even projected any new plan of a civil or religious, of a sober or visionary nature, were denominated Anabaptists. This circumstance is suggested by Mosheim, and it is doubtless correct.

* Bishop Burnet in his history of the reformation, as quoted by Crosby, says, " At this time (1549) there were many Anabaptists in several parts of England. They were generally Germans, whom the revolutions there had forced to change their seats. Upon Luther's first preaching in Germany, there arose many, who, building on some of his principles, carried things much farther than he did. The chief foundation he laid down was, that the Scripture was to be the only rule of Christians." This maxim has been generally laid down by all evangelical reformers, and has ever proved dangerous to the cause of infant baptism. The famous Whitefield was a notable example of this kind. He appears to have had no design of undermining infant baptism, and yet I am inclined to think, by what I have learnt in my travels, that some thousands in this country, were led to embrace the sentiments of the Baptists by following his principles up to their legitimate consequences. It is reported of Whitefield, that he once pleasantly said, many of his chickens had turned ducks, and gone into the water.

When we consider that the term Anabaptist was thus indiscriminately applied to such a heterogeneous assemblage of character, it will not appear strange that the number was great, and that many of them were visionary and seditious. But it is grievous to relate that the sword of justice, or rather of persecution, was unsheathed against all who bore the name of Anabaptists, and the innocent and guilty were involved in the same cruel fate. Even Mo-. sheim laments that so little distinction was made between the sober and seditious, by the cruel executioners of persecuting edicts. He acknowledges that those who had no other marks of peculiarity than their administering baptism to adult persons only, and excluding the unrighteous from their communion, met with the same treatment as seditious incendiaries, who were for unhinging all government, and destroying all authority. " It is true indeed," says this writer, " that many Anabaptists suffered death, not on account of their being considered as rebellious subjects, but merely because they were judged *incurable hereticks;* for in this century the error of limiting the administration of baptism to adult persons only, and the practice of rebaptizing such as had received that sacrament in a state of infancy, were looked upon as most flagitious and intolerable heresies."

Thus the old popish doctrine, that obstinate and incurable hereticks ought to die, was adopted into the protestant creed. Some protestant princes appear to have been unwilling to imbrue their hands in the blood of hereticks, but we are obliged to believe that the protestant ministers stimulated them to the practice. While all parties were disputing in defence of their peculiar tenets, the Baptists took the liberty of holding disputations in defence of theirs. " In the years 1532 and 1528, there were public disputations at Berne, in Switzerland, between the ministers of the church there and some Anabaptist teachers ; in the years 1529, 1527, and 1525, Oecolampadius had various disputes with people of this name at Basil, in the same country; in the year 1525 there was a dispute at Zurich, in the same country, about Pedobaptism, between Zuinglius, one of the first reformers, and Dr. Balthasar Hubmeierus, who afterwards was burnt and his wife drowned at Vienna, in the year 1528 ; of whom Meshovius, though a papist, gives this character : that he was from his childhood brought up in learning; and for his singular erudition was honoured with a degree in divinity; was a very eloquent man, and read in the scriptures and fathers of the church. Hoornbeck calls him a famous and eloquent preacher, and says he was the first of the reformed preachers at Waldshut. There were several disputations with others in the same year at this place. And in the year 1526 or 1527, according to Hoornbeck, Felix Mans or Mentz, was drowned at Zurich; this man, Meshovius says, whom he calls Felix Mantscher, was of a noble family; and both he and Conrad Grebel, whom he calls Cunrad Grebbe, who are said to give the first rise to Anabaptism at Zurich, were very learned men, and well skilled in the Latin, Greek, and Hebrew languages.*

But the liberty of defending their sentiments by arguments was soon denied our brethren by the intolerant reformers. The cause of infant baptism lost ground so much that penal statutes were called in to its aid. And Anabaptism prevailed so fast, that to prevent its growth the magistrates of Zurich published a solemn edict against it in 1525, requiring all persons to have their children baptized, and forbidding rebaptization, under the penalty of being fined, banished, or imprisoned. Another was put forth in 1530, making it punishable with death.

A few cases of capital punishments for denying infant baptism are thus related by Mr. Crosby: "In the year 1528, Hans Kaeffer and Leonard Freek, for opposing infant baptism, were beheaded at Schwas in Germany, and Leopald Suyder at Augsburg for the same. At Saltzburg eighteen persons of the same faith were burnt; and twenty-five at Waltzen the same year. In the year 1529, twenty of them were put to death in the Palatinate; and three hundred and fifty at Altre in Germany. The men for the most part beheaded, and the women drowned. In 1533, Hugh Crane, and Margaret his wife, with two more, were martyred at Harlem; the woman was drowned; the three men were chained to a post, and roasted by a fire at a distance till they died. This was the very same year that the rising was at Munster. Likewise, in the protestant cantons in Switzerland, they were used as hardly about the same time. In 1530, two of the baptized breth-

* Ivimey, p. 17.

ren were burnt. In 1531, six more of the congregation of Baptists, were martyred in the same place. In 1533, two persons, Lodwick Test and Catharine Harngen, were burnt at Munster.

But the rustick war now coming on, which concluded with the tragedy at Munster, in which some of the Anabaptists were concerned, the name now became unspeakably odious, and always excited the idea of a seditious incendiary, a pest to human society. All who were called by this name, whatever was their character or sentiments, became the objects of reproach and vengeance, and were every where exposed to ravages and death.

We shall for the present leave our German brethren in the most deplorable situation, every where hunted like savages and exposed to death in its most tormenting and revengeful forms. The Munster affair with its causes and consequences will be considered under a separate head.

It is natural to conclude that while the terrors of death in the most dreadful forms were presented before all, who opposed the baptism of infants, or in the least favoured the Anabaptists, that many deserted them, and especially that promiscuous multitude, which Mosheim describes, who never entered into the spirit of their principles, and who were connected with them by most feeble ties. But on the other hand some excellent characters became members of their communion, among whom Menno Simon appears to have held the most distinguished rank. Menno, for by his first name he appears to have been generally called, was born at Witmars in Friesland, in 1505. He was ordained a popish priest, and continued a famous preacher and disputer in the Catholick connexion until 1531, when he began to suspect the validity of many things in the church of Rome, and among the rest that of *infant baptism.* He first discovered his suspicions to the doctors of his own fraternity, then to Luther, but failing of satisfaction from any, he next betook himself to the study of the New-Testament and ecclesiastical history, and as it generally happens in all such cases, he brought up at last on Baptist ground. Mosheim asserts that he went over to the Anabaptists first in a clandestine manner, and frequented their assemblies with the utmost secrecy ; but in the year 1536, he threw off the mask, resigned his rank in the Romish church and publickly embraced their communion. About a year after this, he began his ministry among the Anabaptists, and " from this period to the end of his days, (that is, during the space of twenty-five years) he travelled from one country to another, with his wife and children, exercising his ministry under pressures and calamities of various kinds, that succeeded each other without interruption, and constantly exposed to the danger of falling a victim to the severity of the laws. East and West Friesland, together with the province of Groningen, were first visited by this zealous apostle of the Anabaptists; from thence he directed his course into Holland, Gelderland, Brabant, and Westphalia, continued it through the German provinces that lie on the coast of the Baltic sea, and penetrated so far as Livonia. In all these places his ministerial labours were attended with remarkable success, and added to his sect a prodigious number of proselytes. Hence he is deservedly looked upon as the common chief of almost all the Anabaptists, and the parent of the sect that still subsists under that denomination. The success of this missionary will not appear very surprising to those who are acquainted with his character, spirit, and talents, and who have a just notion of the state of the Anabaptists at the period of time now under consideration. Menno was a man of genius; though, as his writings shew, his genius was not under the direction of a very sound judgment. He had the inestimable advantage of a natural and persuasive eloquence, and his learning was sufficient to make him pass for an oracle in the eyes of the multitude. He appears, moreover, to have been a man of probity, of a meek and tractable spirit, gentle in his manners, pliable and obsequious in his commerce with persons of all ranks and characters, and extremely zealous in promoting practical religion and virtue, which he recommended by his example, as well as by his precepts."*

* " Menno was born at Witmarsum, a village in the neighbourhood of Bolswert, in Friesland in the year 1505, and not in 1496, as most writers tell us. After a life of toil, peril, and agitation, he departed in peace in the year 1561, in the dutchy of Holstein, at the country-seat of a certain nobleman, not far from the city of Oldesloe, who, moved with compassion at a view of the perils to which Menno was exposed, and the snares that were daily laid for his ruin, took him, together with certain of his associates, into his protection, and gave him asylum. We have a particular account of this famous Anabaptist in the *Cambria Literata* of Mollerus, *tom.* ii. p. 835. See also Hermon

"Menno," says Morgan Edwards, "continued preaching and planting churches in various parts of the low countries, for a course of about thirty years, and died in peace Jan. 31, 1561, after having been hunted like a partridge on the mountain, by both protestants and papists. The faith and order of this eminent reformer may, in some measure, be gathered from the fragments of his works, which are now extant. A *general Baptist* (as that character is understood in Great-Britain) he certainly was; but I have not seen sufficient evidence of his being what is now called an Arian or Socinian. I rather think that the term Arminian or Remonstrant would better suit his religious sentiments."

"Menno," Edwards further observes, "was a man of parts and learning, and carried the reformation one step farther than Luther or Calvin did, and would, no doubt, have been ranked with the chief reformers, had there not been some cross-grained fatality attending the laudable deeds of Baptists, to prevent their having in this world the praise they deserve."

Some farther account of Menno and his sentiments may be found in the account of the American Mennonites.

We have no account of the number of churches founded by Menno, but it was doubtless great; and not only the churches of his planting, but most, if not all, of his sentiments appear from his time to have been distinguished by the name of Mennonites. Ecclesiastical writers, however, have generally affixed to them the old reproachful name of Anabaptists.

About the middle of the sixteenth century, according to Mosheim, there was a warm contest among the Mennonites concerning excommunication, which terminated in the division of their extensive community. One party was distinguished by the name of *rigid*, and the other of *moderate* Anabaptists. The moderate Anabaptists consisted at first of the inhabitants of a district in North-Holland called Waterland, and hence their whole sect was distinguished by the denomination of Waterlandians. The rigid part of the community were, for the most part, natives of Flan-

Schyn *Plenior Deductio Historia Mennonitarum*, cap. vi. p. 116. The writings of Menno, which are almost all composed in the Dutch language, were published in folio at Amsterdam, in the year 1561."

Mosheim, Vol. IV. p. 441.

ders; and hence their sect acquired the denomination of Flemingians or Flandrians. The rigid Anabaptists were again divided on the subject of excommunication, into Flandrians and Frieslanders, who differed from each other in their manners and discipline. And to them a third denomination was added, who took the name of their country, like the former, and were called Germans; "for the Anabaptists of Germany passed in shoals into Holland and the Netherlands." But the greatest part of these three sects came over by degrees to the moderate community of the Waterlandians, &c. Thus the great body of the Mennonites about the middle of the last century, the time Mosheim's history was published, had come into the moderate class of Anabaptists. Mosheim considers the change was much for the better, but we may safely conclude the contrary. What this author would esteem a mark of wisdom and charity, others would count a worldly compromise, the natural consequence of a defection in evangelical zeal and purity. The rigid Anabaptists undoubtedly carried some of their principles to extremes, but I think there is no hazard in concluding that of the two they had the most evangelical creed.

The Mennonites have established a college in Amsterdam, for the benefit of their society, which is called *the College of the Sun.* I conclude from an expression in Mosheim, that it was founded in the former part of the last century. But I have not been able to obtain any particulars respecting the nature or extent of the establishment.

The Mennonites were, at first, every where persecuted and destroyed. "But after being a long time in an uncertain and precarious situation, they at length obtained a fixed and unmolested settlement in the United Provinces, under the shade of a legal toleration procured for them by William, prince of Orange, the glorious founder of Belgic liberty. This illustrious chief, who acted from principle in allowing liberty of conscience and worship to christians of different denominations, was moreover engaged by gratitude to favour the Mennonites, who had assisted him in the year 1572, with a considerable sum of money, when his coffers were almost exhausted."*

* Mosheim, vol. IV. p. 461.

The doctrinal sentiments of the people we have been describing, are differently represented. They have published a number of confessions of faith; the most ancient and respectable, in Mosheim's opinion, was published by the Waterlandians. Robinson says the Dutch Baptists have published creeds, which for the fundamental points, even Luther and Calvin might have subscribed; he also intimates that they have published others less orthodox in their contents. It seems evident, that the Dutch and German Baptists have, generally speaking, been of an Arminian cast. Arminianism originated in Holland, and all parties seem to have been more or less infected with it.

Dr. Rippon gives an account of a church of Mennonites in Dantzic, who were Calvinists. "In consequence of letters and registers," says he, "sent to the Rev. Messrs. Henry Roots, Isaac Van Duhrin, Erdmann Stobbe, and Peter Klein, the four ministers of a Baptist church at Dantzic, in Polish, otherwise in Royal Prussia, the following information has been communicated: Dantzic is a place of great commerce, very populous, and perhaps about the size of Liverpool. The Dantzicers have numerous places of worship for Lutherans and Calvinists, the steeples of which, as you come from sea, begin to appear at the distance of about five leagues from the city. They have also an English place of worship, and a Baptist or Mennonist congregation. Your letters to the ministers of the last named society, I delivered with my own hand. Their place of worship of about 40 feet by 32 is very neat. Mr. Roots, the elder or pastor of the church, is the youngest man of their four ministers. They have one deacon, an organ in their meeting, and one service in a day, which begins at about half after eight in the morning, and ends at eleven. They enter on worship with singing, then pray, sing again, and preach about three parts of an hour, and conclude nearly as our Baptists congregations do in England. On Lord's day evening, by a previous appointment, I was introduced to them at Mr. Roots': All the four ministers were present, the deacon, and also an attorney, who understood and spoke English as well as myself. I was received in a very friendly way, and, according to the custom of the place, saluted with a kiss. All five, the ministers and deacon saluted me. Your letters were read to them, and I observed peculiar emotions in their countenances at your question; "Whether internal piety or the religion of the heart flourished among them, or in any part of Poland or Prussia?" In the conversation, which was maintained between us by the attorney our interpreter, they asked how the Baptists administered ordinances in England? How often the death of Christ was celebrated? Whether there were collections made for the poor? How we sing, and what psalms? Whether the psalms of David only, or other compositions? I shewed them Dr. Watts' hymns and psalms, some of which the gentleman read off in Dutch; and some of theirs to me in English, consisting of psalms, and also of hymns suited to the Lord's supper. They asked if we had organs in our chapels? I told them that they were not approved of; and was informed that in general they were not used in their congregations. They wished also to know how long the sermons of our ministers are? Whether most of our preachers are learned men? Whether they are in business, or receive salaries from the congregations? I replied as well as I could. By the questions I proposed to them I find that they are Calvinistic Baptists, and are quite clear in this truth, that it is impossible for any man to be saved without a real change of heart. They are enemies to all war, and asked me, If any part of England was besieged, whether the Baptists would fight? I said, to be sure they would defend themselves against their enemies. But they said, Christ has told us we should love our enemies. I then asked, what is the difference between my going to war, and sending another in my room? as I gathered from their conversation they had provided substitutes. They replied that both were totally disagreeable to them; but the laws of the country *forced* them to the latter."*

The Germans and Dutch Baptists appear always to have held some sentiments peculiar to themselves. *They neither admit civil rulers into their communion, nor allow any of their members to perform the functions of magistracy. They deny the lawfulness of repelling force by force, and consider war, in all its shapes, as unchristian and unjust. They are averse to capital punishments*, and feeling themselves bound to swear not at all, *they will not confirm their testimony with an oath.*

* Rippon's Register, No 10, for April, 1795.

Number of the Dutch Baptists....Their Defections.

Respecting the number of communicants in the Dutch or Mennonite Baptist churches, I have obtained no information whatever. According to a list in Rippon's Register, there were, in 1790, in and out of the Netherlands, two hundred and fifty-two churches of the Dutch and Mennonite Baptists, in all of which were five hundred and thirty three ministers. Of these a hundred and seventy-five churches, and two hundred and seventy-one ministers were in the Netherlands and Generalities' Lands. Fifteen churches, in which were ninety-six ministers, were in Prussia. Twenty-seven churches and ninety-two ministers were in Upper Saxony. Twenty-seven churches and forty-nine ministers were in France. The rest were in Switzerland, Poland, and Russia.

It is to be feared that vital religion is at a low ebb in these ancient churches of Baptists, and I wish I were able to say they had all maintained the ordinances of the gospel in their primitive purity, and in the manner they were maintained by their persecuted ancestors. The American Mennonites have adopted pouring instead of immersion, and it is probable that many, and I know not but most of the European Mennonites, have done the same. It is certain that the ancient German Anabaptists practised dipping, and it is probable that the magistrates of those times, with a view of proportioning their punishment to their crimes, caused many of them to be drowned. Robinson says, that "Luther bore the Zuinglians' dogmatizing; but he could not brook a further reformation in the hands of the dippers." Menno taught the doctrine of dipping exclusively. "After we have searched ever so diligently," said he, "we shall find no other baptism besides DIPPING IN WATER, which is acceptable to God, and maintained in his word." After which he adds, "Let who will oppose, this is the only mode of baptism that Jesus Christ instituted, and the Apostles taught and practised."*

We find in the history of the English Baptists, that about a hundred years after Menno made this declaration, a company of christians about London became convinced of believer's baptism by immersion; but because they could not be satisfied about any administrator in England to begin the practice, and hearing that some in the Netherlands

* Morgan Edwards' History of the Baptists in Pennsylvania, p. 93.

practised immersion, they sent over one Richard Blount, who was immersed by a Dutch minister, by the name of John Batte; that on his return he administered the baptismal rite in the same mode to Samuel Blacklock a minister, and that these two baptized the rest of the company to the number of fifty-three.* At what time pouring instead of immersion was introduced among the Mennonites, I do not find. The cause of this change, according to Morgan Edwards, was as follows: "When they made proselytes in prisons, or were hindered from going to rivers, they made the best shift they could, and practised pouring when they could not immerse. But as in Africa so in Europe, what was done at first out of a supposed necessity, became afterwards to be practised out of choice."

I have thus endeavoured to give a brief account of the rise of the Anabaptists in Germany, of their sufferings, progress and character. Every Baptist will find many things in their character which he can but approve, but their defection from their ancient principles and practice he will lament. But it is some consolation to reflect that the principles of the ancient Baptists in Germany have spread extensively in other countries both in Europe and America.

Every party must have its share of mortification. Geneva, once the seat of Calvin and his orthodox compeers, is now overrun with French philosophy. Geneva, the source of Presbyterianism, has renounced the religion of its ancestors. "The present clergy of Geneva, by a public act of shameless apostasy, from pretended gratitude to France, have abandoned their religion, and betrayed their Saviour. Voluntarily they have exchanged the Sabbath of christians for the decade of Atheists."*

The primitive christians maintained baptism aright for a number of ages, and then they fell into error. The ancient Waldenses were doubtless for a long time uniform in their ideas of baptism, but in process of time some of them got to baptizing their children. The Dutch Baptists held to dipping believers at first; they still retain the subjects of the ordinance, but by a surprising change, some, I know not how many, have departed from the Apostolick mode. And although they still retain the name of Bap-

* Ivimey, p. 143.   † Morse and Parish's Gazetteer, article of Geneva.

tists, yet we can have no fellowship with their present mode of administering baptism; for with every real Baptist, pouring as well as sprinkling is null and void.

BOHEMIA.

I shall not attempt to give any thing like a connected history of the people of whom we are inquiring under this and the following heads. The want of materials would render such an attempt altogether impracticable. The most that I can learn is, that there have been at different periods large numbers of christians in Bohemia, Moravia, Poland, Transylvania, and other parts of Europe, which have not yet been mentioned, who maintained believer's baptism by immersion, but who, at the same time, were much divided in their doctrinal sentiments. All I shall now attempt, will be to give some extracts of their history, and then collect some brief biographical sketches of some of their most distinguished characters.

Bohemia, before the late revolutions in Europe, was a distinguished member in the great Germanic body. The king of Bohemia was one of the eight electors of the Emperor, and was cup-bearer to his imperial majesty. The present situation of this kingdom I am not able to state.

In Bohemia, properly so called, were comprehended the dutchy of Silesia and the marquisate of Moravia. There appears to be no information of any importance respecting the Baptists in Silesia; but of those in Moravia we have some interesting accounts. And as the Bohemian and Moravian brethren all originated from the same source, we shall connect their history under the present head.

Bohemia received the gospel from the eastern church, and not from the church of Rome. Popery, however, was introduced into this kingdom in the ninth century by two Greek monks, but it was not fully established here till the fourteenth century, and then not by the consent of the Bohemians, but by the power and artifice of the emperor Charles IV. About this time, it appears there was an attempt made for a reformation by two of the emperors' chaplains, whose names were Milicius and Janovius. But the attempt proved unsuccessful, and the reformers were suppressed with disgrace. But from this period multitudes withdrew themselves from the publick places of worship, and followed the dictates of their own consciences by worshipping God in private houses, woods, and caves. Here they were persecuted, dragooned, drowned, and killed, and thus they went on till the appearance of John Huss and Jerome of Prague.

The names of John Huss and Jerome of Prague are generally mentioned in connection, and Bohemia is rendered famous in ecclesiastical history, on account of their labours. Under the ministry of Huss and Jerome, a work commenced in this kingdom, more than a hundred years before the rise of Luther and Calvin, which, in some respects, was similar to the reformation under them; for it began upon spiritual principles, and arose to a thing of political consequence. Both Huss and Jerome were destroyed by the council of Constance, in 1415. Jerome is said to have been a far more distinguished man than his friend Huss; but, for what reason I have not learnt, the followers of both were called Hussites.

Huss was professor of divinity in the university of Prague, a preacher in one of the largest churches in the city, and a man of eminent abilities and more eminent zeal. He taught much of the doctrine of Wickliff. His talents were popular, his life was irreproachable, and his manners the most affable and engaging. He was the idol of the people, but execrated by the priests. He was not a Baptist, but as his sermons were full of what are called Anabaptistical errors, Wickliffites, Waldenses, and all sorts of hereticks became his admirers and followers; and as he, in the spirit of a true Bohemian, endeavoured to curb the tyranny of the churchmen, who the nobles knew were uniting with the house of Austria to enslave the state, he was patronized by the great, and all Bohemia was filled with his doctrine and his praise.

The cruel fate of these two eminent men produced very astonishing effects in Bohemia. The news of their death flew like lightning all over the kingdom, and it was soon all in an uproar.

The barbarous conduct of the council of Constance was considered (as all other events are) in very different lights by different people, according to their various interests and passions. The pious mourned the loss of these two eminent servants of God, while others were filled with resentment for the insult offered to their nation.

We cannot trace in order the proceedings which followed; but it is sufficient to observe that a prodigious multitude possessing different characters and views collected, and chose John de Trautenau, surnamed Ziska, that is one-eyed, for their general. Fugitives from all parts daily resorted to him, and put themselves under his protection, till his army amounted to forty thousand. Ziska was esteemed a man of religion, but he was distinguished mostly for his skill in war. He seems to have been much such a character as Oliver Cromwell, and his army was probably not much unlike the one which was headed by the famous Protector. Some were bent on political changes, and others were aspiring at religious freedom. The martial spirit of the age undoubtedly induced many sober christians to engage in this military campaign, who under other circumstances might have taken a different course. They probably, however, soon fell out with Ziska's warlike operations; for not long after this, we find a set of christians in this country, who made it one article of their creed not to bear arms. Ziska demolished idols, discharged monks, who, he said, were only fatting like swine in sties, converted cloisters into barracks, took towns, and strongly guarded one, Cuthna, which, as it commanded the mines, he called anti-christ's purse. He routed armies, tolerated and protected all religions, and encamped his followers on a rocky mountain, about ten miles from Prague, which he soon fortified with a wall, within which the people built houses, and to which he gave the name of Tabor, in allusion to the mount of transfiguration, where the apostle Peter would have erected tents, saying, " it is good to be here." Here the feeble found shelter, and from this fortress the army sallied forth to repulse their enemies. The army continued its operations thirteen years, five under Ziska, and the rest under his successor Procopius. It resisted the power of Rome and Germany united, laughed at the bulls of the pope, and routed the armies of the empire. Ziska fought eleven battles, and won them all. When he was dying, a friend asked him where he would be buried? To which he replied, " When

I am dead let the brethren take off my skin, let them give my flesh to the fowls of the air, and make a drum of my skin, the Germans will flee at the sound of it when you approach them in battle."*

The Taborites, for by this name the company was now called, chose Procopius to succeed Ziska in the command of their army. He was also a brave general, and conducted the army with courage and success. At length Sigismund, loaded with titles and misfortunes, opened a conference, and proposed an accommodation, which was accepted, preparatory to a council, which the pope had engaged to hold at Basil, for the final settlement of all religious disputes. Indeed it was high time to put a stop to the barbarous outrages committed in this distracted country, in which all parties had their share.

The council met, and among the delegates for the Taborites, Procopius was one. The general's patience was often put to the trial in the course of their discussions. He was extremely offended with one of the orators, who was a Bohemian, and who called the delegates hereticks. He started up in the council, and exclaimed, "That countryman of ours insults us by calling us hereticks." Cardinal Julian, who presided, endeavoured to pacify him, and told him he had been informed that his party differed from the Roman church in many other articles beside the four that had been mentioned; he had heard they taught that the fraternities of the monks were the inventions of the devil, which was an offence to christian ears. "Very true," replied the general, "for if neither the patriarchs, nor Moses, nor the prophets, nor Christ, nor the apostles appointed monkery, who does not see that the devil was the author of it?" The council set up a loud laugh at the Bohemian captain's logic.

A part of the Taborites were won over at the council and united with the papal party; but a great part of them persisted in their claims and continued their warlike operations after the council was over. But in about two years after the council, Procopius was slain, the officers of his army, and several thousand, who were taken prisoners,

---

* Ziska was probably slain in battle, but I cannot find any particular account of it.

were destroyed in the most perfidious manner, and the army was disbanded and dispersed in different directions.

In Cromwell's army there were many Baptists, and we have reason to believe there were many in this.

At one time, four hundred poor men, who had lived in the mountains for the sake of enjoying religious liberty, came down with their wives and children to Prague, and committed themselves to Ziska. It is highly probable that these were Waldenses, or Picards, the descendants of those who had come and settled in remote parts of the kingdom, more than two hundred and fifty years before, for even then in the reign of Frederick Barbarossa, Bohemia was accounted the sink of all heresies.

Æneas Sylvius, afterwards pope Pius II. visited mount Tabor for the purpose of diverting himself with the hereticks. The following is a part of his description of the people and the place ; " They have a sort of wooden house like a country barn, which they call a church. Here they preach to the people, here they every day expound the law, here they have one altar neither consecrated, nor fit to be consecrated, and here they give the sacrament to the people. The people are not of one faith, but every one believes what he pleases. There are as many heresies as heads, for all the heresies that have infected the church from the first ages to this day have found a way into this synagogue of satan. Here are Nicolaitans, Arians, Manicheans, Armenians, Nestorians, Berengarians, and the poor people of Lyons. The Waldenses are accounted the chief, and while they remain enemies of the vicar of Christ, and the apostolical see, while they reject all superiority and preach liberty, they must necessarily countenance all kinds of errors. When I quitted the city, I seemed as if I came out of hell."

Æneas Sylvius was one of the most accomplished men of his age. He arose from one high station to another, until he arrived at the popedom. When he visited the Taborites, he was an archbishop. In the visit above described, he tarried all night at the house of a concealed Catholick, who resided there for the sake of getting money. In his second visit, he tarried but a few hours, but all the time was busily employed in conversing and disputing with the Taborites. He reproved them for their heresy, and exhorted them to return to the church which he described as the immaculate spouse of Christ, the spotless dove, &c. One of the Taborites at length became impatient with his harangue, and rising up exclaimed, "Why do you decorate the apostolical see with such fine language? We know that the popes and the cardinals are slaves to avarice, impatient, arrogant, ostentatious, devoted wholly to gluttony and lasciviousness, ministers of sin, priests of the devil, and heralds of antichrist, whose god is their belly, and whose heaven is their wealth." This man was corpulent, and had a very prominent belly, and the arch-bishop, who was never at a loss, rose up, went to him, and putting his hand lightly on his belly, said with a smile, "Whence came this swelling? Why do you reduce yourself to such a skeleton by fasting and prayer?" This well-timed jest produced a loud laugh, and they all with many compliments parted in great good humour.

Out of this company of Taborites arose a church, which was denominated *Unitas Fratrum*, the unity of brethren. One article of their creed was, *not to bear arms;* and another was, *that the Scripture without tradition was a perfect rule of life for christians.*

This church composed of Waldenses, Taborites, and others, was formed at Lititz, twenty miles from Prague, probably about 1430. Not long after they had united into a church, they sent into Austria, where they found an old Waldensian preacher, from whom their newly elected ministers, received what they supposed a true apostolical ordination.

Not long after this, we find the United Brethren had two hundred congregations in Bohemia and Moravia. "Authors," says Robinson, "disagree as much concerning the end of this church, as they do about the rise of it. Some affirm that it fell into the reformed churches in the time of Luther. Others say that it subsisted in Bohemia, till the reign of the emperor Ferdinand II. and that it was then scattered and lost. The people among us, who are called Moravians, contend that they are the descendants of the Bohemian brethren, and therefore they denominate themselves as the ancient Bohemians did, *unitas fratrum.* It is not to our purpose to investigate this dispute. It is certain the ancient church subsisted at the reformation, and afterwards left off baptizing adults, on their own profession of faith."

"The Baptists," says the same writer, "ought always to honour this church; it was a cradle in which many of their denomination were cherished. And all allow that the Anabaptists of Moravia proceeded from a schism in it."

Leaving then the church of the *unitas fratrum*, let us turn our attention to that of the Baptists in this country; for though they were increased and multiplied by parties, who withdrew from the unitas fratrum, yet none of these parties were their founders. All Bohemian historians say, Picards or Waldenses settled in Bohemia in the twelfth century at Satz and Laun on the river Eger. Many affirm that there was a set of Arian vagrants there long before, who had fled from Mesopotamia from the Athanasian persecution, and who were joined by others fleeing from persecution in successive ages from all parts of Europe. On this account most Bohemian Catholick historians call their country a sink of heresy, and Prague the metropolis, a common and safe asylum for all sorts of hereticks.

This account of the Waldenses in Bohemia is similar to those which we have of this dispersed people in other countries. We trace them in their flight, we find where they settled, and then a cloud comes over their history. Waldo, the famous patron of the Waldenses, after being every where persecuted, fled to Bohemia, where he ended his days, about the year 1179, and according to Cranz's history of the United Brethren, as quoted by Ivimey, the company of which we are speaking, emigrated hither at the same time. This was more than two hundred years before the rise of Huss and Jerome. "These two men were not Baptists, but they taught what are called Anabaptistical errors. The following are a few of this sort: "The law of Jesus Christ is sufficient of itself for the government of the church militant." "The church is the mystical body of Christ, of which he is the head." "They are not of the world as Christ was not of the world." "The world hates them, because it hates Christ; that is, the virtue and the truth of God." "Christians ought not to believe in the church." "All human traditions savour of folly." "A multitude of human doctrines and statutes is useless, and on many accounts pernicious." "No other law beside the rule of scripture ought to be prescribed to good men." "The devil was the author of multiplying traditions in the church." "Deacons or elders by the instinct of God, by the gospel of Jesus Christ, without any license from a pope or a bishop, may preach and convert spiritual children." We do not say these reformers followed their principles whither they led, but we do contend that some of their hearers reasoned consequentially from them, and so became Baptists."

In the time of Ziska we are informed, that about Prague and in various parts of Bohemia and Moravia, hereticks obtained a settlement. Some had long ago lived in remote parts of the kingdom about the forests and the mines. These were now multiplied by an accession of foreigners, and by converts of Huss and Jerome, who, reasoning on the principles laid down by their teachers, entertained the same ideas of religion as the old Vaudois did. They were all indiscriminately called Waldenses and Picards,* and they all rebaptized; but they were of very different senti-

* Picards or Beghards was a term of very general meaning, and was applied in different ages to people of very different descriptions, to the pious and profligate, to monks in the church of Rome, and others who separated from it. These people were found in many different countries in Europe. They were sometimes called *Adamites*, and at others, the *Brethren and Sisters of the Free Spirit*, and many incredible tales are told about them. I am fully persuaded that the Beghards, properly so called, originated from France. A Beghard and a beggar were synonymous terms, and probably a scoffing world applied the name to a set of christians, on account of their poverty. They were undoubtedly a branch of the Waldenses, and of the same faith with the poor men of Lyons. The Bohemians, by a change in the pronunciation of the word, called them Picards; and it seems evident they were at different times very numerous in that kingdom. Two very pleasant anecdotes, with regard to the Picards, are related in the history of Maximilian II. Maximilian, after he became emperor, openly declared to Henry III. of France, as he passed through Vienna, that such princes as tyrannize over the consciences of men, attacked the Supreme Being in the noblest part of his empire, and frequently lose the earth by concerning themselves too much with celestial matters. He used to say of Huss, they very much injured that good man. His physician, Crato, was one day riding with him in his carriage, when his imperial majesty, after much lamenting the contentions of mankind about religion, asked the doctor, what sect he thought came nearest the simplicity of the apostles? Crato replied, "I verily think the people called Picards." The emperor added, "I think so too." During this reign every body enjoyed liberty of conscience, and when it was attacked, the effort came to nothing. A faction of catholicks at Prague, envying the happiness of the Picards, formed a cabal of senators, who sent the chancellor of Bohemia to Vienna to entreat the emperor to empower them to restrain these hereticks. By some means the chancellor succeeded, and set out for Prague with the instrument; but attempting to pass a bridge over the Danube, the bridge gave way, and he and his company fell into the river and were drowned. His corpse was taken up by some fishermen, but the diploma was never found. *Robinson.*

ments, some held the divinity of Christ, others denied it, some believed more, others less, but all were obliged to act with caution, for though they were generally connived at, yet they were not allowed to hold their assemblies publickly by law.

The Baptists continued to increase so much that when the disciples of Luther, went into Bohemia and Moravia, they complained, that between Baptists and papists they were very much straitened, though they grew among them like lilies among thorns.

There are two events, which we must not pass over, because they cast light on two articles of some consequence. The first is, that a deputation from the Baptist churches in Poland was sent to those in Moravia. Philipowski, collector of the taxes in Poland, Simon Rouemberg, the druggist, George Schoman, the minister, and several others, who will be mentioned more at large in Poland, came to hold a conference with the brethren in Moravia, concerning both doctrine and discipline, and honoured them for their piety and good morals; but they did not approve of their doctrine, for they contended warmly for the trinity, which the Poles did not believe, however they departed in peace. This may serve to shew how inconclusively they reason, who infer from the doctrine of Lewis Hetzer, that all the Moravian Baptists were Anti-trinitarians. The second event is, that some Jesuits, having got into the councils of the too easy emperor, procured an edict to enforce that which was made in the reign of Uladislaus against the Picards an hundred years before. This had no effect, for the emperor signed it with great reluctance; and as he had a little turn towards superstition, when the news was brought him immediately after he had signed the edict, that the Turks had taken Stuhl Weissenberg, one of his towns in Hungary, he exclaimed, " I expected some such blow from the moment I began to usurp dominion over the consciences of men, for they belong to God alone."

I have not been able to learn any thing respecting the number of Baptist churches in Bohemia and Moravia; nor indeed can I gain much information respecting their history. Most of what has been said and what will follow, is taken from Robinson's Ecclesiastical Researches, and

A General Account of Moravian Baptists. 161

the article relating to Bohemia and Moravia, was left in an unfinished state at his death. From what few sketches we can collect, it is evident there were many among the evangelical dissenters in these countries, who held to the leading sentiments of the Baptists. They differed among themselves on doctrinal points. In some of their maxims and modes of life, they differed somewhat from the Baptists in other countries, and large companies of them seem to have been, in their civil economy, similar to the present Moravians. They were scattered in different parts of the kingdom, and Mr. Robinson is of opinion, that multitudes lived around and within the vast herycenian forest, of whom neither friends nor enemies have obtained much information.

But Bohemia, after long and violent struggles for liberty, at length fell under the despotick and uncontrolled reign of the emissaries of Rome, and heresy, in all its shapes, was banished from the kingdom.

The pope and the court of Spain embarked in the cause, and assisted Ferdinand the emperor of Germany, to extirpate heresy and civil liberty under the opprobrious character of sedition. Having prepared matters, by reinstating the Jesuits, it was thought proper to begin with that part of the Baptists whose principles would not allow them to make any resistance, and who would remove at a word, without giving his majesty the trouble of putting them to death.

The Bohemian and Moravian Baptists were then divided into two classes, the one consisted of Cavinist Picards, and resided at different places all over the kingdom. Some of their ministers kept school; others practised physic. The other class lived all together in Moravia, and are called in the edict by the new German name, Anabaptists. These people lived in forty-five divisions, called colleges or fraternities, exactly as their ancestors had done before their banishment from France, about four hundred and fifty years before this period. Each of these little corporations consisted of many families, who held all things common. It is extremely difficult, not to say impossible, to determine the number of the inhabitants. Carafa, the Jesuit, who was the immediate cause of their banishment, mentions the least number, and he says they consisted of more than twenty thousand. Others say, that each fraternity contained between some hundreds and a thousand, and thence it is inferred that they were about forty thousand. Some of these houses carried on manufactories, others were factors and merchants, and others were employed in agriculture, and a wine trade. All were busy, peaceable, and happy, under regulations of their own making, having none of that class of mankind among them, who live on the vices and follies of their fellow-creatures. They were no burden to any body; on the contrary, they served and enriched the community. They had founded liberty on independence, and independence on industry.

It was not an easy matter to get rid of these Baptists. The emperor's chaplains, who were privy counsellors, talked of heresy; but it was difficult to bring a direct charge against a people, who had no public faith, and who never attacked any religion by publishing creeds. They could not be charged with perjury, for they had never taken any oaths, and one of their maxims was, "*swear not at all.*" Sedition could not be pretended, for they never bore arms. They could not be awed by one another, for they had no masters. They could not be bribed, for they had no necessitous gentry. Filled with that unsuspicious freedom, which innocence inspires, they had not one patron at the imperial court, and their whole expectation was placed on the superintending providence of God. Prince Lichtenstein, on whose domain they lived, and to whom they paid rent, and many other noblemen, endeavoured to save these people, on account of the benefits which they derived from them; so that the Jesuit, who effected their banishment, might well compliment himself for surmounting the seemingly insuperable difficulties. "When I thought," says he, " of proscribing the Anabaptists of Moravia, I well knew that it was an arduous undertaking; however, by the help of God, I surmounted many obstacles, and obtained an edict for their banishment, though it was against the consent of some princes and governors, who had a worldly interest in supporting these profitable rascals."

Comenius says this cruel act was coloured with a pretence that king Frederick, when he passed through Moravia, visited these people, and was hospitably entertained by them. It might be reported so at the time, but this is not mentioned in the edict. The truth is, government stood in no fear of these people, and they were banished first only by the way of trial. It was intended to rid all the emperor's dominions of all denominations except Catholicks, who, as they are nursed in ignorance, and habituated to an implicit confidence in their priests, are the only subjects fit for despotical governments; but Lutherans and Calvinists were very numerous, and powerfully supported by protestant princes in the empire, and it was not time to provoke them; but the expulsion of the Anabaptists would offend no body, for all protestant princes had been taught by their priests to do them the same honour.

Ferdinand wrote first to prince Lichtenstein and cardinal Dietrichstein, the first general of the army in Moravia, and the last governor of the province, to inform them of his design, and to require their concurrence on pain of his displeasure. Then followed the edict, in which his majesty expresses his astonishment at the number of the Anabaptists, and his horror at the principal error, which they embraced; which was, that according to the express declarations of holy scripture, they were to submit to no human authority. He adds, that his conscience compelled him to proscribe them, and accordingly he did banish them, both natives and foreigners from all his hereditary and imperial dominions on pain of death. The jesuits contrived to publish this edict just before harvest and vintage came on for two reasons, first, that the neighbouring gentry would be absent, and next, that the people might not carry away the produce of the present year. They allowed them only three weeks and three days for their departure; it was death to be found even on the borders of the country beyond the expiration of the hour.

It was autumn, the prospect and the pride of husbandmen. Heaven had smiled on their honest labours, their fields stood thick with corn, and the sun and the dew were improving every movement to give them their last polish. The yellow ears waved an homage to their owners, and the wind, whistling through the stems and the russet herbage, softly said, *put in the sickle, the harvest is come.* Their luxuriant vine-leaves too hung aloft by the tendrils mantling over the clustering grapes, like watchful parents over their tender offspring; but all were fenced by an imperial edict, and it was instant death to approach. Without leaving one murmur upon record, in solemn, silent submission to the power that governs the universe and causes *all things to work together for good* to his creatures, they plucked up and departed. In several hundred carriages they conveyed their sick, their innocent infants sucking at the breasts of their mothers, who had newly lain in, and their decrepit parents whose work was done, and whose silvery locks told every beholder that they wanted only the favour of a grave. At the borders they filed off, some to Hungary, others to Transylvania, some to Wallachia, others to Poland and Saek-hel; greater, far greater for their virtue, than Ferdinand for all his titles and for all his glory.

The Jesuit, who executed this business, says, ten thousand staid in Moravia, and became Catholicks. That numbers eluded the search of their persecutors, and remained in the country is evident; but it is not so clear that any conformed. The persecution was carried on for seven successive years; and as persecution drives people of different sentiments together, probably they mixed with the Calvinist Baptists, and were confounded all together in subsequent edicts, in which hereticks of all descriptions, Lutherans, Calvinists, Picards, and all other dissenters were confounded together, and punished with unremitted fury. All the following edicts are full of complaints that hereticks met for divine worship in woods, mills, lone houses and castles, and as they could be caught, were tried for both rebellion and heresy. Many suffered and probably some remained, for in time the Austrian family found that persecution would absolutely depopulate and destroy the country; and when their power was well established, and there were no competitors, they found it politic to lighten the people's burdens; but as liberty by connivance is only eligible when no better can be had, the Baptists seem to have quitted Bohemia and Moravia, or to remain only in some feeble scattered companies.

To recapitulate the histories of these Baptists—Authentic records in France assure us, that a people of a certain description were driven from thence in the twelfth century. Bohemian records of equal authenticity inform us, that some of the same description arrived in Bohemia at the

The Character of the Moravians. 165

same time, and settled near a hundred miles from Prague, at Satz and Laun, on the river Eger, just on the borders of the kingdom. Almost two hundred years after, another undoubted record of the same country, mentions a people of the same description, some as burnt at Prague, and others as inhabiting the borders of the kingdom, and a hundred and fifty years after that we find a people of the same description, settled by connivance in the metropolis, and in several other parts of the kingdom. About one hundred and twenty years lower, we find a people in the same country, living under the protection of law, on the estate of prince Lichtenstein exactly like all the former, and about thirty or forty thousand in number. The religious character of this people is so very different from that of all others, that the likeness is not easily mistaken. They had no priests, but taught one another. They had no private property, for they held all things jointly. They executed no offices, and neither exacted nor took oaths. They bore no arms, and rather chose to suffer than resist wrong. They held every thing called religion in the church of Rome in abhorrence, and worshipped God only by adoring his perfections, and endeavouring to imitate his goodness. They thought that christianity wanted no comment, and they professed the belief of that by being baptized, and their love to Christ and one another by receiving the Lord's supper. They aspired at neither wealth nor power, and their plan was industry. We have shewn how highly probable it is that Bohemia afforded them work, wages, and a secure asylum, which were all they wanted. If these be facts, they are facts that do honour to human nature, they exhib it, in the great picture of the world, a few small figures in a back ground, unstained with the blood, and unruffled with the disputes of their fellow creatures. It was their wisdom in their times not to come forward to deliver apologies to the world; and creeds with flattering prefaces to princes, the turbulence of the crowd would have caused the still voice of reason not to be heard.

Here we must leave these persecuted and dispersed brethren. We know but little of what became of them in other countries. It is probable, however, that as the fathers died off, their posterity, by degrees, departed from their principles, until they became absorbed, in the great mass of professors, with which they were surrounded.

We shall close this article with a part of a famous letter written to Erasmus out of Bohemia, in 1519. This letter describes a set of christians then in that country, in the following manner : " these men have no other opinion of the pope, cardinals, bishops, and other clergy, than as of manifest antichrists. They call the pope sometimes the beast, and sometimes the whore, mentioned in the Revelations. Their own bishops and priests, they themselves do choose for themselves, ignorant and unlearned laymen, that have wife and children. They mutually salute one another by the name of brother and sister. They own no other authority than the Scriptures of the Old and New-Testament. They slight all the doctors both ancient and modern, and give no regard to their doctrine. Their priests when they celebrate the offices of mass (or communion) do it without any priestly garments ; nor do they use any prayer or collects on this occasion, but only the Lord's prayer, by which they consecrate bread that has been leavened. They believe or own little or nothing of the sacraments of the church. Such as come over to their sect, must every one be *baptized anew, in mere water*. They make no blessing of salt, nor of water ; nor make any use of consecrated oil. They believe nothing of divinity in the sacrament of the eucharist, only that the consecrated bread and wine do by some occult signs represent the death of Christ ; and, accordingly, that all that do kneel down to it, or worship it, are guilty of idolatry : That that sacrament was instituted by Christ to no other purpose but to renew the memory of his passion, and not to be carried about or held up by the priests to be gazed on. For that Christ himself, who is to be adored and worshipped with the honour of Latreia, sits at the right of God, as the christian church confesses in the creed. Prayers to saints, and for the dead, they count a vain and ridiculous thing ; as likewise auricular confession and penance enjoined by the priest for sins. Eves and fast-days are, they say, a mockery and the disguise of hypocrites."

" This description," says Crosby, " does almost in every thing fit the modern Baptists, especially those in England. Their saluting one another by the name of brother and sister ; their choosing their own ministers, and from among the laity ; their rejecting all priestly garments, and refusing to kneel at the sacrament ; their slighting all authorities but that of the scriptures, but especially their baptizing again all that embraced their way, does certainly give the Baptists a better right than any other protestants, to claim these people for their predecessors."

POLAND.

Mr. Robinson has entered largely into the ecclesiastical history of Poland, and has brought to light much information respecting the Baptists in this kingdom ; but we are sorry to find that the doctrinal sentiments of many, if not the most of them, were not such as the Baptists generally approve.

We know but very little respecting the Polish Baptists before the reformation. Could we come at their history we should doubtless find a people of whose doctrine and practice a pleasing account might be given. From several historical hints it is evident that the Waldenses spread into Poland, not long after they settled in the adjoining kingdom of Bohemia ; and we have already shown that wherever these people went, they carried along with them the principles on which all the Baptist churches are founded.

Cardinal Hosius, who was a Pole, thought it a kind of miracle, that as Bohemia and Moravia were so near Poland, and the language the same, Poland should continue uninfected with the heresy of the Waldenses, for one hundred and forty years. If records were silent, appearances would be very much against such a miracle ; but records the most authentic assure us that this heresy did infect Poland long before the days of John Huss, and much more after his death.

In the twelfth century, as was observed in the history of Bohemia, some Waldenses settled in Satz and Laun, and there they found many of the Greek church, who associated with them, and whom, as they were well skilled in the scriptures, they improved in religious knowledge. In the fourteenth century the Waldenses of Bohemia and Poland sent money collected among themselves, to their persecuted brethren in Lombardy. In later times, on every gust of persecution, they stepped out of one kingdom into another, and so continued to do until the reformation. The vicinity of Poland to Moravia and Bohemia, the election of two of the reigning family of Jagellon in Poland to be kings of Bohemia, and other similar events, rendered such a migration perfectly easy."

" Formerly, (says bishop Cromer) the heresy of Wickliff and Huss infected Poland, and within my memory those of Berengarius, Luther and Calvin, found their way into the country by means of merchants coming hither, and young gentlemen going into Germany for education, by which means the minds of many were infected, and now after the example and under the patronage of some noblemen, we abound with Picards, Anabaptists, Arians, and hereticks of all sorts ; and, O, what lamentable depravity ! every one is master of his own religion, a law and a king to himself, and thus multitudes pretend liberty and become licentious."

Thus we see that Poland was infected with heresies of different kinds, long before the reformation, and that among the hereticks were the Waldenses, Picards, and Anabaptists ; but I find no materials from which their history can be obtained.

Popery was the established religion of Poland, but its bands were not so strong here, as in other kingdoms ; and as the Polanders were in those times passionately fond of freedom, it is highly probable that the Baptists lived openly in many places by connivance, and where this could not be done, that they retired to the forests and obscure retreats, where they followed their own regulations, and maintained the purity and simplicity of their principles. As yet the tide of Socinianism had not began to prevail in this northern kingdom.

During the long reign of Sigismund, who governed Poland forty-two years, the German reformers poured disciples into Poland ; and Lutherans, assisted by Bohemian brethren, taught with so much success that popery was reduced to the lowest ebb. Several noblemen became their patrons, and the senate itself was filled with friends to reformation. It was at the latter end of this reign, that the party of which we are going to speak was formed by a Dutch Baptist.

The party which Mr. Robinson here alludes to was formed in the following manner. While the different parties of Catholicks, Lutherans, Calvinists, and the Bohemian brethren, were each disputing in defence of their peculiar tenets, John Tricessius, a nobleman of Cracow, who had devoted himself to no party, collected a large library and formed a society of men of his own character, who professed to pursue an unbiassed course in search of truth. The members of this society were all distinguished either by their literary merit, their sagacity, or their rank in life. We soon find among them a Dutch Baptist minister, who was soon after excommunicated from his own church for Arianism. He was called by different names, by some Rudolph Martin, by others Adam Pastoris, and by this company, Spiritus. Spiritus started some objections against the doctrine of the Trinity. His arguments were at first opposed; but it appears that the company took them up afterwards, and followed them on with a speculative curiosity, till they settled down on Arian and Unitarian principles. Tricessius continued to hold religious conferences at his house, and the company was increased by new members. Others of the nobility followed his example, and many societies of this kind were formed. We cannot trace in order the progress of these societies, but it is sufficient to observe that they finally centered at Pinckzow, and were hence called Pinckzovians. Here they enjoyed the patronage of prince Nicholas Olesnicki, lord of Pinckzow, by whose means the monks were expelled out of a monastery, which was converted into a seminary of learned men. From this period the Pinckzovians went on with great success; and as in these times princes and great men thought it necessary to attach themselves to some religious party or other, many espoused the cause of the Pinckzovians, and thereby emboldened them to prosecute their exertions. Pinckzow now became the residence of many famous men, who differed widely in their doctrinal speculations. Some were engaged in writing and publishing their sentiments, and others in travelling and preaching in different parts of the country. The Pinckzovians were at first an assemblage of many different characters, among whom there existed a great variety of opinions on doctrinal points. Most of them were natives of Poland, but many among them had fled hither from other European kingdoms, to escape the persecuting hands of their enemies, and find an asylum where they might enjoy and propagate their opinions. Some believed more and others less of the fundamental points of the christian system. The doctrine of the Trinity and the divinity of the Saviour were maintained by some, denied by others, and doubted by the rest; but infant baptism was denied by all. The whole body was of course honoured with the title of Anabaptists. But this term was used in as vague a sense in Poland as in Germany. The Pinckzovians were, properly speaking, ANTI-pedobaptists, but they were not all Baptists. They agreed to reject infant baptism, as a popish tradition; but they were, as a body at first, far from having clear and consistent views of this ordinance. The doctrine of believer's baptism by immersion seemed however generally to prevail; but it was sometime before any of them reduced it to practice. These people adopted good maxims with regard to religious freedom, but they acted absurdly when they attempted to unite in one church such a discordant assemblage of religious opinions. Their discussions were often warm and pointed, and are thus humorously described by their Catholick opposers. " Good heavens!" said they, " what a racket was there at Pinckzow! The question was put, was Poland to be reformed by rules taken from the fathers. or from Saxony, or from Geneva, or from the simple scripture? One pulled out his creed, and another his list; but the vote was carried for reforming by the simple word of God. Then the table being cleared, forth came the Bible, and that was to be the standard. Then a dust was stirred up about what the Bible had to say. One cried, it says there are three Gods. No such thing, replied another, it says there is but one God. Then down they went to the very foundations, and free-will, and justification, and faith, and works, and sacraments, and every article of the church, was overhauled. This comes of casting off the sovereign pontiff. Good heavens! what a dust was there at Pinckzow!"*

These people met often in assemblies, which they called synods, in which subjects of importance were discussed, and plans of proceeding agreed upon. They some-

---

* Robinson's Researches, p. 577.

times met by themselves, and at other times in conjunction with the other bodies of Protestants in Poland. In a synod held at Brest in Lithuania in 1568, two very able speeches were delivered against infant baptism, the first by Peter Goniadzki, commonly Gonesius, and the other by Jerom Piescarski. The latter " affirmed that infant baptism had no place in scripture; that in the two first centuries it was not mentioned; that it rose in Africa in the third century, and was opposed by Tertullian; that the first canons to enjoin it were made at a council at Mela, in Africa, in the year 418; that infant communion came in at the same time ; that before this people were put into the state of catechumens, and instructed in the christian faith, that then they were examined concerning their faith, and on confessing it were baptized by immersion ; that in the fourth and fifth centuries, while the papal power continued feeble though increasing, the children of believers, even those of bishops, were not baptized till they were adults, and some, as Ambrose, not till they had been elected, and were going to accept the office of bishops, and that some deferred it till they were just ready to die." He concluded by saying, " Why then, brethren, do you rise up against me for rejecting this relick of popery ? Why do you impose silence on me under such severe injunctions in regard to a subject, which deserves a fair and full hearing ? Is this the forbearance, the love, the liberty of christians ? Shall I, whom conscience compels to teach the truth, be silent ? Rather let me seriously exhort and beseech you to cast out every thing that popery hath brought into the church, and to cleanse the house of God from all fragments of papal rubbish. For my part I most sincerely pray, that the God and Father of our Lord Jesus Christ may instruct, replenish and establish you by his Holy Spirit." These declarations produced a great deal of reading, conversing, and disputing, both in public and private, and a great number of converts of all ranks to believer's baptism. It is difficult to say, and not very material, who of these Polanders first administered baptism by immersion. Some say, that Matthias Albinus, minister of Ivanowitz, who was a Trinitarian, and continued so till his death. Others say, Stanislaus Paclesius, who was pastor of an Arian church, at Lublin, under the patronage of the palatine Tenckzynski, where he died in sixty-five. In the province of Cujavia, Martin Czechovicius was a warm advocate for it, and published, first in Polish and afterward in Latin, an admirable treatise, concerning the origin of the *errors* of the Pedobaptists, &c.

The doctrine of the Pinckzovians was spreading far and wide, and a great number of people of all ranks declared for it. Magistrates, noblemen, knights, governors, palatines, officers of the crown, ministers, rectors of schools of great and little Poland, Lithuania, Russia, Podolia, Volhinia, Prussia, Silesia, and Transylvania, openly professed their belief of it.

There were at this time three large parties of protestants in Poland, beside the Pinckzovians. There were Calvinists, Lutherans, and the Bohemian Brethren. The Pinckzovians were denominated Arians and Anabaptists, and were the common objects of aversion to all parties, particularly the Catholicks, Calvinists, and Lutherans, who, forgetting their own dissensions, united their endeavours to suppress and extirpate them, and they at length in part effected their purpose.

The Pinckzovians had hitherto gone on with great success, their converts were many and respectable, their patrons were also numerous and great, but the patronage of the great is as uncertain as the weather, and variable as the wind. These people as yet had no settled plan of procedure, their doctrinal notions were vague and fluctuating, and many of them were intermixed among all the other denominations of protestants. But at length they were driven to a separation from them, and the Catholicks and Calvinists obtained a royal edict to drive them from the kingdom. " The king was obliged to yield to the torrent, and he issued, at the request of the Catholick lords and Calvinist ministers, who were then holding a synod with the Lutherans at Lublin, an edict to banish all foreign Arians and Anabaptists, and to suppress domestic heresy and blasphemy upon pain of death. Foreigners quitted the kingdom ; but such was the constitution of Poland, so little do the great lords in such an aristocracy regard laws, and so powerful were the patrons of the Arians, that though they retired as if they paid some respect to authority, yet they met, held synods among themselves, and having been driven from all other parties, formed the first churches in these troublous times. It was about this time they began to read and study the writings of the late Laelius Socinus, who had died at Zurich in 1562, in the 37th year of his age, and had left some of his papers in Poland. Pauli retired from Cracow, some patrons expelled their ministers, others resigned, and several kept close at home, for they feared the fate of Servetus. Albinus, the Trinitarian Baptist minister, sheltered many, and Olesnicki and Philipowski more.

The Pinckzovian confederation was thus broken up and scattered, many of their members left the kingdom, but most of them remained in a dispersed condition, until they were again collected at Racow, under the patronage of the palatine John Sieninski. Here they were called Racovians, and flourished much for a time; but at length an unlucky event exposed them to censure, banishment, and ruin. Mosheim appears to have made no distinction between the Pinckzovians and Racovians; one would think by his account that they were both the same people, under other circumstances and different names. But Mr. Robinson has unravelled this part of the history of the Anabaptists in Poland, and has shown that while they were called Pinckzovians, their notions of church discipline were peculiarly vague and incorrect. Many of their ministers were put into livings by lordly patrons, who had them at their disposal. Their churches were built in some measure after the old popish model, which the other protestants had adopted; and both ministers and churches were under masters whose patronage often involved them in snares and distress. They were all opposed to infant baptism, but as yet few of their ministers or members had been baptized.

"Happy for these people," says Robinson, "all parties agreed to detest and expel them; for then they formed a new church without a master, and agreed that each should be the lord of his own conscience. This event took place after the dispersion of the Pinckzovian confederacy. It is supposed that the famous Baptist, Ronemberg, received his ideas of founding independent churches of baptized believers, on his journey to Moravia, by conversing with the Baptists there. It is evident that by his advice and persuasion, a few professed their faith and repentance, were baptized by immersion, and formed themselves into a regular independent church. The trial succeeded, the scattered flock repaired to fold, they increased every day, and multiplied so amazingly in a few years, that all parties found they must be allowed the rights of citizens, and put under the protection of clear explicit law. Their great men were innumerable, they had power, and they would be heard. They formed flourishing congregations at Cracow, Lublin, Pinckzow, Lucclaw, Smigla, Racow, and other places, where they lived in as much peace as they could wish.

Not long after this, these people formed an establishment at Racow in the following manner: " The family of the palatine Sieninski, nearly related to Olesnicki, had always favoured the Baptists. The palatine, John Sieninski, who was a Lutheran, sometimes heard their sermons, and was once extremely affected under a discourse preached by one of their plain popular teachers, John Securinius. Being asked, what he thought of the sermon? he said, we shall certainly perish, unless we live as the pious man hath been teaching us. The lady of this palatine was a member of a Baptist church. About the year 1569, he had founded a town in the palatinate of Sendomir, about one mile from Sidlow, and in compliment to his lady had named it Racow. In this pleasant spot he had allured, by granting many privileges, various classes of foreigners and natives to settle. Among the rest Securinius, Schoman, and the Baptist church of Cracow came and settled here, and lived happy and easy under the patronage of their lord. This induced more to come, and Racow became a sort of Baptist town, where the principal men resided, taught, and held synods. After the decease of the patron, his son James Sieninski, palatine of Podolia, then in the thirty second year of his age, having entertained some doubts of the Lutheran religion, desired a conference to be held between them and the Baptists. They complied. After he had heard the arguments of both parties, he thought reason was on the side of the latter, and following his own convictions he joined the church. This was a great accession of honour, and wealth, and power to the Racovians, (for so now we must call them) and, though the patron's munificence continued as long as his life, very much to the credit of both him and them, there is no instance, with all their heresy, of their employing power to oppress conscience. They seem to have adopted an opinion, which a son of peace in Germany long after expressed aptly enough by saying, " of all heresies in the world, the most dangerous are a man's own depraved passions."

The Racovians flourished much for a time. Many famous characters resorted hither from different parts of the kingdom, and some by their wealth, and others by their abilities, contributed to aid the progress of this new establishment. Their patrons founded a school for them, and provided them with a printing office. The school was thronged with pupils from different parts of the kingdom. The press was employed in printing the works of their learned men; and here I conclude was published that famous work in six volumes folio, entitled *Fratres Poloni*, or the works of the Polish Brethren, which is in the library of Brown University at Providence.

Thus out of the Pinckzovian party originated a new set of churches, which were more decidedly of a Baptist character. They were called by the different names of Arians, Anabaptists, Racovians, and finally, Socinians. These churches were at first composed wholly of baptized believers, but some of them in a short time adopted open communion, and particularly the one at Racow. This revolution is said to have been brought about by the younger Socinius, who also led the Polish Baptists farther into doctrinal errors. For himself he was an Antipedobaptist, but not a Baptist, He rejected infant baptism as a manifest error, but he was never baptized, nor did he think baptism a scriptural ordinance; but if it were to be administered at all, it was to those who were converted from other religions to the christian. It is strange indeed that the Baptists should listen to such a teacher; but so it was, that by the superiority of his genius and address, he became the oracle of the Polish Baptists, and in time brought the greatest part of them to embrace his doctrinal sentiments, and from him they acquired the name of Socinians.

While the Racovians were going on with great prosperity, and the Baptists increasing in different parts of the kingdom, an unexpected event blasted all their prospects, and involved the whole community in a scene of the deepest distress. In the year 1638, some students of the academy at Racow very rashly and improperly vented their aversion to popery by throwing stones at a wooden crucifix, that stood out of town, till they had beaten it out of its place. A complaint was lodged not against the offenders, as in a well regulated state, but against the religion which their tutors professed. The palatine, who was president of the academy, cleared himself by oath, but neither that, nor his services to the state, nor his age, (he was near seventy) nor any other consideration could prevail with the diet at Warsaw, which was now a mere faction, to admit of any excuse, or accept any amends. It was proved to be a mere freak of boys, without the knowledge of their tutors, and for which they had been corrected by their parents. Several of equestrian rank of all denominations protested against their arbitrary proceedings; but all in vain. The powerful party enacted, that the Racovian academy should be destroyed, the professors banished, the printing office demolished, and the places of worship shut up. All these decrees were executed without any alleviating circumstances, and the afflicted palatine, whom the senate had often honoured with the title of father of his country, saw his city vanish like a dream, and the labour and pleasure of his whole life blasted by one order of this relentless despotism. He survived the cruel act only one year.

For twenty years succeeding this event, Mr. Robinson informs us, persecution was carried on with unrelenting severity against the Baptists in different parts of Poland, and dreadful havock was made with these obnoxious people. The Cossacks invaded the kingdom, and the Baptists were the first to* be plundered by the consent of all parties. Next they were terribly harassed by an army of Swedes. The Catholicks were hearty in promoting their destruction, and the Lutherans and Calvinists, who might have prevented their sufferings, had no small share in helping them forward. But they did not foresee that they were preparing chains for themselves, for they, in process of time, were also expelled from Poland. Civil liberty halted only a little while, for the kingdom was dismembered, and the Poles enslaved by their powerful neighbours.

Recapitulation of the History of Polish Baptists.

Among the patrons and members of the Baptist churches were several palatines and vice-palatines, castellans and their inferior officers, judges and practitioners in the law, members of the lower house in the diet, officers of the crown and gentlemen of the army, lords of manors, physicians, citizens, merchants, tradesmen, and people of all ranks. The rusticks were bound to the soil, and no more notice was taken of them than of the salt-mines, or the forests, for they were all alike real immovable property. Of the rest some staid and worshipped God in private; others strained a point and fell into the other reformed congregations. Numbers fled, some found an asylum in Transylvania, Silesia, Brandenburg, Prussia, and the adjacent places, others of them lurked in Holland, England, Denmark, and Holstein. The king of Denmark would have granted them a settlement in his dominions, and so would some other princes, but all their humane endeavours were frustrated by the Catholick prelates of every state. They were therefore dispersed all over Europe, and the Baptist and Arminian churches of the United Provinces received many of them into their bosom.

To recapitulate the history of the Baptists in Poland. We find that the Waldenses spread into this kingdom not long after they settled in Bohemia, which was more than three hundred years before the rise of Luther and Calvin. We have no account of their proceedings, but we may safely conclude that they carried Baptist sentiments along with them. A long time after this a Catholick bishop complains, that the Anabaptists among other sects abounded in Poland. While the reformation was going on in Germany and Switzerland, and other European kingdoms, Poland was infected with its principles. Infant baptism was doubted at first by some of the followers both of Luther and Calvin; but as these two distinguished champions took a decided stand in its favour, all inquiries upon the subject were hushed within the circles of their immediate influence; and they, instead of reforming the article of baptism, carried it farther from its original mode than the papists had done; for they had continued to dip, except in cases of necessity; but the reformers left off dipping altogether, and first enjoined pouring and then sprinkling. But among many of the reformers in Poland, infant baptism underwent a very fair and able discussion, and was by them rejected as a relick of popery. These people are very properly described by the term Antipedobaptists, that is, opposers of infant baptism, for we have no account that many of them went any farther. But they were generally denominated by their enemies, Anabaptists. They, it is true, countenanced some of the Anabaptistical errors, but we have reason to believe that multitudes of them lived and died without any other baptism, than that which they received in their infancy in the church of Rome. Many of these opposers of infant baptism, were distinguished by their learning, wealth, and princely titles, and we have no reason to believe that they were generally acquainted with the principles of vital piety. Believer's baptism by immersion is always a cross-bearing duty, and this was probably the reason, why no more of them submitted to it. Their notions of baptism were in the main clear and consistent, but their practice was defective. I know not, however, but as many submitted to the ordinance as were fit subjects for it.

In a catechism or confession of faith published at Cracow in 1574, which is said to have been drawn up by a Baptist minister, by the name of George Schoman, the article of baptism is very well defined. "*Baptism,*" says this catechism, "*is the immersion into water and emersion of one who believes in the gospel, and is truly penitent, performed in the name of Father, Son and Holy Ghost, or in the name of Jesus Christ alone.*"*

Infant baptism is well fitted for a church composed of different materials, dead and alive, for it is administered to those who know nothing of the matter. But Believer's baptism will not do for such churches, and wherever it has been adopted it has produced embarrassment at first, and division in the end. And so it happened with the people of whom we are speaking. And the genuine Baptists among them doubtless often found themselves involved in much perplexity. Had they sought instruction of the old Waldenses, many of whom we have reason to suppose maintained the simplicity of the gospel in their obscure retreats, they might have been set right at once. But they were ambitious of worldly honour, they found themselves

* Mosheim, vol. iv. p. 491.

associated with great men, and protected by noble patrons, who thwarted their principles and led them astray. But as tempests dispel the fogs and clear the atmosphere, so the dispersion of the Pinckzovian party, opened the way for their founding independent churches of those who had been baptized on a profession of their faith. For a while the Baptists in Poland appear to have stood right as it respected the discipline of their churches, but before long they plunged into the inconsistent and embarrassing practice of open communion, and admitted into their churches Pedobaptists, and those who held that baptism was not a perpetual ordinance. They had before adopted some fundamental errors in doctrine, and although they enjoyed worldly prosperity for a time, yet at length a terrible gust of persecution blasted all their prospects, and overwhelmed them with distress and ruin.

Hitherto we have said but little respecting the doctrinal sentiments of the Polish Baptists, and I am sorry that a more pleasing account of them cannot be given. They styled themselves Unitarians, and were first of an Arian and afterwards of a Socinian cast. When they first began to tamper with the doctrine of the Trinity, and the divinity of Christ, their notions were vague and fluctuating. They gave an exalted character to the Son of God, and did not entirely divest him of his divinity, and they also defended a kind of trinity for several years. They were unwilling to admit the proper deity of the Saviour, and yet they knew not how to get over some of the strong expressions of scripture which advance it, and some of them professed to adore and invoke him. There is a work, published not long since in New-England, by a Pedobaptist divine, entitled *Bible News*, which I am sorry to find is well received by some of our Baptist ministers. The author of this work professes to hold to the divinity of Christ, but adopts a new method of explaining that sublime and important subject. I am inclined to think that the Baptists in Poland, in the beginning of their speculations, had not arrived much farther in their descent towards Socinianism, than those Baptists in America, who have adopted the Bible News above mentioned. But they went down one step after another, until they landed in the Socinian system, so fatal to every thing pertaining to christianity but the name.

180 Socinian System formed....Objections against it.

Lelius Socinus came first into Poland, where it is supposed he sowed the seeds of Socinianism about the middle of the sixteenth century. After tarrying here awhile, he went to Zurich, where he died in 1562. He had acquired no determinate plan of doctrine, but Faustus Socinus, his nephew, came into Poland in 1579, and from the papers which his uncle left behind him, is supposed to have drawn the system which now bears the name of *Socinian*.

This man was bold and assiduous in the propagation of his sentiments; he went among the Baptists and other Polish dissenters, who were inclined to Arian and Unitarian principles, and multitudes became his admirers and followers. The leading Baptist ministers were too well prepared to embrace his dangerous errors, and of course were the more easily converted; and by their influence, and the insinuating address of Socinus, the churches one after another, were won over to his sentiments, and adopted his creed. But it must be observed, that we have hitherto spoken only of the leading men among the Polish Baptists. The great mass of professors in the churches were altogether illiterate, and could not of course understand the subtle arguments, by which Socinianism is supported. We have no account at all of them, nor are we informed what they said and thought of those chilling doctrines, which disrobed their Saviour of his peculiar attributes, and reduced him to a level with mortals. Robinson, who seems generally well enough pleased with the doctrine of Socinus, acknowledges that Socinianism consists in refined reasonings beyond the abilities of great numbers who joined the Baptist churches in Poland, and that it is therefore unlikely that they understood or embraced the sentiments, which were adopted by their leaders. This is an important concession, and one would think must be an insuperable objection in the mind of every candid man, against the Socinian system. The gospel of Jesus Christ is designed for the ignorant as well as the wise. The wayfaring man though a fool shall not err in the gospel path. That system of doctrine therefore which none but men of philosophical acuteness can comprehend, I think we may safely conclude is not of divine origin, but an invention of speculative and unhumbled men.

TRANSYLVANIA.

The principles of the reformation were first introduced into this little State, which as its name imports, lies beyond the woods or forests on towards the Turkish dominions, by a Lutheran minister, who was chaplain to the prince of the country. He was succeeded in the chaplainship by Francis Davidis, a seventh-day Baptist minister, who afterwards became superintendant of the Baptist churches in Transylvania. We have seen in the account of the Moravian Baptists, that in the time of their banishments, some went into Transylvania, and it is highly probable that many of them were scattered in this country long before the times of which we are speaking.

Both Baptist and Unitarian principles appear to have been carried into Transylvania from Poland. In 1563, George Blandratta, a celebrated physician, was invited into Transylvania by Sigismund, at that time sovereign of the country, in order to the restoration of his health. Davidis, whose name has already been mentioned, accompanied him in his removal.*

Mosheim calls these men Socinians, but gives us no information respecting their sentiments in other respects. But we learn from Robinson that they were both Baptists. Davidis was a preacher, but Blandratta was not. The first became the chaplain of the court, and the other physician to the prince. About this time several other foreigners came into Transylvania by the invitation of prince Sigismund, for the purpose of helping forward the reformation. Among them was John Somer, celebrated for his knowledge of the Greek language, and Jacob Palæologus, a famous Hebrician. Somer was a Saxon, and Palæologus was a native of the isle of Chios, and is said to be of the imperial family. Several other foreigners, who had been persecuted elsewhere, sought refuge in Transylvania, where persecution for religion was unknown. These refugees were Unitarian Baptists, and through their indefatigable industry and address the prince, the greatest part of the senate, a great number of ministers, and a multitude of the people went heartily into their plan of reformation. This was effected by private tuition, by publick preaching,

* Mosheim, vol. 4. p. 496.

by conferences held in publick by appointment with such as desired information, and by debates in the presence of the senate. The prince and the senators attended one of these successively for ten days. In the end the Baptists became by far the most numerous party, and were put in possession of a printing office, and an academy, and the cathedral was given them for a place of worship.

The year after a synod was held at Thorda, at which were present three hundred and twenty-two Unitarian ministers, who unanimously agreed to renounce infant sprinkling as a prostitution of primitive baptism, and published thirty-two theses against it.*

From this period Baptist principles prevailed, and many Baptist churches were founded in Transylvania; and Davidis, who was considered half a Jew by his opposers, because he kept holy the seventh day, became the superintendant of them all. It is probable that there were many other Sabbatarians in this country, but we have no accounts respecting them. The progress of the Baptists in this kingdom we cannot describe with any degree of minuteness. We are informed however that in process of time, they, like their brethren in Poland, adopted open communion, and tolerated infant sprinkling in their churches. They were connected with a court and with courtly characters, by whom they were corrupted and ensnared. We may furthermore observe that the Baptists have always been outwitted, when they have attempted to vie with others in worldly policy. It is an art which they do not understand, and for which, when they keep to their original principles, they have no need.

The Transylvanian Baptists were, as to their doctrinal sentiments, termed Unitarians and Socinians. But Socinianism was not then what it has arrived to since, nor were the Baptists agreed among themselves in their doctrinal opinions. Davidis thought that Christ ought not to be called God, nor invoked in prayer. Dr. Blandratta, it seems, believed both, and he and Davidis had warm disputes upon the subject. And the doctor, hoping to recover the old superintendant to his former belief, invited Socinus, who was then at Basil, to come into Transylvania. Socinus came, and he and Davidis disputed together eigh-

* Robinson's Researches, p. 630—1—2.

teen weeks, and ended where they begun. Davidis thought Jesus an ordinary man; but both Blandratta and Socinus, and many other Socinians of that day, gave him a much more exalted character. But all of them were wrong, and they had set out in a path which led them by degrees to a cold, comfortless, and dangerous region.

I do not find that the Transylvanian Baptists met with any remarkable scenes of persecution, but still their course was unprosperous. Davidis was imprisoned on account of his opinions, and died in prison, and both Socinus and Blandratta were accused of having a hand in the business. Blandratta, to whom the Baptists looked up for assistance, was now old and rich, and spent his latter days as many other old men have done, in hoarding up money. He had made a will in favour of a nephew, but the impatient youth stifled him in his bed. Davidis was succeeded in the superintendency of the churches by Hunyedine, and he by Enyedine, but who was his successor we are not informed. The Baptist churches here were protected by law, and enjoyed external tranquillity, but we have no information of the state of vital piety amongst them. At the times we have been describing, I am much inclined to believe there were, in obscure retreats, many genuine Baptists, the descendants of the old Moravians, who chose to keep away from the splendour and bustle of the great, and who, of course, avoided their speculations and snares.

The Baptists of whom we have been speaking, both Polish and Transylvanian, were injured by the very means from which they hoped to derive advantage. Their noble converts and patrons elevated them above their common level, which excited their ambition, and also rendered them the more conspicuous objects for the shafts of their enemies. Their learned men, by pursuing a course of speculative reasoning, corrupted their faith and led them into error.

Finally, it will be acknowledged by all, who have studied the history of the Baptists, that they like sheep flourish best in short pasture and in rocky places.

It is now proper that we should give some brief sketches of a few distinguished Baptist characters, who have not been mentioned.

Bernard Ochin or Ochinus. This man was an Italian, he had been a monk and confessor to the pope, but he offended his holiness by preaching too freely before him against his pride. Fearing the consequences of the pope's displeasure, he fled for safety, and finally settled at Pinckzow. Robinson says he became a Unitarian Baptist, but it is doubted by Mosheim whether he ever adopted the doctrine of Socinus.

Stanlius Lutomirski. I find no account of the birth of this eminent man. He had been in priest's orders in the church of Rome, and secretary to the king of Poland, who intended to have preferred him to be lord primate, but his conscience, says Robinson, spoiled him for a cardinal archbishop, and converted him into a teacher of a Baptist church. He wrote the circular letter for the synod held at Wengrovia by the Pinckzovians, which is said to be a master-piece in its kind. He informed the churches that the synod had judged infant baptism an error, and had resolved to renounce it—he added that though some one had mentioned the affair at Munster, yet believer's baptism had nothing to do with it, and that as they had always obeyed magistrates, so they had resolved to do in future for conscience' sake—he closes with exhortations to brotherly kindness, and with adoring God, who had brought them out of the Babylonish captivity of the papal church.

Michael Servetus. This unhappy man was a Spaniard by birth, and lost his life at Geneva by means of the famous John Calvin. He was not immediately connected with the Baptists we have been describing, but as no account of him has yet been given, this seems the most proper place to say a few things respecting him. The death of this unfortunate man produced very lively emotions both of pity and resentment in the breasts of many, who were not altogether in favour of his religious opinions.

Many have written accounts of this much injured man, and uttered the severest rebukes against Calvin and his party by whom he was committed to the flames. Robinson has entered somewhat largely into his history in his Researches, under the Article, *The Church of Navarre and Biscay*; but our limits will permit us to give only the brief outlines of the character and sufferings of this famous Baptist. He was born at Villa Neuva in Arragon, in

Spain, not long after the year 1500. He was bred to physic, but he was early inclined to religious studies, and at the age of eighteen he became an author. His first publication was designed to oppose the doctrine of the Trinity. The errors of Servetus on this and some other subjects we lament. But this does not hinder us from pitying his fate, and detesting the persecuting intrigues which cost him his life. Servetus passed through various fortunes, and published a number of works, all of which we must pass over. While he was studying at the University at Paris, he became acquainted with Calvin, who was nearly of his age. This was about twenty years before he was burnt at Geneva.

From Paris, Servetus went to Lyons, where he met with Peter Palmier, a Catholick and Archbishop of Vienna in Dauphine. The Archbishop being a lover of learned men, and fond of Servetus, pressed him to go to Vienna and practise physic, and offered him an apartment in his palace. The doctor accepted his invitation, and thirteen years lived safe and happy, under the auspices of his Catholick patron. This prelate seems to have been one of those, of whom there have been numbers in the Catholick church, who think freely, but who do not act consistently, who inwardly disapprove of their own corrupt system, but who, for reasons best known to themselves, continue to defend it. The reformers of that day could not conceive how a Catholick Archbishop and an Anabaptist doctor, could live in peace in different apartments in the same palace. The enemies of Servetus envied his felicity, and plotted his ruin. A prosecution was commenced against him, and he was cast into prison; but he soon, by the indulgence of the jailer, made his escape and concealed himself four months, no body knows where. The prosecution was carried on in his absence, he was condemned to be burnt alive in a slow fire, and he was actually burnt in effigy. Being thus hunted by his enemies, this persecuted man next determined on going to Naples, in hope of settling there in the practice of his profession. It is supposed that he was induced to this measure by a Spanish nobleman, named John Valdesius, who was then secretary to the king of Naples, and who had embraced the principles of the Anabaptists.* He took his way through Geneva, but kept close for fear of discovery. While he waited for a boat to cross the lake, Calvin, by some means, got intelligence of his arrival, and although it was Sunday, yet he prevailed upon the chief syndich to arrest and imprison him. The proceedings against him are too lengthy to be related here, but the issue of them was, that on the 27th of October, 1553, this unfortunate man, with many aggravating circumstances, was burnt alive at Geneva for heresy.

A multitude of testimonies go to prove that Calvin was at the head of this barbarous affair. But omitting all others, I will transcribe a part of a letter written by him in 1561, to the Marquis Paet, high chamberlain to the king of Navarre. "Honour, glory, and riches," said he to the Marquis, "shall be the reward of your pains; but above all, do not fail to rid the country of those scoundrels, who stir up the people to revolt against us. Such monsters should be exterminated, as I have exterminated Michael Servetus the Spaniard."†

Servetus was a confirmed Baptist, and censured with great severity the custom of infant baptism, and this was probably one of the principal things which provoked the resentment of his enemies. His doctrinal sentiments were unquestionably very exceptionable. He opposed the doctrine of the Trinity, and adopted the Unitarian scheme, but his views upon this mysterious subject were singular, and in a great measure peculiar to himself.‡ He also opposed the proper divinity of Christ, but like Paul of Samosata, he could never get over the first chapter of John, and therefore he sometimes called him God, and accounted for do-

* Robinson's Researches, p. 348.   † Robinson's Researches, p. 348.

‡ Servetus' notion of the Trinity according to Mosheim was as follows: "The Deity, before the creation of the world, had produced within himself, two *personal representations*, or *manners of existence*, which were to be the *medium* of intercourse between him and mortals, and by whom, consequently, he was to reveal his will, and to display his mercy and beneficence to the children of men; that these two representatives were the *Word* and the *Holy Ghost*; that the former was united to the man Christ, who was born of the virgin Mary by an omnipotent act of the divine will; and that on this account, Christ might properly be called God; that the Holy Spirit directed the course, and animated the whole system of nature; and more especially produced in the minds of men wise councils, virtuous propensities, and divine feelings; and finally, that these two *representations* were to cease after the destruction of this terrestrial globe, and to be absorbed into the *substance* of the Deity, from whence they had been formed.

ing so by some sublime sort of inhabitation of the Deity in the man Jesus.

Andrew Dudith was, according to Mosheim, one of the most learned and eminent men of the sixteenth century. He was born in Buda in Hungary, in 1533. He had a most accomplished education, and went an extensive round of honours and preferments. He set out in his career of worldly glory, with the bishoprick of Tinia, and was in succession privy counsellor to the emperor Ferdinand, his imperial embassador to the court of Sigismund, king of Poland, a delegate in the famous council of Trent for Hungary, and finally bishop of Chonat. But tired of the fopperies of the church of Rome, he left her communion, became a protestant, and in the end a member, and an occasional teacher of a Baptist church at Smila, a town belonging to him in Poland. " It is said that he shewed some inclination towards the Socinian system ; some of his friends deny this ; others confess it, but maintain that he afterwards changed his sentiments in that respect."

" The greatest man, says Robinson, among the Baptists at the reformation, was the celebrated, the amiable, the incomparable Dudith, a man to be held in everlasting remembrance, much for his rank, more for his abilities and virtue, but most of all for his love of liberty,"* and so on. Never, says the same writer, was a finer pen than that of Dudith. " You contend," says he to Beza, " that scripture is a perfect rule of faith and practice. But you are all divided about the sense of scripture, and you have not settled who shall be judge. You have broken off your yoke, allow me to break mine. Having freed yourselves from the tyranny of popish prelates, why do you turn ecclesiastical tyrants yourselves, and treat others with barbarity and cruelty for only doing what you set them an example to do ? You contend that your lay-hearers, the magistrates, and not you, are to be blamed, for it is they who banish and burn for heresy. I know you make this excuse ; but tell me, have not you instilled such principles into their ears ? Have they done any thing more than put in practice the doctrine that you have taught them ? Have you not told them how glorious it was to defend the faith ? Have you not been the constant panegyrists of such princes

* History of Baptism, p. 556.

as have depopulated whole districts for heresy? Do you not daily teach, that they who appeal from your confessions to scripture ought to be punished by the secular power? It is impossible for you to deny this. Does not all the world know, that you are a set of demagogues, or (to speak more mildly) a sort of tribunes, and that the magistrates do nothing but exhibit in publick what you teach in private? You try to justify the banishment of Ochin, and the execution of others, and you seem to wish Poland would follow your example. God forbid! When you talk of your Augsburg confession, and your Helvetic creed, and your unanimity, and your fundamental truths, I keep thinking of the sixth commandment, THOU SHALT NOT KILL. Farewell, most learned and respected Beza. Take what I have said in good part, and continue your friendship for me." This is only a sketch of a letter, but these hints may serve to shew the temper and the turn of the man.

This eminent Baptist fell asleep at Breslaw, in Silesia, in 1589, about the 57th year of his age.

CHAP. V.

ENGLAND.

WE have now arrived to a country, where we shall not be obliged to rely altogether on the accusations of enemies, and the records of courts of inquisition for information respecting our brethren. The English Baptists have paid considerable attention to their own history, and have furnished materials from which we can gain clear and explicit accounts of their character, progress, sufferings, and circumstances, for between two and three hundred years; they have also collected from the writings of their adversaries many valuable hints respecting their brethren at a much earlier period.

About seventy years ago, Mr. Thomas Crosby, a deacon of the old church in London, formerly under the care of Dr. Gill, but now of Dr. Rippon, published, in four volumes, *A History of the English Baptists*. This history is something like that of our late venerable Backus; it contains a vast fund of valuable information, but is deficient in style and arrangement. About the beginning of the present century a periodical work was commenced by Dr. Rippon of London, entitled *The Baptist Annual Register*. This work was continued to forty one numbers, and contains many interesting accounts of the Baptists both in England and elsewhere.

A History of the English Baptists has been lately undertaken by Mr. Ivimey, a Baptist minister in London. This history, I conclude, is intended to be both an abridgment and continuation of Crosby. The first volume which closes with the seventeenth century, I have obtained of Dr. Baldwin of Boston; it is the only copy I have heard of in this country.

In the English Baptist Magazine, a few scattering numbers of which have been loaned me by my friend Dr. Baldwin, I find a few detached portions of what are entitled *Memoirs of the English Baptists*, written by the late Josiah Taylor of Calne, Wiltsshire, England. I very much regret that I cannot get the whole of these ingenious and somewhat singular *Memoirs*, as they would, I have reason to believe, furnish to my hands the substance of the sketch which I am preparing to give. But they are not probably to be obtained this side the Atlantic, and it is now too late to seek them from the other.

The affairs of our English brethren furnish materials for a lengthy article, but it belongs to them to write their own history. It is now taken in hand, and perhaps finished by a gentleman, who appears well qualified for the undertaking. How large the work will be I am not informed, but I hope and am inclined to believe, it will soon be reprinted in this country.

The plan of this work admits only of summary statements and abridged accounts, and but very brief sketches can be given of the Baptists in England. I should have endeavoured to reserve a larger place for them, were it not that those, who may wish to peruse their history at large, will probably soon have the opportunity of doing it, either by the importation or republication of Ivimey's work.

The Baptists in England are divided into *General* and *Particular*, and have been since soon after the reformation. Their principal difference is in points of doctrine. It will be difficult, and indeed unnecessary, to pay a strict regard to these distinctions throughout the following sketch. Both parties have had their share of sufferings, and among them both we find a number of very worthy and distinguished characters.

About sixty years after the ascension of our Lord, christianity was planted in Britain, and a number of royal blood, and many of inferior birth, were called to be saints. Here the gospel flourished much in early times, and here also its followers endured many afflictions and calamities from pagan persecutors. The British christians experienced various changes of prosperity and adversity until about the year 600. A little previous to this period, Austin the monk, that famous Pedo-baptist and persecutor, with about forty others, were sent here by pope Gregory the great, to convert the pagans to popery, and to subject all the British christians to the dominion of Rome. The enterprise succeeded, and conversion (or rather perversion) work was performed on a large scale. King Ethelbert and his court, and a considerable part of his kingdom, were won over by the successful monk, who consecrated the river Swale, near York, in which he caused to be baptized ten thousand of his converts in a day.

Having met with so much success in England, he resolved to try what he could do in Wales. There were many British christians who had fled hither in former times to avoid the brutal ravages of the outrageous Saxons. The monk held a synod in their neighbourhood, and sent to their pastors to request them to receive the pope's commandment; but they utterly refused to listen to either the monk or pope, or to adopt any of their maxims. Austin, meeting with this prompt refusal, endeavoured to compromise matters with these strenuous Welshmen, and requested that they would consent to him in three things, one of which was that they should give christendom, that is, baptism to their children; but with none of his propositions would they comply. " Sins therefore," said this zealous apostle of popery and pedobaptism, " ye wol not receive peace of your brethren, ye of other shall have warre and wretche," and accordingly he brought the Saxons upon them to shed their innocent blood, and many of them lost their lives for the name of Jesus.

The first British Christians were Baptists. 191

The Baptist historians in England contend that the first British christians were Baptists, and that they maintained Baptist principles until the coming of Austin. "We have no mention," says the author of the Memoirs, "of the christening or baptizing children in England, before the coming of Austin in 597; and to us it is evident he brought it *not from heaven* but *from Rome*. But though the subject of baptism began now to be altered, the mode of it continued in the national church a thousand years longer, and baptism was administered by dipping, &c." From the coming of Austin the church in this island was divided into two parts, the *old* and the *new*. The old or Baptist church maintained their original principles. But the new church adopted infant baptism, and the rest of the multiplying superstitions of Rome.

Austin's requesting the British christians, who opposed his popish mission, to baptize their children, is a circumstance which the English and Welsh Baptists consider of much importance. They infer from it, that before Austin's time, infant baptism was not practised in England, and that though he converted multitudes to his pedobaptist plan, yet many, especially in Wales and Cornwall, opposed it; and the Welsh Baptists contend that Baptist principles were maintained in the recesses of their mountainous Principality all along through the dark reign of popery.

Popery was the established religion of England almost a thousand years; and although the people paid Peter's pence, and were involved in darkness, ignorance, and the shadow of death, yet some of these islanders were refractory subjects of the papal see, and some of the kings occasioned much trouble to his holiness. They had much rather be pope themselves, than submit to a foreign ecclesiastical jurisdiction.

William the Conqueror ascended the British throne in 1066. During his reign, the Waldenses and their disciples from France, Germany, and Holland, began to emigrate to and abound in England. About the year 1080, they are said to have propagated their sentiments throughout England; so that not only the meaner sort in country villages, but the nobility and gentry in the chiefest towns and cities, embraced their doctrines, and of course adopted the opinions of the Baptists, for we have no information that any of the Waldenses at this period, had fallen off to infant baptism. For more than a hundred years, that is, from 1100 to 1216, during the successive reigns of Henry I. Stephen, Henry II. Richard I. and John, the Waldenses increased and were unmolested. The two last of these kings were much engaged in foreign affairs. Richard was long absent in the holy war, and John had great contests with the pope, who laid his kingdom under an interdict, and forbid all publick worship for the space of six years, only admitting of private baptism to infants.

In the reign of Henry III. about 1218, the order of the friar Mennonites were sent over from the continent to suppress the Waldensian heresy, and many, doubtless, suffered by their means.

We must now pass on to the reign of Edward II. in 1315, when Walter Lollard, a German preacher of great renown among the Waldenses, and a friend to believer's baptism, came into England and preached with great effect. His followers and the Waldenses generally in England for many generations after him were called Lollards,* and Crosby has quoted authorities to show that they rejected infant baptism as a needless ceremony. In the reign of Edward III. about the year 1311, John Wickliff began to be famous in England, and multitudes embraced his doctrine, and entered heartily into his views of reformation. Wickliff was famous both for writing and preaching. His writings were carried into Bohemia, and his sentiments were there propagated extensively by Huss, Jerome, and others, and among the followers of this great man in Bohemia and England we find many Baptists. There can be no dispute that Wickliff taught Anabaptistical errors, that many who built in his principles rejected infant baptism; and indeed the evidence is very strong that he himself *became a Baptist.*†

Dr. Hurd in his *History of all Religions* says, "It is pretty clear from the writings of many learned men, that Dr. John Wickliff, the first English reformer, either considered infant baptism unlawful or at best unnecessary." The author of a *History of Religion*, published in London

* Ivimey, p. 56.

† We do not contend that he was one at first.

in 1764, in four volumes octavo, says, "it is clear from many authors that Wickliff rejected infant baptism, and that on this doctrine his followers agreed with the modern Baptists." Thomas Walden and Joseph Vicecomes, who had access to his writings, have charged him with denying pedobaptism, and they brought their charge at a time when it might have been easily contradicted, if it had not been true.

"Walden before mentioned calls Wickliff one of the seven heads that came out of the bottomless pit, for denying infant baptism, that heresy of the Lollards, of whom he was a great ring-leader.*"

There were now in England Lollards and Wickliffites, and a number of testimonies go to prove they rejected infant baptism. They were numerous throughout the kingdom, and for some time continued in the established church. But Rapin says that in 1389, the Lollards and Wickliffites began to separate from the church of Rome, and to appoint priests from among themselves, to perform divine service after their way.

In the year 1400, Henry IV. enacted the cruel statute for the burning of hereticks. And the first that suffered by this infernal law was William Sawtre, a Lollard, and supposed to be a Baptist. The signal was now given for bloody men to execute their cruel purposes in a legal way. The sufferings of the Baptists and all evangelical dissenters, from this period till the reformation, were very great. "The Lollards' tower," says Ivimey, "still stands a monument of their miseries, and of the cruelty of their implacable enemies. This tower is at Lambeth palace, and was fitted up for this purpose by Chicheley, Archbishop of Canterbury, who came to his see in 1414. It is said that he expended two hundred and eighty pounds to make this prison for the Lollards. The vast staples and rings to which they were fastened, before they were brought out to the stake, are still to be seen in a large lumber-room at the top of the palace, and ought to make protestants look back with gratitude upon the hour which terminated so bloody a period."†

* Ivimey, p. 71—2. † Page 69.

From the death of William Sawtre to the time when Henry VIII. renounced the dominion of the pope, and became head of the English church, was upwards of a hundred and thirty years. During this period many Baptists were found in this kingdom, many were obliged to flee from it, and many more were martyred in it. In about three years from 1428, to 1431, one hundred and twenty persons were committed to prison for Lollardy; some of them recanted, others did penance, and several of them were burnt alive.

In 1535, twenty-two Baptists were apprehended and put to death, and in 1539, thirty-one more of the same people, sixteen men and fifteen women, were banished the country, who, going to Delf in Holland, were there put to death, the men beheaded and the women drowned. In the same year two others of their brethren were burned beyond Southwark, in the way to Newington; and a little before five Dutch Anabaptists were burned at Smithfield. By a speech which Henry VIII, delivered to his parliament in 1545, it appears that many of his subjects went under the name of Anabaptists. And Bishop Latimer, in a sermon preached before the young and amiable Edward VI, son and successor of the popish protestant Henry, mentions that he had lately been informed by a credible person, that there was at that time, one town in England, which contained more than five hundred hereticks, who held the erroneous opinions of the Anabaptists.

The change, which took place under Henry VIII, was in the end favourable to the cause of religion in England; the fetters of popery were broken; the scriptures in the English language were sanctioned by parliament, and by their means evangelical principles were diffused throughout the land. In a short time the Puritans arose, and pushed on the reformation beyond the bounds which the courtly reformers had set. They professed to take the Bible for their only rule, and many building on their principles, rejected the remains of popish rubbish, and embraced the principles of the Baptists. But persecuting laws were still in force, and the ruling party both in church and state had a disposition to put them in execution. Popery was indeed abolished and protestantism established, but the Baptists soon found that the protestant power was as much determined on their ruin as the popish had ever been. In 1549, a kind of Protestant inquisition was established which consisted of the Archbishop of Canterbury, a number of bishops, noblemen, and others, any three of whom being a quorum, were instructed to examine and search after all Anabaptists, hereticks, &c. Many Baptists were apprehended, how many were executed we are not informed; but we are sure that two of considerable eminence, viz. Joan Boucher, commonly called Joan of Kent, and George Van Pare, a Dutchman, were committed to the flames. Great exertions were made to save from the stake the unfortunate Joan, who appears to have been a woman of distinction, but who had been compelled by her Bible and conscience to become a Baptist. A person, supposed to be Fox, the author of the Book of Martyrs, earnestly entreated the famous John Rogers, who was afterwards burnt at Smithfield, to use his interest with the Archbishop to save the poor woman from the cruel death to which she had been doomed. But Rogers answered, that burning alive was no cruel death, but easy enough. Fox, astonished at such an answer, replied, "*Well, perhaps it may so happen that you yourselves shall have your hands full of this mild burning.*" And so it came to pass, for Rogers was the first man who was burned in Queen Mary's reign.

Not long after this, we are informed that "the Anabaptists began wonderfully to increase in the land;" whether they founded many churches we cannot learn; but if they did, such was the vigilance of their enemies, they were probably soon broken up. In former times it appears many Baptists had fled from the continent, and for a time found shelter in this kingdom; but now they were hunted out by watchful inquisitors, and either destroyed or driven from the realm. A congregation of Dutch Anabaptists was discovered on Easter-day, probably about 1570, without Aldgate in London, seven and twenty of whom were taken and imprisoned, four of them recanted, and the rest were probably either banished or destroyed. One month after this, eleven other Baptists, one Dutchman, and ten women, were apprehended and condemned. One was persuaded to renounce his error, eight were banished the land, and two of the company,

John Wielmaker and Henry Tor Woort were burnt at Smithfield.

Very scanty accounts have been obtained of the Baptists in England in the times of which we are speaking, and but a few of the sketches which our English brethren have preserved can be inserted here. But it is sufficient to observe that for almost a century after the church of England was established by law, our Baptist brethren throughout the kingdom were every where persecuted and distressed, and many were exposed to tortures and death.

The last man who was put to death in England for religion was a Baptist. His name was Edward Wightman, and is supposed to be the progenitor of a large family of that name in America, many of whom have been members of different Baptist churches in Rhode-Island, and the neighbouring States of Connecticut and Massachusetts, and not a few of them worthy ministers in our churches. Mr. Wightman was of the town of Burton upon Trent, he was convicted of divers heresies before the bishop of Litchfield and Coventry, and being delivered over to the secular power, was burnt at Litchfield, April 11th, 1612. This poor man was accused by his persecutors with Arianism, Anabaptism, and almost every other heretical *ism*, that ever infected the christian world. He was condemned for holding the wicked heresies of the Ebionites, Cerinthians, Valentinians, Arians, Macedonians, of Simon Magus, Manes, Manicheus, Photinus, and of the Anabaptists, and of other heretical, execrable, and unheard of opinions. "If," says Crosby, "Wightman really held all the opinions laid to his charge, he must have been either an idiot or a madman, and ought to have had the prayers of his persecutors rather than been put to a cruel death."

From the death of William Sawtre, who was burnt in London, to the time that Edward Wightman perished in the flames at Litchfield, was a period of two hundred and twelve years. We have very good grounds for believing that Sawtre was a Baptist, we are sure that Wightman was, and thus it appears that the Baptists have had the honour of leading the van, and bringing up the rear, of that part of the noble army of English martyrs, who have laid down their lives at the stake.

It is now about two hundred years since Wightman, with his enormous load of heresies, was committed to the purifying flames. Almost half of this time, the Baptists in England were, for the most part, in an uncertain state; what earthly enjoyments they possessed were held by a precarious tenure, and persecution and distress were their common lot. They had indeed some short intervals of repose, but these were succeeded by tempestuous seasons, and the cup of affliction was dealt out to them by their enemies in plenteous measure.

We have observed that Edward Wightman was the last man who suffered death for religion in England. But this statement needs some qualification. He was indeed the last who suffered death for conscience' sake by a direct course of law; but multitudes since him, both Baptists and others, have died in prisons, and came by their ends by the various methods of legal persecutions, and lawless outrage, with which implacable adversaries pursued them. Thousands have suffered by fines, scourging, and imprisonment, been driven to exile, starvation, and wretchedness, by a protestant power, which professed to have separated from the mother of harlots, and to have renounced the works of darkness. Of many of these sufferers we have obtained some information, but the history of many others must remain unknown, until that tremendous day, when the righteous Judge of the universe shall make IN-QUISITION FOR BLOOD.

We shall now pass on to the founding of Baptist churches in this kingdom, and then take notice of their increase from time to time. I find that Crosby and Ivimey are not entirely agreed respecting the time when the first Baptist churches were founded in England. Crosby's account is as follows: "In the year 1633, the Baptists, who had hitherto been intermixed with other protestant dissenters, without distinction, and who consequently shared with the Puritans in the persecutions of those times, began to separate themselves, and form distinct societies of their own. Concerning the first of these, I find the following account collected from a manuscript of Mr. William Kiffin.

" There was a congregation of protestant dissenters of the Independent persuasion in London, gathered in the year 1616, of which Mr. Henry Jacob was the first pastor, and after him succeeded Mr. John Lathrop, who was their minister in 1633. In this society several persons, finding that the congregation kept not to its first principles of separation, and being also convinced that baptism was not to be administered to infants, but to such as professed faith in Christ, desired that they might be dismissed from the communion, and allowed to form a distinct congregation in such order as was most agreeable to their own sentiments.

" The church, considering that they were now grown very numerous, and so more than could in those times of persecution conveniently meet together, and believing also that those persons acted from a principle of conscience, and not from obstinacy, agreed to allow them the liberty they desired, and that they should be constituted a distinct church, which was performed, Sept. 12, 1633. And as they believed that baptism was not rightly administered to infants, so they looked upon the baptism they had received at that age as invalid, whereupon most or all of them received a new baptism. Their minister was a Mr. John Spilsbury. What number they were is uncertain, because in the mentioning of about twenty men and women, it is added, *with divers others.*

" In the year 1638, Mr. William Kiffin, Mr. Thomas Wilson, and others, being of the same judgment, were upon their request dismissed to the said Mr. Spilsbury's congregation. In the year 1639, another congregation of Baptists was formed, whose place of meeting was in Crutchedfriars, the chief promoters of which were Mr. Green, Mr. Paul Hobson, and Captain Spencer."

There can be no dispute but that these churches were founded at the time, and in the manner above related. But Mr. Ivimey contends that they were not the *first* which were established in England. He has produced a passage from the writings of Dr. Some, which states that as early as 1589, "there were several Anabaptist conventicles in London and other places." " Some persons," adds the doctor, " of these sentiments have been bred at our universities."

It is highly probable that the churches or conventicles mentioned by Dr. Some, were General Baptists, as they doubtless founded many churches in England before the

Particular Baptists had any. But the reader must keep in mind, that the following statements respect the Particular Baptists only. The General Baptists will be taken notice of under a separate head.

As our brethren in this insulated kingdom were constantly loaded by their enemies with opprobrious epithets, both from the pulpit and the press, and were accused of holding many dangerous opinions, they at length put forth a confession of their faith for the purpose of clearing themselves from such unjust aspersions. An instrument of this kind was published by the Particular Baptists about ten years after their first churches were founded.* It was signed in the name of seven congregations, or churches of Christ in London; as also by a French congregation of the same judgment. The ministers' names are Thomas Gunne, John Mabbitt, Benjamin Cockes, Thomas Kilicop, John Spilsbury, Samuel Richardson, Thomas Munden, George Tipping, Paul Hobson, Thomas Goare, William Kiffin, Thomas Patient, Hansard Knollys, Thomas Holmes, Christopher Duret, Denis Le Barbier. Several editions of this confession were published in 1643, 1644, and 1646. It was put into the hands of many of the members of parliament, and produced such an effect, that some of their greatest adversaries, (and even the bitter and inveterate doctor Featly) were obliged to acknowledge, that excepting the articles against infant baptism, it was an orthodox confession.

Although but seven churches put forth this confession, yet it appears that there were many more then in being, and before the year 1646, they had increased to forty-six, which Ivimey supposes were situated in and about London. The Anabaptists, said Robert Baille, in 1646, in a work entitled, *Anabaptism the true fountain of error*, have lifted up their heads and increased their number above all the sects in the land.

I do not find any particular account of the number of churches from this period until 1689. About this time, William, Prince of Orange, ascended the throne of England. One of the first measures of government was, to

* I find Dr. Rippon, on the cover of No 8, of his Register, under the head of *Materials wanted*, makes mention of a Confession of Faith, published as early as 1611.

pass the *Act of Toleration,* the Magna Charta of the protestant dissenters ; and but a few months after the coronation of that illustrious prince, we find the delegates from upwards of a hundred churches in England and Wales, met in London for the purpose of inquiring into the state of their churches, and adopting measures for their future prosperity. This was in 1689, and by this assembly was published the confession of faith, which has often been distinguished by the name of the Century Confession. This great Association of churches continued its annual sessions for a few years, when finding it inconvenient for delegates to travel so far, it was divided, and associations appear to have been kept up by the English Baptists from that to the present time. " It must not be supposed, says Ivimey, that this general assembly, consisting of a hundred and seven churches, contained all the Baptist churches in England. There were, at the same time, a great number of General Baptists, who had no concern with this assembly. There were also a number of churches of the Particular Baptists, or who, at least, held to their doctrinal sentiments, who, for particular reasons, did not unite in this great association. Some of them held to open communion, and among these were a number in Bedfordshire, which had been founded by the famous John Bunyan, who was a great advocate for that practice. Others probably had some scruples respecting the propriety and utility of Associations.

Among the manuscript writings of Morgan Edwards, I find a list of the Baptist churches in England, which appears to have been made out about the year 1768. At that time the number of Particular Baptist churches was two hundred and seventeen. Dr. Rippon in his Annual Register published a list for 1790, by which it appears that their number had increased to three hundred and twelve. Eight years after, we learn from the same Register that their number amounted to three hundred and sixty-one.

We shall now collect from the wide range of materials before us, brief accounts of the principal scenes of sufferings, which our brethren passed through from the time their first churches were founded, up to the close of their persecutions for conscience' sake. We shall also, as we go along, take notice of some of those distinguished events which transpired in the land during the times of their afflictions, by which their reputation and tranquillity were affected, or in which they were implicated or concerned.

While the bigotted and cruel Archbishop Laud had the government of the church of England, dissenters of every class, and particularly the Baptists, experienced a continual scene of vexation and trouble. About the year 1638, many ministers were apprehended and shut up in prison. And among them was a Mr. Brewer, a Baptist minister, who lay in prison fourteen years.

In these times, the High Commission Court and the Star Chamber were two of the chief engines of wrong both in church and state ; but they were terminated by an act of parliament in 1641. But other means of oppression and cruelty remained, and the Baptists were made continually to feel their force. Baptist meetings were frequently disturbed and broken up, and many eminent ministers were punished with fines and imprisonment. Some slanderous pieces were published against them, and among the rest was one by the famous Richard Baxter. This eminent man, whose name on many accounts ought always to be mentioned with respect, and who was himself afterwards persecuted with much severity, vented the most virulent invectives against the watery Anabaptists. In a piece entitled Plain Scripture Proof, &c. we find the following astonishing accusations against the dangerous and indecorous dippers. " My sixth argument," said he, " shall be against the usual manner of their baptizing, as it is by dipping over head in a river, or other cold water. That which is a plain breach of the sixth commandment, *Thou shalt not kill*, is no ordinance of God, but a most heinous sin. But the ordinary practice of baptizing over head, and in cold water, as necessary, is a plain breach of the sixth commandment, therefore it is no ordinance of God, but a heinous sin. And as Mr. Cradock shows in his book of gospel liberty, the magistrate ought to *restrain* it, to save the lives of his subjects— That this is *flat murder*, and no better, being ordinarily and generally used, is undeniable to any understanding man—And I know not what trick a covetous landlord can find out to get his tenants to die apace, that he may have new fines and heriots, likelier than to encourage such preachers, that he may get them all to turn Anabaptists. I wish that *this device* be not it which countenanceth these men; and covetous physicians, methinks, should not be much against them. Catarrhs and obstructions, which are the two great fountains of most mortal diseases in man's body, could scarce have a more notable means to produce them where they are not, or to increase them where they are. Apoplexies, lethargies, palsies, and all other comatous diseases would be promoted by it. So would cephalalgies, hemicranies, phthises, debility of the stomach, crudities, and almost all fevers, dysenteries, diarrhæas, cholics, iliac passions, convulsions, spasms, tremors, and so on. All hepatic, splenetic, and pulmonic persons, and hypochondriacs would soon have enough of it. In a word, it is good for nothing but to dispatch men out of the world, that are burdensome, and to ranken church yards—I conclude, if murder be a sin, then dipping ordinarily over head in England is a sin; and if those who would make it men's religion to murder themselves, and urge it upon their consciences as their duty, are *not to be suffered* in a commonwealth, and more than highway murderers; then judge how these Anabaptists, that teach the necessity of such dipping, are to be suffered. My seventh argument is also against another wickedness in their manner of baptizing, which is, their dipping persons *naked*, which is *very usual* with many of them, or next to naked, as is usual with the modestest that I have heard of. If the minister must go into the water with the party, it will certainly tend to his death, though they may scape that go in but once. Would not vain young men come to a baptizing to see the nakedness of maids, and make a mere jest and sport of it?"*

"Poor man!" says Mr. Booth, "he seems to be afflicted with a violent hydrophobia! For he cannot think of any person being immersed in cold water, but he starts, he is convulsed, he is ready to die with fear. Immersion, you must know, is like Pandora's box, and pregnant with a great part of those diseases, which Milton's angel presented to the view of our first father. A compassionate regard therefore to the lives of his fellow creatures compels

---

* Baxter's Plain Scripture Proof, p. 134—137

Mr. Baxter to solicit the aid of magistrates against this destructive plunging, and to cry out in the spirit of an exclamation once heard in the Jewish temple, *Ye men of Israel, help!* or Baptist ministers will depopulate your country! Know you not that these plunging teachers are shrewdly suspected of being pensioned by avaricious landlords to destroy the lives of your liege subjects? Exert your power! Apprehend the delinquents! Appoint an *Auto da Fe!* Let the venal dippers be baptized in blood, and thus put a salutary stop to this pestiferous practice!— What a pity it is that the celebrated History of Cold Bathing, by Sir John Floyer, was not published half a century sooner! It might, perhaps, have preserved this good man from a multitude of painful paroxysms occasioned by the thought of immersion in cold water. Were I seriously (adds Mr. Booth) to put a query to these assertions of Mr. Baxter, it should be with a little variation in the words of David, "*What shall be given unto thee, or what shall be done unto thee, thou* FALSE *pen?* Were the temper, which dictated the preceding caricature to receive a just reproof, it might be in the language of Michael, *The Lord rebuke* thee!"*

When a circumstance is related, which took place in the year 1646, it will not be thought that Mr. Booth has treated the misrepresentations of Mr. Baxter with too great severity. In this year Samuel Oates, a very popular preacher among the Baptists, by whom many hundreds were baptized, was indicted for the murder of Anne Martin, who died a few weeks after she was baptized by him. He was tried at Chelmsford, and great endeavours were used to bring him in guilty. But many credible witnesses were produced, and among others the mother of the young woman, who all testified, that the said Anne Martin was in much better health for several days after her baptism, than she had been for several years before. And in the end the jury pronounced *not guilty*. But so great was the enmity against Mr. Oates, that he was, not long after, dragged out of a house where he was visiting, and thrown into a river, his persecutors boasting that they had thoroughly dipped him.

* Pedobaptism Examined, vol. I. p. 263—265.

During the reign of Cromwell, the Baptists experienced a respite from their troubles, many of them found favour with the Protector, were elevated to posts of honour and profit, and their number greatly increased throughout the land.

Charles II. was restored to the throne of his ancestors, May 29, 1660. In his Majesty's declaration from Breda, before his return, it was said, "We do also declare a liberty to tender consciences, and that no man shall be disquieted or called in question for differences of opinion in matters of religion, which do not disturb the peace of the kingdom." How far his conduct accorded with these professions, the events of his reign will abundantly show.

The first who suffered for religion in the reign of this profligate prince, was the famous John Bunyan, author of the Pilgrim's Progress and many other excellent works. He had been a preacher of the gospel about five years, and was exceedingly popular, though he still followed his business as a travelling tinker. While preaching at a village in Bedfordshire in 1660, he was apprehended and committed to Bedford jail, where he remained twelve years. Seven years of the time he was kept so close, that he could not look out of the door of his prison.

The year 1661, says Rapin, was ushered in by an extraordinary event which gave the court a pretence for breaking through the declaration of indulgence, which had been published. The event here alluded to was, in short, as follows: About fifty of those who were called fifth monarchy men, under the conduct of one Thomas Venner, assembled in the evening in St. Paul's church yard, and killed a man, who, upon demand, had answered for God and the King. This gave an alarm, the company was pursued by military force to some distance from the city, where some were taken prisoners. They afterwards returned and fought furiously in several positions until they were all either killed or taken prisoners. The prisoners were shortly after condemned and executed. This was an unfortunate event for dissenters, for the crime of a few furious fanaticks was laid to the charge of all. The king took occasion from this insurrection to publish a proclamation forbidding all meetings and conventicles under pretence of religion, and commanding the oath of allegiance and supremacy to be tendered to all persons disaffected to the government; and in case of refusal, they were to be prosecuted. The consequence was, that numbers of Baptists and other dissenters were imprisoned, and their meetings every where disturbed.

This insurrection, like the Munster tragedy, was improved against the turbulent dippers. But "Mr. Jessey preaching soon after, declared to his congregation that Venner should say, he believed there was not one Baptist among them ; and that if they succeeded, the Baptists should know that infant baptism was an ordinance of Jesus Christ. Mr. Gravener was present at Venner's meeting house in Coleman street, and heard him say this; from whose mouth (says the writer) I had this account."

Troubles now gathered thick upon our English brethren. In 1662, the Act of Uniformity was passed, in consequence of which, upwards of two thousand eminently godly, learned, and useful ministers were obliged to leave their livings, and were exposed to many hardships and difficulties. Amongst these were a number of the Baptist denomination, but how many cannot be determined with certainty. We are sure, however, that among the Baptist ministers were Henry Jessey, A. M. William Dell, M. A. Francis Bampfield, M. A. Thomas Gennings, Paul Frewen, Joshua Head, John Tombes, B. D. Daniel Dyke, A. M. Richard Adams, Jeremiah Marsden, Thomas Hardcastle, Robert Browne, Gabriel Camelford, John Skinner, ——— Baker, John Gosnold, Thomas Quarrel, Thomas Ewins, Lawrence Wise, John Donne, Paul Hobson, John Gibbs, John Smith, Thomas Ellis, Thomas Paxford, Ichabod Chauncey, M. D.

Crosby has mentioned the names of a number of these ejected ministers, of whom it was doubtful whether they were Baptists, and Ivimey has omitted the names of some of whom it has been determined that they had become Baptists before this event. And among them was John Miles, who founded the Baptist church at Swansy in Massachusetts.

" It is rather wonderful," says Ivimey, " that any Baptists were found in the churches at this time, when it is considered that the first act, which was passed, after the restoration of the king, contained an exception of all, who had declared against infant baptism from being restored to their livings. It is probable also that amongst those, who had been expelled to make room for the old incumbents, some were of this denomination. The Act of Uniformity completed the business, and after this we do not find that any person who rejected the baptism of infants continued in the establishment."

Some may be surprised that so many Baptist ministers should accept of livings in the parish churches. But it appears to have been a very common custom before these times. It is not unfrequent in this country for Baptist ministers to preach to, and receive salaries from Pedobaptist congregations; they do not administer ordinances amongst them, unless that now and then they find some disposed to go into the water, and they commonly preach more or less to Baptist churches at the same time. And in much the same way these 'ministers conducted of whom we have been speaking. Whatever fault a Baptist may be disposed to find with such a procedure, it is sure that the Pedobaptists have generally the most reason to complain in the end.

The reign of Charles II. exhibited a series of profligacy, cruelty, and oppression. But as the divine judgments do not always slumber, the nation was visited with very sore calamities. In 1665, a plague broke out, which was then the most dreadful within the memory of man. The number of those who died in London only, amounted to about one hundred thousand. Eight or ten thousand died in the city and suburbs in a week. This calamity was preceded by an unusual drought, and it was succeeded in 1666, by a most destructive fire, which, in three or four days, consumed thirteen thousand and two hundred dwelling houses, eighty nine churches, and many other publick buildings. Thus this guilty nation, which had committed to the flames so many of the saints of the Lord, which had starved and tormented so many others in various ways, was, in quick succession, visited with three of the terrible messengers of divine vengeance, famine, plague, and fire.

In 1673, among other vile attempts to render the Baptists odious and contemptible, a pamphlet was published entitled, *Mr. Baxter baptized in blood.* This scandalous piece professed to give an account of the murder of Mr. Josiah Baxter, at Boston in New-England, by four Anabaptists, &c. This Baxter was said to be a godly minister, whom the bloody Anabaptists had murdered, in the most barbarous and horrid manner, merely because he had worsted them in argument. The writer of this detestable libel took much pains to conceal his fraud, and to make the story credible among the enemies of the Baptists. But providence favoured our brethren to defeat the design of this base fictitious performance. The lord mayor published an interdict to prevent the sale of the pamphlet ; and many of the publishers were committed to prison. Through the influence of Mr. Kiffin, at court, the matter underwent a rigid examination at the council board, when upon finding it a falsehood, the following order was published in the gazette :

" By order of council."

" Whereas there is a pamphlet lately published, entitled, *Mr. Baxter baptized in blood*, containing a horrible murder committed by four Anabaptists upon the person of Mr. Josiah Baxter, near Boston in New-England : the whole matter having been inquired into, and examined at the council board, is found altogether false and fictitious.

Edward Walker."

That the reader may have a view of the circumstances in which the Baptists, in these times were placed, and how their enemies conducted towards them, I will transcribe the following summary statements from the Memoirs of the English Baptists."*

" Lord's day, May 29, 1670, a congregation of Baptists, to the amount of five hundred, met for divine worship near Lewes in Sussex. Two of their enemies observed them go to their meeting house, and informed against them, upon which Sir Thomas Nutt, a violent persecutor, and three other justices, convicted the minister and above forty of the hearers. The minister was fined 20*l.* and his fine laid upon five of his hearers, and the rest of the company was fined five shillings each. Warrants were issued under the hands of the justices, for the recovery of the

---

* These accounts relate to the Baptists in the country. Their sufferings in London are related in those numbers of the Magazine which I have not obtained.

fines by distress and sale of goods, and directed to the constables of the hundred, and the church wardens and overseers of the parish. In the month of June the distresses were made. From Richard White, fined 3*l*. 15*s*. they took value 10*l*. 13*s*. From John Tabret, fined 2*l*. 14*s*. they took a cow. From Walter Brett, a grocer, fined 6*l*. 5*s*. they took two casks of sugar, which cost him 15*l*. From Thomas and Richard Barnard, fined 11*l*. 10*s*. they took six cows, upon which the dairy-maid told them she believed they would *have a store of syllabubs*, having taken so much sugar from Mr. Brett! From Thomas Tourle, fined five shillings, they took a horse, and another from Richard Mantle for a like fine. From others for similar fines they took bacon, cheese, kitchen furniture, wearing apparel, and other goods, to about treble the amount of their fines. The cattle and other property taken from the said several sufferers, were publickly sold for about half their value.

" On the aforesaid 29th of May, a meeting of Baptists was held in Brighthelmstone, at the house of Mr. William Beard, who was fined 20*l*. for which fine the constable of the place and two assistants took *sixty-five bushels of malt, and sold it for twelve shillings per quarter!*

" At Chillington, three miles from Lewes, Mr. Nicholas Martin was convicted of having a meeting at his house, and fined 20*l*. for which fine the officer of injustice took from him six cows, two young bullocks, and a horse, being all the stock he had, all of which he recovered again, but not till he had taken a great deal of trouble, and been at more than 23*l*. expense.

" The magistrates at Dover began early to shew their unrighteous zeal against the Baptists. Many of them were violently taken from their meeting house, committed to prison, and detained in confinement, to the ruin of their circumstances, and great distress of their families. These hardships urged them to petition the King and Duke of York for redress, but no relief was given. At Aylesbury in Buckinghamshire, the justices endeavoured to revive the old practice of punishing hereticks with death. By virtue of a dormant statute made in the reign of Queen Elizabeth, Mr. Stephen Dagnal, pastor of a Baptist congregation that met at Aylesbury, and eleven of his people, being taken at a meeting, were sentenced to be hanged, and as soon as sentence was passed against them, officers were sent to their several houses to seize their goods, and whatever effects of theirs could be found ; which order was executed immediately, and great havock was made of what possessions they had ; but powerful intercession being made for them at court, by Mr. Kiffin, the king granted them a pardon, and sometime afterward they were all set at liberty again.

" Great were the sufferings of the Baptists in Gloucestershire, particularly in the neighbourhood of Fairford, Bourton on the water, Stow, and some other places. The most eminent cavaliers, embittered persecutors, rode about armed with swords and pistols, ransacked their houses and abused their families in a most violent manner.

" In the county of Wilts, and diocess of Salisbury, our brethren were persecuted with great severity. Bishop Ward often disturbed their meetings in person, and encouraged his clergy to follow his example. Informers were every where at work, and having crept into religious assemblies in disguise, levied great sums of money upon ministers and people. Soldiers broke into honest farmers' houses, under pretence of searching for conventicles, and where ready money was wanting, plundered their goods, drove away their cattle, and sold them a great deal under their value. Many of these sordid creatures spent their profits in ill houses upon lewd women, and then went about again to hunt for more prey.

" The Baptist church at Calne suffered much; having been often disturbed when they assembled in their meeting house ; in order to avoid fresh troubles they sometimes met at a mill, called Moses' Mill, a little distance from the town, and at other times under a large white-thorn bush upon the brow of a hill, in a field called Shiepfield, about two miles from the town. The bush has ever since been called *Gospel Bush ;* but only some very small branches of it remain.

" The Baptists in Lincolnshire were persecuted with savage rage. Not less than one hundred of them were imprisoned, some for hearing, and others for preaching the word of God. They endured not less than three hundred levies for fines. Some for two pence a week, others for 10, 20, 40, and 60 l. whereby many were reduced to great poverty, and others driven from home. Presentments and excommunications, they had several hundreds, and indictments at the assizes and sessions upon the statute for two pence per week, and twenty pounds a month, not less than a thousand.

" Mr. Robert Shalder, of Croft, in the said county, was long confined in prison, and dying soon after his release from it, was interred in the common burying ground amongst his ancestors. The same day he was buried, certain of the inhabitants of Croft, opened his grave, took up his corpse, and dragged it upon a sledge to his own gates, and there left it unburied !

" In short, there was not a protestant dissenting congregation in the kingdom but were grievously harassed, not a zealous Baptist but had a double mess of persecution. From the restoration of Charles II. to the revolution under William III. a space of twenty-nine years, more than sixty thousand people suffered for religion, were plundered of two millions of money,* and eight or ten thousand of them died in gaol. Very many of the sufferers were Baptists ; but they cheerfully endured the cross, despising the shame, stood fast in the Lord, and served God acceptably with reverence and godly fear."

These legal robberies and outrageous proceedings appear to have been carried on under the sanction of a Conventicle Act, which received the royal assent in 1670. By this act it was decreed that the preachers or teachers in any conventicle should forfeit twenty pounds for the first and forty for the second offence. And those who suffered any conventicles in their houses, barns, yards, &c. were to forfeit twenty. Smaller fines were levied upon all over sixteen years of age, who were found at conventicles. One third of the money collected of the conventicleers, was to go to the informer or his assistants. This held out a powerful motive to avaricious bigots to pillage their innocent neighbours, and some acquired considerable fortunes from the spoils of the poor afflicted people of God. One Thomas Battison, an old church warden, engaged with much assiduity in this unrighteous mode of procuring wealth. But

* Neal, in his history of the Puritans, vol. ii. p. 759, mentions that the damages sustained by the non-conformists, were two millions in three years And if they were in the same proportion from the restoration to the revolution, Crosby is not mistaken when he computes the sum total at near twenty millions.

Eminent Men among the Baptists. 211

the indignation of the populace was excited against him, and while he was attempting to distrain the goods of one John Burdolf, in which, however, he did not succeed, they tied a calf's tail to his back, and then derided him with shouts and halloos, as he was going off to another place. Soon after he took a brass kettle from one Edward Covington; but when he had brought it to the street door, none of the officers would carry it away; neither could he hire any to do it in two hours time, though he offered money to such needy persons among the company as wanted bread. At last he got a youth for sixpence to carry the kettle less way than a stone's throw, to an inn-yard, where he had before hired a room to lodge such goods under pretence to lodge grain; but when the youth had carried the kettle to the inn-gate, being hooted at all the way by the common spectators, the inn-keeper would not suffer the kettle to be brought into his yard; and so his man set it out in the middle of the street, none regarding it, till towards night a poor woman that received alms was caused by an overseer to carry it away.

These proceedings were in the town of Bedford, and although the people were against the distrainers, yet they had law on their side, and made terrible havock with the property of all, who had been guilty of the atrocious crime of meeting in houses and barns to worship the God of heaven.

Our limits forbid us to pursue any further the narrative of the sufferings of our English brethren in these times of cruelty and oppression.

We shall now take notice of some of the most distinguished characters among the English Baptists, from the beginning to the present.

" It was not long after the Particular Baptists had founded distinct churches, when Mr. Hansard Knollis, who had been graduated at Cambridge, formed a Baptist church in London, in the year 1641, and presided over it till his death in 1692. About the same period Mr. Francis Cornwell, M. A. of Emanuel College, Cambridge, embraced the Baptist sentiments, and became pastor of a church at Marden in Kent.

" Before this, Mr. Benjamin Coxe, a bishop's son, and a graduate of one of the universities, had joined the Baptists, by which he lost all the preferments he might have obtained in the church.

"There were also at this time Mr. Henry Denne, Mr. Christopher Blackwood, Mr. Daniel Dyke, Mr. Francis Bampfield, and others ; who were much distinguished for their learning and usefulness, in the reign of Charles I.

" Another eminent person was Mr. John Tombes, B. D. of whom even his enemies speak in terms of high commendation. Dr. Wall, in his history of infant baptism, says, " of the professed Antipedobaptists, Mr. Tombes was a man of the best parts in our nation, and perhaps in any other.

" All these, and many besides, had good livings in the Established Church, but left it either before or at the passing the Act of Uniformity in 1662.

" Another learned man was Mr. Henry Jesse, who had been for several years the pastor of the first Independent Church, but being convinced of the error of infant baptism, was baptized in 1645, and was a very useful minister in London for many years. He had undertaken and almost completed a new translation of the Bible, being dissatisfied with the present received version, on account of the ecclesiastical words introduced or retained by the ecclesiastical divines, at the command of James I. This work he made the master study of his life, and would often exclaim, " O, that I might finish it before I die." This, however, was denied him.

" Another person of great reputation was Charles Maria Duveil, D. D. by birth a Jew, but embracing christianity. After passing through the church of Rome, and the church of England, he settled as pastor of a Baptist church in Gracechurch street, London. He was much supported by many of the dignified clergy, notwithstanding the change of his sentiments ; among whom were Dr. Stillingfleet, bishop of Worcester, Dr. Sharp, dean of Norwich, Dr. Tillotson, dean of St. Paul's, afterwards archbishop of Canterbury, Dr. Simon Patrick, bishop of Ely, and William Lloyd, bishop of St. Asaph. He published a literal exposition of the gospels of Mark and Luke ; also of the Acts of the Apostles and the minor prophets.

" There was Mr. John Gosnold, pastor of a church in Barbican, London ; who was eminently learned, and a very popular preacher, much esteemed and valued by men of note and dignity in the established church. He was intimately acquainted with Dr. Tillotson, who was frequently his hearer. Dr. Calamy says, he was bred in the Charter-house school, and in Pembroke-hall, Cambridge; and was afterwards chaplain to Lord Grey.

" Another learned man of this denomination, was the famous Thomas Delaune, who was a minister and schoolmaster in London; and who, it is well known, fell a victim to the cause of non-conformity in the reign of Charles II."

William Kiffin was one of the earliest promoters of the Particular Baptists, and a distinguished minister among them. He was one of the few Baptist ministers, on whom the Disposer of all events saw fit to bestow much of the possessions and honours of the world. He was personally known to both Charles II, and James his successor. Crosby informs us that it was currently reported, that when Charles wanted money, he sent to Mr. Kiffin to borrow of him *forty thousand pounds*; that Mr. Kiffin pleaded in excuse he had not so much, but told the messenger, if it would be of any service to his majesty, he would present him with *ten thousand;* that is, upwards of forty thousand dollars; the which was accepted, and Mr. Kiffin afterwards said he had saved thereby *thirty thousand pounds.* Mr. Kiffin had great influence at court, and was enabled to render essential service to his brethren. By his means the wicked and scurrilous pamphlet, entitled, *Baxter baptized in blood,* was examined and condemned; and by his intercession also, twelve Baptists, who had been condemned to death at Aylesbury, received the king's pardon. But with all his wealth and influence he was a meek and modest man.

Two of his grandsons, viz. Benjamin and William Hewling, young gentlemen of great fortunes, of accomplished education, and of eminent piety, were concerned in the ill-timed and ill-fated expedition of the Duke of Monmouth, which terminated in the destruction of almost all who had any hand in it. The grandfather and father of the late Dr. Gifford of London, were also deeply engaged in this unhappy affair. And at this time perished in the flames a distinguished Baptist woman by the name of Elizabeth Gaunt. Her crime was that of harbouring one of the rebels, who, with the basest ingratitude, turned evidence against her. She was condemned for treason, and therefore died rather a patriot than a martyr. But it is said by bishop Burnet, that there was no evidence that she knew that her traitorous guest was a rebel except his own.

But many of the church of England, of Presbyterians, Independents, and Baptists, were zealously engaged for the Duke of Monmouth, and many fell by the means of the cruel Jeffries and others.

But to return to Mr. Kiffin: He was nominated by James II. for one of the aldermen of the city of London in his new charter. But this was an honour which the old Baptist Elder by no means desired. Waiting on the king by his request he addressed him as follows: " Sire, I am a very old man, and have withdrawn myself from all kinds of business for some years past, and am incapable of doing any service in such an affair to your majesty in the city. Besides, Sire"——the old man went on, fixing his eyes steadfastly on the king, while the tears ran down his cheeks——" the death of my grandsons gave a wound to my heart which is still bleeding, and never will close but in the grave."

The king was deeply struck by the manner, the freedom, and the spirit of this unexpected rebuke. A total silence ensued, while the galled countenance of James seemed to shrink from the horrid remembrance. In a minute or two, however, he recovered himself enough to say, " Mr. Kiffin, I shall find a balsam for that sore," and he immediately turned about to a lord in waiting.

Mr. Kiffin was now in great trials; to accept the office of alderman was much against his inclination, and to refuse, he had learnt, would be dangerous. " I went," says he, " to the ablest council for advice, and stating my case to him, he told me my danger was every way great, for if I accepted to be an alderman, I ran the hazard of five hundred pounds, and if I did not accept, as the judges then were, I might be fined by them ten, or twenty, or thirty thousand pounds, even what they pleased. So that I thought it better for me to run the lesser hazard of five hundred pounds, which was certain, than be exposed to such fines as might be the ruin of myself and family."

Accordingly after waiting some time in suspense, he accepted the office; but things were soon changed by the coming of the Prince of Orange, and this aged minister was relieved from his burdens and snares. Crosby mentions that there were four other Baptists made aldermen at the same time, but I have not learnt their names.

Among the judges and regicides of Charles I. were two eminent men, who afterwards became Baptists. These were Major General Harrison and Col. Hutchinson.

Harrison arose from obscurity to an elevated rank among the heroes of the Commonwealth. He was very desirous to bring the king to trial, and was the officer who conducted the English monarch before the tribunal which sentenced him to lose his head on the scaffold. It was not till some time after this tragical event that he became a Baptist. The same may be said of Colonel Hutchinson. Both of these great men were executed on the restoration of Charles II.

About this time lived the famous Benjamin Keach, author of the Scripture Metaphors, and many other valuable works. In 1664, he was prosecuted and sentenced to the pillory, for publishing a work entitled *The Child's Instructer*, or a *New and Easy Primer*. While in the pillory, he among other things said to the spectators, "Good people, I am not ashamed to stand here this day, with this paper on my head. My Lord Jesus was not ashamed to suffer on the cross for me, and it is for his cause that I am made a gazing-stock. Take notice, it is not for any wickedness that I stand here; but for writing and publishing his truths, which the Spirit of the Lord hath revealed in the Holy Scriptures." A clergyman, who stood by, could not forbear interrupting him, and said, "It is for writing and publishing errors; and you may now see what your errors have brought you to." Mr. Keach replied, "Sir, can you prove them errors?" But before the clergyman could return an answer, he was attacked by some of the people, who told him of his being "pulled drunk out of a ditch." Another upbraided him with having been found "drunk under a hay-cock." Upon this the people, turning their attention from the sufferer in the pillory, laughed at the drunken priest, insomuch that he hastened away with the utmost disgrace and shame.

Mr. Keach was the author of eighteen practical works, some of them large, sixteen polemical, and nine poetical, making in all forty-three; besides a number of prefaces and recommendations for the works of others.

Dr. Gill, who was afterwards pastor of the same church, was the author of upwards of sixty different works, and among them was an Exposition of the Old and New Tesment in nine volumes folio. Dr. Rippon, his biographer, assures us, that had the writings of this eminent man been uniformly printed in the size of his Old and New Testament, they would have made the astonishing sum total of TEN THOUSAND folio pages of divinity. Well might Mr. Shrubsole give him the title of *Dr. Voluminous*.

I much regret that I cannot give a more general account of the eminent characters, who have appeared at different times among the English Baptists. They, I find, mention among the skilful defenders of their doctrinal sentiments, Piggot, the Stennetts, the Wallins, the Wilsons, Evans, Brine, Gill, Day, Beddome, Francis, Ryland, and Gifford.*

But few of our American Baptists know that John Canne, author of the marginal references in the Bible, Dr. Ash, author of a Dictionary and other classical works, which bear his name, Thomas Wilcox, author of an excellent little piece entitled a Drop of Honey from the Rock Christ, and Winterbottom, author of the View of America, were of their sentiments. Miss Steele, the author of those excellent hymns, which appear in our collections, was, I find by a hint in Morgan Edwards's list, the daughter of a Baptist minister in the county of Hampshire.

At different periods in the seventeenth century, there were many long public disputes held by appointment between the Baptists and Pedo-baptists on the subject of baptism; the last dispute of this kind of any considerable consequence, appears to have been held at Portsmouth, in 1699. Mr. John Tombes, Dr. Russel, Mr. Jeremiah Ives, and others, were famous disputants for the Baptists, and Dr. Featley, Mr. Baxter, and Mr. Chandler and others, for the Pedo-baptists.

There is a pleasant anecdote related of Jeremiah Ives, in one of his public disputations, of which in the History of

* English Baptist Magazine, No. 21, p. 187.

Baptism, we promised to give some more particular account. Mr. Ives by his many disputations became so noted that Charles II. sent for him to dispute with a Romish priest. He accepted the invitation and maintained a dispute before the king, and many others, in the habit of a clergyman. " Ives pressed the priest closely, shewing, that whatever antiquity they pretended to, their doctrine and practices could by no means be proved apostolical, since they are not to be found in any writings, which remain of the apostolic age. The priest, after much wrangling, in the end replied, " That this argument of Mr. Ives' was of as much force against *infant baptism*, as against the doctrines and ceremonies of the church of Rome." To which Mr. Ives replied, " that he readily granted what he said to be true." The priest upon this broke up the dispute, saying, " he had been cheated, and that he would proceed no farther, for he came to dispute with a clergyman of the established church, and it was now evident that this was an Anabaptist preacher." This behaviour of the priest afforded his majesty and all present not a little diversion. Mr. Ives was pastor of a *baptized* congregation in the *Old Jewry*, between thirty and forty years; was well beloved, and bore a fair character to his dying day.*

We read of another dispute held between a Baptist minister whose name is not mentioned, and a clergyman of the established church. The clergyman insisted that the dispute should be in *Latin;* but the Baptist minister pleaded for its being in *English*, that it might be to the edification of the audience. But the clergyman still persisted in his demand, and laid down his arguments in *Latin*. Fortunately the illiterate Baptist was an *Irishman*, and answered in *Irish*. The clergyman, surprised at the learning of his antagonist, ingenuously confessed that he did not understand *Greek*, and therefore desired him to reply in *Latin*. " Well," says the Baptist, " seeing you *cannot* dispute in Greek, I *will not* dispute in Latin; let us therefore dispute in English, and leave the company to judge." But the pedantic priest still plead for an unknown tongue, and thus the dispute was frustrated.

* Crosby, vol. iv. p. 248.

A little while after the year 1670 it appears a controversy arose among the Baptists in England about the practice of laying on of hands, which occasioned no little trouble among them. The famous Danvers wrote against the practice. But Keach wrote in defence of it, as did Thomas Grantham, a General Baptist. Others doubtless wrote on both sides of the subject, but these men seem to have taken the lead in the controversy. How many churches now practise the laying on of hands, I am not informed, but I conclude not many.

Sometime after this there was a controversy among our English brethren, respecting the propriety of singing in public worship, and many pieces were written for and against it. But by pursuing prudent measures, this controversy was quieted, and the practice of singing was adopted by many churches, which had formerly neglected it, and I conclude now generally prevails. Some of the Baptists, who emigrated to America, brought over with them from their mother country, a prejudice against singing in public worship, and in some places, especially in Rhode-Island, there have been found, until within a few years past, a few ministers, who would not adopt the practice.* They did not, like the Quakers, oppose singing altogether; they held christians should sing to themselves, &c. but not with *conjoined voices* in public assemblies.

I know not what arguments those Baptists brought against singing in public, who omitted the practice. I am inclined to think, however, that the custom originated in times of persecution, when they were obliged to hold their meetings with the greatest secrecy. Singing was then from necessity dispensed with, and it is probable, that those who came after thought it inexpedient and improper.

Open communion is now generally opposed by the Particular Baptists, and although the General Baptists are more lax than they in their doctrinal sentiments, yet I believe they are equally strenuous in their terms of communion. But before the Baptists began to form churches, and indeed for some time after, it was a very common thing

---

* I know not as there is now any Baptist minister in Rhode-Island, that opposes singing, or any Baptist congregation that neglects it; but their posterity remain in different parts of the State, by whom I have been asked if I was a *Singing Baptist*.

for them to travel in communion with Pedo-baptist churches. Different reasons may be assigned for their so doing. At first there were no Baptist churches for them to join. And after churches began to be established, many were brought to embrace believer's baptism in situations remote from them. And others doubtless continued in their old churches after they had been baptized, without much consideration on the subject. We do not find that many churches founded by the Baptists held to open communion, and had they, no harm nor benefit would have resulted from it, for they were generally so despised and persecuted, that few Pedo-baptists would be seen in their churches.*

In the times of which we are speaking, the Baptists were not stunned with a continual din of entreaties to unite in the Pedo-baptist communion, but they were admitted to it as a mere matter of favour and indulgence, which but few would grant. But we are informed that the good Doctors Watts and Doddridge, admitted Baptists to their communion, and treated them with kindness and respect.†

That wealthy and benevolent Baptist, Thomas Hollis, the liberal benefactor of Cambridge College, near Boston, was a member of a Pedo-baptist church.

In the early times of the Baptists in England, some few, who had been created Doctors in Divinity, and a number who had received inferior titles, left the establishment, and united with these despised people. In later times a considerable number have been honoured with the diploma of D. D. and a few with L. L. D. from Scotland and America. By the English Universities no honour of this kind can be bestowed upon any dissenters whatever.

We have thus endeavoured to bring to view a few of the ancient worthies among the English Baptists. A great many others, eminent for learning, piety, suffering, and usefulness, we are obliged from the scantiness of our limits to omit. I am inclined to think there are at present three or four hundred ministers in the churches of the Particu-

---

* " The people of this persuasion" says Neal, in his history of the Puritans, vol. ii. p. 112, " were more exposed to the public resentment, because they would hold communion with none but such as had been *dipped*. All must pass under this cloud before they could be received into their churches ; and the same narrow spirit prevails too generally among them even to this day." (1733)

† Rippon's Register.

lar Baptists. Many of them, probably, like their brethren in America, have had but moderate advantages for education, and receive but a scanty support for their services. But there are some, whose talents, learning, popularity, and usefulness, are not excelled by any ministers in the kingdom.

Many of the Baptists in England have for a long time made laudable exertions to promote the cause of learning among their denomination, and, besides smaller institutions, have established three seminaries, to which they have given the name of Academies. The oldest is at Bristol, the second at Bradford, and the third at Stepney-Green, near London.

BRISTOL ACADEMY.

In 1795, Dr. Rippon read before *The Bristol Education Society*, a brief essay towards the history of the Baptist Academy at Bristol, which is inserted in his Register. From this essay I shall select a few sketches of the history of this institution. Its foundation appears to have been laid by the General Assembly of Baptists in 1689. At this convention they resolved to raise a fund or stock for different purposes, one of which was to assist in the education of young men of promising gifts, &c. The first student, who was educated at Bristol, was Richard Sampson, a member of the church at Plymouth. After he had finished his studies he became pastor of the church at Exeter where he died in 1716. Mr. Sampson was much esteemed by Sir Isaac Newton; and so strong was his memory, that one day when the conversation turned on the depriving good men again of their Bibles, Sir Isaac said, "they cannot possibly deprive Mr. Sampson of his, for he has it all treasured up within him." The first students of the Academy of which we are speaking were assisted by yearly collections from the churches, and they studied not always at Bristol, but sometimes at London, at Taunton, Tewkesbury and elsewhere, for as yet no permanent society had been formed to direct the infant institution, nor was it confined to any particular place. Mr. Edward Terrill is considered the father and founder of the Academy, which his benevolence was the means of fixing in the city of Bristol. " He left something considerable to the pastor of the church in Broadmead, for the time being, provided that he were qualified for the business, and devoted a part of his time to the instruction of young students, &c." We soon after learn that Caleb Jope was chosen to educate young men ; but with the names of the students who were under his care, says Dr. Rippon, I am totally in the dark.

Bernard Foskett was the next tutor of this rising seminary, and acted in that capacity between twenty and thirty years. The number of students under him was sixty four, just half of them were Welshmen, and the other English. Among these students were Benjamin Beddome, A. M. Benjamin Francis, A. M. Morgan Jones, L. L. D. Thomas Llewelyn, L. L. D. John Ash, L. L. D. Robert Day, A. M. John Ryland, A. M. and Hugh Evans, A. M. who succeeded Mr. Foskett in the presidency of the Academy. Next to him was his son Caleb Evans, D. D. and his successor was John Ryland, D. D. who is still at the head of this important establishment. Respecting the usual number of students in the Bristol Academy, its funds, its library, and other usual appendages of literary institutions, I have not been able to gain any satisfactory information. Neither am I acquainted with its internal economy and regulations. I conclude, however, that none are admitted to this Academy, but such as have either began to preach or are promising for the ministry, and that those, who are needy, are supported either wholly or in part, as their circumstances require. Connected with this Academy is the Bristol Education Society, which was formed in 1770, and has contributed greatly towards augmenting its pecuniary resources.*

* The following statement is found in Rippon's Register, No xiv.

A *Copy of the Table of Benefactors, in the Museum belonging to the Bristol Education Society.*

Those marked thus (*) subscribed annually 1*l.* 1 *s.* The sums directly after the names were also annual subscriptions ; the larger sums were original benefactions.

		£	s.
1770	Frederick Bull, Esq. London, 5*l.* 5*s.* annually,	150	00
	Thomas Sparry, sen. Upton,	100	00
	Rebekah Lippincott, Wellington,	50	00

Bristol Education Society.

From this Academy have proceeded many useful ministers and eminent characters. Many of them have gone

		£.	s.
1770	Robert Houlton, Esq. Grittleton, 5l. 5s.	21	00
	Joseph Tomkins, Esq. Abingdon, 5l. 5s.	25	5
	William Tomkins, Esq. do. 5l. 5s.	25	5
	Joseph Butler, Esq. do. 5l. 5s.	41	00
	John Bull, Esq. Bristol, 2l. 2s.	15	15
	Francis Bull, Esq. do. 2l. 2s.	10	10
	John Collett, do. 10l. 10s.		
	John Stock, do. 5l. 5s.	10	10
	Thomas Bunn, Frome,*	10	10
	William Steele, Esq Broughton, 2l. 2s.	10	10
	Baptist Church, Lymington,	10	10
	Rev. Hugh Evans, M. A.* ⎫		
	Rev. Caleb Evans, M. A.* ⎬ Tutors to the Institution.	31	10
	Rev. James Newton, M. A.* ⎭		
1772	John Houlton, Esq. Seagry, 5l. 5s.	10	10
	Rev. Thomas Dunscombe, Coate,*	10	10
1774	Ann Callwell, Chesham,	50	00
	Susannah Callwell, do. 10l. 10s.	100	00
	Thomas Llewelyn, Esq. L. L. D. London,	60	00
	Stephen Williams, do.	10	00
	Rev. Samuel Stennett, D. D.* do.	20	00
1775	Ebenezer Hollick, Esq. Witser, 2l. 2s.	20	00
	Elizabeth Durban, Bristol,	21	00
1777	Abraham Elton, Esq. do.	10	10
	John Crammont, Leicester, (a legacy.)	10	00
1778	Rev. Isaac Woodman, Sutton, (a legacy.)	40	00
1779	John Holmes, Esq. Exon,	16	6
1780	Rev. Andrew Gifford, D. D. London,	100	00
	John & William Parsons, Esqrs. Chichester, 2l. 2s.	10	00
1781	George Wilkinson, London,	10	10
1782	William Deane, Plymouth, (a legacy.)	150	00
	John Reynolds, Barbican, 2l. 2s.	20	00
1783	Rev. Andrew Bennett, Barbadoes,	10	00
1784	Diana Munt, Tiverton, (a legacy.)	20	00
	James Hewardine, Arnsby, (a legacy.)	10	00
	Hester Bull, Bristol,*	10	00
	Thomas Llewelyn, Esq. L. L. D. London, ⎫		
	(a legacy) consisting of his library, which ⎬	1500	00
	cost more than ⎭		
	Rev. Andrew Gifford, D. D. London, ⎫		
	(a legacy) consisting of his library, ⎬	1000	00
	pictures, coins, &c. estimated at ⎭		
	Frederick Bull, Esq. the reversionary Bequest of	1000	00
1785	John Thornton, Esq. Clapham,	10	00
	John Austic, Esq. Devizes,	10	10
1787	John Davis, Calne, a reversionary legacy of	50	00
1789	John Cook, Bristol, (a legacy.)	50	00
1790	Rev. James Newton, M. A. do. (a legacy.)	50	00
1791	William Thomas, Hutchin, (a legacy)	50	00
	John Edmunds, Fairford, a Reversionary ⎫	200	00
	legacy of 200l. 3 per cent. Consols-Stock, ⎭		
1792	Ann Moore, Bristol,	20	00
	Rev. John Poynting, Worcester, (a legacy.)	200	00
1793	Rev. Abraham Booth, London,	5	00
1794	Mrs. Simpkin, Balby,	5	00
1795	Rev. Peter Reece, Warwick, (a legacy.)	100	00

to rest, many are now labouring among the churches in England, and a few of them are in America.

NORTHERN EDUCATION SOCIETY.

THIS society appears to have commenced about 1804 or 1805. In the last mentioned year it had raised by subscription and contribution a little móre than eighteen hundred pounds sterling, not far from *eight thousand dollars*. The resources of this society were then considered sufficient to support eight or nine students besides discharging all other expenses. Rev. William Steadman, formerly of Plymouth Dock, was chosen President of the Academy, which was fixed " for the present at Bradford," a town in Yorkshire, 36 miles S. W. of York, and 193 N. N. W. of London.

I have obtained the proceedings of the annual meeting of this society for 1805, to which is annexed a list of the names of donors and subscribers; the highest upon this list is James Bury of Pendle-hill, who gave the liberal sum of five hundred pounds sterling.

STEPNEY-GREEN—*near London.*

A Baptist Academy was founded at this place, probably about 1810. We learn from the Massachusetts Baptist Missionary Magazine, that a house and premises at Stepney Green, near the metropolis, well fitted for an Academy, had been given by a liberal individual, and that exertions were making to establish a third literary institution for the benefit of the Baptist denomination. But what success has attended these exertions I have yet to learn; but it is probable there is, before this time, a well-endowed and flourishing Academy at Stepney-Green.

The exertions of the Baptists in England to promote the missionary cause will be noticed in the account of the India Mission. And besides sending missionaries abroad they have made exertions to promote itinerant preaching in destitute places at home. Itinerant societies have been formed, and by them many have been assisted to travel and labour with success in different parts of the kingdom.

We shall now close this account with some general observations respecting the number of churches, Associations, ministers, and members of the Particular Baptists in England.

We have already shown that the number of churches in 1798, was 361; and in 1790, it was 312, and in 1768, it was 217. If they have increased in the same proportion for fifteen years past, they must now amount to about four hundred and fifty, which, I conclude is not far from their number. I know of no method by which we can determine, with any degree of certainty, the number of members in these churches. Dr. Rippon, in the notes which are subjoined to his list for 1798, has given the number of upwards of seventy of the smaller churches, which run from eleven to a hundred and forty, but average about fifty-five. But he informs us that the ancient churches in London, Bristol, and elsewhere, contained then from a hundred and fifty, to three and four hundred, and some more. If we compute the number of churches at four hundred and fifty, and these upon an average to contain eighty members, it will make the sum total of thirty-six thousand; which is probably not far from the number of Particular Baptists in England.

The number of Associations in 1790, was seven, viz. York and Lancashire, Northampton, Midland, Kent and Sussex, Western, Norfolk and Suffolk, and Northern. Since then, have been formed two others called Oxfordshire and Shropshire. In 1790, when there were but three hundred and twelve churches, one hundred and ninety of them were not associated. How many stand unassociated at present, I have not learned.

Many of the churches have no pastors, but in other churches there are a number of ministers besides the pastor, so that on the whole it is probable there are as many ministers as churches.

GENERAL BAPTISTS.

This term has, from the beginning of the reformation, been applied to that class of Baptists in England, who have held universal redemption. The Particular Baptists are strictly Calvinistic in their creed. But those who are called General, lean to the Arminian system. The former hold that Christ died for the elect only, while the latter plead that the Saviour by his death and sufferings, has made salvation possible for all. Dr. Fuller, the author of *The Gospel worthy of all Acceptation*, is a Particular Baptist; some of his brethren have adopted his notion of the atonement, others have opposed it, and the time has been, when he would probably have been turned over to the General side.

Respecting the General Baptists in England, I have been able to gain but a very little information. They do not appear to have taken much pains to record their own history, and as no others have paid much regard to them, but very brief sketches can be given of them.

Mr. Ivimey is of opinion that the General Baptists began to found churches in England in the sixteenth century. The church at Canterbury of this persuasion, he observes, is thought to have existed for two hundred and fifty years, and that Joan Boucher, who was burnt in the reign of Edward VI, was a member of it. This is in the county of Kent, and the church at Eyethorn, in the same county, is, according to this author, supposed to have been founded more than two hundred and thirty years.

How the General Baptists progressed for about a hundred years from the founding of their first churches, I find no particular information, only that they, with their brethren of the Particular belief, were loaded with reproaches, and every where exposed to havock and death.

In 1661, soon after the restoration of Charles II. the General Baptists among other dissenters, presented an address to his majesty, and petitioned for some alleviation of their miseries. This address was presented by Thomas Grantham; it was signed by forty-one elders, deacons, and brethren, on behalf of themselves and many others in several counties of the same faith with them, and was said to be owned and approved by more than *twenty thousand*, whether of their communicants or of their friends and adherents does not appear. But it is evident that the General Baptists were at this time a large and respectable community, and among their ministers were some of great distinction and usefulness.

By Morgan Edwards' list beforementioned, it appears that in 1768, when there were two hundred and seventeen of the Particular, there were but sixty-nine of the General Baptists, and thirty-three of them were in Kent and Lincolnshire, the rest were scattered in different parts of the kingdom.

I have not seen any later list of the General Baptists, and have no data by which I can form a very accurate estimate of the number of their churches, ministers, or members. But I conclude that they are much below the Particular Baptists in numbers, energy, and influence.

In 1790, they had three Associations, the Kentish, the Lincolnshire or Old-Connexion, and the Leicestershire or New-Association. And besides these I find mention made of a General Assembly; but whether this Assembly is composed of delegates from the three Associations, or is a distinct connexion, I am at a loss to determine. There are, moreover, a number of churches of the General Baptists which are not in any associate connexion.

The New or Leicestershire Association in 1790, contained thirty-two churches, twenty-two pastors, twenty-one unordained ministers, and two thousand eight hundred and forty-three members. The church at Loughborough in Leicestershire was the largest, and contained three hundred and eight. Its ministers were Benjamin Polland and William Parkinson. The church of London, of which Dan Taylor was pastor, consisted of two hundred and twenty-five. Allowing the other Associations to be as large as this, and that there are a considerable number of churches unassociated, the sum total of the General Baptists may amount to ten or twelve thousand.

" The General Baptist churches are not all properly united in one close body any more than the Particulars." Some believe more and some less of the leading maxims of the General creed. And this may be said of all sects and parties whatever.

The General Baptists appear to have had more learned men, and distinguished characters amongst them in former times than they have at present. Dr. William Russell, Thomas Grantham, Dr. John Gale, and other eminent men, were of this connexion.

Russell and Grantham were cotemporaries and fellow-sufferers with Bunyan, Keach, Kiffin, and other distinguished ministers of the Particular Baptists.

The following Memorial of Mr. GRANTHAM, in Golden Capitals, is hung up in the Meeting-house belonging to the General Baptists, in the Priory of the White Friars, in the Parish of St. James, in the city of Norwich.

A MEMORIAL,

Dedicated to the singular merits of
A faithful Confessor, and laborious Servant of Christ:
Who with christian fortitude, endured persecution
Through many perils, the loss of friends and substance,
And ten persecutions for conscience' sake,
A Man endowed with every christian grace and virtue,
The Rev. Mr. THOMAS GRANTHAM,
A learned Minister of the baptized Churches,
And pious Founder of this Church of Believers baptized:
Who delivered to King Charles II. our Declaration of Faith;
And afterwards presented to him a Remonstrance against Persecution.
Both were kindly received, and redress of grievances promised.
He died xvii. Jan. MDCXCII, aged LVIII. years,
And, to prevent the indecencies threatened to his corps,
Was interred before the west doors,
In the middle Aisle of St. Stephen's Church, in this City;
Through the interest, and much to the credit of
The Rev. Mr. JOHN CONNOULD,
By whom, with many sighs and tears
The burial service was solemnly read to a crowded audience.
When, at closing the book, he added,
This day is a very great man fallen in our Israel;
For after their Epistolary Dispute, in sixty letters, ended,
That very learned Vicar retained
The highest esteem and friendship for him whilst living,
And was, at his own request, buried by him, May MDCCVIII.
That Mr. GRANTHAM was a very great man, appears
In those Letters, and in numerous printed works.
Also, when engaged in public disputations,
Successfully displaying the well accomplished Logician:
For to such exercises of skill and literature
He was often called in that disputing age.
Blessed are the dead which die in the Lord, yea, saith the Spirit,
They rest from their labours, and their works do follow them.

WALES.

WE have briefly related under the preceding head the account of the ancient British Christians retiring into Wales, to avoid the persecutions of the pagan Saxons, and of their being visited by the bloody emissary of Rome, St.

Austin, who requested them to receive the commandment of the pope, and baptize their children. These christian refugees are upon very good ground supposed to have been Baptists. After they were driven into Wales they enjoyed tranquillity for a length of time, and religion flourished by their means. They formed two large societies of a somewhat peculiar nature, one at Bangor in the north, and the other at Cear-leon in the south. According to Danvers the society or college at Bangor contained two thousand one hundred christians, who dedicated themselves to the Lord, to serve him in the ministry, as they became capable, to whom was attributed the name of *the monks of Bangor.* But this writer assures us they were no ways like the popish monks, for they married, followed their different callings, those who were qualified for the ministry engaged in the holy employment, while the others laboured with their hands to support them, and to provide for the great spiritual family. We have seen that the Moravian Baptists lived in confraternities much like the one we are now describing, and the Baptist Missionaries at Serampore, as we shall soon show, have founded an institution of a similar nature, where from one fund, the wants of all, however differently engaged, are supplied. The Mission house at Serampore would doubtless be called a monastery, and the missionaries monks by a popish writer. But the two great societies at Bangor and Cear-leon, were broken up, and all the Baptists in Wales, who rejected St. Austin's commission, were terribly harassed, and most of them destroyed about the year 600, by the army of Saxons, which the sanguinary saint procured to carry war and wretchedness among them.

For many centuries after this the history of Wales is covered with great obscurity. Our English and Welsh brethren seem inclined to think that Baptist principles lived in this country through all the dark ages of popery, although they do not pretend that those who maintained them remained in a congregated state. The supposition is not altogether improbable, but until some clearer historical evidence can be adduced, it must rest as a matter of opinion. We know that Wales, for a long time, has been a nursery of Baptists. Multitudes have emigrated to this country from that principality, and many of the

American churches were founded either wholly or in part by these emigrants. Wales has also supplied the American churches with many useful ministers, many of whom are gone to receive their reward, but some of them are yet actively engaged in this western department of the Lord's vineyard. Roger Williams, the founder of Rhode-Island, Morgan Edwards, Dr. Samuel Jones of Lower-Dublin, (Penn.) Mr. David Philips, of Washington county in the same State, Mr. Lewis Richards of Baltimore, and Mr. John Williams of New-York, were all born in Wales. The names of many other ministers of Welsh extraction will occur in the course of this work.

The first Baptist church in Wales, of which we can give any clear account, was founded at Swansea in that country in 1649. The principal man among them was John Miles, who afterwards came to America and founded the church at Swansea, in Massachusetts. The Swansea church in Wales had increased to about three hundred members by the year 1662. Other churches arose in this country soon after the one was founded at Swansea, and in the time of the Commonwealth, they maintained an Association, and published a Confession of Faith, which was publicly opposed by George Fox, the Quaker. But on the restoration of Charles II. their Association was broken up, and they with all other non-conformists were made to feel the rod of a persecuting church. When the General Assembly of Baptists met in London, in 1689, it appears there were delegates from only seven churches in Wales. It is probable, however, that there were more churches in the principality at that time, which could not conveniently send delegates so far, or who might not have been convinced of the expediency of the measure.

In Morgan Edwards' list for 1768, the number of Baptist churches in Wales was twenty-three, only one of which was of the General persuasion. In all these churches were about twenty ministers, and two thousand one hundred and ten communicants.

In Rippon's list for 1790, the number of churches had increased to forty-eight, and the number of ministers was much greater. In 1798, the number of churches amounted to eighty-four, in which were ninety-one ministers, who had a pastoral charge, forty-seven who were not ordained, and not less than nine thousand members.

If the Baptists in Wales have increased as fast since the last mentioned date, as they did for a number of years preceding it, there must now be considerably more than a hundred churches, twelve or fourteen thousand members, and not far from two hundred ministers, including such as are not ordained.

There are three Associations in Wales, which are called the East, West, and North.

In Rippon's latest list of the Welsh churches, he has specified the year in which each one was constituted. The one at Olchon is dated in 1633, sixteen years before the one at Swansea.

IRELAND.

This catholic kingdom has never contained many Baptists, but yet there appears to have been a few respectable churches in it for more than a hundred and sixty years. At what period Baptist churches began to be founded in Ireland, I cannot learn, but it was probably not far from the year 1650. Ivimey has given an account of a correspondence, which was maintained between the Baptists in Ireland, and England, a little after this period. By a letter from Ireland, in 1653, it appears there were ten Baptist churches in the following places, viz. Dublin, Waterford, Clonmell, Kilkenny, Cork, Limerick, Galloway, Wexford, Kerry, and near Carrick Fergus. Three years after, another letter was sent, signed by Patient, Blackwood, Roberts, Lawern, Seward, Jones, Cudmore, Hopkins, and Thomas, all of whom, I conclude, were ministers. The Baptists appear to have flourished in Ireland during the existence of the Commonwealth; but on the restoration of the persecuting and inglorious Charles II, they doubtless met with trouble, and it is supposed that those ministers, who had gone over from England to that kingdom, were then obliged to return home.

Among the papers left by Mr. John Comer, and preserved by Mr. Backus, I find a letter written from Dublin in 1731, by a Baptist minister, whose name was Abdiel Edwards. By this letter it appears there were then eight or ten churches in Ireland, of the Particular Baptists, besides one of Arminian principles, and another which held to open communion. Mr. Edwards informs his correspondent that the church in Swift's Alley, Dublin, of which he was pastor, consisted of about two hundred members, that it was, for ought he could learn, the oldest in the kingdom, and was formed, as he supposed, about eighty years before, that is, about 1650. He also mentions that the whole number of Baptist communicants then in Ireland, did not exceed four hundred. The number of both churches and members has been less since that time, but of late years they begin to increase.

Ireland has produced some famous statesmen and literary characters, and it also gave birth to that famous Baptist, that champion of non-conformity, Thomas Delaune, whose immortal plea for the non-conformists was re-published a few years since, by Elias Lee, pastor of the Baptist church at the Ballston Springs, in the state of New-York.

SCOTLAND.

"IT was supposed till very lately, that there never had existed in Scotland a religious society of the Baptist denomination, before the year 1765; but it now appears that this was a mistake, and that such a society did really exist there as far back as about the middle of the seventeenth century, and which used to meet at Leith and Edinburgh. What led to this discovery was a book which lately fell into the hands of a certain person at Edinburgh, entitled, "A confession of the several congregations or churches of Christ in London, which are commonly (though unjustly) called Anabaptists; published for the vindication of the truth, &c. Unto which is added, Heart-bleedings for professors' abominations, or a faithful general epistle, (from the same churches) presented to all who have known the way of truth, &c. The fourth impression corrected. Printed at Leith, 1653." To this edition a preface is prefixed by some Baptists at Leith and Edinburgh, which, however, contains nothing of the history of the church, only that they were of the same faith and order with the churches in London. It is dated, "Leith, the tenth of the first month, vulgarly called March, 1652-3," and "signed in the name, and by the appointment of the church of Christ, usually meeting at Leith and Edinburgh, by Thomas Spencer, Abraham Holmes, Thomas Powell, John Brady."

"It is more than probable that this church was composed of English Baptists, who had gone into that country, during the civil wars. In that case it may be supposed that they were chiefly soldiers, as we know of no other description of men so likely to have emigrated from England to Scotland; and it is well known that there were many Baptists in the army which Cromwell led into that country, a good part of which was left behind for the purpose of garrisoning Edinburgh, Leith and other places.

"This church, it is supposed, continued in existence down to the era of the restoration, when, in all probability, it was dissolved and dispersed, owing either to the garrisons of Leith and Edinburgh, being then withdrawn and replaced by other troops, or else to the violence of the persecution, which so notoriously distinguished the execrable reign of the second Charles. Be that as it may, there do not appear, as far as is now known, the slightest traces of so much as one single Baptist church in North-Britain, for more than a hundred years from that period. It was not till the year 1765, that the Baptist profession began again to make a public appearance in that country; its first rise, however, may be traced a little further back."*

In 1763, Robert Carmichael and Archibald M'Lean, conversing together upon the subject of infant baptism, were at a loss to find any proper ground for it in the word of God; but being unwilling to relinquish it hastily, it was agreed that each of them should carefully consult the scriptures upon that subject, and communicate their thoughts upon it to each other. Carmichael had been for several years pastor of an Antiburgher congregation, the strictest class of seceders, but had now joined the Glassites. M'Lean was a printer at Glasgow. The result of these examinations was, that both of these men were led to renounce infant baptism. Carmichael was now at Edinburgh. He had been pastor of an Independent society in that city; but for certain reasons, he and seven others had separated from that society, before he became a Baptist. Soon after this separation he became fully convinced of the

* Rippon's Register.

scripture doctrine of baptism, and preached it publickly. Five of the seven who adhered to him declared themselves of the same mind, among whom was Mr. Robert Walker, surgeon. To obtain baptism in a regular way, it was judged proper that Mr. Carmichael should first go to London and be baptized himself. He accordingly went and was baptized by Doctor Gill, at Barbican, October 9, 1765, and, returning to Edinburgh, administered that ordinance to the five above mentioned, and other two, in November following. Archibald M'Lean, then residing at Glasgow, was not baptized for some weeks after; and while at Edinburgh upon that occasion he was much solicited to write an answer to Mr. Glass's Dissertation on Infant Baptism, which he did in the spring following, but it was not published till the end of that year. A publication of this nature being a novelty in Scotland, awakened the attention of many in different places to the subject. In December, 1767, Archibald M'Lean removed to Edinburgh, the church then consisting of about nine members; and in June, 1768, he was chosen colleague to Mr. Carmichael. Soon after this the church increased considerably.

This was the beginning of the present Baptist churches in Scotland. In 1769, Mr. Carmichael removed from Edinburgh, and settled at Dundee, where a church was organized immediately, and he and Thomas Boswel became its elders. About the same time Dr. Walker was chosen joint-elder with Archibald M'Lean of the church at Edinburgh. The same year (1769) several persons came from Glasgow, and were baptized. Afterwards, when their number increased, they were set in order, and Neil Stuart was appointed their elder. In 1770, a small society arose at Montrose, and John Greig, David Mill, and Thomas Wren, officiated as its elders. From this period Baptist sentiments spread around in many different places, and a number of small societies were formed. Some acquired a permanent standing, while others were broken up in a short time by disputes among themselves about the *order of the house, &c.* I am inclined to think there were not more than ten or twelve Baptist churches in Scotland, in 1800. But since that time they have increased greatly. Many Pedobaptist ministers have espoused the Baptist cause, and the doctrine of believer's baptism has had an extensive prevalence within a few years past in the Scottish realm. The converts seem to have come more from the Independent connexion, than the fast-bound Kirk. Among the distinguished characters, in Scotland, who have embraced the principles of the Baptists, we may reckon Robert Haldane, Esq. and Rev. James A. Haldane his brother. The former of these is a gentleman of fortune, and has, for many years, devoted his revenues to the promotion of the cause of truth. By his means many pious young men have been educated and sent forth into the ministry in different directions; and a considerable number of them, have with their patron been buried in baptism, and espoused the principles of the despised Baptists.

I very much regret that I am not able to give a more particular account of the late progress of the Baptist sentiments, and of the present number of the denomination in Scotland.

Mr. Maclay of New-York informs me, that before he left Scotland, he foresaw what has since come to pass, and gave his Independent brethren to understand that he expected many of them would become Baptists. And so it has happened that many of their ministers, multitudes of their members, and in not a few instances almost whole churches have embraced the Baptist principles. The Independents and Baptists are very nearly related. Their notions of church government are alike, in doctrine they generally agree, and it is only for an Independent to go into the water, and he is a Baptist at once. The Independent churches have always been Baptist nurseries. The Independents are upon the brink of gospel order, and when they are immersed in Jordan they are completely in it.

The present number of Baptists in Scotland I am not able to state; but from all accounts it must amount to many thousands. Should any further accounts come to hand in season, they shall be inserted in the Appendix.

INDIA MISSION.

This mission originated in England, and is supported and directed by a society, which was formed about twenty years ago, by the Baptists in that kingdom.

Missionary Society formed.

An interesting account of this important establishment was not long since published in a small volume by Dr. Staughton of Philadelphia, under the title of THE BAPTIST MISSION IN INDIA, containing a narrative of its rise, progress, and present condition. Very interesting communications from the Missionaries in India, are also frequently inserted in the Baptist Magazine, edited by Dr. Baldwin of Boston. But for the benefit of those of our brethren, who have not had access to these sources of information, I shall here give a brief account of this noble institution.

As early as 1784, it was resolved by an Association held at Nottingham, in England, to set apart an hour the first Monday evening in every month, for extraordinary prayer for the revival of religion, and for the extending of Christ's kingdom in the world. This was three years before Mr. Carey was ordained. This distinguished man from his first entering on the work of the ministry, directed all his thoughts, plans, and studies towards enterprises of a missionary kind. In 1790, he visited Birmingham and became acquainted with the late Samuel Pearce, whose kindred soul entered with ardour into all his views. Others at the same time were animated with a missionary zeal, and in 1792 the society was formed at Kettering, which has since, by its wonderful acts, astonished the christian world, and made the word of God accessible to millions in India's benighted realm. Its funds at first were only 13*l.* 2*s.* 6*d.*

About this time, Mr. John Thomas returned from India to England. He went out as a surgeon of an East Indiaman in 1783. Before he left England he had embraced the gospel under Dr. Stennet; while he was in Bengal, he felt a desire to communicate it to the natives, and being encouraged to do so by a religious friend, he obtained his discharge from the ship, and after learning the language, continued from the year 1787 to 1791 preaching Christ in different parts of the country. But it does not appear that the Baptists in England were at the time acquainted with Mr. Thomas' proceedings. But now they were happy to find that while they had been praying at home for the spread of the gospel among the heathen, one of their brethren had been making the attempt among the wretched Hindoos, and that some success had attended his exertions.

From information received from Mr. Thomas, the committee of this infant society, which at first consisted of John Ryland, Reynold Hogg, William Carey, John Sutcliff, and Andrew Fuller, were fully of opinion that a door was now open for a mission in the East-Indies. They accordingly resolved to invite Mr. Thomas to go out as one of their missionaries. Mr. Carey, whom God, in his wise providence, had fitted for the important part he has since acted, and had brought him into his vineyard at this eventful juncture, was asked if he were willing to accompany Mr. Thomas; to which he readily answered in the affirmative. Thus two missionaries stood ready to depart for the dark and distant coast. "The next step was to calculate the expense of sending them out, and to obtain the means of defraying it. The expense was estimated at 500*l.* which sum required to be raised in about three or four months. To accomplish this the committee frankly stated to the religious public their plan, requesting that so far as it appeared to be deserving of encouragement, they would encourage it. Letters were also addressed to the most active ministers of the denomination throughout the kingdom, requesting their concurrence and assistance. The result was, that more than twice the sum which had been asked for was collected; yet, when the work was finished, the actual expense had so far exceeded the estimate, that there were only a few pounds to spare. One principal cause of this was the circumstance of Mr. Carey's whole family, with Mr. Carey's sister, being induced to accompany him."

In June, 1793, on board the princess Maria, a Danish Indiaman, these missionaries set sail for India, and after the usual passage safely arrived at the place of their destination. During the first years of their residence in this heathen land, they experienced a mixture of trials and encouragements, but on the whole they found sufficient motives for perseverance in the arduous work which they had undertaken.

In the spring of 1796, Mr. John Fountain offering himself as a missionary was accepted, and sent out to join the brethren in India.

More Missionaries sent out.

As repeated requests had been made for more missionaries, and particularly for one, who should understand the printing business, the committee paid every possible attention to this object. In the spring of 1799, they were enabled to send out four men and four women; namely, Mr. and Mrs. Marshman, Mr. and Mrs. Grant, Mr. and Mrs. Brunsdon, Mr. William Ward and Miss Tidd. Mr. Ward understood the printing business, and Mr. and Mrs. Marshman had kept a school.

In 1802 Mr. Chamberlain and wife departed for India under the patronage of the society.

In 1804 four more young men with their wives, who had previously been set apart for the work of the ministry, viz. John Biss, Richard Mardon, William Moore, and Joshua Rowe, set sail for India by way of America. After a tedious and perilous voyage, during which they received much kindness from friends, both in America and at Madrass, they all arrived safe at the place of their destination.

The next missionaries were Messrs. Chater and Robinson. These men met with difficulty from government; they were commanded to return to Europe, and Capt. Wickes was refused, at the same time, a clearance, unless he took them back, but after considerable parley, the Captain was furnished with his passports, and a way was devised by the other missionaries to retain Messrs. Chater and Robinson in the country.

In 1812, Messrs. Johns and Lawson with their wives, who had been some time in America, set sail for India. They were accompanied by four Pedobaptist missionaries, viz. Messrs. May, Nott, Hall and Rice. Messrs. Judson and Newell of the same denomination had sailed before them. They all landed safely in India, but some of them met with troubles on account of the vexatious policy of the East-India Company. Of these Pedobaptists Mr. Judson and wife, and Mr. Rice embraced the Baptist sentiments, and were baptized not long after they landed in India. These worthy young men have turned their attention to their Baptist brethren in America for assistance, and they are making exertions to afford it.

I am not sure but other missionaries besides those we have named, have been sent to India by the society in

England. But these are all of which I have gained any information. Some of them have died. Those who remain are now actively engaged in the great business for which they submitted to a voluntary exile to a heathen and unhealthy land.

A considerable number of those who have been brought to the knowledge of the truth by means of these missionaries, have become preachers of the gospel. Some of these also have died. In 1811, Dr. Carey wrote to Dr. Rogers of Philadelphia as follows: "The Lord has been very gracious in raising up labourers in this work. There are about ten persons, formerly idolaters or mussulmans, who now preach the gospel of our Redeemer, and seven others, native Portuguese or Armenians, who are either called to the work of the ministry, or are now on trial for it. Two of our native brethren, Hindoos, are employed in Calcutta and its precincts, where they preach at twelve or fourteen different places every week, and have been the instruments of the conversion of many. Indeed, I think they are the most useful persons now employed in the work of God at Calcutta, or in India."

We shall now give a brief account of the great things our brethren in India have been enabled to perform.

The missionaries on their first arrival in this country resided at different places, but in 1800, they settled at Serampore, and this place became henceforward the head quarters of all who were concerned in the mission. The first object of attention was to settle a plan of family government. All the missionaries were to preach and pray in turn; one to superintend the affairs of the family a month, and then another; Mr. Carey was appointed treasurer, and keeper of the medicine chest; Mr. Fountain, librarian; Saturday evening was devoted to adjusting any differences which might arise during the week, and pledging themselves to love one another; finally, *it was resolved, that no one should engage in any private trade; but whatever was done by any member of the family, should be done for the benefit of the mission.*

The rent of lodgings which they at present occupied was very high. They therefore purchased a house, by the river side, with a pretty large piece of ground. It had va-

The printing of the Bengalee New Testament begun. 239

rious accommodations, but the price alarmed them ; yet the rent in four years would have amounted to the purchase.

In 1801 the missionaries purchased the house and premises adjoining their own. The garden and out-buildings contained more than four acres of land. By this addition they had room not only for the schools, and for the printing and binding business, but also for any new missionaries that might arrive. They made themselves trustees for the society, as they had done in the first purchase.

The missionaries have also purchased a large real estate at Calcutta. Whatever property they obtain, belongs to the mission family, and is held in trust by them for the society in England. These are some of the temporal advantages of the missionaries, but those of a spiritual kind are far greater. They found it a laborious task to learn the languages of the country. They first, it appears, made themselves masters of the Bengalee. About the time the mission-house was established at Serampore, Dr. Carey had nearly finished the translation of the Old and New-Testament into that language, and preparations for printing having previously been made, in May, 1800, the first sheet of the Bengalee New-Testament was struck off. From that period the missionaries have gone on with great assiduity and success, in learning other languages and presenting the precious word of life to the idolatrous natives of the East in their own tongues.

From a statement furnished by Mr. Johns while in America, it appears that translations were making in 1811, in twelve languages, viz. 1st. The Bengalee. 2d. The Orissa. 3d. The Telinga. 4th. The Guzerattee. 5th. The Kurnata. 6th. The Mahratta. 7th. The Hindoosthanee. 8th. The Seek. 9th. The Sungskrit. 10th. The Burman. 11th. The Chinese. 12th. The Thibet or Bootan. Besides the printing of the Malayala and the Tamul.

" The present state of the translations," says Mr. Johns, " is highly encouraging, and marks the zeal and perseverance of the persons engaged in the work. The Bengalee Bible, in 5 vols. 8vo. has been completed for some time, and has reached even to a third edition. This work was the result of " sixteen years labour." The New-Testament and Pentateuch are printed in Sungskrit ; the New-Testament and the Old-Testament, from Job to Malachi in the Orissa. The New-Testament in the Mahratta and in the Hindoosthanee, is printed. In the Chinese, the Gospels by Matthew and Mark are printed off, and the New Testament will shortly be published :—In 1809, the translation had proceeded to the end of Ephesians. The printing in the Burman, and also in the Seek, is begun. The Telinga and Kurnata, may be commenced this present year, (1811 ;) the Kurnata and Guzerattee have been hitherto delayed by circumstances, chiefly of a pecuniary nature. The translations of all are much further advanced than the printing ; and the missionaries express a hope, that ere long, All the nations of the East will hear in their own tongues the wonderful works of God. Besides the above, the Serampore missionaries are printing the Malayala, translated from the celebrated Syriac version, under the direction of Mar Dionysius, bishop of the Syrian Christians ; and also the Tamul, translated by a valuable deceased missionary from the London Society."

The Sungskrit, or Sangskrit, as it is sometimes written, is read all over India ; it is the learned language of the country. The Bengalee is spoken by a population equal to that of the United States of America ; the Hindoosthanee, to France and Italy ; the Chinese by three hundred millions ; the Burman by seventeen millions ; and the other languages by many millions each. The missionaries are yearly studying new languages and making preparations to make the Oracles of Truth legible to the remaining idolatrous millions of the East.

The missionaries have hitherto devoted most of their attention to the translating of the Scriptures into the numerous languages of India, but they have at the same time laboured much among the natives, and a considerable number of them have been hopefully born into the kingdom of God. A number professed a serious regard for the gospel from the first preaching of the missionaries in India, but it was not until the year 1800, that any one of the natives came out and made a publick profession of it. In December of that year Kristno was baptized, the first native, who had ever in Bengal publickly renounced *cast*, and owned Jesus Christ. This was an important event. The chain of the East was now broken, and the missionaries saw what they had been waiting and hoping for many years, and concerning which they had met with so many disappointments.* From this period a few were from time to time brought to make a public profession of christianity, and by the close of the year 1808, about a hundred and fifty had been baptized in different parts of India. About thirty of these were Europeans, who had settled in the country, the rest were natives. Of the natives about ten were Bramins, a few were mussulmans, and the remainder were Hindoos of different descriptions. It is now about five years since this statement was made, which is found in Staughton's India Mission, and it is probable that a much greater number has been converted in this time, than had been before.

From a letter from Dr. Carey we learn that last year there were, in different parts of India, twelve missionary stations, viz. at Agra, Digga, Patna, Goamalti, Dinagepore and Sadamahl, Cutwa, Changach'ha in Jessore, Serampore, Calcutta, Balasore in Oorissa, Rangoon, and at Columba in Ceylon. And at that time Mr. Robinson was waiting for a conveyance to Java and Mr. Carapeit Aratoon to Bombay, where they hope to found stations. Besides preaching at the stations, the missionaries and many of the native christians spend much time in travelling in different parts of the country, to preach the gospel, to distribute the Scriptures and religious tracts, and to converse upon the great things of the kingdom with all who will hear him.

* The Hindoos from time immemorial have been divided into tribes or casts. The four principal casts are the Bramins, Soldiers, Labourers, and Mechanics, and these are divided into a multiplicity of inferior distinctions. The Bramins are the most noble tribe, they alone can officiate in the priesthood, like the Jewish tribe of Levi. All the different casts are kept distinct from each other by insurmountable barriers ; they are forbidden to intermarry, to cohabit, to eat with each other, or even to drink out of the same vessel with another tribe. Every deviation from these points subjects them to be rejected by their tribe, renders them polluted forever, and obliges them from that instant to associate with a herd, who belong to no cast, but are held in utter detestation by all others, and are employed only in the meanest and vilest offices. The members of each cast adhere invariably to the profession of their forefathers ; from generation to generation the same families have followed one uniform line of life.

To lose cast is to become subject to an excommunication of the most terrible kind, and for this reason a superstitious Hindoo will suffer torture and even death itself rather than do it.

From this we see that the infernal cast, as Dr. Fuller calls it, was a most formidable barrier against the introduction of the gospel among the heathen in India. Well might the missionaries exult when the chain of the *cast* was broken by Kristno, and the door of faith was opened to these perishing Gentiles.

These itinerant excursions are often the most profitable parts of their labours.

The plan of the Serampore mission is thus stated by Mr. Judson in a letter to Dr. Baldwin, 1812. " All the pecuniary avails of the brethren, as well as monies received from the society in England, belong to the common treasury. Dr. Carey's salary, in the college, of 12,000 rupees per annum ;* Dr. Marshman's income from the school, and Mr. Ward's avails of the printing-press, are as much devoted to the common cause, as receipts from England. Out of the public treasury, each man, woman, and child, belonging to the mission, receives a monthly allowance for clothes, &c. which varies according to age and circumstances from 20 to 40 rupees. The whole family, as well as the boarders, eat at a common table. The table expenses, as well as all the expenses of the mission, arising from building, repairs, servants, pundits, native preachers, &c. are defrayed by appropriations from the public fund. The fund for translating and printing is preserved distinct, in order to secure the subscriptions of some who might be unwilling to contribute to the common object. A missionary in an out-station receives an allowance proportioned to the expense of his situation. Should he be able to lessen this by a school, or by any other means, he is obliged to do so ; and should his avails exceed his expenditure, the surplus reverts to the public treasury. Still farther, all the lands and buildings, belonging to the mission at Serampore and elsewhere, are deeded to the society in England. Thus, Sir, you see, that the whole system in all its parts is disinterested. No missionary has any private property. All opportunities, and therefore all temptations to *lay up money* are effectually precluded. The society at home have the utmost security for the honest application of the money which they remit ; and should any wish to satisfy themselves on this

* The College of Fort-William at Calcutta was founded in 1800, about a year after Mr. Carey was honored by Marquis Wellesley with an appointment of teacher of the Bengalee, Sangskrit and Mahratta languages in that institution. His salary was 500 rupees a month, that is, 3000 dollars a year. When the College was new modelled in 1807, Mr. Carey was made professor of Bengalee and Sangskrit, with a salary of six thousand dollars a year. Calcutta is fifteen miles from Serampore ; at this place there is a Baptist church, and here Mr. Carey mostly resides, pursuing with unwearied assiduity his professional and missionary duties, which so harmoniously correspond with each other. Well might he say " The earth helpeth the woman."

point, the cash accounts of the mission are always open to examination."

Mr. Judson states in the same letter that the expenses of supporting a missionary in India, are much greater than people here would generally expect. Mr. Robinson and wife, who were then bound to Java, were allowed an hundred and forty rupees, that is, seventy dollars a month, or eight hundred and forty dollars a year. Mr. Chater and wife and two children in the island of Ceylon were allowed eighty dollars a month, or nine hundred and sixty-dollars a year.

Great charges have attended the prosecution of this mission, the sum total of which I am not able to state. The fund for translating and printing the Scriptures we see is preserved distinct. The giving of the word of life to the heathen in their own languages, is a cause in which party feelings can have no influence; all denominations may, therefore, heartily engage in it, and many benevolent christians have cordially lent their aid. Many wealthy individuals resident in India have contributed towards carrying forward this noble undertaking. A late Mr. Grant in that country a few months previous to his decease bequeathed five thousand dollars for the translations.

The friends of the Holy Scriptures in Scotland, of all denominations, have repeatedly and liberally contributed towards this object.

The British and Foreign Bible Society, that grand and peculiar institution of modern times, had, previous to 1811, voted annually for three preceding years, nearly five thousand dollars. The New-York Bible Society have also aided this design. In the years 1806 and 1807, the religious friends in America of different persuasions furnished our brethren in India with about six thousand dollars. From 1801 to 1809, the money received from various sources for the translations expressly, amounted to thirty-nine thousand, five hundred and eighty four dollars and seventeen cents. Great sums have been forwarded since, the amount of which I have not been able to learn. But Mr. Johns, previous to his leaving America, collected nearly five thousand dollars, mostly in Boston and Salem. Among the donors in Boston, the Honorable William Phillips gave the liberal sum of one thousand dollars.

The manner in which the Scriptures have been received by the natives will afford satisfaction to the contributors, as it has served to encourage the hearts of the unwearied labourers. Often is the poor Hindoo seated under the shade of the trees, reading "this wonderful book." They come to Serampore from a great distance to inquire about *the new Shaster.* This *Shaster,* say they, will be received by all India, and the Hindoos will become *one cast.* What heart can remain unaffected at the news of these wonderful events.

The expenses of supporting the missionaries exclusive of the translations, have been great ; but they have been able to do much for themselves, and what has been wanting has been communicated by the society under whose patronage they labour. The brethren in England know how to solicit, and what is still better, the religious public know how to give.

In the beginning of 1812, the missionaries experienced a very heavy affliction by the loss of their printing office, and most of its valuable contents. This building, which was two hundred feet in length, was totally consumed by fire, together with large quantities of books, manuscripts, types, and other printing apparatus. The loss was estimated at thirty thousand dollars to the mission, and five thousand to the Bible Society. " This," says Dr. Carey, " was a heavy blow, not only on account of the pecuniary loss, but as it totally stopped our printing the scriptures in the Oriental languages. The manuscripts consumed will not be all replaced in a long time to come, however hard we labour at them. We however immediately began to recast the types, and to labour to begin printing again as soon as possible. May the Lord stand by us, and enable us to hold on in this great work till it be accomplished,&c."

From these accounts we see that the Baptist missionaries in India have met with great encouragement and success ; but they have all along met with many troubles and embarrassments, both from the natives, and many of the unbelieving Europeans who are settled in the country. From the superstitious Indians they had reason to expect opposition, but from their own countrymen they rather hoped for friendship and encouragement. But contrary to this, many have ridiculed their attempts, defamed their characters, and laboured hard to defeat their benevolent designs. But their most serious troubles have arisen from the embarrassing policy of the English East-India Company. This company has advanced from a society of merchants to the sovereignty of the country, and its revenues are superior to that of many crowned heads.* It is a notorious and lamentable fact, however differently it may be explained, that this Company has opposed the introduction of christianity in India. Of this the missionaries have often complained.

In 1806, Mr. Ward thus wrote to a friend in Philadelphia : " You know the English Company don't like the Hindoos to be converted ; and it is a part of their charter, that they will not do any thing to change their religion. They also allow none, (except by sufferance) but their own servants to settle in the country. We have been also lately prohibited by the governor from interfering with the prejudices of the natives, either by preaching, distributing tracts, sending out native itinerants, &c. In short, the governor said, as he did not attempt to disturb the prejudices of the natives, he hoped we should not. Thus if we were to obey this request, in its literal meaning, we must give up our work altogether, and instead of wanting fresh missionaries, we might reship those we already have. But it is impossible to do this. We avoid provoking the government, but we dare not give up our work at the command of man. We have written home on the subject, and sought relief from these painful restrictions ; but what will be the result we know not."

By the authority of this company missionaries have been ordered back ; but we believe that God has ordered them there, and will open ways for their stay and success. Serampore, where the mission house is established, is under the Danish government, which has always protected the missionaries, and shown a friendly disposition towards their design. It was with a view to these advantages that our brethren fixed on this place for the residence of the mission family.

This company has found means to collect a revenue from the detestable superstitions of the Hindoos, and like

* Morse's Geography, Vol. II. p. 555.

Demetrius of Ephesus, they fear their craft will be in danger by the reforming influence of gospel light. The benighted Indians are obliged to pay a tax for the privilege of worshipping the obscene and bloody Juggernaut, the Moloch of the East. Dr. Buchanan, after witnessing the horrid scenes exhibited at the worship of this cruel deity, observes, " How much I wished that the proprietors of India Stock could have attended the wheels of Juggernaut, and seen this peculiar source of their revenue."*

In reviewing the progress of the Baptist mission in India, may we not exclaim with gratitude, *What hath God wrought!* Here we see that a small company of men, aided only by the voluntary contributions of religious friends, beset with hosts of adversaries, thwarted often by the unfriendly policy of government, opposed by idolatrous superstitions of immemorial antiquity, have planted the gospel in many parts of India's benighted realm, have presented multitudes, and are ready soon to present multitudes more with the everlasting word of God. May this effulgent lamp of truth dispel the mists of Bramin darkness. May this sharp two-edged sword demolish the Moloch of the East, and lead to the worship of the true God the millions of that land of ignorance and error.

CHAP. VI.

MUNSTER.

THE Munster affair, like an evil genius, has followed the Baptists all over the world, or at least, wherever they have been found. As all, who have done the Anabaptists the honour of writing their history, have begun and ended with the mad men of Munster, it seems proper that we should say something respecting them, before we close the accounts of the Baptists in foreign countries and ancient times.

We shall in the first place give some account of the insurrection in Germany, and then endeavour to show what hand the Baptists had in them.

The condition of the peasants in Germany in the year 1524, about the time they began to meditate a revolt from the galling yoke of their tyrannical masters, was deplorable

* Researches in Asia, p. 197.

indeed, if there be any thing to deplore in a deprivation of most of the rights and liberties of rational creatures.

"The feudal system, that execration in the eyes of every being, that merits the name of man, had been established in early ages in Germany in all its rigour and horror. It had been planted with a sword reeking with human gore in the night of barbarism, when cannibals drank the warm blood of one enemy out of the skull of another, and it had shot its venomous fibres every way, rooted itself in every transaction, in religion, in law, in diversions, in every thing secular and sacred, so that the wretched rustics had only one prospect for themselves and all their posterity, one horrid prospect of everlasting slavery.

"The great principle of the feudal system, that all lands were derived from, and holden mediately or immediately of the crown, was always productive of unjust and oppressive consequences, tyranny in a thousand shapes, under the names of fines, quit-rents, alienations, dilapidations, wardships, heriots, and the rest, fleeced the unhappy people, deprived them of their property, depressed their spirits, and drove them sometimes to despair and distraction. To these innumerable evils must be added another innumerable mass brought in by popery. Tithes great and small, christenings, churchings, marriage dues, offerings, mortuaries, with a thousand other servile appendages of a horrible system of oppression, were incorporated in a pretended religion, itself the greatest affront that ever was offered to the reason of mankind.

"At the beginning of the sixteenth century, Germany was divided into six circles, and governed by sovereign princes, whose tyrannical oppressions would exceed belief, were they not well attested. Of the great number of good historians, who speak of the rustic war, we have not seen one, who pretends to deny the excessive and insupportable tyranny of the nobility and gentry, or one, who does not expressly affirm, that the peasants groaned under intolerable grievances, which they were no longer able to bear.

"The love of liberty, which is natural to every human being, is of itself an ingenuous and active principle, but it is not unfrequently invigorated by circumstances, and the peasants were emboldened by several favourable circumstances now. The attempt was not only just in itself, and an obedience to an universal and almighty impulse; but in the present case it was countenanced by precedents, and could not be taxed with even the paltry plea of novelty. " There is," says Hume, "an ultimate point of depression, as well as of exaltation, from which human affairs naturally return in a contrary progress, and beyond which they seldom pass, either in advancement or decline." The German peasants sunk to this ultimate point of depression in different places at different periods, and then they took a contrary direction, and made noble efforts to recover their freedom. Within the memory of the present insurgents, there had been many insurrections, as one against the oppressions of the bishop and canons of Spire, in 1502, another against the tyranny of a neighbouring abbot, in 1491, and several more. The recollection of these encouraged the present peasants to rise. This was their first motive. In the second place, good authors assure us, that they expected aid from their neighbours the Swiss. A third circumstance was the lamentable condition of both church and state. The whole of their wretched lives were spent in earning money for a cruel, profligate, and quarrelsome set of gentry to consume in luxury or war; and as to religious privileges, they had none. A fourth event that animated them, was the example of Luther. Within the last seven years, Luther and his associates had broke out of prison and set tyranny at defiance. All Europe knew this, and as all had as many reasons and as much right as he had, all were agitated, and some acted. Luther had published in 1520 a small tract in German on christian liberty, which was read with the most astonishing avidity, and the contents communicated by such as could read, to others who could not. Many, it appears, carried Luther's maxims of liberty as well as those relating to baptism farther than he did, and much farther than he intended they should. He had renounced the authority of the pope, and at Wittemberg, in the presence of ten thousand spectators, committed to the flames both the bull that had been published against him, and the decretals and canons relating to the pope's supreme jurisdiction. The writings and examples of the Saxon Reformer could not but stimulate the miserable peasants to throw off the enormous load of tyranny under which they groaned. Their plan was fast maturing, and many, who were neither mad men nor monsters, favoured their cause. And as Germany was now agitated by disputes of various kinds, and the ancient barriers of oppression were in many places shaken, this seemed a favourable juncture for the wretched rustics to put in their claim for some portion of that freedom, which is the natural right of every rational being. They were not exclusively Anabaptists, nor Lutherans, nor Catholicks; but they were a mixture of different religious opinions, who had been galled to the quick by the horrid tyranny of their masters, and who, uniting their efforts in one common cause, were determined to be free or perish in the attempt. But a wise providence saw fit not to favour their designs; they were defeated and ruined, and their names, by a thousand writers, have been loaded with infamy and disgrace.

"In the summer of 1524, the peasants of Suabia, on the estate of count Lutfen, sounded the alarm of a revolt. The counts Lutfen and Furstenberg, and the neighbouring gentry in Suabia, who had all a mutual interest in suppressing the insurrection, and who had entered into a confederacy for another purpose, agreed to suppress them, and Furstenberg, in the name of all the confederates, went to inquire into their grievances. They informed him that they were Catholicks, that they had not risen on any religious account, and that they required nothing but a release from those intolerable secular oppressions, under which they had long groaned, and which they neither would, nor could any longer bear. The second insurgents were the peasants of a neighbouring abbey, and they declared as the first had done, the oppression of the abbot, and not religion, was the cause of their conduct. The news, however, flew all over Germany, and the next spring three hundred thousand men, having more reason to complain than the first had, left off work, and assembled in the fields of Suabia, Franconia, Thuringia, the Palatinate, and Alsace. They consisted of all sorts of peasants, who thought themselves aggrieved in any manner.

"Of all the teachers in Germany at this time, the Baptists best understood the doctrine of liberty; to them therefore the peasants turned their eyes for counsel. Of the Baptists one of the most eminent was Thomas Muncer of Mulhausen in Thuringia. He had been a priest, but he became a disciple of Luther, and a great favourite with the reformed. His deportment was remarkably grave, his countenance was pale, his eyes rather sunk as if he was absorbed in thought, his visage long, and he wore his beard. His talent lay in a plain and easy method of preaching to the country people, whom (it should seem as an itinerant) he taught almost all through the electorate of Saxony. His air of mortification won him the hearts of the rustics. It was singular then for a preacher so much as to appear humble. When he had finished his sermon in any village, he used to retire either to avoid the crowd, or to devote himself to meditation and prayer. This was a practice so very singular and uncommon, that the people used to throng about the door, peep through the crevices, and oblige him sometimes to let them in, though he repeatedly assured them, that he was nothing, that all he had came from above, and that admiration and praise were due only to God. The more he fled from applause, the more it followed him. The people called him Luther's curate, and Luther named him his Absalom, probably, because *he stole the hearts of the men of Israel.* Muncer's enemies say, all this was artifice. It is impossible to know that. The survey of the heart belongs to God alone. This was not suspected till he became a Baptist. They say he was all this while plotting the rustic war; but there was no need to lay deep plots to create uneasiness, the grievances taught the peasants to groan, and rise, and fight before Muncer was born, and nobody ever taxed him with even knowing of the first insurrections now. The truth is, while Luther was regaling himself with the princes, Muncer was preaching in the country, and surveying the condition of their tenants, and it is natural to suppose he heard and saw their miserable bondage, and that on Luther's plan there was no probability of freedom flowing to the people.

"Luther wrote to the magistrates of Mulhausen, to advise them to require Muncer to give an account of his call, and if he could not prove that he acted under human authority, then to insist on his proving his call from God by working a miracle. The magistrates fell into this snare, and so did the monks, for persecution is both a catholick and a protestant doctrine, and they set about the work. The people resented this refinement on cruelty, especially as coming from a man, whom both the court of Rome, and the diet of the empire had loaded with all the anathemas they could invent, for no other crime than that for which he accused his brother, and they carried the matter so far in the end, that they expelled the monks, to which the Lutherans had no objection, and then the magistrates, and elected new Senators, of whom Muncer was one. To him, as to their only friend, the peasants all looked for relief.

" Muncer's doctrine all tended to liberty; but he had no immediate concern in the first insurrections of the peasants. It was many months after they were in arms before he joined them; but knowing their cause to be just, he drew up for them that memorial or manifesto, which sets forth their grievances, and which they presented to their lords, and dispersed all over Germany. This instrument is applauded by every writer who mentions it, as a master piece of its kind. Mr. Voltaire says, *a Lycurgus would have signed it.* It was the highest character he could have given it. Some, by mistake, ascribe it to Stapler.

" This manifesto consists of twelve articles, in which are set forth the grievances of the peasants, and the redress which they required, and on the grant of which they declared themselves ready to return to their labours.

I. The first sets forth the benefit of public religious instruction, and they pray that they may be permitted to elect their own ministers to teach them the word of God without the traditions of men; and that they may have power to dismiss them, if their conduct be reprehensible.

II. The second represents that the laws of tithing in the Old-Testament ought not to be enforced under the present economy, and praying that they may be allowed to pay the tithe of their corn, and be excused from paying any other; and that this may be divided by a committee into three equal parts, the first to be applied to the support of their teachers, the second to the relief of poor folks, and the third to the payment of such public taxes and dues as had been exacted of people in mean circumstances.

III. The third sets forth, that their former state of slavery was disgraceful to humanity, and inconsistent with the condition of people freed by the blood of Christ, who extended the benefits of his redemption to the meanest as well as to the highest, excepting none:

that they were determined to be free, not from the control of magistrates, whose office they honoured as of divine appointment, and whose just laws they would obey ; that they did not desire to live a licentious life after their own sinful passions ; but they would be free and not submit to slavery any longer, unless slavery could be proved right from the Holy Scripture.

IV. The fourth shews, that they had hitherto been deprived of the liberty of fishing, fowling, hunting, and taking animals wild by nature ; which prohibition was incompatible with natural justice, the good of society, and the language of Holy Scripture ; that in many places they had not been suffered even to chase away the wild animals that devoured their herbage and their corn, which was a great injury to them, contrary to all principles of justice, and to that free grant of wild animals, which the Creator of the world bestowed on all mankind at the beginning ; that they did not desire to enter by force on any man's private property great or small, under any pretence of right to fish, but they prayed that pretended private privileges might yield to equal publick benefit.

V. The fifth sets forth, that the forests were in the hands of a few great men, to the inexpressible damage of the miserable poor, who had been obliged to pay double the value of what little wood they wanted for firing or repairs ; they therefore prayed, that such woods and forests, as had not been purchased and become private property, either of individuals, or of corporate bodies, ecclesiastical or civil, might hereafter be reserved for the public use ; that they might be allowed to cut wood for necessary building, repairs, and firing, without any expense, under the direction, however, of a board of woodwards duly elected for the purpose ; that in case the forests could all be proved to be private property, then the matter should be amicably adjusted between themselves and the proprietors.

VI. The sixth sets forth the various hardships of base and uncertain villenage, the innumerable and ill-timed services, which the lords obliged their tenants to perform, which kept increasing every year, and which had become absolutely intolerable ; they pray that these services may be moderated by the princes, according to laws of equity, and the precepts of the gospel, and that no other burdens might be imposed on them, than such as were warranted by ancient custom.

VII. The seventh complains of abuses in regard to such tenures of farms, lands, and tenements, as were called beneficiary, and originally held on certain terms fixed in the first grants, as then agreed on between the grantors and the grantees, but which were now charged with a great many oppressive fines, fees, and payments detrimental to the tenants ; they pray that these tenures may be held in future on the terms of the original grants.

VIII. The eighth article regards the rents of the farms, held from year to year ; they complain that these annual rents far exceeded the worth of the lands, and they pray that honest and indifferent men may be employed to survey the estates, and report the fair value, and that the princes, if the rents should appear enormous, would remit a part, so that the husbandmen might be allowed a certain livelihood, and not reduced as they had been to extreme indigence, as every workman is worthy of his meat.

IX. The ninth complains of the wanton exercise of the power of making and executing penal statutes; they say that new laws were daily published, creating new crimes, and inflicting new fines and penalties, not for the improvement of society, but merely for pretences to extort money, and for the gratification of private resentment, or partial attachment; they pray, therefore, that justice may not be left to the care of discretion or affection, but administered according to ancient written forms.

X. The tenth sets forth, that formerly there was reserved in every village in Germany, commons which had been granted to the inhabitants; that now they were monopolized and held as private property to the total exclusion of the poor; that the lords had seized them under pretence, that they were only indulgencies, which former lords in times of security had granted for a little while to their tenants for pasturage only; that they were employed now only to maintain a great number of useless horses for luxury or for needless wars; that they reclaimed these commons, and did not allow this late prescription the value of a good title, and therefore they required the holders to restore them, unless they would rather choose to make a purchase of them, and in that case they engaged to settle the business on friendly and brotherly terms.

XI. The eleventh complains, that the demand of heriots is the most unjust and inhuman of all oppressions; that the affliction of the widow and children for the loss of their father and friend, appointed by Heaven to be their guardian, made no impression on the officers; that instead of pitying the survivors, and supplying the place of the deceased, they increased their wretchedness, by swallowing up all their property; they required therefore that the custom of claiming heriots should be utterly abolished.

XII. The last article says, that this memorial contains their present grievances; that they are not so obstinately attached to these articles, as not to give up any one on receiving conviction that it was contrary to the word of God; that they were ready to admit any additions agreeable to truth and scripture, tending to promote the glory of God, and the good of mankind; and that though this memorial contained a list of their present grievances, yet they did not mean by this to preclude the liberty of making such future remonstrances as might be found necessary.

These are the infernal tenets, the damnable anabaptistical errors, (garbled and recorded by their enemies too) which the Pedobaptists of all orders, from Luther to the present time, have thought fit to execrate under all the most monstrous names that malice and rage for persecution could invent. For almost three hundred years hath this crime of the Baptists been visited upon their descendants.

Thus we see that the Rustic War was not a wanton and heedless rebellion of unprincipled men, but was, on the contrary, a serious and patriotic attempt to throw off a cruel and excessive yoke, which could no longer be borne. "And had they succeeded, ten thousand tongues would have celebrated their praise. Indefatigable writers would have sifted every action to the bottom, tried the cause by rules of equity, examined the credibility of every witness, and would not have suffered improbable, contradictory, and even impossible tales, told by ignorant and interested men, to have seized the credit and honour, which are due to nothing but impartial truth. If the procuring of liberty for three hundred thousand wretched slaves, and their posterity, had been accompanied with some imperfections, and even with some censurable actions, the latter would have been attributed to an unhappy fatality in human revolutions, and in comparison with the benefits thrown into the great scale of human happiness, they would have diminished till they had totally disappeared."

Great political struggles have always been attended with acts more or less unjustifiable upon the principles of war, reason, or humanity. Many will attach themselves to large bodies of warriors, who voluntarily rise in defence of their rights, whom neither the voice of reason, nor the authority of generals can restrain from acts of violence and injustice. Many such acts were undoubtedly committed in different parts of Germany, by the wretched rustics, who had been provoked by enormous oppressions, to a high degree of resentment; but we may also conclude, that their censurable actions have been greatly exaggerated by a set of prejudiced and defaming historians.

We shall now go back to the beginning of these insurrections, and endeavour briefly to describe the progress of insurgents till they were defeated and dispersed.

In the spring of 1525, we are informed, that three hundred thousand men left off work, and assembled in the fields of Suabia, Thuringia, the Palatinate, and Alsace. They soon after published a manifesto, setting forth their grievances and stating their demands. Men in power viewed them as an ignorant herd, who might be easily brow-beaten out of their demands, and terrified into submission. Luther began to be greatly alarmed, for he found himself deeply implicated in the affair. Many pretended that they had received their notions of liberty from his writings, and that they were stimulated in their present attempts by his example of throwing off the papal yoke. Luther, in this critical situation, wrote four pieces on the subject of the threatening affairs. The first was an answer to the peasants' manifesto. The second was addressed to the German princes, and in it he taxes them with having caused all the present ills by their excessive tyranny. To this he added a third, addressed to both princes and peasants, setting forth the wickedness of tyrannical governors, and the calamities of seditious insurrections, and he advised both parties to settle their disputes, and be at peace for the public good of Germany. This was good advice, but neither party gave heed to it. The princes continued their oppressions and the peasants persisted in their demands, which they had determined to support, *peaceably* if they *could*, *forcibly* if they *must* ; and now they begun their operations. When Luther found nobody minded his papers, he drew up a fourth, addressed to the princes, in which he conjures them to unite their force to suppress sedition, to destroy these robbers and parricides, who had thrown off all regard for magistracy, &c. About this time, Mosheim informs us, " kings, princes, and sovereign states, exerted themselves to check these rebels and enthusiasts in their career, by issuing out first, severe edicts to restrain their violence, and by employing at length, capital punishments to conquer their obstinacy." But their number was too powerful to be easily restrained or soon reduced. In different places, under different leaders, they drove forward in those destructive measures always attendant on war. This army of the peasants was a promiscuous assemblage of various characters, some were Anabaptists, some Lutherans, some Catholicks, some christians, and some republicans, but the greater part, we have reason to suppose, had no fixed principles either in religion or politics, but were determined to throw off the oppressive yoke of their tyrannical masters.

They, it seems, first made themselves masters of Mulhausen, an imperial city in Alsace ; here they expelled the monks and magistrates, and elected new senators, of whom Muncer was one ; and it was in a pitched battle near this town that the peasants were defeated and Muncer was slain.

The populous city of Munster was taken by these revolutionists in 1533, and held by them about three years. " Munster is the capital city of the bishoprick so called in the circle of Westphalia. It is the largest of all the Westphalian bishopricks and yields the bishop, who is a prince of the empire, seventy thousand ducats a year. There are in the city five collegiate and six parish churches, a college belonging to the jesuits, a great number of convents, and other religious houses. The chapter consists of forty noblemen, and maintains seven regiments of soldiers."

Such was the state of this city, according to Robinson, before the late revolutions. Munster is rendered famous in the history of the Baptists, both by the censures of their enemies, and the apologies of their friends ; but after all that has been said on both sides, I am sorry to find that so imperfect an account has been given by either, of the memorable tragedy which was acted here, and which has been handed down to posterity by a thousand Pedo-baptist writers, as an everlasting monument of infamy to the Baptists, and a thundering memento against the dangerous principles of believer's baptism. At Munster was brought to a close the Rustic War, not by treaty, but by the defeat, and the indiscriminate slaughter of the rustics, and the utter extirpation of their confederacy. I find no description of the scenes, which were transacted here, except that given by Mosheim ; and as his account of the Rustic War is throughout peculiarly unfair, we have good reasons for concluding that his history of the Munster affair is of the same character. According to this prejudiced author, " certain Dutch Anabaptists chose this city for the scene of their horrid operations, and committed in it such deeds, as would surpass all credibility, were they not attested in a manner that excludes every degree of uncertainty. A handful of mad-men, under the guidance of John Matthison, John Bockhold, or John Leyden, and one Gerhard, made themselves masters of the populous city of Munster, deposed the magistrates, committed enormous crimes—made this city the seat of their New-Jerusalem, and proclaimed John of Leyden, who was a tailor, king of their new hierarchy." Thus Mosheim ascribes the whole of the Munster affair to a handful of mad Anabaptists. They must indeed have fought like the band of Leonidas to have taken this famous capital. No, it was not a handful of mad Anabaptists; it was a powerful, and probably the main division of the army of the peasants, that besieged and took this city, which henceforward became their principal place of rendezvous, and from which they sent forth agents and detachments to other places. What were the horrid crimes they committed we are not informed, but we may conclude they were such as are always attendant on war and conquest. They are complained of for deposing the magistrates, &c. This is truly a ridiculous charge. They must have been fools indeed, not to have taken the government of the city, which they had fairly conquered, out of the hands of their enemies, and put it in those of their friends. They made John Bockhold king or chief legislator. But what was there novel, or wicked, or ridiculous in this? Every one acquainted with the history of Germany, knows that it abounded with free imperial cities, which were independent of any foreign power, and were governed by their own legislators and laws. The peasants, in making Munster an independent sovereignty, acted in perfect conformity with the maxims and examples of their country, and they doubtless had sufficient reasons for making John of Leyden, though a tailor by trade, their chief magistrate. " But the reign," says Mosheim, " of this tailor king was transitory, and his end deplorable. For the city of Munster was, in the year 1536, retaken after a siege of fourteen months, by Count Waldeck, the bishop and sovereign of the place, &c." This worldly ecclesiastic was doubtless assisted by the other princes of Germany. John of Leyden was put to a most painful and ignominious death, the confederacy of the peasants was broken, and multitudes of them suffered death in the most cruel and tormenting forms. Vengeance and havock every where pursued those who had been any ways concerned in the Rustic War.

We shall now close with some general observations on this unhappy affair. We have thus seen that the Rustic War lasted about eleven years, and that the number of the first insurgents was three hundred thousand. Many of them were doubtless either persuaded or terrified soon to return to their former stations and employments. And we may reasonably suppose that according to the success or adversity which attended the measures of the peasants, so their number increased or diminished.

Mosheim has ascribed the whole of this unhappy war to the influence of religious fanaticism, and has cast the whole odium of it on the German Anabaptists. This statement is certainly both erroneous and unfair. That much fanaticism mingled with the operations of this war, and that many Anabaptists were concerned in it, we do not deny; but it was the freedom of their country, and not the defence of their creed, which led them to unite with the struggling peasants.

Dr. Isaac Milner, the brother, and continuator of the history of the late Joseph Milner, has touched upon the tumults of Germany, and his account, though by no means free from the prejudice of his party, is by far more candid and probable than Mosheim's. He acknowledges that " the causes of the Rustic War, or the war of the peasants, were *purely secular.*"*

A writer in the Encyclopedia observes, " It must be acknowledged that the rise of the numerous insurrections of this period ought not to be attributed to religious opinions. The first insurgents groaned under the most grievous oppressions. They took up arms principally in defence of their civil liberties; and of the commotions that took place, the Anabaptist leaders, viz. Muncer, Stubner, Stork, &c. seem rather to have availed themselves, than to have been the prime movers." This writer concludes that " a great part of the main body was Anabaptists;" this may be true when we consider in how vague and indefinite a sense the term was then used ; " that a great part also were Roman Catholicks, and a still greater of persons who had no religious opinions at all." " Bishop Jewel, in his defence of the Apology of the church of England in reply to Harding, &c. answers thus: The hundred thousand Boors in Germany of whom you speak, for the *greatest part*, were adversaries unto Luther, and under-

* Vol. V. p. 319.

stood no part of the gospel; but conspired together as they said against the cruelty and oppression of their lords," &c.*

Most writers compute the number of those, who perished in these insurrections, at a hundred thousand, and that they were nearly all Anabaptists. If this statement be correct, the German Anabaptists were literally a church militant, engaged in a very unsuccessful campaign. And this church was truly large, for besides the hundred thousand slain in war, many thousands were left to be dragooned, tortured, burnt, drowned, confined in prisons, and driven into exile. This statement gives the dippers much more than they ask. They do not pretend that there ever were at one time in Germany, any where near a hundred thousand advocates for their sentiments.

But Dr. Milner from Beausobre has made a statement which seems very likely to be near the truth. He supposes that this unfortunate war cost Germany the lives of more than fifty thousand men;† that is, of both sides, for many of the oppressors were slain, although the peasants were the greatest sufferers.

It is not our wish to justify acts of violence in men, by whatever name they are called, nor to apologize for the censurable acts of these rising peasants, whom oppression had made mad. We do not deny that many, who bore the name of Anabaptists, were found in their ranks. Many of them were doubtless such Anabaptists as we have found in Poland, who had rejected infant baptism, but who had never been baptized, nor were fit subjects for the ordinance. And multitudes, who were reputed Anabaptists, we have good reasons for believing, had no religious principles at all, but were so called by way of reproach, because they had adopted their notions of civil liberty. Although some of the measures pursued by the peasants cannot be justified, yet they set out in a righteous cause as their Manifesto shows. Baptist ministers were induced from this consideration, to encourage their attempts, to become chaplains in their armies, and this again induced many of their brethren to enlist under the standards of the strugglers for freedom. Many who were Baptists both in principle and practice, appear to have entertained the

* Ivimey in a note p. 561.   † Vol. V. p. 357.

erroneous opinion so prevalent at a certain time in England among those who were called fifth monarchy men, that dominion is founded in grace, that the pure church establishment to which they were aspiring, was to be under the protection and guidance of religious rulers, who were to found a pure christian republick, to be governed wholly by the laws of Christ. Those who had not imbibed this opinion, were induced to hope that some good would come out of the struggles of the peasants, and that the present commotions of Germany would settle down in some system favourable to their views. Many others doubtless united with the revolutionary party, either of their voluntary accord, or by the persuasion of their friends, without much reflection on the subject, only they knew their present condition was wretched, and they hoped that it might be made better in the end. But some of the Baptists of these times, it appears, were opposed to the Rustic War altogether. We are informed that a teacher by the name of Peter was beheaded at Amsterdam as guilty of the late insurrection, who had used his utmost endeavours to hinder it. But the whole crime of the civil war was laid to the charge of the Anabaptists, and all, who bore their name, whether they were such or not, were marked out as the objects of vengeance and death. If they had not taken a part in the insurrections, it was considered their principles lead to them, and therefore they were every where extirpated with fire and sword.

But why has the whole balance of the tumults in Germany been always cast upon the Baptists? It has been their unhappiness to have some hand in other scenes of a similar nature. Many Baptists were in Ziska's army in Bohemia, which besieged towns and took them, pulled down monasteries, expelled monks, and seized upon their revenues, and dealt out destruction and death to all who opposed them. In the army of Cromwell were many who had espoused the Baptist principles, and two of the regicides of Charles the first, viz. Harrison and Hutchinson, became Baptists after the death of the king. Harrison was at one time but a little below the Protector in authority and influence, Hutchinson was governor of Nottingham. Baptists were in the Parliament, in the navy, and army of the Commonwealth. Some were also engaged in the ill-fated expedition of the Duke of Monmouth, the rival of James the second. But for all these overt acts they have received a public pardon. Why have they not been charged with being the promoters of the civil wars in England, of the tumults of the commonwealth, and the murder of the English monarch? This would be as just as to charge them with being the authors of the insurrections in Germany. Why have not historians dealt as fairly in the case of Germany, as in that of England, and given to each party its due proportion of blame?

The following seems the only satisfactory solution of this mysterious affair. All parties are anxious to clear themselves of the reproach of an unsuccessful and unpopular enterprize.* Such an one was that of the German peasants. The Catholick historians of the times excuse all their brethren, who were concerned in it, and lay the whole blame at the door of Luther and the reformation. The Lutheran historians, from whom the English took their accounts, endeavoured to clear themselves by accusing the Anabaptists of being the prime movers and principal promoters of the insurrections. The papists were doubtless very unfair and erroneous, in charging the reformation with being the direct cause of the troubles, wars, and commotions, of which it was certainly no more than the indirect and innocent occasion; but they were not mistaken when they charged the Lutherans with being deeply engaged in the Rustic War. The Lutherans have conceded

* The American war terminated in a glorious manner, and all who were concerned in it were loaded with applauses, and hailed as the deliverers of their country. But the grievances of the American people were trifling compared with those of the German peasants But suppose the fortune of war had turned against th struggling Americans, how different would have been their fate! What, in such a case, would have been said of those Baptist brethren, who enlisted under the revolutionary standard, whose eulogium was pronounced by the immortal Washington? What character would have been given of those ministers, who promoted the war by every means in their power, who became chaplains in the armies, and dwelt in the camps of the warriors? Backus, Gano, Stillman, Manning, Smith, Rogers, and others, instead of being the subjects of eulogium for the part they took in the war, would have been loaded with infamy, and branded with the odious names of rebels, fanaticks, and the ring-leaders of a seditious multitude. They would have been the Muncers, Stubners, Storks, Bockholds, Phiffers, and Knipperdolings of America.

The American people took up arms in defence of their civil rights, but it is well known that many of our Baptist brethren had their eye upon advantages of a religious nature, which actually arose to them, especially in New-England, out of the principles and agitations of the war, as will be more fully illustrated in the next chapter.

that some of their party perverted and misconstrued the reformers' doctrine of christian liberty, and flocked to the standard of the rebels. But the papists are not content with these concessions, they have constantly laid the WHOLE mischief of this intestine dissension at the door of Luther and his disciples, &c. " This," say they, " is the fruit of the new doctrine ! This is the fruit of Luther's gospel !"*

It is certain that the disturbances, in the very city of Munster, were begun by a Pedobaptist minister of the Lutheran persuasion, whose name was Bernard Rotman or Rothman ; that he was assisted in his endeavours by other ministers of the same persuasion ; and that they began to stir up tumults, that is, teach revolutionary principles, a year before the Anabaptist ring-leaders, as they are called, visited the place.†

These things the papists knew, and they failed not to improve them to their advantage. They uniformly insisted that Luther's doctrine led to rebellion, that his disciples were the prime movers of the insurrections, and they also asserted that a hundred and thirty thousand Lutherans perished in the Rustic War.‡

Such were the aspersions cast upon the Lutheran party by the papists. And though many Catholicks were engaged in the war, yet the Lutherans knew it would be unavailing to retort upon them ; for whatever resistance the oppressed Catholicks had shown, the Catholick doctrine did not lead to it, for that taught nothing but blind and dumb submission to every law of their superiors, whether civil or religious. But as the Anabaptists were the advocates for liberty, and as many of them had taken a part in the war which they hoped would set them free, the Lutherans found it easy to cast all the blame upon them. And they having no one to tell their story as it was, nor put in any plea for them, which could be heard, the Munster affair, as it was first related by the Lutheran historians, has been transmitted from one generation to another, without any correction or amendment ; it has been transcribed by a thousand Pedobaptist pens, as a salutary

---

* Milner, Vol. V. p. 320. Ibid, p. 327.

† Ivimey, p. 16. Mosheim in a note, Vol. IV. p. 438.

‡ Milner, Vol. V. p. 327.

memento for the seditious dippers ; it is the dernier resort of every slanderous declaimer against them ; it is the great gun, the *ultima ratio* of every disputant, which they keep in reserve against the time of need.

But why all this din about Munster and the War of the Peasants, since every body knows, who knows any thing of the matter, that it was not a quarrel about baptism, but about the feudal system; that it was not for water, but in opposition to the horrid oppressions of the princes, that the German peasants rose.

Why are not the Independents and the Congregationalists their offspring, visited from age to age with the deeds of a few of their zealous predecessors, and of the promiscuous multitude, who attached themselves to their cause, and bore their name ? They were accused by their enemies of every thing horrid and flagitious. " The most eminent English writers, not only among the patrons of episcopacy, but even among those very Presbyterians, with whom they are now united, have thrown out against them the bitterest accusations and the severest invectives, that the warmest imagination could invent. They have not only been represented as delirious, mad, fanatical, illiterate, factious, and ignorant both of natural and revealed religion, but also as abandoned to all kinds of wickedness and sedition, and as the only authors of the odious parricide committed on the person of Charles I. Rapin represents the Independents under such horrid colours, that were his portrait just, they could not deserve to enjoy the light of the sun or breathe the free air of Britain, much less to be treated with indulgence and esteem by those who have the cause of virtue at heart."*

But Mosheim could discover the tongue of slander in these representations ; he could apologize for the Independents so far, that Dr. Maclaine has thought it necessary to give him a check. He could, in giving their history, adopt " the wise and prudent maxim, not to judge of the spirit and principles of a sect, from the actions or expressions of a handful of its members, but from the manners, customs, opinions, and behaviour of the generality of those who compose it, &c." But no such things could be thought of in treating of the German Anabaptists.

* Mosheim, vol. v. p. 381—2. Ibid. p. 382.

Why this partiality in cases so exactly alike? The answer is plain, the Independents held to infant baptism, which the Anabaptists rejected.

The respectable body of Presbyterians have at different times been loaded with the foulest aspersions. A certain writer observes, that "the Presbyterians in England, in the meridian of their strength, differed from popery only as a musket differs from a cannon, or as a kept mistress from a street-walking prostitute." Millot, in speaking of the Parliament army, says " it breathed only the fervour of Presbyterianism and the rage of battle; and knew no pleasures but *prayer* and *military* duty." We forbear to select examples of the kind, and these we have related with no other view, than to show the reader the impropriety of judging of the character of a sect or party from the accounts of its adversaries.

We shall now close our observations on the affair of Munster. The sum and substance of the matter as represented by the adversaries of the Baptists, is, that they had no existence in the christian world until the beginning of the sixteenth century; that then they originated all at once, in a stormy, seditious period, out of the scum of the reformation, and increased so rapidly, that in a very short time, they led about a quarter of a million into the field to defend and propagate their opinions, and that a hundred thousand of them were slain ! ! ! The sum and substance of the matter as understood and conceded by the Baptists, we have already stated. We have shown before, that our denomination did not originate with the tumults of Germany, but with John the Baptist, in the land of Palestine, fifteen hundred years before they happened. It is hoped that no Pedobaptist will in future follow us with the riot of Munster, or the seditions of Germany; but if they do, we can only inform them, that we shall consider, as we always have done, that for the want of argument they resort to slander.

We have thus endeavoured to give a general view of our Baptist brethren in countries abroad and in times of old, and we have seen that they have generally been described by all historians, as a dangerous set of men, whose principles lead to rebellion and sedition, and that for this reason they have been proscribed in some governments, banished from others, and in others burnt and drowned, and allowed to live no where only as a matter of favour and indulgence. Why should they thus be universally abhorred and persecuted? Baptism is a thing so inoffensive in itself, that if it were repeated every month, no serious consequences could follow to any one, except to the person baptized. There must be something more than water in this affair; and that something is, that the Baptists have held from time immemorial that the civil magistrate hath no right to give or enforce law in matters of religion and conscience. This principle has been at the bottom of all their sufferings in every age. And this principle hath subjected the Quakers and Independents, properly so called, to the terrible persecutions, which they have at different times endured. The Baptists, Independents and Quakers have each their peculiarities, but they are the best qualified to live together of any three sects in christendom; for they all separate religion from civil patronage, they are each willing that every one should be his own judge in matters of conscience, and all that either of them has ever asked of civil government is to be let alone.

This article has been extended to a much greater length than was first intended; but it is hoped that it will not, on that account, be the less acceptable to the reader. We shall now turn our attention to the American shore.

CHAP. VII.

A GENERAL HISTORY OF THE BAPTISTS IN AMERICA.

EPOCH FIRST.

IN the Proposals for this work, it was suggested that the history of the American Baptists would be preceded by four Epochs or General Divisions, in which their progress and circumstances would be comprehensively related in a chronological order. These Epochs were intended to be nothing more than brief compendiums of the history of our brethren from time to time. The preparation of them has been deferred until the history of each State has been made out, and as most historical facts of importance have been already related, they will be shorter than it was at first expected.

The first Epoch was to begin with the banishment of Roger Williams, and to end with 1707, when the Philadelphia Association was formed. But it has been thought best under this head to go back to the discovery of America, to give a brief account of the settlement of its different parts, and to take a general view as we go along of its religious affairs.

In the year 1492, October the 12th, this part of the world, since called America, was discovered by Christopher Columbus, a Genoese, in the service of the king of Spain. The first land made by this adventurer, was one of the Bahama Islands, to which he gave the name of San Salvador. Thus a new world was discovered, in which much cruelty and oppression has been practised, especially by the merciless Spaniards; in which much liberty and happiness has been enjoyed; and in which there have been many signal displays of the grace of God. Settlements were made in many parts of the American continent before any were effected in that portion of it which is now included in the United States.

Discovery of America. 267

The following table, taken from Morse's Geography, exhibits in one view the settlements of the different States, and the names of those by whom they were effected.

Names of places.	When settled.	By whom.
Quebec,	1608	By the French.
Virginia,	1610 or 1611	By Lord De la War.
Newfoundland,	June, 1610	By Governour John Guy.
New-York, New-Jersey,	about 1614	By the Dutch.
Plymouth,	1620	By part of Mr. Robinson's congregation.
New-Hampshire,	1623	By a small English colony near the mouth of Piscataqua river.
Delaware, Pennsylvania,	1627	By the Swedes and Finns.
Massachusetts Bay,	1628	By Capt. John Endicot and company.
Maryland,	1633	By Lord Baltimore, with a colony of Roman Catholicks.
Connecticut,	1635	By Mr. Fenwick, at Saybrook, near the mouth of Connecticut river.
Rhode-Island,	1635	By Mr. Roger Williams and his persecuted brethren.
New-Jersey,	1664	Granted to the Duke of York by Charles II. and made a distinct government, and settled some time before this by the English.
South-Carolina,	1669	By Governour Sayle.
Pennsylvania,	1682	By William Penn, with a colony of Quakers.
North-Carolina,	about 1728	Erected into a separate government. Settled before by the English.
Georgia,	1732	By General Oglethorp.
Kentucky,	1773	By Col. Daniel Boon.
Vermont,	baout 1764	By emigrants from Connecticut and other parts of N. England.
Territory N. W. of Ohio river,	1787	By the Ohio and other companies.
Tennessee,	1789	Became a distinct government, settled many years before.

The above dates are mostly from the periods when the first permanent settlements were made."

By this table it appears that a permanent settlement was effected in Virginia, ten years before the fathers of New

England landed at Plymouth. Some temporary settlements had been made in the country about twenty years before.

Most of the first settlers of America were merely worldly adventurers, who were induced to encounter the dangers of a distant voyage, and the hardships of a wilderness from the prospects of temporal advantages. Those who came from England, which was by far the greatest number, were for the most part Episcopalians. There were however, intermixed in almost all the different companies of emigrants, dissenters of different names, and among them we have reason to believe there were of the Baptists a few.

It does not appear that there were in any of the colonies, any religious establishments, which acquired much permanency, or that carried their acts of intolerance to any considerable degree, except in Virginia, Massachusetts, and Connecticut. The Episcopal church was the established religion of the Carolinas, but it had neither the spirit nor power of persecuting dissenters, to any great extent. Maryland was founded by Roman Catholicks, but they, different from their brethren in the old world, were always tolerant and mild. Pennsylvania was founded by Quakers, who, like the Baptists in Rhode-Island, would never establish any religious laws, and of course there could be no religious persecutions. New-York and New-Jersey were settled by a mixture of people of many nations and religions, but it is probable a majority of the settlers were Episcopalians. I do not find that there ever was any religious establishment in New-Jersey; but I am inclined to think that Episcopacy was for a time the established religion of New-York. Mr. Wichenden of Providence, Rhode-Island, was imprisoned there four months for preaching the gospel, sometime before the year 1669; and in the year 1728, the Baptist meeting-house, then newly built, was licensed and entered as the toleration act required. These things scent of Babylon, and indicate an ecclesiastical establishment, but I do not find that it was prosecuted with much rigour, and it has now been so long done away, that there are probably but few who know that it ever existed.

Episcopacy took deep root in the strong soil of Virginia, and an account of its spirit, its measures, and end, will be given in the history of the Baptists in that State. Rhode-

In what States Religious Establishments were formed. 269

Island has always from first to last maintained, and gloried in maintaining, liberty of conscience, in the strictest and most unqualified sense ; and accordingly none of its records are stained with laws to regulate religious worship, or with acts to oppress or favour dissenters.

New-Hampshire and Vermont have done but little in the outrageous business of distressing the persons and spoiling the goods of dissenters ; and the newer States have altogether let alone this wretched work. We must now come to Massachusetts and Connecticut, and with pain we must relate that these States, which were planted by a religious Colony, and which have been the nurseries of much piety and virtue, have, notwithstanding, been the most distinguished of any in the Union, for intolerance and oppression. In these States, ecclesiastical establishments have taken the deepest root of any part of the American empire ; they have been defended by the civil power, and have manifested an unwavering and obstinate perseverance in enforcing their iniquitous maxims, and in encroaching on the liberties, and despoiling the goods of dissenters.

The spirit of the church was sometimes high in Virginia, and for a while persecution raged with violence ; but it was carried on chiefly by a band of unprincipled churchmen, whose main object seems to have been, to molest the persons and disturb the meetings of dissenters.

But the New-England persecutors have taken generally a different course. They have had their eyes on the goods of dissenters more than on their persons. If they would but pay their parish taxes, they might worship when and how they pleased. But if any one was so heretical as to refuse his money towards building a meeting-house within the parish lines, which might happen to encircle him, or to support a preacher which he never chose, nor wished to hear, then he must look out for writs, constables, sheriffs, courts, priests and lawyers, stripes, prisons, and forfeitures, and the whole sanctimonious procession of ecclesiastical tormentors. So rigorous were the New-Englanders in enforcing their taxing laws, that Esther White of Raynham, about thirty miles from Boston, was thrown into prison for a ministerial tax of *eight-pence*, which she refused to pay, because she had separated from the parish worship. After lying in prison almost a year, she was let out without paying the tax, by the religious gentry, who put her in.*

The American war was peculiarly auspicious to the cause of religious liberty in Massachusetts, and the other Colonies, where religious establishments were enforced with rigour. All denominations unitedly engaged in resisting the demands of Great-Britain. But her demands were no more unreasonable nor unjust, than those which the predominant party, whether Congregational or Episcopalian, made on dissenters. The Baptists and other dissenters did not fail to make a proper use of this argument. And although many attempted to explain it away, yet many others saw and acknowledged its force.

Many of the first settlers of New-England were pious and worthy men, among them however were many of a different character ; but they all united in building up the New-England church establishments.

The first Pedobaptist churches here required the candidates for admission, to give a verbal account of their religious experience. But in process of time they were permitted to give in their relations in writing, and this practice is still continued by those churches which require any experience at all. The ancient church of Plymouth changed their way of receiving members from verbal to written relations in 1705.† Others had probably done it before.

The great mistake of the New-England fathers lay in taking the laws of Moses for the commands of Christ, and blending the Jewish and Christian dispensations together. And indeed, from this source have originated all the evils which have overrun the christian world, and deluged it with blood. By this means, unholy men are entrusted with the regulation of religious concerns. They know nothing of its nature, they feel nothing of its power, and under their dominion the saints of God have always had occasion to say, " for thy sake we are killed all the day long."

The New-England fathers were certainly men of understanding, and yet many of their legislative acts and eccle-

* Backus' Church History, Vol. II. p. 194.   † Vol. I. p. 47. Vol. II. p. 29.

siastical proceedings were absurd and ridiculous in the extreme.

In 1638, the Assembly of Massachusetts passed a law to compel excommunicated persons to seek to be restored to the churches which had cast them out. " Whosoever shall stand excommunicated for the space of six months, without labouring what in him or her lieth to be restored, such person shall be presented to the Court of Assistants, and there proceeded with by fine, imprisonment, banishment, or further for the good behaviour, as their contempt and obstinacy upon full hearing shall deserve."*

In 1656, a famous dispute arose upon this question, Whether the children of those, who are not immediate members of churches, should be baptized. The Connecticut people took the lead in this affair. They sent twenty one questions to their brethren in Massachusetts respecting it; an ecclesiastical assembly was called, which set fifteen days, in deliberating upon this weighty matter. They answered the Connecticut questions, but did not settle the dispute. It raged throughout the country a number of years, and many churches were divided by it. A considerable party contended that if parents who were not church members, should own the covenant, which their parents made for them when they were ☞*initiated into the church*, then they should have the privilege of getting their children baptized.† And in this way originated what is called *the half way covenant*, which is still practised upon by many Congregational churches. What a pity, that any anxious parent should have so much trouble about the christening of his dear babes. If it is such a peculiar advantage, as their ministers contend for, it is certainly hard, that any poor child should be debarred from it. While this dispute was going on, some, it appears, found a way of getting rid of all difficulties, by having *the children baptized* on their grand-parents account; but it was contended on the other hand, that in such a case, they would be bound to take the charge of their education. Such frivolous controversies were agitated by the renowned fathers of New-England. They arose

---

* Backus, Vol. I. p. 98.
† This statement is paraphrased a little, but the sense is retained.

not from a want of ability in the men, but from the absurdity of the principles, which they had adopted.

The witchcraft affair was the most melancholy and degrading of any ever acted in New-England. It began in 1692, in the house of Mr. Parris, a Congregational minister of Salem, where two girls of ten or eleven years of age were taken with uncommon and unaccountable complaints. A consultation of physicians was called, one of whom was of opinion that they were bewitched. An Indian woman, a servant in the family, was accused of being the witch. From small beginnings, the bewitching distemper spread through several parts of the province, till the prisons were scarcely capable of containing the number of the accused. This distressing affair lasted about fifteen months, nineteen persons were executed, one was prest to death, and eight more were condemned; the whole number amounted to twenty eight, of whom above a third part were members of some of the Pedobaptist churches in New-England. Among the sufferers was a Mr. Burroughs, formerly minister of Salem.

The New-England people at first supported their ministers in a voluntary way, probably by weekly contributions. But in 1638, a law was made that every inhabitant, who would not voluntarily contribute his portion, &c. should be compelled thereto by assessment and distress, to be levied by the constable or other officer of the town as in other cases. This was the beginning of that iniquitous policy which has caused the Baptists in New-England so much vexation and distress.

The beginning of our brethren in America will be related under the head of each respective State, and the banishment of Roger Williams may be found under that of Rhode-Island. The church which he founded at Providence, in 1639, was the first of the Baptist denomination in the American continent. The first church in Newport, Rhode Island, founded in 1644, by Dr. John Clark, was the second; the second in that town, formed in 1656, was the third; the church in Swansea, begun by John Miles, in 1663, was the fourth; and the first in Boston, founded first in Charlestown, in 1665, by Thomas Gould, was the fifth. In forty years from the founding of the last mentioned church, there arose eleven more in the following order : Seventh-Day, Newport, 1671 ; Tiverton, Rhode Island, 1685 ; Middletown, New-Jersey, 1688 ; Pennepeck, now called Lower-Dublin, Pennsylvania, 1689 ; Piscataway, New-Jersey, the same year; Charleston, South-Carolina, 1690 ; Cohansey, New-Jersey, 1691 ; 2d Swansea, 1693 ; Welsh-Tract, Delaware, 1701 ; Groton, Connecticut, 1705 ; Seventh-Day, Piscataway, New-Jersey, 1707 ; The first church in Philadelphia was in reality formed in 1698, although it has generally been dated in 1746, when it was re-organized.

Thus in almost a hundred years after the first settlement of America, only seventeen Baptist churches had arise in it. Nine of them were in New-England. Of these seventeen churches, only four, that is, the three in Massachusetts, and the one in Connecticut, were put to any trouble on account of their religious principles ; and of these four, the one at Boston felt most of the hard hand of civil coercion. This church was treated in a most oppressive and abusive manner, as will be shown in the history of Massachusetts.

EPOCH SECOND.

In 1707, the Philadelphia Association was formed of the five following churches, viz. Pennepeck, Middletown, Piscataqua, Cohansey, and Welch Tract. This Association was the first in America ; it has always maintained a regular and respectable standing, and has been from its commencement to the present time one of the most important institutions of the kind.

From 1707 till 1740, about twenty new churches were raised up in different parts of the United States ; some were of an Arminian cast ; but most of them adopted the Calvinistic faith. Three or four became extinct in a few years, but the rest remain till the present time.

During the period under consideration, no very remarkable event appears to have occurred. The churches in New-England, except those in Rhode-Island, were persecuted and fleeced ; those in other parts were left at liberty to serve God, and dispose of their property as they pleased.

EPOCH THIRD.

About 1740, a very powerful work of grace began in New England, and prevailed much in other parts of the United States. It was, by way of derision, called the *New Light Stir*. This work commenced under the ministry of that honoured servant of God, the famous George Whitefield, who was then travelling as a flaming itinerant along the American coast. "The most remarkable things," says a late writer, "that attended the preaching of Mr. Whitefield was the power of the Holy Ghost." Multitudes were awakened by his means and brought to bow to the sceptre of Immanuel. Many ministers opposed his course, but many others caught his zeal, ran to and fro with the tidings of salvation, and knowledge was almost every where increased. This work began generally among the Pedobaptists, and where they opposed it, separation ensued. And here originated the term Separates, which was first applied to Pedobaptist and afterwards to Baptist churches. Separate churches were formed all over New-England. In many parts of the country there was hardly a town or parish in which they were not to be found. Some pushed on their zealous measures to an enthusiastic extreme, but most of them acted a sober and rational part; their views were highly evangelical, and their maxims of gospel discipline were generally clear and consistent. They permitted all to exhort, who had gifts to edify their brethren; they ordained ministers of those who were instructed in the mysteries of the kingdom, whether they were learned or not. They took the Bible alone for their guide, and of course, Baptist principles soon prevailed amongst them. Very singular scenes were soon exhibited in New-England. Pedobaptists were seen persecuting their brethren, and casting them into prison because they were too religious The clergy of Connecticut determined that the *New Light Stir* was not *according to law;* they therefore stimulated their rulers to attempt its regulation. A law was actually made to prohibit one minister from going into the parish of another, to preach and exhort the people, unless he were particularly invited. Upon this law a number of their own ministers were prosecuted, and Mr afterwards Dr. Finley, President of Princeton College, New-Jersey, was transported as a vagrant person, from one constable to another, out of the bounds of the land of *steady habits*.

We have already observed that Baptist principles soon began to prevail among the Pedobaptist Separates. All their doctrine tended that way, and those who followed it whither it led embraced believers' baptism. Many Baptist churches arose out of those Separate societies, and the late venerable Backus of Middleborough, Hastings of Suffield, and a number of other Baptist ministers, were at first of their connexion.

Towards the conclusion of the American war, and for a number of years subsequent to the termination of that serious conflict, there were very extensive revivals of religion in different parts of the land, and Baptist principles almost every where prevailed. In the year 1780, according to Mr. Backus, there were not less than two thousand persons baptized in the New-England States only. In ten years, beginning with 1780, and ending with 1789, considerably over two hundred churches were organized in different parts of the United States. During this period a number of ministers, and with them a considerable number of brethren, fell in with Elhanan Winchester's notion of Universal Restoration. The rage for this doctrine prevailed for a time to a considerable extent; but it was at length found to be easier to let sinners down into a disciplinary purgatory, than it was to get them out again, and this visionary scheme is now generally exploded by all, among the Baptists at least, who profess any regard for gospel truth. Those ministers who embraced it, generally descended to other errors of a blasting nature, or else sunk into obscurity and insignificance. Mr. Winchester, the author or rather reviver of it in modern times, was for a while a very popular preacher among the Baptists. He was indeed in some respects, and particularly in memory, a prodigy of nature, and his talents and address were such, that he was sure to command followers and applause of some kind or other, wherever he went, and whatever he preached. His theory of Universalism was borrowed from a German author, to which he added some things from the reveries of his own eccentric imagination. His scheme appears never to have been well digested, and it is thought by many, that he would have abandoned it, had it not been for the difficulty of saying, *I was mistaken.* But he died rather suddenly in the midst of his singular career, and those, who knew him best, entertain different opinions, respecting his acquaintance with the religion of the heart.

In 1790, John Asplund published his first Register of the Baptist denomination in America. This singular man had, in eighteen months, travelled about seven thousand miles, chiefly on foot, to collect materials for this work. It was a new attempt of the kind in America, and is as correct as could be expected. By this it appears, there were, at the date of it, in the United States, and in the Territories, eight hundred and sixty eight churches, eleven hundred and thirty two ministers, including those who were not ordained, and sixty-four thousand nine hundred and seventy-five members.

EPOCH FOURTH.

Mr. Asplund continued travelling after he published his first Register, until 1794, when he published a second. By this it appears, that our brethren in some States had increased greatly, in others they remained pretty much as they were in 1790. Since Asplund published his last Register, a number of computations have been made of the extent of the Baptist interest in America, but no list of the churches has been attempted, until it was undertaken by the author of this work. It will be inserted at the end of the second volume.

Since the close of the war, not many of our brethren have been troubled on account of their religious opinions. In Connecticut and Massachusetts, they are in many cases still obliged to lodge certificates, &c. and by complying with this small but mortifying requisition, they may remain unmolested, and be entirely excused from all imposts of a religious nature.

Formerly, the opposers of the Baptists reasoned continually against their mode of baptizing, but this is now so generally acknowledged to be scriptural, that they have turned their whole force against what they are pleased to call *close communion.*

It is doubted whether any considerable number of the Baptists would be admitted to the Pedobaptist communion, if they were disposed for it; but they may safely offer them the privilege, because they know beforehand that they will not accept it. But why should we be continually reproached for a practice, which arises not from the want of affection towards christians of other denominations, but from our principles of the pre-requisites to communion? We believe that none have a right to partake of the Lord's Supper, until they are baptized ; nothing, in our opinion, short of immersion, is baptism; we cannot, therefore, consistently commune with those who have only been sprinkled. We have a right to believe the two first propositions, and we must take the liberty to practise upon the third, all opposition notwithstanding. Many Pedobaptists have acknowledged, that we cannot with consistency do otherwise, and have therefore ceased to reproach us.

Out of the *New Light Stir* arose a considerable number of churches, which adopted the plan of open communion. The Groton conference in Connecticut was at first founded altogether of churches of this opinion. But very few of these open communion churches remain ; some were split to pieces by the embarrassing policy, and others have adopted the practice of communing with baptized believers only. The zealous New-Lights kept together, as long as they could ; but opposite principles about baptism, necessarily lead them to divide into distinct communities. Most of those, which did not become Baptists, have fallen in with the parish churches, so that very few of the ancient Separate churches remain.

Believer's baptism by immersion has prevailed much in the United States, within ten or twenty years past. Multitudes of the Methodists have adopted it, and not a few of the Congregational ministers in New-England have condescended to go into the water with those candidates, who could be contented with nothing short of immersion. In Virginia and the southern States, there has been a great schism in the Methodist church. A large party has come off, which denominate themselves *Christians*. A similar party has separated from the Presbyterians and Methodists in Kentucky, and the western States, and a great number of these *Christian* people have lately been buried in baptism.

On the whole it appears, that baptism is fast returning to its primitive mode. A general conviction seems to be prevailing, that infant sprinkling is an invention of men, and ought to be laid aside; and that believers are the only subjects of the baptismal rite, and that immersion is the only way in which it ought to be administered. Of late years a considerable number of ministers of the Pedobaptist order, have come over to the Baptist side; some whole churches, and many parts of others have done the same; and we look forward to the time, when there shall be with the saints of God, but *one Lord, one faith, and one baptism.*

CHAP. VIII.

NOVA-SCOTIA AND NEW-BRUNSWICK.

THESE two British provinces occupy a large extent of territory to the east and north-east of the District of Maine. There are now, in both of them, upwards of forty Baptist churches, most of which have been organized within the course of twenty years past.

At the close of the French war, about fifty years ago, many families emigrated from New-England, and settled in different parts of these two provinces, which, at that time, were all included under the name of Nova-Scotia. Among these emigrants were some Baptists, and from that period there have always been a few of the denomination in the country.

In 1776, and a few succeeding years, there was a very great attention to the things of religion in Nova-Scotia; the work was promoted chiefly by a zealous young preacher, whose name was Henry Alline, whose history will be more fully related in its proper place. This work, in some respects, resembled the New-Light Stir in Whitefield's time. By the labours of Henry Alline and his zealous associates, many churches were formed of the Congregational order; most of them, however, have now become extinct, and Baptist churches have arisen in their stead.

For most of the historical facts respecting the Baptist interest in Nova-Scotia, I am indebted to Mr. Edward Manning, pastor of the Church at Cornwallis. Some sketches have, however, been forwarded by Messrs. Burton and Dimock ; some verbal communications were made by Mr. Ries, now on a mission to New-Orleans, and a few facts have been ascertained from Backus' history and Leland's M. S. S.; but most of the following statements are made upon the authority of Mr. Manning, who has taken much pains to furnish materials for this work.

According to the best information, the first Baptist church, which ever existed in either of these provinces, was transported and established in the following manner.

In the year 1763, immediately after the conclusion of the French war, Nathan Mason and wife, Thomas Lewis and wife, Oliver Mason and wife, and a sister by the name of Experience Baker, all of the 2d church in Swansea, Bristol county, Mass. Benjamin Mason and wife, Charles Seamans and wife, and Gilbert Seamans and wife, from some of the neighbouring churches, resolved on removing to Nova-Scotia. And with a view to their spiritual benefit, these thirteen persons were formed into a church, on the 21st of April, 1763, and Nathan Mason was ordained their pastor. Soon after, this little church sailed in a body for Nova-Scotia, and settled at a place now called Sackville in New-Brunswick.* Here they continued almost eight years, enjoying many spiritual blessings, and witnessing much of the goodness of the Lord, in this new and remote situation. Elder Mason laboured here with good success, and the little church increased to about 60 members, and Mr. Job Seamans, formerly pastor of the church in Attleborough, Mass. now of that of New-London, N. H. was converted and began to preach among them. But the lands and government not meeting their

* This account is found in Backus' History, vol. iii. p. 146. Mr. B. says, this emigrant church settled at the head of the Bay of Fundy ; but Mr. Manning assures me, that Mr. Mason settled at Sackville, which is on the Cumberland Bay. But still, both of these statements may be correct. Mr. Backus is general, Mr. Manning particular. As near as I can undertand by maps, at the head of the great Bay of Fundy, are two other smaller Bays ; one is called the Bason of Minas, and the other Cumberland Bay. Mr. Mason and his company, therefore, sailed up the Bay of Fundy to its head, and then entered the Bay of Cumberland, and on its north side made their settlement. The place was then called Tantarramar.

approbation, and finding themselves uncomfortable in other respects, in 1771 the founders of the emigrating church with Elder Mason removed back again to Massachusetts, and settled at a place called New-Providence, now in the township of Cheshire, in Berkshire county.

This account of Elder Mason's success in Nova-Scotia, was furnished some years ago by Mr. John Leland of Cheshire, which I found among Mr. Backus' papers. What became of the converts, whom Mr. Mason left behind, I do not find; but it is probable that they were scattered, and the church broken up after the founder had left them. Some further account of the Baptists in this place will be given in its due order.

HORTON. Not long after the settlement of the church at Sackville, an Elder Moulton from one of the New-England States, probably from Massachusetts, began to preach at Horton. His preaching was attended with success, and in a short time a church was formed consisting of Baptists and Congregationalists. What became of Mr. Moulton I do not find; but the church did not enjoy much prosperity, until it was revived under the ministry of Henry Alline. This zealous minister was cordially received among them, and the church adopted his maxims of discipline. They travelled but a short time, however, in fellowship with his New-Light connexion, before they made choice of a Mr. Piersons, a native of England, for their minister, who induced them to give up their mixed communion plan, and settled them on consistent ground. But in a short time, by the influence of one of their deacons, they broke down all their bars, and again admitted unbaptized persons to their communion. In this practice they continued until 1809, when a reformation was again effected, which is likely to be permanent.

About the year 1790, Elder Piersons removed to Hopewell, New-Brunswick, where he died shortly after.

David George, in speaking of Horton church, (Rippon's Register, vol. I. p. 481) mentions that a Mr. Scott was their minister. He probably succeeded Mr. Piersons, and continued with them but a short time. But I can gain no further account of him.

A few years after Mr. Piersons' removal, the church made choice of Elder Theodore S. Harding, for their pastor, in which office he continues to the present time. He had been a Methodist preacher, but was baptized and ordained by Mr. Burton of Halifax, soon after his settlement in that city.

NEWPORT.—This town received its name from Newport on Rhode-Island, from which most of the planters of it emigrated. While Mr. John Sutton was in Nova-Scotia, he preached some time in Newport and baptized a few persons; but he soon left the country, and returned to New-Jersey. Shubal Dimock is said to have been one of the principal promoters of religion in this town. He was a native of Mansfield in Connecticut, and was brought up a Presbyterian. But when he was brought into the light of the gospel, he found himself under the necessity of dissenting from the parish worship, for which he was oppressed and plundered, and this oppression lead him to seek an asylum elsewhere. Accordingly in 1760, he removed to Nova-Scotia, and settled at Falmouth, where he tarried about a year. He then removed to Newport, where he spent the remainder of his days. He became a Baptist about the year 1775. He was a man of eminent piety, and occasionally preached. His eldest son Daniel was a Baptist in sentiment before he left Connecticut, but was not baptized till he settled in Nova-Scotia, when that rite was administered to him by Mr. Sutton about 1763. This man was also a preacher, and preached until within a few days of his death. Joseph Dimock, pastor of the church in Chester, is his oldest son.

The two Dimocks, Shubal and his son Daniel, united with the church in Horton, but laboured much to promote religion in their own town. But it does not appear that any Baptist church was formed here until the year 1800. The father died about ten years before this period, and the son about four years after it. Mixed communion was the prevailing custom among most of the Nova-Scotia Baptists, when the church in this town was formed, and it fell in with the practice, continued it a short time, and then gave it up.*

* I have given the history of this church a place here, for I supposed it was amongst the oldest in the country. Morgan Edwards, in a Catalogue of American churches, which he wrote in 1764, mentions one in this town. Mr. Edwards probably had his information from Mr. Sutton, who had preached in the place. But since writing the account, Mr. Manning has informed me

The Newport church has waded through many trials, from its disputes respecting the terms of communion, but more on account of the ill conduct of its late pastor, William Delany, whose labours were, for a while, attended with much success, but who, a short time since, fell into the sin of drunkenness, and was excommunicated from the church. This shipwreck of their pastor, by causing divisions, had like to have destroyed their visibility as a church; but they have since recovered, in a good degree, from this painful shock, and although they have no settled minister, bid fair to be one of the most flourishing churches in the province.

CORNWALLIS.—This church is situated in a large township of the same name in King's county, on the southern shore of the strait, which connects the Basin of Minas with the Bay of Fundy. The history of this church will lead us back to the year 1776, when Henry Alline began his New-Light ministry in Nova-Scotia, and established a church here upon his plan, over which he was ordained pastor; and under this head it may be proper to say what we propose to of this extraordinary man, and of the mixed and zealous community, which he was instrumental in raising up.

Henry Alline was born of respectable and pious parents, in Newport, R. I. June 14, 1748. In 1760, the family removed from Newport to Nova-Scotia, and settled at Falmouth. Henry was the only son, and was early instructed in the principles of the christian religion, and when about 8 years old, according to his own account, as stated in his journal, his mind was seriously impressed with a sense of divine things. From this early period it appears that convictions followed from time to time, until they terminated in a sound conversion; which happened in March, 1775, when he was almost 27 years old. Soon after his conversion his mind was lead to the work of the ministry. Having always been taught to believe that learning was absolutely necessary to qualify men for this important undertaking, he resolved on going to New-England to solicit the aid of his friends and relations there, to-

---

that Mr. Edwards' Catalogue must be incorrect. He is positive there never was a Baptist church in this town until 1800. I have, therefore, corrected the statement, which I at first made, but left the article to stand in its present place.

wards obtaining it. Pursuant to this resolution, he took leave of his friends, and actually proceeded some distance on his journey. But Providence hedged up his way by a number of insurmountable obstacles, and he returned. This was in the close of the year in which he was converted. After passing through many trials, occasioned by the struggles of his own mind, and the solicitations of his friends, some urging him to go in pursuit of learning, others to engage in the ministry without it, he, the next spring, began to preach. His first efforts were crowned with such remarkable success, that he was encouraged to proceed. He soon began to travel extensively, revivals of religion almost constantly attended his ministry, and for about eight years he was abundantly owned of God, as the instrument of the conversion of souls ; he was much beloved by his friends, and was much abused and persecuted by many, who unreasonably became his enemies. And notwithstanding some errors in his creed, he was a bright and shining light through the dark regions of Nova-Scotia.

Mr. Alline was brought up a Congregationalist, and from that community he never separated ; but he outstripped most of his brethren in his ardent zeal, and evangelical exertions, which soon procured for him the appellation of a New-Light.

His notions of gospel discipline were confused and indefinite. The external order of the gospel, and particularly baptism and the mode of it, he professed to view with great indifference. He baptized but little himself, and never condescended to go into the water ; but was willing his followers should practise what mode they chose ; and if they could be easy in their minds, under the entire omission of the ordinance, he considered it rather their felicity than neglect ; but if their minds dwelt much upon baptism, he advised them to go forward in what mode they chose, that they might thereby quiet the troubles of their minds, and so forget the things which were behind, and be prepared for the calm and undisturbed enjoyment of the things of God.

Such instructions from a leader, we might naturally suppose would lead to confusion among his followers.

Mr. Alline also plunged into some speculations on theological points, which he could not have fully understood, as it would have puzzled a Jesuit to define them. But with all the exceptions to his maxims and doctrine, he was undoubtedly a man of God, and his labours were crowned with remarkable success; he was unquestionably the instrument of the conversion of many hundreds of souls in the provinces of Nova-Scotia and New Brunswick.

Having preached in this country about eight years, viz. from 1776 till 1784, he travelled into the United States, and sickened and died, at the house of Rev. David M'Clure, in the town of North-Hampton, State of New-Hampshire, Feb. 2, 1784, in the 36th year of his age.

As he lived in a country where he had but little opportunity of doctrinal instruction, and was almost incessantly employed, during his short ministry, in travelling and preaching, it is not strange that his sentiments were hastily adopted. Had he lived to have maturely reviewed his system, he would probably have pruned it of many of its exceptionable parts.

His principal business was to roam through the forests, and hew down the trees, spending but little time in preparing and arranging them; and he raised up many communities, which were afterwards, (some during his life, and others after his death) organized into distinct churches, of the New-Light or Congregational order; the most distinguished of which were those of Cornwallis, Newport, Horton, and Upper-Granville.

There were, at this time, the remains of a few Baptist churches, and besides them there were many Baptist members, scattered in different parts of the country. Many, but not all of them, fell in with the New-Light party. But in a short time, many of the New-Light Pedobaptists took to the waters, but all continued in communion together. But Baptist sentiments made rapid advances; some of the New-Light ministers were baptized, and were thus qualified, with more consistency, to baptize their converted brethren. Some great revivals of religion took place, and the converts almost uniformly became Baptists, and followed their Redeemer into the watery tomb. The Baptist leaven thus intermixed, produced a gradual fermentation, and in the course of a few years, many of the

New-Light Congregational were in reality transformed into New-Light Baptist churches. But the Baptists, either without much thought upon the subject, or from a principle of reciprocal charity, continued on the mixed communion plan, long after they had become a large majority in the churches.

But what are called *close communion* principles were at length broached among them, and caused no small stir in the churches. The Pedobaptist, and indeed a number of the Baptist members, were much opposed to the restrictions which they imposed. But as light and consistency prevailed, prejudice and tradition gave way, and in process of time, a reformation, as to external order, was effected ; so that now, most of the churches in Nova-Scotia and New-Brunswick have adopted what our enemies call the monstrous doctrine of close communion.

But to return to Cornwallis : After Henry Alline's death, a Congregational minister of the New-Light connexion, by the name of Payzant, was ordained to the pastoral office here, in which situation he continued a number of years, when he removed to the town of Liverpool, where he now resides. Their next, who is also their present pastor, was Rev. Edward Manning, who has furnished me with much information of Nova-Scotia, and the following respecting himself. He was ordained as their pastor, Oct. 19, 1795, being then an unbaptized New-Light minister. But his mind soon became disturbed about baptism, and for three years subsequent to his ordination, was much agitated on the subject; during which time he continued a motley mixture of administrations, sometimes immersing, and at other times sprinkling both adults and infants, constantly endeavouring to prove from the scriptures the eligibility of his subjects for the ordinance, and the validity of his different administrations. But at length his mind was brought to a stand ; the only gospel baptism was clearly exhibited to his view, and he was made willing to obey. He accordingly went to Annapolis, and was baptized by the Rev. Thomas H. Chipman, the former pastor of the church in that place. This measure, as might be expected, produced some agitation in the church, but it was finally agreed, that he should continue their pastor, without being obliged to sprinkle any more, either infants or adults; but open communion both pastor and people conscientiously maintained. About this time, a very refreshing season was granted to the church, and many believers were added by being baptized in the gospel mode. The church, however, was far from being harmonious for many years, but was in an agitated and divided state. Mr. Manning was obliged, after a few years, to relinquish open communion, and in 1807, soon after the church was reformed to its present unmixed and consistent plan, he was lead to call in question the validity of his former ordination. This brought on him a new and peculiar trial, for his brethren were not unanimous in their opinions about the matter. In the midst of their inquiries, Elders Isaac Case and Henry Hale, two missionaries from the Massachusetts Baptist Missionary Society came among them; by their advice and assistance a unanimity was obtained, and his re-ordination was effected. Since that time they have moved on in order and harmony.

CHESTER.—This church was formed in 1788, upon the open communion plan, most of the members at that time being Congregationalists. One article in their Confession was: " We believe baptism to be a divine institution, yet, as there are different opinions as to the subjects and outward administration of the ordinance, we give free liberty to every member to practise according to the dictates of their consciences, as they profess to be directed by the word of God."

Different ministers laboured among them with success. Rev. John Secomb, a very godly minister of the Congregational order, became their pastor, and continued in that office till his death. Rev. Joseph Dimock, who was then a Baptist minister, and who is now their pastor, made them a number of visits during Mr. Secomb's life, and soon after his death, viz. in 1793, he accepted a call and settled among them. Under his ministry they have been a prosperous and generally a happy people. They had, however, for a while, some severe trials, occasioned by their disputes about the terms of communion. In 1809, a partial reformation was effected, so that no more were to be received into the church, unless they were baptized. But still a few good people, who had not been baptized, were admitted to their communion. Thus matters continued until 1811, when the reformation was completed, and the church was received into the association.

The limits prescribed for this work will not permit us to give a full account of the remaining churches, which once stood in the New Light connexion. But it is sufficient to say, that they have passed through struggles and changes, in many respects, similar to those already mentioned.

SHELBURNE.—This church was formed mostly of black people, under the ministry of a black man, whose name was David George. At the close of the American war, Mr. George with many other people of colour, and a large number of whites, fled from the southern States, and settled at Shelburne. An account of the settlement of the church, its progress and breaking up, and the trials of Mr. George, are related in Rippon's Register, vol. I. p. 473—483. The first part of the narrative I shall abridge, the latter part I shall give entire.

David George was born a slave in Essex county, Virginia, about 1742. His master was very severe with his negroes, which induced him to run away, when he had grown to manhood. He went first to Pedee river in South Carolina, where he tarried but a few weeks, before he found he was pursued. He next went towards the Savanna river, and let himself to a Mr. Green, with whom he laboured about two years, when he was again heard of, and to escape his pursuers, he fled among the Creek Indians, and became the servant of their king, who was called *Blue Salt*. He was now about 800 miles from his master; it was, however, but a few months, before his master's son, who pursued him with unremitting diligence, came where he was, and took him; but before he could get him out of the Creek nation, he escaped from him, and fled to the Nantchee or Natchez Indians, and got to live with their king *Jack*. As there was much trading between the Indians and white people, he was soon heard of here, and was purchased by a Mr. Gaulfin, who lived on Savannah river, at Silver Bluff. Mr. Gaulfin had an agent among the Indians, whose name was John Miller, and into his custody, the poor hunted refugee was delivered. After serving him a few years, he by his own request, went to live with his master Gaulfin at Silver Bluff. It does not appear that he experienced any unkind usage from any of these masters, whether Indians or white people. And although he appeared peculiarly unfortunate, in being so often detected, yet he soon saw that a kind Providence directed his path, and brought him in due time, to receive that mercy which was laid up in store for him. He was, all this time, a thoughtless and wicked man. After living at Silver Bluff about four years, his mind was awakened to religious concern by the conversation of a man of his own colour, whose name was Cyrus. His convictions were deep and distressing, but his deliverance was clear and joyful. Soon after his conversion, he began to pray and exhort among the black people. He received instruction and encouragement from two preachers of his own colour, George Liele, who afterwards went to Jamaica, and "——Palmer, who was the pastor of a church of black people, at some distance from Silver Bluff," probably at Augusta. He was now entirely illiterate, but he soon set about learning; he got a spelling book, and by his own unwearied exertions, and the instruction of the little white children, he soon learnt so much, that he could read in the Bible. This was before the American war, during the whole of which he continued to preach in different places, under many embarrassments, but with a good degree of success.

The remaining part of the history of this worthy man, I shall give in his own words as related to Dr. Rippon of London, and the late Samuel Pearce of Birmingham.

" When the English were going to evacuate Charleston, they advised me to go to Halifax, in Nova-Scotia, and gave the few black people, and it may be as many as 500 white people, their passage for nothing. We were 22 days on the passage, and used very ill on board. When we came off Halifax, I got leave to go ashore. On shewing my papers to General Patterson, he sent orders by a serjeant for my wife and children to follow me. This was before Christmas, and we staid there till June; but as no way was open for me to preach to my own colour, I got leave to go to Shelburne, (150 miles, or more, I suppose, by sea,) in the suite of General Patterson, leaving my wife and children, for a while, behind. Numbers of

Mr. George began to preach at Shelburne.

my own colour were here, but I found the white people were against me. I began to sing, the first night, in the woods, at a camp, for there were no houses then built; they were just clearing and preparing to erect a town. The black people came far and near, it was so new to them; I kept on so every night in the week, and appointed a meeting for the first Lord's day, in a valley, between two hills close by the river, and a great number of white and black people came, and I was so overjoyed with having an opportunity once more of preaching the word of God, that after I had given out the hymn, I could not speak for tears. In the afternoon we met again, in the same place, and I had great liberty from the Lord. We had a meeting now every evening, and those poor creatures who had never heard the gospel before, listened to me very attentively; but the white people, the justices, and all, were in an uproar, and said that I might go out into the woods, for I should not stay there. I ought to except one white man, who knew me at Savannah, and who said I should have his lot to live upon as long as I would, and build a house if I pleased. I then cut down poles, stripped bark, and made a smart hut, and the people came flocking to the preaching every evening for a month, as though they had come for their supper. Then Governor Parr came from Halifax, brought my wife and children, gave me six months provisions for my family, and a quarter of an acre of land to cultivate for our subsistence. It was a spot where there was plenty of water, and which I had before secretly wished for, as I knew it would be convenient for baptizing at any time. The weather being severe and the ground covered with snow, we raised a platform of poles for the hearers to stand upon, but there was nothing over their heads. Continuing to attend, they desired to have a meeting house built. We had then a day of hearing what the Lord had done; and I and my wife heard their experiences, and I received four of my own colour; brother Sampson, brother John, sister Offee, and sister Dinah; these all were well at Sierra Leone, except brother Sampson, an excellent man, who died on his voyage to that place. The first time I baptized here was a little before Christmas, in the creek which ran through my lot. I preached to a great number of people on the occasion, who behaved very well. I now formed the church with us six, and administered the Lord's supper in the meeting-house, before it was finished. They went on with the building, and we appointed a time every other week to hear experiences. A few months after, I baptized nine more, and the congregation very much increased. The worldly blacks, as well as the members of the church, assisted in cutting timber in the woods, and in getting shingles; and we used to give a few coppers to buy nails. We were increasing all the winter, and baptized almost every month, and administered the Lord's supper first of all once in two months; but the frame of the meeting-house was not all up, nor had we covered it with shingles, till about the middle of summer, and then it had no pulpit, seats, nor flooring. About this time, Mr. William Taylor and his wife, two Baptists, who came from London to Shelburne, heard of me. Mrs. Taylor came to my house, when I was so poor that I had no money to buy any potatoes for seed, and was so good as to give my children somewhat, and me money enough to buy a bushel of potatoes, which one produced thirty-five bushels. The church was now grown to about fifty members. At this time, a white person, William Holmes, who, with Deborah his wife, had been converted by reading the Scriptures, and lived at Jones's harbour, about twenty miles down the river, came up for me, and would have me go with him in his schooner to his house. I went with him first to his own house, and then to a town they called Liverpool, inhabited by white people. Many had been baptized there by Mr. Chipman, of Annapolis, in Nova-Scotia. Mr. Jesse Dexter preached to them, but was not their pastor. It is a mixed communion church. I preached there; the christians were all alive, and we had a little heaven together. We then returned to brother Holmes'; and he and his wife came up with me to Shelburne, and gave their experiences to the church on Thursday, and were baptized on Lord's day. Their relations, who lived in the town, were very angry, raised a mob, and endeavoured to hinder their being baptized. Mrs. Holmes' sister especially laid hold of her hair to keep her from going down into the water; but the justices commanded peace, and said that she should be baptized, as she herself desired it. Then they were all quiet. Soon after this the persecution increased, and became so great that it did not seem possible to preach, and I thought I must leave Shelburne. Several of the black people had houses on my lot; but forty or fifty disbanded soldiers were employed, who came with the tackle of ships, and turned my dwelling house and every one of their houses quite over; and the meeting-house they would have burned down, had not the ring-leader of the mob himself prevented it. But I continued preaching in it, till they came one night and stood before the pulpit, and swore how they would treat me if I preached again. But I stayed and preached, and the next day they came and beat me with sticks, and drove me into a swamp. I returned in the evening, and took my wife and children over the river to Birchtown, where some black people were settled, and there seemed a greater prospect of doing good than at Shelburne. I preached at Birchtown from the fall till about the middle of December, and was frequently hearing experiences, and baptized about twenty there. Those who desired to hear the word of God, invited me from house to house, and so I preached. A little before Christmas, as my own colour persecuted me there, I set off with my family to return to Shelburne; and coming down the river the boat was frozen, but we took whipsaws, and cut away the ice till we came to Shelburne. In my absence, the meeting-house was occupied by a sort of tavern-keeper, who said, "The old negro wanted to make a heaven of this place, but I'll make a hell of it." Then I preached in it as before, and as my house was pulled down, lived in it also. The people began to attend again, and in the summer there was a considerable revival of religion. Now I went down about twenty miles to a place, called Ragged Island, among some white people, who desired to hear the word. One white sister was converted there while I was preaching concerning the disciples, who left all and followed Christ. She came up afterwards, gave her experience to our church, and was baptized, and two black sisters with her. Then her other sister gave in her experience, and joined us without baptism, to which she would have submitted, had not her family cruelly hindered her; but she was the only one in our society, who was not baptized.

By this time, the Christians at St. John's, about 200 miles from Shelburne, over the bay of Fundy, in New-Brunswick, had heard of me and wished me to visit them. Part of the first Saturday I was there, was spent in hearing the experiences of the black people; four were approved, some of whom had been converted in Virginia; a fortnight after, I baptized them in the river, on the Lord's day. Numerous spectators, white and black, were present, who behaved very well. But on Monday, many of the inhabitants made a disturbance, declaring that no body should preach there again, without a license from the Governor. He lived at Frederick-town, about an hundred miles from thence up St. John's river. I went off in the packet to him. Colonel Allen, who knew me in Charleston, lived but a few miles from the Governor, and introduced me to him; upon which his Secretary gave me a license.* I returned then to St. John's, and preached again, and left brother Peter Richards to exhort among them. He afterwards died on the passage, just going into Sierra Leone, and we buried him there. When I got back to Shelburne, I sent brother Sampson Colbart, one of my elders, to St. John's, to stay there. He was a loving brother, and the Lord had endowed him with great gifts. When the experiences of nine or ten had been related there, they sent for me to come and baptize them. I went by water to Halifax, and walked from thence to Horton, about 80 miles from Annapolis, and not far from New-Brunswick. There is a large church at Horton, I think the largest in Nova-Scotia. They are all Baptists; Mr. Scott is their minister. We spent one Sabbath together, and all day long was a day to be remembered. When I was landing at St. John's, some of the people, who intended to be baptized, were so full of joy, that they ran out from waiting at table on their masters, with the knives and forks in their hands, to meet me at the water side. This second time of my being at St. John's, I staid preaching about a fortnight, and baptized ten people. Our going

---

* Secretary's Office, Frederick-town, 17th July, 1792.

I do hereby certify, that David George, a free negro man, has permission from his Excellency the Lieutenant-Governor, to instruct the black people in the knowledge, and exhort them to the practice of the Christian religion.

JON. ODELL, *Secretary.*

down into the water, seemed to be a pleasing sight to the whole town, white people and black. I had now to go to Frederick-town again, from whence I obtained the license before ; for one of our brethren had been there, and heard the experiences of three of the people, and they sent to me, entreating that I would not return until I had been and baptized them. Two brethren took me to Frederick-town in a boat. I baptized on the Lord's day, about 12 o'clock ; a great number of people attended. The Governor said he was sorry that he could not come down to see it ; but he had a great deal of company that day, which also hindered one of his servants from being baptized. I came back to St. John's, and home to Shelburne. Then I was sent for to Preston, it may be four miles from Halifax, over against it, on the other side of the river. Five converted persons, who lived there, desired to be baptized and join the church. I baptized them, and administered the Lord's supper to them at Preston, and left brother Hector Peters, one of my elders, with them. In returning to Shelburne, with about 30 passengers, we were blown off into the sea, and lost our course. I had no blanket to cover me, and got frost bitten in both my legs up to my knees, and was so ill when I came towards land, that I could not walk. The church met me at the river side, and carried me home. Afterwards, when I could walk a little, I wanted to speak of the Lord's goodness, and the brethren made a wooden sledge, and drew me to meeting. In the spring of the year, I could walk again, but have never been strong since.

The next fall, Agent (afterwards Governor) Clarkson came to Halifax, about settling a new colony at Sierra Leone. The white people in Nova-Scotia were very unwilling that we should go, though they had been very cruel to us, and treated many of us as bad as though we had been slaves. They attempted to persuade us, that if we went away, we should be made slaves again. The brethren and sisters all round, at St. John's, Halifax, and other places, Mr. Wesley's people, and all consulted what was best to do, and sent in their names to me, to give to Mr. Clarkson, and I was to tell him that they were willing to go. I carried him their names, and he appointed to meet us at Birchtown the next day. We gathered together there, in the meeting-house of brother Moses, a blind man, one of Mr. Wesley's preachers. Then the Governor read the proclamation, which contained what was offered, in case we had a mind willingly to go, and the greatest part of us were pleased and agreed to go. We appointed a day over at Shelburne, when the names were to be given to the Governor. Almost all the Baptists went, except a few of the sisters whose husbands were inclined to go back to New-York; and sister Lizze, a Quebec Indian, and brother Lewis, her husband, who was an half Indian, both of whom were converted under my ministry, and had been baptized by me. There are a few scattered Baptists yet at Shelburne, St. John's, Jones'Harbour, and Ragged Island, besides the congregations at the other places I mentioned before. The meeting-house lot, and all our land at Shelburne, it may be half an acre, was sold to merchant Black, for about £7.

We departed and called at Liverpool, a place I mentioned before. I preached a farewell sermon there; I longed to do it. Before I left the town, Major Collins, who, with his wife, used to hear me at this place, was very kind to me, and gave me some salted herrings, which were very acceptable all the way to Sierra Leone. We sailed from Liverpool to Halifax, where we tarried three or four weeks, and I preached from house to house, and my farewell sermon in Mr. Marchington's Methodist meeting-house.

Our passage from Halifax to Sierra Leone was seven weeks, in which we had very stormy weather. Several persons died on the voyage, of a catching fever, among whom were three of my Elders, Sampson Colwell, a loving man, Peter Richards, and John Williams.

There was great joy to see the land. The high mountain at some distance from Freetown, where we now live, appeared like a cloud to us. I preached the first Lord's day, it was a blessed time, under a sail, and so I did for several weeks after. We then erected a hovel for a meeting-house, which is made of posts put into the ground, and poles over our heads, which are covered with grass. While I was preaching under the sails sisters Patty Webb and Lucy Lawrence were converted, and they, with old sister Peggy, brother Bill Taylor, and brother Sampson

Haywood, three, who were awakened before they came this voyage, have since been baptized in the river.

On the voyage from Halifax to Sierra Leone, I asked the Governor if I might not hereafter go to England? and sometime after we arrived there, I told him I wished to see the Baptist brethren who live in his country. He was a very kind man to me and to every body; he is very free and good natured, and used to come and hear me preach, and would sometimes sit down at our private meetings; and he liked that I should call my last child by his name. And I sent to Mr. Henry Thornton, O what a blessed man is that! he is brother, father, every thing! he ordered me five guineas, and I had leave to come over. When I came away from Sierra Leone, I preached a farewel sermon to the church, and encouraged them to look to the Lord, and submit to one another, and regard what is said to them by my three Elders, brethren Hector Peters, and John Colbert, who are two exhorters, and brother John Ramsey."

Mr. George was on a visit to London when he gave this account of himself; he returned to Sierra Leone, not far from the time that Messrs. Radway and Grigg went as missionaries into that country. Whether he is yet alive, and what progress the Baptist cause has had at Sierra Leone, since about 1792, I have not been able to learn. If David George be yet living, he must be upwards of 70 years old.

The church at Shelburne was broken up when Mr. George and his followers left the place. There were, however, a few scattered Baptist members left, who were formed into a church a few years after, by Mr. Burton of Halifax. William Taylor and his wife, who are respectfully mentioned in David George's narrative, came from Dr. Rippon's church in London, and were, for many years, the principal members in the church at Shelburne. Mr. Taylor was a wealthy and liberal man. By his generosity, and, it is said, by some considerable assistance from the church, from which he emigrated, this small people built a very commodious meeting-house, which is now in a great measure unoccupied. Mr. Taylor died a few years since. During his life he was the deacon of the church, and had the care of the meeting-house. His widow is yet alive. There is yet a small church in Shelburne, but without a pastor.

HALIFAX.—This church was founded by Rev. John Burton, its present pastor, in the following manner. Mr. Burton is a native of England, was initiated into the Episcopal church in infancy, and never entirely left that establishment, until he became a Baptist. He was, however, licensed in England, as a dissenting minister. He arrived at Halifax, May 20, 1792, but he had no design of tarrying there, for he left England with an intention of settling in the United States. At this time, there was a Mr. Marchington in Halifax, who had built a meeting house for the Methodists, to which denomination he belonged ; but on account of a disagreement between him and the society, his meeting house was unoccupied when Mr. Burton arrived. Into this house he was invited, where he preached for more than a year after his arrival in Halifax. In the fall of 1793, Mr. Burton travelled into the United States, and at the town of Knowlton, in New-Jersey, he was baptized in December of this year, and the next month was ordained at the same place. In June, 1794, he returned to Halifax a Baptist minister, to the astonishment of all his friends. He was now entirely alone, there not being an individual Baptist in the town beside himself. He continued preaching in Mr. Marchington's meeting house, until the next year ; and by this gentleman he was much befriended, until after he had become a Baptist. But now being left without patronage, his prospects were truly gloomy and discouraging, being low in his temporal circumstances, and almost destitute of the society of his brethren, as the province was then much overrun with error and enthusiasm, and the few Baptists who were scattered in it, were so much intermixed with the Pedobaptist New-Lights, that he could have but little fellowship or communion with them. But his prospects soon became more encouraging ; liberal helpers were raised up for the supply of himself and family ; in a short time a number were baptized, and in 1795 a small church was constituted, which has never been large, but is respectable and well established. A respectable congregation has been collected, from which Mr. Burton receives a comfortable support. They have purchased a lot $55\frac{1}{2}$ by $36\frac{1}{2}$, on which they have erected a commodious house of worship, and also a dwelling house for the accommodation of their pastor. Both of the buildings are of brick, and they, with the lot, cost about 900*l.* in the currency of the province, which is about 3600 dollars. The meeting house is 36½ feet by 25¼, with galleries; towards the defraying the expenses of this estate, Mr. Burton collected considerable sums in different parts of the United States.*

Besides the churches, whose history has been given, there are the following in this province, which have established unmixed communion: viz. Sissiboo, in the township of Digby, Upper Granville, Lower Granville, Ragged Island, Clements, Onslow, Amherst, Lunenburgh, Digby-Neck, Nictau, and Wilmot, and a small church on Jordan and Pleasant rivers, in a new settlement between Nictau and Liverpool. On the Isle of St. John's, in the Gulf of St. Lawrence, and which island is attached to the province of Nova-Scotia, there is a small church under the care of Elder Isaac Bradshaw. Some of these churches were nearly as old, in their beginning, as those whose history has been given at large, and were formerly mixed in their communion; others are of later date, and were established, at first, on their present foundation.

There are also four churches in this province, which still admit unbaptized members to their communion; viz. Yarmouth, Argyle, Barrington, and Cockweet. There are also about 20 Baptist members in the town of Liverpool, some of whom are in the communion of a Congregational church, under the pastoral care of a Mr. Payzant. Yarmouth church is said to consist of almost 300 members: Rev. Harris Harding is their pastor. It was first planted by Henry Alline. For many years it consisted of Pedobaptists and Baptists indiscriminately. In 1807, they effected a partial reformation, so that none but Baptists are permitted to sign their articles, and enjoy the privileges of complete membership, but about 20 or 30 Pedobaptists are admitted to their communion; this they call not *open*, but *occasional communion*.

ARGYLE.—In this place, there was also a church established by that successful planter of churches, Henry

---

* The substance of this account was communicated by Mr. Burton.

Alline ; but it had become broken or dissolved, before the present one was erected. About 1806, there was a very pleasing and extensive revival in this place, and the present church was gathered under the ministry of Mr. Enoch Tower, their present minister ; their number is about 70. One Pedobaptist, who is a very old and pious person, is admitted to their communion. The church generally are convinced of the propriety of unmixed communion, but the old disciple is not inclined to go into the water, and they are waiting, (with patience, it is hoped) until some escorting angel shall bear him beyond the bars of communion tables, and thus complete the reformation which they have brought to such a hopeful period.

All the churches in Nova-Scotia are to the westward and northward of Halifax, along the Atlantic shore on the Bay of Fundy, the Basin of Minas, and on the creeks and rivers, which empty into these respective waters—the church of Amherst only excepted, which is on the Cumberland Bay.

NEW-BRUNSWICK.

THIS province was formed by a division of that of Nova-Scotia in 1784, and is situated between it and the District of Maine. New-Brunswick contains a greater number of churches than Nova-Scotia, but they are of much later date, having been mostly formed within the present century, and furnish fewer materials for a historical narrative.

SACKVILLE.—This church claims our first attention. This place was formerly called Tantarramar, which name it is said to have received from the French. It has been the resort of Baptists for about fifty years. We have already seen that Elder Mason and his company from Swansea settled in this place, in 1763, where they continued about eight years, and then returned again to the United States. Two Baptist ministers, whose names were Windsor and Rounds, are mentioned as having laboured here in early times, but what became of them I cannot learn. By their names one would think they went from Rhode-Island, or Rehoboth, or Swansea.

A Mr. Joseph Reed was called to the ministry in this church, probably after Mr. Mason left the place. He laboured here awhile with much success, and then removed to Horton and died. But the first Baptist church here was entirely dissolved before Henry Alline's time. Under his ministry there was a revival of religion in this place, and a Congregational church established. But this church was also scattered before the present one was established, which was raised up under the ministry of Mr. Joseph Crandall, the present pastor, in the year 1800.

Salisbury, Waterbury, and Prince-William churches were all likewise constituted in 1800. These churches, together with those of Wakefield and Springfield, belong to the Nova-Scotia and New-Brunswick Association. The following churches, I believe, have all been constituted since those abovementioned, viz. Fredericktown, Mangerville, Shepody, city of St. John's, Nashfork or Nashwalk, Woodstock, King's Clear, Long Reach, Sussex, St. Mary's, St. Martin's, St. George's, St. Andrews, and St. Stephen's. Very little information has been obtained respecting the time when, or the circumstances under which these churches were formed, except that a number of them were gathered and others were enlarged and strengthened, by Elders Isaac Case, Henry Hale, Daniel Merrill, and Amos Allin, who have travelled hither, under the patronage of the Massachusetts Baptist Missionary Society, and that most of those in the parishes are on the western boundary of the province, adjoining the District of Maine.

By the foregoing sketches it appears that the Baptists are in a flourishing condition, generally speaking, in the two provinces of Nova-Scotia and New-Brunswick, and although they began here almost fifty years ago, yet they never prevailed much until within fifteen or twenty years past.

In the midst of the ardent zeal of the New-Lights there was no small portion of enthusiasm and error, too much of which was retained by them after they became Baptists. And, indeed, amongst the Baptists, there has been propagated a system of speculations, called the New Dispensation, of a very fantastic nature. This system consists in a mystical explanation of many passages of scripture, and illustrates many theological points in a fanciful and highly ludicrous manner. This Dispensation was, at one time, advocated by some Baptist ministers, who have since abandoned it, and who now hold a very respectable standing among the churches in this country. The Dispensation itself is waxing old and unpopular, and vanishing away.

Many of the churches in this country have enjoyed very precious seasons of revival, within a few years past, some accounts of which have been published in the Massachusetts Baptist Missionary Magazine, edited by Dr. Baldwin of Boston. The following extracts will give the reader a better view of these revivals, than we can otherwise exhibit.

EXTRACT OF A LETTER FROM REV. THOMAS H. CHIPMAN, TO THE EDITOR OF THE M. B. M. MAGAZINE.

"*Yarmouth, Shelburne county, Nova-Scotia, Dec. 5, 1806.*

"REVEREND AND DEAR SIR,

"I have been in this town and Argyle, five weeks, and such glorious times I never saw before. Multitudes are turned to God. It is about three months since the work began in Yarmouth. Brother Harding is the minister of this place, who stands clear in the doctrines of the glorious gospel, and in the order and discipline of God's house. Since the work began, there have been about one hundred and fifty souls brought to own Jesus. But a number of these had probably been born again before, but had received no satisfying evidence until now. Before I came to this place, brother Harding had baptized seven persons; since I came he and myself, on one Sabbath, baptized eighteen. The Sabbath after but one, we baptized forty. We have had two church meetings, and surely I never saw such meetings before. The last Saturday we began at ten in the morning, and continued till eight in the evening, to hear persons relate the dealings of God with their souls. Some of them have been great enemies to the truth, and never went to meeting until God converted their souls. Some would inform the enemies of religion, that they could not say, that this or that preacher or person had influenced or turned them; for God had done the work for them at home. A great many of the subjects of this work have been young people and children.

"Monday, Dec. 8. Yesterday brother Harding and myself baptized twenty-two persons, and there are a considerable number now waiting that have been approved of by the church. The work is still spreading.

"At Argyle, twenty miles from this, there has been a glorious work the summer past. God has visited Tuscut-river, a village between this and Argyle, where brother Harding and myself have baptized four. There is an Esquire L——, a member of the House of Assembly, who is a christian, whom God hath blessed with a handsome property, and a heart to devote it to his service. His wife is of the same spirit : Two of their children, I believe, are sealed to the day of redemption,

" Yours, with great esteem,
THOMAS H. CHIPMAN."

EXTRACT OF A LETTER FROM REV. ENOCH TOWNER, TO THE SAME.

Argyle, Nova-Scotia, April 13, 1807.
" REVERED AND DEAR SIR,

" On the 16th of July last I sat out from Digby, Annapolis county, my place of residence, on a journey to Argyle, where I arrived on Saturday the 18th, late in the evening. The people not having notice of my coming, and the next morning being very rainy, but few attended the meeting. I was requested to stay another Sabbath, which I did, and preached several times in the course of the week. Religion was at a very low ebb among the few professors, who belonged to a church formerly established by a Mr. Frost, a New-Light Congregational minister. After his death the church was re-established and increased under the ministration of other preachers ; they still holding the baptism of believers non-essential to fellowship in the church of Christ. The broken and scattered state of this church was great ; all discipline was done away. Nevertheless there were a few mourning souls, that would not be comforted, because God's heritage lay waste.

" Here I tarried the next Lord's day and preached from Solomon's Song, v. 16. *His mouth is most sweet : yea, he is altogether lovely. This is my beloved, and this is my friend, O daughters of Jerusalem*; and in the afternoon from chap. i. 8. *If thou know not, O thou fairest among women, go thy way forth by the footsteps of the flock, and feed thy kids beside the shepherds' tents.* The set time was now come to raise his people from the dust. A young woman, who had been awakened the winter before, by hearing some young people sing and discourse upon the happiness of religion, in the township of Digby, the impression of which had never left her, till this Sabbath evening, when she found peace and joy in the gospel. Her feelings led her to exhort her young companions to turn to the Lord. Many were brought to bow to the sceptre of King Jesus, and proclaim salvation in his blessed name. Here I saw the Lord had begun his work. The young professors manifested a desire to follow their Lord's commands, and be buried with him by baptism. There being no church here for them to covenant with, as most of the old professors could not see the expediency of baptism, I was at a loss how to proceed ; but resolved to follow the Lord's command to teach and baptize. Accordingly a conference meeting was appointed to hear their experiences, when nine came forward, two old professors, and seven young converts, and were baptized the fourth Lord's day after my first arrival. After this, the work spread with great power, and people assembled from all parts of the town, and some from the adjoining towns. I thought proper to send for brother Harris Harding, as he was more acquainted with the old professors than I was, as many had professed under his ministry, in order to see if we could settle a church ; but it proved to no purpose at this time. However, ten came forward and were baptized. I now thought it proper to form those, who had been baptized, into some order ; and for that purpose offered them a covenant which they cherrfully signed. In a few days from this time, there were twenty-two of the old professors, who came forward to baptism. Here was seen a mother, son and wife, and grand-daughter, all following their Lord into the water ! Here was one man seventy years of age, and a little boy of only ten ! Baptism was administered five Lord's days successively, until seventy-eight joined the church. After staying here thirteen Sabbaths, I was under the necessity of returning to my people. I tarried there four weeks, and then returned to this place again. I found the Lord was still at work, though not so powerfully as when I left them. But the cloud seemed to return again ; for there being a number of men, who follow the seas, on returning home to winter, seeing such an alteration in the place were struck with deep solemnity. Many were wounded to their hearts, and made to groan under the weight of their sins. The last Sabbath in March, twenty came forward and were baptized. I must conclude with adding, that one hundred and twenty have been baptized. There were five baptisms in the winter season. Twenty-four have told their experiences, who are not yet baptized, and a number of others are under hopeful impressions. The work is still going on in this place, and spreading rapidly in different parts of the province.

" I am, Sir, your unworthy brother in Christ,

ENOCH TOWNER."

Notwithstanding the extent of the foregoing extracts, yet I am unwilling the reader should be without the pleasing intelligence contained in the two following communications.

EXTRACT OF A LETTER FROM THE REV. ISRAEL POTTER, TO THE EDITOR OF THE SAME.

" *Clements, Annapolis county, Nova-Scotia, May* 12, 1810.

" DEAR AND REV. SIR,

" In the beginning of March last, a most wonderful and powerful reformation began in the lower part of this town, which seemed to pervade the minds of old and young, and many, we hope, were brought to the knowledge of the truth. About ten days after, the good work made its appearance in the middle of the town. The people assembled from every quarter, and it seemed that it might be truly said, that God was passing through the place in a very powerful manner. The glorious work has since spread through every part of the town, and some of all ages have been made to bow to the mild sceptre of the Redeemer.

"The ordinance of baptism has been administered for five Sabbaths successively. Forty-five have been admitted to this sacred rite, and a church has been constituted upon the gospel plan, consisting of sixty five members, to which we expect further additions. If I should say that two hundred have been hopefully converted to the Lord in this town since the reformation commenced, I think I should not exceed the truth. The good work is still spreading eastward very rapidly, and looks likely to spread through the province.

"The opposition has been great, and many oaths have been sworn even in the time of divine service. But the Lord has triumphed gloriously over the horse and his rider, and blessed be his name.

"At Round-hill I understand there is a number to be baptized to-day. The province of Nova-Scotia has been highly favoured with the gospel. We beg an interest in your prayers, that the Lord would give us strength to contend earnestly for the faith that was once delivered to the saints.

"Your unworthy friend,
ISRAEL POTTER."

EXTRACT OF A LETTER FROM THE REV. DANIEL MERRILL, TO THE EDITOR OF THE SAME.

"*Sedgwick, Maine, Aug.* 17, 1810.

" MY DEAR BROTHER,

"A fortnight to day, I returned from my eastern expedition. My route lay through part of his Britannic Majesty's dominions, and hard by some of the strong holds of satan; I was every where, however, received with sufficient attention and civility.

It was very pleasing to me, to behold my beloved brethren of Nova-Scotia and New-Brunswick, who have so lately emerged into gospel liberty, so expert in discipline, so determinate in christian order and communion, and so well marshalled in battle array. They appear in a very good degree, like *veterans,* whilst they are, in age, but very children. Fourteen years only have elapsed, since but one *baptized* church was to be found in both provinces. Now they can count nearly forty, and some of them are large and flourishing.

"Their Association, which I visited as a messenger from the Lincoln, was holden at Sackville on the 25th and 26th of June. It was a good season. Tokens of the Chief Shepherd's kindness and presence appeared specially manifest. The elders and messengers of the churches were solemn, cheerful, and of good courage. The letters from the different churches were refreshing, and fraught with much good news. In one county, (Annapolis, if I mistake not) between two and three hundred had put on Christ the present year, by being baptized into him. Babylon appears to be in full retreat, yet her pursuers should be very wary, for she is very subtle, and by no means in a very good mood. She thrust one of Christ's ministers* into prison, the week before I left those regions, and their evil

* Mr. Ennis. See an account of him towards the close of this chapter.

eye was fixed on brother Hale, to take him the same week ; but he being a " Gospel Ranger," they were not, and I presume they will not be able to incarcerate him.

" Zion's God is *so generally* lengthening her cords, and making her stakes stronger, that I cannot, in one short letter, descend to particulars, without leaving the larger half behind. However, that my letter be not altogether in generals, I will particularize a few instances.

" I will begin with Brier-Island. The place was notorious for irreligion, perhaps as much so, in proportion to its magnitude, as was Sodom, on the morning of Lot's escape. Last autumn or winter, brother Peter Crandal visited the Island, and preached to as many of the shy Islanders, as he could collect within hearing of his voice. He was threatened with death if he ventured to preach on this Island again. However, he loved their salvation, more than he feared their threatenings ; he ventured, the people collected, he spoke, and the Lord spoke too. At a late hour the assembly was dismissed. He retired, but ere soft sleep had closed his eyes, a messenger requested he would visit a house distrest. Without gainsaying he arose and followed him. Whilst on his way, in the first house he passed, he discovered a light ; it came into his mind just to call and see how they did. He found them in the agonies of dying unto sin ; an household distrest for sins committed and salvation infinitely needed. He saw their anguish manifestly such, as all must feel, or die forever ; and observing their exercises and situation such as he judged not expedient to be interrupted, retired in silence. The next house he found and left in a very similar condition. Going a little further, he heard a person in the field, manifesting, by his sighs and groans, bitterness of spirit. Mr. Crandall turned aside, and in silent wonder beheld, and left the sin-sick man. He was soon at the house whence they had sent for him. Here he found a company sorely opprest with their load of sin, burdened by it, and longing to be free. Here he broke silence, and pointed dying sinners to a living Saviour. On this never to be forgotten Island, in sixteen of the eighteen families which reside on it, were thirty-three hopefully born from above. The reformation had reached the main, so that when I saw him, he had baptized between fifty and an hundred.

" Before this shall reach you, brother Hale's to brother Collier will probably be handed to you. In addition to what he has communicated, I will add, that he has given but a very modest account of what the Lord hath wrought on Belisle Bay by him. I know not whether I ever saw or heard of any one garrison, being so largely harassed by a single gospel ranger in the compass of one campaign, and that too a winter one. It is true brother Ansley, who is no mean soldier, was there one evening, in which the Lord wrought wonderfully. An account of this evening, with one preceding it, is nearly as much as I have now time to relate. On an evening preceding the two, and in which brother Hale delivered his first discourse to the then idle people on Belisle Bay, a Polly Davis was arrested by the Spirit of truth, and, before the next rising sun, was set at liberty. The next day being a militia muster, the young men came to see their changed associate, and wondered at but hated the change. Another lecture was appointed for the following evening. Not far from the time of meeting, two of the foremost young men, taking the inn on their way, called for half a pint of ardent spirits each, and drank it, observing that they would raise the devil at the meeting. The religious exercises began, and sleep prevailed over the young men, till little more was to be heard. However, they awoke from their drunkenness, and in season to hear a sentence or two, and what they heard was as a nail in a sure place. They had rest no more, till they found it in believing. Soon after this, at an evening lecture, brother Ansley preached, and when brother Hale had observed what he judged expedient, and the assembly were dismissed, the people all sat down. A solemn silence now prevailed for nearly an hour, when a young woman, of about 20, who had been baptized ten years before, arose, and, filled with a sense of her backsliding heart, spake in such a feeling and solemn manner, as greatly to affect the whole assembly. It was now a time of weeping, mourning, and lamentation. The saving health of our Immanuel soon appeared in healing the broken hearted, and setting the poor captives free. Before the morning light, nine young converts were chanting forth their young hosannas.

"You can hardly imagine how suddenly and deeply these things waked the enemies of reformation, and roused all their powers of opposition. The church priest now visited where he had never walked before. The dialogues between him and his now converted, but heretofore deluded parishioners, would be sufficiently entertaining, had I time to relate them.

"From Belisle Bay, I came down the river to the city of St. John's, where I preached three times, twice on the commons, and baptized one worthy man and two honourable women.

"In bonds of perpetual friendship, I am sincerely yours,

"DANIEL MERRILL,"

NOVA-SCOTIA AND NEW-BRUNSWICK ASSOCIATION.

So much has been said of the churches of which this body is composed, that its history will, of consequence, be short. It commenced and has progressed in the following manner.

In 1797, four ministers, whose names were Pazant, Chipman, James and Edward Manning, met in Cornwallis and devised the plan of an Association. According to their request, six churches, by their delegates, met the next year, among whom were six ministers, some of whom were Congregationalists, and some Baptists, and all the churches were, at this time, composed of a mixture of both denominations. At this time the Association was formed, and mixed communion, at that day, was a thing of course, and continued to be practised in this body, for eleven years, viz. until 1809. The Association had now become considerably large; it had enjoyed many prosperous seasons, and believer's baptism had almost supplanted the doctrine of infant sprinkling. The reader will perceive by the preceding history of the churches, that the terms of communion had been previously much agitated among them. Many had come to a point on the subject, and the Association at its annual session in 1809, found itself so much straitened and embarrassed, that a vote was then passed, that for the future, no church should be considered as belonging to it, which admitted of open communion. On account of this vote, four churches were dropped or else withdrew.

It was a trying circumstance in the minds of many, to shut their doors against so many of their pious and beloved Pedobaptist brethren, who had so long travelled in communion with them. And under these delicate circumstances, some were doubtless over-zealous in pushing the reformation, while others, probably from the tenderness of their feelings, declined promoting a measure, of the propriety of which they were most fully convinced. The reader must not suppose, that all the unbaptized persons, whom these churches admitted to their communion, were zealous for Pedo-baptism. Many of them were what some have called *Upland* Baptists, who profess to be convinced of the duty of believer's baptism, but live through life in the neglect of it. Some of these persons were so fully convinced of the propriety of unmixed communion, that they said to their brethren, " Do not wait for us, but go forward and do your duty, and leave us to do ours." And many of these who had long been halting, and who felt in a measure easy in their minds, while their baptized brethren sanctioned their neglect, by admitting them to the same church privileges with themselves, now were awakened to a sense of their duty, come forward and were baptized.

Many, who had been for a long time much embarrassed on their former plan, were now relieved, and viewed themselves as standing on tenable ground; and many individuals throughout the country, and the whole church at Halifax, who had refused communing and associating with the mixed communion connexion, as soon as they were reformed, most cordially united with them. The discipline of the churches has been much better regulated on the new plan than on the old one. The Association has opened a correspondence with the Associations in the District of Maine, from which it has derived much comfort and advantage. The new churches which have been formed, have been established on the gospel plan. So that the reformation in the terms of communion was an important era in the history of the Nova-Scotia churches.

There are now about eighteen or twenty ordained, and eight or ten unordained ministers in these two provinces, and besides them there are a number of gifted brethren, who bid fair for the ministry. Some of these ministers are natives of the country, and the others have emigrated hither from the United States, and from different parts of Europe. Mr. Chipman was born in Newport, Rhode-Island. The two Mannings are natural brothers; they were born in Ireland, and were brought to this country when they were small. Mr. Ries, who has recently been on a mission to New-Orleans, is a native of France; he was brought a prisoner to Halifax, when he was quite young. Messrs. Ansley and Towner are both natives of the State of New-York. Mr. Burton's history has already been related. Mr. Easterbrooks was born in one of the United States, which, I have not learnt. I believe that all the remaining ministers are natives of one or the other of these two provinces.

Some of their ministers are in part supported by the churches which they serve, and others receive but little. A number of them have good estates. The Baptist churches in this country, as in all others, are pretty careful how they pamper their ministers, but they are said, notwithstanding, to be very liberal to strangers who travel among them; and the fame of this liberality has induced many impostors to visit them.

Mr. Daniel Dodge, pastor of the Baptist church in Wilmington, Delaware, was born at Port-Royal in Nova-Scotia. Mr. Job Seamans of New-London, New-Hampshire, began preaching in this country, as did Mr. John Grant, late of Middleton, Connecticut, now of Chester, Massachusetts.

The list of churches and ministers in these two provinces will be given in the general table.

The church of England is the established religion in these two provinces, but dissenters are tolerated, and suffer but few restrictions or embarrassments; and what is much for their comfort, " They are excused from any rates or taxes for the support of the established church." In Nova-Scotia, no person is obliged to get a license from the Governor, except he be an alien. In that case it is necessary. Mr. Ries, because he is a Frenchman, has been apprehended four times, by the authority of what is called the Vagrant Act, if I mistake not the name. Once he was taken two hundred miles from Halifax, and conducted a prisoner thither, but he easily obtained a release; for these molestations were not from the spirit of the laws or magistrates, but from the malicious spirit of ill-natured people who found an old law which suited their purpose.

In New-Brunswick, although there is a general toleration for dissenters, yet there is an old law, which prohibits all dissenters, except Presbyterians, from doing many things, and among the rest from performing the ceremony of marriage, and preaching without the Governor's license. I do not know as all take pains to solicit this permission from his Excellency, but if they do, it is easily obtained. The Episcopal priests are the most interested in this old law, and they care but little who preaches; but the concerns of matrimony they guard with more care on account of the fees. Some time ago an old Baptist minister by the name of Innes presumed to marry a couple who lived forty miles from where any Episcopal clergyman resided. For this act he was complained of, and thrown into prison, where he lay, I believe, more than a year; but he is now out upon bail, and the brethren, I am informed, are about to petition for a repeal of the law. The fine for this transgression is not less than fifty, and not more than a hundred pounds.

CHAP. IX.

DISTRICT OF MAINE.

THIS is a large tract of country of two hundred miles square, belonging to the State of Massachusetts, from which it is separated by the State of New-Hampshire. It lies along the Atlantic coast, extends east to the British Province of New-Brunswick, and is bounded on the north by Lower Canada.

As early as 1681, there were some Baptists in Kittery on Piscataqua River, in the south-west part of this District, who united at first with the church in Boston, then under the care of Elder Hull. The year after, they were formed into a church, which was soon broken up by the persecutions of its enemies, and by the removal of its members to other parts. The constituents of this church were William Scriven, elder, Humphrey Churchwood, deacon, Robert Williams, John Morgandy, Richard Cutts, Timothy Davis, Leonard Drown, William Adams, Humphrey Azell, George Litten, and a number of sisters. Scriven went to South-Carolina, and founded the church at Charleston, and probably some of the others went with him.

After the dispersion of this little company we hear no more of Baptists in this region, nor indeed in this District; until about 1767, when there was a revival of religion in Berwick, which, like Kittery, is in the county of York, just over the line of New-Hampshire, and Mr. Smith of Haverhill went and baptized a considerable number of persons, who were formed into a church by his assistance the next year.

The next church formed in this District was at Gorham, near Casco Bay, in the county of Cumberland. This church was also organized by the assistance of Mr. Smith of Haverhill. Joseph Moody, a member of it, had his horse taken from him for a ministerial tax of about six dollars. Not long after he petitioned the Assembly at Boston, that they would, like the good Samaritan, set him on his own beast. But the legislators, like the Priest and Levite, passed him by without compassion.

In a few years after, other churches arose in the western part of this District, in Sanford, Wells, Shapleigh, Coxhall, Parsonsfield, New-Gloucester, Harpswell, &c. in the counties of York and Cumberland. These were all founded by the year 1785. In the course of ten years following, other churches had arisen in the same counties at Waterborough, Fryeburg, Cornish, Hebron, Buckfield, Paris, Livermore, and Raymondstown; and since them a great many others have been formed in their respective vicinities. Still farther eastward in this District, in the county of Lincoln, churches began to be formed about 1784, by the labours of James Potter, Job Macomber, Isaac Case, and others.

Mr. Potter was born at Brunswick, in this District, in 1754; Mr. Macomber is a native of Middleborough, and Mr. Case of Rehoboth, in Massachusetts. They all began labouring in this part of Maine, when it was in a wilderness condition, and soon churches were formed in Bowdoinham, Thomastown, Edgecomb, Bowdoin, Vassalborough, Ballston, and many other places. Elder Simon Lock, from Wells, was very useful in his ministerial visits in these parts, and as the churches increased, a number of useful ministers were raised up to supply them, among whom were Elisha Snow, Humphrey Purinton, William Stinson, Asa Wilbour, Lemuel Jackson, Andrew Fuller, Ephraim Hall, Mephibosheth Cain, Nehemiah Gould, Job Chadwick, and others.*

As the settlements extended, the Baptists carried their principles eastward until they reached the British line, and a considerable number of churches have been planted by the ministers of this District, in the Provinces of New-Brunswick and Nova-Scotia.

So great has been the increase of the Baptists in the District of Maine, that it now contains three large Associations, not far from a hundred and thirty churches, and some where between six and seven thousand members. This great increase has been partly by emigrants from other places, but mostly by those many and precious revivals, which, for about thirty years past, have been granted to different parts of this highly favoured District.

* Backus, vol. iii. p. 201—212.

Mr. Merrill and his Church become Baptists. 311

BOWDOINHAM ASSOCIATION.

This Association was begun in 1787, of only the three churches of Bowdoinham, Thomastown, and Harpswell. It took its name from that of the town where it was formed, which is on the Kennebeck River, about 170 miles northeast of Boston. This Association had increased to forty-eight churches by the year 1804. Nothing special appears to have occurred in this body during this period, only it experienced an almost uninterrupted scene of prosperity and enlargement.

The churches of which it was composed, were now scattered over a great extent of country, and a division was thought advisable, which was accordingly amicably effected.

LINCOLN ASSOCIATION.

This was formed by the division of the Bowdoinham just mentioned, in 1804. This like the mother body has had a very prosperous course, and has extended its bounds far beyond the Penobscot River, in the new towns and plantations, which have there been settled. It has increased to fifty churches, in which are about two thousand seven hundred members.

An event took place within the bounds of this Association, the year after it was formed, which excited no small attention throughout the United States.

In 1805, Rev. Daniel Merrill, pastor of a Congregational church in Sedgwick, about 300 miles north-east of Boston, embraced the doctrine of believer's baptism, and preached seven sermons in defence of it. These sermons have passsed through many editions, and have had an extensive circulation throughout the United States. The church at Sedgwick was then in a flourishing condition, and had before been famed in its connexion for its piety and purity. As soon as Baptist principles began to be examined among them, many were convinced of their former errors, and embraced them, and by the assistance of Dr. Baldwin of Boston, Mr. John Pitman of Providence, and Mr. Elisha Williams of Beverly, Mr. Merrill and wife, and others of his church, to the number of sixty-six, were buried in baptism, May 13, 1805. Nineteen

312   *A baptismal Controversy ensues.*

more were baptized the day following, and the whole were formed into a Baptist church, and Mr. Merrill was ordained their pastor. The Congregational church continued to repair to the water until about a hundred and twenty of them were baptized !

The fame of these proceedings spread far, and produced unusual sensations among different parties. The Baptists had every reason to believe that Mr. Merrill and his church had embraced their sentiments from a sober conviction of their truth. A number of their most judicious ministers had visited them, heard their account, and given them fellowship. But many of the Pedobaptists wondered and reproached. Their *Dear Brother Merrill*, whom they had always before spoken of in high terms of respect as an evangelical and laborious minister of the cross, was assailed from every quarter. Pamphlet after pamphlet was written against him, to most of which he replied. Others got concerned in the baptismal controversy on both sides of the question, and a watery war raged extensively for a number of years.

The Sedgwick church, after its renovation, united with the Lincoln Association, in which it still continues. The churches of Blue-hill and Deer-isle, one to the north and the other to the south of it, have been formed from it. It has sent forth into the ministry, Phinehas Pillsbury, Henry Hale, Dr. John Burnham, John Roundy, and Amos Allen. All of these ministers, except Dr. Burnham, belonged to it while it was on the Pedobaptist plan. Amaziah Dodge, another of its members, has been approbated to preach.

On east of the bounds of the Lincoln Association, towards the British line, are a number of churches, which, on account of their remote situation, have not yet united with any Association.

CUMBERLAND ASSOCIATION.

THE Bowdoinham Association by 1810, only six years after the Lincoln was taken from it, had increased to fifty-one churches, and had again become too large to meet with convenience in one body ; it was therefore agreed in that year to divide it, and the Androscoggin or Amoriscoggin River, was fixed upon as the dividing line. The churches east of this line remained with the old Association; those to the west of it, united in a new one, to which they gave the name of Cumberland. This Association is in the south-west corner of Maine, and comprehends some of the first churches which were organized in it, particularly Harpswell, Hebron, Buckfield, Paris, Livermore, &c.

The church in Livermore was formed in 1793. It is remarkable for having approbated eleven ministers in the course of a few years. Their names were Elisha Williams, Otis Robinson, Henry Bond, Zebedee Delano, Sylvanus Boardman, William Goding, Thomas Wyman, John Simmons, Ebenezer Bray, Perez Ellis, and Ransom Norton. Williams is now at Beverly, Robinson at Salisbury, New-Hampshire, Delano at Berwick, Boardman at North-Yarmouth, Wyman at Livermore, Norton with the second church in that town, Bray is at Bethel; respecting the others I am not informed.

The church in Portland on account of its singular origin and local situation deserves a brief description. In 1796, five or six persons in this town were hopefully born into the kingdom of God, and became zealously engaged in religious pursuits. The preaching they had usually attended was not sufficiently evangelical to meet their views; they therefore in a short time declined attending it. For a time, some went over to Cape Elizabeth, where they were comforted by the ministry of Rev. Mr. Clark, a Congregational preacher, who died not long after. Among this little company of inquirers for truth, were Benjamin Titcomb, now pastor of the church in Brunswick, and Thomas Beck, one of the deacons of the church, which arose by their means. After the death of Mr. Clark, Mr. Titcomb opened his own house for the reception of his pious associates, and there, for a time, they conducted a little meeting, which frequently did not consist of more than six persons, by singing, praying, and reading sermons. They next proceeded to read the scriptures only, and those who were able expounded them to the rest. All this time they had no thoughts of becoming Baptists, nor was the subject of baptism any part of their study. But having taken the Bible for their guide, believers' baptism followed of course.

Mr. Titcomb was baptized in 1799, by Dr. Green of North-Yarmouth, twelve miles south-east of Portland, and united with the church then under the Doctor's care. Others, not long after, followed his example, until ten persons were baptized, and of this number the church, whose history we have in view, was formed in 1801, and Mr. Titcomb, who had previously been called to the ministry by the church in North-Yarmouth, became its pastor. He continued here until 1804, and then he removed to his present situation in Brunswick. Twenty were added to the Portland church under his ministry. After his removal it remained destitute of a pastor until 1807, when Mr. John Convers was ordained to the care of it, in which he continued about three years. By this time it increased to over a hundred. Soon after his removal, Mr. Caleb Blood was, by the unanimous voice of the church, settled in the pastoral office, in which he still remains. This church made an early purchase of a lot in a central part of the town, ninety feet front, and seventy back, on which they erected a low temporary building, which they occupied until 1811, when it was removed to make room for their present more spacious edifice, which is sixty-one feet by sixty-four. Thus Mr. Blood, in an advanced age, is settled with a young church under promising circumstances.

A number of churches, and some of the oldest in Maine, belong to the New-Hampshire Association. There are a considerable number scattered in different parts of the District, which are not associated, and besides, there is a large body of what are called Free-will Baptists, whose history will be related under a separate head.

The Baptists, in this District, are preparing to erect a college, for the benefit of their community. Considerable sums have already been subscribed towards it, and for a new thing under the sun, the Legislature of Massachusetts very lately granted them a township of unsettled land, for the purpose of carrying forward their design. This was obtained principally by the means of Mr. Merrill of Sedgwick, who was a member of the House of Assembly at the time.

CHAP. X.

NEW-HAMPSHIRE.

THE first settlements in this State were begun in 1623, only three years after the fathers of New-England landed at Plymouth. But we do not find that any Baptists were settled here, until more than a century after. The oldest and most distinguished Baptist establishments in New-Hampshire, were formed in the south-east corner of the State, between the Merrimack and Piscataqua rivers, in the counties of Rockingham and Strafford. Not far from the time that churches began to be gathered here, a few were raised up in the western part of the State, along the Connecticut river, in the counties of Cheshire and Grafton. The third group of churches was gathered in the county of Hillsborough, which lies, for the most part, west of the Merrimack river, and extends from the southern line of the State far up into its middle regions.

But one church was formed in New-Hampshire, previous to the year 1770; that was the one at Newtown, which was gathered in 1755. From 1770, until 1779, nine other churches were planted. From this period they began to increase with great rapidity, so that nine more were established in the year 1780.

This rapid increase of the Baptists in this State aroused the jealousies and resentment of some of the neighbouring Congregational clergy, to such a degree, that one of them wrote a letter against them the next year, which he published in one of the Boston papers. This invidious and arrogant letter contained the following clause: "Alas! the consequence of the prevalence of this sect! They cause divisions every where. In the State of New-Hampshire, where there are many new towns, infant settlements, if this sect gets footing among them, they hinder, and are like to hinder, their settling and supporting learned, pious, and orthodox ministers; and the poor inhabitants of those towns must live, who knows how long! without the *ministry of the gospel and gospel ordinances.*"* But this slanderous epistle had but little effect; the Baptists still continued their zealous and successful exertions,

---

* Backus' History of New-England, vol. III. p. 278.

their sentiments prevailed, and their churches increased, so that by the year 1795, there were, within the bounds of New-Hampshire, 41 churches, 30 ministers, and 2562 communicants, and these churches were scattered in almost every part of the State.

From the last mentioned date to the present time, the Baptist sentiments have probably prevailed with as much rapidity as at any former period ; but as many Baptist members have emigrated to other States, and the Free-will Baptists (as they are called) having of late years proselyted many to their communion, and divided and overrun a number of the Calvinistick churches, their numbers, which may be seen in the table at the end of this work, is not so great as it might otherwise have been. A number of the oldest churches in this State, mentioned by Mr. Backus in his Catalogue for 1784, have either become extinct, or exist under different names.

The New-Hampshire, the Meredith, the Woodstock, and Dublin Associations, are all of them either partly or wholly in this State ; and there are also a few churches in this State, which belong to the Boston and Leyden Associations in Massachusetts, and those of Barre and Danville in Vermont.

Some brief sketches of the history of these Associations, and of some of their most distinguished churches, we shall now attempt to give.

The first Baptist church, which ever existed in New-Hampshire, was gathered at Newtown in 1755, as has already been mentioned. Mr. Backus, who must be our guide in most of the following observations, has not related, with any degree of precision, the circumstances of its origin. This omission, in that scrutinizing researcher, was, doubtless, for the want of materials. He merely informs us, that this church was small in its beginning, was gathered out of a society of *Separate* Pedo-baptists in 1755, and was the only church in the State for fifteen years. He also states that Walter Powers, the father of the present Walter Powers of Gilmantown, was ordained its pastor the same year it was constituted, that it increased for a while under his ministry, and then fell into difficulties and divisions, which interrupted its harmony, and finally terminated in its dissolution. Soon after the church was formed at Haverhill, by Dr. Hezekiah Smith, which was only seven miles off, a number of members united with that body, and the Newtown church lay waste until 1796, when it was revived under Mr. John Peak, now of Newburyport.

But long before the Newtown church arose, there resided at some distance to the north of this town, a woman, who, after living forty years a solitary life, as to communion with her brethren, was finally the means of spreading the Baptist sentiments in this part of the State, and of laying the foundation for some of the oldest churches in the New-Hampshire Association.

The story of this remarkable woman is thus related by Mr. Backus in his history of New-England, Vol. II. p. 265, 266.

About the year 1720, a man by the name of Scammon, of Stratham, on Piscataqua river, married Rachel Thurber, of Rehoboth, Massachusetts, and removed her to his own town. Mrs. Scammon was a woman of piety, and firmly and understandingly established in the Baptist principles. But she was now removed at a distance from her brethren, and settled in a place where the Baptists were not known, and where their sentiments were not named, except by way of censure and reproach. In this lonely situation she remained most of her days, and although she frequently conversed with her neighbours respecting the propriety of her peculiar opinions, yet so strong were their prejudices against them, that for the space of forty years she gained but one proselyte. That was a woman, who being convinced of her duty repaired to Boston, the distance of more than fifty miles, and was baptized by Elder Bound, the pastor of the second church in that town.

Mrs. Scammon, towards the close of her life, fell in with Norcott on Baptism. The arguments in that little work appeared so clear and convincing, that she was firmly persuaded they would have an enlightening effect on the minds of her neighbours and friends, if they could be prevailed upon to read them. She accordingly carried the piece to Boston, with a view of getting it reprinted. But when she come to propose the matter to the printer, he informed her that he had more than a hundred copies of the work then on hand. These she immediately purchased, carried them home, and distributed them around her neighbourhood, to all who would accept of them. She, however, did not live to see much of the fruits of her benevolence and zeal; but she used often to say to her neighbours, that she was fully persuaded that a Baptist church would arise in Stratham, although she might not live to see it. And so it happened that a Baptist church actually arose there soon after her death, and others were gathered in different parts of the country not long after, and the light which was reflected from Norcott's little book, which this pious lady had dispersed abroad, was the means either directly or indirectly of producing them.

"Thus," says Mr. Backus, "Mrs. Scammon's bread, cast upon the water, seems to have been found after many days; the books which she freely dispersed, being picked up, and made useful to many."

The most remarkable instance of this kind, was in the case of Samuel, generally distinguished by the title of Dr. Shepard, who has long been extensively known as an eminent preacher amongst the Baptists, in this part of New-Hampshire. He was, at this time, a young man, engaged in the practice of physick, and being at the house of one of his patients, he took up one of the little books above-mentioned; and on reading it through, he found his mind much impressed with the force of the sentiments which it advocated. He had been converted when very young, but remained in the Pedobaptist connexion. But the light, which he now received, increased, until he was brought fully to embrace the Baptist sentiments; and in a short time became a Baptist minister, and besides all his other labours, planted a church in Brentwood, which now contains almost seven hundred members.

About the time of Mrs. Scammon's death, a revival commenced in this part of New-Hampshire, which prevailed to a considerable extent, and many were led to embrace the Baptist sentiments.

Dr. Smith was now settled in Haverhill, near the borders of New-Hampshire. He frequently made excursions into this State, and zealously engaged in the work, which was then going on, and by the eloquence of his preaching, and the weight of his character, bore down the strong prejudices against the Baptists, and was the means of abundantly extending their cause. During one week, in June, 1770, Mr. Smith baptized thirty-eight persons, who belonged mostly to Nottingham, Brentwood, and Stratham. Among this number were a Congregational minister, two deacons, and the majority of a Congregational church. This minister's name was Eliphalet Smith ; he was the pastor of a Congregational church in a part of Nottingham, called Deerfield. In this place a Baptist church was formed soon after this great baptism, and Mr. Eliphalet Smith was ordained their pastor, who after continuing with them a number of years, removed to the county of Lincoln, in the District of Maine, and the church, I conclude, is now included in that of Brentwood. Dr. Shepard was one of the number baptized by Dr. Smith, in this excursion ; he began to preach soon after, and was ordained at Stratham, the next year, by Drs. Stillman of Boston, Smith of Haverhill, and Manning of Providence.

The church at Deerfield, we have already observed, was formed in 1770 ; a church was planted in Stratham the same year, and those in Brentwood and Nottingham were gathered the year after. Thus in a very short time after Mrs. Scammon's death, four Baptist churches were formed, and the Baptists had become numerous in these parts. If it be a fact that the angels inform the inhabitants of heaven, of the prosperity of Zion on earth, what joyful tidings must they have carried to this once mourning and anxious, but now glorified spirit.

The remaining part of the history of New-Hampshire, we shall now exhibit under the heads of the Associations which it contains.

NEW-HAMPSHIRE ASSOCIATION.

THIS body was begun under the name of a Conference, in 1776, and did not assume the name and standing of an Association, until 1785. The churches of which this Conference was at first composed, were those of Brentwood, Berwick and Sanford ; the two last were in the District of Maine. Dr. Shepard and William Hooper, then of Berwick, now of Madbury, were the principal promoters of this little Association. At their first interview, they were visited by Mr. Backus, the historian, who was then travelling through the country. This small community soon began to increase; some churches, which had been formed before they began to associate, soon fell in with them, others were raised up soon after, and united with them in their progress, and in a harmonious and prosperous manner, they have travelled on from their beginning to the present time. And although their number has, at various times, been diminished by different causes, yet they remain, in some measure, a large, and in every sense, a respectable body.

From the beginning of this Association some of its churches were in the District of Maine, and in that District, a considerable portion of them have ever been, and are still situated. Some account of these churches has already been given.

Of those churches in this Association which are situated in New-Hampshire, the one called Brentwood is by far the largest, and in many respects, the most distinguished; and, indeed, this is the only church in this region, of which I have been able to collect any historical sketches, of any considerable importance.

Brentwood is in the county of Rockingham, about twenty miles westward of Portsmouth. The church here was organized in May 1771, with only thirteen members; but it has now increased to almost seven hundred. This great increase has been partly by means of revivals with which this body has been favoured in a remarkable manner, and partly by collecting in its fold other churches, and the broken remains of other churches in its vicinity, some of which had been formed before it.

The Brentwood church at present, comprehends all the Baptists throughout an extensive circle around it; and consists, besides the main establishment at Brentwood, where Dr. Shepard resides, of five other branches, which are distinguished by the names of Epping, Lee and Nottingham, Hawke and Hampstead, Northwood, and Salisbury. These branches extend over a territory, whose diameter is upwards of thirty miles, and whose circumference, of course, is not far from a hundred. They are mostly supplied with preachers, and all of them enjoy the privileges, and exercise, in some measure, the power of distinct churches. Brentwood is their Jerusalem, to which they frequently repair. Here, like a bishop, in the midst of his diocess, resides the venerable elder, who is considered as the pastor of this extensive flock, and who, in his active days, spent much of his time in visiting among them, and whose popularity has probably been the means of collecting this extensive and unwieldy body, this church of churches, whose affairs must certainly be managed with peculiar inconvenience.

This wide spread church, not long since, projected a plan of becoming an association by itself. This plan has not yet been carried into effect, and it would certainly be a preposterous measure. For what is an association, according to the Baptist phraseology, but an assembly of churches? But the Brentwood church proposes to associate with itself.

This church, from its various branches, has sent forth a considerable number of preachers, and among them was Joshua Smith, the author of a little hymn book, which has been much esteemed, and had an extensive circulation. This worthy minister, after labouring much, with good success in various places, died with a consumption in 1795.*

As Dr. Shepard, the founder, father and pastor of this extensive community, is now apparently just upon the verge of time, it may not be improper to give some sketches of his character. He was born at Salisbury, Massachusetts, near Newburyport, in 1739. Some account of his early life, until he engaged in the ministry, has already been given. For many years after he began his ministerial course, his labours were abundant and remarkably successful; and, indeed, he has never been idle in the Lord's vineyard. For besides his labours in the ministry, he has continued more or less through life, to exercise the functions of his medical profession, and he has also been the author of a number of little works, which we shall mention at the close of this account. The calls of his profession, and the extensiveness of his flock, made it necessary for him almost incessantly to lead an itinerant life. The reader may form some idea of the extent and success of the labours of this eminent minister, from the following letter, which he wrote to Mr. Backus in 1781.

* His Excellency William Plumer, Esq. Governor of New-Hampshire, who lives in Epping, was formerly a minister in this church.

Extract from one of Dr. Shepard's Letters.

"I rejoice, Sir, to hear, that in the midst of judgment, God is remembering mercy, and calling in his elect, from east to west. You have refreshed my mind with good news from the west and south, and in return I will inform you of good news from the north and east. Some hundreds of souls are hopefully converted in the counties of Rockingham, Strafford, and Grafton, in New-Hampshire, within about a year past. In the last journey I went before my beloved wife was taken from me, I baptized seventy-two men, women, and some that may properly be called children, who confessed with their mouths the salvation God had wrought in their hearts, to good satisfaction. Meredith, in Strafford, has a church gathered the year past, consisting of between sixty and seventy members. I baptized forty three in that town in one day, and such a solemn weeping of the multitude on the shore, I never before saw. The ordinance of baptism appeared to carry universal conviction through them, even to a man. The wife, when she saw her husband going forward, began to weep, to think she was not worthy to go with him; in like manner the husband the wife, the parent the child, the children the parent; that the lamentation and weeping, methinks, may be compared to the inhabitants of Hadadrimmon, in the valley of Magiddon. Canterbury, in Rockingham county, has two Baptist churches gathered in the year past, one in the parish of Northfield; the number I cannot tell, but it is considerably large. I baptized thirty-one there, and a number have been baptized since by others. The other is in the parish of Loudon, in said Canterbury, containing above one hundred members. Another church, of about fifty members, is gathered in Chichester; another in Barrington, consisting of a goodly number, and one in Hubbardston, all three in Strafford county. Two churches in Grafton county, one in Holderness, the other in Rumney. The church in Rumney had one Haines ordained last August, much to the satisfaction of the people. All these seven churches have been gathered in about a year past. One church was gathered last fall in Wells, over which brother Nathaniel Lord, late of Berwick, is ordained. There appears to be a general increase of the Baptist principles, through all the eastern parts of New-England."

For the want of sufficient materials, and a more intimate acquaintance, I must forbear pursuing the biography of this distinguished servant of Christ. His writings are,

1st. A Scriptural Inquiry respecting the ordinance of water baptism. This piece was answered at different times, by three Pedobaptist ministers.

2d. A Reply to these answers in defence of the Inquiry, &c.

3d. A Scriptural Inquiry concerning what the Friends or Quakers call spiritual baptism. Being an answer to a work, published by Moses Brown, of Providence, Rhode Island.

4th. The Principle of Universal Salvation, examined and tried by the Law and Testimony.

5th. An Examination of Elias Smith's two pamphlets, respecting original sin, the death Adam was to die the day he eat of the forbidden fruit, and the final annihilation of the wicked.

It would doubtless be gratifying to the members of this Association, to read some historical sketches of a number of remaining very respectable churches; but as no adequate materials have been received from them, what has already been said, must suffice for its history. It may, however, be proper to observe, respecting its boundaries, that it extends along the sea coast about eighty miles, from about twenty miles west of Portsmouth, in New-Hampshire, almost to Portland in the District of Maine, where it meets the Cumberland Association. The churches extend back from the sea coast generally about sixty miles.

MEREDITH ASSOCIATION.

THIS body was formed in 1789. It was small at first, and for some cause has never appeared to enjoy much prosperity or enlargement. It has, however, at different times, contained almost twice as many churches as it does at present. Some of the churches, which formerly belonged to it, have united with the Woodstock and Barre Associations, and others have been overrun by the Free-will Baptists, who have now become numerous in its vicinity.

The town of Meredith from which this Association received its name, is in the county of Strafford, on the west side of Winnipisseogee lake, fifteen miles north of Gilmanton, and seventy north-west of Portsmouth. The church here, which is one of the oldest in this body, was gathered in 1780, when Dr. Shepard, of Brentwood, baptized forty-four persons in one day. Mr. Nicholas Folsom, who went from Brentwood, was ordained the pastor of this church in 1782; and in that office, though far advanced in age, he still continues. This venerable elder has long been considered the father of this little Association.

The church in Sandbornton is also one of the oldest in this body; it was formed in 1780. Mr. John Crockett, their present pastor, was settled among them in 1794.

The church in Rumney, in the county of Grafton, was also formed in 1780. Mr. Cotton Haines was their first pastor, but he was, not long after, rejected from the fellowship of the Baptists. Under the ministry of Mr. Ezra Willmarth, lately pastor of this church, it experienced a great revival; in 1811, it received the addition of about one hundred and forty members, which increased its whole number to upwards of three hundred. Rev. Peletiah Chapin, formerly a Congregational minister, was baptized in this place, by Mr. Willmarth, in 1806. He received Baptist ordination immediately after, and is now preaching some where in this region, to good acceptance.

DUBLIN ASSOCIATION.

THIS little body was organized as an Association in 1809, in the town from which it received its name, which is in the county of Cheshire, upwards of sixty miles west of Portsmouth, and near the southern borders of New-Hampshire. It consisted, at the time of its formation, of six churches, which were dismissed from the Woodstock Association.

The churches of Temple, Mason, and Dublin, are the oldest in this community, and were among the first, which were formed in this part of the State. The first of these bodies is now destitute of a pastor, but the other two are supplied by Elders William Elliot, and Elijah Willard. These two ministers have been labouring with good success in this part of the vineyard for many years, and they are now the only ordained preachers in this Association.

This Association is situated in the southern parts of the counties of Hillsborough and Cheshire.

On the western side of New-Hampshire, along the Connecticut river, and extending some distance back in the country, is a large group of very respectable churches, which are supplied by a number of eminent ministers. These churches mostly belong to the Woodstock Association; and, indeed, they compose about half of that body, and some of them are almost as old as any in New-Hampshire.

We shall now attempt to give some general account of the beginning of the Baptists in this region, and then proceed to some historical sketches of a few individual churches.

About the year 1770, and during a few succeeding years, a considerable number of Baptist brethren, and some ministers of the denomination, removed from different parts of Massachusetts and Connecticut, and some from other parts, and settled along the western side of New-Hampshire, in the counties of Cheshire and Grafton, on, and at no great distance from, Connecticut River, which divides this State from Vermont.

Some of the ministers, who settled in this region, were Matturin Ballou, Ebenezer Bailey, Jedidiah Hibbard, Eleazer Beckwith, Thomas Baldwin, now of Boston, Isaac Kenny, &c. The oldest churches, along or near to the river, are those of Richmond, Westmoreland, Marlow, and Newport.

In 1779, Elders Job Seamans, of Attleborough, Massachusetts, and Biel Ledoyt, of Woodstock, Connecticut, were appointed by the Warren Association, to travel, and spend a few weeks in preaching in these new and destitute plantations. Their appointment was in consequence of an affecting letter from Mr. Caleb Blood, who was at that time preaching at Marlow. Mr. Blood informed his brethren of the destitute situation of the people around him, and earnestly entreated the Association to send some ministering brethren over into this Macedonia to help him. Messrs. Seamans and Ledoyt were selected for the mission, which they performed in 1779. In their journey, they travelled up the Connecticut river as far as Woodstock, in Vermont, before the church was raised in that place ; they preached both sides of the river, but mostly on the New-Hampshire side ; their coming was refreshing to the hearts of many, and an evident blessing followed their zealous and evangelical labours. Both of these ministers afterwards removed to this State, and settled not far from the scene of their labours in this missionary excursion. Mr. Ledoyt, who settled in Newport, has returned to Woodstock, in Connecticut, where he was settled before his removal hither, but Mr. Seamans still remains at New-London, the aged and much respected pastor of the large and flourishing church which was planted, and which hath been built up under his ministry.

A number of ministers, whose names ought to be mentioned with respect, have settled on this side of New-Hampshire, still later than those we have already named. Among these are Jeremiah Higbee, Ariel Kendrick, Joseph Wheat, Thomas Brown, Nathan Leonard, and Joseph Elliot.

Near the southwest corner of this State are two churches belonging to the Leyden Association, one of them is called Richmond, and the other Hinsdale and Chesterfield. The Richmond church was formed in 1770, and the same year, Mr. Matturin Ballou was ordained their pastor. The next year they joined the Warren Association, and continued in connexion with that body a great number of years. This church has passed through a variety of scenes, both prosperous and adverse. For a number of years they were harassed with ministerial taxes. In 1780, they experienced a revival, by which more than forty members were added. But soon after this joyful event, a division ensued, and another church was formed, and Artemas Aldrich was ordained as its pastor. In 1790, these churches, which had long been low and in broken circumstances, were refreshed by a copious shower of divine grace, and in the course of two years, upwards of a hundred members were added ; the two churches laid aside their bickerings and united as one ; their two former pastors were dismissed, and Mr. Isaac Kenny was ordained to the pastoral care of the united body. How matters have been with them, from the last mentioned period, to the present time, I have learnt no more, than that they, at present, are reduced to a small number, and are destitute of a pastor.

The church at Hinsdale and Chesterfield has, for its pastor, a young man, by the name of Joseph Elliot, a son of William Elliot of Mason.

We shall now proceed to give some brief sketches of a few of the churches on the west side of New-Hampshire, which belong to the Woodstock Association.

The church in Westmoreland being the oldest, demands our first attention. Westmoreland is on the east bank of Connecticut river, in Cheshire county, directly opposite Putney in Vermont. Many of the first settlers in the town, removed from Mr. Backus' congregation in Middleborough. The church here was formed in 1771. Mr. Ebenezer Bailey was its first pastor; he was ordained among them about two years after they were constituted, and continued with them until a few years past. But he has now become a member of the church in Alstead, and is succeeded in the pastoral office by Mr. Nathan Leonard.

The same year the church in Westmoreland was formed, there was one gathered in Lebanon, a town in Grafton county, which also lies on the river, but a few miles below Dartmouth College. Mr. Jedidiah Hibbard was ordained the pastor of this church not long after it was formed, and continued in that office until 1784, when he removed from them. Soon after he left them, the church was so much reduced by the removal of others, that, in a few years, it became extinct.

In this county are also two churches of considerable age, distinguished by the names of Canaan and Grafton. The first was formed in 1783, and was, for a number of years, under the pastoral care of Dr. Baldwin; the other was gathered in 1785; its first pastor was Oliver Williams, who died among them in 1790. He was from Rhode-Island, and is supposed to have been a descendant of the famous Roger Williams, the founder of that State. This church is now under the care of Mr. Joseph Wheat.

The church in Marlow was formed in 1777. Mr. Eleazer Beckwith was its pastor many years. He, and many of the members of the church, removed from Lyme, in Connecticut. In this church, Mr. Caleb Blood, who was afterwards in Shaftsbury, then in Boston, and now in

Portland, was ordained. This has, at times, been a large and flourishing body. In 1790, it contained almost two hundred members; but it has now become so much reduced, that it has almost, if not entirely lost its visibility as a church.

The church, which is now called Newport, according to Mr. Backus, was first established in Croydon, a neighbouring town, in 1778. But in 1790, the brethren here united with those in Newport, and settled among them Mr. Biel Ledoyt, from Woodstock, Connecticut, whose name has, not long since, been mentioned. From that period the church has been known by the name of Newport, which name suggests, that some of its first settlers removed from one of the principal towns in Rhode-Island. Mr. Ledoyt resided here about fourteen years, and then returned again to Woodstock. While resident in Newport, he prosecuted his ministry with that evangelical ardour, for which he has, from the commencement of it, been peculiarly distinguished, and he had the happiness of seeing that his labours were not in vain in the Lord. In 1793, he thus wrote to a friend: "It hath been a long, dark, and cloudy night with me and the people here; but glory to our God, the cloud is dispersing fast. His work is begun among us. Newport and Croydon are greatly blest. There have been forty souls hopefully converted in a few weeks among us. I have baptized twenty-nine in four weeks. The work appears still going on. I cannot be idle, it is out of my power to answer all the calls I have at this time; but I endeavour to do all I can. Being favoured with health, and the spirit of preaching, I ascend the mountains easy. There is a prospect of a glorious reformation in these parts. O may it spread far and wide! God hath remembered my family also for good; my three eldest daughters, I hope, are converted; the oldest seventeen years, and the youngest ten years old, are baptized."

NEW-LONDON. This church is in the northwest corner of the county of Hillsborough, about twenty miles east of Connecticut river. It was planted in 1788, by Mr. Job Seamans, who still remains its aged and much respected pastor. Mr. Seamans was born in Swansea, Massachusetts, in 1748. He was one of the company, which went to Nova-Scotia, with Elder Nathan Mason, in 1763,

Here he was converted and began to preach. After his return he became pastor of the church in Attleborough, in his native State, now under the care of Mr. James Read, in which station he continued fourteen years. From this place he removed to his present residence, when the country was very new, and much uncultivated in every respect. Here he soon planted a little church, which immediately began to increase, and has now arisen to a large and flourishing body. Mr. Seamans has had the happiness of witnessing, in this field of his labours, many precious and extensive revivals. A work broke out among his people in 1792, of which he gave the following account in a letter to Mr. Backus : " This town consists of about fifty families, and I hope that between forty and fifty souls have been translated out of darkness into God's marvellous light, in this town, besides a number in Sutton and Fishersfield, who congregate with us. Fifteen have been baptized, and joined to the church, and I expect that a number more will come forward in a short time. Indeed, I know not of one of them but what is likely to submit to gospel order, nor one person in the town, who stands in any considerable opposition. We have lectures or conferences almost every day or evening in the week. Our very children meet together to converse and pray with each other ; and I believe I may safely say, that our young people were never a quarter so much engaged in frolicking, as they now are in the great concerns of the soul and eternity. Some things in this work have exceeded every thing I ever saw before. Their convictions have usually been very clear and powerful, so that industrious men and women have had neither inclination nor strength to follow their business as usual. And they freely acknowledge the justice and sovereignty of God. They also have desires beyond what I have ever before known, for the universal out-pouring of the Holy Spirit." This letter was written in 1793. This work progressed so fast, that by the next year, the church, which, at its commencement, consisted of only eighteen members, had increased to a hundred and fifteen. Some of all ages, from seventy down to eight years old, had been brought in ; and what was remarkable, there were, at that time, in this church, thirty seven men and their wives.*

Another revival, which prevailed to a considerable extent, took place among this people, but a few years ago.

Our limits forbid us to make any particular mention of but two more of this cluster of churches, and of these we can give but very brief accounts. These churches are Cornish and Alstead, both in the county of Cheshire.

The town of Cornish is on Connecticut river, directly opposite Windsor in Vermont. In this town a church was established in 1788. Mr. Jedidiah Hibbard was pastor of it some years after he left Grafton, but it is now supplied by Mr. Ariel Kendrick, and is a large and respectable body.

Alstead is situated still lower down the river, eight miles below Charlestown, formerly called No. 4. The church was formed here in 1790 of fifteen members, but it has now increased to about a hundred and fifty. Its pastor is Jeremiah Higbee, a native of Middletown, Connecticut, who was ordained among them in 1794.

In the county of Hillsborough, and towards the lower part of this State, are three churches which formerly belonged to the Warren, but now to the Boston Association. These churches are distinguished by the name of Weare, New-Boston, and Nottingham-West. The church at Weare was formed in 1768. An account of its origin and early progress I have not obtained; but about 1787, Mr. Amos Wood, who was educated at Rhode-Island college, was ordained among them, and continued their pastor until his death. Mr. Wood was a minister of considerable eminence and usefulness, and under his ministry this church became a large and respectable body. But since his death, it has, for the most part, been destitute of preaching, and in other respects in a tried and broken situation. But lately, they were supplied, a part of the time, by a young man, by the name of Evans, from the church in Reading, near Boston, and their circumstances became more comfortable and prosperous. The church is now under the care of Elder Ezra Willmarth.

Respecting the church in New-Boston, I have obtained no historical sketches. It has not, however, been formed

* Backus' History, Vol. III. p. 284, 285.

many years, and it is now under the pastoral care of a very worthy minister, whose name is Isaiah Stone, who was once at Dummerston, in Vermont.

The church in Nottingham-West was formed in 1805. It is said to owe its origin to the labours of Mr. Daniel Merrill, now of Sedgwick, Maine, while he was a Pedobaptist minister. In the winter of 1793, Mr. Merrill spent a number of months in this place. A revival commenced under his ministry, in which about thirty were hopefully converted, and professed religion, at that time, in the Pedobaptist connexion. But most of them became Baptists afterwards, and were the principal materials in building the Baptist church in this place.

In the neighbourhood of these three churches, are the broken remains of some others, particularly at Londonderry and Hopkinton. The churches of Bow and Goffstown, have lately been revived; they have united into one, and are under the pastoral care of Elder Gates.

Thus we have given a general view of the Calvinistic Associated Baptists in New-Hampshire. There are a few churches of the same faith and order, which are not associated, which will be brought to view in the general list of Associations and churches.

There is, also, in this State, a considerable number of churches of the Free-will Baptists, of whom some information will be given in the history of that community.

The Congregational church is the established religion of New-Hampshire. But dissenters of various denominations form a large body of its inhabitants. I do not find that the Baptists have suffered much in this State, from religious oppression, or been much harassed with those fretting plagues to New-England dissenters, ministerial taxes.

This moderation we may attribute partly to the spirit of the established church, but mostly to other causes. While New-Hampshire was a provincial government, its Governors and Counsellors were appointed by the Crown of England. This circumstance was favourable to dissenters, and operated as a check to the monopolizing views of the Congregational clergy, and was the reason, as Mr. Backus informs us, why that denomination was not exalted to such an overbearing pre-eminence here, as in Massachusetts and Connecticut.

Another reason why ecclesiastical publicans, or ministerial tax-gatherers have not been so troublesome to the Baptists and other dissenters in this State, as in some of the neighbouring ones, may be, that under the government of Benning Wentworth, while a large portion of the State was unsettled, there were grants of ministerial lands in all the unsettled townships. These grants provided one lot for the first settled minister, and another for the support of the ministry. A few Baptist ministers obtained these lands by right of being the first settled ministers, for they were not exclusively promised to any one denomination ; but most of them have fallen into the hands of Congregational ministers ; and have, in many places, precluded the need of religious taxation.

By the Constitution of New-Hampshire, " all towns, parishes, bodies corporate, or religious societies, &c. are empowered to make adequate provision for public protestant teachers of piety, morality and religion." But it also *provides*, " that no person of any one particular religious sect or denomination, shall ever be compelled to pay towards the support of the teachers of another persuasion, sect, or denomination."*

This article promises all that dissenters would ask. But notwithstanding these strong and unqualified terms of exemption, the Baptists and other dissenters, have, in a few instances, been obliged to lodge certificates, or make some formal declaration of their faith to get clear of parish *rates*. But these instances have not been numerous, and, at present, our brethren in this State generally enjoy all the religious privileges, which they have ever asked from the civil power, viz. *to be let alone.*

* Bill of Rights, Art. VI.

CHAP. XI.

VERMONT.

THIS is wholly an inland State, and is bounded north by Lower Canada, east by Connecticut river, which divides it from New-Hampshire, south by Massachusetts, and west by New-York. This State began to be settled about 1725 or 1730; the south part of it, at that time, was claimed by Massachusetts. After the year 1741, the whole territory was considered as lying within the jurisdiction of New-Hampshire; but in 1764, it was by order of the King of Britain, annexed to the province of New-York. This occasioned a long series of altercation between the settlers and claimants under New-Hampshire and the government of New-York. But these tedious controversies were finally adjusted, and in 1791, Vermont was admitted a member of the federal union.*

There were but two Baptist churches established in this State, previous to the year 1780. The first of these was gathered in Shaftsbury in 1768, and the other at Pownal in 1773. An account of these churches will be given when we come to treat of the Association, to which they belong. About the year 1780, and during a few succeeding years, a number of Baptist ministers from different parts of the neighbouring States removed and settled amidst the lofty forests of this then uncultivated territory. These ministers were preceded in their settlement here, by a few families of their brethren, they were attended in their removals by a considerable number more, and multitudes shortly followed after them, who dispersed in almost every direction on both sides of the Green Mountains, in the lower and middle regions of the State, and thus laid the foundation for the large number of churches, which shortly afterwards arose.

Between the years 1780 and 1790, thirty-two churches were planted in Vermont, so that together with the two which had been planted before, there were at the last mentioned date, thirty-four churches in this State, in which were twenty-eight ordained, and fifteen licensed preach-

---
* Morse's Geography, vol. I. p. 361.

ers, and their whole number of communicants was about sixteen hundred. Elisha Ransom, Elisha Rich, Joseph Cornell, Thomas Skeels, Hezekiah Eastman, William Bentley, John Hibbard, John Peak, Caleb Blood, Aaron Leland, Isaac Beal, John Drew, Isaac Webb, Henry Green, Isaiah Stone, and Joseph Call, were among the first Baptist ministers, who settled in this State, and by whose laborious and evangelical exertions, the early churches were planted. But few of these ministers moved into the State, with the immediate expectation of taking the pastoral care of churches, for at the time of their removal very few churches had been gathered; but most of them came by the invitation of the few scattering inhabitants, who had just commenced the settlement of their plantations, and were desirous of having the gospel preached among them. And some of them were merely adventurers into a new country for the purpose of obtaining lands on which they might plant their families, and provide for their support. But that wise Providence, which led them in the wilderness, not only made a way for their temporal comfort and advantage, but soon opened a door for peculiar usefulness in their ministerial labours; showers of grace were soon sent down on many of the infant settlements; the calls for their labours became numerous and importunate, and the Lord inspired his servants with diligence and delight in his service, and crowned their labours with abundant success.

In the churches, which were planted by these men, have been raised up a number of ministerial sons, who have long been and still continue to be successful labourers in this part of the Lord's vineyard. Their names will be mentioned in the history of the churches and Associations with which they are respectively connected.

There are, at present, within the bounds of this State about 80 churches, most of which are connected with the Shaftsbury, the Woodstock, the Vermont, the Richmond, the Barre, and the Danville Associations, all of which bodies were organized within this State; none of them, however, are exclusively in it, and the Shaftsbury and Woodstock have the majority of their churches in the States of New-York, Massachusetts and New-Hampshire.

As the churches, in this State, began to associate soon after they were planted, and have, with a very few exceptions, always travelled in an associated capacity, it may be best to exhibit what the limits of this work will permit us to say of them, in connection with the histories of the Associations to which they belong.

SHAFTSBURY ASSOCIATION.

This Association was formed in the town from which it received its name, in the year 1780. It contained at first the five following churches, viz. two in Shaftsbury, the first in Cheshire, then called, now New-Providence, one in Stillwater, and one at White-Creek. The principal ministers were Peter Warden, William Wait, Lemuel Powers, and Joseph Cornell. Lemuel Powers was ordained at this first meeting of the Association.

For a few years after this body was formed, it embraced some churches, which now belong to the Vermont Association. At present, though this Association contains thirty-two churches, yet but four of them are in the State of Vermont, viz. the first and fourth in Shaftsbury, the first in Pownal, and the church in Stanford; sixteen are in the State of New-York, eight in that of Massachusetts, and four in Upper Canada.

Some sketches of those churches belonging to this body, which are situated in Massachusetts, New-York, and Upper Canada, will be given in the history of the States and Province to which they belong. Although there are so few churches in this community situated in Vermont, yet, as it was formed in this State, this may be the most proper place to give a general view of its movements. We shall first, however, give some brief sketches of the few churches which belong to it in this State.

SHAFTSBURY. This town is in Bennington county, near the south-west corner of the State. It joins the town of Bennington on the south, and the State of New-York on the west. Such is its local situation, being near to the place where the three States of New-York, Vermont, and Massachusetts meet, that it has never been at any great distance from the centre of the Association, and here its sessions have very frequently been held.

It has already been observed, that the oldest church in Vermont was formed in this town in 1768; this was but four years after Bennington began to be settled. I can find no particular account of the origin of this church. Mr. Backus merely mentions, that Mr. Bliss Willoughby, who was ordained as the pastor of a Separate church, at a place called Newent, in the town of Norwich, Connecticut, in 1753 ; who went to England in the character of an agent for the Separate churches in 1756, became a Baptist after the year 1764, was a leader in early times amongst the Baptists in this place.* He also mentions that his son Ebenezer Willoughby, preached among this people, although neither he nor his father had the pastoral care of them ; and that in 1774, the church consisted of 39 members. This town appears to have abounded with Baptists ; a second church was formed here in 1780, a third in 1781, and a fourth in 1788. The third church was composed of brethren, mostly from Rhode-Island, who were strenuous for the imposition of hands, and their church was founded upon what are called *The Six Principles.* This church united with the fourth in 1798. At present there are three churches in this town, called the first, second, and fourth. Two of them belong to the Association, and one does not. The first church is under the pastoral care of a young man, a native of the place, whose name is Isaiah Mattison.

The second church has no pastor, and never had ; but they have a worthy exhorter among them, by the name of Downer, who is now 80 years old.

The fourth in this town has flourished more than any of the rest. It was many years supplied by Mr. Caleb Blood, and under his ministry it experienced some precious revivals and prospered greatly. The most distinguished of these refreshing seasons, was in the years 1798 and 1799, at which time, about 150 persons were baptized. An interesting account of this revival was written by Mr. Blood, and after being inserted in a number of pamphlets and Magazines, it was published in Mr. Woodward's Surprising Accounts, &c. After administering to this church about nineteen years, Mr. Blood, in 1807, by the request of the 3d church, then newly formed in Boston, removed

---

* Backus' History, Vol. III. p. 296. I find the account of Mr. Willoughby's being a leader, &c. is disputed by some, and supposed probable by others. And so I must leave it.

and settled with them. There he continued about three years, and then he removed to Portland, in the District of Maine, where he now resides. The church, which he left in Shaftsbury, has had some refreshing seasons since his removal; they are still a large and respectable body; but as yet remain destitute of a pastor.

His Excellency Jonas Galusha, Esq. the present Governor of Vermont, resides in the neighbourhood of this church, of which a number of his family are members. One of his sons, who was bred to the law, has lately embraced the gospel, has united with this church, and by it has been approbated to preach.

POWNAL.—This town is also in the county of Bennington, and lies in the south-west corner of Vermont, having Massachusetts on the south, and New-York on the west. Through it runs the Hoosuck river, on which some Dutch people from the State of New-York, formed settlements, as early as any which were made in Bennington.

In 1764, a Baptist minister by the name of Benjamin Garner, from West-Greenwich, in the State of Rhode-Island, travelled into these parts, and preached among the few inhabitants through the summer of that year; and the year following he removed his family and settled in the place. Nothing of a religious nature appeared here, until 1772, when Mr. Garner, having found five Baptist members besides himself, he united with them, and embodied them into a church. The next year the place was visited with a distressing sickness, which was the means of awakening many to the concerns of religion, and the church, this year, was increased to sixty members.

Mr. Garner made high pretensions to godliness, but his profession and practice were far from corresponding with each other. The foul sin of uncleanness easily beset him. Of this sin he had been accused while in Rhode-Island, and a repetition of it here, plunged him into disgrace, and the new-formed church into embarrassment and confusion. This affair happened soon after the enlargement just mentioned, and in a broken and disconsolate situation, this infant church remained, until the winter of 1781, when they were visited by Francis Bennet from Foster in Rhode-

Island, whose labours were blessed among them, and the church soon after resumed its visibility and travel.*

In 1788, Elder Caleb Nichols, who was also from Rhode-Island, settled in Pownal, and became the pastor of this church, in which station he laboured with much acceptance and success for many years. Mr. Nichols was born in Exeter, R. I. March 12, 1743. He was a vain and thoughtless youth, much attached to the violin and merry company. At the age of twenty-four, he was brought to embrace the Saviour, and soon after was baptized by Elder Nathan Young. Not long after he began to preach, he was ordained to the pastoral care of the second church in Coventry in his native state, which had been constituted a few months before. Under Mr. Nichols' ministry, this church prospered greatly, so that in the course of eight or ten years it increased to 350 members; but in the time of the war the members scattered abroad, and the church became so broken and feeble, that Mr. Nichols thought best to remove from them, at the time already mentioned.

In a MS. of Mr. John Leland's, written while Mr. Nichols was alive, I find his character thus given : " Elder Nichols moved into Pownal in 1788, bringing with him not only fair paper credentials, but what far exceeds, a heart glowing with love to God and men ; and now, instead of using his violin to captivate the thoughtless throng, he is engaged with successful zeal in sounding the gospel trumpet. His life and conversation are exemplary ; his preaching is spiritual and animating, pretty full of the musical *New-Light tone.* But his gift in prayer is his great excellency ; for he not only prays as if he was softly climbing Jacob's ladder to the portals of heaven, but his expressions are so doctrinal, that a good sermon may be heard in one of his prayers."

Under the ministry of this excellent man, the Pownal church was edified and enlarged. The year after he removed among them, a revival attended his labours. In

---

* Mr. Garner died at Pownal, in the autumn of 1793, in the 78th year of his age. For a long time before his death he was, to use his own words, " A poor object of despair." But a little before he died, he manifested some comfortable views in the prospect of eternity, and once said to a friend " That he believed that all the punishment he should ever endure would be in this life."

Second Pownal Church....Saratoga Association. 339

1793, another powerful work of God broke out among them, and in a short time about seventy were added to their number. This worthy minister finished his course in 1804. Since his death, the church has experienced some refreshing seasons, and been supplied with different preachers, but have not as yet settled any one among them in the pastoral office.

The 2d church in Pownal was gathered in the west part of the town in 1790, by Mr. Bennet, whose name has already been mentioned. This church has never been large, and has never united with the Association.

Concerning the church in Sanford, I have received no information.

We shall now proceed to give some brief sketches of the body whose history we have under consideration.

The Shaftsbury Association, although of a recent date, compared with some of its sister communities, yet on account of its almost continual prosperity and enlargement, the number and size of its churches, and the number of eminent ministers amongst them, must be considered as one of the most important establishments of the kind, amongst the American Baptists.

In 1788, the number of its churches had increased to sixteen, at which time the total number of members was about 800.

In 1796, the number of churches was twenty eight, and in this year upwards of four hundred were added by baptism, which made the whole number of members almost eighteen hundred.

In the year 1800, this Association contained upwards of forty churches, and more than four thousand members. In this year there were added by baptism 767. In this prosperous manner, this body progressed, until the year 1804, when its number amounted to between five and six thousand. It had now become so large and extensive, that a division which had previously been proposed was amicably effected.

The churches in this Association, at the time of its division, were scattered over the counties of Berkshire and Hampshire in Massachusetts, and in those of Columbia, Rensselaer, Washington, and Saratoga, in New-York. It had in former years been much more extensive in its boundaries, but many churches had been dismissed before this period, to unite with Associations which had been established within their respective vicinities.

Most of the churches which were dismissed in 1804 were situated to the westward of the Hudson river, in the counties of Washington and Saratoga in the State of New-York; these united in forming the Saratoga Association.

About the time of this division, the Association probably contained as great a number of Elders of distinguished abilities and eminent usefulness, as any other Association in the United States. But the Saratoga Association took off some of these men, others, not long after, were taken away by death, and some removed to other parts; and thus this extensive and influential establishment, was not only reduced in its numbers but enfeebled in its energies. But at present it appears to be resuming its former character, and is travelling on with reputation and strength.

For a number of years, this Association was considerably occupied in discussing the question, " Whether church members ought to be tolerated in uniting with, and continuing to frequent, Masonick Societies, to the grief of their brethren ?" This was a question of much importance, and at the same time of a very embarrassing nature. It appears to have been started in the Association in 1798, and continued to be agitated more or less for five or six years. It is stated in their Minutes, that there were, in some of their churches, at the time this matter was taken up, brethren, who had united with Masonick Societies, and who continued to frequent their Lodges in opposition to the remonstrances, and to the continual grief of their brethren. When this matter was brought before the Association, the brethren generally were puzzled to know what advice to give. They could by no means approve of the grievous conduct of the brethren complained of; and at the same time, as it could not be proved that they had, by uniting with the Masonick Fraternity, violated any moral rule, they could find no law by which they could be made the subjects of church discipline and censure. The Association, at first, said but little on the matter, but the question being agitated from year to year, they at length became somewhat animated with their own discussions, and expressed themselves with more energy and decision on the subject. In 1803, a committee, who had been appointed for the purpose, after a short preamble, made the following report: "In order to prevent any further difficulty on the subject, we wish now to be fairly and fully understood; that as to the propriety or impropriety of Free Masonry, we do not, as an Association, undertake to determine. Yet we freely say, that inasmuch as our brethren do not pretend they are bound in conscience, by any rule in the word of God, to unite with that fraternity, for them to form a connexion with them, or frequent their Lodges, when they know it is a grief to their christian brethren, and makes disturbance in the churches; it (in our opinion) gives sufficient reason for others to conclude they are not such as follow after the things that make for peace, and things wherewith one may edify another, Rom. xiv. 19; but rather are such as cause divisions and contentions, contrary to the doctrine we have learned, Rom. xvi. 17; and, of course, if they continue obstinately in such practices, ought to be rejected from fellowship; and consequently it is not reasonable for us to invite them to a seat in our Association. We therefore answer the query from the church at Providence, in the negative.

"Yet we do not wish, at present, to have this resolution so construed, as to interrupt our correspondence with sister Associations, but to have it continued.

"If there be any brethren, in any of our churches or sister Associations, who live in the practice of frequenting the Masonick Lodges, we flatter ourselves, that such churches and Associations, after hearing our minds on the subject, will not feel disposed to grieve brethren among us, by sending such of their members as delegates to this Association."

This report was received by the Association and inserted in their minutes for 1803, page 9. The broad hints towards the close of it were not the most grateful to some members of corresponding Associations, who had been let farther into the secrets of Masonry, than their proscribing brethren, and who had never considered that the meeting with Masonick Lodges was, in itself, a crime of sufficient magnitude to interrupt christian fellowship and communion.

But to make short the history of this affair, it is sufficient to observe, that it proved in the end, to be much labour and time spent to little purpose. The Association, notwithstanding their spirited resolves, left the question pretty much as they found it. They, it is true, manifested some portion of wisdom in their discussion of the matter, but they showed by far the most when they gave it up.

WOODSTOCK ASSOCIATION.

THIS Association lies on both sides of the Connecticut river, in the States of Vermont and New-Hampshire. It was organized with a very few churches, February, 1783, in Woodstock, which is one of the principal towns in Windsor county, a few miles above Windsor in Vermont, and not far below Hanover in New-Hampshire, and no great distance west of Connecticut river.

Some of the oldest churches in this body are situated on the eastern side of the river in the counties of Cheshire, Grafton and Hillsborough, in New-Hampshire. An account of these churches has already been given in the history of the State to which they belong. As this body originated in Vermont, we shall, under this head, give a brief narrative of its proceedings, together with some historical sketches of the most distinguished churches which it contains.

This Association has never been large compared with the Shaftsbury and some others; but it has generally been in a flourishing state, its movements have been harmonious and regular; its churches have been well established and respectable, many of which have been, and still are, supplied with ministers eminent for their abilities and usefulness.

Dr. Baldwin, now the pastor of the 2d Baptist church in Boston, was, for a number of years, the pastor of the church in Canaan, (N. H.) one of the constituent members of this Association, and the most remarkable event, which I find in its history is, that by their request, he exhibited before them, a small treatise, entitled, " *The Baptism of Believers only, and the Particular Communion of the Baptist Churches, explained and vindicated.*" This performance, being approved by the Association was, at their instance, forwarded to the press. " This work was intended rather as an apology for the particular communion of the Baptists, than as an attack upon the sentiments and practice of others." But it was, however, viewed by the Pedobaptists, as a work of too much importance to pass unnoticed. Accordingly, in 1791, the Rev. Noah Worcester, pastor of a Congregational church in Thornton, (N. H.) published a reply to it, entitled, " *A Friendly Letter,*" &c. This called forth a reply from Dr. Baldwin in 1794, after he had settled in Boston. In a word, the little tract which Dr. Baldwin wrote amidst the forests and mountains of New-Hampshire, laid the foundation for that baptismal controversy, which he has since, with much ability, maintained against a number of opposers.

Amongst the oldest churches in the Woodstock Association, on the Vermont side of the river, we must reckon those of Woodstock, Hartford, Bridgewater, Westminster, Dummerston, Royalton, Windsor, Putney, Chester, Rockingham, and Reading. Dummerston, Putney, and some other churches in the south-east corner of Vermont, now belong to the Leyden Association. Of a few of the remaining ones it may be proper to give some brief accounts.

The Woodstock church was planted in 1780, by Elder Elisha Ransom, who had removed from Sutton, Massachusetts, and settled in this town a short time before. This church joined to the Warren Association the same year in which it was gathered, and continued with it, until the Woodstock Association was formed. The Woodstock church prospered much for some time. In the course of three years from its beginning, it increased to eighty members, and became so extensive that another church was formed from it in the same town, about 1785, which, however, was not long afterwards re-united to the mother establishment. Mr. Ransom continued in the pastoral office here, upwards of twenty years. And after him, Mr. Jabez Cottle administered to the church a few years ; but he has removed from thence ; and the followers of Elias Smith have prevailed so much, that the church has now nearly or quite lost its visibility.

344 Chester Church....Its Enlargement and Division.

The church in Chester, Windsor county, was formed in 1789. It originated in the following manner. In 1786, Aaron Leland, a native of Holliston, Massachusetts, who had been approbated to preach a little before, by the church in Bellingham, then under the care of Elder Noah Alden, received a letter from fifteen persons living in Chester, none of whom however were Baptist' members, requesting him to come and preach among them for a short time. Conformable to this request, he took a journey to the place a few months after. But when he arrived, he found it so much uncultivated, both in a natural and moral point of view, and the prospect so unpromising, that he was unwilling to think of tarrying with them long. But after being here a short time, he felt a powerful application to his mind of this passage, "The Lord hath much people in this city." This scripture afforded him much comfort then, and he has had the happiness since of seeing it abundantly verified. After preaching with the people a few weeks, he returned; visited them again not many months after, and in a short time settled among them. He had been previously ordained by the church in Bellingham.

In 1789, he had the happiness of seeing a small church gathered, which consisted of only ten members, including himself. This little body travelled on in harmony and order, experiencing a gradual increase, but no remarkable ingathering for ten years after it was founded. But in 1799, a revival commenced, which became very powerful and extensive, and spread, not only throughout Chester, but prevailed in a number of the neighbouring towns. At the close of this work, the church had become so numerous and extensive, that they thought proper to make a division, and by the advise of their brethren, who were called for the purpose, on the 31st of August, 1803, four churches were set off from the original body, which were named from the towns in which they were situated, Andover, Grafton, Wethersfield, and Cavendish. This was an interesting day, and the circumstance is probably unexampled in the annals of our churches. These detached churches are now all supplied with pastors, and are well established and flourishing bodies. Two of their pastors had been deacons in the mother church before its division, the other two came from other parts. Mr. Jonathan Going, pastor of the church in Cavendish, was educated at Brown University. Besides planting so many daughters around her, and furnishing two of them with pastors, the Chester church has sent out three other ministers, who are labouring in other parts.

Notwithstanding this great and sudden reduction, this fruitful body was left with between 70 or 80 members. It experienced no great addition, from the time of its division, until 1811, when another revival commenced within its bounds, by which a goodly number have been added.

Mr. Leland, the worthy pastor of this church, has, in addition to his ministerial duties, filled a number of civil offices in the State. He was nine years a Representative from the town of Chester in the State Legislature, four of which he was Speaker of the House of Assembly. In 1803, he was appointed Judge of the County Court for the county of Windsor. This office he still holds. He has also held a number of minor offices, all of which he has now resigned. He was at one time, so loaded with civil offices and honours, that many of his friends were much concerned for his religious and ministerial character. And, indeed, he at length became concerned about himself, and that not without cause. Although he had been enabled to maintain an unspotted character, in the midst of all his worldly elevations, yet he found such a want of religious enjoyment, and such a defection in the zeal and success of his ministry, that he, a few years ago, gave up all his civil employments, except that of officiating on the bench, which occupies his attention but a few weeks in the course of a year, and he is now once more very zealously and affectionately engaged in the most honourable, and at the same time the most despised employment amongst men. Mr. Leland is distantly related to John Leland of Cheshire.

The county of Windham, in the southeast corner of this State, has been in some measure a distinguished resort and nursery of Baptists, for upwards of forty years. In this county are twelve churches, belonging to the Leyden Association, the seat of which body is considered to be in Massachusetts. The first church in Guilford, and the church in Dummerston, are the oldest among them; the Guilford church appears to be the oldest on this side of the Green Mountains, the origin of which was in the following manner : About the year 1770, a number of persons from different parts, moved into this town, many of whom were soon afterwards awakened to religious concerns, and embraced the Baptist sentiments. These persons, to the number of thirty-three, were embodied into a church in 1776. This church increased so much that another was formed out of it in 1783. But the next year, for some reason, these two churches were again united into one, and a revival commenced among them soon after, by which a large number were added, and the church moved on in harmony, until the famous dispute between the States of New-York and New-Hampshire disturbed its tranquillity. As the church was established on disputed land, the members imbibed the spirit of controversy, and soon fell into an unhappy contention, insomuch that the church was scattered and nearly dissolved. But in 1790, after the interfering claims of the contending States were adjusted, and the territory of Vermont was restored to tranquillity, this church recovered from its dispersion, and re-commenced its travel. The town of Guilford has abounded with Baptists, and it now contains three churches, but I have not gained sufficient information to give an account of their origin or movements.

The ministers, who have laboured here at different times, were Whitman Jacobs, a native of Bristol, Rhode-Island, who planted the church in Thompson, Connecticut; Peleg Hix, from Rehoboth, Massachusetts, and Richard Williams, from Groton, Connecticut. The first church is now under the pastoral care of Jeremy Packer; the one called Guilford United Church, is supplied by Lewis Allen ; the third church is destitute of a pastor.

Dummerston church was constituted in 1783. The next year after it was formed, Mr. Isaiah Stone, who is now at New-Boston, New-Hampshire, settled in the town, and preached a part of the time with this church for a number of years. When he removed from them, the church contained only thirty-one members. Soon after his removal, a revival commenced, by which about a hundred were added to their number.

In 1793, Rufus Freeman settled among them, and soon after he was ordained their pastor, in which office he continued many years. Mr. Freeman was a native of Providence, Rhode-Island, where he was born in 1762. His father died at sea when he was an infant, his mother died while he was yet a child. At six years of age he was carried to Fitzwilliam, in New-Hampshire, by a man who brought him up. In this town he was converted in the seventeenth year of his age, and here, also, he began to preach in 1789. From Fitzwilliam he went to Hardwick, and from that place to Dummerston. His next remove was to Colerain, and farther than this I cannot trace him. Mr. John Leland, in his MS. History of this church, speaks of Mr. Freeman in respectful terms.

The present pastor of this church is Jonathan Hunt, who has been with them a number of years. Of the remaining churches in this county, I have not obtained sufficient information, to form any interesting details.

VERMONT ASSOCIATION.

This was the third confederacy of the kind established in this State. It was organized in Elder Joseph Cornell's barn, in the town of Manchester, May, 1785. The country was then so new, and the houses so small, that a mansion similar to that in which the Saviour was first seen by mortals, was the most convenient place in which they could assemble. This body, at the time of its constitution, comprized only five small churches, in which were but four elders, and 231 members. In five years from its beginning, it increased to thirteen churches, and 740 members. The number of churches is now twenty-two, which contain about 1900 communicants.

This Association lies wholly west of the Green Mountains, and is mostly in the counties of Rutland and Addison. Two of its churches, viz. Salem and Granville, are in Washington county, New-York. This body now comprises a number of large and respectable churches, which are supplied by a number of ministers, eminent for their abilities and usefulness; but as to its movements we cannot say that they have, at all times, been harmonious and comfortable. For many years the Association travelled in peace and love, but at length it fell into a dispute about the prerogatives which it possessed. Some were for constituting it a board of trial for ministers, churches, &c. others opposed these measures as an infringement on the independency of the churches, and an usurpation of power, to which they had no constitutional claim. And thus, to use a familiar figure, while some were endeavouring to plant *horns* on their body, which in their opinion was wanting in energy, others stood by with their weapons to beat them off ; and at length the contest arose so high, that the Association was rent asunder, and the two parties, for a short time, met in separate companies ; thus the body, about which they were contending, was left without either *head* or *horns*. It is not intended, by this familiar manner of treating these measures, to trifle with the feelings of those worthy brethren, by whom they were promoted. These unhappy proceedings must not be reckoned among their wisest and most condescending acts. But it is pleasant to learn, that a spirit, conciliatory and forbearing, soon succeeded that which was so discordant and painful; a convention composed of delegates from both parties came to an amicable adjustment of their differences, the powers of an Association were unanimously agreed upon, the dissevered members of this body were happily united, and it has, from that period, travelled on in harmony and love. The substance of these remarks was communicated by a minister who has long held a respectable standing in this Association.

Respecting the history of the churches in this connexion, some very brief sketches must suffice. I was not enabled to travel amongst them. I have, however, taken much pains to ascertain their history, a few things have been communicated, but many more which were expected have, for some reason, not come to hand.

The five constituent churches of this Association were those of Clarendon, Granville, Manchester, Danby, and Mapletown. The churches in Wallingford, Ira, Middletown, and Pittsfield, were constituted before the Association was formed; and those of Poultney, Orwell, Hubbardston, Brandon and Paulet, but a few years after.

The church in Wallingford was gathered in 1780, and is the oldest within the bounds of the Vermont Association. It was named after Wallingford in Connecticut, from which town many of the first settlers emigrated,

Mr. Henry Green, now in Cornwall, was its first pastor. The Wallingford church withdrew from the Association in the time of its contentions, and has never united with it since. It is still in respectable standing, though destitute of a pastor.

The next church in point of seniority, is that of Manchester, in the county of Bennington, which was planted by Elder Joseph Cornell, in 1781. Mr. Cornell is a native of Swansea, Massachusetts, from which place he removed to Cheshire, in the same State, in 1770, where he was ordained ten years after. Immediately after his ordination, by the request of more than seventy heads of families in Manchester, he removed and settled among them, and continued upwards of thirteen years, pastor of the church which he established there.

This church, like that of Wallingford, wishing to let alone contention, before it is meddled with, left the Association at the same time, and yet remains out of it. Mr. Cornell left them before this time. Its circumstances are prosperous, being under the care of a worthy minister, whose name is Calvin Chamberlain.

There is also an unassociated church in East-Clarendon, which is now supplied by an Elder M'Culler.

MIDDLETOWN. The church here was constituted, October, 1782. It remained without a pastor until 1790, when Mr. Sylvanus Haynes, a native of Princeton, Massachusetts, was settled among them, under whose ministry they have been edified and built up to a large and respectable body.

POULTNEY. This church was constituted in 1785. It was formed upon Calvinistick principles, but on the plan of open communion, which plan was continued a number of years, but has long since been given up. This church was small, and in a measure destitute of preaching for many years. In 1801, it was reduced to fifteen members, who thought best to attach themselves to the church in Middletown, under the character of a branch of that body. But the next year, having Mr. Clark Kendrick to preach among them, they again resumed their travel as a distinct church; Mr. Kendrick was, soon after, ordained over them, and still continues their much respected pastor. Mr. Kendrick was born in Hanover, New-Hampshire, in

1776, and is a brother of Ariel Kendrick, of Cornish in that State.

I have not received accounts from any other churches in this Association, except the one in Middlebury, which was formed in 1809, and is now under the care of Nathaniel Kendrick, who was formerly in Lansingburg, New-York. Some sketches of a number of others would doubtless be as interesting as those which have been given, but as they have not been forwarded as was expected, they must of necessity be omitted.

RICHMOND ASSOCIATION.

This Association is situated northward of the Vermont, and extends from Onion river to the northern boundaries of the State, and three of the churches are in the province of Lower Canada. It is bounded on the west by lake Champlain, and extends eastward to the Green Mountains, and is in the counties of Chittenden, Franklin, and Orleans.

This Association was begun with not more than four or five churches, in 1795, and although it has been gradually increasing from its beginning, it has not yet become large. Respecting the history of the churches in this establishment, I have obtained scarcely any information, except that some were raised up by the labours of Elders Jedidiah Hibbard, from New-Hampshire, and Joseph Call, from Woodstock, in this State. I find, also, that Elders Ezra Willmarth, now of Weare, New-Hampshire, Samuel Rogers, at present in Galway, New-York, and Elisha Andrews, of Templeton, Massachusetts, were preaching within the bounds of this Association, in the early part of its movements.

Elder Ezra Butler, who has long been in the State Legislature, a member of the Senate, a county Judge, and who is now a member of Congress, belongs to this Association, and resides at Waterbury, on Onion river. Three churches in the Richmond Association, viz. Sutton, Hatley, and Stanstead, and St. Armond, are in the province of Lower Canada.

I have lately been informed that this Association has changed its name to that of Fairfield, and that the churches in Canada which contain about two hundred members, are not included in it.

The ecclesiastical Laws of Vermont all done away. 351

Besides those already mentioned, there are two other small Associations in this State, which are situated on the east side of the mountains. These Associations are Barre and Danville.

The Barre Association lies immediately north of the Woodstock. It was formed about 1807, of six or seven churches, and is yet very small. It is situated in the counties of Orange, Caledonia, and Jefferson. The churches of Hanover and Lyme are in the county of Grafton in New-Hampshire.

The Danville Association lies still north of the Barre, mostly in the county of Caledonia. It was formed of four or five small churches, about 1810. This Association is mostly the fruits of Missionary labours.

The unassociated churches in this State will be brought into the list of Associations and Churches.

There are a number of Baptist churches in this State of the Freewill order, which will be taken notice of in the history of that community.

Although many of our brethren were amongst the first settlers, in most parts of this State, yet the greater part of the settlers were of the Congregational order, from the States of Massachusetts and Connecticut. These people carried with them the religious maxims of their native States, and by their influence the country was divided into parishes, in most of which Congregational churches were established, and a law was passed similar to those in the other New-England States, empowering these parishes to levy a general tax for building meeting-houses, and supporting their ministers. The Baptists in a few instances, and but a few, have been oppressed with these taxes. But now, all laws, regulating religious worship, are done away, and the gospel is left in Vermont as it is in all the other United States except three, and as it ought to be every where, and as we believe it finally will be, to be supported by the voluntary contributions of its advocates and friends.

A brief account of the nature, progress, and abrogation of these laws will now be given.

I do not find that any laws were made in Vermont, with regard to religion, until 1797. Then an act was passed for the support of the gospel, &c. the substance of which was to empower the inhabitants of every town or parish in the State, (in which there should be twenty-five voters) to associate for religious purposes, to levy and collect taxes, to build meeting-houses, and to hire and support religious teachers of such denomination, as a majority of such town or parish thought proper. And every person of "adult age, was, by said act, considered as being of the religious opinion and sentiment of such society, and liable to be taxed, after residing in said town or parish one year, unless he should, previous to the vote for raising taxes, &c. obtain, and procure to be recorded in the Town Clerk's office in said town, a certificate of his different belief, signed by some minister of the gospel, deacon, elder, moderator, or clerk of the church, congregation, sect or denomination, to which he belonged."

This statute remained in force, until the 3d of November, 1801, when the Legislature passed an act, repealing so much of the former act, as related to procuring certificates; but still considered the voters in such town or parish of the religious opinion of such society, and made them liable to be taxed for religious purposes; unless they should, individually, previous to any vote of said society, &c. deliver to the clerk of such town a declaration in writing, with their names thereto subscribed, in the following words, "I do not agree in religious opinion, with a majority of the inhabitants of this town," or parish, &c.

Thus stood the law until the 24th day of October, 1807, when the Legislature passed an act, repealing all the statutes on the subject, except the section relating to voluntary associations, and contracts individually entered into."*

The bill which proposed this law, which is so congenial with every principle of religious freedom, was two sessions before the Vermont Assembly, and was supported by the united exertions of the great body of dissenters. Messrs. Aaron Leland and Ezra Butler were at this time members of the State Legislature. Leland was Speaker of the Lower House, and Butler was an active member of the Senate. It is generally thought that our ministering brethren had better keep at home, than to engage in the bustle of political affairs. But on this occasion, these

* This information was communicated by Cephas L. Rockwood, Esq. of Chester.

two ministers did much good. This bill was much contested. In the Lower House it was debated by a committee of the whole, which brought Mr. Leland on the floor. Both he and Mr. Butler zealously and ably advocated it, and exhibited with much perspicuity and effect those unanswerable arguments, which the Baptists always urge against supporting religion by law. They were seconded by many gentlemen of different persuasions. But their arguments were, at the same time, violently opposed by many powerful adversaries. But the spirit of freedom prevailed, and the bill, to the honour of the valiant Green Mountain men, finally passed into a law.

Many had very alarming apprehensions of the levelling consequences of this law; none of them, however, have been realized. There were, at this time, about a hundred Congregational ministers settled in this State, but not one of them was displaced in consequence of this law. They were a worthy set of men, and as soon as their churches and congregations saw the law was repealed, which empowered them to raise money for their support, they set about raising it in other ways, and all of them were supported as well without law, as they had been with.

This would doubtless be the case generally in the other New-England States. But the ministers there have so long been accustomed to lean on the strong arm of the civil power for their support, that they are afraid to stand up and trust to the voluntary contributions of their flocks. And it is highly probable that many of them would make out poorly indeed. But those who are worth having, would be supported, and those, who are not, ought to dig for themselves, and it is no matter how soon they are displaced.

CHAP. XII.

MASSACHUSETTS.

THERE was not any church of the Baptist order founded in this State, until more than forty years after its settlement; but there were at first, and all along during this period, some persons of the Baptist persuasion, or to speak in the language of that day, persons tinctured with Anabaptistical errors, intermixed with the inhabitants. And before we proceed to the churches and associations in this Commonwealth, we shall exhibit in one view, the number, names, circumstances, and sufferings of our brethren, and of those who were baptistically inclined, in this boasted asylum of religious freedom, up to the year 1663, when the first church in Swansea was founded.

It is asserted by Dr. Mather, in his Magnalia, that "some of the first planters in New-England were Baptists;" and this assertion is corroborated by some of the laws and letters which will be mentioned in the following sketches. Roger Williams was not a Baptist practically while he resided in this government, but he, nevertheless, began here his baptistical career, and it is evident that the fear of the consequences of his popular ministry induced the priest-led magistrates to pass the cruel sentence of banishment against him. While he was at Plymouth, it was feared "that he would run the same course of rigid separation and Anabaptistry, which Mr. John Smith of Amsterdam had done;" and after he went to Salem, it is said, that "in one year's time he filled that place with principles of rigid separation, tending to *Anabaptism*."*
Anabaptism, in the view of the Massachusetts people, was a heretical monster, of which they were most terribly afraid.

It has always been found that the leading principles of the first reformers, when carried forward to their legitimate consequences, will endanger the cause of infant baptism. "Bishop Sanderson says, that the Rev. Archbishop Whitgift, and the learned Hooker, men of great judgment, and famous in their times, did long since for-

* Backus, Vol. 1. p. 56.

see, and declare their fear, that if ever Puritanism should prevail among us, it would soon draw in Anabaptism after it.—This, Cartwright and the Disciplinarians denied, and were offended at.—But these good men judged right, they considered only as prudent men, that Anabaptism had its rise from the same principles the Puritans held, and its growth from the same course they took; together with the natural tendency of their principles and practices toward it; especially that *one principle,* as it was then by them misunderstood, that the Scripture was *adequata agendorum regula,* so as nothing might be lawfully done without express warrant, either from some command or example therein contained; which clue, if followed as far as it would go, would certainly in time carry them as far as the Anabaptists had then gone." "This, says Mr. Callender, I beg leave to look on as a most glorious concession, of the most able adversaries. One party contend, that the scripture is the adequate rule of worship, and for the necessity of some command or example there; the other party say this leads to Anabaptism."

The Archbishop and Mr. Hooker were by no means mistaken in their conjectures; for so many of the Puritans as adhered strictly to that one principle, that the scripture is the adequate rule of worship, did become Anabaptists, as they were called; and the reason why all did not, was, that they would not allow 'this one powerful principle, which is sufficient to demolish the whole fabrick of human inventions, to operate in all its force against infant baptism, but threw in its way Abraham's covenant, and the traditions of the fathers.

The first settlers of New-England knew by what they had seen at home, the danger of the Puritans running into Anabaptism; or to speak correctly, their disposition to revive to its apostolic purity the ordinance of baptism; they therefore continually made use of every precaution, to hush all inquiries, and to close every avenue of light upon the subject; and although we condemn their methods, we must at the same time confess that they were attended with too much success.

It was a long time before the Baptists could gain much ground in either of the colonies of Plymouth or Massachusetts. It is probable, however, that they would have gained establishments here much sooner than they did, notwithstanding the vehement zeal with which they were opposed, had not the glorious liberties of the little colony of Rhode-Island offered them an asylum so much to their mind.

But notwithstanding all their attempts to keep them out and to beat them down, it is evident there have been Baptists in this state, from its first settlement, which is now a period of upwards of a hundred and ninety years; and some distinguished persons resided here for a time, who became Baptists after they left the colony and settled in other parts.

Hansard Knollys, who afterwards became a very distinguished Baptist minister in London, came over to this country in 1638, and landed at Boston, but afterwards went to Dover on the Piscataqua river, where he tarried a few years, and then went back to England.

In 1639, it seems there was an attempt to found a Baptist church at Weymouth, a town about fourteen miles south-east of Boston, which was, however, frustrated by the strong arguments of interposing magistrates. John Smith, John Spur, Richard Sylvester, Ambrose Morton, Thomas Mackpeace, and Robert Lenthal, were the principal promoters of this design. They were all arraigned before the General Court at Boston, March 13, 1639, where they were treated according to the order of the day; Smith, who was probably the greatest transgressor, was fined twenty pounds, and committed during the pleasure of the Court. Sylvester was fined twenty shillings and disfranchised. Morton was fined ten pounds, and counselled to go to Mr. Mather for instruction. Mackpeace had probably no money; he was not fined, but had a modest hint of banishment, unless he reformed. Lenthal it seems compromised the matter with the court for the present; consented to appear before it at the next session; was enjoined to acknowledge his fault, and so on. How matters finally terminated with him I do not find; but it is certain he soon after went to Mr. Clark's settlement on Rhode-Island, and began to preach there before the first church in Newport was formed.

The court having thus dispersed the heretical combination, " thought fit to set apart a day of humiliation, to seek the face of God, and reconciliation with him by our Lord Jesus Christ, &c."*

In 1640, Mr. Charles Chauncey came over to this country; he was an advocate for the doctrine of dipping in baptism, but at the same time held that infants were proper subjects of the ordinance. He was esteemed a great scholar and a godly man. The church in Plymouth were anxious to settle him amongst them; but they were as strenuous for sprinkling as he was for immersion. "There was much trouble about the matter. The magistrates and the elders there, and the most of the people, withstood the *reviving of that practice*, (that is immersion) not for itself so much as for fear of worse consequences, as the annihilating our baptism, &c."† The church finally proposed that Mr. Reyner, their other minister, with whom he was to be associated, should do all the sprinkling, so that he should not be obliged to administer the sacred rite, only in his own way; but with this temporizing proposal, "he did not see light to comply." For although he was but half right, yet he was strong so far as he had gone. From Plymouth, Mr. Chauncey went to Scituate, a town on the Massachusetts Bay, about twenty-eight miles southeast of Boston, where he was settled and resided many years. We are told that "here he persevered in his opinion of *dipping in baptism*, and practised accordingly, first upon two of his own children, which being in very cold weather, one of them swooned away; another having a child about three years old, but fearing it would be frightened, as others had been, carried it to Boston, with testimonials from Chauncey, where the seal of the covenant was impressed upon it in a milder form."

Mr. Backus well observes, that "Mr. Chauncey's grand difficulty in *burying in Baptism*, was his admitting subjects, who had not the faith or discretion necessary for such an action."‡

There is, it must be acknowledged, a conformity between *babes* and *sprinkling*. Both of them are puerile things, and seem well fitted for each other.

* Backus' History, &c. Vol. I. p. 113, 114.
† Winthrop's journal as quoted by Backus.
‡ Backus' History, &c. vol. I. p. 115 and 145, 146.

The same year in which Mr. Chauncey came over, a female of considerable distinction, whom Governor Winthrop calls the lady Moody, and who, according to the account of that candid statesman and historian, was a wise, amiable, and religious woman, "was taken with the error of denying baptism to infants." She had purchased a plantation at Lynn, ten miles northeast of Boston, of one Humphrey, who had returned to England. She belonged to the church in Salem, to which she was near, where she was dealt with by many of the elders and others; but persisting in her error, and to escape the storm which she saw gathering over her head, she removed to Long-Island and settled among the Dutch. "Many others infested with Anabaptism removed thither also." Eleven years after Mrs. Moody's removal, Messrs. Clark, Holmes, and Crandal, went to visit some Baptists at Lynn, by the request of an aged brother, whose name was William Witter. This circumstance makes it probable, that although many Anabaptists went off with this lady, yet there were some left behind. We shall soon have occasion to take more particular notice of the Baptists in this place.

In 1644, we are informed by Mr. Hubbard, that "a poor man, by the name of Painter, was suddenly turned Anabaptist, and having a child born would not suffer his wife to carry it to be baptized. He was complained of for this to the court, and *enjoined* by them to suffer his child to be baptized. But poor Painter had the misfortune to dissent both from the church and court. He told them that infant baptism was an antichristian ordinance, for which he was tied up and whipt. He bore his chastisement with fortitude, and declared that he had divine help to support him. The same author who recorded this narrative, intimates that this poor sufferer "was a man of very loose behaviour at home." This accusation was altogether a thing of course; it would have been almost a miracle, for a poor Anabaptist to have been a holy man. Governor Winthrop tells us he belonged to Hingham, and says he was whipt "for reproaching the Lord's ordinance." Upon which Mr. Backus judiciously inquires, "did not they who whipt this poor, conscientious man, reproach infant sprinkling, by taking such methods to support it, more than Painter did?"*

* Backus' Hist. vol. I. p. 147, 148.

About this time Mr. Williams returned from England, with the charter for Rhode-Island, and landed at Boston. He brought with him a letter, signed by twelve members of Parliament, addressed to the Governor, Assistants, and people of Massachusetts, exhorting them to lenient measures towards their dissenting brethren, and towards Mr. Williams in particular. The sentence of banishment yet lay upon him, which these noble advocates for liberty besought them to remove. But every avenue of compunction and mercy was closed; "Upon the receipt of this letter the Governor and magistrates of Massachusetts found, upon examination of their hearts, no reason to condemn themselves for any former proceedings against Mr. Williams, &c."[*]

The Baptists and those inclined to their sentiments were, doubtless, emboldened by the favour which Mr. Williams had obtained at home, and by knowing that he had obtained the royal assent for a colony which would afford them an asylum in time of danger. About this time, we are told by Winthrop, that "the Anabaptists increased and spread in Massachusetts." This increase was a most fearful and ungrateful sight to the rulers of this colony, and was doubtless the means of leading the General Court to pass the following act for the suppression of this obnoxious sect.

" Forasmuch as experience hath plentifully and often proved, that since the first rising of the Anabaptists, about one hundred years since, they have been the incendiaries of commonwealths, and the infectors of persons in main matters of religion, and the troublers of churches in all places where they have been, and that they, who have held the baptizing of infants unlawful, have usually held other errors or heresies therewith, though they have (as other hereticks use to do) concealed the same, till they spied out a fit advantage and opportunity to vent them, by way of question or scruple; and whereas divers of this kind have, since our coming into New-England, appeared amongst ourselves, some whereof (as others before them) denied the ordinance of magistracy, and the lawfulness of making war, and others the lawfulness of magistrates, and their inspection into any breach of the first table; which opinions, if they should be connived at by us, are like to be increased amongst us, and so must necessarily bring guilt upon us, infection and trouble to the churches, and hazard to the whole commonwealth; it is ordered and agreed, that if any person or persons, within this jurisdiction, shall either openly condemn or oppose the baptizing of infants, or go about se-

---

[*] Hubbbard, as quoted by Backus, vol. I. p. 155—6.

cretly to seduce others from the approbation or use thereof, or shall purposely depart the congregation at the ministration of the ordinance, or shall deny the ordinance of magistracy, or their lawful right and authority to make war, or to punish the outward breaches of the first table, and shall appear to the court wilfully and obstinately to continue therein after due time and means of conviction, every such person or persons shall be *sentenced to banishment.*"

This was the first law which was made against the Baptists in Massachusetts. It was passed November 13th, 1644, about two months after Mr. Williams landed in Boston as above related. Two charges, which it contains, Mr. Backus acknowledges are true, viz. that the Baptists denied infant baptism and the ordinance of magistracy ; or as a Baptist would express it, the use of secular force in religious affairs ; but all the other slanderous invectives he declares are utterly without foundation. He furthermore asserts, that he had diligently searched all the books, records, and papers, which he could find on all sides, and could not find an instance then (1777) of any real Baptist in Massachusetts being convicted of, or suffering for any crime, except the denying of infant baptism, and the use of secular force in religious affairs.

If a Puritan Court in the seventeenth century, professing to be illuminated with the full blaze of the light of the Reformation, could thus defame the advocates for apostolic principles, will any think it strange if we suspect the frightful accounts which were given of them in darker ages by a set of monkish historians, who believed that fraud and falsehood were christian virtues, if they could be made subservient to the good of the church?

Mr. Hubbard, one of their own historians, speaking of their making this law says, "but with what success it is hard to say ; all men being naturally inclined to pity them that suffer, &c." The clergy doubtless had a hand in framing this shameful act, as they, at this time, were the secretaries and counsellors of the Legislature.

Mr. Backus' observations upon these measures, and the men by whom they were promoted, are very judicious. "Much (says he) has been said to exalt the characters of the good fathers of that day : I have no desire of detracting from any of their virtues ; but the better the men were, the worse must be the principles that could ensnare them in such bad actions."

Mr. Hubbard informs us, that "at a General Court in March, 1645, two petitions were preferred, one for suspending (if not abolishing) a law made against the Anabaptists the former year ; the other was for easing a law of like nature made in Mrs. Hutchinson's time, forbidding the entertaining of any strangers, without license of two magistrates, &c. But some, continues the same author, at this time were much afraid of the increase of Anabaptism. This was the reason why the greater part prevailed for the strict observation of the aforesaid laws, although peradventure a little moderation as to some cases might have done very well, if not better. Many books, coming out of England in this year, some in defence of Anabaptism and other errors, and for liberty of conscience as a shelter for a general toleration of all opinions----led the ministers----of all the United Colonies to meet at Cambridge, &c." One of the Anabaptist books above referred to was sent by the famous John Tombes. It was an examination of a sermon in defence of infant baptism, preached by Stephen Marshall, and dedicated to the Westminster Assembly. Soon after the news reached England of the law to banish the Baptists, Mr. Tombes sent a copy of his work to the ministers of New-England, and with it an epistle dated from the Temple in London, May 25, 1645, " hoping thereby to put them upon a more exact study of that controversy, and to allay their vehemency against the Baptists." " But the Westminster Assembly, says Backus, were more ready to learn severity from this country, than these were to learn lenity from any."

Soon after Mr. Tombes sent over his book and letter, Sir Henry Vane, whose interest was then very great in Parliament, wrote to Governor Winthrop as follows :

" HONORED SIR,

" I received yours by your son, and was unwilling to let him return without telling you as much. The exercise and troubles which God is pleased to lay upon these kingdoms, and the inhabitants in them, teaches us patience and forbearance one with another in some measure, though there be difference in our opinions, which makes me hope, that from the experience here, it may also be derived to yourselves, lest, while the Congregational way amongst you is in its freedom, and is backed with power, it teach its oppugners here, to extirpate it and root it out, from its own principles and practice. I shall need say no more, knowing your son can acquaint you particularly with our affairs. Sir, I am your affectionate friend, and servant in Christ,

H. VANE.

JUNE 10, 1645.

All these remonstrances, however, were unavailing, and the bigoted New-Englanders persisted in their persecuting career. And lest their exterminating laws should not effect the business, the press was set to work to prevent the alarming progress of Anabaptistical errors. In this year, three pieces were written for this purpose by Messrs. Cotton of Boston, Cobbet of Lynn, and Ward of Ipswich, then called by its Indian name Agawam. Cotton and Cobbet lay some strange charges against the devil, for seeking to undermine the cause of infant baptism, because it is not commanded in the Scripture. The reader will doubtless be astonished at this assertion; but let him read the following quotations fairly made, and then he may judge whether it is not correct. Mr. Cotton says, Satan, despairing of success by more powerful arguments, "chooseth rather to play small game, as they say, than lose all. He now pleadeth no other argument in these stirring times of reformation, than may be urged from a main principle of purity and reformation, viz. *That no duty of God's worship, nor any ordinance of religion is to be administered in the church, but such as hath just warrant from the word of God.* And in urging this argument against the baptism of children, Satan transformeth himself into an angel of light,"* and so on. This was the great Mr. Cotton, who, for many years, was the bishop and legislator of New-England. He was doubtless a great and good man; he reasoned well on many subjects, and the absurdity of his arguments here must be ascribed to the weakness of the cause which they were intended to support. His successors have made great improvements in arguing this point, but we must acknowledge that the Baptists

* Cotton's Grounds and Ends of Children's Baptism, p. 3, 4, as quoted by Backus, vol. I. p. 176.

have made none at all. What was their main principle *then*, is their main principle *now*. They wish it not to be altered or amended, but are willing it should stand just as Mr. Cotton has stated it. It has ever proved an insurmountable barrier against all the assaults of their enemies, and so far as it is permitted to operate, is sure to beat down all the inventions of men. But the greatest curiosity is, that this Reverend Divine accuses the devil of helping them to it.

Mr. Cobbet accuses Satan of having a special spite at the seed of the church. He says it is one of Satan's old tricks to create scruples in the hearts of God's people about infant baptism. And *Thus it is written*, and *Thus saith the Lord*, according to this singular divine, are nothing but " *satanical suggestions.*"

The Baptists feel perfectly secure against this kind of logic, and the deceivers of mankind would doubtless be much obliged to his adversaries if they would never assault his kingdom with any more powerful weapons.

The last of this mighty triumvirate does not lay so much of the blame to satan; but his arguments are, if possible, still more weak and contemptible. He accuses the Anabaptists of a " high pitch of boldness in cutting a principal ordinance out of the kingdom of God." He also charges them with the crime of " *dislocating*, *disgooding*, *unhallowing*, *transplacing*, and *transtiming* a stated institution of Jesus Christ." " What a cruelty is it," says he, " to divest children of that only external privilege, which their heavenly Father hath bequeathed them, to interest them visibly in himself, his Son, his Spirit, his covenant of peace, and the tender bosom of their careful mother, the church. What an inhumanity it is, to deprive parents of that comfort they may take from the baptism of their infants dying in their childhood!"*

Had the Pedobaptists in Massachusetts assaulted our brethren with no weapons more powerful than their pens, they would have had nothing to fear. But if the arguments of their divines were weak and contemptible, those of their magistrates were strong and cruel, as we shall soon have occasion to observe.

* Backus, vol, I. p. 184.

Hitherto but few instances of corporal punishments had taken place among our brethren in the Massachusetts colony. Most of the fathers of it were yet alive, and had grown gray in the midst of their persecutions at home, and their labours here. It is charitably doubted by some, whether they had it in their hearts at first to imitate the bloody scenes from which they had fled. Such would suppose that their threatening legislative acts were intended merely to be hung out as a terror to dissenters from the idol uniformity which they had set up. But be that as it may, they had established a principle fraught with blood. Roger Williams, secure in his little colony at Providence, foresaw the sanguinary storm, which was approaching, and which, according to his prediction, soon burst upon this Commonwealth, and blotted its annals with an indelible stain. With a view to open the eyes of his old neighbours and associates to the tendency of their maxims, he published his piece, entitled, " *The bloody Tenet,*" &c. as early as 1644. But remonstrances were vain. The bloody tenet was scrupulously maintained, and hurried forward to its baneful consequences, so that in 1651, the Baptists were unmercifully whipped, and not long after, the Quakers were murderously hung.

We are now prepared to give an account of a scene of suffering peculiarly cruel and afflictive.

We have already seen that there were some Baptists at Lynn, in 1640, when the lady Moody left the place, and it is probable that a little band remained there until the period now under consideration. In July, 1651, Messrs. Clark, Holmes, and Crandal, "being the representatives of the church in Newport, upon the request of William Witter of Lynn, arrived there, he being a brother in the church, who, by reason of his advanced age, could not undertake so great a journey as to visit the church." This account is found among the records of the ancient church at Newport. The circumstance of these men being representatives, leads us to infer that something was designed more than an ordinary visit. Mr. Witter lived about two miles out of the town, and the next day after his brethren arrived, being Lord's day, they concluded to spend it in religious worship at his house. While Mr. Clark was preaching from Rev. iii. 10, " *Because thou hast kept the word of my patience, I also will keep thee from the hour of temptation, which shall come upon all the world, to try them that dwell upon the earth,*" and illustrating what was meant by the hour of temptation and keeping the word with patience, " two constables, (says he,) came into the house, who, with their clamorous tongues, made an interruption in my discourse, and more uncivilly disturbed us than the pursuivants of the old English bishops were wont to do, telling us that they were come with authority from the magistrate to apprehend us. I then desired to see the authority by which they thus proceeded, whereupon they plucked forth their warrant, and one of them with a trembling hand, (as conscious he might have been better employed) read it to us; the substance whereof was as followeth:

" By virtue hereof, you are required to go to the house of Wil-
" liam Witter, and so to search from house to house, for certain er-
" roneous persons, being strangers, and them to apprehend, and in
" safe custody to keep, and to-morrow morning at eight o'clock to
" bring before me,
" ROBERT BRIDGES."

" When he had read the warrant, I told them, Friends, there shall not be, I trust, the least appearance of a resisting of that authority by which you come unto us; yet I tell you, that by virtue hereof, you are not strictly tied, but if you please you may suffer us to make an end of what we have begun, so may you be witnesses either to or against the faith and order which we hold. To which they answered they could not. Then said we, notwithstanding the warrant, or any thing therein contained, you may. They apprehended us and carried us away to the alehouse or ordinary, where at dinner one of them said unto us, Gentlemen, if you be free I will carry you to the meeting. To whom it was replied, Friend, had we been free thereunto we had prevented all this; nevertheless we are in thy hand, and if thou wilt carry us to the meeting thither will we go. To which he answered, Then will I carry you to the meeting. To this we replied, If thou forcest us into your assembly, then shall we be constrained to declare ourselves, that we cannot hold communion with them. The constable answered, That is nothing to me, I have not power to command you to speak when you come there, or to be silent. To this I again replied, Since we have heard the word of salvation by Jesus Christ, we have been taught, as those that *first trusted in Christ,* to be obedient unto him both by word and deed ; wherefore, if we be forced to your meeting, we shall declare our dissent from you both by word and gesture. After all this, when he had consulted with the man of the house, he told us he would carry us to the meeting; so to their meeting we were brought, while they were at their prayers and uncovered; and at my first stepping over the threshold I unveiled myself, civilly saluted them, and turned into the seat I was appointed to, put on my hat again, and sat down, opened my book and fell to reading. Mr. Bridges being troubled, commanded the constable to pluck off our hats, which he did, and where he laid mine, there I let it lie, until their prayers, singing, and preaching was over ; after this, I stood up and uttered myself in these words following : I desire as a stranger to propose a few things to this congregation, hoping in the proposal thereof, I shall commend myself to your consciences to be guided by that wisdom that is from above, which, being pure, is also peaceable, gentle, and easy to be entreated ; and therewith made a stop, expecting that if the Prince of peace had been among them, I should have had a suitable answer of peace from them. Their pastor answered, We will have no objections against what is delivered. To which I answered, I am not about at present to make objections against what is delivered, but as by my gesture at my coming into your assembly, I declared my dissent from you, so lest that should prove offensive unto some whom I would not offend, I would now by word of mouth declare the grounds, which are these : First, from consideration we are strangers each to other, and so strangers to each other's inward standing with respect to God, and so cannot conjoin and act in faith, and what is not of faith, is sin. And in the second place, I could not judge that you are gathered together, and walk according to the visible order of our Lord. Which, when I had declared, Mr. Bridges told me I had done, and spoke that for which I must answer, and so commanded silence. When their meeting was done, the officers carried us again to the ordinary, where being watched over that night as thieves and robbers, we were the next morning carried before Mr. Bridges, who made our mittimus, and sent us to the prison at Boston."

About a fortnight after, the court of assistants passed the following sentences against these persecuted men, viz. that Mr. Clark should pay a fine of twenty pounds, Mr. Holmes of thirty, and Mr. Crandal of five, or be publickly whipped. They all refused to pay their fines, and were remanded back to prison. Some of Mr. Clark's friends paid his fine without his consent. Mr. Crandal was released upon his promise of appearing at their next court. But he was not informed of the time until it was over, and then they exacted his fine of the keeper of the prison. The only crime alleged against Mr. Crandal was his being in company with his brethren. But Mr. Holmes was kept in prison until September, and then the sentence of the law was executed upon him in the most cruel and unfeeling manner. In the course of the trial against these worthy men, Mr. Clark defended himself and brethren with so much ability, that the court found themselves much embarrassed. " At length (says Mr. Clark) the Governor stepped up and told us we had denied infant baptism, and being somewhat transported, told me I had deserved death, and said he would not have such trash brought into their jurisdiction ; moreover he said, " you go up and down, and secretly insinuate into those that are weak, but you cannot maintain it before our ministers. You may try and dispute with them." To this I had much to reply, but he commanded the gaoler to take us away. So the next morning, having so fair an opportunity, I made a motion to the court in these words following :

" *To the honourable court assembled at Boston.*

" Whereas it pleased this honoured court yesterday, to condemn the faith and order which I hold and practise ; and after you had passed your sentence upon me for it, were pleased to express, I could not maintain the same against your ministers, and thereupon publickly proffered me a dispute with them : Be pleased by these few lines to understand, I readily accept it, and therefore desire you to appoint the time when, and the person with whom, in that public place where I was condemned, I might with freedom, and without molestation of the civil power, dispute that point publickly, where I doubt not by the strength of Christ to make it good out of his last will and testament, unto which nothing is to be added, nor from which nothing is to be diminished. Thus desiring the Father of lights to shine forth, and by his power to expel the darkness, I remain your well-wisher,

"JOHN CLARK.

"*From the prison, this 1st day, 6th mo.* 1651.

"This motion, if granted, I desire might be subscribed by their Secretary's hand, as an act of the same court, by which we were condemned."

This motion was presented, and after much consultation, one of the magistrates informed Mr. Clark, that a disputation was granted to be the next week. But on the Monday following, the clergy held a consultation, and made no small stir about the matter, for although they had easily foiled these injured men in a court of law, yet they might well anticipate some difficulty in the open field of argument, which they were absolutely afraid to enter, as will soon appear. Near the close of the day, the magistrates sent for Mr. Clark into their chamber, and inquired whether he would dispute upon the things contained in his sentence, &c. " For," said they, " the court sentenced you, not for your judgment and conscience ; but for matter of fact and practice." To which Mr. Clark replied, " You say the court condemned me for matter of fact and practice : be it so. I say that matter of fact and practice was but the manifestation of my judgment and conscience ; and I make account, that man is void of judgment and conscience, with respect unto God, that hath not a fact and practice suitable thereunto. If the faith and order which I profess do stand by the word of God, then the faith and order which you profess must needs fall to the ground ; and if the way you walk in remain, then the way that I walk in must vanish away ; they cannot both stand together : to which they seemed to assent ; therefore I told them, that if they please to grant the motion under the Secretary's hand, I would draw up the faith and order which I hold, as the sum of that I did deliver in open court, in three or four conclusions, which conclusions I will stand by and defend, until he, whom you shall appoint, shall, by the word of God, remove me from them ; in case he shall remove me from them, then the disputation is at an end. But if not, then I desire like liberty by the word of God, to oppose the faith and order which he and you profess, thereby to try whether I may be an instrument in the hand of God to remove you from the same. They told me the motion was very fair, and the way like unto a disputant, saying, because the matter is weighty, and we desire that what can, may be spoken, when the disputation shall be, therefore would we take a longer time. So I returned with my keeper to prison again, drew up the conclusions, which I was resolved, through the strength of Christ, to stand in defence of, and through the importunity of one of the magistrates, the next morning very early I shewed them to him, having a promise I should have my motion for a dispute granted under the Secretary's hand."

Mr. Clark's resolutions were four in number, and contain the leading sentiments of the Baptists, which have been the same in every age respecting positive institutions, the subjects and mode of baptism, and gospel liberty and civil rights. But while he was making arrangements and preparing for a public dispute, his fine was paid, and he was released from prison.

Great expectations had been raised in Boston and its vicinity respecting this dispute, and many were anxious to hear it. And Mr. Clark, knowing that his adversaries would attribute the failure of it to him, immediately on his release drew up the following address :

" Whereas, through the indulgency of tender hearted friends, without my consent, and contrary to my judgment, the sentence and condemnation of the court at Boston (as is reported) have been fully satisfied on my behalf, and thereupon a warrant hath been procured, by which I am secluded the place of my imprisonment, by reason whereof I see no other call for present but to my habitation, and to those near relations which God hath given me there ; yet, lest the cause should hereby suffer, which I profess is Christ's, I would hereby signify, that if yet it shall please the honoured magistrates, or General Court of this colony, to grant my former request under their Secretary's hand, 1 shall cheerfully embrace it, and upon your motion shall, through the help of God, come from the island to attend it, and hereunto I have subscribed my name,

JOHN CLARK.

" 11*th day,* 6*th mo.* 1651."

370 The Magistrates address Mr. Clark.... His Answer.

This address was sent next morning to the magistrates, who were at the commencement at Cambridge, a short distance from Boston, and it was soon noised abroad that the motion was accepted, and that Mr. Cotton was to be the disputant on the Pedobaptist side. But in a day or two after, Mr. Clark received the following address from his timorous adversaries :

MR. JOHN CLARK,

" We conceive you have misrepresented the Governor's speech, in saying you were challenged to dispute with some of our elders ; whereas it was plainly expressed, that if you would confer with any of them, they were able to satisfy you, neither were you able to maintain your practice to them by the word of God, all which we intended for your information and conviction privately ; neither were you enjoined to what you were then counselled unto ; nevertheless, if you are forward to dispute, and that you will move it yourself to the court or magistrates about Boston, we shall take order to appoint one, who will be ready to answer your motion, you keeping close to the questions to be propounded by yourself, and a moderator shall be appointed also to attend upon the service ; and whereas you desire you might be free in your dispute, keeping close to the points to be disputed on, without incurring damage by the civil justice, observing what hath been before written, it is granted ; the day may be agreed, if you yield the premises.

                JOHN ENDICOTT, *Governor.*
                THOMAS DUDLEY, *Dep. Gov.*
                RICHARD BELLINGHAM,
                WILLIAM HIBBINS,
                INCREASE NOWEL.

11*th day of the* 6*th mo.* 1651."

This communication Mr. Clark answered in the following manner :

" *To the honored Governor of the Massachusetts, and the rest of that Honorable Society these present.*

" WORTHY SENATORS,

" I received a writing subscribed with five of your hands, by way of answer to a twice repeated motion of mine before you, which was grounded as I conceive sufficiently upon the Governor's words in open court, which writing of yours doth no way answer my expectation, nor yet that motion which I made ; and whereas (waving that grounded motion) you are pleased to intimate that if I were forward to dispute, and would move it myself to the court, or magistrates about Boston, you would appoint one to answer my motion, &c. be pleased to understand, that although I am not backward to maintain the faith and order of my Lord the King of saints, for which I have been sentenced, yet am I not in such a way so forward to dispute, or move therein lest inconvenience should arise. I shall rather once more repeat my former motion, which, if it shall please the honored General Court to accept, and under their Secretary's hand shall grant a free dispute, without molestation or interruption, I shall be well satisfied therewith ; that what is past I shall forget, and upon your motion shall attend it ; thus desiring the Father of mercies, not to lay that evil to your charge, I remain your well-wisher,"

JOHN CLARK.

" *From prison, this* 14*th day,* 6*th month,* 1651."

Thus ended Mr. Clark's chastisement and the Governor's challenge. The last communication, which he had from his fearful opponents, was indeed signed by the heads of departments, but it was not made in official manner. Mr. Clark all along kept in view the law which had been made seven years before, which threatened so terribly any one, who should oppose infant baptism. This was the reason of his requesting an order for the dispute in a legal form. But it was abundantly evident to him, as it will be to every impartial reader, that neither the great Mr. Cotton, nor any of his clerical brethren, dared to meet him in a verbal combat. Infant baptism was safe while defended by the sword of the magistrate, but they dared not risk it in the field of argument. Mr. Clark therefore left his adversaries in triumph ; but poor Mr. Holmes was retained a prisoner, and in the end experienced the full weight of their cruel intolerance. An account of his sufferings is thus related by himself.

" Unto the well-beloved brethren, John Spillsbury, William Kiffen, and the rest that in London stand fast in the faith, and continue to walk stedfastly in that order of the gospel, which was once delivered unto the saints by Jesus Christ : Obadiah Holmes, an unworthy witness that Jesus is the Lord, and of late a prisoner for Jesus' sake, at Boston, sendeth greeting.

Dearly beloved and longed after,

" My heart's desire is to hear from you, and to hear that you grow in grace, and in the knowledge of our Lord and Saviour Jesus Christ, &c.

" Not long after these troubles (at Rehoboth which he relates in the first part of this letter) I came upon occasion of business into the colony of the Massachusetts, with two other brethren, as brother Clark being one of the two can inform you, where we three were apprehended, carried to Boston, and so to the court, and were all sentenced; what they laid to my charge you may here read in my sentence;* upon the pronouncing of which, as I went from the bar, I expressed myself in these words : I bless God I am counted worthy to suffer for the name of Jesus. Whereupon John Wilson (their pastor, as they call him) struck me before the judgment seat, and cursed me, saying, the curse of God or Jesus go with thee : So we were carried to the prison, where not long after I was deprived of my two loving friends, at whose departure the adversary stept in, took hold of my spirit, and troubled me for the space of an hour, and then the Lord came in and sweetly relieved me, causing to look to himself, so was I stayed, and refreshed in the thoughts of my God ; and although during the time of my imprisonment, the tempter was busy, yet it pleased God so to stand at my right hand, that the motions were but sudden, and so vanished away ; and although there were that would have paid the money, if I would accept it, yet I durst not accept of deliverance in such a way, and therefore my answer to them was, that although I would acknowledge their love to a drop of cold water, yet could I not thank them for their money, if they should pay it. So the court drew near, and the night before I should suffer according to my sentence, it pleased God I rested and slept quietly ; in the morning my friends came to visit me, desiring me to take the refreshment of wine and other comforts ; but my resolution was not to drink wine nor strong drink that day, until my punishment was over; and the reason was, lest in case I had more strength, courage, and boldness, than ordinarily could be expected, the world should either say he is drunk with new wine, or

* " The sentence of Obadiah Holmes, of Seaconk, the 31st of the fifth mo. 1651.

" Forasmuch as you, Obadiah Holmes, being come into this jurisdiction about the 21st of the 5th mo. did meet at one William Witter's house, at Lynn, and did here privately (and at other times, being an excommunicate person, did take upon you to preach and baptize) upon the Lord's day or other days, and being taken then by the constable, and coming afterward to the assembly at Lynn, did, in disrespect to the ordinance of God and his worship, keep on your hat, the pastor being in prayer, insomuch that you would not give reverence in vailing your hat, till it was forced off your head, to the disturbance of the congregation, and professing against the institution of the church, as not being according to the gospel of Jesus Christ ; and that you, the said Obadiah Holmes, did, upon the day following, meet again at the said William Witter's, in contempt to authority, you being then in the custody of the law, and did there receive the sacrament, being excommunicate, and that you did baptize such as were baptized before, and thereby did necessarily deny the baptism that was before administered to be baptism, the churches no churches, and also other ordinances, and ministers, as if all were a nullity ; and did also deny the lawfulness of baptizing of infants ; and all this tends to the dishonour of God, the despising the ordinances of God *among us*, the peace of the churches, and seducing the subjects of this commonwealth from the truth of the gospel of Jesus Christ, and perverting the straight ways of the Lord, the court doth fine you 30 pounds, to be paid, or sufficient sureties that the said sum shall be paid by the first day of the next Court of Assistants, or else to be well whipt, and that you shall remain in prison till it be paid, or security given in for it.

" By the Court,

" INCREASE NOWEL."

else that the comfort and strength of the creature hath carried him through; but my course was this: I desired brother John Hazel to bear my friend's company, and I betook myself to my chamber, where I might communicate with my God, commit myself to him, and beg strength from him. I had no sooner sequestered myself, and come into my chamber, but satan lets fly at me, saying, Remember thyself, thy birth, breeding, and friends, thy wife, children, name and credit; but as this was sudden, so there came in sweetly from the Lord as sudden an answer, ' Tis for my Lord, I must not deny him before the sons of men, (for that were to set men above him) but rather lose all, yea, wife, children, and mine own life also: To this the tempter replies, Oh, but that is the question, is it for him? and for him alone? is it not rather for thy own or some other's sake? thou hast so professed and practised, and now art loth to deny it; is not pride and self at the bottom? Surely this temptation was strong, and thereupon I made diligent search after the matter, as formerly I had done, and after a while there was even as it had been a voice from heaven in my very soul, bearing witness with my conscience, that it was not for any man's case or sake in this world, that so I had professed and practised, but for my Lord's cause and sake, and for him alone; whereupon my spirit was much refreshed; as also in the consideration of these three scriptures, which speak on this wise, *Who shall lay any thing to the charge of God's elect? Although I walk through the valley of the shadow of death, I will fear no evil, thy rod and thy staff, they shall comfort me. And he that continueth to the end, the same shall be saved.* But then came in the consideration of the weakness of the flesh to bear the strokes of a whip, though the spirit was willing, and thereupon I was caused to pray earnestly unto the Lord, that he would be pleased to give me a spirit of courage and boldness, a tongue to speak for him, and strength of body to suffer for his sake, and not to shrink or yield to the strokes, or shed tears, lest the adversaries of the truth should thereupon blaspheme and be hardened, and the weak and feeble-hearted discouraged, and for this I sought the Lord earnestly; at length he satisfied my spirit to give up, as my soul, so my body unto him, and quietly to leave the whole disposing of the matter to him; and so I addressed myself in as comely a manner as I could, having such a Lord and Master to serve in this business. And when I heard the voice of my keeper come for me, even cheerfulness did come upon me, and taking my Testament in my hand, I went along with him to the place of execution, and after a common salutation there stood. There stood by also one of the magistrates, by name Increase Nowel, who for a while kept silent, and spoke not a word, and so did I, expecting the Governor's presence, but he came not. But after a while Mr. Nowel bade the executioner do his office. Then I desired to speak a few words, but Mr. Nowel answered, it is not now a time to speak. Whereupon I took leave, and said, men, brethren, fathers, and countrymen, I beseech you give me leave to speak a few words, and the rather because here are many spectators to see me punished, and I am to seal with my blood, if God give strength, that which I hold and practise in reference to the word of God, and the testimony of Jesus. That which I have to say in brief is this; although I confess I am no disputant, yet seeing I am to seal what I hold with my blood, I am ready to defend it by the word, and to dispute that point with any that shall come forth to withstand it. Mr. Nowel answered me, now was no time to dispute. Then said I, then I desire to give an account of the faith and order I hold, and this I desired three times, but in comes Mr. Flint, and saith to the executioner, *Fellow, do thine office, for this fellow would but make a long speech to delude the people.* So I being resolved to speak, told the people, that which I am to suffer for is the word of God, and testimony of Jesus Christ. No, saith Mr. Nowel, it is for your error, and going about to seduce the people. To which I replied, not for error, for in all the time of my imprisonment, wherein I was left alone, (my brethren being gone) which of all your ministers in all that time, came to convince me of an error; and when upon the Governor's words a motion was made for a publick dispute, and upon fair terms so often renewed, and desired by hundreds, what was the reason it was not granted? Mr. Nowel told me, it was his fault that went away and would not dispute; but this the writings will clear at large. Still Mr. Flint calls to the man to do his office: so before, and in the time of his pulling off my clothes, I continued speaking, telling them, that I had so learned, that for all Boston I would not give my body into their hands thus to be bruised upon another account, yet upon this I would not give the hundredth part of a *wampum peague** to free it out of their hands, and that I made as much conscience of unbuttoning one button as I did of paying the £30 in reference thereunto. I told them moreover, the Lord having manifested his love towards me, in giving me repentance towards God, and faith in Jesus Christ, and so to be baptized in water, by a messenger of Jesus, into the name of the Father, Son, and Holy Spirit, wherein I have fellowship with him in his death, burial and resurrection, I am now come to be baptized in afflictions by your hands, that so I may have further fellowship with my Lord, and am not ashamed of his sufferings, for by his stripes am I healed. And as the man began to lay the strokes upon my back, I said to the people, though my flesh should fail, and my spirit should fail, yet my God would not fail. So it pleased the Lord to come in, and so to fill my heart and tongue as a vessel full, and with an audible voice I broke forth, praying unto the Lord not to lay this sin to their charge; and telling the people, that now I found he did not fail me, and therefore now I should trust him forever, who failed me not; for in truth, as the strokes fell upon me, I had such a spiritual manifestation of God's presence, as the like thereof I never had nor felt, nor can with fleshly tongue express, and the outward pain was so removed from me, that indeed I am not able to declare it to you, it was so easy to me, that I could well bear it, yea, and in a manner, felt it not, although it was grievous, as the spectators said, the man striking with all his strength (yea, spitting in his hands three times, as many affirmed) with a three corded whip, giving me therewith thirty strokes. When he had loosed me from the post, having joyfulness in my heart and cheerfulness in my countenance, as the spectators observed, I told the magistrates, you have struck me as with roses; and said moreover, although the Lord

---

* A *wampum peague* is the sixth part of a penny with us. Backus.

hath made it easy to me, yet I pray God it may not be laid to your charge. After this, many came to me rejoicing to see the power of the Lord manifested in weak flesh ; but sinful flesh takes occasion hereby to bring others in trouble, informs the magistrates hereof, and so two more are apprehended as for contempt of authority ; their names were John Hazel and John Spur, who came indeed and did shake me by the hand, but did use no words of contempt or reproach unto any ; no man can prove that the first spoke any thing, and for the second, he only said thus, blessed be the Lord ; yet these two for taking me by the hand, and thus saying after I had received my punishment, were sentenced to pay forty shillings, or be whipt. Both were resolved against paying their fine ; nevertheless, after one or two days' imprisonment, one paid John Spur's fine, and he was released ; and after six or seven days' imprisonment of brother Hazel, even the day when he should have suffered, another paid his, and so he escaped, and the next day went to visit a friend about six miles from Boston, where the same day he fell sick, and within ten days ended his life. When I was come to the prison, it pleased God to stir up the heart of an old acquaintance of mine, who with much tenderness, like the good Samaritan, poured oil into my wounds, and plaistered my sores ;* but there was present information given what was done, and inquiry made who was the surgeon, and it was commonly reported he should be sent for, but what was done I yet know not. Now thus it hath pleased the Father of mercies so to dispose of the matter, that my bonds and imprisonments have been no hindrance to the gospel, for before my return, some submitted to the Lord and were baptized, and divers were put upon the way of inquiry. And now being advised to make my escape by night, because it was reported there were warrants forth for me, I departed ; and the next day after, while I was on my journey, the constable came to search at the house where I lodged, so I escaped their hands, and was, by the good hand of my heavenly Father, brought home again to my near relations, my wife and eight children. The brethren of our town and Providence, having taken pains to meet me four miles in the woods where we rejoiced together in the Lord. Thus have I given you as briefly as I can, a true relation of things ; wherefore my brethren, rejoice with me in the Lord, and give glory to him, for he is worthy, to whom be praise forevermore ; to whom I commit you, and put up my earnest prayers for you, that by my late experience who have trusted in God, and have not been deceived, you may trust in him perfectly. Wherefore my dearly beloved brethren, trust in the Lord, and you shall not be ashamed nor confounded ; so I also rest,

Yours in the bond of charity,

OBADIAH HOLMES."

* In a manuscript of Governor Joseph Jenks, wrote near one hundred years ago, he says, " Mr. Holmes was whipt thirty stripes, and in such an unmerciful manner, that in many days, if not some weeks, he could take no rest but as he lay upon his knees and elbows, not being able to suffer any part of his body to touch the bed whereon he lay."

Warrants were issued out against thirteen persons, whose only crime was showing some emotions of sympathy towards this innocent sufferer. Eleven of them escaped, and two only were apprehended; their names were John Spur and John Hazel. Spur was probably the man who had been apprehended at Weymouth. Hazel was one of Mr. Holmes' brethren of Rehoboth. Both of these men were to receive ten lashes or pay forty shillings apiece. The latter they could not do with a clear conscience, and were therefore preparing for such another scourging as they had seen and pitied in their brother Holmes. But some without their knowledge paid their fines. Mr. Backus has given an account of their trial, and the depositions which were preferred against them, in which nothing more was pretended than that they took Mr. Holmes by the hand when he came from the whipping-post, and blessed God for the strength and support he had given him. But this was "a heinous offence," and called for the vengeance of the civil arm. Mr. Hazel was upwards of sixty years old, and died a few days after he was released, before he reached home.

Mr. Clark went to England this same year, where he published a narrative of these transactions, from which the preceding sketches have been selected.

These measures of intolerance and cruelty tended to promote rather than retard the Baptist cause. And many Pedobaptists, both here and in England, remonstrated with much severity against the intemperate zeal of their persecuting brethren. And among the rest, Sir Richard Saltonstall, one of the Massachusetts magistrates then in England, wrote to Mr. Cotton and Wilson of Boston in the following manner:

"Reverend and dear friends, whom I unfeignedly love and respect,—It doth not a little grieve my spirit to hear what sad things are reported daily of your tyranny and persecutions in New-England, as that you fine, whip, and imprison men for their consciences. First, you compel such to come into your assemblies as you know will not join you in your worship, and when they shew their dislike thereof, or witness against it, then you stir up your magistrates to punish them for such (as you conceive) their public affronts. Truly, friends, this your practice of compelling any in matters of worship to do that whereof they are not fully persuaded, is to make them sin, for so the apostle, (Rom. xiv. 23.) tells us, and many are made hypocrites thereby, conforming in their outward man for fear of punishment. We pray for you, and wish you prosperity every way, hoped the Lord would have given you so much light and love there, that you might have been eyes to God's people here, and not to practise those courses in a wilderness, which you went so far to prevent. These rigid ways have laid you very low in the hearts of the saints. I do assure you I have heard them pray in the public assemblies that the Lord would give you meek and humble spirits, not to strive so much for uniformity, as to keep the unity of the spirit in the bond of peace."

MR. COTTON'S ANSWER.

Honoured and dear Sir,

"My brother Wilson and self do both of us acknowledge your love, as\otherwise formerly, so now in the late lines we received from you, that you grieve in spirit to hear daily complaints against us. Be pleased to understand we look at such complaints as altogether injurious in respect of ourselves, who had no hand or tongue at all to promote either the coming of the persons you aim at into our assemblies, or their punishment for their carriage there. Righteous judgment will not take up reports, much less reproaches against the innocent. We are amongst those, whom (if you knew us better) you would account peaceable in Israel. Yet neither are we so vast in our indulgence or toleration, as to think the men you speak of, suffered an unjust censure. For one of them, (Obadiah Holmes) being an excommunicate person himself, out of a church in Plymouth patent, came into this jurisdiction, and took upon him to baptize, which I think himself will not say he was compelled here to perform.* And he was not ignorant that the rebaptizing of an elder person, and that by a private person out of office and under excommunication, are all of them manifest contestations against the order and government of our churches established, *we know*, by God's law, and, he knoweth, by the laws of the country. As for his whipping, it was more voluntarily chosen by him than inflicted on him. His censure by the court, was to have paid, as I know, 30*l*. or else be whipt; his fine was offered to be paid by friends for him freely, but he chose rather to be whipt; in which case, if his suffering of stripes was any worship of God at all, surely it could be accounted no better than will-worship.† The other, (Mr. Clark) was wiser in that point, and his offence was less, so was his fine less, and himself as I hear, was contented to have it paid for him, where-

---

* What an evasion is this! Sir Richard spake of compelling persons into their worship, and Cotton here turns it as if he meant a compelling persons out of one government into another to worship in their own way.

† "Although the paying of a fine seems to be but a small thing in comparison of a man's parting with his religion; yet the paying of a fine is the acknowledging of a transgression; and for a man to acknowledge that he has transgressed when his conscience tells him he has not, is but little, if any thing at all, short of parting with his religion; and it is likely that this might be the consideration of those sufferers." GOV. JENKS.

upon he was released.* The imprisonment of either of them was no detriment. I believe they fared neither of them better at home, and, I am sure, Holmes had not been so well clad for many years before.

"But be pleased to consider this point a little further. You think, to compel men in matter of worship is to make them sin. If the worship be lawful in itself, the magistrate compelling him to come to it, compelleth him not to sin, but the sin is in his will that needs to be compelled to a christian duty. If it do make men hypocrites, yet better be hypocrites than profane persons. Hypocrites give God part of his due, the outward man, but the profane person giveth God neither outward nor inward man. You know not, if you think we came into this wilderness to practise those courses here which we fled from in England. We believe there is a vast difference between men's inventions and God's institutions; we fled from men's inventions, to which we else should have been compelled; we compel none to men's inventions. If our ways (rigid ways as you call them) have laid us low in the hearts of God's people, yea, and of the saints, (as you style them) we do not believe it is any part of their saint-ship. Nevertheless, I tell you the truth, we have tolerated in our churches some Anabaptists, some Antinomians, and some Seekers, and do so still at this day. We are far from arrogating infallibility of judgment to ourselves or affecting uniformity; uniformity God never required, infallibility he never granted us."

Such was Mr. Cotton's logic in support of persecution, and Mr. Ivimey well observes, " that we have happily arrived at a period when arguments are not necessary to prove the absurdity of his reasoning ;" and he also observes, " that the severities were not so much the result of the disposition of these New-England persecutors, as of the principles which they had adopted."

What on earth can be more shocking to any being, who has human feelings, than to see a humble and devout christian, who renders to Cesar what is his due, merely for not believing some things which his brethren believe, arrested in his peaceful and pious course, sentenced to be tied to a public whipping post like a malefactor, and there to have his body barbarously scourged, to chastise and cure the conscientious scruples of his mind; and all this by his countrymen, his neighbours; yea, by his fellow christians, who profess to worship the same God, and trust for salvation in the same Redeemer! Who can contemplate such a scene of barbarity without being sickened at the sight, and retiring from it with disgust and horror! To say noth-

* If the reader will look back to page 369 and read Mr. Clark's letter to the magistrates, he will see how contrary this is to truth.

ing of hanging, burning, and torturing to death, with all the murderous engines, which hellish ingenuity can invent, the circumstance merely of one christian beating another thirty strokes with a three-corded whip, for conscience' sake, is a scene on which heaven must frown, the earth on which it is perpetrated must groan, and candid devils (if such there are) must be astonished and confounded at the folly and absurdity of men.

In the period now under review, I find but one more event, of any considerable importance as it respects the Baptists or their sentiments, and that was the case of President Dunstar. This learned gentleman was the first President of Cambridge College or Harvard University. He was a native of England, but when and where he was born I do not find ; he became the President of this then infant institution in 1640, in which office he continued with much reputation and success about thirteen years. By the united testimonies of Johnson, Hubbard, and Prince, he was a man of profound erudition, and "an orthodox preacher of the truths of Christ." This eminent man, in 1653, was brought so far on to the Baptist ground, that " he not only forbore to present an infant of his own unto baptism, but also thought himself under some obligations to bear his testimony in some sermons, against the administration of baptism to *any infant* whatever." For this defection he was immediately opposed with violence, and soon after removed from the town, and settled at Scituate in Plymouth Colony, where he spent the remainder of his days. What progress President Dunstar made in his pursuit of Baptist principles I do not find, but it does not appear that he ever openly espoused the Baptist cause. Capt. Cudworth, writing to Mr. John Brown of Rehoboth, then in England, in 1658, says, "Through mercy we have yet among us worthy Mr. Dunstar, whom the Lord hath made boldly to bear testimony against the *spirit of persecution*." Morton says that he fell asleep in the Lord, in 1659.

It is said by Mr. Backus, that President Dunstar was led to inquire into the Baptist sentiments, by the persecutions against Messrs. Holmes, Clark, and Crandal, and that his preaching against infant baptism set Thomas Gould to examining the subject ; and his examination issued in the founding of the first Baptist church in Boston. While this learned advocate for apostolical baptism was yet in Cambridge, Mr. Jonathan Mitchel, the minister of the place, went to converse with him on the subject. " When I came from him, (says he) I had a strange experience ; I found hurrying and pressing suggestions against *Pedobaptism*, and injected scruples and thoughts, whether, the other way might not be right, and infant baptism an *invention of men ;* and whether I might, with a good conscience, baptize children, and the like." But all these " unreasonable suggestions," he ascribed to the devil, and resolved with Mr. Hooker, that " he would have an argument able to *remove a mountain* before he would recede from, or appear against a truth or practice received among the faithful !" What an expeditious way of silencing one's doubts and convictions ! How many have we reason to believe, in order to avoid going over to the despised Baptists, have entrenched themselves with barriers equally irrational and strong ! " But sure I am," says Mr. Backus, " that if any Baptist minister had told such a story, and made such an absurd resolution, our adversaries would then have such grounds to charge us with *wilfulness* and *obstinacy* as they never yet had."*

From these brief sketches of the early Baptists in this commonwealth, we shall proceed to a more systematical narration of their subsequent affairs, and give some detailed accounts of the churches and Associations, which have arisen within its bounds.

It is highly probable, that the late severities exercised towards our brethren in this jurisdiction, set many to examining into their principles, and we may also suppose, that those Baptists, who had hitherto travelled in communion with the Pedobaptist churches, some of whom were accused of the *profane trick* of turning their backs, when infants were sprinkled, were now constrained to come out and separate themselves from a church, whose tenets were bloody, and which had now begun its persecuting career. These events I state as probabilities, not being in possession of authentic details. But certain it is that the Baptists now began to be more numerous ; they were also encouraged to take a bolder stand against the encroachments

* Backus, vol. I. pp. 282, 284, 320, 321.

of their adversaries, their terrible legislative threatenings, and their merciless scourgings notwithstanding.

In 1663, a church was founded in Swansea, and two years after the church was begun, which afterwards took the name of the first in Boston. In 1685, a church was begun in Dartmouth, about seventy miles southwesterly from Boston. But so slow was the progress of the Baptists in this government, that in a hundred years from the organization of the church in Swansea, they had planted but eighteen churches, which had acquired a permanent standing. Some few besides had arisen during the century which had lost their visibility before its close. Many were the oppressions and privations, which our brethren suffered in this boasted asylum of liberty, until the American War. That calamitous scene, so distressing to the country otherwise, was nevertheless peculiarly auspicious to the cause of religious liberty in this commonwealth, as well as in other colonies, where religious establishments were domineering with tyrannic sway.

Although the war shook very sensibly the system of religious oppression, it was not the cause of its demolition here as it was the case in Virginia. Many of its bands were indeed broken, yet some by the vigilance of a watchful priesthood were preserved entire. In the unsettled state of affairs, which succeeded the war, the Baptists with Mr. Backus at their head preferred a petition to the Legislature, praying "that ministers should *in future* be supported by Christ's authority, and not at all by assessment and secular force." And had statesmen been let alone in their discussions, it is highly probable that this petition would have been regarded ; but the clergy, poor men, were afraid to be left on this precarious ground ; they therefore put forth their cries ; legislators heard them, pitied their dangerous condition, and disgraced their State Constitution with an article to regulate religious worship, and so on.

But notwithstanding the failure of this righteous request, our brethren, under the new government, found their circumstances materially improved. The predominant party, it is true, still had the power of oppressing them in certain cases, but it was used less frequently than formerly ; many became convinced of the truth of Baptist sentiments, and embraced their communion, and many others, who went not so far, were constrained to let them alone. Many new churches soon arose in different parts of the State, so that by the year 1784, their whole number amounted to sixty-four. Twenty more were added to this number during the ten succeeding years. And the number of churches, as well as communicants, have been increasing in about the same proportion, from the last mentioned period to the present time. Their number will be exhibited in the General Table.

In this commonwealth are a part of the Warren Association, all the Boston except one or two small churches, part of those named Sturbridge, Leyden, Westfield, and Shaftsbury. Four of these six associations, viz. the Boston, Sturbridge, Leyden, and Westfield, are considered as having their seat in Massachusetts, and those of Warren and Shaftsbury have always had a large portion of their members and influence in this State.

I have thought proper in farther prosecuting the history of this State, to consider it under two divisions; and the line, which we shall fix upon, will be drawn from about the northeast corner of the State of Rhode-Island, and extend northerly to the State of New-Hampshire. That portion of the State which lies east of this line, I shall consider the first division, and that which lies west of it the second.

FIRST DIVISION.

This division comprehends the oldest settlements as well as the oldest churches in the state, and in it are situated the Warren and Boston Associations. It embraces the counties of Essex, Middlesex, a part of Worcester, the whole of Suffolk, Norfolk, Bristol, Plymouth, Barnstable, Dukes, and Nantucket. It is bounded east and south by the Atlantic ocean.

In this division we find a number of churches distinguished for age and sufferings, and those now called the first in Swansea and Boston, stand the foremost on the list; their history will of necessity occupy more room than that of the rest. They are dated, the first in 1663, and the other in 1665; but both of them were in reality begun a number of years before. Although the Swansea church is the oldest, yet as we shall regard the local and relative situation of the churches about to be described, we shall begin with the one in Boston, and then take notice of the other churches in the northern part of this division, before we come to Swansea and those in the southern.

First Church in Boston. The date of this church has already been given; it existed a few years in Charlestown,* where it was founded, and then its seat was removed to Noddle's Island, a little out in the Massachusetts Bay, where it remained some time before it was established in the town from which it received its name.

We have given a general account of the Baptists in this government up to about the time of the founding of this body, which originated as follows:

Mr. Hubbard, one of the Massachusetts historians, observes, that " while some were studying how baptism might be enlarged and extended to the seed of the faithful in their several generations, there were others as studious to deprive all unadult children thereof, and restrain the privilege only to adult believers."†

" Infant baptism," says Dr. Mather, "hath been scrupled by multitudes in our day, who have been, in other points, most worthy christians, and as holy, watchful, fruitful, and heavenly people, as perhaps any in the world." Some few of these people, he says, were among the first settlers in New-England. Some of their names have been mentioned, and many things make it probable that there were many more who never happened to fall under the lash of the law, and whose names for that reason do not appear on the page of history; for the Baptists at this time had no one to tell their story, and we never get a view of them, except at the tribunals of their adversaries, in their prisons, or at their whipping-posts.

After being long harassed in courts and churches, a few of our brethren, despairing of better times, and being prepared for the worst, took the bold step of embodying themselves into a church of the Baptist order. The constituents were nine in number; their names were Thomas Gould, Thomas Osburn, Edward Drinker, John George,

---

* Charlestown is separated from Boston by Charles river.
† Backus, vol. I. p. 355.

Richard Goodall, William Turner, Robert Lambert, Mary Goodall, and Mary Newell. Gould and Osburn were members of the Pedobaptist church in Charlestown. Goodall was a member of a Baptist church in London, of which Mr. Kiffin was pastor. His wife was probably a member of the same church. Turner and Lambert were members of a church in Dartmouth, England, whose pastor was a Mr. Stead. Of the others we have not so particular information. Turner accepted a captain's commission in king Philip's war, and lost his life in the defence of a colony, in which he was most cruelly oppressed.

The founding of this church was considered by the Massachusetts people, as a most heinous and heaven-daring offence, and many of the members of it spent most of their time in courts and prisons; they were often fined, and some of them were banished, or at least were ordered to depart out of the jurisdiction, or desist from the error of their way; neither of which however would they do; they were of course denounced obstinate hereticks, and suffered accordingly. " It would take a volume," says Morgan Edwards, "to contain an account of all their sufferings for ten or twelve years."

The ostensible reason, which their enemies urged for distressing them, was, that they had formed a church without the approbation of their ministers and rulers. "This principle," says Mr. Neal, "condemns all the dissenting congregations, which have been formed in England since the act of uniformity in the year 1662." The fact was they were determined that no churches should be formed only upon their own plan. Our brethren well knew that no such permission would be granted, and, besides, they could not in principle solicit the favour. And finding by experience that the churches, established by law, would not suffer them to live quietly in their communion, nor peaceably separate from it, they resolved to set up a standard of their own, and united " in a solemn covenant in the name of the Lord Jesus Christ, to walk in fellowship and communion together, in the practice of all the holy appointments of Christ, which he had, or should further make known to them."

" The king's commissioners being here," says Mr. Backus, " caused the court not to lay hold of these people so soon as otherwise they might have done. But in August a note was entered in Roxbury church records, and published in an Almanack, which has been communicated to me in these words : " The Anabaptists gathered themselves into a church, prophesied one by one, and some one among them administered the Lord's supper after he was regularly excommunicated by the church at Charlestown; they also set up a lecture at Drinker's house, once a fortnight."

Thomas Gould was the founder of this church, and for many years had the principal share of the sufferings it underwent. The manner in which he came to embrace the Baptist sentiments, and the treatment of the church in Charlestown towards him are thus related by himself:

"It having been a long time a scruple to me about infant baptism, God was pleased at last to make it clear to me by the rule of the gospel, that children were not capable nor fit subjects for such an ordinance, because Christ gave this commission to his apostles, first to preach to make them disciples, and then to baptize them, which infants were not capable of; so that I durst not bring forth my child to be partaker of it; so looking that my child had no right to it, which was in the year 1655, when the Lord was pleased to give me a child ; I staid some space of time and said nothing, to see what the church would do with me. On a third day of the week when there was a meeting at my house, to keep a day of thanksgiving to God, for his mercy shown to my wife, at that time one coming to the meeting brought a note from the elders of the church to this effect, that they desired me to come down on the morrow to the elder's house, and to send word again what time of that day I would come, and they would stay at home for me ; and if I could not come that day, to send them word. I looking on the writing with many friends with me, I told them I had promised to go another way on the morrow. Master Dunstar (probably President Dunstar) being present, desired me to send them word that I could not come on the morrow, but that I would come any other time that they would appoint me ; and so I sent word back by the same messenger. The fifth day, meeting with elder Green, I told him how it was ; he told me it was well, and that they would appoint another day when he had spoken with the pastor, and then they would send me word. This lay about two months before I heard any more from them. On a first day in the afternoon one told me I must stop, for the church would speak with me. They called me out, and Master Sims told the church, that this brother did withhold his child from baptism, and that they had sent unto him to come down on such a day to speak with them, and if he could not come on that day, to set a day when he would be at home; but he refusing to come, would appoint no time, when we writ to him to take his own time, and send us word. I replied that there was no such word in the letter, for me to appoint the day; but what time of that day I should come. Mr. Sims stood up and told me, *I did lie,* for they sent to me to appoint the day. I replied again that there was no such thing in the letter. He replied again, that they did not set down a time, and not a day, therefore he told me it was a lie, and that they would leave my judgment, and deal with me for a lie; and told the church, that he and the elder agreed to write, that if I could not come that day, to appoint the time when I could come, and that he read it after the elder writ it, and the elder affirmed it was so; but I still replied there was no such thing in the letter, and thought I could produce the letter. They bid me let them see the letter, or they would proceed against me for a lie. Brother Thomas Wilder, sitting before me, stood up and told them, that it was so in the letter as I said, for he read it when it came to me. But they answered, it was not so, and bid him produce the letter, or they would proceed with me; he said I think I can produce the letter, and forthwith took it out of his pocket, which I wondered at; and I desired him to give it to Mr. Russel to read, and so he did, and he read it very faithfully, and it was just as I had said, that I must send them word what time of that day I would come down; so that their mouths were stopped, and master Sims put it off and said he was mistaken, for he thought he had read it otherwise; but the elder said, this is nothing, let us proceed with him for his judgment. Now let any man judge what a fair beginning this was, and if you wait awhile you may see as fair an ending. They called me forth to know why I would not bring my child to baptism? My answer was,

I did not see any rule of Christ for it, for that ordinance belongs to such as can make profession of their faith, as the Scripture doth plainly hold forth. They answered me, that was meant of grown persons and not of children. But that which was most alleged by them was, that children were capable of circumcision in the time of the law, and therefore as capable in the time of the gospel of baptism; and asked me, why children were not to be baptized in the time of the gospel, as well as children were circumcised in the time of the law? My answer was, God gave a strict command in the law for the circumcision of children; but we have no command in the gospel, nor example, for the baptizing of children. Many other things were spoken, then a meeting was appointed by the church the next week at Mr. Russell's.

"Being met at Mr. Russell's house, Mr. Sims took a writing out of his pocket, wherein he had drawn up many arguments for infant baptism, and told the church that I must answer those arguments, which I suppose he had drawn from some author, and told me I must keep to those arguments. My answer was, I thought the church had met together to answer my scruples, and to satisfy my conscience by a rule of God, and not for me to answer his writing. He said he had drawn it up for the help of his memory, and desired we might go on. Then I requested three things of them. 1st. That they should not make me offender for a word. 2d. They should not drive me faster than I was able to go. 3d. That if any present should see cause to clear up any thing that is spoken by me, they might have their liberty without offence; because here are many of you that have their liberty to speak against me if you see cause. But it was denied, and Mr. Sims was pleased to reply, that he was able to deal with me himself, and that I knew it. So we spent four or five hours speaking to many things to and again, but so hot both sides, that we quickly forgot and went from the arguments that were written. At last one of the company stood up and said, I will give you one plain place of Scripture where children were baptized. I told him that would put an end to the controversy. That place is in the 2d of the Acts, 39th and 40th verses. After he had read the Scripture, Master Sims told me that promise belonged to infants, for the Scripture saith,

The promise is to you and your children, and to all that are afar off; and he said no more; to which I replied, *Even so many as the Lord our God shall call.* Mr. Sims replied that I spoke blasphemously in adding to the Scriptures. I said, pray do not condemn me, for if I am deceived, my eyes deceive me. He replied again, I added to the scripture, which was blasphemy. I looking into my Bible, read the words again, and said it was so. He replied the same words a third time before the church. Mr. Russell stood up and told him it was so as I had read it. Ay, it may be so in your Bible, saith Mr. Sims. Mr. Russell answered, yea, in yours too if you will look into it. Then he said he was mistaken, for he thought on another place; so after many other words we broke up for that time.

" At another meeting, the church required me to bring out my child to baptism. I told them I durst not do it, for I did not see any rule for it in the word of God. They brought many places of Scripture in the Old and New-Testament, as circumcision and the promise to Abraham, and that children were holy, and they were disciples. But I told them that all these places made nothing for infant baptism. Then stood up W. D. in the church and said, " Put him in the court! Put him in the court!" But Mr. Sims said, " I pray forbear such words." But it proved so, for presently after they put me in the court, and put me in seven or eight courts, whilst they looked upon me to be a member of their church. The elder pressed the church to lay me under admonition, which the church was backward to do. Afterwards I went out at the sprinkling of children, which was a great trouble to some honest hearts, and they told me of it. But I told them I could not stay, for I looked upon it as no ordinance of Christ. They told me that now I had made known my judgment, I might stay, for they knew I did not join with them. So I stayed and sat down in my seat when they were at prayer and administering that service to infants. Then they dealt with me for my irreverent carriage. One stood up and accused me, that I stopped my ears; but I denied it.

" At another meeting they asked me if I would suffer the church to fetch my child and baptize it? I answered, if they would fetch my child and do it as their own act, they might do it ; but when they should bring my child, I would make known to the congregation that I had no hand in it ; then some of the church were against doing of it. A brother stood up and said, " Brother Gould, you were once for children's baptism, why are you fallen from it ?" I answered, " It is true, and I suppose you were once for crossing in baptism, why are you fallen from that ?" The man was silent, but Mr. Sims stood up in a great heat, and desired the church to take notice of it, that I compared the ordinance of Christ to the cross in baptism ; this was one of the great offences they dealt with me for. After this, the deputy-governor, Mr. Bellingham, meeting me in Boston, called me to him and said, " Goodman Gould, I desire you that you would let the church baptize your child." I told him that " if the church would do it upon their own account, they should do it, but I durst not bring out my child." So he called to Mrs. Norton of Charlestown, and prayed her to fetch Goodman Gould's child and baptize it. So she spake to them, but not rightly informing them, she gave them to understand I would bring out my child. They called me out again, and asked me if I would bring forth my child ? I told them " No, I durst not do it, for I see no rule for it."

In much the same manner the church proceeded with their obnoxious brother, until Master Sims, who was not only a petulant but an ignorant priest, put on him the second admonition. "This," says he, "continued a long time before they called me out again. In the mean time, I had some friends, who came to me out of old England, who were Baptists, and desired to meet at my house on a first day, which I granted ; of these was myself, my wife, and Thomas Osbourne, that were of their church. Afterward they called me forth, and asked why I kept the meeting in private on the Lord's day, and did not come to the publick ? My answer was, " I know not what reason the church had to call me forth." They asked me if I was not a member of that church ? I told them they had not acted toward me as a member, who had put me by the ordinances of Christ seven years ago ; they had denied me the privileges of a member. They asked whether I looked upon admonition as an appointment of Christ ? I told them, "yes, but not to lie under it above seven years, and to be put by the ordinances of Christ in the church ; for the rule of Christ is first to deal with men in the first and second place, and then in the third place before the church ; but the first time that ever they dealt with me, they called me before the whole church." Many meetings we had about this thing, whether I was a member or not, but could come to no conclusion ; for I still affirmed that their actings rendered me no member. Then Mr. Sims told the church that I was ripe for excommunication, and was very earnest for it ; but the church would not consent."

It was not till some time after this, that they "delivered him up to Satan for not hearing the church."

This account was found by Mr. Backus among Mr. Callender's papers. It gives the reader a view of the spirit of the times, and also of the deliberate manner in which Mr. Gould proceeded amidst a constant scene of irritation and abuse. It appears from a number of expressions in different parts of the narrative, which have not been extracted, that he would have preferred remaining with his Pedobaptist brethren, if they would have permitted him to enjoy his Baptist principles in peace ; but because he could not in conscience bring out his babe to be christened, they drove him on to a separation, which he did not meditate at first. The names of the first members of the Baptist church which he founded, have already been mentioned. The sufferings which they endured for a number of years are related by Mr. Backus in a more extensive manner than we can do it here. But it is sufficient to say, that they were many and grievous, and were similar to those to which the Baptists of that day were every where exposed, where the defence of the church was entrusted with the civil power. This little Anabaptist church consisting of only nine members, a part of whom were females, and the rest illiterate mechanics, made full employ for the rulers of Massachusetts a number of years. The innocent people, who gave them so much trouble, were accused of no other crime than that of forming a church without their permission, and of meeting in their own houses to worship their Maker according to the dictates of their consciences. And for these heinous offences, they were incessantly stunned with the harangues of the priests and lawyers, and distressed and ruined by courts, legislatures, forfeitures, and prisons.

The New-England persecutors we would charitably believe, were actuated more by their principles than dispositions. They certainly conducted the business in a bungling and ridiculous manner, and at times manifested some misgivings for their injustice and absurdity.

After Mr. Gould and his companions had been condemned as heretics and law-breakers, fined and imprisoned for non-conformity, they were challenged to a public dispute upon their peculiar sentiments, that it might be determined whether they were erroneous or not! The six following divines, viz. Messrs. John Allen, Thomas Cobbet, John Higginson, Samuel Danforth, Jonathan Mitchell, and Thomas Shepard were nominated to manage the dispute on the Pedobaptist side, which was appointed to be April 14, 1668, in the meeting house in Boston, at 9 o'clock in the morning. But lest these six learned clergymen should not be a match for a few illiterate Baptists, the Governor and magistrates were requested to meet with them. The news of this dispute soon spread abroad, and Mr. Clark's church in Newport sent William Hiscox, Joseph Tory, and Samuel Hubbard, to assist their brethren in Boston in it, who arrived there three days before it was to come on. No particular account of this dispute has been preserved. Mr. Backus has made an extract of considerable length from a paper supposed to have been written by Mr. Gould's wife, in which some things respecting it are mentioned, and by which it appears that the Baptists instead of having full liberty to vindicate their sentiments, were called together only to be tantalized and abused. "When the disputants were met, there was a long speech made by one of them of what vile persons the Baptists were, and how they acted against the churches and government here, and stood condemned by the court. The others desiring liberty to speak, they would not suffer them, but told them they stood there as delinquents, and ought not to have liberty to speak. Then they desired they might choose a moderator as well as they; but they denied them. Two days were spent to little purpose. In the close, Master Jonathan Mitchell pronounced that dreadful sentence against them in Deuteronomy, 17th chapter, from the 8th to the end of the 12th verse." The passage is as follows : *If there arise a matter too hard for thee in judgment, between blood and blood, between plea and plea, and between stroke and stroke, being matters of controversy, within thy gates ; then shalt thou arise, and get thee up into the place, which the Lord thy God shall choose : And thou shalt come unto the priests, the Levites, and unto the judge that shall be in those days, and inquire ; and they shall shew thee the sentence of judgment. And thou shalt do according to the sentence which they of that place, which the Lord shall choose, shall shew thee ; and thou shalt observe to do according to all that they inform thee : According to the sentence of the law, which they shall teach thee, and according to the judgment which they shall tell thee, thou shalt do : thou shalt not decline from the sentence which they shall shew thee, to the right hand nor to the left. And the man, that will do presumptuously, and will not hearken unto the priest, that standeth to minister there before the Lord thy God, or unto the judge, even that man shall die : and thou shalt put away the evil from Israel.*

This was the same Mitchell, who was afraid to converse with President Dunstar, lest his mind should be shaken upon infant baptism ; who found such satanical scruples against it, that he had much ado to write his sermons for Sunday ; and who, in the end, resolved that he would have an *argument able to remove a mountain*, before he would give it up.

So far as we can gain information of the management of this dispute, on the part of the Pedobaptists, it exceeded in cowardly and contemptible tyranny, any thing of the kind we read of in England.* We will excuse in part the men, and lay the most of the blame at the door of their popish, ever hurtful principles of confounding together the Jewish and Christian dispensations, of placing Aaron and Moses in the same chair, and of committing the defence of the church to the civil power.

* Neal somewhere mentions that an English Bishop got so exasperated against the dissenters around him, that he appointed a day in which he would dispute with them, and prove them all hereticks, &c. When the day came, a vast concourse assembled, and when the bishop began to rail, the Quakers paid him in his own coin, and brow-beat him so hard that he was forced to yield ; as he was going to his house, they followed him with shouts, *The hireling fleeth ! The hireling fleeth !*

A singular Act of Assembly.

This curious disputation was in April. The May following the Assembly enacted, that

"Whereas the council in March last did for the further conviction, &c. appoint a meeting of divers elders, and required the said persons to attend the said meeting, which was held in Boston with a great concourse of people. This court, being sensible of their duty to God and the country, and being desirous that their proceedings in this great cause might be clear and regular, do order that the said Gould and company be required to appear before this court, on the seventh instant, at eight in the morning, that the court may understand from themselves, whether upon the means used, or other considerations, they have altered their former declared resolution, and are willing to desist from their former offensive practice, that accordingly a mete effectual remedy may be applied to so dangerous a malady. At the time they made their appearance, and after the court had heard what they had to say for themselves, proceeded. Whereas, Thomas Gould, William Turner, and John Farnum, sen. obstinate and turbulent Anabaptists, have sometime since combined themselves with others in a pretended church estate, without the knowledge and approbation of the authority here established, to the great grief and offence of the godly orthodox; the said persons did, in open court, assert their former practice to have been according to the mind of God, that *nothing that they had heard convinced them to the contrary;* which practice, being also otherwise circumstanced with making infant baptism a nullity, and thereby making *us all* to be unbaptized persons, and so consequently no regular churches, ministry, or ordinances; as also renouncing *all our churches,* as being so *bad and corrupt,* as they are not fit to be held communion with; denying to submit to the government of Christ in the church, and entertaining of those who are under church censure, thereby making the discipline of Christ to be of none effect, and manifestly tending to the disturbance and destruction of these churches; opening the door for all sorts of abominations to come in among us, to the disturbance not only of ecclesiastical enjoyments, but also contempt of our civil order, and the authority here established; which duty to God and the country doth oblige us to prevent, by using the most compassionate effectual means to attain the same; all which considering, together with the danger of disseminating their errors, and encouraging presumptuous irregularities by their examples, should they continue in this jurisdiction; this court do judge it necessary that they be removed to some other part of this country, or elsewhere, and accordingly doth order, that the said Thomas Gould, William Turner, and John Farnum, sen. do before the twentieth of July next remove themselves out of this jurisdiction; and that if after the said 20th of July, either of them be found in any part of this jurisdiction, without license had from this court or the council, he or they shall be forthwith apprehended and committed to prison by warrant from any magistrate, and there remain without bail or mainprise, until he or they shall give sufficient security to the Governor or any magistrate, immediately to depart the jurisdiction, and not to return as above said. And all constables and other officers are required to be faithful and deligent in the execution of this sentence. And it is further ordered, that the keepers of all prisons, whereto the said Thomas, or any of them shall be committed, shall not permit any resort of companies of more than two at one time to any of the said persons. And our experience of their high, obstinate and presumptuous carriage, doth engage us to prohibit them any further meeting together, on the Lord's day or other days, upon pretence of their church estate, or for the administration or exercise of any pretended ecclesiastical functions or dispensation of the seals or preaching; wherein, if they shall be taken offending, they shall be imprisoned until the tenth of July next, and then left at their liberty within ten days to depart the jurisdiction upon penalty as aforesaid. And whereas Thomas Gould is committed to prison in the county of Middlesex, by the last court of assistants, for non-payment of a fine imposed, this court judgeth it meet, after the sentence of this court is published, this day *after the lecture to them,* that the said Gould shall be discharged from imprisonment in Middlesex as to his fine, that so he may have time to prepare to submit to the judgment of this court."

It is truly difficult to preserve one's patience while reviewing these tyrannical proceedings. We would gladly draw a veil over the faults of the fathers of Massachusetts; but what is history, but a relation of facts, whether pleasant or painful? The injuries sustained by Thomas Gould and his associates excited the compassion of many, who did not think with them, both in Europe and America. While they were suffering in prison because they would not go into exile, a petition was presented to the court in their favour, signed by sixty-six persons, among whom are said to have been Capt. Hutchinson, Capt. Oliver, and others of note in the country. But the court was under the influence of the clergy; "and so far were they," says Backus, "from listening to the petition, that the chief promoters of it were fined, and the others were compelled to make an acknowledgment for reflecting on their honours." About this time, the following letter was sent from England, which exhibits a very correct view of the iniquity of these measures.

"MY DEAR BROTHER,

"The ardent affection and great honours that I have for New-England transport me, and I hope your churches shall ever be to me as the gates of heaven. I have ever been warmed with the apprehension of the grace of God towards me in carrying me thither. I have always thought that of the congregational churches of New-England in our days. But now it is otherwise, with joy as to ourselves, and grief as to you, be it spoken. Now the greater my love is to New-England, the more am I grieved at their failings. It is frequently

Mr. Mascall's Letter.

said here, that they are swerved aside towards Presbytery ; if so, the Lord restore them all. But another sad thing, that much affects us is, to hear that you, even in New-England, persecute your brethren ; men sound in the faith ; of holy life ; agreeing in worship and discipline with you ; only differing in the point of baptism. Dear brother, we here do love and honour them, hold familiarity with them, and take sweet counsel together ; they lie in the bosom of Christ, and therefore they ought to be laid in our bosoms. In a word, we freely admit them into churches ; few of our churches, but many of our members are Anabaptists ; I mean baptized again. This is love in England ; this is moderation ; this is a right New-Testament spirit. But do you now (as is above said) bear with, yea, more than bear with the Presbyterians ? yea, and that the worst sort of them, viz. those who are the corruptest, rigidest, whose principles tend to corrupt the churches ; turning the world into the church, and the church into the world ; and which doth no less than bring a people under mere slavery ? It is an iron yoke, which neither we nor our congregational brethren in Scotland were ever able to bear. I have heard them utter these words in the pulpit, that it is no wrong to make the independents sell all they have, and depart the land : and many more things I might mention of that kind ; but this I hint only, to shew what cause there is to withstand that wicked tyranny which was once set up in poor miserable Scotland, which I verily believe was a great wrong and injury to the reformation. The generality of them here, even to this day, will not freely consent to our enjoyment of our liberty ; though through mercy, the best and most reformed of them do otherwise. How much more, therefore, would it concern dear New-England, to turn the edge against those, who, if not prevented, will certainly corrupt and enslave, not only their own, but also their churches ? Whereas Anabaptists are neither spirited nor principled to injure nor hurt your government nor your liberties ; but rather these be a means to preserve your churches from apostasy, and provoke them to their primitive purity, as they were in the first planting, in admission of members to receive none into your churches but visible saints, and in restoring the entire jurisdiction of every congregation complete and undisturbed. We are hearty and full for our Presbyterian brethren enjoying equal liberty with ourselves. Oh, that they had the same spirit towards us ! But, oh, how it grieves and affects us, that New-England should persecute ! Will you not give what you take? Is liberty of conscience your due? and is it not as due unto others that are sound in the faith ? Read the preface to the declaration of the faith and order, owned and practised in the Congregational churches in England. Amongst many other scriptures, that in the 14th of Romans much confirms me in liberty of conscience thus stated ; *to him that esteems any thing unclean, to him it is unclean.* Therefore, though we approve of the baptism of the immediate children of church members, and of their admission into the church when they evidence a real work of grace ; yet to those that in conscience believe the said baptism to be unclean, to him it is unclean. Both that and mere ruling elders, though we approve of them, yet our grounds are mere interpretations of, and not any express scripture. I cannot say so clearly of any thing else in our religion, neither as to faith or practice. Now must we force our interpretation upon others pope-like! In verse 5th of that chapter, the Spirit of God saith, *let every one be fully persuaded in his own mind;* therefore this being the express will of God, who shall make a contrary law, and say, persuaded or not persuaded, you shall do as we say, and as we do! And verse 23d, *what is not of faith is sin;* therefore there must be a word for what we do, and we must see and believe it, or else we sin if we do not. And Deut. xii. and last, as we must not add, nor may we diminish. What is commanded we must do. Also 28th of Matthew. And what principles is persecution grounded upon? Domination and infallibility. This we teach is the truth. But are we infallible, and have we the government? God made none, no not the apostles, who could not err, to be lords over faith; therefore, what monstrous pride is this! At this rate, any persuasion getting uppermost may command, and persecute them that obey them not; all non-conformists must be ill-used. Oh wicked and monstrous principle! Whate'er you can plead for yourselves against those that persecute you, those whom ye persecute may plead for themselves against you. Whatever they can say against the poor men, your enemies say against you. And what! is that horrid principle crept into precious New-England, who have felt what persecution is, and have always pleaded for liberty of conscience! Have not those run equal hazards with you for the enjoyment of their liberties; and how do you cast a reproach upon us, that are congregational in England, and furnish our adversaries with weapons against us? We blush and are filled with shame and confusion of face, when we hear of these things. Dear brother, we pray that God would open your eyes and persuade the hearts of your magistrates, that they may no more *smite their fellow-servants*, nor thus greatly injure us their brethren; and that they may not thus injure the name of God, and cause his people to be reproached, nor the holy way of God (the congregational way) to be evil spoken of. My dear brother, pardon my plainness and freedom, for the zeal of God's house constrains me. What cause have we to bless God who gives us to find favour in the eyes of his Majesty? and to pray God to continue him, and to requite it graciously to him in spiritual blessings. Well, strive I beseech you with God by prayers, and use all lawful ways and means even to your greatest hazard, that those poor men may be set free. For be assured, that this liberty of conscience, as we state it, is the cause of God; and hereby you may be a means to divert the judgments of God from falling upon dear New-England, for our Father in faithfulness will afflict us if we repent not. Doth not the very gospel say, *what measure we mete to others, shall be measured to us?* God is not unrighteous. What is more provoking to him than the persecuting of his saints! *Touch not mine anointed, and do my prophets no harm;* did he not *reprove kings for their sake?* Those who have the unction the apostle John speaks of, and the spirit and gift of prophecies. With what marvellous strength did holy Mr. Burroughs urge that place against persecution? Persecution is bad in wicked men, but it is most abominable in good men, who have suffered and pleaded for liberty of conscience themselves. Discoun-

Account of the First Church in Boston. 397

tenance men that certainly err, but persecute them not. I mean gross errors. Well, we are travelling to our place of rest. With joy we look for new heavens and new earth. We shall ere long be in the fulness of bliss, holy, harmless in the bosom of Christ. Let us pray the earth may be filled with the knowledge of the Lord, that they may not hurt nor destroy in all his holy mountain. The Lord grant we may by the next hear better things of the government of New-England. My most hearty love to your brother and to all the brethren. My respects and service to my dear cousin Leveret and to Mr. Francis Willoughby. The Lord make them instrumental for his glory, in helping to reform things among you. I shall be glad to hear from you. I remember our good old sweet communion together. My dear brother, once again pardon me, for I am affected! I speak for God, to whose grace I commit you all in New-England, humbly craving your prayers for us here, and remain,

" Your affectionate brother,

" ROBERT MASCALL.

" *Finsbury, near Morefield,* }
the 25th of March, 1669." }

Another letter of a similar import was about this time addressed to the Governor, signed by twelve dissenting ministers in London, among whom were the learned Dr. Goodwin, Dr. Owen, Mr. Nye, and Mr. Caryl.

But all remonstrances were without effect, and Mr. Backus concludes from the best information he could gain, that these *turbulent Anabaptists* were imprisoned more than a year after the sentence of banishment was pronounced against them. After Mr. Gould was released, he went to live on Noddle's Island in Boston harbour, where the church assembled for some years. At what time it was removed to Boston, is not certain; but it was not till after the year 1672.

The next members, who were added to it after its constitution, were Isaac Hull, John Farnum, Jacob Barney, John Russell, jun. John Johnson, George Farlow, Benjamin Sweetser, and Ellis Callender, all before 1669. After them were added Joshua Turner, Thomas Foster, John Russell, sen. William Hamlit, James Loudon, Thomas Skinner, John Williams, Philip Squire, Mary Gould, Susanna Jackson, Mary Greenleaf, &c.

Mr. Gould died in 1675. I can learn nothing more of his history than what has been related in the preceding sketches. It is much to be regretted that a more particular account of him has not been preserved; his name ought to be recorded on the tallest page of the history of the New-England Baptists; and when the reader considers that the church, which he founded, included the whole of the Baptist interest in the colony of Massachusetts, for about seventy years, he will not think it improper to give this lengthy and particular account of its origin.

Mr. Gould was succeeded in the pastoral office by Isaac Hull. How long he continued among them, their records do not show.

John Russell was his successor, and it seems probable that both of these ministers preached in the church at the same time. They were companions in sufferings, having both been fined and imprisoned for non-conformity. Of Mr. Hull, we have scarce any account. Of Mr. Russell, the following sketches have been preserved. He was ordained in 1679, but died the next year. Previous to his death he wrote a narrative of the sufferings of this little flock, which was sent over to London, and printed in 1680, with a preface to it by Messrs. William Kiffin, Daniel Dyke, William Collins, Hansard Knollys, John Harris, and Nehemiah Cox. These eminent Baptist ministers made some very severe but judicious reflections on the unaccountable conduct of the New-England fathers. It seems strange, said they, that christians in New-England should pursue the very same persecuting measures, which they fled from Old-England to avoid! This argument they knew not how to withstand, and their reasonings against it were altogether frivolous and contemptible. *Protestants*, said they, *ought not to persecute Protestants, yet that Protestants may punish Protestants cannot be denied!* Because Mr. Russell was by occupation a shoe-maker, many low, abusive reflections were made upon him, even after he was dead. One of the Boston divines published an answer to his narrative, with a Latin title, the English of which was, *Cobler keep to your Last.* Dr. Mather published a piece in which he accused the Baptists of the sin of Jeroboam, in making priests of the lowest order of the people, &c. Mr. Willard said, " Truly if Goodman Russell was a fit man for a minister, we have but fooled ourselves in building colleges and in instructing children in learning." Hubbard, who was generally more candid and fair than the rest, in speaking of the narrative, &c. observed, " One John

Russell, a wedder drop'd shoe-maker, stitched up a pamphlet, wherein he endeavours to clear the innocency of those commonly (though falsely he says) called Anabaptists." In this scurrilous manner was this honest and worthy minister treated by his impotent adversaries. But had he and his associates met with nothing more than the revilings of priests, their case would have been less deplorable, but to these were added forfeitures, stripes, and prisons.

Those three eminent ministers of Swansea, Job, Russell, and John Mason, were great-grand-children of this worthy but much despised man. From him also descended the Russells of Providence, Rhode-Island; and Jonathan Russell, Esq. late Charge de Affairs in France and England, is one of his descendants.

In 1678, this church built them a house for worship, out of which, however, they were soon shut, and a long difficulty ensued upon the matter. They had been often reproached for meeting in *private houses*, "but since," said they, "we have for our convenience, obtained a *public house*, on purpose for that use, we are become more offensive than before." Their leaders were convented before the General Court, who not finding any old law to suit their purpose, made a new one, which forbid their assembling, and they furthermore enacted that their house, and all houses for worship, which were built without legal permission, together with the premises, appurtenances, &c. should be forfeited to the use of the county, and be disposed by the county-treasurer, by sale or demolishing, as the court that gave judgment in the case should order.

This affair went the whole round of courts and legislatures. The patient little flock submitted quietly to the orders of the sanctimonious court, and "waited to see what God would do for them."

Not long after this, the king of England wrote to the Massachusetts rulers, "requiring that *liberty of conscience* should be allowed to all protestants, so as that they might not be discountenanced from sharing in the government, much less that no good subjects of his, for not agreeing in the Congregational way, should by law be subjected to *fines* and *forfeitures*, or other incapacities for the same, which, said his majesty, is a severity the more to be wondered at, whereas liberty of conscience was made a principal motive for your transportation into those parts." But this remonstrance from the throne was disregarded by the priest-led magistrates.

Deplorable indeed, says Mr. Backus, was the case of these brethren; but having information of the king's letter in their favour, they again presumed to meet in their house, which they had done but a few times before they were again called before the canting, vexatious court to answer for their high offence of worshipping God contrary to law. But being emboldened by the royal mandate in their favour, they began to take a bolder stand against the unrighteous encroachments of their adversaries.

But the next thing we hear of, the doors were nailed up by the Marshall, and a paper put on them, which said,

" All persons are to take notice, that by order of the court, the doors of this house are shut up, and that they are inhibited to hold any meeting, or to open the doors thereof without license from authority, till the General Court take further order, as they will answer the contrary at their peril. Dated at Boston, 8th March, 1680.

" EDWARD RAWSON, *Secretary*."

The church thought fit to regard this paper blockade, and accordingly the next Lord's day assembled in their yard; and in the ensuing week erected a shed for their covering. But when they came together the second Lord's day, they found their doors opened, and since then they have been left to the care of the sexton, and not constables and sheriffs. But the leaders of the church were convented before the Assembly, the May following, where they plead, 1st, *That the house was their own.* 2d, *That it was built when there was no law to forbid it, therefore, they were not transgressors.* 3d, *That it was the express will and pleasure of the king, that they should enjoy their liberty.* After some reviling speeches were cast upon them, they were publicly admonished by the Governor, pardoned for their past offences, but prohibited from meeting in their house for the future without permission from the authority. But it does not appear that this prohibition was regarded either by the church or the rulers.

These scenes transpired during the lives of Elders Hull and Russell. They were the principal leaders of the church through all this perplexing affair, and for that reason we have thought proper to relate it in connexion with their history.

Mr. Hull survived Mr. Russell nine years, and how much longer the records of the church do not show; but being aged and feeble, and often incapable of ministerial work, they sent over to England, and obtained for their next pastor John Emblen, who arrived here in 1684, and continued in office until 1699, when he died. Nothing farther can be learnt of his character, than that he was well esteemed.

After Mr. Emblen's death, this church wrote again to England for another minister, but could not obtain one. They next applied to Mr. Screven, of Charleston, South-Carolina, who had been one of their number; but he informed them that he could by no means be spared. "But if," said he, "the Lord do not please to supply you, in the way you expected, your way will be to improve the gifts you have in the church. Brother Ellis Callender and Joseph Russell, I know have gifts that may tend to edification, &c." Pursuant to this advice, the church called Mr. Callender to the ministry shortly after, and in 1708, he was ordained their pastor, which office he sustained to the edification of his flock a number of years. He had been a member of the church thirty-nine years before he was ordained, and "continued in high esteem among them, till 1726," when he must have been not far from eighty years of age.

His son, Elisha Callender, became his successor, and continued in the pastoral office, until his death, which happened in 1738. He appears to have been the first learned pastor of this flock, and was distinguished for a pious and successful ministry. He was educated at Cambridge, and was ordained in 1718, by the assistance of three Pedobaptist ministers, viz. Dr. Increase Mather, Dr. Cotton Mather, and Mr. John Webb. This was a singular event in those days, and probably no great good came out of it in the end. Both parties must have strained a point in order to unite on such an important occasion. The sermon was preached by the younger Dr. Mather, which was entitled, *Good Men United*. In it are some very respectful addresses to the Baptist church, and a number of very severe reflections on their persecutors. *Happy*, says Backus, *is he that condemneth not himself in that thing which he alloweth.*

This temporary expression of catholicism promised more than was afterwards realized. The report of it in England, induced Thomas Hollis, Esq. a wealthy merchant of the Baptist persuasion, to become one of the most liberal benefactors to Cambridge College, that it ever enjoyed. *

Mr. Callender was succeeded by Jeremiah Condy, who was ordained in 1739. He was educated at Cambridge College, where he graduated in 1726. He went over to England not long after, and tarried there until he was called by this church to become its pastor. His doctrinal sentiments were less orthodox than those of his predecessors ; and four years after his settlement a number of his members withdrew and founded the Second Church in this town, as will be more particularly related when we come to their history. The church did not flourish under his ministry, but was in a declining state, when the care of it devolved on the renowned

Samuel Stillman, D. D. This eminent minister, who afterwards shone as a star of the first magnitude among the American Baptists, became the pastor of this church

---

* His benefactions to this Institution were astonishingly great : for besides making large additions to its library, he founded two professorships, one of Theology and one of Mathematicks and Experimental Philosophy, with a salary of eighty pounds each. In addition to these, he endowed the College with funds to the amount of a hundred pounds a year, to be distributed among ten scholars of good character, four of them should be Baptists, if any such were there. He also provided ten pounds a year to the College Treasurer for his trouble, and ten pounds a year to supply accidental losses, or to increase the number of students. Thus it appears, that this worthy and munificent Baptist must have bestowed upon this Pedobaptist University, funds to the amount of almost five thousand pounds. A philosophical apparatus which cost £150 sterling was sent over in 1726.

These endowments have doubtless been of much use to the college ; but the advantages which Mr. Hollis expected the Baptists to derive from his unexampled generosity, have never been realized.

What a pity that this generous Baptist had not appropriated these princely endowments exclusively to his own brethren ; as they would have founded an institution from which they could have derived peculiar benefit !

Mr. Hollis held to open communion, and the account of Dr. Mather the then President at Cambridge, together with two other Pedobaptist ministers uniting with a Baptist church in ordaining a pastor, doubtless opened to his imagination a pleasing prospect of an extensive union between the two denominations, and moved upon his benevolent feelings to afford the College the astonishing patronage already mentioned.

in 1765, just a hundred years from its beginning. Mr. Condy from that period retired to a private station, and died in 1768, aged 59 years. Dr. Stillman's ministry was long and prosperous, and whatever peculiar events transpired, during its continuance, will be related in his biography.

He was succeeded by Joseph, more commonly called Judge Clay. This eminent man, as he said to a friend a little before his death, had in the ministry *a rapid and peculiar course*. He was born in Savannah, Georgia, August 16, 1764. He graduated at Princeton College, New-Jersey, in 1784, and after preparatory studies commenced the practice of law, in which profession he continued until 1795. The year following he was appointed Judge of the District of Georgia, and continued on the bench until 1801. Although he had been instructed in the Holy Scriptures from a child, and had manifested an habitual reverence for the christian religion, it was not until the year 1803, that he made a publick profession, and joined the Baptist church at Savannah, under the pastoral care of the Rev. Mr. Holcombe. This church called him to the ministry, and in 1804, he was ordained in their fellowship as an assistant pastor with Mr. Holcombe. In September, 1806, Mr. Clay made a visit to the New-England States, and preached in most of the principal towns to very general satisfaction. And as this church had, for a considerable time, been contemplating an *assistant pastor*, (on account of the advanced age, and increasing infirmities of Dr. Stillman, and by his particular desire) they unanimously agreed to invite him to come and take upon him that office, and in the event of the Doctor's death, to become their sole pastor. To this invitation he signified his acceptance the December following, so far as to consent to come and spend one year with them, and then be at liberty to act as duty might appear. While the church was anxiously waiting the period of his arrival, Dr. Stillman was suddenly removed from his pastoral office by death. On the 16th of June following, Mr. Clay arrived in Boston with his family, to the great joy of that afflicted people. The favourable impressions under which he commenced his publick labours, seemed to presage his future usefulness and prosperity. Mr. Clay continued his ministrations with this people, until the beginning of November, 1808 ; when agreeably to his previous engagement, he left them, and sailed for Savannah, expecting to return to them again in the spring. But soon after, finding his health declining, he wrote to the church, proposing to them to look out for another pastor, and soon after requested a dismission from his pastoral care. On the 27th of October, 1809, the church addressed an affectionate letter to him, in which they signified their compliance with his request. As part of the family were resident in Boston, Mrs. Clay came with the remainder on a visit in November of that year, having left him much as usual, excepting a depression of spirits occasioned by her coming away. But finding his complaints increasing, and urged by a desire to be with his family, he soon after embarked for Boston, and arrived there, December, 1810. Although in a very feeble, debilitated state, no serious apprehensions were at first entertained respecting his recovery. But it was soon perceived that his complaints became daily more and more alarming, notwithstanding the continued efforts of the best medical aid. Exhausted nature at length gave up the conflict, and on the 11th of January, 1811, he gently fell asleep in Jesus, being in the 47th year of his age. Mr. Clay was above the middling stature ; his form elegant, his countenance comely, and his manners, though somewhat reserved, were easy and graceful. As a christian, his deportment was modest, grave, and humble. Though accustomed to move in the higher circles of life, yet, as a christian minister, he cheerfully condescended to men of low estate. As a public speaker he held a respectable rank. His voice was pleasant and harmonious, his gestures natural, and his language generally classical and pure. His system of doctrine was highly Calvinistical, and it is believed he never shunned to declare what he thought to be the *whole counsel of God.* The divinity of Christ, his obedience and death, together with the work of the Holy Spirit in renewing the heart and in comforting the saints, were sentiments, which he enforced with much interest and ability.

    Judge Clay lived but about seven years after he entered the ministry, most of which time he spent in itinerating in different parts of the United States. The novelty of such a distinguished statesman becoming a Baptist minister, collected large assemblies wherever he preached, and many learned characters flocked to hear their professional brother. Some of his discourses were of the most masterly kind, and displayed, in a very attracting manner, the splendid resources of his devout and highly cultivated mind. At other times that nervous affection and depression of spirits, of which he was frequently the unhappy subject, in a measure unfitted him for the labours of the pulpit; " but his most desultory performances were pious and affectionate, and in many instances truly eloquent. His preaching was blessed to the awakening and comforting of numbers in different places. He left behind him a large circle of sincere friends to mourn his early removal."

This honourable preacher possessed an estate in Georgia, which placed him above the need of any reward for his ministerial services, and he had conceived the benevolent design of planting his family in an eligible situation in one of the middle States, and bestowing his labours on destitute churches, which were not well able to support preachers among them. For this employment he was well fitted. But the solicitations of Dr. Stillman and his respectable church, induced him to alter his plan, and settle among them. But in this situation, as has been stated, Providence saw fit that he should not long continue. By the decease of this eminent minister, in the meridian of life, all the flattering expectations of the christian publick were cut off. He left behind him an amiable widow, and a number of children. His oldest daughter had, a little before his death, married into the family of the Hon. William Gray, lately Lieutenant-Governor of Massachusetts.

For about four years past this church has been destitute of a pastor. It has had many candidates, but no one as yet has appeared to meet their united views.

The lot in the possession of this church, is of the following dimensions: On Back-Street, $37\frac{1}{2}$ feet; on Stillman-Street, about 250 feet; 114 feet of this distance it continues the same width as on Back-Street. This space forms a handsome court in front of the meeting-house. 40 feet further it is about 70 feet wide, and the remainder of it is 80. This spacious lot has been enlarged at different times to its present convenient size.

The original house built in 1678 was small; but I do not find by any records or tradition that any alteration was made in it until 1771; then it was removed, and a new one built, 53 feet by 57. This house was enlarged in 1791, to its present dimensions, which are 77 feet by 57. It is built of wood, has a porch in front, and a small vestry in the rear. Besides this vestry, there is one almost adjoining the house on the north side, 46 feet by 19, built in 1799.

Second Church in Boston. This Church proceeded from the First in 1743. As it arose after the storm of persecution was over, and has never experienced any vicissitudes except what are common in the progress of such churches, its history will be short compared with the one we have just related.

While Mr. Condy was pastor of the first church, a number of its members became dissatisfied with his doctrinal sentiments, which appear to have been different from those on which that body was founded, or which it has maintained since his time. These brethren sent in a protest to the church, in which they stated many articles of grievance; but the substance of all was, that their pastor was what they called an Arminian; and that if matters remained as they were, they should be under the painful necessity of proceeding to a separation. This was in September, 1742, and as they obtained no satisfaction, in July of the next year, seven brethren, viz. James Bound, John Proctor, Ephraim Bosworth, John Dabney, Thomas Boucher, Ephraim Bound, and Thomas Lewis, formed themselves into a new church, and elected Ephraim Bound their pastor. James Bound and Mr. Dabney were from England; Boucher was from Wales; Proctor was of Boston; Bosworth was of Hull near to Boston, and having no children, he gave the church a good estate, the remains of which they still enjoy. Of the other brethren we have no particular account. Not long after this church began its progress, one Philip Freeman came over from London and united with them. He sent over an account of their principles and conduct to Dr. Gill, which met the approbation of that illustrious divine, and induced him to make them a generous donation of the following articles, viz. one large cup, four smaller ones, two dishes, two plates and a large damask cloth for the communion table; 7 sets of baptismal garments, viz. one for the minister, three for men, and three more for women, and books to the amount of about fifty dollars.* At the same time they received a further gift of forty-eight volumes of the sermons of the then late Rev. Mr. Hill, an Independent minister of London, successor to Dr. Ridgley. The sermons were sent by the author's father, to be given away at the direction of the church.

Mr. Bound's ordination was a matter of some difficulty, as no ministers could be found near to assist on the occasion. The church applied to the aged Mr. Wightman, of Groton, Connecticut, but he was too old and infirm to undertake such a journey. Finally, Mr. Bound went to Warwick, Rhode-Island, where he met the venerable Elder from Groton, and was ordained by him, Dr. Green of Leicester, and an Elder Whipple. "Mr. Bound was a plain, unlettered man, but an able minister of the New-Testament: Like Apollos he was mighty in the Scriptures, and the want of human learning was abundantly made up by that gracious unction, with which God was pleased to favour him. Numbers came from considerable distance to hear the word, and additions were made to the church, not only of the inhabitants of Boston, but also from Hull, Newton, Needham, Medfield, Chelmsford, Lynn, and other places."† Under his ministry the church increased from seven to a hundred and twenty, and many were awakened by his means who joined to Pedobaptist churches. But in the midst of prosperity and usefulness, in the 20th year of his ministry, he was seized by a paralytic shock, from the effects of which he never fully recovered. He died 1765, much lamented by his flock and friends, but with a comfortable assurance of a blessed immortality. During his feeble state, the church obtained occasional assistance from others, particularly from the late Dr. Stillman,

---

* These communion vessels have been given away to churches in the country, but the church has supplied their place with an elegant new set consisting of twelve cups, two large flaggons and four plates, which together are reputed to be worth 600 dollars.

† Dr. Baldwin's Sermon at the opening of the New Meeting-House, in 1811, p. 25, 26.

who, at their invitation, removed from Bordentown, New-Jersey, and served them as an assistant to Mr. Bound, for the space of one year.

The second pastor of this church was Mr. John Davis, a native of the State of Delaware, and a son of David Davis, one of the pastors of the Welsh Track church, in that State. He was educated in the University of Pennsylvania, and commenced his labours here in the spring of 1770. His ministry in Boston was short, but highly respectable. He, in company with Mr. Backus, took an active part against the oppressive measures of the ruling party, and in 1771, he was chosen by the Warren Association, as their agent, to use his influence both in Massachusetts and in London, to obtain the establishment of equal religious liberty in the land. In the prosecution of this agency, the nature of which will be explained in Mr. Backus' biography, he met with the cordial approbation of his friends, but with much abusive treatment from the opposite party. Every thing in Mr. Davis presaged a course of distinguished usefulness. His learning, abilities, and zeal, were adequate to any services to which his brethren might call him. Mr. Backus had now begun his history, and had the promise of assistance from this literary companion; but a mysterious Providence saw fit to cut him down almost in the beginning of his course. In about two years after his settlement in Boston, he went into a decline. By the advice of his friends he returned to his native state, hoping that a softer atmosphere might remove his complaints. And having in some measure recovered his health, with a view of confirming it, he set out on a journey into the western country, in company with Dr. David Jones, of Pennsylvania, and near the Ohio River, December 13th, 1773, after an illness of three weeks, finished his earthly course, in the 36th year of his age. His last words, according to Mr. Jones' account, were, " In a little time I expect to be with Christ, to see and know him as he is known, and as he is not known. My faith in my Saviour is unshaken." Mr. Davis was a member of the Philosophical Society of Philadelphia; and was also one of the Fellows of the Baptist College at Providence.

The third pastor of this church was Isaac Skillman, D. D. a native of New-Jersey, and a graduate of Princeton College. Mr. Skillman was sent out into the ministry by the first church in New-York, and having been ordained there, it was mutually agreed that he should discharge the pastoral duties here, without a formal installation.* He commenced his labours in 1773, and continued them until 1787, a period of fourteen years. At his own request, he was then dismissed, and returned to New-Jersey. He afterwards took the charge of the Salem church in that State, where he closed his life and ministry together a few years since. Dr. Skillman was a man of learning and abilities, but never very popular as a preacher.

The fourth in office here, was Thomas Gair, a native of the town, and a graduate of Providence College. Mr. Gair was awakened under the ministry of Dr. Stillman, when about sixteen years of age, and soon after joined the church of which he was pastor. Not long after he had finished his education, in which he was assisted by his friends, he was settled in Medfield, where he continued about ten years. Peculiar circumstances then making it necessary for him to leave that people, he, upon the removal of Dr. Skillman, began to labour here, and in a few months after was publicly installed in the pastoral office. "To undissembled piety and respectable talents, Mr. Gair added a dignified deportment, and a gentleness of manners, which rendered him highly acceptable to all classes of people." But while rising into eminence and usefulness, he was suddenly arrested with a nervous, putrid fever, of which he died, April 27th, 1790, in the 36th year of his age.

Thomas Baldwin, D.D. the present pastor of this body, was the immediate successor of Mr. Gair, and was in-

* This installation will need some explanation to our brethren abroad, as we read nothing of it in the New-Testament, nor in the history of the Baptists in other countries. It is nothing more nor less than going over the same ceremonies with an ordained minister, when he takes the pastoral care of a church, as were practised when he was first set apart for the ministry. If a minister has not been a subject for the ordaining ceremony, he is ordained into office; if he has, he is installed into it Both is the same thing in form, although called by different names. This sacred installing is practised uniformly by the New-England Pedobaptists, and from them the Baptists seem to have borrowed it. It was, however, never practised but by a comparatively few churches; among some of them it is going into disuse, and by all it is hoped it will soon be laid aside. If those, who practise installation, are not *Re*-baptizers, they are constantly *Re*-ordainers.

vested with the pastoral office, November, 1790. He was born at Norwich in Connecticut, the birth place of Mr. Backus, December 23, 1753. He was ordained in Canaan, New-Hampshire, in 1783, and laboured in that town, and adjoining ones, until he removed to his present situation. He has been the pastor of this flock over twenty years, which has increased under his successful ministry, from ninety to upwards of four hundred, besides suffering large diminutions in different ways. By Dr. Baldwin have been baptized 478 persons who have united with this church. About the time he commenced his pastoral labours, a revival began, in which not far from seventy were added to this church, and about the same number to the old one.

In 1803, another revival commenced, which became more extensive in its prevalence ; it continued for more than two years, in which time about two hundred were added to this church, and nearly the same number to the First.

The lot in the possession of this church was, in its original form, the gift of Mr. Bosworth : additions have been made to it at different times, so that it is now of the following size. On Back-Street (not far from the old church) 90 feet, and continues the same width 270 feet to within 12 feet at one corner and upwards of 30 at the other of Margin-Street, which was lately made by filling up a Mill Pond. This lot would be one of the handsomest in town were it not for the incumbrance of one of considerable size near its middle, on which are a cluster of old unsightly buildings, which they hope soon to purchase and move off. Adjoining Back-Street is the parsonage-house which is reputed in common times worth about 200 dollars a year. This house was built with the avails of Mr. Bosworth's estate. The meeting-house stands back almost 200 feet, and has an alley leading to it 12 feet wide.

The first house of worship erected by this church was small, and was finished in 1746. This was enlarged during the ministry of Mr. Gair, in 1789. Another addition was made to it in 1797, which made it 69 feet by 53 ; but this large building was generally well filled, and often crowded to an uncomfortable degree. The Congregation continuing to increase, and the house, which was built of wood, needing considerable repairs, it was, in 1810, removed to make room for their present spacious edifice, of brick, covered with slate, and is eighty feet by seventy-five, exclusive of the tower, which is thirty eight feet by eighteen. This house, exclusive of some costly appendages, was built at the expense of more than 22,000 dollars.

Third Church in Boston.—This body was formed in 1807, of 24 members, 19 of whom were from the Second Church, and 5 from the First. Nothing very special has occurred during its progress. The motives which led to its formation were, that the great revival in this town in 1803, and onward, increased the two churches so much, that many were unable to get seats in their houses, and they conceived, that the state of religion in the town rendered it peculiarly desirable, that another place should be erected, where the name of Jesus, and the discriminating truths of of the gospel might be proclaimed.

In 1806, a house for worship was begun, which was opened August 5th, 1807, the same day the church was formed. This house is situated on Charles-Street, in the west part of the town; it is built of brick, 75 feet square, exclusive of the tower. It is an elegant edifice, adorned with a cupola and bell, and cost 27,000 dollars. The lot is but a little larger than the house, most of which was given by the Mount Vernon Company.

The same year this church was formed, Mr. Caleb Blood, of Shaftsbury, Vermont, became its pastor, which office he sustained about three years, when he removed to his present situation at Portland, Maine.

Successor to him was Mr. Daniel Sharp, who was born at Huddersfield, in Yorkshire, England, in 1783; his father is pastor of the Baptist church at Forsley, near Leeds, in the same county. Mr. Sharp came to America in 1805, and was sent into the ministry by the Fayette-Street Church, New-York, the year following. After studying about two years with Dr. Staughton, of Philadelphia, he became pastor of the church in Newark, New-Jersey, where he continued until the autumn of 1811, when he came on to Boston; and the ensuing spring was invested with the pastoral care of this body.

African Church.—This community of sable brethren arose in 1805; their number at first was twenty, most of whom were the fruits of the ministry of Mr. Thomas Paul, a man of their own colour, who is their present pastor. The year after this church was formed, they began to make exertions towards building them a place of worship. They chose a committee to make collections; among whom was Cato Gardiner, a native of Africa, who had long been one of Dr. Stillman's respectable members. Cato was all alive in the business; by his importunity Dr. Stillman drew a subscription paper, which he circulated in different places, and obtained about fifteen hundred dollars. Cato, notwithstanding his age, had faith to believe that his brethren would have a house for their use, and that he should live to see it finished, which he did, and soon after died. Others of the church made collections to a considerable amount, and having received encouragement to go forward in their design, they chose a committee of white men to superintend their building, which was finished in 1806. This committee consisted of Messrs. Daniel Wild, John Wait, William Bentley, Mitchell Lincoln, Ward Jackson, and Edward Stevens. Some of these gentlemen made large advances towards the house, which with the lot they hold in trust for the church, until the debts are discharged, then they are to give a deed of it to the body for whom it was built. This house is built of brick 40 feet by 48, three stories high. The lower story is fitted up for a school room, for coloured children, and has been occupied for that purpose from the time it was finished. The instructer is Prince Saunders, a man of colour of education; his school generally consists of about 40 scholars. The two upper stories are well finished with pews, pulpit, galleries, &c. the lot is small, and that with the house cost 8,000 dollars. Debts of considerable amount have been upon this establishment till lately, but by Mr. Paul's collections they are now nearly all discharged.

Mr. Paul, the pastor of this flock, was born in Exeter, New-Hampshire, in 1773; he was sent into the ministry by the church in Limerick, Maine, at the age of 28; he has preached successfully in various places both before and after he was settled in Boston.

Notwithstanding our brethren in Boston were so severely persecuted at first yet the storm was soon over, and they lived in the undisturbed enjoyment of their rights, while their brethren, in different parts of the country, were fleeced, imprisoned, and distressed in various ways. The reason for this difference was, that in this town all monies for religious purposes are collected by a tax on the pews, and not on the estates of the worshippers. This custom has prevailed from early times, and Mr. Backus assures us, that no one of the Baptist persuasion has been obliged to pay any money to the Congregationalists since about 1690.

From the First Church in Boston have originated, 1st, The church at Kittery, in the District of Maine, in 1682, as has been related in the account of that District. 2d, The Second Church in this town. 3d, Most of the church in Charlestown, which was formed in 1801. Other churches around have probably received a part of their members from this, but I have not received sufficient information on this point to make any authentic statements.

Charlestown Church was embodied in 1801 of twenty members, most of whom were dismissed from the church then under the care of Dr. Stillman. The same day the church was organized, a very commodious house which had just been finished was opened for publick worship. Dr. Stillman preached on the occasion from, *Behold, how good and pleasant it is, for brethren to dwell together in unity.* At the close of his discourse, he made the following interesting address to the new formed church:

" DEARLY BELOVED IN OUR LORD JESUS CHRIST,

" In the year 1665, the First Baptist Church in Boston, from which most of you have been dismissed, originated in this town. To-day she sends you back at your own desire, in conjunction with our friends from the Second Baptist Church in Boston, to form a church where she began. But how great the difference between that period and this! Then the right of private judgment was denied; now all is candour, love and friendship. This event is surely providential: to human agency alone it cannot be ascribed.

" The churches you have left have dismissed you with all that christian affection, which has arisen from a long and pleasing acquaintance with you, and from your constant endeavour to behave as becomes the gospel: believing, at the same time, that this event will terminate in the better accommodation of yourselves and families, and the advancement of the interests of religion and morality. Go and prosper, and the Lord be with you."

The first pastor here was Mr. Thomas Waterman from England, now at Woburn, who tarried with them but a short time. In 1804 they obtained for their pastor Mr. William Collier, who still continues with them. Mr. Collier was born at Scituate a little below Boston in 1771; was educated at Brown University; sent into the ministry by the Second Church in Boston, and was for about four years pastor of the First Church in New-York. The church under consideration moved on in harmony from the commencement of Mr. Collier's ministry until 1809, when a series of difficulties began respecting church order, &c. which issued in the division of the church and the founding a new one, of which we shall give some account when we come to speak of the churches which hold to Weekly Communion.*

At the time of this division a question arose respecting the meeting house. This had been built by an association of gentlemen of the Baptist persuasion previous to the founding of the church. It is fifty feet by seventy-five, with a tower, cupola, bell, &c. and cost upwards of 11.000 dollars. It was expected the pews would pay the expense of it. The fee of it was in Mr. Oliver Holden, who gave the lot, was treasurer to the association, by whom it was built, and had made large advances towards its erection. No deed had been conveyed either to the original undertakers or the church, and matters were left in a loose way, until the division took place. The church, desirous of retaining the house for their use, inquired of Mr. Holden the lowest terms on which he would give them a deed—

* The reason assigned by the seceding party for their separation, was, that the church retained in her bosom a number of members who held doctrinal errors of different kinds. The leaders of the church acknowledge that they were then infested with errors, but they also contend that they had previously commenced a course of discipline, which after some interruptions was carried through, and those erroneous members who could not be reclaimed were excluded, so that they are now united in the faith and fellowship of the gospel.

which were not such as they saw fit to comply with. They next proposed to relinquish all their right in the house, provided he would exonerate them from all debts upon it, which proposal he accepted, it being then expected that a minister would come on from the southward to occupy it. The church was thus rendered destitute of a house for worship. By Mr. Holden's permission they occupied his, until, by their own exertions, and the assistance of others, they erected the one which they now occupy, which is a commodious brick building, one story high, 70 feet by $47\frac{1}{2}$. The fee of it is in the church, where it ever ought to be. Mr. Holden and his associates meet in a school house, and thus, by their going out, one after another, the great house is left alone.

Respecting the branches of the Second Church in Boston, we have already observed, that during the ministry of Mr. Bound additions were made to it from Hull, Newton, Needham, Medfield, Chelmsford, Lynn, &c. In most of these places churches afterwards arose, and these members doubtless laid the foundations for them. In Chelmsford a church was formed in 1771, and Elisha Rich, who afterwards went to Vermont, was its first pastor. After him was Samuel Fletcher and Abishai Crossman, who were only sojourners, and soon went to other places. In 1792, John Peckens was settled among them, and yet remains in the pastoral office. The church in Medfield was formed in 1776, and Thomas Gair was its pastor ten years. After him they were a long time destitute, but have lately settled among them, much to their satisfaction, a young man by the name of William Gammell, from the First Church in Boston. The church in Newton, only nine miles from Boston, was formed in 1780, partly of members from the Second Church, and partly from the remains of two *Separate* churches, one of Newton and the other of Brookline. Mr. Caleb Blood, now of Portland, Maine, became its pastor the year after it was formed, and continued in that office about seven years, when he went to Shaftsbury, in Vermont. In 1788, Joseph Grafton was settled among them, and still continues their worthy and much respected pastor. Mr. Grafton was born in Newport, Rhode-Island, June 9, 1757. Under his ministry in this place a number of precious revivals have been experienced, and the church has been built up to a large and respectable body.

In Cambridge, adjoining Boston, there was a Baptist church as early as 1751; but it seems never to have flourished much, and after experiencing a number of painful vicissitudes, it was broken up, and the members scattered in different ways. In 1781, a new church arose of members in Cambridge, and the adjoining towns of Woburn and Lexington. The seat of the church has since been transferred to Woburn, and it is now supplied by the labours of Mr. Thomas Waterman, from England.

HAVERHILL.—This town is on the Merrimack River, thirty miles north of Boston. The Baptist church here was founded in troublesome times, under the ministry of its late renowned pastor, Hezekiah Smith, D. D.

In the New-Light Stir in Whitefield's time, a small society of Separates was formed in Haverhill, which, however, did not continue long; but the savour of this New-Light spirit probably remained after the society was broken up. Sometime after this, one of the parish ministers of the town became obnoxious to his people; controversies and councils ensued, and in the end he was shut out of his meeting-house, and dismissed from his office, and the parish remained destitute of a preacher, until Mr. Smith, who was then travelling as an itinerant through New-England, paid them a visit, and preached among them so much to their acceptance, that they invited him to tarry and supply them awhile. This was in the summer of 1764. He had calculated on returning to New-Jersey the ensuing autumn; but finding his labours blessed, he consented to remain and labour for the present in this vacant parish. He had been treated with respect by the Pedobaptist ministers around, and some of them had invited him to preach in their pulpits; but as soon as he was stationed in one of their folds, which their quarrels had made vacant, they dismissed their civilities, and exerted all their influence against him. They doubtless feared the prevalence of Baptist principles in this Pedobaptist flock, and that not without just grounds; for in May, 1765, a Baptist Church was founded in the centre of the town, Mr. Smith became its pastor, and continued in the successful and dignified discharge of that office forty years. A number of the first members of this church and congregation were, for a while, harassed with sheriffs and *parish rates;* but their oppressors, finding them not easy of management, were induced soon to let them alone.

As no very remarkable occurrences appear to have transpired in the progress of this church, we shall confine our attention principally to the history of its founder and late distinguished pastor.

Mr. Smith was born on Long-Island, in the State of New-York, April 21, 1737. He was a happy instance of early piety, as appears by his making a publick profession of religion before he was nineteen years of age. He was educated at Princeton College, New-Jersey, that distinguished seminary of illustrious men, where he graduated in 1762. He was a companion of Dr. Manning from early years, and during the President's life, though stationed seventy miles apart, they were generally called together on all important occasions, which regarded the Baptist interest. They were both taught the rudiments of science at Mr. Eaton's Academy at Hopewell, and they were also class-mates in College. Mr. Smith, soon after he began to preach, took a journey to the southward, in which he was gone over a year; he went as far as Georgia, preached much in South-Carolina, was ordained, and laboured a while at a place then called Cashaway, now Mount Pleasant, on the Pedee River, in that State, and in different places made collections of considerable amount for the College, which his friend Manning was about establishing in Rhode-Island. His beginning at Haverhill has already been mentioned. At first he was treated here with much abuse by a set of outrageous zealots, who equalled the rude Virginians in their mode of defending their established worship. The most scandalous reports were circulated against his character; and in addition to these, he was personally insulted, and his life endangered. A beetle was cast at him one evening as he was walking the street, which he took up and carried to his lodging. After he was in bed, a stone was thrown through his window, and struck near his head, of sufficient size to have proved fatal had it hit him. His horse was disfigured in the same way that many other Baptist ministers' horses have been, and a paper put on the door of the house where he lodged, which threatened him with worse treatment if he did not depart. He was once assaulted at a private house in Bradford, where he had appointed to preach, by a sheriff and his gang. As he got up to speak, the chair on which he leaned was snatched away, and much tumult ensued; but the rioters shortly withdrew, and he proceeded in his discourse. Some of them, however, laid wait for him on his return home; but he, without knowing their cruel design, providentially tarried till the coldness of the air forced them from their stand. These were some of the opposing measures which at first attended this intruder upon parish lines. But such was his undaunted courage, his patient forbearance, and powerful eloquence, that his impotent adversaries were soon put to shame, and he arose to pre-eminent esteem among all around him. He made frequent excursions in the neighbouring towns, and a number of churches arose mostly by his means. He also often journied in his active days considerable distances around in New-Hampshire, Maine, and other places, and a large circle of his most cordial friends, and many of the seals of his ministry, are to be found in almost every part of the surrounding country. As he advanced in years, his labours were mostly confined to his own congregation. During most of the revolutionary war he served as a chaplain in the American army, where his dignified and exemplary deportment gained him the confidence and esteem of both officers and soldiers. Like Mr. Gano, often did he expose his own life to danger in the field of battle, while animating the soldiers and soothing the sorrows of the wounded and dying.

The preceding sketches of the life of Dr. Smith have been selected mostly from Backus' History, and from a brief memoir in the Baptist Magazine. The following description, &c. was drawn by Dr. Baldwin, to whom we are also indebted for what has been selected from the Magazine.

"As a preacher Dr. Smith was equalled by few. His subjects were well chosen, and always evangelical. His voice was strong and commanding, and his manner solemn and impressive. He was often led to pour the balm of consolation into the wounded conscience, but the general tenor of his preaching was calculated to arouse the careless and secure.

" In stature, Dr. Smith was considerably above the middling size, being about six feet in height, and well proportioned. His countenance, though open and pleasant, was peculiarly solemn and majestic. In his deportment, he was mild, dignified and grave, equally distant from priestly hauteur, and superstitious reserve. He never thought religion incompatible with real politeness; hence the gentleman, the scholar and the christian were happily blended in his character. And such was the urbanity of his manners, that many who differed from him in his religious opinions, honoured and respected him as a gentleman and companion. While the wicked were awed by his presence, it was impossible for a good man to be in his company, without being pleased and edified. In a word, he lived beloved and respected, and died greatly lamented."

Dr. Smith was one of the fellows of Brown University, and was, through life, a zealous promoter of that institution. Dr. Messer, who now presides over it, was brought up under his ministry.

Successor to Dr. Smith is Mr. William Batchelder, who was born in Boston, 1769; commenced his ministry in Deerfield, New-Hampshire, but removed hither from Berwick, in the District of Maine. Under his ministry the church has had large additions, and now contains about three hundred members.

As we proceed eastward from Boston, we find the churches of Malden, Reading, Salem, Marblehead, Beverly, Danvers, Ipswich, Newburyport, &c. of only a part of which some brief sketches can be given.

SALEM.—This town lies about thirteen miles eastward of Boston. In it Roger Williams began his *Anabaptistical career* about 1635 ; but very few of his sentiments have been found here from the time of his banishment until within a few years past. The Salem church is yet in its infancy, but it has arisen to a distinguished rank among her sister communities, and originated in the following manner: In the winter of 1803—4, a Baptist meeting was set up in a small private house by eight or ten professors of the denomination who belonged to a number of the neighbouring churches. They conducted the meeting mostly in a social manner, but procured preachers to come among them as often as convenient. Perceiving a disposition in many to attend their worship, they often lamented that their meeting place was not more commodious. The matter lay so heavily upon their minds, that they soon held a special prayer meeting, to make known their wants unto God. And their fervent supplications were answered in a most remarkable manner; in two weeks from this time, the following gentlemen, viz. Capt. Edward Russel, and Michael Webb, Esq. came forward and offered to erect for them a place of worship. This proposition was as grateful as it was unexpected. By these gentlemen a one story wooden building, fifty-five feet by thirty-six, was set forward, and was so far finished, that by the last of April, 1804, the first sermon was preached in it by Mr. Lucius Bolles, who was at that time studying with Dr. Stillman of Boston, and labouring with him as an assistant. Spiritual as well as temporal blessings were poured upon this little band, and the number of baptized believers increased so much, that on the 9th of January, 1805, they were embodied into a church, and the same day Mr. Bolles was ordained their pastor. Since that time they have enjoyed many refreshing seasons, and have advanced rapidly to a large and flourishing community. Their congregation increased so fast, that the house, with which Providence had so remarkably furnished them, soon became too small for their convenience. They therefore soon began a more spacious one, which was opened for worship, January, 1806. This is a very neat, commodious brick building, seventy-two feet by sixty-two. It is built on a lot of 100 feet by 250,* and cost 16,000 dollars. Their former house is converted into a vestry. This latter spacious building is well filled with worshippers, and the church has increased to upwards of 300. One hundred and thirty were added to them in about eight months, in the year 1809.

This infant church and congregation have often excited the astonishment and gratitude of surrounding older communities, by their spirited exertions and surprising acts of

* This lot extends to the tide water, which furnishes a delightful place for baptizing, immediately back of the meeting house. The lot is 250 feet to high water mark, probably 500 or 600 to low water.

munificence in promoting the cause of Zion. They, from their beginning, began to display a liberality worthy of imitation, and in one year, very lately, they contributed for charitable and missionary purposes about twelve hundred dollars.

Mr. Bolles was born in Ashford, Connecticut, in 1779. He was educated at Brown University, and was, for about three years previous to his settlement here, a pupil and assistant to Dr. Stillman.

Most of the members of the Marblehead church were dismissed from Salem. This body is only four miles distant; its pastor, Mr. Ferdinand Ellis, is a graduate of Brown University; was formerly a tutor in that institution, and a minister of the Pedobaptist persuasion.

BEVERLY.—This town is connected to Salem by a bridge fifteen hundred feet in length. The church in it is of recent origin, and was formed in 1801, of nineteen members. Joshua Young was its pastor about two years. After him was Elisha Williams, under whose ministry they have enjoyed two very considerable revivals. In the first about sixty were added to their number; in the second between forty and fifty. Upwards of a hundred and sixty were added to the church while under his care. But notwithstanding these successes of this worthy pastor, some members raised a difficulty against him, and he has been dismissed from office, but still resides in the town.

Mr. Williams is a son of the late Dr. Williams, a Pedobaptist minister of East-Hartford, Connecticut; he was educated at Yale College, New-Haven, began to preach at Livermore, in the District of Maine, was for some years pastor of the church in Brunswick, in that District; and removed from that place to Beverly, in 1803.

DANVERS.—This town also joins to Salem. The church here was formed in 1793; Morgan Edwards would call it a grand-daughter of Haverhill, as it came out of the church at Rowley, which was a branch of that body. Danvers is distinguished for giving birth to James Foster, D. D. who died pastor of the first church in New-York. Mr. Jeremiah Chaplin, who now officiates here, is a native of the place, and was for a short time pastor of the same church in New-York.

NEWBURYPORT.—In 1805, a church was formed in this town, (which lies upwards of thirty miles northeast of Boston) of only nineteen members. Mr. Joshua Chase, one of their number, was called to the ministry, and preached among them a short time, when he removed to the District of Maine. Not long after his removal, the church obtained for its pastor, Mr. John Peak, who had preached in divers places in New-England, but who removed hither from Barnstable on Cape Cod. Soon after his settlement, this little body, mostly by the assistance of others, erected a large brick building, 70 feet by 60, which cost upwards of sixteen thousand dollars. Thus they were put in possession of a costly commodious building, which, however, they occupied under some peculiar embarrassments. The pewholders were to govern the house and elect their teacher; and at a certain time, the Baptists came within one vote of being turned out of it, and having it applied to another denomination. But all their prospects and embarrassments, all the benevolent designs of their friends abroad, and of spectators at home, were suddenly closed by a destructive fire in 1811, in which this stately edifice was consumed. As it was detached from other buildings, it was, at the commencement of the fire, made a place of deposit for furniture, goods, &c. But the flames spread so rapidly, and soon became so vehement, that it was enveloped by them, and every combustible part of it was reduced to ashes. After this, Mr. Peak travelled as far as Philadelphia and Baltimore, and in various places collected sufficient sums to erect for them a neat, commodious, brick house, which, if not so splendid as their former one, is held by a more substantial and consistent tenure, and occupied without the fear of molestation.

BOSTON ASSOCIATION.

THIS Association was formed in 1812 by a division of the Warren. That body had become so numerous and extensive, that but few churches could conveniently provide for the large assemblies which convened on its interesting anniversaries. A division was therefore thought necessary, and was amicably agreed upon in 1811. The line was to run from Boston westward as far as the Association extended; those churches, which were near this line on either side, were considered at their option to fall in with either the new or old Association, as best suited their convenience. The general table will exhibit a view of the churches in each body.

As this Association has been formed so lately, its movements do not furnish articles for an historical narrative; but it ought to be observed, that a considerable number of its churches and ministers have long been among the main pillars and active promoters of the respectable body from which it proceeded.

We shall now turn our attention to the southern part of this First Division, in which it will be perceived most of the churches south of Boston are included.

First Church in Swansea.—This is the oldest church in Massachusetts, and was the fourth which was formed in America. It is dated in 1663; but it was begun about 13 years before by Obadiah Holmes and others. The account of Mr Holmes' persecution at Boston has already been related; some further information of his character will be given, when we come to Newport, in Rhode-Island. He was for some years after he came to this country in the Pedobaptist connexion, first at Salem, and then at Rehoboth, where one Samuel Newman was pastor. This Newman undertook a domineering course of discipline, different from what had been taught in the old Puritan school, and Holmes and some others withdrew from his church, and set up a meeting by themselves, about 1649. Soon after this they fell in with Baptist principles, and were baptized, it is supposed, by Mr. Clark of Newport, as they joined his church. Mr. Holmes became the leader of this little company, against whom Mr. Newman pronounced the sentence of excommunication, and stirred up the civil power to take them in hand. They were in the Plymouth colony, and before the court in that town Mr. Holmes and two of his associates were cited to appear, where they found four petitions had been lodged against them. One from Rehoboth signed by thirty-five persons; one from the church at Taunton, the adjoining town eastward; one from all the clergymen but two in the Plymouth colony; and a fourth from the meddling court at Boston, under their Secretary's hand, urging the Plymouth rulers speedily to suppress this growing schism. But the rulers of this colony appear to have been more mild and tolerant than those of Massachusetts, and probably did no more than they found absolutely necessary to keep the teasing clergy in humour. With all these stimulations to severity, they only charged them to desist from their practice, which was offensive to others, and Obadiah Holmes and Joseph Tory were bound the one for the other, in the sum of ten pounds, for their appearance at court. No imprisonment was inflicted, and no other bonds or sureties were required. One of the company it seems promised to comply with their requisition, and was dismissed. This was in June, 1650. At the next October court, the Grand Jury found a bill against them, and by their presentment we learn that the company consisted of John Hazel, Edward Smith and wife, Obadiah Holmes, Joseph Tory and wife, the wife of James Mann, and William Buell and wife. They were charged with the crime of continuing a meeting from house to house on the Lord's day, contrary to the order of court, &c. but no sentence appears on record against them. Not long after this Mr. Holmes removed to Newport, and became pastor of the old church there, and a part of his company removed with him. But before his removal, that scene of suffering at Boston, which has already been related, was experienced.

In 1663, John Miles came over from Wales and began the church, which has continued to the present time. He had founded a Baptist church in Swansea, in his native country, in 1649, and was one of about two thousand ministers who were ejected from their places by the cruel Act of Uniformity in 1662. He brought to this country the records of the Swansea church in Wales, which, being in the Welsh language, can be of no use to the present generation; but large extracts were made from them by Mr. Backus, and sent over to Mr. Tommas of Leominster, England, the historian of the Welsh Baptists.

Some of Mr. Miles' company in Wales came over with him, and at the house of John Butterworth in Rehoboth, they, to the number of seven, united in a solemn covenant together. Their names were John Miles, elder, James Brown, Nicholas Tanner, Joseph Carpenter, John Butterworth, Eldad Kingsley, and Benjamin Alby.

First Church in Swansea.

This measure became offensive to the orthodox churches of the colony ; the court was solicited to interpose its influence ; and the members of this little church were fined five pounds each, for setting up a publick meeting without the knowledge and approbation of the court, to the disturbance of the peace of the place ; ordered to desist from their meeting for the space of a month, and advised to remove their meeting to some other place, where they might not prejudice any other church, &c. Rehoboth, at this time, included nearly all the present county of Bristol. In what part of this large township this church was formed, I do not find ; but not long after, its seat was removed to near Kelly's bridge, at the upper end of Warren, on a neck of land, which is now in the township of Barrington, where their first meeting-house was built. Afterwards its seat was removed to the place where its present meeting-house stands, which is only three miles from Warren, and about ten from Providence. In 1667, the Plymouth court, instead of passing the sentence of banishment against this little company of Baptists, as the men of Boston had done against Thomas Gould and his associates, made them an ample grant of Wannamoiset, which they called Swansea. It then included the extensive territory, which has since been divided into the towns of Swansea, Warren, and Barrington. Barrington and Warren, now in Rhode-Island, were then claimed by the Plymouth colony, and afterwards by the Massachusetts government until 1741. What is now the town of Swansea became the residence of the Baptists ; a second church arose in it in 1693, and no church of the Pedobaptists has ever been established here to perplex and fleece them. Some of their members, who resided in other towns around, were at times harassed with ministerial taxes ; but their sufferings of this kind were trifling, compared with what their brethren in other places endured. Besides the constituent members of this church, there were families by the name of Luther, Cole, Bowen, Wheaton, Martin, Barnes, Thurber, Bosworth, Mason, Child, &c. among the early planters of Swansea, whose posterity are still numerous in the surrounding country.

Mr. Miles continued pastor of this church until his death, which happened in 1683. What few sketches have been preserved of his life go to show that he bore an excellent character, and was eminently useful in his day. He lived near a bridge, which still bears his name, but a small distance from the present meeting-house. He laboured frequently with his brethren in Boston, in the time of their sufferings, and at one time there was a proposition for his becoming their pastor, which was not, however, carried into effect. We are told that being once brought before the magistrates for preaching, he requested a Bible, and opened to these words in Job, *But ye should say, Why persecute we him? seeing the root of the matter is found in me;* which, having read, he sat down; and such an effect had the sword of the Spirit, that he was afterwards treated with moderation, if not with kindness. All I can learn of his posterity is, that a son went back to England, and a grandson of his was an Episcopal minister in Boston, (Mass.) in 1724.

Next to Mr. Miles was Samuel Luther, who was ordained here in 1685, by the assistance of Elders Hull and Emblen of Boston. He was much esteemed, both at home and abroad, until his death in 1717. His posterity are numerous in these parts, and many of them are of this and the neighbouring churches.

After him was Ephraim Wheaton, who had been his colleague thirteen years. He lived in the bounds of Rehoboth, and faithfully discharged the pastoral duties of this church until he died in 1734, aged 75. His posterity are numerous in these parts, in Providence and other places. His ministry in Swansea was attended with good success; in five years from 1718, he baptized and received into his church fifty members. That was, in those days, a remarkable circumstance, of which he wrote an account to Mr. Hollis of London, who sent him a letter of gratulation on his ministerial success, with a present of books.

Samuel Maxwell was ordained a colleague pastor with Mr. Wheaton in 1733; but five years after he became a Sabbatarian, and was dismissed from his office. He was esteemed a pious man, and lived to a good old age, but does not appear to have had much success in the ministry.

After him was Benjamin Herrington from the Narraganset country. He had a crowded audience for a few years; but being accused of the sin of uncleanness, which charge he never cleared up, he went off to Canterbury, in Connec-

Second Church in Swansea. 427

ticut, where he preached to a few people, and lived in obscurity to old age.

In 1751, Jabez Wood of Middleborough became the pastor of this church, in which office he continued without much success about thirty years, when he was dismissed and removed to Vermont, where he died in 1794. He was a grandson of Thomas Nelson, who then belonged to this church, whose history will be related when we come to Middleborough.

Next to Mr. Wood was Charles Thompson, one of the first graduates of the Institution, which has since taken the name of Brown University. As the necessary materials for the history of this valuable man are not now at hand, we shall defer his biography till we come to Warren, Rhode-Island, where he began his pastoral labours.

After he removed from Swansea, the church was, for some years, under the care of Mr. Samuel Northup, a native of North-Kingston, Rhode-Island, who died lately in the care of a church in Rehoboth.

The present pastor of this body is the aged and respectable Mr. Abner Lewis, who has preached in different places, but removed hither from Harwich in Cape Cod.

Second Church in Swansea.—This church was begun by some members from Providence and other places, who settled to the eastward of the old church, and set up a meeting by themselves, which their gifted brethren carried on until the church was formed, and Thomas Barnes, one of their number, was ordained their pastor in 1693. This office he filled with respect till his death, which happened in 1706. One of the leaders of this church was Samuel Mason, who was a soldier in Cromwell's army, but came over to America on the Restoration of Charles II. He settled in Rehoboth, where, and in the adjoining towns, and also in remoter places, his posterity is very numerous. His sons were Noah, Samson, James, John, Samuel, Joseph, Isaac, Peletiah, and Benjamin. James and John went to Boston, but the remaining six lived in Rehoboth and Swansea, until the youngest of them was seventy years of age. Isaac was ordained a Deacon in the church at the same time that Mr. Barnes became its pastor, and continued in the faithful discharge of that office until his death in 1742.

Joseph, another of the brothers, was ordained a pastor of this body in 1709, and six years after John Pierce was ordained his colleague. These two elders ministered to this church, as long as they were capable of ministerial service, and both of them lived to about the age of ninety. Mr. Pierce was the grand-father of Mr. Joseph Cornell, late pastor of the second church in Providence. He began preaching among a few Baptists in Scituate, where President Dunster spent his last days; but being persecuted for worshipping God in his own house, he with others of the company removed to Swansea about 1711.

Next to these venerable elders were in succession three by the name of Mason, grand-children on the father's side of the famous Samson Mason, and on the mother's, of John Russell once pastor of the old church in Boston. Job was ordained in 1738, Russell in 1752, and John in 1788. The last of them died but a short time since. They were all highly esteemed for their piety and usefulness. Next to them was Elder Benjamin Mason; but whether he was a brother of his predecessors I have not learnt. The church is now under the care of Mr. Philip Slade; it abounds with members; but in point of doctrine and discipline, it has probably seen better days. From this church have proceeded a considerable number of ministers, who have removed to other parts, among whom are Nathan Mason, who went to Nova-Scotia, as is related in the history of that Province; Joseph Cornell, whose name has just been mentioned; Nathaniel Cole, now of Plainfield, Connecticut; and a number of others, whose names and stations cannot be accurately ascertained.

This church was founded on what some of the Rhode-Island brethren call the *Six Principle* plan, as stated in Hebrews vi. 1, 2, and made the laying-on-of-hands on every baptized member a term of communion; they also opposed the practice of singing in public worship, which was not introduced until after the year 1780, almost a hundred years from their beginning. The laying-on-of-hands they still strenuously hold, and belong to the Rhode-Island Yearly Meeting. They have a commodious place of worship a few miles from the old church.

REHOBOTH.—This township, before its late division,* was not far from twelve miles square. For a number of miles on its western side, it joins the State of Rhode-Island, and is separated from Providence only by the Pawtucket River.

It is probable there have been Baptists in this town from about 1650, when Obadiah Holmes separated from the parish worship, but no church was gathered in it until 1732, when one arose near its southeast corner under the ministry of Mr. John Comer, of whom more will be said when we come to Newport. By the year 1794, no less than seven Baptist churches had been formed in Rehoboth, most of them were small, and hardly any two of them were united in their views of doctrine and discipline. Elhanan Winchester, who afterwards distinguished himself by the propagation of the doctrine of Universal Restoration, was, for a few years, pastor of one of them. The youngest of these churches is that at the lower end of the great Seekhonk plain, within about three miles of Providence, which is supplied by Mr. John Pitman of that town.

Rehoboth has been a fruitful nursery of Baptists for many years, and from it multitudes have emigrated to almost every part of New-England.

MIDDLEBOROUGH.—The first church in this town was formed in 1756; some account of its origin and progress may be found in the biography of Mr. Backus, who was, for about fifty years, its worthy pastor. After his death Mr. Ezra Kendall had the care of it a few years, and next to him was Mr. Samuel Abbot, a native of New-Hampshire, who is its present pastor.

Second Church in Middleborough.—This church arose in the following manner : Thomas Nelson, formerly a member of the first church in Swansea, removed in 1717 to the south part of Middleborough, to a place called Assawamset, his being the first English family which settled there. He set up a meeting at his house, and procured preachers to visit him as often as he could. One of whom

---

* A short time since, this township was divided into two, and the new one was called Seekhonk, after the name of a very large singular plain, which is within three or four miles of Providence, and on which, it appears by ancient records, Obadiah Holmes and his little company of Baptists, set up their meeting in 1649. This was but about four miles from the village of Pawtucket, a part of which was formerly in Rehoboth, but is now in Seekhonk.

Sufferings of the Church at Kingston.

was the late Ebenezer Hinds, who began to preach there statedly in 1758. By these means a little company of baptized believers was collected. The remains of a Pedobaptist church of the Separate order, at a place called the Beech Woods, embraced the Baptist principles after the death of their pastor, Mr. James Mead, and in 1757, the church under consideration was formed, and Mr. Hinds soon after became its pastor. Thomas Nelson, who must be considered the father of this church, died at the age of eighty, a short time before it was founded. His widow lived to the age of a hundred and five years and seven months, and died in 1780. She had living of her posterity at her death, as near as could be ascertained, three hundred, thirty and seven. Of her grandsons, William, Samuel, and Ebenezer Nelson, became Baptist ministers. Two of them are yet living ; one in this town, and the other at Reading near Boston. Among her great-grand-children are Stephen S. Nelson, of Mount Pleasant, New-York, and Dr. Thomas Nelson, of Bristol, Rhode-Island.

Mr. Hinds continued in office here not far from forty years, when he removed from them, and died, a short time since, on Cape Cod, at the age of about ninety. He retained his mental and bodily powers to a very singular degree. But two or three years previous to his death, he could mount his horse with the greatest ease, and ride off journies of a number of weeks, to preach among his old acquaintances, or rather in places where his old acquaintances *had lived*. Beside these churches two others have been formed in this town, which is very large in its boundaries, and from it great numbers of Baptists have emigrated to the District of Maine and other places. The four churches in it are all of respectable standing, and contain together upwards of four hundred members. Middleborough is in Plymouth county, and but a few miles from the place where the fathers of the Plymouth Colony landed in 1620. Around it a number of churches have been established, most of whom have, at different times, been distressed for religious or rather irreligious taxes for the support of the established clergy.

Kingston Church, only 4 miles from Plymouth, has suffered most severely by these vexatious things, while their sister communities all around have enjoyed an exemption from their tormenting and ruinous effects. This church was formed in 1805, under the ministry of Ezra Kendall, who was then pastor of the old church in Middleborough. For about six years its members, together with those of the congregation, were annually harassed for the support of the parish preacher. A considerable number of them have had their property attached and sold at auction, to satisfy the outrageous and unrighteous demands of the Congregational party. As late as 1810, one of their number was dragged from his house, bound fast, carried and lodged in Plymouth gaol, because he refused to pay his money for the support of a minister, which he did not wish to hear. The most grievous and wanton havock was made of the property of the Kingston Baptists down to the year 1811, and from that period they have been spared, not for the want of a disposition in the Pedobaptist oppressors, but in consequence of a late law of the Massachusetts Legislature, which will be noticed at the close of this chapter. Such coercions have been practised in the nineteenth century in a State whose Constitution declares, that ☞ *No subject shall be hurt, molested, or restrained, in his person, liberty, or estate, for worshipping GOD, in the manner and season most agreeable to the dictates of his own conscience, &c.* Samuel Glover is the present pastor of this body. He was sent into the ministry by the first church in Boston, and was educated at Brown University.

In Harwich and Barnstable, on Cape Cod, are two large respectable churches of considerable age, both of which have, in former times, been distressed in consequence of imposts for religious purposes. Both of these churches arose out of Pedobaptist ones of the Separate order. The one at Harwich was formed in 1757; that at Barnstable in 1771; they have had different preachers to labour among them, some of whom are dead, and others are now settled in other places. The Harwich church is under the care of Mr. James Barnaby, a graduate of Brown University; the one at Barnstable has for its pastor Barnabas Bates, a native of England, who was educated a Roman Catholick; came to this country when fifteen years of age, and was sent into the ministry by the first church in Boston.

There are yet remaining in the region under consideration a considerable number of churches, of which our limits will not permit us to give any particular account. Most of them belong to the Warren Association, where their names, numbers, and pastors will be exhibited.

SECOND DIVISION.

THIS division comprehends a considerable part of this State, and extends from a line drawn north and south, between twenty and thirty miles west of Boston to its western side. It is bounded south by Rhode-Island and Connecticut, west by New-York, and north by Vermont and New-Hampshire. In it are about sixty churches, which belong to the Boston, Warren, Sturbridge, Leyden, Westfield, Danbury and Shaftsbury Associations. Of these seven Associations, three only, viz. Sturbridge, Leyden, and Westfield, are considered as having their seat in the region now under consideration; and of these we shall, in the first place, give some brief account.

STURBRIDGE ASSOCIATION.

THIS body was formed at the place from which it took its name in 1802, of churches which had belonged to the Warren Association. Nothing remarkable has occurred in its progress. Of a few of its most ancient churches we shall relate a few particulars.

STURBRIDGE.—This church arose in the following manner: In 1747, a Separate church was formed in this town, and Mr. John Blunt was ordained its pastor. In about two years after, Baptist principles began to prevail amongst them, and Elder Moulton of Brimfield baptized 13 of their number, among whom was Daniel Fisk, one of their deacons. John Newell was their other deacon, and Henry Fisk and David Morse were their ruling elders. It was not long before these officers, with Mr. Blunt their pastor, and others to the number of upwards of sixty, were baptized, and in 1749 they began to travel in a Baptist church. For three years from that period, they were oppressed for parish taxes in a most grievous manner; five of them were imprisoned in Worcester gaol, and property of different kinds was taken from them to a large amount.*

* Mr. Moulton, for preaching here, was seized by the constable, dragged out of the town and thrust into prison, as a stroller and vagabond. In 1750 and 1751, the assessors took from Abraham Bloyce a spinning-wheel; from

Some of the principal brethren in Boston endeavoured in vain to allay the vengeance of their oppressors; but the crime of dissenting was not to be forgiven, and the havock which followed, may be seen in the note below. The storm of persecution was furious, but not of long continuance. The Baptists soon arose to respect, and were let alone by the established party; and deacon Fisk, who was so cruelly treated at first, became afterwards a representative of the town, and died a member of the House of Assembly, in 1778. This church has had a number of teachers, but for some time past it has been under the care of Zenas L. Leonard, who was educated at Brown University, and who has, for a number of years, been a member of the State Legislature.

Before the church at Sturbridge was formed, there had arisen three of our denomination in Sutton, Brimfield, and Leicester. The Sutton church was formed in 1735; the first promoters of it removed hither from Danvers, near Salem, in which town it was then included. One Peter Clarke, being minister of that place, preached so much upon infant baptism, that a number of his people adopted the opposite opinion, and because they did not relish the continual brow-beating of their minister, removed from the sound of his declamations, and began a settlement in this place. But no sooner were they settled here, than the Sutton minister began in Mr. Clarke's strain, and by this means a number of his people became convinced of Baptist sentiments; then the emigrants from Danvers and the converts in Sutton united in forming the church

deacon Fisk, five pewter plates and a cow; from John Pike, a cow; from Jonathan Perry, a saddle and steer; from Mr. Blunt, the pastor, a trammel, andirons, shovel, tongs, &c. and a heifer; from John Streeter, a kettle, pothooks, &c. from Benjamin Robbins, a warming-pan, quart pot, broad-axe, saw, and other tools; from Henry Fisk, ruling elder, five pewter plates and a cow; from John Perry, a cow; from David Morse, ruling elder, a cow, in 1750, for a tax of £. 1 1s. 4d, and in 1751, a yoke of oxen valued at not less than thirty-six dollars, for a tax of less than five dollars; from Phineas Coller, a kettle, two pewter plates, a tankard, and a young cow; from John Newel, deacon, all his pewter plates, a cow, and a flock of geese; John Draper's goods were distrained, but the kind is not mentioned. And besides this despoiling of goods, deacon Fisk, John Cory, Jeremiah Barstow, Josiah Perry, and John Draper, were imprisoned in Worcester gaol, twenty miles from their homes. This havock of property was made for the support of Rev. Caleb Rice, the minister of the town; and if that greedy divine received all these spoils of his neighbours, his house must have been well furnished, his nest well feathered, and his flocks and herds considerably increased.——*Edwards'* *MS. Materials for a History of the church in Sturbridge.*

at the time above mentioned, and two years after, Benjamin Marsh and Thomas Green were ordained its pastors. This church was long since dissolved. Mr. Marsh continued its pastor about forty years, and died in 1775, at the age of ninety. He was a native of Salem, and was esteemed a godly and exemplary man, but his gifts were not great. There are, at present, three churches in this town, one belonging to the Warren Association, one to the Groton Conference, and the other to the Association whose history we now have in view. This last church was formed in 1768, partly out of the remains of a Congregational, Separate one, which was gathered in 1751, which had been previously broken up and scattered. Its present pastor is Samuel Waters who is a native of the place.

In 1783, the old church in Sutton was divided by mutual agreement, and the one at Leicester was formed, of which Thomas Green became pastor. He was a native of Malden near Boston, but was an early settler in Leicester. He was not only a useful minister, but a skilful physician; and being often called abroad both to preach and practise in his medical profession, he disseminated his principles throughout a wide circle around, and his church became very extensive. After spending a life of eminent usefulness, he finished his course in 1773, aged 73. The late John Green, M. D. of Worcester, was a son of this eminent minister, whose son, Dr. Thomas Green, was many years pastor of the church in North-Yarmouth, Maine. His successor was Benjamin Foster, afterwards pastor of the first church in New-York. Next to him was Isaac Beals, who is now in Vermont. Since his removal they have had Nathan Dana and Peter Rogers, but now are destitute of a pastor.

The Brimfield church was gathered in 1736, and a few years after, Ebenezer Moulton was ordained its pastor, in which office he continued until 1768. He then went to Nova-Scotia, where he continued about fifteen years, and then came back and died among his old people in 1783. After him this church had two pastors from Middleborough; the first was James Mellen, who died in 1769; the second was Elijah Codding, who is still with them.

In the shire town of Worcester, the Baptists have never made much progress until within a short time past. But now they have a flourishing church there which was raised amidst much opposition in 1812. It belongs to the Warren Association, and is under the care of Mr. William Bentley, a native of Boston, who came out from the first church in that town.

A number of churches belonging to the Sturbridge Association are in the north-east corner of Connecticut; some account of them will be given, when we come to that State.

LEYDEN ASSOCIATION.

THIS body was formed in Leyden, in 1763, of thirteen churches, which are situated at no great distance from the Connecticut River, in the three States of Massachusetts, New-Hampshire, and Vermont. Leyden is about thirty miles above North-Hampton, and upwards of a hundred north-west of Boston. The church here was formed in 1780, and Joseph Green, from Norwich, Connecticut, became its pastor. Most of the settlers of the town and the constituents of this church came from Rhode-Island and the adjoining parts of Connecticut. As there was no church of the established order in the place, they were not troubled with ministerial taxes; but a considerable number of churches throughout this region, in the counties of Hampshire and Berkshire, were, for a time, unmercifully harassed with those scourges to dissenters.

The Ashfield church formerly belonged to the Warren Association, but for some reason it does not now associate with any connexion. It was formed in 1761, and Ebenezer Smith became its pastor. For a number of years this church and its adherents were persecuted with great severity by the predominant party. In 1770, about four hundred acres of their land were disposed of at publick sale by the furious parish tax-gatherers. For a demand of less than four dollars, Mr. Smith was dispossessed of ten acres of his home lot. From his father was taken twenty acres, containing his orchard and burying ground, which was struck off to one Wells for less than seven dollars. This coveting of fields, and taking them by force, goes beyond any thing we read of in England. There is an account of the pope taking land in a similar way from the Waldenses in France; but in Protestant countries no example of the kind appears. In these distressing circumstances the Baptists petitioned the Boston Assembly for relief; a number of fair promises were made, but no assistance was afforded them, until they, by the assistance of Governor Hutchinson, addressed the king and council, by whom the law, which sanctioned their oppressions, was disannulled, and their lands were ordered to be restored. The business was not finally settled until 1774, by which time the minister, who had been the occasion of all this oppression, became obnoxious to his own people, and went off with the avails of the estate which had been settled upon him.*

The church in Montague and Leverett was formed in 1765. They gave in certificates to the parish assessors according to law; but these certificates were no better than American protections; and they were, notwithstanding, taxed and distressed. In a short time Samuel Harvey had a cow and calf and yoke of oxen taken from him for the support of the parish minister; and for the same purpose a cow was taken from a Mr. Sawyer. Major Richard Montague was carried six miles towards the prison, and kept all night; in the morning the officer released him, and went back and took out of his pen a large valuable animal of that species into which the devil once entered, in the country of the Gergesenes. Major Montague was a principal leader in this church, and his son Elijah has for many years been its pastor.

In a similar way have many other churches in this vicinity been robbed of their property, for the support of a set of clergy, who were well contented to fatten on the spoils of their neighbours. There is, however, one honourable exception to this general remark. A Mr. Cook of Bernardston was settled with a salary of £75 a year; at the time of his settlement he gave a written instrument, which was registered in the town book, binding himself to deduct that part of his salary, which fell to the share of the Baptists, which was annually about sixteen pounds.

* Backus, vol. i. p. 248, 261.

WESTFIELD ASSOCIATION.

This is a small body, which was formed of only six churches in 1811. In the town from which it received its name, which is about a hundred miles west of Boston, a church was formed in 1784. Adam Hamilton, a native of England, was for a time its pastor, and was highly esteemed in the Baptist connexion wherever he preached; but on account of his misconduct he sometime since was rejected from their fellowship, and sunk into disrepute. The church is now destitute of a pastor.

WEST-SPRINGFIELD.—As early as 1727, some persons were baptized in this town by Mr. Elisha Callender, then pastor of the first church in Boston. Their names were John Leonard, Ebenezer Leonard, William Scott, Abel Leonard, and Thomas Lamb. These people set up a meeting, and, as often as they could, obtained Baptist ministers to come among them; and in 1740, they, with others who had joined them, were formed into a church, and Edward Upham became their pastor. He was born at Malden in 1709, and educated at Cambridge College, where he graduated in 1734. After ministering at Springfield about nine years, he removed to Newport and became the successor of John Callender, the author of the Century Sermon. Here he remained about twenty years, when he went back to his old flock at Springfield, and continued his labours among them till he was turned of eighty, when a violent disorder confined him to his bed. After remaining in this condition about five years, he died in 1795, at the good old age of eighty-seven. Mr. Upham was one of the earliest and most zealous friends of Rhode-Island College, of which he was an original Trustee and Fellow.

This church appears to have been once dissolved and formed anew, as it is now dated in 1789. Its present pastor is Jesse Wightman, a grandson of the founder of the Groton church in Connecticut. A second church has arisen in this town, whose pastor is Thomas Rand, who was educated at Brown University.

West-Springfield is on the west side of Connecticut River, twenty-eight miles above Hartford. Opposite is Springfield, in which a small church was formed in 1811

Chesterfield is the largest church in this association ; it was formed in 1780 of only ten members, which have now increased to about two hundred. This body, by giving annual certificates, has from its beginning escaped the rapacious hands of the sacred constables. Its first pastor was Ebenezer Vining ; its present is Asa Todd, an elder of good repute, who was born in North-Haven, Connecticut, in 1756.

The Hinsdale church in this body has been much distressed even within the present century for taxes towards building a meeting-house for the Congregational society.

On west of these churches, in the county of Berkshire, are eight belonging to the Shaftsbury Association. South of them are some connected with the Danbury Association in Connecticut. And interspersed among all of these are a considerable number of good repute, which for different reasons do not belong to any associate connexion. As correct a view of them as can be obtained will be exhibited in the General Table.

A few sketches of the churches in Cheshire must close the history of this State. This town has been a distinguished nursery of Baptists for many years. Great numbers have been baptized in it, who have removed to other places ; but there yet remain two churches, which, together, contain upwards of two hundred and fifty members.

In 1766, some men of Providence and Coventry in Rhode-Island, purchased a large tract of land, near the head of Hoosack River, which was afterwards settled by people from that State, from Swansea, and other places near ; the settlement was at first called New-Providence. Afterwards a part of it was incorporated with the town of Adams, and probably some of it fell into other towns. In 1793, the town of Cheshire was incorporated out of part of Adams, Lanesborough, and a number of surrounding towns. These frequent subdivisions of townships has led to some confusion in this part of our narrative, as there is no one at hand to give explanations on the matter ; but it is sufficient to observe that in this region have arisen a number of churches, which were begun by people mostly from Rhode-Island, Swansea, and Rehoboth ; the oldest of them are now called the first and second in Cheshire, and belong to the Shaftsbury Association. The first of these was, in its beginning, called Adams, and was begun by Peter Werden from Rhode-Island, of whom a farther account will be given in the biographical department. The second was planted by Nathan Mason of Swansea, who previously founded a church in Nova-Scotia, as has been stated in the history of that Province.

These two churches have passed through various changes, and have been favoured with refreshing seasons of a remarkable kind. The first is, by the emigrations of its members to other parts, reduced to a small number, and is under the care of a young man by the name of Bartemus Braman. The other is still large, and has for its minister Mr. John Leland, whose name is well known throughout the United States. Mr. Mason was born in Swansea, 1726, and was baptized in the 24th year of his age, by Job Mason, then pastor of the second church in that town. In 1763 he, with a company of his brethren, went to Nova-Scotia, where they tarried about eight years, when he came back and settled in this place, where he spent the remainder of his useful life. The company, which came back from Nova-Scotia, consisted of twelve; they found here six more of their Swansea brethren, and these eighteen were formed into a church in 1771, and united with the Rhode-Island Yearly Meeting. In ten years from that time they increased to about two hundred members, which were scattered in many of the surrounding towns, and laid the foundations for some of the neighbouring churches. Among the number added in this period was Mr. Joseph Cornell, late pastor of the second church in Providence, Rhode-Island. This church was founded on the *Six Principle Plan*, which lays peculiar stress upon the Laying-on-of-hands. But disputes upon this doctrine at length crept in among them, and finally arose so high, that in 1788 the church was divided. The greater part, among whom was Elder Mason, held that the Laying-on-of-hands ought not to be a bar of communion. Those, who held this doctrine, maintained a church a number of years, but it appears now to have become extinct.

Mr. Mason died a short time since in a good old age, and left behind a character fair and irreproachable. " He was," says Mr. Leland, " a man of peace and godliness, preaching seven days in a week by his life and conversation." Sometime previous to his death, Mr. Leland returned from Virginia, settled in Cheshire, and took a part with him in the ministry. Under his labours a revival commenced in 1799, which prevailed in such an astonishing manner, that from the first of September, 1799, to the first of April, 1800, two hundred and twenty were added to the church, which increased its number to three hundred and ninety six. Since that time some have been added, but great numbers have removed from them to the western country.

Mr. Leland was born in Grafton, Worcester county, Massachusetts, 1754; at the age of twenty he was baptized by Mr. Noah Alden, joined the church in Bellingham, and not long after began to preach. In 1776, he went into Virginia, where he remained about fourteen years. Some account of his labours in that state will be given when we come to its history. In 1791, he returned to New-England and settled in Cheshire, as has been related. Mr. Leland has made great and successful exertions for liberty of conscience, both in Virginia and New-England. For the vindication of this important subject he published his *Virginia Chronicle, Jack Nips, Blow at the Root, Stroke at the Branches, Yankee Spy, &c.* His speech in the Massachusetts Assembly will be given in the Appendix.

Cheshire is famous for its excellent cheese, and in 1801, a number of farmers united their efforts, and made one of the astonishing weight of *thirteen hundred pounds !** This was called the *Mammoth Cheese* ; it was designed as a present to Mr. Jefferson, then President of the United States, and Mr. Leland was commissioned to conduct it to Washington. In the journey he was gone four months, in which time he preached seventy-four times, and multitudes every where flocked to hear the *Mammoth priest.* Mr. Leland is remarkable for his singularities, and also for his success in the ministry. In 1810, he had baptized eleven hundred and sixty-three persons, about seven hundred of them in Virginia.

From this Cheshire church have proceeded, besides Mr. Cornell, Josiah Goddard, now of Conway, the compi-

---

* The Author saw one in this town a few years after, which weighed fifteen hundred pounds. It was, if I am rightly informed, sold for a large sum, to be put into a Museum.

ler of a Hymn Book, which is well esteemed; Aaron Seamans, now of North-Hampton, New-York, and a number of other ministers. It was with this church that the late worthy Lemuel Covel was settled as an assistant to Mr. Leland a little before his death.

We have thus given a general view of the progress of our brethren in Massachusetts, and from the foregoing sketches it appears that their sufferings and successes have both been great.

We shall now give a brief account of the laws, which have operated against them, and also those by which they have been exempted from time to time.

In the writings of Dr. Cotton Mather we find the following correct statement; " The reforming churches, flying from Rome, carried, some of them more and some of them less, all of them something of Rome with them, especially in that spirit of *imposition* and *persecution*, which too much cleaved to them all."* This remarkable concession explains the whole subsequent conduct of the Massachusetts rulers. They legislated by the advice and with the assistance of their ministers, who desired that their government might be considered a *theocracy*, and that the Lord would lead his people by the hand of Moses and Aaron. At first, none but church members were allowed to vote in the election of rulers, and as none could be admitted into their churches but by the ministers, they had, in effect, the keys of the state as well as the church in their hands.† Thus, in the beginning of their government, church and state were united by the strongest ties; the ministers assisted in legislation, and the magistrate, in return, lent his aid in ecclesiastical affairs.

The Massachusetts people seem to have been ambitious from the first of erecting a peculiar government for themselves, in which no dissenter should be permitted to remain. They compared their Colony to the land of Canaan, the Congregational party were the chosen people of God, and all, who differed from them in opinion and practice, were like the seven nations of the Canaanites, who were to be driven out of the land which the Lord their God had

* Backus, vol. i. p. 63. † Hannah Adams' Hist. of New-England, p. 34, 35.

given them.* At first their ministers were supported by the voluntary contributions of their flocks; but in 1638, a law was made, empowering the parish officers to distrain the due proportion from those who would not contribute in a voluntary way. This law was much opposed by some of their own party, and one Nathaniel Briscoe, of Watertown, wrote a book against it, for which he was fined ten pounds; and one John Stowers, for reading some of it before a company of his friends, was fined forty shillings.† But notwithstanding the murmurs of some, this law prevailed, and has been the source of unspeakable trouble and damage to the Baptists and other dissenters in this commonwealth. We are informed, in 1657, the people of Ipswich settled a minister, and voted to give him a hundred pounds to build him a house, and taxed all the inhabitants to pay it. "This being a new thing, several persons would not comply with the scheme," and one, who had his pewter seized for the tax, prosecuted the collector, and recovered his furniture with cost and damages. The reason rendered by the judge for this decision, was just such as every advocate for liberty would give.‡ In these squabbles none but Pedobaptists were concerned; but the opposing efforts of a few soon gave way to the prevalence of an iniquitous and tyrannical custom, and for more than a hundred and fifty years past, all the towns and parishes throughout this commonwealth, with the exception of Boston and a few other places, have raised all monies for supporting their ministers, building their meeting-houses, and for other religious purposes, by a general assessment upon all rateable poles of every description, and upon all taxable property, which happened to lie within the parish bounds. The taxing laws go upon the supposition that all are of the predominant party, and if any are exempted, it is not because it is their right, but in consequence of a special act of favour from the government. According to Mr. Backus, the first law of the Massachusetts Assembly to exempt any denomination from sacred taxes, was passed immediately after the great earth-

* According to Capt. Johnson the seven nations or sectaries were *Gortonists, Papists, Famalists, Seekers, Antinomians, Anabaptists,* and the *Prelacy.* Backus, vol iii. p, 238.

† Backus vol. i. p. 100.

‡ Backus, vol i. p. 310, 311.

Baptists, Quakers, and Episcopalians imprisoned. 443

quake in 1727.* This was in favour of the Episcopalians. The next year a law was passed to exempt Anabaptists and Quakers, *provided*, that they usually attended the meetings of their respective societies, and *lived within five miles* of the place of meeting ; otherwise their taxes must be paid. This law was to continue in force no longer than till May, 1733. And between the time of its passing and expiration, twenty-eight Baptists, two Quakers, and two Episcopalians, were imprisoned at Bristol by the constables of Rehoboth, for ministerial taxes. The pretext for this oppression was, that the law of 1727 was not to go into operation until the next year. But the Governor and Council decided the contrary.† As soon as this law expired, taxes were again imposed upon our brethren, and some were imprisoned ; but by applying to the Legislature they were again exempted until 1740. Fresh troubles breaking out at the expiration of that term of grace, they were again obliged to beg for mercy, and obtained a respite of seven years more. After that an exempting law was passed for ten years, which brings us down to 1757. Then another one was passed, which lasted thirteen years, that is, until 1770 ; but so was it framed, that no tongue nor pen, says Mr. Backus, can fully describe all the evils that were practised under it : Such was the precarious and ever failing tenure, by which the Baptists, Quakers, and others, held their liberty and preserved their horses, cows, swine, poultry, furniture, &c. from the destructive hands of ministerial collectors. The rulers in this government, instead of enacting a perpetual law for the exemption of dissenters in case they would give certificates as they did in Connecticut, chose rather to hold the rod continually over their heads, and keep them forever in uncertainty and fear.

In 1770, another act was passed, which appears to have continued until the State Constitution was formed. Soon after this period, the disputes came on which terminated in the American war, and until its close all parties were so much engaged in its struggles, that the business of parish taxes does not appear to have been prosecuted in a very rigorous manner. The exertions, which our brethren of this Commonwealth made to secure to themselves

---

* Backus, Vol. II. p. 85. † Backus, vol. II. p. 88.

and descendants the enjoyment of religious freedom, under the new form of government, have already been in part related, and will be more fully brought to view in the biography of Mr. Backus.

All the exempting acts, which we have referred to, were qualified with requisitions of an humiliating nature, which some refused to comply with ; most, however, to avoid greater evils, consented to make, what Mr. Leland calls, the Certificate Bow.

We have seen that the law of 1728 exempted only those who lived within five miles of the place of meeting. This limitation was afterwards left out, but it was still necessary that a long perplexing certificate should, upon oath or solemn affirmation, be annually presented to the county clerk, who must give it to the parish assessors, before any one could be excused from paying the sacred rates. This certificate was to be signed by " Meet persons in each respective society," and was to contain a list of all who professed themselves Anabaptists, &c. and usually attended their meetings.*

The law of 1752† enacted that certificates in future should be signed by the Baptist minister, and two principal members of the church ; but it was, at the same time, furthermore enacted, that no minister or church should have power to give lawful certificates, until they should have obtained " *From three other churches, in this or the neighbouring provinces, a certificate from each respectively, that they esteemed such church to be of their denomination, and that they conscientiously believed them to be Anabaptists.*"‡ This was truly adding insult to injury, since it was well known that our brethren had never acknowledged the term Anabaptists as descriptive of their sentiments, but had always understood it as the language of either ignorance or malice. But now they were obliged to heap certificate upon certificate, and in the end to testify a conscientious belief of a point which they had ever contended was erroneous and false. It is difficult to conceive how any could obtain certificates under these detestable reg-

* Backus, vol. ii. p. 87.
† At this time they broke over their own law with particular reference to the Church in Sturbridge. *Backus.*
‡ Backus, vol. ii. p. 193.

ulations: it is probable, however, they qualified the matter by saying, *commonly called Anabaptists*, &c.

The next law modified matters a little by requiring the certifiers to say they conscientiously believed the persons in question to be of their persuasion,&c.

The law of 1770 enacted that certificates should be signed by three or more principal members of the church, and minister, if any there were. The word conscientious was retained, but the term church was exchanged for congregation, and Anabaptist for Antipedobaptist. By this law, and all former ones, certificates were to be annually procured. At the same time this law was passed, it was further enacted, that parishes might, if they pleased, vote the Baptists clear without any certificates. But it does not appear that any vote of this kind was ever passed.

These statements will give the Baptists in other parts, a view of the vexatious entanglements in which their brethren in this boasted asylum of liberty were continually involved.

When the State Constitution was adopted, the Baptists, and other dissenters, hoped for a full relief from their long scene of affliction on account of religious imposts. The Bill of Rights apparently secured to them the peaceable enjoyment of that religious freedom, which they had so long and ardently desired, and for the attainment of which, they had made every exertion, which prudence could dictate and diligence perform. This Bill declares that in this Commonwealth, " no subordination of any one sect or denomination to another shall ever be established by law." And that " no subject shall be hurt, molested or restrained in his person, liberty, or estate, for worshipping God in the manner and season most agreeable to the dictates of his own conscience," &c. What more could any subject ask of his government? and we may further inquire, by what unaccountable process has this Bill of Rights been so often contradicted and violated? The only solution of this mysterious affair is, that the same Bill, (Article III.) declares that, " As the happiness of a people, and the good order and preservation of civil government essentially depend on piety, religion, morality, &c. the Legislature shall, from time to time, authorise and require the several towns, parishes, and precincts, &c. to make suitable provision, at their own expense, for the institution of the publick worship of God, and for the support and maintenance of publick protestant teachers of piety, religion, morality, &c." The way in which this provision was to be made was prescribed in an act of 1786, which empowers " The qualified voters of any parish or precinct, at every annual meeting, to grant such sum or sums of money as they shall judge necessary, for ministers—meeting-houses—or other parish charges, to be assessed on the poles and property, within the same, as by law provided."* The Congregational denomination, it is true, is not named in this act, nor any other which regards the support of religious teachers, &c. The power was given to the majority of every parish, precinct, &c. and it was well known to the law-makers, that the Congregationalists, with a very few exceptions, composed this majority, so that they without being named as such, became, in fact, the established party, and had without appearing to ask the favour, a control of all other sects put into their hands. If it should so happen that in any town, parish, &c. the Baptists should be a majority, they also had the power of assessing taxes and collecting them by law. But this power they rather deprecate than desire ; they do not thank any government to sanction among them a mode of procedure so contrary to all their notions of regulating religious affairs.

Thus we see that the Bill of Rights with all its strong assurances of impartiality, with all its expressions of paternal care, was counteracted by subsequent acts of the Legislature. The major party was put in possession of a religious establishment ; the Congregationalists composed this majority, and of course conducted the business of parish taxes as they pleased ; and all minorities were obliged to submit to their regulations. But there was still one avenue left for the escape of dissenters. The Bill of Rights declares, that " all monies paid by the subject, to the support of publick worship, &c. shall, if he require it, be uniformly applied to the support of a public teacher or teachers of his own religious sect or denomination, provided there be any on whose instructions he attends ;" otherwise his money is forfeited to the use of the parish. The construction put upon this article was, that the money

* Laws of Mass. Vol. I. p. 327.

must be paid into the treasury, and then be drawn out by an order on the treasurer, &c. And in this way the business was conducted from the adoption of the State Constitution, until 1811, that is, about thirty years. The Baptists and all others, excepting the Quakers, *must* pay their proportion towards the support of religion, and then they *might* draw their money back again, if they *could*, for their own ministers. Those communities of the established order, who were condescending upon the matter, paid over these monies without hesitation ; but in many cases difficulties ensued, and the money, once deposited in the treasury, could not be drawn back without a legal process, and not always then. It would be tedious to go over the whole history of this perplexing economy ; it is sufficient to observe, that in a multitude of cases, the Baptists as well as others, were treated in a churlish, fraudulent, and abusive manner. After all their precautions and attempts for justice, they were shuffled out of their rights, and obliged to sit down and console themselves for their losses as well as they could. Assessors, collectors, treasurers, judges, and jurors, were generally against them, and of course their attempts at redress were easily defeated.

In this posture the business of taxes for religious purposes remained, until the beginning of 1811, when an event took place, which awakened the fears and called forth the energies of the united body of dissenters. At the time referred to, the late Judge Parsons, then the Chief Justice of the State, in a trial of one of these cases respecting drawing back money,&c. decided, that no society, except those which were incorporated by law, could be entitled to the privilege. Immediately upon the news of this decision, a Circular Address, signed in behalf of others, by Dr. Baldwin of Boston, Mr. Williams of Beverly, and Mr. Bolles of Salem, was distributed through the State ; accompanying it was the following petition to the Legislature :

TO the Honorable Senate, and House of Representatives of the Commonwealth of Massachusetts in General Court assembled, the Petition of the Subscribers, being of the religious denomination of Christians, called (Baptists, or as the case may be.)

HUMBLY SHEWETH,

THAT whereas it appears to have been the wise and equitable intention of the *framers* of the Constitution of this state, to secure to the citizens individually, the equal enjoyment of their religious rights and privileges; and to bar in the most effectual manner every attempt to introduce, or maintain a " subordination of any one sect or denomination of Christians to another." And whereas it is also expressly declared in the third article of the Bill of Rights, which makes a part of the said Constitution, that " all monies paid by the subject to the support of the publick worship and of the publick teachers, shall, if he require it, be uniformly applied to the support of the publick teacher, or teachers of *his own* religious sect, or denomination, provided there be any on whose religious instructions he attends."

In conformity to the construction which has heretofore been given to this Article, many when taxed to the support of religious teachers of a different denomination, have applied for the monies thus collected, and required, that they should be paid over to the religious teacher of their own denomination, on whose ministrations they attended. In some instances, the money thus required, has been paid over to the religious teacher of their choice ; but more frequently it has been detained, until recovered by a *legal process*, notwithstanding the plain provisions of the above article

Your Honors' petitioners beg leave further to state, that by the *late* decisions of the *Supreme Bench*, a new construction, as we conceive, has been given to the above article ; limiting it wholly to *incorporated religious Societies ;* so that no money can be claimed by the subject for the use of the religious teacher on whose instructions he attends, unless he be the teacher of an *incorporated society.* By the above construction, a great proportion of persons who regularly worship in unincorporated societies, will be obliged to pay to th e support of teachers with whom they disagree in principle, and from whose instructions they conscientiously dissent ; and without any legal remedy whatever.

In consequence of the foregoing construction, which we believe to be contrary to the intentions of the framers of the constitution, many worthy conscientious Christians will be subjected to a double proportion of ministerial taxes. Duty, honour, and gratitude, will oblige them to pay to the teacher on whose instructions they attend ; and by the above construction of the laws, they will also be obliged to pay to the support of such as they do not, and cannot conscientiously hear

Your Honors' petitioners beg leave further to observe, that to the unequal operation of the laws, or more especially to the above-mentioned construction of them, may (as we humbly conceive) be attributed, the unusual and increasing number of petitions to the General Court for acts of incorporation. To this mode of procedure, however, many have conscientious scruples ; but even if they had not, it must be acknowledged as but a partial remedy for the evil of which we complain : while the state is subjected to a needless expense in granting acts of incorporation.

IN ORDER, THEREFORE, more effectually to remedy the foregoing evils, and place your petitioners upon an equal footing of privileges with their fellow citizens, we pray your Honors to take this subject into your serious and wise consideration, and cause the several

A Law passed to exempt Baptists from Taxation. 449

existing laws respecting the worship of God, to be so *revised* and *amended*, that all denominations of christians may be exempt from being taxed to the support of religious teachers, excepting those on whose ministrations they voluntarily attend. Or otherways to grant such relief in the premises, as your Honors may deem proper ; and your petitioners, as in duty bound, shall ever pray.

This petition was signed by many thousands of citizens of almost every denomination, for many of the Congregationalists went heartily into this measure. When the business came before the Assembly, it underwent a long and animated discussion ; the Speech of Mr. John Leland, who accepted a seat in the Legislature for the purpose of aiding this measure, will be given in the Appendix. Other able speeches were made by different gentlemen, and particularly by Rev. Mr. Cannon, a Methodist minister from Nantucket.* In the end, a law was passed of the following import. That whenever any person shall become a member of any religious society, corporate or unincorporate, and shall produce a certificate of such membership to the clerk of the town where he dwells, signed by a committee of the society chosen for the purpose, such person shall ever afterwards, so long as he continues such membership, be exempted from taxation for the support of publick worship and publick teachers of religion, in every other religious corporation whatsoever. This law was passed June, 1811. It afforded peculiar relief to the Baptists and other dissenters, but still neither party is altogether satisfied with it. The Congregationalists are afraid that they have given up too much, but the dissenters suppose they have not yet obtained what they claim as their just and indisputable right, viz. a free exemption from all taxes and all certificates. They think it best, however, for the present, to shift along with what they have got, and obtain the rest when Providence shall open a door. The Connecticut rulers, notwithstanding all the reproaches cast upon them for their ancient Blue Laws, have, long ago, done better for dissenters than Massachusetts has at this late period. There a dissenter may write his own certificate ; here we see he must procure one from others.

* See A Blow at the Root of Aristocracy, p. 14, &c.

VOL. I. 57

A few remarks on civil incorporations, and a brief recapitulation shall close this long, perplexing narrative of law affairs. In Rhode-Island, New-York, New-Jersey, and all the middle, southern and western States, churches and religious societies obtain acts of incorporation, merely for the purpose of managing and defending their property. No religious duties are imposed upon them in consequence of these acts, nor is there the least danger of any inconvenience arising from their being known in law as bodies politic and corporate. For these reasons they wonder why our brethren in this State should have any scruples about the business of incorporation. They ought to be informed that as the law of this Commonwealth now stands, every religious society, which becomes incorporated by civil law, is authorized, in case a major vote can be obtained, to assess whatever sums they please on the corporate body, and collect it by a course of law. This is one evil, which many fear from incorporations.

In the second place, every incorporated society, of whatever denomination, is bound by law, to be constantly provided with a preacher, (whether the Lord send them one or not) and in case they are without for the term of three months in any six, they are liable, for the first offence, to a fine of not more than *sixty dollars*, nor less than *thirty*; and for every after offence, their fine cannot be over a *hundred dollars*, nor less than *sixty*: the costs of prosecution they must also pay. The imposing of these fines is left at the discretion of the county court, and the avails of them are to be disposed of to the support of the publick worship of God, &c.* This is the second evil feared from incorporations. But it ought to be observed, that though these evils may arise to incorporate societies, yet there is, at present, no great danger of them.

But a still greater objection to incorporations in the minds of many of our brethren is, that they cannot persuade themselves but that it is blending law and gospel together. They have been so long harassed with this policy, that the very sound of law, in connexion with the gospel, has become offensive to their ears, and awakens their strong suspicions and disgust. And much to their comfort, the law of 1811 has provided that all unincorporate religious socie-

* Laws of Massachusetts, vol. ii. p. 931.

A Recapitulation of the foregoing Sketches. 451

ties shall have the power to manage and defend their property, to prosecute and sue for any right, &c.*

To recapitulate the foregoing sketches : We thus see, that our brethren have had a long scene of adversity and distress in this renowned land of freedom. All taxes for the support of government they have ever cheerfully paid, but those for religious purposes have been as obnoxious to them as the vapours of Babylon, and as ruinous as the locusts of Egypt. They have ever protested against them as unequal and unjust, as not authorized either by the original charter of the colony, by the tenure of their lands, by the State Constitution, or upon any other consideration. Their oppressions have been grievous, but the principle, from which they have proceeded, has ground them to the quick. Their oppressors have, however, held the reins, and led them as they chose. Laws made in their favour were often administered against them ; the course of justice was prevented by the quibbles of lawyers and the connivance of courts ; the interested clergy were always canting against them ; and the petty parish officers always acted upon the principle, that the priests must have their salaries, and they must collect them according to law ; and finally, the important Bill of Rights, as construed by renowned statesmen, became a vague, evasive thing, which, like the Oracle of Delphi, gave answers susceptible of many different meanings.

We have happily arrived at an age, in which the spirit of imposition has lost much of its former force. Many of the prevailing party here, like the Episcopalians of Virginia, have just notions of religious liberty, and are willing all should enjoy it ; but we believe there is a large portion of the ancient leaven remaining, and dissenters need to be on their guard to prevent its operations.†

* Laws of Massachusetts, vol. I. New Series, p. 227

† Most of this lengthy article has been compiled from Backus' History, and though references are not always made, the reader may rest assured that all important statements are grounded on authorities which admit of no dispute.

CHAPTER XIII.

RHODE-ISLAND.

NOW in the twelfth year of the reign of Charles the First king of Great-Britain, and the dominions thereunto belonging, Haynes being Governor of the colony of Massachusetts, and Bradford of Plymouth, Wilson and Cotton being chief priests at Boston, Roger Williams, filled with the spirit of liberty and anabaptism, was banished from their presence and fled to the head of the Narraganset Bay, where he built a town for his persecuted brethren, and founded a State, which is now called Rhode-Island.

As this State was first settled by Baptists, and they have always been the prevailing denomination in it, it may be proper to give a more particular account of its origin and civil affairs, than we shall do of the other States.

Rhode-Island is the smallest State in the Union, its greatest length being forty seven miles, its greatest breadth thirty seven, and containing only about thirteen hundred square miles. It is bounded north and east by Massachusetts, south by the Atlantic, and west by Connecticut. It is divided into five counties, viz. Providence, Kent, Washington, Newport, and Bristol ; these counties are subdivided into thirty-one townships, and contained, in 1810, about seventy-seven thousand inhabitants. This State has not increased very rapidly in population of late years, as it contained about sixty-thousand inhabitants forty years ago. No part of the United States is more healthy, but the territory is so small, that every part of it has long since been taken up, and as the inhabitants increase, they are obliged to remove to other parts for settlements. The manufacturing interest is now very rapidly advancing, and the number of inhabitants will probably increase much faster for the future, than it has done for half a century past.

The island, from which this State receives its name, is about fifteen miles long, and generally about three miles wide, and was, before the American war, called by travellers the Eden of America. It is divided into three townships, by the name of Newport, Middleton and Portsmouth.

The earliest settlements in this little State were made by two separate companies, who do not appear to have had any knowledge of each other's designs. The first was begun by Roger Williams and his persecuted brethren in 1636;* the other by Dr. John Clark,† William Codington, and others, about 1638. The place where Mr. Williams settled, and which in testimony of God's merciful providence to him in his distress, he named Providence, was by the Indians called Mooshausick. Mr. Clark and his company settled on Aquidneck, or Aquetneck, now called Rhode-Island, at a place then named Pocasset, now Portsmouth. This was on the north end of the Island, between twenty and thirty miles from Mr. Williams. Some of the company soon after removed and settled on the south-west part of the Island, where Newport now stands.

In 1644, the inhabitants of Aquidneck named it the Isle of Rhodes or Rhode-Island.

A third settlement was begun on Pawtuxet River, south of Providence, by Samuel Gorton and others, about 1641.

From these brief sketches we shall now proceed to a more circumstantial account of the commencement of these settlements.

Roger Williams was the parent and founder of the State of Rhode-Island. He first planted the standard of freedom and peace among the Narraganset Indians, and all the settlements, which were afterwards made, were by his assistance. He at first by his pacific measures and peculiar skill gained the friendship of the Indian princes, and any favour, which he requested, was easily obtained. He was most thoroughly convinced that the untutored savages were lords of the soil on which the God of nature had planted them, and therefore took the utmost care, that none of the inhabitants of this infant colony should occupy the least part of it until it was fairly purchased of the aboriginal proprietors. The Indians did, indeed, in some instances convey large tracts by deeds of gift, but these were *Indian*

---

* I have followed Mr. Backus' dates in describing these events. Some historians have dated Mr. Williams' settlement in 1634; but no one has investigated this subject more thoroughly than Mr Backus, and I am inclined to think he is the most correct.

† Morgan Edwards observes, that ' Mr. Clark was properly the founder of the Rhode-Island Colony, although Mr. Codington has run away with the praise of it."

gifts, which in the end proved very costly. But the utmost care was taken that every claim should be satisfied, and every pretext for hostility precluded.

The cause of the banishment of this worthy man from the colony of Massachusetts was as follows : He was most firmly persuaded, and like an honest man faithfully defended the two following important propositions, viz. that the Princes of Europe had no right whatever to dispose of the possessions of the American Indians ; and secondly, that civil rulers as such had no authority from God to regulate or control the affairs of religion. A more definite statement of this last proposition will be made in the account of the founding of the church in Providence. It is sufficient to observe here that out of his maxims of religious liberty, and national justice, grew most of the heresies contained in his indictment.* And such were his talents and address, that the magistrates were fearful whereunto his opinions would grow, and after some ineffectual endeavours to convince or quiet him they passed against him the cruel sentence of banishment, October, 1635. He had permission to tarry within their jurisdiction until spring, upon condition " that he would not go about to draw others to his opinions ;" but in January, 1636, the Governor and Assistants were informed that he received and preached to companies in his house at Salem, " even of such points as he had been censured for." Having received this information, they agreed to send him back to England by a ship then ready to depart ; " the reason was, because he had drawn about twenty people to his opinions ; they were intended to erect a plantation about the Narraganset Bay, from whence infection would easily spread into these churches, the people being many of them much taken with the apprehension of his godliness." They sent for him to come to Boston, but he sent an excuse ; upon which they sent a pinnace, with a commission to Captain Underhill, to apprehend him and carry him on board the ship then at Nantasket ; but when they came to his house they found he had been gone three days.

---

* " The sin of the *Patents*, Mr. Williams says, lay heavy on his mind, especially that part by which *Christian* kings (so called) were invested with a right, by virtue of their *christianity*,to take and give away the lands and countries of other men." His sentiments on this subject, Mr. Cotton informs us, formed the first article in his indictment. BACKUS, vol. i. p. 57, 58.

"What human heart," says Mr. Backus, "can be unaffected with the thought, that a people, who had been sorely persecuted in their own country, so as to flee three thousand miles into a wilderness for religious liberty, yet should have that imposing temper cleaving so fast to them, as not to be willing to let a godly minister, who testified against it, stay even in any neighbouring part of this wilderness, but moved them to attempt to take him by force, to send him back into the land of their persecutors !"*

The next we hear of this injured man, was on the Seekhonk plain, since called Rehoboth, a few miles east of Providence. To this place, which was then wholly inhabited by savages, he fled in the depth of winter and obtained a grant of land of Osamaquin, sometimes called Masasoit, chief Sachem at Mount Hope, now in Bristol, R. I. But he was soon informed by a letter and messenger from the men of Plymouth, that this place was within their patent. He next went over Pawtucket River, as will be related in the history of the first church in Providence.

Here he found that favour among the savages which christians had denied him. Many of his friends and adherents soon repaired to his new habitation. He had the happiness to gain the friendship of two powerful Narraganset princes, of whom he made a formal purchase of a territory sufficient for himself and friends. He soon acquired a sufficient knowledge of the Indian language to transact the affairs of trade and negociation, and perhaps no man ever had more influence over the savage tribes than Roger Williams. This influence enabled him to soothe the irritated Indian Chiefs, and break up their confederacies against the English. And the first act of this kind was performed in favour of the colony from which he had been so cruelly banished.

The first deed which he obtained of his lands, or at least the first which is now extant, bears date the same day with that of Aquidneck, and was given two years after his settlement at Providence. It runs in the following style :

"At Nanhiggansick, the 24th of the first month, commonly called March, in the second year of our plantation, or planting at Mooshausick, or Providence : Memorandum, that we Caunannicus and

* Vol. i. p. 72.

Miantinomu, the two chief sachems of Nanhiggansick, having two years since sold unto Roger Williams the lands and meadows upon the two fresh rivers called Mooshausick and Wanaskatuckett, do now by these presents establish and confirm the bounds of these lands, from the rivers and fields of Pautuckett, the great hill of Neoterconkenitt on the north-west, and the town of Mashapauge on the west. As also, in consideration of the many kindnesses and services he hath continually done for us, both for our friends of Massachusetts, as also at Quininkticutt and Apaum, or Plymouth; we do freely give unto him all that land from those rivers reaching to Pautuxett river, as also the grass and meadows upon Pautuxett river;* in witness whereof we have hereunto set our hands in the presence of,

The mark of ‡ Caunannicus,
The mark of ‖ Miantinomu.
The mark of † Seatagh,
The mark of * Assotemewett.

" 1639, Memorandum, 3d month, 9th day, this was all again confirmed by Miantinomu ; he acknowledged this his act and hand ; up the stream of Pautuckett and Pautuxett without limits we might have for our use of cattle ; witness hereof,

Roger Williams,
Benedict Arnold."

This deed must have comprehended all the county of Providence, or the north part of the State, and most of the county of Kent.

A few months after this purchase was made, Mr. Williams admitted as his associates the persons afterwards named by the following instrument :

" Providence, 8th of the 8th month, 1638, (so called.) Memorandum, that I, Roger Williams, having formerly purchased of Caunannicus and Miantinomu this our situation or plantation of New-Providence, &c. the two fresh rivers of Wanasquatuckett and Mooshausick, and the ground and meadows thereupon ; in consideration of thirty pounds received from the inhabitants of said place, do freely and fully pass, grant, and make over equal right and power of enjoying and disposing of the same grounds and lands unto my loving friends and neighbours, Stukely Westcoat, William Arnold, Thomas James, Robert Cole, John Greene, John Throckmorton, William Harris, William Carpenter, Thomas Olney, Francis Weston, Richard Waterman, Ezekiel Holliman, and such others as the major part of us shall admit into the same fellowship of vote with us :

* The Mooshausick river empties into Providence cove from the north, a little below the Mill Bridge ; the Wanaskatuckett is that on which Olney's Paper Mills are situated. The Pawtucket river rises in, or near Rutland in Worcester county, Massachusetts, and empties into the Narraganset Bay at India Point, Providence. The Pawtuxet rises near the borders of Connecticut, and falls into the Bay five miles below the town. On the fields of Pawtucket the author is now writing, but he is not sure where the town of Mashapauge stood.

His Design in founding the Colony explained. 457

As also I do freely make and pass over equal right and power of enjoying and disposing of the lands and grounds reaching from the aforesaid rivers unto the great river Pautuxett, with the grass and meadows thereupon, which was so lately given and granted by the aforesaid sachems to me ; witness my hand,

ROGER WILLIAMS."

The next who were admitted into this company, were Chad Brown, William Field, Thomas Harris, William Wickenden, Robert Williams, brother to Roger, Richard Scott, William Reynolds, John Field, John Warner, Thomas Angell, Benedict Arnold, Joshua Winsor, Thomas Hopkins, Francis Weeks, &c.*

The following passage explains, in a very pleasing manner, Mr. Williams' design in these transactions :

" Notwithstanding I had the frequent promise of Miantinomu, my kind friend, that it should not be land that I should want about those bounds mentioned, provided that I satisfied the Indians there inhabiting, I having made covenant of peaceable neighbourhood with all the sachems and natives round about us, and having, in a sense of God's *merciful providence unto me in my distress,* called the place PROVIDENCE, I desired it might be for a *shelter for persons distressed for conscience ; I then considering the condition of divers of my countrymen,* I communicated my said purchase unto my loving friends, John Throckmorton, and others, who then desired to take shelter here with me, And whereas by God's merciful assistance I was the procurer of the purchase, not by monies nor payment, the natives being so shy and jealous that monies could not do it, but by that language, acquaintance and favour with the natives, and other advantages which it pleased God to give me ; and also bore the charges and venture of all the gratuities which I gave to the great sachems, and other sachems and natives round about us, and lay engaged for a loving and peaceable neighbourhood with them, to my great charge and travel ; it was therefore thought fit that I should receive some consideration and gratuity." Thus, after mentioning the said thirty pounds, and saying, " this sum I received ; and in love to my friends, and with *respect to a town and place of succour for the distressed as aforesaid,* I do acknowledge this said sum and payment a full satisfaction ;" he went on in full and strong terms

---

* " Of these I find Williams (brother to Mr. Roger) among the Massachusetts freemen, but no more of their names upon those records. Perhaps most of them might have newly arrived ; for Governor Winthrop assures us, that no less than three thousand arrived this year in twenty ships ; and Mr. Hubbard tells us that those, who inclined to the Baptists' principles, went to Providence ; others went to Newport. Seven of the first twelve, with Angell, I suppose began the settlement with Mr. Williams in 1636."

Backus.

to confirm those lands to said inhabitants; reserving no more to himself and his heirs than an equal share with the rest; his wife also signing the deed.*

The settlement of Aquidneck was begun in the following manner: Soon after the banishment of R. Williams, the colony of Massachusetts was most violently agitated by religious discords, and a synod held at Newton, now Cambridge, after due examination, found to their grief, that their country was infested with no less than eighty-two heretical opinions, which were all arraigned before the sapient ecclesiastical tribunal, and solemnly condemned. Rev. Mr. Whellwright, and Mrs. Ann Hutchinson, both Pedobaptists, were banished the jurisdiction for what was called Antinomianism, and others were exposed to a similar fate. Mr. John Clark, an eminent physician, made a proposal to his friends to remove out of a jurisdiction so full of bigotry and intolerance. Mr. Clark was now in the 29th year of his age; he was requested with some others to look out for a place, where they might enjoy unmolested the sweets of religious freedom. By reason of the suffocating heat of the preceding summer, they first went north to a place which is now within the bounds of New-Hampshire, but on account of the coldness of the following winter, they resolved in the spring to make towards the south. " So having sought the Lord for direction, they agreed that while their vessel was passing about Cape Cod, they would cross over by land, having Long-Island and Delaware Bay in their eye, for the place of their residence. At Providence Mr. Williams lovingly entertained them, and being consulted about their design, readily presented two places before them; Sowams, now called Barrington, and Aquetneck, now Rhode Island. And inasmuch as they were determined to go out of every other jurisdiction, Mr. Williams and Mr. Clark, attended with two other persons, went to Plymouth, to inquire how the case stood; they were lovingly received, and answered, that Sowams was the *garden of their patent*. But they were advised to settle at Aquetneck, and promised to be looked on as free, and to be treated and assisted as loving neighbours."†

* Backus Vol. I. p. 94.

† Backus' Hist. vol. 1. p. 89. Callender's Century sermon, p. 30.

Williams's Account of the Purchase of R. Island. 459

On their return, the 7th of March, 1638, the men, to the number of eighteen, incorporated themselves a body politic, and chose William Coddington their judge or chief magistrate. The names of these men were William Coddington, John Clarke, William Hutchinson, John Coggshall, *William Aspinwall*, *Thomas Savage*, William Dyre, William Freeborne, Philip Shearman, John Walker, Richard Carder, William Baulstone, *Edward Hutchinson*, *Edward Hutchinson, jun.* Samuel Wilbore, John Sanford, John Porter, and Henry Bull. Those, whose names are in italicks, afterwards went back to Massachusetts; most of the others arose to eminence in the colony, which they established.

" It was not price or money," says Mr. Williams, " that could have purchased Rhode-Island; but 'twas obtained by love, that love and favour, which that honoured gentleman, Sir Henry Vane, and myself had with the great sachem Myantonomo, about the league, which I procured between the Massachusetts English, and the Narragansets in the *Pequot war*. This I mention, that as the truly noble Sir Henry Vane, hath been so great an instrument in the hand of God, for procuring this island of the barbarians, as also for the procuring and confirming the Charter, it may be with all thankful acknowledgments recorded and remembered by us and ours, who reap the sweet fruits of so great benefits, and such unheard of liberties among us." And in another manuscript he tells us, " The Indians were very *shy and jealous of selling the lands to any*, and chose rather to make a *grant of them*, to such as they affected; but at the same time, expected such gratuities and rewards, as made an *Indian gift* oftentimes a very dear bargain." " And the colony in 1666," says Mr. Callender, " avered that though the favour Mr. Williams had with Myantonomo was the great means of procuring the grants of the land, yet the purchase *had been dearer* than of any lands in New-England; the reason of which might be, partly, the English inhabited between two powerful nations, the Wamponoags to the north and east, who had formerly possessed some part of their grants, before they had surrendered it to the Narragansets; and though they freely owned the submission, yet it was thought best by Mr. Williams to make them easy by gratuities to the sachem, his counsellors and followers. On the other side the Narragansets were very numerous, and the natives inhabiting any spot the English sat down upon or improved, were all to be bought off to their content, and oftentimes were to be paid over and over again.*

The colony of Rhode-Island was small, and laboured under many embarrassments. In an address to the supreme authority in England, in 1659, they gave the following account of their circumstances: "This poor colony consists mostly of a Birth and Breeding of the Most High. We being an outcast people, formerly from our mother-nation in the bishop's days, and since from the New-English over-zealous colonies. Our whole frame being much like the present frame of our dearest mother England; bearing with the several judgments, and consciences of each other, in all the towns of the colony; which our neighbour colonies do not; and which is the only cause of their great offence against us."

A third settlement was made below Providence on the western shore of the Narraganset Bay, by Samuel Gorton, and his company. This company suffered for a time most severely by the officious and unrighteous interference of the Massachusetts and Plymouth rulers. Gorton was a very different character from either Williams or Clark, but he was a zealous advocate for liberty of conscience, and sought an asylum where he might enjoy it. He was a man of learning and abilities, but of a satyrical, crusty turn; he was also a preacher, but of a very singular cast. He arrived in Boston in 1636, which place he in a short time left for Plymouth. There he soon fell out with their preacher, was taken in hand by the authority, and bonds were required of him for his good behaviour. From Plymouth he went to Rhode-Island, where, for something in his conduct, what I cannot learn, he was, by Mr. Coddington's order, roughly treated, and according to Callender's account banished the Island. He next went to Providence, where he was kindly received by Mr. Williams and others, and he with others soon settled at Pawtuxet, which was within the bounds of Mr. Williams' grant. But here new troubles followed him, con-

* Century Sermon, p. 31, 32.

tentions were fomented among his company, the weaker party sought assistance from the men of Boston, and some of them actually submitted themselves and their lands to that government. The Boston court had then a specious pretext for meddling with the affairs of an infant distant colony, and they having learnt the peculiar policy of the cabinet of their mother country, to foment quarrels and then profit by them, cited Gorton and his associates to appear at their tribunal, and answer to the complaints which had been exhibited against them. The warrant was signed by the Governor and three assistants ; but Gorton treated it with disdain, and in answer wrote a long, mystical paraphrase upon it, which was signed by himself, Randal Holden, Robert Potter, John Wickes, John Warner, Richard Waterman, William Woodale, John Greene, Francis Weston, Richard Carder, Nicholas Power, and Sampson Shatton. It appears these people, in order to avoid further troubles, removed southward to a place then called Shawwomet, now Warwick, which they purchased of the sachems, Miantinomy,* Pomham, and others, for 144 fathoms of wampum.†

But new complaints soon went to Boston against them, and the petty sachems under Miantinomy and Pomham, for political reasons, were easily induced to become their enemies and accusers, and they were again summoned to appear before the Massachusetts rulers. And upon their refusal, because out of their jurisdiction, a company of armed men were sent to fetch them. They sent word to the company that if they set foot upon their land, it should be at their peril. But a band of soldiers marched on, the women and children, and some of the less resolute, were terrified and dispersed, and the rest, being overpowered by numbers, were carried to Boston, where they were treated in a severe and scandalous manner. Gorton, for being a blasphemous enemy of the religion of our Lord Jesus Christ, &c. was confined to Charlestown, set to hard work, loaded with bolts and irons to hinder his escape ; and in case he should break his confinement, and in the

* The name of this famous Indian chief is spelt many different ways, but Myantinomy seems the most proper, and according to Mr. Callender it was by the Indians pronounced Myantinō\my. *Cent. Ser. p.* 1.

† This was then computed at *forty pounds sixteen shillings* sterling. *Backus.*

mean time publish, declare, or maintain his blasphemous abominable heresies, wherewith he had been charged by the court, after due conviction, he should be condemned and executed. John Wickes was confined to Ipswich, Randal Holden to Salem, Robert Potter to Beverly, Richard Carder to Roxbury, Francis Western to Dorchester, John Warner to Boston, and William Woodale to Watertown. John Green, Richard Waterman, and Nicholas Power, not being found so guilty as the rest, were dismissed after paying costs and hearing an admonition. The rest were confined at their different stations through the winter, eighty head of their cattle were sold to pay the charges of bringing them from their homes, and trying them before a foreign tribunal, which amounted to a hundred and sixty pounds. But the court, finding it impossible to keep them from seducing others, and despairing of reclaiming them from their errors, in the spring released them, and banished them, not only from their jurisdiction, but also from their own lands at Showwomet.* This detestable tyranny came of Mr. Cotton's *Jewish theocracy*, and it is a lamentable fact, that that mistaken divine encouraged the court in this horrid oppression of Gorton and his unfortunate associates. Some of them were, at that very time, members of the church at Providence; they had associated with Gorton, not on account of his religious opinions, but for the purpose of obtaining lands on which they might procure a subsistence for themselves and families. But if Gorton had been that blasphemous, damnable heretick, which his orthodox persecuters pretended; if he had worshipped the sun, moon and stars; what right did that give the Boston rulers to treat him and his company in such an outrageous manner?

These much injured men, being prohibited on pain of death to go to their lands, repaired to Rhode-Island, where they tarried awhile meditating what course to take.

As yet none of the companies of this colony had any patent from the crown for their lands; but they had all purchased them of the Indians, their proper owners, and therefore ought to have been suffered peaceably to enjoy them.

* Backus, vol. I. p. 126—129.

Mr. Williams obtains a Charter in 1644.

About the time that Gorton and his company were released, that is, in 1643, Mr. Williams was sent to England as agent for the two colonies of Providence and Rhode-Island, and by the assistance of Sir Henry Vane, obtained " a free and absolute Charter of Civil Incorporation, by the name of the *Incorporation of Providence Plantations in the Narraganset Bay, in New-England.*" This charter was dated the 17th of March, in the 19th year of Charles I. 1644. It was obtained of the Earl of Warwick, who was then appointed by Parliament, Governor and Admiral of all the plantations, &c. and was signed by him and ten other noblemen his council. It empowered them to rule themselves and such others as should inhabit within their bounds by such a form of civil government as by the voluntary agreement of all or of the greater part should be found most suitable to their estate and condition, &c.

Mr. Williams returned with this charter the September following, and landed at Boston.

As persons of many different sentiments and tempers had resorted to this now asylum of freedom, it was a matter of some difficulty to fix upon a form of government, in which they could be united. But this desirable object was, not long after effected, and no event seems to have occurred, except what are common to the first efforts of new plantations, until 1651, when a very serious difficulty arose, which from the name of its author, was called *Coddington's Obstruction.* But before we proceed, it is proper to observe, that not long after Mr. Williams went to England, Messrs. Gorton, Greene, and Holden, set sail for the same country, and obtained an order to be suffered peaceably to possess their purchase at Showowmet. By this means the claims of the Massachusetts court were defeated. As Mr. Williams's Charter covered their purchase, it was incorporated with the Providence Plantations, and as the Earl of Warwick was their peculiar friend in this affair, they, for that reason, gave their settlement the name of Warwick, and the posterity of its planters are still numerous in different parts of the State. Callender, Backus, and others, who have spoken of Gorton's religious opinions, acknowledge that it is hard to tell what they really were ; but they assure us that it ought to be believed, that he held all the heresies which were ascribed to him. The most we can learn is, that in allegory, and double meanings of scripture, he was similar to Origen; in mystical theology and the rejection of ordinances, he resembled the Quakers; and the notion of visible instituted churches he utterly condemned. He was the leader of a religious meeting at Warwick above sixty years, and says he made use of the learned languages in expounding the Scriptures to his hearers. He was of a good family in England, lived to a great age, was promoted to honour in the Rhode-Island Colony, and left behind him many disciples to his *nondescript* opinions. Some of his posterity have been found among the Baptists, some among the Quakers, but the greater part of them are what Morse would call Nothingarians. But all of them still retain a lively abhorrence of that religious tyranny, by which he was so cruelly oppressed.*

The Charter obtained by Roger Williams in 1644, lasted until 1663, when another was granted by Charles II. by which the incorporation was styled " The English Colony of Rhode-Island and Providence Plantations in New-England." This Charter, without any essential alteration, has remained the foundation of the Rhode-Island government ever since. Previous to its being obtained, that is, in 1651, Messrs. Williams and Clark were sent to England as agents for the Colony, which then consisted of only the four towns of Providence, Portsmouth, Newport, and Warwick. The object of their embassy was to remove the obstructions which had been thrown in the way of their progress by William Coddington, then Governour of their infant settlement. This gentleman had, as they said, " by most untrue information," obtained a commission of the *Council of State*, to govern a part of the colony, that is, the Island, with such a council as the people should choose, and he approve. This they considered as "a violation of their liberties," &c. and by the exertions of these agents the commission was vacated, and the administration progressed in the original form. Mr. Williams soon returned, but Mr. Clark remained in England about twelve years, to watch the motion of affairs, and to be ready to lend his assistance to his brethren here as emergencies should require.

* Callender's Century Sermon, p. 37, 38.—Backus, vol. ii. p. 95.

Form of Government among the Rhode-Islanders.

The form of government established by the Rhode-Islanders was, as to civil affairs, much like those of the other colonies, but in the important article of religion, they differed from them all. Liberty of conscience was, in the first social compact at Providence, established by law, and no one was allowed to vote among them, who opposed it.* This darling principle was planted in the soil of Rhode-Island, before the red men left it, or ever the lofty forests were laid waste, and has been transmitted from father to son with the most studious care ; it was interwoven in every part of the State Constitution, has extended its influence to all transactions, whether civil or sacred, and in no part of the world has it been more inviolably maintained for the space of upwards of a hundred and seventy years. It is the glory and boast of Rhode-Island, that no one within her bounds was ever legally molested on account of his religious opinions, and that none of her annals are stained with acts to regulate those important concerns, which lie wholly between man and his Maker. Hence it was early said of this colony, " They are much like their neighbours, only they have one vice less, and one virtue more than they ; for they never persecuted any, but have ever maintained a perfect liberty of conscience."*

They, among their first Legislative acts, (instead of establishing their own religion by law, and compelling all others to maintain it) determined that " Every man, who submits peaceably to civil government in this colony, shall worship God according to the dictates of his own conscience without molestation." And when in 1656, the colonies of Plymouth, Massachusetts, Hartford, and New-Haven, pressed them hard to give up this point, and join with them to crush the Quakers, and prevent any more from coming to New-England, they, for an answer, made the noble declaration, " We shall strictly adhere to the foundation principle on which this colony was first settled," &c. Accordingly, the Quakers found a safe asylum here, while they were in all places persecuted and destroyed.

* Backus, vol. I. p. 96.
† Edwards' MS. Hist. of Rhode-Island, p. 10.

When these people obtained their second Charter in 1663, they petitioned Charles II. " that they might be permitted to hold forth a lively experiment, that a most flourishing civil State may stand and best be maintained, and that among English subjects, with a full liberty in religious concernments, and that true piety, rightly grounded on gospel principles, will give the best and greatest security to sovereignty ; and will lay in the hearts of men the strongest obligations to true loyalty."—This permission was granted by his majesty, and the tenor of their Charter was, that every person might freely and fully have and enjoy his own judgment or conscience in matters of religious concernment, &c. The inviolable attachment of the Rhode-Islanders to this heaven-born principle of Religious Freedom, was the real cause of all those calumnies and injuries which the other colonies heaped upon them. Connecticut and Massachusetts on either side of them, were now making strong exertions to enforce their religious laws, and could not endure the maxims of this little colony, which were a tacit and standing condemnation of *their* bigotry and intolerance. They therefore stretched their lines if possible to swallow up the little State, and Massachusetts actually took possession of a large share of it one side, and Connecticut on the other ; but failing of their design on this plan, they encouraged the Indians to harass them to the loss of 80 or 100 pounds a year; they refused to let them have ammunition for their money when in imminent danger ; they fomented divisions among them, and encouraged their subjects to refuse obedience to their authority ; they finally laboured hard, after they could not dismember the colony, to gain a party within its bounds, of sufficient strength to outvote them in their elections, and establish among them their abominable system of parish worship, and parish taxes. Their letter writers, preachers, and historians, calumniated them as " the scum and runaways of other colonies, which, in time, would bring a heavy burden on the land : as so sunk into barbarity, that they could speak neither good English nor good sense—as despisers of God's worship, and without order or government," &c.* Dr.

* Edwards' MS. Hist. of Rhode-Island, p. 12, 13.—Backus, vol I.—MS. of Governor Jenks.

Mather,* speaking of this State about a hundred years ago, says, " It has been a Colluvies of Antinomians, Familists, Anabaptists, Antisabbatarians, Arminians, Socinians, Quakers, Ranters, every thing in the world but Roman Catholicks and real christians, though of the latter, I hope, there have been more than the former among them ; so that if a man had lost his religion, he might find it at this general muster of Opinionists." He goes on to describe it as the Gerizzim of New-England, the common receptacle of the convicts of Jerusalem, and the outcasts of the land. " The Island," says he, " is indeed for the fertility of its soil, the temperateness of its air, &c. the best garden of all the colonies, and were it free from *serpents*, I would call it the *Paradise* of New-England." But he finally applies to it the old proverb, *Bona Terra, Mala Gens*, a good land, but a bad people. This is but a part of a long reviling piece of the same character. Among other things he informs us, that the Massachusetts ministers had made a *chargeless* tender of preaching the gospel to this wretched people in their towns and on their *paganizing plantations ;* but these offers had been refused.

The two following letters will give the reader to understand the manner in which these chargeless tenders were made, and also in what point of light the Rhode-Island people viewed them. The first is from an Association of the Massachusetts ministers ; the other from the people of Providence :

" *To the honourable Joseph Jenckes, Esq. late Deputy-Governor, William Hopkins, Esq. Major Joseph Willson, Esq. Joseph Whipple, Esq. Col. Richard Waterman, Esq. Arther Fenner, Esq. ——— Wilkinson, Esq. Philip Tillinghast, Esq. Capt. Nicholas Power, Esq. Thomas Harris, Esq. Capt. William Harris, Esq. Andrew Harris, Esq. ——— Brown, Esq. Jonathan Burton, Esq. Jonathan Spreauge, Jun. Esq. and to the other eminent men in the town of Providence. Pardon our ignorance if any of your honourable christian names, or if your proper order be mistaken.*

" Honourable Gentlemen,

We wish you grace, mercy, and peace, and all blessings for time and for eternity through our Lord Jesus Christ. How pleasing to Almighty God and our Lord and Redeemer, and how conducible to

* Magnalia, Book VIII. p. 20.

the publick tranquillity and safety, an hearty union and good affection of all pious protestants, of whatever particular denomination, on account of some difference in opinion, would be, by the divine blessing, yourselves, as well as we, are not insensible of. And with what peace and love, societies of different modes of worship have generally entertained one another in your government, we cannot think of without admiration. And we suppose, under God, 'tis owing to the choice liberty granted to protestants of all persuasions in the Royal Charter graciously given you ;* and to the wise and prudent conduct of the gentlemen that have been improved as governors and justices in your colony. And the Rev. Mr. Greenwood, before his decease at Rehoboth, was much affected with the wisdom and excellent temper and great candour of such of yourselves as he had the honour to wait upon, and with those worthy and obliging expressions of kind respects he met with when he discoursed about his desire to make an experiment, whether the preaching of our ministers in Providence might not be acceptable ; and whether some, who do not greatly incline to frequent any pious meeting in the place, on the first day of the week, might not be drawn to give their presence to hear our ministers, and so might be won over, by the influence of Heaven, into serious godliness ; and although God has taken that dear brother of ours from his work in this world, yet it has pleased the Lord to incline some reverend ministers in Connecticut and some of ours to preach among you ; and we are beholden to the mercy of Heaven for the freedom and safety they have enjoyed under the wise and good government of the place, and that they met with kind respect, and with numbers that gave a kind reception to their ministration among you. These things we acknowledge with all thankfulness. And if such preaching should be continued among your people, designed only for the glory of God and Christ Jesus in chief, and nextly, for promoting the spiritual and eternal happiness of immortal, precious souls, and the furtherance of a joyful account in the great day of judgment, we earnestly request, as the Rev. Mr. Greenwood in his life time did before us, that yourselves, according to your power and the influence and interest that God hath blessed you with, will continue your just protection ; and that you add such further countenance and encouragement thereunto as may be pleasing to the eternal God, and may, through Christ Jesus, obtain for you the great reward in Heaven. And if ever it should come to pass that a small meetinghouse should be built in your town to entertain such as are willing to hear our ministers, we should account it a great favour if you all, Gentlemen, or any of you, would please to build pews therein ; in which you and they as often as you see fit, may give your and their presence and holy attention. And we hope and pray that ancient matters, that had acrimony in them, may be buried in oblivion ; and that grace, and peace, and holiness, and glory, may dwell in every part of New-England ; and that the several provinces and colonies in it may love one another with a pure heart fervently. So

---

* Be it observed that the same liberty was granted the Massachusetts people by their charters first and last. EDWARDS.

recommending you all, and your ladies and children, and neighbours and people to the blessing of Heaven, and humbly asking your prayers to the divine throne for us, we take leave and subscribe ourselves your servants,
PETER THACHER,
JOHN DANFORTH,
JOSEPH BELCHER."

"By the foregoing paper," says Edwards, "which is the joint act of the Massachusetts ministers, it appears that the people of Rhode-Island government were good people, even while the Mathers, their chief accusers, were alive. And if the Association spake according to knowledge and truth, the characters in the Magnalia and other New-England histories must be false and slanderous. I will here add the answer that was made to the foregoing paper, and then offer two or three remarks."

"*To John Danforth, Peter Thacher, and Joseph Belcher, committee of the Presbyterian Ministry.*

"SIRS,

WE, the inhabitants of the town of Providence, received yours, bearing date, October 27, 1721, which was read publickly, in the hearing of the people, and we judge it uncivil to return you no answer. But finding the matter to be of religious concernment, we counted it our duty to ask counsel of God, lest we should be beguiled as Israel was by the Gibeonites. And inasmuch as the sacred scriptures were given forth by the Spirit of the living God to be our instructer and counsellor, we shall therefore apply ourselves to them. And in the first place, we take notice of the honourable titles you give to many of us. Your view, as we take it, is to insinuate yourselves into our affections, and to induce us to favour your request. But, we find flatteries in matters of religion to be of dangerous consequence ; witness the Hivites, who said, *We are your servants, and have heard of the fame of the God of Israel.* In this way did Joash set up idolatry after the death of Jehoida. Elihu abstained from flattery for fear of offending God, while the enemies of Judah, for want of the fear of God, practised it. By the same means was Daniel cast into the Lion's den, and Herod sought to slay the Lord Christ; and some at Rome sought to make divisions in the church of Christ by flattering words and fair speeches, to deceive the simple ; but, saith the Spirit, *Such serve not the Lord Jesus Christ, but their own belly ;* and saith the apostle Peter, *Through covetousness and feigned words they shall make merchandize of you.* To conclude this article. We see that flattery in matters of worship has been, and now is, a cloak to blind men and lead them out of the way ; and serves for nothing but to advance pride and vain glory. Shall we praise you for this ? We praise you not. Next. You salute all as saints in the faith and order of the gospel, wishing all of us blessings for the time present and to all eternity. It is not the language of Canaan but of Babel to salute men of all characters as in the faith of the gospel. This is the voice of the false prophets, which daub with untempered mortar, sewing pillows under every arm-hole, and crying, peace! peace! when there is no peace. Is this your way to enlighten the dark corners of the world? Surely, this is darkness itself. Moreover, You highly extol liberty of conscience to men of all persuasions, affirming it to be most pleasing to God, and tending most to love and peace, and the tranquillity of any people. And you say, *We are not insensible of this any more than you.* To which we say, *Amen ;* and you well know it hath been our faith and practice hitherto. Fourthly. We take notice how you praise the love and peace that dissenters of all ranks entertain one another within this government; and it is, as you say, *to your admiration:* and you suppose *that* under God, *it is owing to the choice liberty granted to protestants of all denominations in the Royal Charter graciously given us, and to the discreet and wise rulers under whose conduct we enjoy this happiness.* We answer, This happiness principally consists in our not allowing societies to have any superiority one over another, but each society supports their own ministry of their own free will, and not by constraint or force upon any man's person or estate; and this greatly adds to our peace and tranquillity. But the contrary, which takes away men's estates by force, to maintain their own or any other ministry, serves for nothing but to provoke to wrath, envy, and strife. This wisdom cometh not from above, but is earthly, sensual and devilish. In those cited concessions we hope too, that you are real and hearty, and do it not to flourish your compliments; otherwise you make a breach on the third commandment. This is but a preface to make room for your request, which is, *That we would be pleased, according to our power, to countenance, protect, and encourage your ministers in their coming and preaching in this town of Providence.* To which we answer :—We admire at your request! or that you should imagine or surmise that we should consent to either; inasmuch as we know, that (to witness for God) your ministers, for the most part, were never set up by God, but have consecrated themselves, and have changed his ordinances; and for their greediness after filthy lucre, some you have put to death; others you have banished upon pain of death; others you barbarously scourged; others you have imprisoned and seized upon their estates. And at this very present you are rending towns in pieces, ruining the people with innumerable charges, which make them decline your ministry, and fly for refuge to the Church of England, and others to dissenters of all denominations, and you, like wolves, pursue; and whenever you find them within your reach, you seize upon their estates. And all this is done to make room for your pretended ministers to live in idleness, pride, and fulness of bread. Shall we countenance such ministers for Christ's ministers? Nay, verily. These are not the marks of Christ's ministry; but are a papal spot that is abhorred by all pious protestants. And since you wrote this letter the constable of Attleborough* has been taking away the estates of our dear friends and pious dissen-

---

* Only nine miles from Providence

ters to maintain the minister. The like hath been done in the town of Mendon.* Is this the way of peace? Is this the fruit of your love? Why do you hug the sin of Eli's sons and walk in the steps of the false prophets, biting with your teeth, and crying peace? but no longer than they put into your mouth but you prepare war against them. Christ bids us beware of such as come to us in sheep's clothing, but inwardly are ravening wolves ; and your clothing is so scanty that all may see your shame, and see that your teaching is like Gideon's, who taught the men of Succoth with the *briers and thorns of the wilderness.* In the next place : You freely confess that we entertained you kindly at all times. We hope we are all so taught of God *to love our enemies, and to do good to them that hate us, and pray for them who despitefully treat us.* And since you admire the love and peace we do enjoy, we pray you to use the same methods and write after our copy. And for the future never let us hear of your pillaging conscientious dissenters to maintain your own ministers. O, let not this sin be your everlasting ruin. Further. You desire that all former injuries, done by you to us, may be buried in oblivion. We say, Far be it from us to avenge ourselves, or to deal to you as you have dealt to us, but rather say with our Lord, *Father, forgive them, for they know not what they do!* But if you mean that we should not speak of former actions done hurtfully to any man's person, we say, God never called for that nor suffered to be so done ; as witness Cain, Joab and Judas, which are upon record to deter other men from doing the like. Lastly. You desire of us to improve our interest in Christ Jesus for you at the throne of grace. Far be it from us to deny you this, for we are commanded to pray for all men. And we count it our duty to pray for you, that God will open your eyes and cause you to see how far you have erred from the way of peace ; and that God will give you godly sorrow for the same, and such repentance as is never to be repented of; and that you may find mercy and favour of our Lord Jesus Christ at his appearing. And so hoping, as you tender the everlasting welfare of your souls and the good of your people, you will embrace our advice; and not suffer passion so to rule as to cause you to hate reproof, lest you draw down vengeance on yourselves and on the land. We, your friends of the town of Providence, bid you farewell. Subscribed for, and in their behalf, by your ancient friend and servant for Jesu's sake,

" JONATHAN SPREAGUE.

Feb. 23, 1722.

"If it be thought," says Morgan Edwards, "that there is too much tartness and resentment in this letter, they will be readily excused by them, who consider, that the despoiling of goods, imprisonments, scourgings, excommunications and banishments, the slandering of this colony at home and abroad, and attempts to ruin it were yet fresh in the knowledge of the people ; and especially,

* About twenty miles from this town.

that the Massachusetts people were at the time, doing those very things to the brethren in the neighbourhood, which they desire the men of Providence to forget. This was such a piece of uncommon effrontery and insult, as must have raised a mood in the man of Uz. Yet be it further observed, that the people of Providence do not forbid the Presbyterian ministers to come among them, nor threaten them if they should come, but in express terms execrate the thought of *dealing to them as they had dealt to Baptists.*

An anonymous letter in answer to this, was published in Boston a few months after, in which it was insinuated that all these complaints about persecution were groundless, and that those who made them did it in consequence of their being buffetted for their faults. This letter was answered by Mr. Sprague in 1723, at the close of which he inquires, " But why do you strive to persuade the rising generation, that you never persecuted nor hurt the Baptists? Did you not barbarously scourge Mr. Obadiah Holmes, and imprison John Hazel of Rehoboth, who died and came not home? And did you not barbarously scourge Mr. Baker in Cambridge, the chief mate of a London ship? Where also you imprisoned Mr. Thomas Gould, John Russell, Benjamin Sweetser, and many others, and fined them fifty pounds a man. And did you not take away a part of the said Sweetser's land, to pay his fine, and conveyed it to Solomon Phipps, the Deputy Governor Danforth's son-in-law, who after by the hand of God ran distracted, dying suddenly, saying he was bewitched? And did you not nail up the Baptist meeting-house doors, and fine Mr. John Miles, Mr. James Brown, and Mr. Nicholas Tanner?—Surely, I can fill sheets of paper with the sufferings of the Baptists, as well as others, within your precincts; but what I have mentioned shall suffice for the present." Mr. Sprague preached for many years to a small society of Baptists in that, which is now the east part of Smithfield; and died in January, 1741, aged 93. Mr. Comer knew him, and speaks of him as a very judicious and pious man.*

The custom of making chargeless tenders of the gospel to the inhabitants of this benighted realm has been contin-

* Backus, vol. ii. p. 103, 105.—Edwards' M. S. Hist. of Rhode-Island, p. 15—32.

ued to the present time. And now the evangelizing Pedobaptists of Connecticut and Massachusetts are almost constantly sending missionaries with freights of sermons well arranged in black and white to illuminate this heathenish land of dippers; and many wish that more good may follow their labours than has hitherto done. They pass unmolested, the Baptists frequently invite them to preach in their pulpits,* and those, who do not deal out too freely their canting censures are listened to with attention, and they find it convenient to receive the missionary reward for labouring in ancient settlements within a short distance of their homes. Some of these missionaries are doubtless pious, worthy men, but the Rhode-Islanders are not without suspicions that their employers have other ends in view in sending them hither, besides the salvation of souls. Their prejudices, however, whether right or wrong, are strong and unyielding, and all attempts to convert them to Pedobaptism or Law-Religion will be unavailing.

We shall now give a brief account of some of the Baptist churches which have arisen in this State, and begin with

The First Church in Providence.—This church, which is the oldest of the Baptist denomination in America, according to Governor Winthrop, was planted in the year 1639. Its first members were twelve in number, viz. Roger Williams, Ezekiel Holliman, William Arnold, William Harris, Stuckley Westcot, John Green, Richard Waterman, Thomas James, Robert Cole, William Carpenter, Francis Weston, and Thomas Olney. Roger Williams being the chief instrument of this work of God, and also in settling this colony, we shall here give a connected view of his origin, character, banishment, &c. Although many things have already been said of this distinguished man, yet we have purposely omitted the following sketches, that they might stand in connexion with the church which he founded; they are found in its records, from which they are here transcribed.

" Mr. Williams was a native of Wales, born in the year 1598, and had a liberal education, under the patronage of Sir Edward Coke. The occasion of Mr. Williams' re-

* A Reverend Doctor of Massachusetts, a few years since, was invited to preach in the Baptist pulpit at Providence, but when the same favour a short time after was asked of him, it was denied.

ceiving the favour of that distinguished lawyer was very singular. Sir Edward, one day, at church, observing a youth taking notes from the sermon, beckoned and received him into his pew. He obtained a sight of the lad's minutes; which were exceedingly judicious, being a collection of the most striking sentiments delivered by the preacher. This, with Mr. Williams' great modesty, so engaged Sir Edward in his favour, as to induce him to solicit Mr. Williams's parents to let him have the care of their son; which was readily granted. Mr. Williams soon entered on the study of the law, and received all possible assistance from his generous patron; but finding this employment not altogether agreeable to his taste, after pursuing it some time, he turned his attention to divinity, and made such proficiency therein, as encouraged Sir Edward to obtain him episcopal orders. His preaching was highly esteemed, and his private character revered. By embracing the sentiments of the Puritans, he was greatly exposed to suffering, and at last was thereby compelled to leave his native country. He embarked for America, on February 5, 1631, being then in the 32d year of his age. On his arrival, he was called by the church at Salem to join in the ministry with Mr. Skelton; but the Governor and Council not being satisfied with it, the appointment was suspended. This was a means of his being called by the church at Plymouth, where he preached two or three years, and was held in high estimation by Governor Bradford and the people. The former was pleased to give this testimony of Mr. Williams: " He was a man, godly and zealous, having many precious parts. His preaching was well approved, for the benefit of which I still bless God, and am thankful for his sharpest admonitions, so far as they agreed with truth." Mr. Skelton, of Salem, now growing old, a second application was made to Mr. Williams; but many of his Plymouth friends were against his removal. One Mr. Brewster at length prevailed with the church to dismiss him; saying, " If he stayed, he would run the same course of rigid separation and anabaptism which one Smith of Amsterdam had done." He accordingly settled in Salem, and many of the church at Plymouth followed him. The Court again wrote to prevent his settlement, but could not prevail. Morton and Hubbard inform us, " In one year's time, Mr. Williams filled that place with principles of rigid separation, and tending to anabaptism." His favourite topic, *liberty of conscience*, a subject he well understood, gave offence to a few of the leading part of the congregation ; but this would have been borne with, had he not further maintained that civil magistrates, *as such*, have no power in the church, and that christians, *as such*, are subject to no laws or control, but those of King Jesus." This so greatly enraged the magistrates, that they excommunicated and banished him. The town was again enraged at the conduct of the magistrates, and several of the inhabitants followed their minister. This was done in the winter of 1636. When they were out of the Massachusetts jurisdiction, they pitched in a place now called Rehoboth ; but the men of Plymouth hearing thereof, sent to inform them that they were settled on lands within their territories. Now they had no refuge, but must venture among savages ; and it is said, that Mr. Williams and his friend Olney, and Thomas Angel, an hired servant, came over the river in a canoe, and were saluted by the Indian word that signifies, *What cheer?* They then came round Fox Point, until they met with a pleasant spring, which runs to this day, and is nearly opposite the Episcopal Church. Being settled in this place, which, from the kindness of God to them, they called PROVIDENCE, Mr. Williams and those with him, considered the importance of Gospel Union, and were desirous of forming themselves into a church, but met with a considerable obstruction ; they were convinced of the nature and design of believer's baptism by immersion ; but, from a variety of circumstances, had hitherto been prevented from submission. To obtain a suitable administrator was a matter of consequence : at length, the candidates for communion nominated and appointed Mr. Ezekiel Holliman, a man of gifts and piety, to baptize Mr. Williams ; and who, in return, baptized Mr. Holliman and the other ten. This church was soon joined by twelve other persons, who came to this new settlement, and abode in harmony and peace. Mr. Holliman was chosen assistant to Mr. Williams. This Church, according to Chandler, held particular redemption ; but soon after deviated to general redemption. Laying-on-of-hands was held in a lax manner, so that some persons were received without it. And such, says Governor Jenks, was the opinion of the Baptists throughout this colony. Psalmody was first used and afterwards laid aside. These alterations took place about sixteen years after their settlement. The church at first met for worship in a grove, unless in wet and stormy weather, when they assembled in private houses. Mr. Williams held his pastoral office about four years, and then resigned the same to Mr. Brown, and Mr. Wickendon, and went to England to solicit the first charter.* After Mr. Williams' return, he preached among the Indians, whose forefathers were gathered by him. He wrote an account of the Indians, which the then Lords of Trade highly commended ; also a defence of the doctrines controverted by the Quakers, and another piece, called the Bloody Tenet, with some other pieces. He died in the year 1682, aged 84, and was buried under arms in his own lot ; now supposed to be not far from the new house lately built by Mr. Dorr on Benefit-Street.† Mr. Williams's wife's name was Elizabeth, by whom he had children, viz. Mary, Freeborn, Providence, Mercy, Daniel, and Joseph. The third died without issue, aged 48 years. The others married into the Rhodes, Olney, Waterman, Windsor, and Sayles families ; whose descendants, according to Governor Hopkins, had in 1770 been traced to the number of two thousand.

" Mr. Williams' character, given by many, as a man, a scholar, and a christian, was truly respectable. He appears, says Mr. Callender, in his Century Sermon, page 17, by the whole tenour of his life, to have been one of the most disinterested men that ever lived, and a most pious and heavenly minded soul. Governor Hutchinson, reflecting on the life of this good man, says, " Instead of shewing any revengeful temper, or resentment, he was continually employed in acts of kindness and benevolence to his enemies." Vol. 1st, page 38. Mr. Callender observes, " the *true grounds* of liberty of conscience were not understood in America, until Mr. Williams and John Clarke publickly avowed, *that Christ alone*

---

* Some accounts state his ministry in the church to have been but a few months.

† His grave is not certainly known, but tradition makes it to be near some trees to the west of this street.

is king in his own kingdom, and that *no others* had authority over his subjects, in the affairs of conscience and eternal salvation." Governor Hopkins said, "Roger Williams justly claimed the honour of being the first legislator in the world, that fully and effectually provided for, and established a free, full, and absolute liberty of conscience." He not only founded a State, but, by his interest with the Narraganset Indians, broke the grand confederacy against the English, and so became the saviour of all the other colonies.

"Rev. Chad Brown, who succeeded Mr. Williams in the charge of this church, came to Providence the latter end of the year 1636, by reason of the persecution in Massachusetts. He was ordained in the year 1642. Mr. Brown was one of the town proprietors, and the fourteenth in order. He supported a good character, and was prosperous in his ministry.

"Rev. Mr. Wickendon, who was colleague with Mr. Brown, came from Salem to Providence in 1639, and was ordained by Mr. Brown. He died, February 23, 1669, after having removed to a place called Solitary Hill. Mr. Wickendon preached for some time in the city of New-York, and as a reward for his labour was imprisoned four months.

"Rev. Gregory Dexter was next in office. He was born in London, and followed the stationary business with a Mr. Coleman.* It is said, he fled from his native country for printing a piece, which was offensive to the then reigning powers. He came to Providence in 1643, and was the same year received into the church, being both a Baptist and a preacher before his arrival. He took the care of this church on Mr. Wickendon's removal to Solitary Hill. He was the first who taught the art of printing in Boston, in New-England. He was never observed to laugh, and seldom to smile. So earnest was he in the ministry, that he could hardly forbear preaching when he came into a house, or met a number of persons in the street. His sentiments were those of the Particular Baptists. He died in the 91st year of his age.

* This Coleman became the subject of a Farce called *The Cutter of Coleman Street*. *Edwards.*

"Rev. Thomas Olney succeeded to the pastoral office. He was born at Hertford, in England, about the year 1631, and came to Providence in 1654; but when baptized or ordained is not known. He was the chief who made a division about laying-on-of-hands. He and others withdrew and formed a separate church, but it continued only a short time. He died June 11, 1722, and was buried in his own field.

"Rev. Pardon Tillinghast was next in office. He was born at Seven-cliffe, near Beachy-Head in Old-England, about the year 1622. He came to Providence by way of Connecticut, in the year 1645, and was of the Particular Baptist denomination, and remarkable for his piety and his plain dress. At his own expense he built the first meeting house, about the year 1700, on a spot of ground towards the north end of the town; having the main street for the front, and the river to the back. A larger house was erected in its place in the year 1718. He was buried in his own lot, towards the south end of the town; and which is still continued as the burial place of the family.

"Rev. Ebenezer Jenckes succeeded Mr. Tillinghast in office. He was born in Pawtucket, in the township of Providence, 1669, and ordained pastor in 1719; which office he held till his death, Aug. 14, 1726. He was a man of parts and real piety. He refused every publick office, but the surveyorship of the propriety of Providence. He was buried in the family burial ground in Pawtucket.

"Rev. James Brown, grandson to the Rev. Chad Brown, by his eldest son, born at Providence, 1666, was next ordained to the pastoral office in this church, and continued therein till his death, October 28, 1732. He was an example of piety and meekness, worthy of admiration. He was buried in his own lot at the north end of the town, and a stone was erected to his memory.

"Rev. Samuel Windsor succeeded Mr. James Brown. He was born in the township of Providence, 1677, and ordained, 1733. He continued the care of this church, until November 17, 1758, when he died. He was esteemed a worthy man, and had considerable success in his ministry.

"Rev. Thomas Burlingham was in union with Mr. Windsor. He was born at Cranston, May 29, 1688, and was ordained at the same time with Mr. Windsor, but in a measure resigned his care of the church, a considerable time before his death in order to preach to a new church at Cranston. He died January 7, 1740.

"Rev. Samuel Windsor, son to the aforenamed Samuel Windsor, was next in office. He was born, November 1, 1722, in the township of Providence, and ordained June 21, 1759. He continued his office with ease and some success, till towards the year 1770, when he made repeated complaints to the church, that the duty of his office was too heavy for him, considering the remote situation of his dwelling from town. He constantly urged the church to provide help in the ministry, as he was not able to serve them any longer in that capacity, without doing injury to his family, which they could not desire.

"Divine Providence had so ordered, that the Rev. James Manning, President of the Rhode-Island College, was likely to remove from Warren, to settle with the college in the town; and which was esteemed favourable to the wishes of Mr. Windsor and the church. However, at this juncture, Mr. John Sutton,* minister, on his way from Nova-Scotia to the Jerseys, arrived at Newport; when Mr. Windsor and the church invited him to preach as *assistant* for six months; which he did to good acceptance, and then pursued his journey. The attention of the church and Mr. Windsor, was now directed to Mr. Manning; and at a church meeting held the beginning of May, 1770, Daniel Jenckes, Esq. chief judge of the inferior court, and Solomon Drown, Esq. were chosen to wait on Mr. Manning at his arrival, and, in the name of the church and congregation, to invite him to preach at the meeting-house. Mr. Manning accepted the invitation, and delivered a sermon. It being communion-day, Mr. Windsor invited Mr. Manning to partake with them, which the President cordially accepted. After this, several members were dissatisfied at Mr. Manning's partaking of the Lord's Supper with them; but at a church meeting appointed for the purpose, Mr. Manning was admitted to communion by vote of the church. Notwithstanding this, some of the members remained dissatisfied, at the privilege of transient communion being allowed Mr. Manning; whereupon another meeting was called previous to the

---

* Now in Kentucky, ànd is one of those who are known by the name of Emancipators.

next communion-day, in order to reconcile the difficulty. At said meeting Mr. Manning was confirmed in his privilege by a much larger majority. At the next church meeting, Mr. Windsor appeared with an unusual number of members from the country, and moved to have Mr. Manning displaced, but to no purpose. The ostensible reason of Mr. Windsor and of those with him for objecting against President Manning was, that he did not make imposition of hands a bar to communion, though he himself received it, and administered it to those who desired it. Mr. Windsor and the church knew Mr. Manning's sentiments and practice for more than six years at Warren; those, therefore, who were well informed, attributed the opposition to the President's holding to singing in public worship; which was highly disgustful to Mr. Windsor. The difficulty increasing, it was resolved to refer the business to the next association at Swansy. But when the case was presented, the association, after a full hearing on both sides, agreed that they had no right to determine, and that the church must act for themselves. The next church meeting, which was in October, was uncommonly full. All matters relative to the President were fully debated, and by a much greater majority were determined in his favour. It was then agreed all should sit down at the Lord's table the next Sabbath, which was accordingly done. But at the subsequent communion season, Mr. Windsor declined administering the ordinance; assigning for a reason, that a number of the brethren were dissatisfied. April 18, 1771, being church meeting, Mr. Windsor appeared and produced a paper, signed by a number of members living out of town, dated, Johnston, February 27, 1771, in which they say,

" Brethren and sisters,—We must in conscience withdraw ourselves from all those who do not hold strictly to the six principles of the doctrine of Christ, as laid down in Hebrews vi. 1, 2."

" At a church meeting held May 30, 1771, Mr. Samuel Windsor made a second declaration, that he withdrew from the church at Providence, and that he should break bread in Johnston, (an adjacent town) which he accordingly did the first Lord's day in June, and continued so to do.

A Letter from Elders Job and Russel Mason.

" The church remaining in Providence, applied to Rev. Gardner Thurston, of Newport, for advice. In consequence of advice received, it was resolved to apply to Rev. Job and Russel Mason, of Swansy, to come and administer the Lord's supper. Accordingly, a letter was sent signed by Daniel Jenckes, Esq. Deacon, Ephraim Wheaton, and others, bearing date, June 10, 1771. To this letter the following answer was received :

Swansy, June 28, 1771.

" To the Brethren and Sisters in the town of Providence, not long since under the care of Elder Samuel Windsor, but now forsaken by him, we send greeting, wishing all grace, mercy and peace may abound toward you all, through our Lord and Saviour Jesus Christ. Whereas you have sent a request for one of us to break bread among you, we laid your request before our church meeting, and there being but few members present, and we, not being able to know what an event of such a proceeding might be at this time, think it not expedient for us to come and break bread with you. And whereas you have received Mr. Manning into your fellowship, and called him to the work of preaching, (he being ordained) we know not but by the same rule he may administer the Lord's supper. But whether it will be most expedient for you to omit the administration of the Lord's supper, considering the present circumstances of the case, until the association, we must leave you to judge. No more at present, but desiring you would seek God for wisdom to direct you in this affair; hoping you will have the glory of God, the credit of our holy religion, and the comfort of his children at heart, in all your proceedings. Farewell.

JOB MASON,
RUSSEL MASON, } *Elders.*

" In consequence of the above advice, the church appointed a meeting to consider the propriety of calling President Manning to administer ordinances to the church; whereupon the following resolution was formed :

" At a meeting of the members of the Old Baptist Church Meeting in Providence, in church-meeting assembled this 31st day of July, 1771, Daniel Jenckes, Esq. Moderator. Whereas, Elder Samuel Windsor, now of Johnston, has withdrawn himself, and a considerable number of members of this church, from their communion with us who live in town ; and we being destitute of a minister to administer the ordinances amongst us, have met together, in order to choose and appoint a suitable person for that purpose. Upon due consideration, the members present choose and appoint Elder James Manning to preach and administer the communion, according to our former usage."

"To the above resolve Mr. Manning returned the following answer:

"As the church is destitute of an administrator, and think the cause of religion suffers through the neglect of the ordinances of God's house: I consent to undertake to administer *pro tempore;* that is, until there may be a more full disquisition of this matter, or time to seek other help; at least until time may prove whether it will be consistent with my other engagements, and for the general interest of religion."

"This answer being accepted, the Rev. James Manning was appointed pastor of this church, *pro tempore.*

"At the general meeting or association, held September 20, 1771, a question was put "Whether those members who withdrew with Mr. Windsor, or those in Providence, be considered the Old Church?" Whereupon the brethren, meeting in Providence, were acknowledged the Old Church; but it was agreed that the association would hold communion with both churches so long as they walked agreeably to the gospel.

"Mr. Manning preached with general acceptance to an increasing congregation for some time, without any visible success in the conversion of sinners. In the latter end of the year 1774, the sudden death of one Mr. Biggilo, a young man, who was accidentally shot by his intimate companion, playing with a gun, made a very uncommon impression on the minds of many. In December of the same year, it pleased the Lord to make his power known to the hearts of Tamar Clemans and Venus Arnold, two black women, who were soon added to the church by baptism, and who maintained the dignity of their profession. The sacred flame of the gospel began to spread; and in the course of fifteen months, one hundred and four persons confessed the power of the Spirit of Christ, in the conversion of their souls, and entered the gates of Zion with joy. During this time a peculiar solemnity pervaded the whole congregation and town. There was a general attendance on the worship of God; and meetings for conference and prayer were held from house to house to great advantage.

The new Meeting-House built.

The meeting-house was not sufficient to contain the people, who pressed to hear the word; therefore, those whose hearts the Lord opened, were ready to join their hands to build a more convenient place for the worship of God.

" A committee was now appointed to petition the general assembly of the State at their next session to obtain an act, empowering them to sell the meeting-house and ground, and lay out the money arising from the sale thereof, in purchasing and preparing another lot, and building a house for the Baptist church and society. The petition was granted, and the meeting house and lot were sold at publick vendue to John Brown, Esq. for the sum of four hundred and twenty pounds, L. M. A generous subscription was soon obtained, and a lot of ground of large dimensions situated in the centre of the town, was purchased of Mr. William Russel, and Mr. Amaziah Waterman.

" The draught of the new meeting-house was made by Joseph Brown, Esq. a member of this church, and Mr. Sumner, who also superintended the building. The floor was laid 80 feet square. It contains 126 square pews on the ground floor. A large gallery on the south, west, and north, and one other above on the west, for the use of the blacks. The roof and galleries are supported by twelve fluted pillars of the Doric order. The ceiling in the body is a continued arch, and over the galleries it is intersected; the adjustment of which, and the largeness of the building, render it extremely difficult for most who attempt to preach in it. At the east end is a very elegant, large Venitian window, before which the pulpit stands. At the west end is a steeple of the height of 196 feet, supposed to be the best workmanship of the kind of any in America, it was furnished with a good clock and bell, both made in London. The weight of the bell was 2515 lb. and upon it was the following motto :

" For freedom of conscience, the town was first planted ;
Persuasion, not force, was us'd by the people ;
This church is the eldest and has not recanted,
Enjoying and granting bell, temple, and steeple."

" This bell was split by ringing in the year 1787, and afterwards recast by Jesse Goodyear at Hope Furnace; the weight thereof is 2387 lb. The inscription of it is,

"This Church was founded, A. D. 1639, the first in the State, and the oldest of the Baptists in America." The ground and building amounted to about seven thousand pounds, lawful money, that is, over 23,000 dollars. It was opened for publick worship, May 28, 1775, when the President, afterwards Doctor Manning, preached the first sermon from Genesis xxviii. 17. *This is none other but the house of God, and this is the gate of heaven.*

"At this time, a number of the principal members of the church and congregation, sincerely wishing the utmost prosperity to attend the interest of Christ among them, proposed to form themselves into a body politick, to be known by the name of "The charitable Baptist society, in the town of Providence, in the colony of Rhode-Island, and Providence Plantation, in New England." The design of this society was to raise a fund towards the support of the ministers of the church, educate youth, and other laudable purposes. These members petitioned the General Assembly, at their next session, holden at Newport, for a charter, which was readily granted, on the first Wednesday in May, 1774. This society is still continued.

"The church and congregation being happily settled in the new meeting house, and promising themselves great pleasure therein, were soon disturbed by the alarm of war. Many of the young members were taken away to join the army. Families removed for safety to the country; and those who were left behind, were exposed to the fears common to such afflictive seasons. Through divine goodness, the stated worship was continued, and meetings of business regularly preserved. When it pleased the Lord to ordain peace, and to return many of those brethren, who had been separated by publick calamities, it was thought proper to hold two especial meetings; one at Providence and the other at Pawtucket, four miles distant, where a number of the members resided. The design of these meetings was to engage each other to walk in the fear of God, and enjoy the happy privilege of christian communion, which proved of real advantage. However, the church was constrained to experience the sad consequences of their scattered state. Gifts and graces were greatly injured, and that bloom of profession, which ap-

Stephen Gano becomes Pastor of this Church. 485

peared at the time of the general revival unhappily faded away.

" Dr. Manning continued his ministry to good satisfaction, and with success; but his constant employ in the college, not only prevented him from attending the affairs of the church, and from necessary visits, but unavoidably permitted its members to lie in a very unpleasant situation. The Doctor being sensible of these things, repeatedly entreated the church to look out for a minister to take the charge of them; and at length in a most honourable way resigned his pastoral office. He died in a fit of the apoplexy, universally regretted, July 29, 1791, leaving behind an amiable widow, who is yet living in Providence."

Thus far the history of this church has been transcribed from its records, which were set in order in 1775, by Rev. John Stanford, now of New-York, who was then preaching with them. This account, up to Dr. Manning's beginning in Providence, is found almost in the same form as here stated in Morgan Edward's MS. History, &c. prepared in 1771. It was published in Rippon's Register in 1802, and as it is well written, I have chosen to copy it without scarce any alteration.

After Dr. Manning's death, Mr. now Dr. Maxcy, President of Columbia College, South-Carolina, served this church about two years.

Next to him was Mr. Stephen Gano, who is still with them. He is a son of the late John Gano whose history will be related in the biographical department; was born in the city of New-York, Dec. 25, 1762; was bred to physic; was a surgeon in the American army in the latter part of the revolutionary war, and was settled in his medical profession at Orangetown, New-York, before his attention was called to the things of religion. At the age of 23 he commenced his ministry in the First Church in his native city, where he was ordained, May, 1786. From this period he laboured successively at Hudson, Hillsdale, and Nine Partners, until 1792, when, by the call of this ancient church, he removed among them and became their pastor. During the twenty-one years of his pastoral labours here, some very precious and extensive revivals have been experienced, and by him about five hundred persons have been baptized, who have joined this church, besides many others in different parts of the surrounding country.

The branches of this church have been considerably numerous, and it seems probable that from it originated either directly or indirectly most of the churches which have, at different times, arisen in the northern part of the State. Mr. Callender informs us that "this church shot out into divers branches, as the members increased, and the distance of their habitations made it inconvenient to attend the publick worship in the town ; several meetings were thereupon fixed at different places for their ease and accommodation ; and about this time (1730) the large township of Providence became divided into four towns ; their *chapels of ease* began to be considered as distinct churches, though all are yet (1738) in a union of councils and interests."*

The towns taken from Providence were Smithfield, Gloucester, and Scituate ; in each of which large and flourishing churches afterwards arose.

In 1743, a church was formed at Greenwich, partly of members from this body.

The church in Cranston, still nearer home, was formed mostly of members from Providence in 1764. This church was first founded on Calvinistic principles, which, I conclude, did not long prevail among them.

In 1771, a church arose at Johnston, only three miles distant, in consequence of Mr. Windsor's separation, which has already been mentioned.

We must from that time pass on to 1805, in which year were formed from this ancient body and in union with it, the second church in Providence, and the one at Pawtucket. The year after was formed the church at Pawtuxet. Considerably over a hundred members were dismissed to form these three churches, and yet it being a time of revival, the old church increased so fast, that it was larger after they were all formed than before.

This church has experienced some changes as to its doctrinal sentiments : it was, as we have seen, first founded on the Particular or Calvinistic plan ; in process of time they became what our English brethren would call General Baptists, and so continued for the most part more

* Century Sermon, p. 61. 62.

than a hundred years. From the commencement of Dr. Manning's ministry, they have been verging back to their first principles, and now very little of the Arminian leaven is found among them. From first to last the Bible, without comment, has been their Confession of Faith.

The doctrine of Laying-on-of-hands was, at the beginning of this church, held in a lax manner; but it became afterwards a term of communion, and continued so until after Dr. Manning came among them; he prevailed with the church to admit to *occasional* communion those brethren, who were not convinced of the duty of coming under hands; but very few such were received as *members* till after his death. But on August 4, 1791, the church had a full meeting, when this point was distinctly considered, and a clear vote was gained to admit members who did not hold that doctrine. But notwithstanding this vote, the laying-on-of-hands, not as an ordinance, but as a form of receiving new members, was generally practised until 1808, when the pastor of the church, who had been educated in the belief of this ceremony, as his father was an advocate for it, and who had hitherto practised it, not, however, without troublesome scruples of its propriety, found his mind brought to a stand on the subject, and after duly weighing the matter, informed the church, that he could no longer continue the practice, and unless they could excuse him, he must ask a dismission from his pastoral care. After a full discussion of the subject, the church, with but one dissenting voice, voted not to dismiss him, and laying-on-of-hands of course fell into neglect. Some few worthy members were desirous of retaining both their pastor and this ancient ceremony, but not being disposed to act against the voice of the church, no division and but little controversy ensued.

Before we close this sketch, it is proper we should take notice of some things pertaining to this ancient and wealthy congregation, which have not yet been mentioned. The lot, on which their meeting-house stands, is bounded on four streets, and is enclosed with a handsome and costly picket fence. Its dimensions are 150 feet on Main-street, west; 300 feet on Thomas-street, north; 170 feet on Benefit-street, east; and 188 on President-street, south. This spacious lot would occupy an entire square, were it not for two small lots on which are buildings at its south-west corner. This lot is near the centre of the town, and would probably sell for at least thirty thousand dollars. The meeting house, forty years ago, cost not far from twenty thousand dollars; it could not probably be built now under double that sum. Under the floor at the west end is a vestry, which will contain about five hundred persons.

The appendages of this establishment, which have not been mentioned, are, 1st. A large elegant glass chandelier, which cost about four hundred dollars, and was presented by Mrs. Ives, sister of Nicholas Brown, Esq. This lady, about the time she made this present, expended six hundred dollars in painting the inside of the meeting-house. 2d. A parsonage house, built in 1792, which, with the lot, cost about three thousand dollars; two thousand of which were given by the above mentioned Mr. Brown. 3d. Funds at interest, which produce about five hundred dollars a year. This fund was raised by subscription, and a considerable portion of it came from the Brown family. 4th. A legacy of about three hundred dollars, intrusted particularly with the church, for the benefit of the poor coloured members. This, like the widow's mite, seems to be more than all the rest, as it was bequeathed by a black sister lately deceased, whose name was Patience Borden, commonly called Patience Sterry.

Second Church in Providence.—This church arose, as we have already stated, in 1805. It was formed in perfect agreement with the first, and received from it the right hand of fellowship as a sister community. Its seat is some distance from it on the west side of the river. Mr. Joseph Cornell, whose name has frequently occurred in the preceding narratives, became its pastor at the time of its constitution, and continued in that office about seven years. His membership is still with them, but he has been travelling as a missionary most of the time for a year or two past. They have had preaching constantly since his resignation; but the pastoral office is yet vacant. Mr. Cornell, previous to the founding of this church, had preached a short time with the congregation of the late Mr. Joseph Snow, who closed his long and successful ministry in 1803, when he was over 80 years of age. Mr. Snow was one of the zealous New-Lights of Whitefield's time, was ordained at Providence in 1747, and was, in early life, a companion in labours with Mr. Backus, and other successful itinerants of those times. He was a Pedobaptist in principle, but saw fit to administer baptism in any way his disciples chose, and as the Providence people are much inclined to the ancient mode, a considerable number of them were immersed.* Mr. Snow was well esteemed by the Baptists in Providence and elsewhere. His funeral sermon was preached by Dr. Gano from 2 Tim. iv. 7, 8, *I have fought a good fight, I have finished my course, I have kept the faith, &c.*

The church under consideration, by their own exertions, by the assistance of the old church and congregation, and others, built them a convenient house of worship 60 feet by 40. It was completely finished in less than two months after the foundation was begun.

Pawtucket Church.—Pawtucket is four miles north-east of Providence, on the road to Boston. For a hundred and thirty or forty years past, there have at all times resided in this place and its vicinity, a number of the members of the church in Providence. Some of the most distinguished of whom were Ebenezer Jenks, for a number of years pastor of that body, Governor Joseph Jenks, Judge William Jenks, and others. The pastors of Providence used frequently to preach here; but no provision was made for a stated meeting, until about 1793. At that time a number of the inhabitants formed themselves into a Baptist Society, obtained an act of incorporation, built them a house for worship, raised a fund of three thousand dollars for the support of preaching, and obtained supplies from different preachers, until the autumn of 1804, when the Author began to labour among them. A few months after a revival commenced, and in August, 1805, the church was formed of members dismissed for the purpose, from the mother church at Providence. The meeting house stands on a lot of half an acre, the gift of Nicholas Brown, Esq. of Providence; it was at first 45 feet by 36, but has been enlarged this summer, (1813) to 60 feet by 45.

---

* Towards the close of Mr. Snow's ministry, his church was divided; the larger part has for its minister, Mr. James Wilson, who also immerses those, who prefer that mode. The part to which Mr. Cornell preached, is under the care of Mr. Thomas Williams, from Connecticut, who chooses not to go into the water.

Pawtuxet is five miles below Providence, on the western shore of the Narraganset Bay. The church here was formed the year after that at Pawtucket, and is now under the care of a young man by the name of Bela Jacobs. The origin of this church was similar to the one at Pawtucket. Some of the Providence members had long resided in the place, and the inhabitants had, a number of years before the church was established, formed an incorporated Baptist Society, and built them a place of worship, which has since been enlarged.

We have thus given a general view of the origin, progress, appendages, and branches of the oldest Baptist church in America. The number of her ministerial sons cannot be ascertained with any degree of precision; since 1790, she hath given her approbation to the twelve following, whose stations we shall add to their names. Dr. Jonathan Maxcy, President of the college at Columbia, South-Carolina; Dr. Asa Messer, President of Brown University; David Leonard, ———, John M. Roberts, Statesbury, South-Carolina; Abisha Sampson, Harvard, Massachusetts; Ferdinand Ellis, Marblehead, do. Henry Grew, Hartford, Connecticut; Jonathan Going, Cavendish, Vermont; James Barnaby, Harwich, Massachusetts; Hervey Jenks, Hudson, New-York; George Angel, Woodstock, Connecticut; Nicholas Branch, not yet settled.

"This church," said Governor Hopkins, a Quaker, "hath from its beginning kept itself in repute, and maintained its discipline, so as to avoid scandal or schism to this day." And he further adds, " It hath always been and still is a numerous congregation, and in which I have with pleasure observed very lately sundry descendants from each of the founders of the colony, except Holliman."*

This eulogium, which could not have flowed from sectarian partiality, was pronounced forty-eight years ago. This Baptist congregation is still large and respectable in every point of view; and in it are usually found a greater number of men of wealth, of honourable, professional, and literary characters, than are to be found in any Baptist congregation in America, and their estate of different kinds, cannot be estimated at less than eighty thousand dollars. And the church, after fitting out so many daughters around, consists of four hundred and twenty-five members.

* Providence Gazette for March 16, 1765, article, History of Providence.

Such is the history of a Baptist community, which has ever protested against civil coercion in the affairs of conscience, which has always depended on the voluntary contributions of its patrons for its support, and which has existed an hundred and seventy-four years under the influence of those very principles, which many of the New-England declaimers have represented as heretical, licentious, dangerous, and disorganizing.

Among the families, who have been members and distinguished patrons of this church and society, those of the Browns' and Jenks' deserve particular notice. Others are entitled to respectful mention, but a connected history of them I have not been able to obtain.

From Chad Brown, who became the pastor of this church but three years after it was formed, descended that opulent and liberal train of benefactors, who have contributed so much to its splendour and convenience. One of his sons was, according to tradition, a preacher; but I find no record of him. His grandson James, of whom we have given an account, died the pastor of this church in 1732. Grandsons to him were the four brothers Nicholas, Joseph, John, and Moses, under whose superintendance the College was built, and who were, from the beginning of that institution, among its most distinguished patrons. Their mother was a member of the church, but their father was not.

Joseph Brown, L. L. D. was long a member of this church, was distinguished for his attainments in philosophical researches, and held, till his death, the office of Professor of Experimental Philosophy in the College, of which he was a zealous patron. He died December, 1785. Obadiah Brown, Esq. Mrs. Ward, and the youngest daughter of the pastor of this church, are all who remain of his posterity.

Nicholas Brown, Esq. died in 1791, in the 62d year of his age; his funeral sermon was preached by Dr. Stillman of Boston. "He was, from early life, engaged in the mercantile business, by which he acquired an ample fortune; he was from sentiment a lover of all mankind, especially of the good.—His manners were plain and sincere; and in him the publick lost a good citizen, the College a Mæcenas, and the religious society, to which he belonged, an ornamental and main pillar." He was esteemed by his religious friends a man of piety, although he never so far surmounted his doubts, as to make a publick profession of religion. His only surviving children are Nicholas Brown, Esq. and Mrs. Ives, the wife of Thomas P. Ives, Esq.

John Brown, Esq. was a liberal promoter of the Baptist Society and also of the College, the foundation stone of which was laid by him in 1769. He accumulated a vast estate, and left, it is said, half a million of dollars for his heirs, one of whom married James B. Mason, Esq. grandson of John Mason, one of the pastors of the second church in Swansea.

Moses Brown, Esq. is the only survivor of these brothers; he has been a liberal patron of the College, but has, for many years, belonged to the Society of Quakers or Friends.

The Jenks' family for near a century resided mostly in Pawtucket and its vicinity; but they are now widely scattered in many different States, and not so many eminent men are found among them as formerly. They all descended from the Hon. Joseph Jenks, Esq. who was born in Buckinghamshire, England, 1632. When young, he came to America, tarried awhile at Lynn, in Massachusetts, and then emigrated to Pawtucket and erected the first house, which was built in this place. Here he built a forge, which was burnt down in king Philip's War. Whether he became a member of the church at Providence, I cannot learn, but he is reputed to have been a man of piety, and most of his descendants, who have professed religion, have been found in the Baptist connexion. His four sons, Joseph, Nathaniel, Ebenezer, and William, were eminent in their day; each of them built houses in Pawtucket, which are yet standing, and three of them were worthy members of the Providence church.

Joseph Jenks, who filled many important offices in the colony, who was a number of years an ambassador to the court of St. James on the business of the colony, and who was five years its Governor, was born in 1656, and was an active and ornamental member of the church, whose affairs we have in view. He was solicited to remain longer in the chair of State, but for this sage reason he declined : "I now," said he, "perceive my natural faculties abating—if I should continue longer in office, it is possible I may be insensible of their decay, and may be unwilling to resign my post when I am no longer capable of filling it." He was interred in the family burying ground at Pawtucket, where the following epitaph may be seen on his tomb :

"In memory of the Hon. Joseph Jenckes, Esq. late Governor of the Colony of Rhode-Island, Deceased the 15th day of June, A. D. 1740, in the 84th year of his Age. He was much Honoured and beloved in Life and Lamented in Death : He was a bright Example of Virtue in every Stage of Life : He was a Zealous Christian, a Wise and Prudent Governor : a Kind Husband and a Tender Father : a good Neighbour and a Faithful Friend : Grave, Sober, Pleasant in Behaviour : Beautiful in Person, with a Soul truly Great, Heroic, and Sweetly Tempered."

His wife was Martha Brown, daughter of Elder James Brown of Providence, by whom he had children, Obadiah, Catharine, Nathaniel, Martha, Lydia, John, Mary, Esther, who married into the families of the Blakes, Turpins, Scotts, Andrews, Masons, Harendens, and Bucklins. John studied physick, went to England with his father to perfect himself in his profession, where he died with the small pox. It does not appear whom he married, but he left three children.

Major Nathaniel Jenks was born in 1662, and died in 1723, aged 61.

Of Elder Ebenezer Jenks, one of the pastors of the Providence church, we have already given some account.

Judge William Jenks, the youngest of these four brothers, was a worthy member of the church at Providence, and died 1765, in the 91st year of his age.

Judge Daniel Jenks, a son of Elder Ebenezer, settled in Providence, became a member of the church, accumulated a great estate, and was a generous promoter of the Baptist interest in the town. It is said he expended a thousand dollars towards the College, and the same sum upon the meeting-house. He was born in Pawtucket, October 1701, was forty-eight years a member of the church, was forty years in the General Assembly, and nearly 30 years Chief Justice of Providence County Court. He died July, 1774, in the 73d year of his age. The Hon. Joseph Jenks, a member of the Providence church, who has lately removed to the Narraganset country, is a grandson of this eminent man. One of his daughters was also the mother of the present Nicholas Brown, Esq. and Mrs. Ives. The remaining history of the Jenks' family, which will be somewhat more particular than we usually give, may be found in the note below.*

* The house built by Governor Jenks is now owned by his great-grand-son, George Jenks and Dr. Manchester. The part owned by Dr. Manchester is the oldest: in this the Governor died The other part was built while he resided at Newport by one of his sons. The one built by Elder Ebenezer is now owned by James Mason, Esq. Judge William's house is that near to Samuel Slater's, and is now owned by Friend Moses Brown of Providence. Nathaniel's house is now owned by the widow and heirs of the late Ichabod Jenks. In this house the Pawtucket Church first covenanted together. It is said, that the old part at the east end of it, which is now in tolerable repair, is the very house built by Joseph Jenks, the planter of Pawtucket; that it first stood not far from where Mr. Timothy Green's house now stands, and was removed from that place to its present situation. From Governor Jenks descended the Hon. John Andrew, the Hon. Peleg Arnold, and the wife of James Fenner, Esq. late Governor of Rhode-Island.

From Elder Ebenezer Jenks descended, as we have seen, Judge Daniel Jenks, Ebenezer Jenks, Esq. Mr. Esek Esten, who furnished these accounts of this family, and the widow of the late David L. Barns, Judge of the District of Rhode-Island.

From Judge William descended Jonathan Jenks, one of the members of Providence church, who died at Brookfield, but was brought down and buried at Pawtucket. His sons were Gideon, Judge Jonathan, who died at Winchester, and Nicholas, now of Brookfield, the father of Hervy Jenks, now pastor of the church in the city of Hudson, New-York. Samuel Eddy, Esq. Secretary of State, and one of the Providence Church, is connected by blood to both Judge William Jenks of Pawtucket, and Elder Chad Brown of Providence.

From Nathaniel descended a numerous family, many of whom are in Pawtucket and its vicinity, and many have removed to other parts. The descendants of the late Captain Stephen and Mr. Ichabod Jenks all sprang from Major Nathaniel, the second son of the ancient and Hon. Joseph. Of his posterity also is Nicholas Branch, who has lately been approbated as a preacher by the old Providence church. One of Governor Jenks' grand-children, viz. Joseph, belongs to the Pawtucket church, and a great number of the great-grand-children of him and his three brothers, and some of the fifth generation, belong to the churches and congregations of Pawtucket and Providence.

Thus from the ancient and Honourable Joseph Jenks, who was one of the Senators of the colony, or as they call them Assistants of the Governor, have descended a most numerous posterity, which it is supposed would, counting them in the male and female lines, amount to eight or ten thousand.

Among his grand-children were ten widows of remarkable character: viz. Catharine Turpin, ancestor of a gentleman of that name, now in Charleston, South Carolina. At her house the General Assembly of the colony was held for many years. She died at the age of 88. 2d, Catharine Jenks, widow of Capt. Nathaniel, who died in her 96th year. 3d, Bridget, widow of another Nathaniel, who lived to the age of 89. 4th, Experience, widow of Ebenezer Jenks, Esq. who lived to be more than 90. 5th, Joanna, widow of Judge Daniel Jenks, who died in her 93d year. 6th, Rachel, widow of Cornelius Esten, who lived to be 71. 7th, Mercy, widow of Philip Wheeler, who lived to her 80th year, and died a member of the Swansea church. 8th, Freelove, widow of Jonathan Jenks, who lived also to the age of 80. 9th, Mercy, widow

The next cluster of churches, which demand our attention, are those of

NEWPORT.

First Church.—For the origin of this church we must go back to 1644, when according to tradition it was formed. The constituents were Dr. John Clark and wife, Mark Lukar, Nathaniel West and wife, William Vaughan, Thomas Clark, Joseph Clark, John Peckham, John Thorndon, William and Samuel Weeden.

John Clark, M. D. was the founder of this church and also its first minister. He took the care of them at their settlement, and continued their minister until his death, which happened in 1676, in the 66th year of his age. He had three wives, but left no children. The Clarks now in the State sprang from his brothers Thomas, Joseph, and Carew. Where Mr. Clark was born is not certainly known. In some of his old papers he is styled "John Clark of London, Physician;" but tradition makes him a native of Bedfordshire. Neither can we find where he had his education and studied physick; but we meet with proofs of his acquaintance with the learned languages. In his will he gives to his "dear friend, Richard Bailey, his Hebrew and Greek books; also (to use his own words) my Concordance with a Lexicon to it belonging, written by myself, being the fruit of several years' study." His baptism and ordination are also matters of uncertainty; tradition saith, that he was a preacher before he left Boston, but that he became a Baptist after his settlement on Rhode-Island by means of Roger Williams. The cause of his leaving Boston and the Massachusetts colony has been related in the beginning of this chapter. An account of his imprisonment at Boston may be found under the head of Massachusetts. Soon after his release from that scene of affliction, he was appointed with Roger Williams to go to England on the business of the Rhode-Island col-

of Thomas Comstock; she was a Quaker and lived to the age of 90. 10th, Patience, widow of John Olney, Esq. who died at the age of four score. These ten widows were all first cousins, seven by blood, and three by marriage, were all eminent for piety, and most of them were members of the Providence Church.

Some of the eighth generation from this ancient Joseph, are now settled in the State of Ohio.

ony, where he tarried twelve years, and returned with their second charter in 1663. "By which it appears,". says Morgan Edwards, "that Mr. Clark had a hand with Mr. Williams in establishing the polity of this government, that *he without him, might not be made perfect.*" Mr. Clark's character as a christian was unspotted; "as a divine," says Mr. Callender, "he was among the first, who publickly avowed that Jesus Christ alone is king in his own kingdom."* His sentiments were those of the Particular Baptists. His Narrative of the Sufferings of Obadiah Holmes, &c. printed in London in 1652, is the only piece of writings, which has come down to us.

Successor to him was Obadiah Holmes, who had such a terrible scourging at Boston, for preaching the gospel and baptizing some persons at Lynn, an account of which has been related. He had for his assistant Mr. Joseph Tory, of whom we find no more than that he was one of the three who went to Boston in 1668, to assist the Baptists in that curious dispute, of which we have given an account in the history of Massachusetts.

Mr. Holmes was a native of Preston, Lancashire, England; arrived in America about 1639, and continued a communicant with the Pedobaptists, first at Salem, then at Rehoboth, about eleven years, when he became a Baptist and joined to this church. After he had recovered from his wounds inflicted at Boston, he removed his family from Rehoboth to Newport, where he found an asylum from the rage of his enemies, and in 1652, the year after Mr. Clark set sail for England, was invested with the pastoral office which he held till his death in 1682, aged 76 years. He was buried in his own field, where a tomb is erected to his memory. Mr. Holmes had eight children, and his posterity are spread in different parts of New-England, Long-Island, New-Jersey, Pennsylvania, &c. "and it is supposed," says M. Edwards, "could all that sprang from him in the male and female lines be numbered, they would amount (in 1790) to near 5000. His son Obadiah was long a judge in New-Jersey, and a preacher in the Baptist church at Cohansey. Another of his sons, by the name of John, was a magistrate in Philadelphia, at the time of the Keithian separation, which will be mentioned to-

* Century Sermon, p. 16.

wards the close of the second volume. One of his grandsons was alive in Newport in 1770, in the 96th year of his age.

After Mr. Holmes was Richard Dingly and William Peckham, of whom we can learn but little more than that they were men of good characters and useful in their day, and that the former went to South-Carolina in 1694.*

The fifth pastor of this church was John Comer, A. B. He was born in Boston in 1704, began his education at Cambridge, but finished it at New-Haven. Before he entered college he had hopefully experienced a gracious change; while there, one of his intimate young friends, by the name of Crafts, joined the Baptist church in Boston. Comer admonished him for his departure from the faith, and entreated him to recant; but being prevailed on to read Stennett on baptism, he became convinced of the sentiments he had opposed, joined the same church with his friend Crafts, and by it was approbated to preach in 1725.† From Boston he went to Swansea, where he was invited to settle, but was prevented by an invitation from Newport. Hither he came, and was ordained co-pastor with Mr. Peckham, May, 1726. His ministry in this place was short but successful; by his means singing in publick was introduced, which had not before been practised. The laying-on-of-hands was held in a lax manner, and his attempts to urge it as an indispensable duty, though not as a term of communion, gave offence to two leading members in the church, and was the means of his being dismissed from his office. He afterwards settled in that part of Rehoboth called the Oak Swamp, where he gathered a church in 1732; but falling into a decline, he was removed from the scene of his labours, 1734, in the 30th year of his age. His son John is now a member of the church in Warren in this State, between eighty and ninety years of age. Mr. Comer bid fair to be one of the most eminent ministers of his day; his character was unspotted and his talents respectable and popular; he had conceived the design of writing the history of the American Baptists, and for the purpose of forwarding it travelled as far as Philadelphia, opened a correspondence with persons in the different colonies, and also in England and Ireland.

* Backus, vol. iii. p. 228. † Backus, vol. ii. p. 66, 111.

He was curious in making minutes of remarkable events of every kind ; he also collected many useful facts for his intended history. These minutes, in the few years of his ministry, swelled to two volumes folio of about 60 pages each. They are now owned by his aged son of Warren, and were by him loaned to the Author. These minutes, together with his letters upon historical matters (for he preserved copies of them all) have been of singular advantage to Edwards, Backus, and the writer of this sketch of this promising man, whom a mysterious providence saw fit to cut down almost in the beginning of his course.

The next in office in this church was John Callender, A. M. He was a native of Boston, nephew of Elisha Callender, pastor of the old church in that town, was educated at Cambridge, and was one of the very few, who enjoyed the benefit of Mr. Hollis' donation to that Institution. He became pastor of this flock in 1731, and acted the part of a good shepherd till his death, which happened January 26, 1748. He published, 1st, A Funeral Sermon, occasioned by the death of Rev. Mr. Clap, a Congregational minister of Newport. 2d, A Sermon preached at the ordination of Mr. Condy of Boston. 3d, A Sermon to young people. And 4th, A Sketch of the History of Rhode-Island for a hundred years, usually known by the name of *the Century Sermon,* from which much assistance has been derived in the preceding sketches of this State. Mr. Callender's excellent character was thus drawn by Dr. Moffit in an epitaph which may be seen on his tomb in Newport :

" Confident of awaking, here reposeth
JOHN CALLENDER ;
Of very excellent endowments from nature,
And of an accomplished education,
Improved by application in the wide circle
Of the more polite arts and useful sciences.
From motives of conscience and grace
He dedicated himself to the immediate service
Of GOD,
In which he was distinguished as a shining
And very burning light by a true and faithful
Ministry of seventeen years in the first Baptist
Church of Rhode-Island, where the purity
And evangelical simplicity of his doctrine, confirmed
And embellished by the virtuous and devout tenor

Of his own life,
Endeared him to his flock, and justly conciliated
The esteem, love, and reverence of all the
Wise, worthy, and good.
Much humanity, benevolence and charity
Breathed in his conversation, discourses and writings,
Which were all pertinent, reasonable, and useful.
Regretted by all, lamented by his friends, and
Deeply deplored by a wife and numerous issue,
He died,
In the forty-second year of his age,
January 26, 1748;
Having struggled through the vale of life
In adversity, much sickness, and pain,
With fortitude, dignity, and elevation of soul,
Worthy of the philosopher, christian and divine."

Mr. Callender was succeeded by Edward Upham, A. M. who was born at Malden, near Boston, 1709, was educated at Cambridge, and probably received the benefit of Mr. Hollis's donation. He became a minister of this church in 1748, where he continued until 1771, when he resigned his office and returned to West-Springfield, in Massachusetts, where he was first settled, and where he spent the remainder of his days. Some further account of him may be seen in the history of the West-Springfield church.

Next to him was Erasmus Kelly, a native of Buck's County, Pennsylvania, where he was born in 1748. He was educated at the College in Philadelphia, and began to preach in 1769; two years after, he was called to Newport and was ordained the pastor of this church, which prospered much under his ministry until the troubles of the war obliged him to remove to Warren, where the enemy followed him and burnt the parsonage house in which he lived with Mr. Thompson, together with his goods, November 7, 1778. After this he tarried awhile in Connecticut, and then went back to Pennsylvania. On the return of peace he resumed his charge at Newport, which he continued not a year before he was removed by death in 1784.

Mr. Kelly was succeeded by Benjamin Foster, D. D. afterwards pastor of the first church in New-York. He continued with them but about three years.

In 1790, Mr. Michael Eddy, their present pastor, was settled among them. He was born in Swansea, November 1, 1760, and was ordained in the second church in that town in 1785. Two very considerable revivals have been experienced in this church within ten or twelve years; its present number is 250. Its possessions are 1st, A farm of about 150 acres, which now rents for 600 dollars a year. 2d, A lot of 30 acres, rented for 100 dollars a year. 3d, A lot in the town occupied by the pastor as a garden. This property was bequeathed to the church by Mr. John Clark its founder. In addition to these valuable possessions, they have, for a parsonage house, the mansion of Governor Lyndon, which was bequeathed to them by that honourable member of their Society. The Governor was esteemed a man of piety, although he never joined the church; he died 1778, aged 74. The meeting-house to this church is 40 feet by a little under 60. The lot is 73 feet by 64, and was given by Col. Hezekiah Carpenter, and Governor Lyndon.

Second Church.—This church originated in 1656, when twenty-one persons broke off from the first church, and formed themselves into a separate body. Their names were William Vaughan, Thomas Baker, James Clark, Jeremiah Clark, Daniel Wightman, John Odlin, Jeremiah Weeden, Joseph Card, John Greenman, Henry Clark, Peleg Peckham, James Barker, Stephen Hookey, Timothy Peckham, Joseph Weeden, John Rhodes, James Brown, John Hammet, William Rhodes, Daniel Sabear, and William Greenman.

These seceders objected against the old body, 1st. Her use of psalmody. 2d. Undue restraints upon the liberty of prophesying, as they termed it. 3d. Particular Redemption. 4th. Her holding the laying-on-of-hands as a matter of indifference. This last article is supposed to have been the principal cause of the separation. Mr. Clark was now in England on the business of the colony; had he been with his church the division might have been prevented. But this is one of the many cases where similar divisions have been overruled for good.

The three first pastors of this church were William Vaughan, Thomas Baker, and John Harden. The first died in 1677; the second after ministering here awhile, removed and raised up a church at North-Kingston. The third was a native of England, and died in the pastoral care of this people in 1700.

The fourth in succession was James Clark a nephew of Dr. John. He was ordained pastor of this flock in 1701, by Messrs. Dexter, Tillinghast, and Brown of Providence, and continued in good esteem until he died, December 1, 1736, aged 87.

Daniel Wightman was his colleague and successor. He was born in Narraganset, January 2, 1668, was ordained in 1701, at which time he took the joint care of the church with Mr. Clark. He continued in office until he died in 1750 aged 82. He was a man of an excellent character, was related to Valentine Wightman of Groton, Connecticut, and is supposed to have been a descendant of Edward Wightman, who was burnt for heresy at Litchfield in 1612, being the last man, who suffered death for conscience' sake in England.*

The colleague and successor of Mr. Wightman was the famous Nicholas Eyres. He was born at a place called Chipmanslade, Wilts county, England, August 22, 1691; came to New-York about the year 1711; was baptized about three years after by Mr. Wightman of Groton, of which event, and also of his ministry in that city, an account will be given under the head of New-York. October, 1731, he set sail for Newport in compliance with an invitation from this church, and the same month was settled co-pastor with Mr. Wightman. "Mr. Eyres left behind him heaps of manuscripts, some polemical, some doctrinal, some political, for which he was every way qualified." He died February 13, 1759, and was buried in Newport, where a tomb was erected to his memory with the following inscription :

> "From an early institution in the languages
> And mathematical learning,
> He proceeded to the study of the sacred scriptures,
> And from them alone derived
> The true christian science
> Of the recovery of man
> To virtue and happiness.
> This he explained in his pastoral instructions ;
> This he happily recommended in his own example
> Of gravity, piety, and unblemished morals.
> Like his Divine master
> In his daily visitations
> He went about doing good.

* See page 196.

> He was a friend to the virtuous of every denomination,
> But a foe to established error and superstition;
> An enemy to unscriptural claims of superiority
> Among the churches of our common Lord;
> But of protestant liberty and the rights of conscience
> An able and steady defender.
> From these distinguishing strictures
> And ruling principles of his character
> Posterity may know,
> Or at least have reason to judge,
> That while many monumental inscriptions
> Perpetuate the names of those
> Who will awake to shame and everlasting contempt,
> This stone transmits the memory of one,
> Who shall shine as the brightness of the firmament
> And as the stars for ever and ever."

Mr. Eyres was succeeded by Mr. Gardner Thurston, who was ordained the April after his death. The history of this worthy man may be found in the biographical department. During a part of his ministry, his meetinghouse and congregation were the largest among the Baptists in New-England.* He finished his long and successful course in 1802.

Mr. Joshua Bradley, a native of Massachusetts and a graduate of Brown University was, a few years previous to Mr. Thurston's death, ordained as co-pastor with him. Under his ministry large additions were made to the church; but in the midst of a prosperous course he saw fit to ask a dismission, and removed to Connecticut; he has lately settled at Windsor in Vermont.

Successor to Mr. Bradley is Mr. John B. Gibson, who was settled among this people in 1807. He was born in Woodbury, Connecticut, in 1765; was first a Methodist, and a preacher in their connexion about eight years; was, after travelling different circuits, located at Warren, Rhode-Island, where he became fully convinced of believers' baptism, and of the errors of Wesley's creed; was baptized by Mr. Baker in May, 1807, and was ordained in the same place the June following.

The house of worship belonging to this church and congregation is 76 feet by 50. It stands on a lot of 140 feet by 75. Adjoining is another lot 50 feet square, on which is a small building, formerly occupied as a school-house,

* Morgan Edwards.

but now it is used for the accommodation of some of the poor members. Their funds are only 750 dollars ; 400 of which are expressly appropriated for the poor.

The old Sabbatarian church in this town will be noticed under the head of Seventh Day Baptists, towards the close of the second volume.

A fourth church was formed in Newport in 1788. It was, till lately, under the care of Mr. Caleb Green, who is now in Suffield, Connecticut. They have now no one, who is properly their pastor ; they, however, keep up their meetings, and Elder William Moore, who is far advanced in years, and others among them, help to carry them on. Their number is about 75.

In Tiverton, on the east side of this State, are three churches, which arose in the following manner : The first was formed in the adjoining town of Dartmouth about 1685 ; the members at first lived in Dartmouth, Tiverton, and Little Compton. Their first minister was Hugh Mosier, and next to him was Aaron Davis. This was the seventh Baptist church formed on the American continent. In process of time its seat was removed from Dartmouth to Tiverton, where it continues to the present day. Philip Taber succeeded Mr. Davis, and ministered to this people until his death, which happened in 1752. He was a respectable minister and useful citizen. During his ministry an event took place, which made considerable noise both in England and America. Tiverton was then claimed by Massachusetts, and continued to be until 1741. In 1723, the Assembly of that Commonwealth passed an act to raise five hundred and seventy-five dollars, in the towns of Dartmouth and Tiverton, for the support of *their* ministers ; and to blind the eyes of the people in these towns, who were mostly Quakers and Baptists, this sum was put in with the province tax, and was afterwards to have been drawn out of the treasury.* But the assessors of these towns, of whom Mr. Taber was one, getting knowledge of the devise, refused to assess the money, for which they were imprisoned in Bristol gaol about eighteen months, and were then released in obedience to an order from the Court of St. James, dated June, 1724. The names of these sufferers were, besides Mr. Taber, Joseph

---

* Stratagems of this kind were very frequent in these times.

Anthony, John Sisson, and John Atkin. Their petition was laid before the clement prince George I. by Thomas Richardson and Richard Partridge, Quakers, who were set forward and supported in their embassy by the Society of Friends.*

Next to Mr. Taber was David Rounds of Rehoboth, who ministered to the church about thirty years. After him was Benjamin Shelden, and then Peleg Burroughs from Newport, who was settled among them in 1775, and died, after a pious and successful ministry, in 1800. In 1780 and 1781, he had the happiness of receiving to membership in his flock 105 persons. Their next pastor was Mr. Benjamin Peckham from Newport, who was settled among them in 1801. In 1805—6 a refreshing season of an extensive nature was granted to this people, and about 100 were added to their number.

From this church proceeded the second in Tiverton in 1788, which is now under the care of Mr. Job Borden ; and in 1808 another church was formed from the old body, at Howland's Bridge, in the same town.

WARREN.—This church was constituted October 15, 1764, one of the constituents was Dr. Manning, then residing in the town ; most of the other members had previously belonged to the old church in Swansea, only three miles distant. Mr. Manning took the care of this church at its beginning, and continued with them till 1770, when he removed with the College to Providence.

Successor to him was Mr. Charles Thompson, A. M. one of the first graduates of the college, which began its movements in this town. Mr. Thompson was born at Amwell, New-Jersey, April 14, 1748, was ordained at Warren in 1771, by Messrs. Ebenezer Hinds of Middleborough, and Noah Alden, of Bellingham. He was a chaplain in the army almost three years of the first part of the Revolutionary War ; and it was while he was at home on a visit, that the British came up to Warren, burnt the meeting and parsonage houses, carried him to Newport, and confined him in a guard ship, from which he was released in about a month, by what means he never knew. After this he preached a short time in Pomfret, Connecticut, and as the church at Warren was mostly dispersed,

* Backus, vol. ii. p. 70, 73.

and many of them had gone back to the mother church at Swansea, he, by the invitation of that body, became their pastor in 1779 or 1780. In this situation he continued 23 years, when he removed to Charlestown, Massachusetts, where he died, May 1, 1803, in the 56th year of his age. His widow and three of his children are now settled in Warren. Mr. Thompson left behind him an unblemished character, and a large circle of cordial friends. His MS. writings were numerous, but nothing of his has appeared in print.

It was not till after the war that the church, under consideration, resumed its travel as a distinct body; they had, for about eight years after their dispersion, stood as a branch of the church at Swansea.

In 1784, they built their present meeting-house, on the same ground where their former one stood. It is 61 feet by 44, and has a steeple and bell. About two years after this house was built, Mr. John Pitman settled in the town, and ministered to this people till 1790, when he removed to Providence. After him Mr. Nathaniel Cole, now in Plainfield, Connecticut, and others preached here occasionally, till 1793, when Mr. Luther Baker, their present pastor, was ordained. He was born in the town, June 11, 1770. Under his ministry some very considerable revivals have been experienced. In the year 1805, over ninety were added to their number. In September, 1812, immediately after the session of that Association, which took its name from this town, another revival commenced, in which over sixty were baptized in the course of a few months. This church has a fund of about fourteen hundred dollars.

BRISTOL.—This town is five miles south of Warren, and is next in size, and in point of commercial importance, to Providence and Newport. It was, until 1741, claimed by Massachusetts, and, being a shire town, its gaol was the frequent receptacle of Baptists, Quakers, and others, who were so heretical as not to pay their parish taxes. From this, and other causes, the Baptists gained but little influence here, until long after the Pedobaptists had acquired a permanent standing. But the principles of believers' baptism have at length forced their way through the barriers of antiquated errors, and a church has been formed, which bids fair to flourish and prevail. It arose in the following manner : In 1780, Mrs. Hopestill Munro, the wife of Hezekiah Munro, was led to embrace the Baptist sentiments, and was the first person in the town from time immemorial, who submitted to baptism in the Apostolical mode.* A few months after was baptized the wife of Mr. Daniel Lefavour, who died about fifteen years ago, with a well grounded hope of immortality. On her deathbed, she left a solemn injunction on her husband, to give unconditionally seven hundred dollars for the support of the ministry in Bristol, whenever there should arise a church of the same faith and order with the one at Warren under the care of Mr. Baker. This sum her husband bequeathed in his Will, dated May, 1797, was entrusted with the Warren church, and has now increased to near fifteen hundred dollars. The next person baptized in this place was Mrs. Hannah Martin, who is still living. Thus slowly progressed the Baptist interest in Bristol, until 1801, when Dr. Thomas Nelson, whose name has been mentioned in the account of the second church in Middleborough, settled in the place in the practice of his profession. By his means Baptist preachers were procured to visit the town, among whom were Elders Simeon Coombs and Joseph Cornell, whose labours were greatly blessed. And in 1811, a church was formed, which at first consisted of only 23 members, but has since increased to 56. This church has been supplied a year since its constitution by Mr. James M. Winchell, a native of North-Easttown, New-York, who lately finished his education at Providence. Since the history of the first church in Boston was sent to press, Mr. Winchell has gone to visit that people, with whom there is a prospect of his settling. And very lately Mr. Barnabas Bates, of Barnstable, has accepted a call to settle with this church. They meet now in a commodious hall, called the Tabernacle, in Dr. Nelson's house, which he has fitted up for the purpose, but are making exertions to erect a house for worship, and it is sincerely hoped that the neighbouring churches will

---

* According to Mr Comer, a Mr. Carpenter was baptized by immersion in this town by Rev. Mr Usher, an Episcopalian minister, in 1725 The year after, five persons in Rehoboth were baptized in the same mode by Mr. Piggot of that denomination. The year after that, a woman was immersed in Newport by Dr. M'Sparran, of Narraganset. *Backus, vol. ii. p.* 112.

lend them their aid. Mrs. Munro, first mentioned, has lately given them a deed of an estate valued at a thousand dollars. This, with their other funds, amount to two thousand seven hundred dollars.

A short time since there was a very remarkable revival in this town; not far from two hundred were hopefully awakened to religious concern; a considerable number of them were buried in baptism, but few, however, comparatively, united with the Baptists. The additions were made mostly to the Congregational, Episcopalian, and Methodist churches.

On the west side of the Narraganset Bay, in the counties of Kent and Washington, are a considerable number of churches, of which our limits prevent our giving a very particular account. A few of them are of ancient date, some arose in and after the New-Light Stir, and others have arisen within a few years past.

We shall now proceed to some account of the Associations, which have originated in this State, and to which the Rhode-Island churches now belong.

At what time the churches in this State began to associate I do not find, but it was probably at an early period. Mr. Comer gives an account of an Association or General Convention, as it was then called, 1729, which was supposed to have been the largest assemblage of brethren they had ever witnessed. Thirteen churches were represented, and the whole number of messengers was thirty-two. The churches composing this convention were the one in Providence, the second in Newport, two in Smithfield, and one in each of the towns of Scituate, Warwick, North and South-Kingston. In other colonies were the one in Dartmouth, now the first in Tiverton, the second in Swansea, and those of Groton, New-London, and New-York. The ministers belonging to these churches were of Providence, James Brown; of Smithfield, Jonathan Sprague; of Scituate, Peter Place and Samuel Fisk; of Newport, James Clark, Daniel Wightman, and John Comer, then supplying them after his dismission from the first church; of Warwick, Manasseh Martin; of North-Kingston, Richard Sweet; of South-Kingston, Daniel Everett; of Swansea, Joseph Mason; of Dartmouth, Phillip Taber; of Groton, Valentine Wightman; of New-London, Stephen Gorton ; of New-York, Nicholas Eyres. Ten of these ministers were present ; the number of communicants at the convention were 250, and the number of auditors about 1000. The churches were all strenuous for the laying-on-of-hands, and were generally inclined to those doctrinal sentiments, which in England would have denominated them General Baptists. At the same time there were the first churches in Newport, Swansea, and Boston, who held decidedly to particular election, and who did not practise the imposition of hands, and for these reasons were not members of the Association. These sixteen churches comprehended at that time all the Baptists this side of New-Jersey.

It is now (1813) eighty-four years since this great Association, as it was then esteemed, was held ; very considerable changes have taken place in most of the churches of which it was then composed ; but the same body on the same plan of doctrine and discipline, still exists under the name of the Rhode-Island Yearly Meeting. This meeting, on account of its making the laying-on-of-hands a term of communion, and its inclination to the Arminian system of doctrine, has no connexion with any of the neighbouring Associations. It contains thirteen churches, twelve ministers, and over eleven hundred members. Eight of the churches are in this State, the others are in Massachusetts and New-York.

WARREN ASSOCIATION.

This body was formed in the place from which it took its name in 1767, at which time three ministers* from the Philadelphia Association came on with a letter to encourage the measure. Only four churches at first associated, viz. Warren, Haverhill, Bellingham, and the second in Middleborough. The delegates from six other churches were present, but they did not feel themselves ready to proceed in the undertaking. As the annual commencement of the college had been fixed on the first Wednesday of September, the anniversary of the Association was appointed the Tuesday after. This arrangement is still observed. The second and third sessions of this Associa-

---

* Mr. Backus has not mentioned their names. Dr. Jones and Morgan Edwards were probably two of them.

tion were held in the place where it was formed. The fourth was at Bellingham and the fifth at Sutton in 1771, by which time it had increased to 20 churches and over 800 members. This year they began to print their Minutes, and have continued to do so to the present time. The two churches in Boston fell in with this establishment a few years after it was begun, but it was some time before the Providence church, which is now the oldest and largest in it, could be brought into its measures. The doctrine of the laying-on-of-hands was probably the principal cause of this delay. This Association for a number of years included a large circle of churches, which were scattered over a wide extent of country in Rhode-Island, Massachusetts, New-Hampshire, Vermont, and Connecticut. Most of them were however in Massachusetts, and in process of time Boston became not far from its centre. It has, from its beginning, been a flourishing and influential body; has contained a number of ministers of eminent standing in the Baptist connexion; has successfully opposed the encroachments of religious oppression; has aided the designs of the college at Providence; has devised plans of a literary and missionary nature; and has been more or less concerned in whatever measures have had a view to the promotion of the cause of truth, of the Baptist interest in New-England, and remoter regions. By this body were presented many addresses to the rulers of Massachusetts, and some to the continental Congress against civil oppressions for conscience' sake; by it also were issued many publications in defence of religious freedom. It was almost constantly employed in measures of this kind from its formation to the close of the war in 1783; and no small success attended its exertions.

After travelling in union upwards of forty years, and witnessing within its bounds much of the divine goodness, it had become so large that its division appeared indispensable, and accordingly a new one was formed, called the Boston; of which we have already given a brief account. Thus the staff has become two bands, which together contain 65 churches, 53 ministers, and almost 7000 members.

In the south-west part of this State, in the counties of Kent and Washington, are eleven churches, which belong to the Stonington and Groton Associations in Connecticut.

Some of them arose in the New-Light Stir in Whitefield's time. The church at Exeter, belonging to the Stonington Association, was formed in 1750; it has ever been a flourishing body, and now contains over 250 members, and is under the care of Mr. Gershom Palmer.

The large Sabbatarian church at Hopkinton will be noticed under the head of Seventh-Day Baptists towards the close of the second volume.

We shall now close the history of this State with some brief remarks.

We have already quoted some of the calumniating accounts, which have been given of the people in this State, and the following extract will show that they now stand no higher in the estimation of some of their Pedobaptist neighbours than formerly. Dr. Worcester, of Salem, in his epistolary dispute with Dr. Baldwin, of Boston, found it necessary to resort to a State, which was founded by an exile from his own government, for arguments against his opponent. " Was not Rhode-Island," said he, " originally settled on Antipedobaptist principles? Have not those principles there been left to their free and uncontrolled operation and influence? To these interrogations there can be but one answer. If then," continues he, " the principles of Antipedobaptism were true and scriptural, might we not look to Rhode-Island for a more general prevalence of divine knowledge, a more general and sacred observance of divine institutions, more pure and flourishing churches, and more of the spirit of primitive christianity, than is to be expected in almost any other part of the globe? But what is the actual result of this experiment? Alas! let the forsaken, decayed houses of God—let the profaned and unacknowledged day of the Lord—let the unread and even exiled oracles of divine truth—let the neglected and despised ordinances of religion—let the dear children and youth, growing up in the most deplorable ignorance of God, his word, and sacred institutions—let the *few* friends of Zion, weeping in secret places over her *desert*, her affecting and wide-spread *desert* around them— let the deeply-impressed missionaries, who, in obedience to the most urgent calls, have been sent by Pedobaptist societies into different parts of the State—be allowed to testify! *If there be religion there*, is it not almost wholly confined to those places in which Pedobaptist churches are established, and a *Pedobaptist influence* has effect? Witness the late revivals!"

This gloomy and affecting picture was drawn but three or four years ago. It is doubted whether this Rev. Doctor was ever in the State, and it is probable that the outlines of his doleful picture were furnished by those slanderous missionaries, whose urgent calls for eight dollars a week, led them to travel in it.* The candid reader will, doubtless, consider the following statement a sufficient refutation of this ungenerous calumny. There are thirty-six Baptist churches in Rhode-Island in which are over five thousand communicants, who have all been received upon a verbal relation of their religious experience; pertaining to the denomination are about thirty meeting-houses in good repair,† besides a number of others in which meetings are

* We know not what other urgent calls these deeply-impressed missionaries have to travel in Rhode-Island. It is certain the Baptists do not call them, for they have but little faith in their commission—the Quakers will not hear them, because they do not think they are moved by the Spirit to teach—and it cannot be that there are any of Dr. Worcester's Pedobaptists in those "*deserts,*" those affecting wide-spread *deserts,*" which they visit, for their influence would soon convert them into celestial regions. We will not dispute about their urgent calls—but we know well enough, that they roam around the rocks and forests of Burrillville, Gloucester, &c. the most destitute parts of the State, and from their scanty survey represent the whole of it as sunk into the most deplorable condition of profaneness and barbarism.

† In this list of churches, we do not reckon a number, which, by deaths and removals, have so far declined, that they have in a measure lost their visibility, although many worthy members remain to mourn over the broken walls of their Zion. We may add to this account of meeting-houses, that there are many new commodious school-houses, in the neighbourhood of the Factories, built by their owners on purpose for the accommodation of meetings as well as schools. Publick worship is also maintained either statedly or occasionally in academies, court-houses, and halls of different kinds, in divers parts of the State. Besides the meeting-houses we have reckoned in good repair, there are a considerable number which are not so. But it ought to be observed that within this present century, many new houses have been built, and of the remainder a number have been built anew, enlarged, or repaired, since the last war. Of the houses of worship belonging to our churches in some of the principal towns, we have already given brief descriptions; the first which were erected in the country were mostly small, and the structure and finishing of them varied according to the means of the builders. It was not uncommon for churches, as they branched out, to have two or three meeting-houses for their use. Many of these have either fallen or are falling into decay. 1st. Because they were built too slightly to be worth repairing, or were not well contrived for enlargement. 2d Because, in process of time, they were left out of the centre of the congregations. But while they have been left to decay, others more spacious and durable, and in more eligible situations have been erected in their stead. But when Dr. Worcester's missionaries pass one of these old houses, they look——they wonder——they sigh——

held, and which will probably be fitted up in better order, when the gracious Lord shall again revive his work in their vicinities. There are now, and have been for a great many years, over forty stated meetings among the Baptists in this State, besides many occasional ones in school-houses, private dwellings, &c. Of other denominations, there are eighteen congregations of Quakers or Friends, the same number of meeting-houses, in which they statedly assemble twice a week, and in their community they reckon 1150 members; there are eleven churches of Congregationalists, as many houses of worship, and probably not far from 1000 communicants; there are four Episcopal churches, fourteen Methodist Societies, a few churches of those who call themselves Christians, a Moravian Chapel, and a Synagogue for Jews.

Thus it appears there are about 90 religious societies in the thirty-one towns of Rhode-Island, in which publick worship is constantly maintained; and to these societies appertain at least seventy houses of worship, which are neither *decayed* nor *forsaken*. These societies all maintain the ordinances of religion according to their different views of propriety; the *oracles* of *truth* they have neither exiled nor incorporated with their civil code; and their Bible Society lately established can furnish with the word of life all who have need. As to those children for whom this compassionate Doctor shows so much regard, we will only say, they can teach divines of Massachusetts better divinity than to fatten on the spoils of conscientious dissenters, and more civility than to defame their fellow men of whose affairs they are ignorant.

This statement of the religious affairs of Rhode-Island, which is made not from conjecture and vague report, but from actual survey, from absolute, uncontrovertible matters of fact, it is hoped, will, in the view of some at least, dis-

and in their memorandums write against the whole State, MENE, MENE, TEKEL, UPHARSIN. These memorandums doubtless furnished materials for the affecting picture of this ungenerous adversary. Where houses of worship are erected, churches gathered, and ministers supported by the aid of law, they may all remain in a permanent and splendid form. It would be a sad case indeed if some benefits did not arise from the evil of ecclesiastical establishments. In those parts of the United States, where houses of worship are built and ministers supported, not by legal taxes, but by the voluntary contributions of their patrons, changes, similar to those we have described in Rhode-Island, as the Author knows from observation, have been, and are now taking place, not only among the Baptists, but all other denominations.

pel somewhat of the horrid gloom of Dr. Worcester's picture. And as a proof that the Divine Spirit has not withdrawn from the Antipedobaptist churches, whose principles he would represent as blasting and pestiferous as the tree of Java, we would state, with gratitude to the Father of mercies, that over a thousand persons have been hopefully born into the kingdom, buried in baptism, and added to their number within six or seven years past. To a number of other societies there have also been large additions.

The reader must keep in mind that this State is but about as large in extent as the adjoining county of Worcester ; its number of inhabitants is but about twice as large as Boston and Charlestown together, and not equal to the city of New-York. And it is believed by those best acquainted with it, that there are as many real christians, if not so many professors of religion, in this, as in any territory of the same extent in any of the neighbouring States.

It is acknowledged that in some of the country towns in this State, too many of the inhabitants live a careless, irreligious life, disregard the Sabbath, and neglect the worship of God. But Pedobaptists are mistaken when they ascribe the conduct of these people to the influence of Baptist principles. The accusation is unfounded, unfair, and egregiously false. These people are under the influence of no principles of a religious kind, and many of them are the descendants of progenitors of the same character, who fled to this asylum of freedom during the reign of ecclesiastical terror in the neighbouring colonies. It has always been found that men of no religious principles are as desirous of liberty of conscience as real christians, and we may furthermore add, it is just they should enjoy it. From ecclesiastical establishments there always have been a multitude of dissenters of this character, and not a few of them were found amongst the early settlers of Rhode-Island. The maxims of the government were suited to their views ; their money was not distrained for the support of religious teachers, neither were they fined for not attending the worship of God. Mr. Cotton of Boston taught that men had " better be hypocrites than profane persons," that " hypocrites give God part of his due, the outward man," &c.* But the Rhode-Island rulers had

* See page 378.

no belief in this logic. If the subjects of their government performed the duty of citizens, they required nothing more; the regulation of religious opinions they left to the Searcher of hearts, and all were free to possess what religion best accorded with their views, or none at all, if they chose. They could not maintain the foundation principle of the colony, and do otherwise. But this same principle subjected them to inconveniences for which there was no remedy. And the same inconvenience has happened in every country where the standard of freedom, whether civil or religious, has been set up. With the Taborites of Bohemia, under Ziska and Procopius, with the Independents of England, in the time of the Commonwealth, among the Baptists of Germany, in their struggles for religious freedom, as well as with the planters of Rhode-Island, were associated many characters, who understood not their principles, either civil or religious, but who perverted them to purposes, which were never intended. Roger Williams, on a certain occasion, in imitation of a noble *Greek*, thanked God, that he had been the author of that very liberty by which his enemies dare to abuse him. A letter of this renowned legislator, explaining more fully this subject, will be given in the Appendix.

I find Mr. Callender in his Century Sermon, delivered seventy-five years ago, in repelling the calumnies, which were then cast upon Rhode-Island, on account of these irreligious people, observes, that among the first settlers of the State, who were "a pious generation, men of virtue and godliness," some intruded themselves of a very different genius and spirit. He also assures us, that "there scarcely ever was a time, the hundred years (then) past, in which there was not a weekly publick worship of God attended at Newport and in the other first towns of the colony."

Governor Hopkins, about fifty years ago, speaking of this circumstance, has a train of observations similar to those of Mr. Callender.*

We do not pretend that all the careless people of the State descended from those unprincipled settlers, whom the persecutions of the other colonies drove to this asylum. Some of them are the descendants of pious progenitors,

* Providence Gazette, for March, 1765.

who have not inherited their virtues, but have run counter to their instructions, and happy for Pedobaptists if they have no occasion to mourn on the same account.

If the Rhode-Island people had established religion by law, they would have been excused from all the reproaches which are now cast upon them.

It would be an easy but invidious task, to find places enough in Massachusetts, notwithstanding all their laws, as destitute of religion, and as careless of publick worship, as any of the back towns of Rhode-Island.* But we are now engaged only on the defensive.

It is worthy of notice, that the two Baptist churches in Providence and Newport, founded by Roger Williams and John Clark, have always maintained a respectable standing, have had a regular succession of worthy pastors, now together contain almost seven hundred members, have congregations large and opulent, and possess each of them larger estates than any Baptist church in America, except the first in Philadelphia.

While new churches have arisen in some parts, in others, those, which were once large and flourishing, have become small or extinct. This circumstance may appear strange, and may furnish matter of reproach to those, who fine religious societies, " not under sixty nor over a hundred dollars a year," for being " without a teacher of piety, morality, and religion, three months out of six," and who impose fines on individuals for not attending publick worship a certain number of times in a year. But with the Baptists this matter is easily accounted for. Their churches cannot long flourish nor exist without the reviving influence of the Holy Spirit; but those churches, which depend on the civil arm for their support, may continue and flourish even

---

* " Were a serious Baptist from Rhode-Island," says Dr. Baldwin in reply to Dr. Worcester, " to visit the metropolis of Massachusetts, ' the headquarters of good principles,' would he not be led, from your observations, to suppose that no person would be seen in the streets on Lord's day, unless going or returning from church or meeting ? But while he could scarcely credit his senses, would he not be ready to ask, *What meaneth this prancing of the horses, and this rattling of the carriage wheels in my ears ?* And should he be informed, that more horses and carriages of every kind were let to visiting and other parties of pleasure on that day than on any other in the week, what would be his astonishment ? What would he think of the " influence of Pedobaptist principles ?" Would he not suppose there were some besides the ancient Pharisees, who could *strain at a gnat and swallow a camel* "

Series *of Letters,* p. 211.

when there is not a christian nor a spark of grace among them. Many of the Rhode-Island churches have been greatly reduced, and some in a measure broken up, by their members emigrating to other States. We observed in the beginning of this chapter, that this State is so small and so fully settled, that as the inhabitants increase, they are obliged to remove to other parts for settlements. And here it is proper to observe, that by ministers and members from this State were founded the oldest church in Pennsylvania in 1684; the oldest in Connecticut in 1705; the first church in the city of New-York was much assisted by the Rhode-Island brethren about 80 years ago; and by emigrants from this nursery of Baptists have been founded and enlarged many other churches in Connecticut, Hampshire, and Berkshire counties in Massachusetts, and also in New-Hampshire, Vermont, and New-York.

Of the ministers, to whom Rhode-Island has given birth, who have settled in other States, we may name Valentine Wightman, Joshua Morse, Peter Werden, Clark Rogers, Caleb Nichols, Wightman Jacobs, and others, who have all rested from their labours. Of those now on the stage of action, are Dr. Rogers of Philadelphia, Mr. Grafton of Newton, Mr. Thomas H. Chipman of Nova-Scotia, and many others in different parts of the surrounding States. From certain information, from the affinity of names, &c. I am confident that not less than forty, and probably over fifty Baptist ministers of the First and Seventh-Day order, have, within half a century past, gone out from this little territory, and acted, or are now acting, successful parts in various departments of the Lord's vineyard.

The reader is left to make his own comments on the prevalence of those religious principles, on which Rhode-Island was founded, and which she has ever considered it her boast and glory to maintain.

The fathers of the colony, as we have already shown, desired permission from the powers at home to try the experiment, whether a flourishing civil State might not stand and best be maintained with a full liberty in religious concernments. The experiment has been tried, and has answered their most sanguine expectations. A flourishing State has arisen on a little spot of earth in this western world, whose ships when not embargoed nor blockaded,

An Act for the Security of religious Freedom. 517

traverse every sea, whose artificers and manufacturers are spreading to every State,* and in which from first to last, every individual has been left free to profess what religion he chose, without fear or molestation. The proposal of this experiment, and its issue in Rhode-Island, is worthy of being recorded in capitals of gold, and ought to be hung up in the most conspicuous place in the Vatican at Rome, and in every Ecclesiastical Court in Christendom.

The principal acts of the Rhode-Island Legislature in defence of religious freedom have already been given.

In 1716 a law was passed, which has not yet been mentioned. The closing part of the preamble together with the act, are as follow:

" THE present Assembly being sensible by long experience, that the aforesaid privilege (that is of entire toleration) by the good providence of God, having been continued to us, has been an outward means of continuing a good and amicable agreement amongst the inhabitants of this colony: And for the better continuance and support thereof, as well as for the timely preventing of any and every church, congregation and society of people, now inhabiting, or which shall hereafter inhabit within any part of the jurisdiction of the same, from endeavouring for preeminence or superiority one over the other, by making use of the civil power, for the enforcing of a maintenance for their respective ministers:

" *Be it enacted by the General Assembly, and by the authority hereof it is enacted,* That what maintenance or salary may be thought necessary by any of the churches, congregations, or societies of people, now inhabiting, or that hereafter shall or may inhabit within the same, for the support of their respective minister or ministers, shall be raised by free contribution, and no otherwise."†

---

* The manufacturing of cotton on Arkwright's plan was begun in Pawtucket in 1790, by Samuel Slater, Esq. from England. There are now in this village, and near, almost 7000 spindles in operation, and within a mile and a quarter of it, including both sides of the river, are buildings erected, capable of containing about 12,000 more. In 1810, according to an account taken by Mr. John K. Pitman of Providence, in the State of Rhode-Island only, were 39 factories, in which over 30,000 spindles were running, and the same factories were capable of containing about as many more. The number of spindles in operation in this State only, is now (1813) probably not far from 50,000.

In 1810, the gentleman above mentioned ascertained, that within thirty miles of Providence, which includes a considerable territory in Massachusetts, and a small portion of Connecticut, there were 76 factories, capable of containing 111,000 spindles. The number of spindles now in actual operation within this circumference are said to be 120,000. The amount of yarn spun each week, is not far from 110,000 pounds, or 5,500,000 a year. This side of the river Delaware the number of cotton factories of different dimensions, built and in building is estimated at 500.

† Laws of Rhode-Island, edition of 1767, p. 194.

This law was passed under the administration of Governor Cranston, a Quaker, and when Joseph Jenks, afterwards Governor, had great influence in governmental affairs. The Rhode-Island people had many suspicions about this time, that the taxing and distraining policy of the neighbouring colonies, would be attempted among them, and this law was doubtless intended to counteract, and be a standing barrier against any manœuvres of the kind. It has been thought by many in later times, that it rendered invalid all contracts between a minister and people for his support, but I cannot find that it was ever so construed. Subscriptions were recoverable by law while this act was in force, and voluntary contracts individually entered into for the support of ministers are now, and for ought that appears to the contrary, always have been as much binding in law in this, as in any other State, where there are no religious establishments. If a minister here were in his own name to attempt to recover his salary in a legal way, it is not certain how he would succeed; the case I believe was never tried by any—it surely never was among the Baptists, and it is hoped it never will be; for the preacher, who is reduced to the necessity of suing his people, had better dig for his bread, or else decamp to some place where they will be more punctual.

The last act of the Rhode-Island Assembly has a preamble somewhat lengthy, but high in the strain of religious freedom, and closes thus:

"Whereas a principal object of our venerable ancestors, in their migration to this country, and settlement of this State, was, as they expressed it, *to hold forth a lively experiment, that a most flourishing civil State may stand, and best be maintained, with a full liberty in religious concernments* :

"*Be it therefore enacted by the General Assembly, and by the authority thereof it is enacted,* That no man shall be compelled to frequent or support any religious worship, place, or ministry whatsoever; nor shall be enforced, restrained, molested, or burthened in his body or goods, nor shall otherwise suffer on account of his religious opinions or belief; but that all men shall be free to profess, and by argument to maintain, their opinions in matters of religion, and that the same shall in no wise diminish, enlarge, or affect their civil capacities."* [*Laws of Rhode-Island edition of* 1798, *p.* 83, 84.

* The following is a brief statement of the Governors of Rhode-Island. Under their first charter, which lasted nineteen years, their chief magistrates were called Presidents, of these there were seven: some were Baptists, some

CHAPTER XIV.

CONNECTICUT.

THIS State began to be settled by some of the famous Robinson's congregation in 1633, but we do not find any Baptists in it for more than seventy years from that period. In 1705, Mr. Valentine Wightman removed from North-Kingston in Rhode-Island to Groton, seven miles from New-London, where he the same year planted a church of which he became pastor. This remained the only Baptist church in this province for about twenty years: But in 1726 another was gathered in the township of New-London, on the ground which is now occupied by the Seventh-Day Baptists, and a minister by the name of Stephen Gorton became their pastor. He was a man of some eminence as a preacher, and ministered to this people for many years; but he at length fell into some scandalous conduct, for which he was deposed from his pastoral office, and the church in a short time became extinct.

In 1729, some people in Saybrook at the mouth of Connecticut river, embraced Baptist sentiments; but no church was gathered there until fifteen years after.

Quakers, the religious opinions of a number are not known. Three years of this time, the Presidential Chair was filled by Roger Williams. From the time the second charter was obtained, viz. in 1663, is now a period of 150 years. During this period there have been 25 Governors, counting his Excellency the present Chief Magistrate. Eight of these were Quakers or Friends, about the same number Baptists by education or profession, and of the remainder some were Episcopalians, some Congregationalists; the religious opinions of a number are not known. Governor Cook was baptized by immersion, but belonged to a Congregational church, and the same may be said of the present Governor Jones. For more than a century the Baptists and Quakers had the lead in the affairs of government. They at first had some disputes about ordinances and inward light, but these soon subsided, and they have, with very few exceptions, from time immemorial, harmoniously agreed to differ. While they feared the introduction of the religious laws of the surrounding governments, they endeavoured to keep a preponderating balance of power in their own hands. For Pedobaptism and law-religion they both disbelieved, and have ever strenuously opposed. The Quakers now in many places serve as judges, magistrates, legislators, &c. but their pretensions to the gubernatorial chair they have long since resigned, on account of the danger of its subjecting them to military duties, incompatible with their views of religion and morality. The Baptists still fill many offices of different kinds, but more native citizens of other States hold offices and have influence in governmental affairs, than formerly.

In 1731, some of the Pedobaptists in Wallingford, thirteen miles north of New-Haven, by reading Delaune's Plea, &c. became convinced of the error of their former creed, were baptized, and united with the church at New-London, but usually met for worship in their own town, where a church was soon afterwards established.

These were some of the first efforts which our brethren made amongst the rigid Pedobaptists in this fast-bound State.

Their progress was at first extremely slow and much embarrassed; they had to work their way against the deep-rooted prejudices of a people, who had been always taught, with a sanctimonious tone, that these were the vile descendants of the mad men of Munster; that they propagated errors of a pestilential and most dangerous kind; that they were aiming to subvert all the established forms of religion in the land, and on the ruin of the Pedobaptist churches to plant their heretical and disorganizing principles; that for the people to hear them preach, or for the magistrates to tolerate or connive at their meetings in any of their towns or parishes, was a crime of peculiar enormity, which would expose them to the famishing and revengeful judgments of Heaven.

Such were the sentiments of most of the Connecticut people, at the period of which we are speaking. But this host of prejudices was only a shadowy obstacle to the progress of the Baptist cause, compared with those religious laws with which the Connecticut rulers had fenced in their ecclesiastical establishment.

In the New Light Stir the foundations of this establishment were very sensibly shaken; many ministers opposed the progress of that extraordinary work of grace, as being only the fruit of error and fanaticism; divisions ensued; separate meetings were set up in many towns and parishes; Baptist principles almost every where prevailed; and many of the zealous New Lights, who began upon the Pedobaptist, brought up on the Baptist plan.

About the time, and a little after this distinguished epoch in the religious affairs of New-England, small churches were formed in Stonington, Colchester, Ashford, Lyme, Killingly, Farmington, Stratfield, and Horseneck, some of which acquired a permanent standing, while others were soon scattered and became extinct.

So slow was the increase of the Baptists in this government, that in 1760, fifty-five years after Mr. Wightman erected his standard at Groton, they had only eight or nine churches, which had acquired any degree of permanency, and most of these were small and feeble bodies.

In 1784 their number had increased to about thirty, in which were about twenty ministers. From this date, the denomination began to increase much faster than it had formerly done, so that in 1795 the number of churches amounted to sixty, the ministers were about forty, and the communicants a little over *three thousand, five hundred*. These churches were scattered in every county, and in almost every township in the State.

From 1795, Baptist principles have prevailed in this populous territory as rapidly as at any former period. But as many brethren have emigrated to other parts, the clear increase of members has not been so great as it would otherwise have been.

The River from which this State receives its name divides it into two sections nearly equal in size. The churches east of this River, belong mostly to the Stonington, Groton, and Sturbridge Associations. The Danbury Association comprehends most of those to the west of it; a few churches towards the south-west part of the State belong to the Union and Warwick Associations, in New-York.

STONINGTON ASSOCIATION.

This body was formed at the place from which it received its name in 1772. Its progress does not appear to have been marked with any peculiar events; it has now increased to twenty-two churches, five of which are in Rhode-Island, the remainder are in the south-west part of this State.

Groton.—This church was planted by Valentine Wightman in 1705, being the first Baptist church in Connecticut. The members' were harassed for a while by the predominant party; but no account of their sufferings has been obtained. Mr. Wightman was born at North-Kingston, Rhode-Island, in 1681, and finished his course in a joyful manner in 1747. We have already stated that he is supposed to have been a descendant of Edward Wightman, the last man who was burnt for heresy in England. According to a tradition in his family, five brothers came to Rhode-Island in the early settlement of that colony; two of them were preachers, two were deacons, and the fifth was a professor of religion, all of the Baptist persuasion. The subject of this memoir was a son of one of these men, but nothing more particular respecting his progenitors can be learnt. He settled in Groton at the age of twenty-four, when there were but six or seven Baptists in the place.

In 1727, Mr. Wightman, being called to preach at Lyme, was opposed by Rev. Mr. Bulkly of Colchester, who challenged him to a publick dispute, which was first maintained in a verbal manner, and was afterwards kept up in writing. Mr. Bulkly, after ransacking the records of slander for arguments against his opponent, and the Baptists generally, concludes, "They are but of yesterday, and consequently the truth cannot be with them, as being not known in the world till about two hundred years past." Mr. Wightman replied, "I never read of a Presbyterian longer than said term, how then can the way of truth be with them?" &c.*

Mr. Wightman was succeeded by Mr. Daniel Fisk, who served the church about seven years, when Timothy Wightman, one of the sons of the founder of this body, was elected its pastor. He discharged the duties of his office till a good old age, and was succeeded by his son John Gano Wightman, who was ordained in 1800. Jesse Wightman, another of his sons, is pastor of a church in West-Springfield. John Wightman, a brother of Timothy, was an eminent minister in his day, and died at Farmington in this State. From a daughter of Valentine Wightman descended four Baptist ministers, by the name of Rathbun; one of them, by the name of Valentine Wightman Rathbun, died this present year, pastor of the church in Bellingham, Massachusetts.

STONINGTON.—This town is in the south-east corner of Connecticut, adjoining Rhode-Island, and directly east of Groton. In it, as it stood before its late division, were three churches belonging to the Association under consideration. The oldest of the three is situated in what is now

* Backus, vol. II. p. 89, 90.

called North-Stonington, and is under the care of Mr. Peleg Randal. It was formed in 1743; its first members were baptized by Mr. Wightman of Groton. The foundation for the second church in this town was laid by Simeon Brown, now its aged pastor, and Stephen Babcock of Westerly, Rhode-Island. In the remarkable revival so often referred to, these two men caught the New-Light flame, and zealously engaged in promoting the work, which was then going on in the land. Mostly by their means a church was formed in Westerly, on the plan of open communion, in 1750, of which Mr. Babcock was soon ordained pastor, and Mr. Brown a deacon. They travelled together about fourteen years, held meetings sometimes in Westerly, but often in Stonington, and the church increased abundantly, and spread into many of the surrounding parts. But the pastor and deacon at length fell out upon sundry points, both of doctrine and discipline, their disputes, however, turned principally upon what, in that day, was called the *divine testimony*. By this testimony, which consisted of certain impulses and spiritual manifestations, Mr. Babcock was for regulating those acts of discipline, which Mr. Brown would govern by moral evidence. As all attempts at reconciliation proved ineffectual, the deacon, who had not yet been baptized, had the ordinance administered to him by Elder Wait Palmer, the same who had baptized Shubeal Stearns; gathered a church in his own town in 1765, to the pastoral care of which he was ordained the same year. Mr. Brown was born in Stonington, January, 1723, and if still living, is turned of 90.

This church has been a flourishing body, and has now become large; by it were sent into the ministry, John and Valentine Rathbun, Robert Staunton, Eleazer Brown, Amos Wells, Simeon Brown, jun. Asa Spaulding and Jedidiah Randal.

A third church was gathered at Stonington harbour in 1775. Mr. Rathbun, late of Bellingham, was for a number of years its pastor; it is now under the care of Mr. Elihu Cheeseborough.

A fourth church was formed in this town in 1793, which has since been dissolved.

NEW-LONDON.—This town once included Montville and Waterford. In the last place a church was formed in 1726, whose pastor was Stephen Gorton, of whom we have given some account. In the same place has arisen a Sabbatarian church, and also one of the First-day order, whose ministers are Zadock and Francis Darrow. It was formed in 1767. The ancient church, in what is now called Montville, was gathered in 1750, under the ministry of Mr. Joshua Morse, who removed to Sandisfield, Massachusetts, in the time of the war, and his flock appears to have been scattered. The present church is dated in 1786, and is now under the care of Mr. Reuben Palmer.

A church in the city of New-London was gathered in 1804, under the ministry of Mr. Samuel West.

The church in Lebanon, Windham county, arose out of a Pedobaptist quarrel, about an old meeting-house ; the affair made a considerable noise at the time, and is thus briefly related by Mr. Nehemiah Dodge, under whose ministry the church was built up :

" MANY things complicated and perplexing took place in this town, relative to taking down one old meeting-house, and building two new ones ; concerning which many wrong reports have been spread abroad. And since a number of christians have been baptized in this place and formed into a church, some have been ungenerous enough to cast many hard reflections upon the denomination. They have said, that the Baptists had been the cause of the tumults and distressing divisions which took place in the parish anterior to our existence as a church, or to there being any Baptists here, excepting a few individuals, who lived recluse, and had nothing to do with the existing controversy."

This controversy turned principally upon the place where a new meeting-house should be set, and as the parties could not agree, they built two in places they respectively chose. Some measures taken by the party, who became Baptists, it would seem, did not receive the sanction of the Legislature, which accounts for what follows :

" After a meeting-house was-erected, the people, who built it, made application to Presbyterian ministers, under whose ministry they had been brought up, to come and preach to them. But these gentlemen replied, that they could not in conscience preach to them, nor fellowship those that would. Why ? Because the people were immoral or scandalous in their lives ? No. But because they said they had gone contrary to *law* in building their house. They said it

Origin of the Lebanon Church.

did not become them as leaders of the people and examples of piety, to have so much fellowship with a people, who had paid so little regard to the voice of the General Assembly, and who had been governed no more by civil law in the management of their affairs, relative to their meeting-house. It is understood that a vote to this import passed in their Association.

" Many of the people by these means became convinced that *law religion* might, in some instances, operate unjustly, by depriving individuals of their unalienable rights. Or in other words, they became convinced, that civil law and civil rulers had an undue influence over ministers and churches. Feeling the injuries produced by this legal influence, they were led to seek an acquaintance with those christians, who acknowledge no other *Lawgiver* in the church but Jesus Christ, and no other *law-book* to govern them *in their religious concerns* but the Bible. And notwithstanding the many reproaches they had heard cast upon the Baptist denomination, for refusing to be dictated in their religious affairs by civil law, and for trusting alone to the spirit and providence of God to support their cause, they thought best to examine for themselves, and see, if what had so long been deemed foolishness and enthusiasm were not a virtue. Accordingly in October, 1804, application was made to the Stonington Baptist Association by some of the aggrieved people of Lebanon, requesting some of their ministers to visit them and preach the gospel to them. It being in our view consistent with the great commission to preach the gospel to every creature, whether they be governed by civil law in their religion or not, eight of our ministers agreed to visit them in their turns between that time and the next spring.

" When it came to my turn according to appointment to visit this people for the first time (which was about a year ago) I perceived so much solemnity and candour among them, and such a spirit of inquiry after the apostolic truth and practice, as could not fail to interest my feelings in their behalf. I also found how grossly mistaken many people abroad had been about them, by reason of their circumstances having been misrepresented. *Their* ideas were no less incorrect with respect to the Baptists. I therefore thought it my duty to pay more attention to them than just to preach a single day, and then leave them. Hence I appointed to visit them again in February, and continue with them eight or ten Sabbaths. During this visit God was pleased to move upon the minds of some by the influences of his Spirit, as I have reason to hope. While some, who had never experienced the truth, felt the pangs of conviction, a number of backsliders seemed disposed to return to the great Shepherd and Bishop of their souls. Some, who had been members of the Presbyterian church, obtained light upon Bible baptism, and the doctrine of the covenants. Many others began to inquire whether they had not taken that for granted, which ought first to have been proved, in supposing that baptism was appointed by God as a substitute for circumcision, and for a sign and seal of the same covenant. And whether in the case of infant sprinkling they had not acted without any positive or fairly implied evidence. Our assemblies were large and solemn as they have ever since continued. And on Fast day, last spring, three persons were baptized, which, I conclude, were the first ever baptized in this parish.

" As my time of engagement was near expiring, the proprietors of the new house, with others, met and requested me to remove my family, and make my home with them. With this request I thought it duty to comply, and agreed to stay and preach with them as long as they and I should think it duty ; leaving it for them to do for me whatever Bible and conscience should dictate, and nothing more. They accordingly removed my family from Middletown to this place in May last, and have hitherto done for me and my family as well as the principles of honour and christian friendship require, without the aid of civil law to enforce their obligations. A people, who are governed by the religion of Christ, will do their duty in these respects much more cheerfully and uniformly, than those who are goaded to it by civil penalties.

" Since I commenced my stated labours here, God has been pleased graciously to continue his favour to the people. Some have been hopefully converted to God, and baptized. Several brethren and sisters from the Presbyterian church have put into practice the light they have obtained upon this ordinance. Some backsliders have been waked up to purpose, and put on the Lord Jesus Christ.

NEHEMIAH DODGE.

LEBANON, DECEMBER 27, 1805."*

This revival continued until a sufficient number of baptized believers were collected for the purpose, who received the fellowship of a large number of ministers as a distinct church, September, 1805. Among these ministers were Dr. Baldwin of Boston, Dr. Gano of Providence, and others. This church has since increased to eighty members. The meeting-house, thus unexpectedly built for Baptist use, is 73 feet by 48 with a steeple and bell.

By this church was sent into the ministry Mr. Jonathan Goodwin, pastor of the church in Mansfield, founded by Mr. Joshua Bradley in 1809.

GROTON UNION CONFERENCE.

THIS name was given to an Association, which was formed in 1785. The churches of which it is composed are intermixed with those of the Stonington ; they at first held pretty generally, if not uniformly, to open communion, which accounts for its being formed in the neighbourhood of that body. But this practice I believe they have all now given up, and are in fellowship with the surrounding churches.

* Massachusetts Baptist Missionary Magazine, vol. i. p. 186—8.

The Groton church, from which this body took its name, is the second in the town ; it was formed in 1765 ; its first pastor, Silas Burrows, is still living, though far advanced in years. His son, Roswell Burrows, has been ordained his colleague, and will doubtless succeed him. This is a large and flourishing church, has had many refreshing seasons, and contains between two and three hundred members. Mixed communion they held till 1797, when the practice was relinquished without opposition. A few members of this community had lived a number of years at a place called Preston city, considerably to the north of it, where a revival commenced in 1811, in which forty or fifty were brought to put on Christ by a publick profession. They have built them a commodious house of worship, and will probably soon become a distinct church.

LYME.—In this town a church arose in early times under the ministry of an Elder Cooley, which was long since dissolved. The wife of this Elder was a Rogerene, and gave her husband no little trouble in the prosecution of his ministry, but more especially in his family devotions. One of his deacons was a brother of the late Governor Griswold.

The present church in Lyme was formed in 1752, by the labours of Elder Ebenezer Mack, who was for some years its pastor. It arose out of a church of the Pedobaptist New-Lights, which was formed in 1749. Mr. Mack removed to Marlow, in New-Hampshire, in 1768, where he tarried many years, but in his old age came back and died among this people.

The second pastor of this flock was Elder Jason Lee, who died among them at an advanced age in 1810.

The church is now under the care of Mr. Asa Wilcox from Rhode-Island. Their number is between four and five hundred ; they have a farm and parsonage house, the gift of Capt. Miller, estimated at about twelve hundred dollars.

A second church was formed in this town in 1812. Their preacher is Mr. Mathew Bolles from Ashford.

In NORWICH a church was formed in 1800 ; their pastor is Mr. John Sterry ; they have lately received a legacy of real estate supposed to be worth about six thousand dollars. It was given by a Mr. Hatch, who was not a Baptist, and had never manifested any peculiar regard for the denomination. It is said that he had been heard to lament that the Baptists were no more able to support the ministry among them ; but no one knew what he had done until his Will was opened. His widow is a member of the church, and is to have her support out of the property during her life.

From the preceding sketches it appears that the county of New-London has been a fruitful nursery of Baptists for more than a century. The towns of Groton and Stonington have been the most distinguished for the prevalence of the denomination. In these two towns are now five churches, which contain about one thousand communicants. Our brethren here have met with but little opposition from the ecclesiastical powers of the State, compared with what they have experienced in other parts. Their contiguity to the State of Rhode-Island has probably been a principal cause of the prevalence of their opinions and of the toleration they have enjoyed. This Baptist corner of Connecticut is generally represented in as deplorable a state of darkness and ignorance as Rhode-Island, and ministers are frequently sent to teach and enlighten it.

A number of the churches in this body are in Rhode-Island and a few in Massachusetts.

In the north-east corner of this State in the counties of Windham and Tolland, are ten churches belonging to the Sturbridge Association. Some of them arose out of Separate Pedobaptist churches, but most have had their origin at a later period. A church in Thompson was formed on the *Six Principle Plan*, under the ministry of Mr. Wightman Jacobs from Rhode-Island, in 1750. And upon this plan was formed an Association about the same time, which increased to eight or ten churches, when it began to decline and has long since been dissolved. The churches of this Association were mostly in Rhode-Island, which Thompson joins. The first church we find here was dissolved, and the present arose out of its ruins in 1773 ; Mr. John Martin became its pastor ; after him was Mr. Parson Crosby, who is still with them. In 1811, a revival commenced among this people, during which about a hundred were added to their number by baptism. They have a farm with buildings for the accommodation of their pastor, estimated at about two thousand dollars.

The first church in Woodstock was formed in 1766, by the labours of that distinguished man of God, Biel Ledoyt, who spent fourteen years of his ministry in New-Hampshire, and who died among his own people this present year.

The dates of the remaining churches, their pastors, &c. will be exhibited in the General Table.

In this region are a few churches not associated, one of which in Ashford was once under the care of Mr. Thomas Ustick, afterwards pastor of the first church in Philadelphia. It now has for its pastor Mr. Frederick Wightman from Rhode-Island.

DANBURY ASSOCIATION

Was formed in 1790 in the town from which it received its name. It extends from the line of Massachusetts south to the sea-coast; it also extends to the State of New-York, and a few churches are in that State. Its movements have been harmonious and respectable, but nothing very remarkable has attended them. Of only a few of its churches shall we be able to give much account.

SUFFIELD. This town is on the Connecticut River eighteen miles above Hartford. In the time of the religious agitations in New-England, two Separate churches were formed here, whose pastors were Holly and Hastings. Holly wrote first against the Connecticut establishment; then against the Baptists, and afterwards turned back and became a parish minister. Hastings persisted in his separation, and towards the close of his life became a Baptist. Some time before the year 1770, a church of the denomination arose partly out of the remains of the two Separate ones, and partly of those who had newly professed religion, and John Hastings, son of the minister just named, was ordained its pastor in 1775. He was one of the most eminent ministers among the Connecticut churches in his day, and under his labours a large and extensive church arose, which spread its branches throughout a wide extent of towns. It is said that during the whole of his ministry he baptized eleven hundred persons. He finished his course with much serenity, March 17, 1811, aged 68. His successor is Mr. Asahel Morse, late pastor of the church in Stratfield in this State.

From this church, according to a statement of its clerk, originated those of Westfield, Russell, Wintonbury, Hartford, Windsor, Enfield, Granville, Southwick, and Granby, in Massachusetts and Connecticut. Great numbers have also emigrated from this fruitful community to different and distant parts.

In 1804, a second church was formed in this town, partly of members from this body, but not in fellowship with it. Its minister is Mr. Caleb Green from Newport, Rhode-Island.

In COLEBROOK, west of Suffield, adjoining Massachusetts, a church was formed in 1794, and was the first of any denomination gathered in the town. Their pastor is Mr. Rufus Babcock, a descendant of a family of that name in Westerly, Rhode-Island.

HARTFORD.—In this city a church was established in 1790, mostly of members from the Suffield. For a few years after they embodied, they were supplied part of the time by Elders Winchell, Moffit, and others. In 1795, Mr. Stephen S. Nelson was settled in the pastoral office, in which he continued until 1800, when he removed to Mount Pleasant in the State of New-York. Under his ministry a revival took place, in which about seventy-five were added to their number.

For about seven years from Mr. Nelson's removal, this church remained destitute of a pastor, but was generally supplied with neighbouring ministers, and two years of the time by the late Mr. David Bolles of Ashford, who, during that time, resided in the city.

In 1807, they settled among them Mr. Henry Grew from Providence. His ministry was acceptable and prosperous about four years, when he withdrew from his office, and formed a new church on the plan of weekly communion, &c.

Next to him is their present pastor, Mr. Elisha Cushman, a native of Kingston, Massachusetts.

The house of worship belonging to this church stands at the corner of Dorr and Theatre-streets, in a central part of the city; it is 51 feet by 41, with a steeple fourteen feet square. The lot is but a little larger than the house, and is the gift of deacons John Bolles and Samuel Beckwith. Both house and lot were at first owned by the church and society in connexion, but in January, 1813, the society made a generous transfer of their claim to the church, with whom the estate is now wholly vested. This was a rare instance of reformation in the embarrassing tenure of property for religious purposes too common in New-England. It is hoped that other *societies* may follow the example of the accommodating one at Hartford.

This church has lately had a reversionary bequest of bank stock, to the amount of over eight thousand dollars from Mr. Caleb Moore, one of their members.

In MIDDLETOWN a church was formed in 1795. They have a commodious house of worship, and are in a promising condition. Their first pastor was Elder Stephen Parsons, formerly a Pedobaptist minister of the Separate order, who is now settled in the Black River country, New-York. After him they were supplied at different periods by Elders Enoch Green, John Grant, Asa Niles, Joshua Bradley, and others. Last year they settled among them Mr. George Phippen, a graduate of Brown University, who was sent into the ministry by the church in Salem, Massachusetts.

At a place called the Upper Houses in this town, a church was formed in 1800, mostly of members from Hartford.

STRATFIELD.—This is an ancient and respectable church. Like many others in this State, it arose out of a Pedobaptist community of the Separate order, and was formed in 1751. Mr. Joshua Morse, then of New-London, made frequent visits to the place, and baptized most of the first members in it. About six years after they were set in order as a church, Mr. John Sherwood, one of their number, was ordained their pastor, by Messrs. Morse and Timothy Wightman of Groton. He served them about ten years, when his health declined, and the pastoral office devolved on Mr. Benjamin Coles, from Oyster-Bay, Long-Island, who, after tarrying here about six years, removed to Hopewell, New-Jersey. Since then, they have had in succession Elders Seth Higby, Stephen Royce,* and Asahel Morse, now of Suffield. Unless they have settled

* By Mr. Royce the Author was baptized in 1798.

a minister lately, the pastoral office is now vacant. This church has two houses of worship about ten miles apart; it is scattered in many of the surrounding towns, and has extended its branches to Wilton and New-Canaan on towards the line of New-York. They have a small estate estimated at about eight hundred dollars.

In STAMFORD, near the south-west corner of this State, a church was formed in 1773. Most of the first members were baptized by John Gano from the city of New-York, and added to the church under his care, where they continued until their number was sufficiently large to become a distinct body. Mr. Ebenezer Ferris one of their number was ordained their pastor not long after they began their movements, and is still with them, though far advanced in years. A few other churches have, at other times, arisen in this part of the State, of which we shall give a list in the table of Associations, &c.

From this State have emigrated multitudes of the Baptist denomination to New-York, Vermont, and all the surrounding States. This land of steady habits has also given birth to a great number of ministers, who have settled without its bounds. Among these are Messrs. Isaac Backus, the historian, John Waldo, Dr. Thomas Baldwin, Aaron Drake, Justus Hull, Elias Lee, Jeremiah Higbee, Stephen Parsons, Henry Green, Peter P. Roots, and many others. The maxims of the land do not well suit the genius of our Order, and besides, the country is so fully settled, as population increases, the surplusage must go abroad for settlements.

The religious laws of Connecticut are not much unlike those of Massachusetts. The Pedobaptist, frequently called the Presbyterian party, was taken under legal patronage in early times. The whole State was divided into parishes, in which houses of worship were built, ministers settled, and maintained all *according to law*. Some ministers here as well as in Massachusetts are supported from funds, pew rents, &c. but by far the greater part have their living by a direct tax according to the civil lists, which every human being within the parish bounds, whether Jew or Gentile, Infidel or Christian, possessed of a rateable poll or taxable property, is obliged to pay, unless he gives a certificate of his different belief.

An Act for the Relief of the Baptists.

The first certificate law in Connecticut was passed in favour of the Quakers, May, 1729. It provided that those who should produce from a society of that denomination a writing, certifying that they had united with them, and did attend their meetings of worship, should be exempted from ministerial taxes, &c.

In the autumn of that year a similar act was passed in favour of the Baptists of the following tenor :

UPON the Memorial of the people called Baptists, praying that they may be discharged from the payment of rates and taxes for the support of the gospel ministry in this government, and for building meeting-houses,

"*It is resolved by the Governor, Council, and Representatives, in General Court assembled, and by the authority of the same,* That for the future, the same privilege and exemption from the charges aforesaid, as was granted by this Assembly in May last, unto the people called Quakers, is hereby allowed unto them, under the same regulations ; any law, usage, custom, to the contrary notwithstanding."

This act appears to have been obtained principally by the friendly assistance of the Rhode-Island brethren. At an Association of their churches held in North-Kingston, September, 1729, they drew the Memorial above-mentioned, which was signed by Richard Sweet, Valentine Wightman, Samuel Fisk, John Comer, Elders, and brethren Timothy Peckham, Joseph Holmes, Ebenezer Cook, Benjamin Herenden and others, to the number of eighteen, all of Rhode-Island except two. To this Memorial was added the following :

"WE the subscribers do heartily concur with the Memorial of our brethren on the other side, and do humbly request the same may be granted, which we think will much tend to christian unity, and be serviceable to true religion, and will very much rejoice your Honors' friends, and very humble servants,

JOSEPH JENKS, *Governor.*
JAMES CLARK, } *Elders.*
DANIEL WIGHTMAN, }

Newport, Sept. 10, 1729."

This law continued in force without much variation over sixty years. The Quakers and Baptists were the only denominations exempted till about 1756, when the same privileges granted to them were extended to dissenters of all classes, provided they *ordinarily* attended meetings in their respective societies, and paid their due proportion, &c. otherwise they should be taxed.

The words *ordinarily*, &c. were intended to restrain those, who might go off to dissenting sects from motives of economy only, but on the strength of the clause, collectors found pretexts to frequently distrain taxes from church members. A number of Baptists in Stafford had united with the church in Willington under the care of Elder Lillibridge from Rhode-Island. The distance being great and the way rough, they did not meet with the church so often as they could have wished, or the law required. The Presbyterians in Stafford, to pay the expense of a new meeting-house, taxed them all, distrained their goods, and disposed of them at public sale. The brethren then set about seeking redress, commenced an action against the distrainers for their goods, damages, &c. The affair went through two courts; in the second the counsel for our brethren plead, that they were Baptists *sentimentally*, *practically*, and *legally*. To this statement the counsel on the other side acceded, but still continued his plea against them because they did not *ordinarily* attend their own meeting. While the lawyers were disputing, the Judge, who was an Episcopalian, and not very well affected towards the predominant party, called the attention of the court by inquiring, how long a man, who was a Baptist *sentimentally*, *practically*, and *legally*, must stay at home to become a Presbyterian? His Honor's logic produced the same effect upon the whole court as it must upon the reader, and the Baptists easily obtained the case.

In May, 1791, the ruling party thinking probably that certificates were too easily procured, passed a law that they should in future be signed by two magistrates before they could be valid and effectual. This law set all the dissenters in motion. Remonstrances and memorials poured into the Assembly from every quarter, and the act was repealed the October following, when the present certificate law was passed, which reads thus:

"Be it enacted by the Governor and Council and House of Representatives in General Court Assembled, That in future, whenever any person shall differ in sentiments from the worship and ministry, in the ecclesiastical societies in this State, constituted by law within certain local bounds, and shall choose to join himself to any other denomination of Christians, which shall have formed themselves into distinct churches or congregations, for the maintenance and support of the publick worship of God, and shall manifest such his choice, by a certificate thereof, under his hand, lodged in the office of the Clerk of the Society to which he belongs,—such person shall thereupon, and so long as he shall continue ordinarily to attend on the worship and ministry, in the church or congregation, to which he has chosen to belong as aforesaid, be exempted from being taxed for the future support of the worship and ministry in such society.*

This law is probably as favourable as any one of the kind can be framed. A dissenter has nothing to do but to write his own certificate, and then he becomes of another sect. This facility has been the cause of multitudes leaving the established order, who are of no use to any other denomination. No man can be a neuter in religion neither here nor in Massachusetts; unless he gives a certificate of dissent, he is known and dealt with in law as a Presbyterian or Congregationalist.

To the certificate law of this State as it now stands, our Baptist brethren object principally, that it presupposes a subordination, which they do not well relish, and obliges them, in Leland's phraseology, *to lower their peek to the national ship.* They have made several attempts to get it repealed, but the established clergy have hitherto had influence enough to prevent it. In one of the petitions of the Baptists to the Assembly, dated February, 1803, is the following clause : " We are frequently told that giving a *certificate* is a *mere trifle* : if it be so, we would desire that the law would not intermeddle with such *a trifling business*, or that those, who consider it as a mere trifle, may be the persons to do this trifle themselves, and not the dissenters, who consider it in a far different point of light."

Some will not give certificates at any rate, and so much are matters mollified, that very few at present meet with much trouble whether they do or not.

The Pedobaptist communities have found by experience, that it will not do to push their measures, for wherever they have, swarms have deserted from them.

* Statutes of Connecticut.

CHAPTER XV.

NEW-YORK.

THIS State contains almost a million of inhabitants. It stretches from the Atlantic ocean north to the River St. Lawrence, and north-west and west to the lakes Ontario and Erie.

The first appearance of Baptists in this State was in the city from which it takes its name ; they were next found on Long-Island, and a third company settled in dutchess county up the Hudson River.

So late as 1764, it does not appear that there were more than four Baptist churches in this extensive territory ; in 1790, they had increased to sixty, their preachers were about seventy, and their communicants not far from four thousand. There are now of the denomination somewhere between two and three hundred churches, and probably over sixteen thousand members.

NEW-YORK CITY.

BAPTIST churches of late years have increased in this famous metropolis something faster than the materials needful for their construction, and of course some have become extinct, others are small and declining, while a few have gained a good degree of maturity, and are large and flourishing bodies.

First, or Gold-Street Church. This church was founded on its present plan, in 1762, but a community of General or Arminian Baptists had existed on the ground long before, of which it may be proper to give a brief account. William Wickenden of Providence, Rhode-Island, during his ministry there, frequently preached in this city, where, at one time, as a reward for his services, he was imprisoned four months. At what time this event took place, cannot be ascertained ; it must have been before 1669, for in that year Mr. Wickenden died. From this period we hear nothing of Baptists here until about 1712, when Mr. Valentine Wightman of Groton repaired to the place, by the invitation of Mr. Nicholas Eyres, and continued his visits about two years. " His preaching place was Mr.

Eyres' house. Under his ministry many became serious, and some hopefully converted. Their names were Nicholas Eyres, Nathaniel Morey, Anthony Webb, John Howes, Edward Hoyter, Cornelius Stephens, James Daneman, Elizabeth Morey, Hannah Wright, Esther Cowley, Martha Stephens, and Mrs. —— Miller. Some time in 1714, Mr. Wightman baptized the five women in the night, for fear of the mob, who had been very troublesome, while the seven men stood by. The following text dropped into Mr. Eyres' mind, *No man doeth any thing in secret, when he himself seeketh to be known openly.* Accordingly he and the six brethren put off their design till morning, when Eyres waited on the Governor (Burnet,) told the case, and solicited protection, which the Governor promised, and was as good as his word, for he and many of the gentry came to the water side, and the rite was performed in peace. The Governor, as he stood by, was heard to say, " This was the ancient manner of baptizing, and in my opinion much preferable to the practice of modern times." The above twelve persons called Mr. Eyres to preach to them, by whose ministry the audience so increased, that a private house would not hold them. Accordingly they purchased a lot on Golden Hill, (not far from the lot where the present meeting-house now stands) and thereon built a place of worship some time in the year 1728.* The house was in being in 1774, but by mismanagement had become private property. Thus they went on to the month of September, 1724, when Messrs. Valentine Wightman, of Groton, and Daniel Wightman of Newport, formed them into a church and ordained Mr. Eyres to be their minister. To the before mentioned twelve were added, under Mr. Eyres' ministry, William

---

* Among Mr. Backus' papers I found a letter addressed to the church in Providence by Elder James Brown, soliciting some assistance towards defraying the expense of this house. In this address it is stated that the brethren in New-York had purchased a lot and built them a place of worship which cost them dear. That one of their company, a man of property, on whom they much depended, had left them, and the rest being poor, they were now incumbered with a debt which they were utterly unable to discharge. It is furthermore stated that contributions had been made for these people among the Rhode-Island brethren the year before, but as farther aid was still needed, it was thought that about *five and twenty or thirty pounds* would be a suitable proportion to be raised by the church in Providence. At the close of this address there is subscribed by Mr. Brown *one pound*, and by a number of others *thirteen barrels of cider,* which was then valuable in that market.

Ball, Ahasuerus Windall of Albany, Abigail and Dinah North of Newtown, Martha Walton of Staten-Island, and Richard Stillwell, jun. Seven years after, that is, October, 1731, Mr. Eyres resigned the care of them to go to Newport on Rhode-Island. After him Mr. John Stephens preached to them, and baptized Robert North, Mary Morphy, Hannah French, Mary Stillwell, and two more whose names are not known. But Mr. Stephens quitting them to go to South-Carolina, and their house being taken from them, the church dissolved away after having increased to twenty-four members, and existed about eight years.

The present church originated in the following manner : About the year 1745, Mr. Jeremiah Dodge, a member of Mr. Holstead's church at Fishkill, settled in New-York, and opened a prayer, reading, and singing meeting at his own house, to which some of Mr. Eyres' church resorted; but as they were Arminians, and Dodge a strict Calvinist, no good came of it, except that the aforementioned Robert North and he agreed to invite Mr. John Pine, an unordained preacher in the church of Fishkill, to come and preach to them. His ministry took effect partly in reconciling some of the old church to Calvinism, and partly in the conversion of others, particularly John Carman and Nehemiah Oakly, who were baptized by said Holstead ; but Mr. Pine dying in 1750, Mr. James Carman of Cranberry, New-York, visited them and baptized, so as to increase their number to thirteen ; then they were advised to join themselves to Scotch-Plains, so as to be considered a branch of that church, and to have their minister, Mr. Benjamin Miller, to preach and administer the Lord's Supper to them once a quarter; this was effected in 1753. Mr. Miller had not ministered to them many months before the audience grew too large for a private house, therefore they hired a rigging loft in Cart and Horse Lane, and made it convenient for publick worship ; but being refused continuance there after three years, they were obliged to meet in Mr. Joseph Meeks' house in William Street, where they continued about one year ; then they purchased a part of a lot on Golden Hill, and thereon built the meeting-house before described, and for the first time met in it, March 14, 1760. Having now a place of worship, and the number of members increasing to twenty-seven, they petitioned the Scotch Plains for a dismission, which was granted them June 12, 1762, and on the 19th of the same month, they were constituted a church by the assistance of Miller and Gano, and the same year joined the Association."*

Mr. John Gano became the pastor of this church at the time of its constitution, and continued in that office about twenty-six years, when he removed to Kentucky, as will be related in his biography. During his ministry, the church received by baptism about 300 members, and excepting the interruptions of the war, it enjoyed an almost continual scene of prosperity and enlargement. Three men of dividing principles, viz. John Murray, now of Boston, John Allen or Junius Junior, and one Dawson, a censured member, from Dr. Gifford's church in London, each in their turns attempted divisions, caused no little trouble, but in the end failed of success.

The next year after Mr. Gano's removal this church had the happiness to settle in the pastoral office Mr. afterwards Dr. Benjamin Foster, who ministered to them with much reputation and success till 1798, when he died with the yellow fever. For a further account of this distinguished character, the reader is referred to his biography.

Successor to Dr. Foster was Mr. William Collier, now of Charlestown, Massachusetts, who officiated here about four years.

After him was Mr. Jeremiah Chaplin, now pastor of the church in Danvers, the birth place both of Dr. Foster and himself. He served this people about one year. Of these two pastors something has already been said under the head of Massachusetts.

The next in office here was the present pastor, Mr. William Parkinson. He was born near Fredericktown, Maryland, November 8, 1774, served a number of years as pastor of the church in that town, was three sessions chaplain to Congress, and was settled in his present station in the beginning of 1805. Under Mr. Parkinson's ministry this church has enjoyed peculiar prosperity and enlargement; it has also on account of some grievous allegations against his moral character, been called to pass through an afflictive

* Morgan Edwards' MS Materials, &c. For a further account of Mr. Eyres, see Newport, Rhode-Island.

scene of trial and adversity. Twice he has been indicted for an assault and battery; two long expensive law-suits have been maintained, in both of which he was acquitted for want of evidence; but still the minds of not a few of his brethren and friends remain burdened. The crimes laid to his charge by his female accusers he denies; imprudent conduct with some of the tempting daughters of Eve, he has confessed to his church, who have received his confession as satisfactory, and resolved to retain him in office. Further than this, the relation of this unhappy affair may better be omitted.

The house of worship built by this church in 1760 was enlarged during the ministry of Mr. Gano, but the whole was removed, together with the parsonage house adjoining, in 1801, to make room for their present spacious edifice, which was erected the year after. It is built of stone, 80 feet by 65, and cost, including its furniture, about 25,000 dollars. It is situated in Gold-Street on a lot of 125 feet by 100.

From this church have originated the Bethel, the next to be named, the one at Peekskill up the Hudson River, those of King-Street and Stamford in Connecticut, one at Newtown on Long-Island, the Abyssinian or African Church, and North Church, both in this city.

The ministers, who have been sent out from this ancient establishment, are Messrs. Thomas Ustick, late of Philadelphia, Isaac Skillman, D. D. once pastor of the Second Church in Boston, Stephen Gano of Providence, Rhode-Island, Thomas Montanye of Southampton, Pennsylvania, Cornelius P. Wyckoff, James Bruce deceased, and John Seger.*

BETHEL CHURCH.—This church was formed from the Gold-Street not altogether harmoniously in 1770. But as the dispute was about matters of no great interest, it was soon settled, and the two churches have long travelled in fellowship together. This church in the beginning was called the second in New-York, its first pastor was Dr. John Dodge, who is now settled with the church in Canton, above Poughkeepsie. He was born on Long-Island, February 22, 1738, was bred to physic, became a Baptist in Baltimore, by means of the late John Davies, became

* Jubilee Sermon, &c.

the pastor of this church soon after it arose, and continued with it a number of years. After him they had for a number of years Mr. Charles Lahatt, now of Pittstown in this State. Successor to him was their present pastor, Mr. Daniel Hall. The first house of worship belonging to this body was in Rose-Street, where they met until 1803, when they sold that and built their present house in Broome-Street, 44 feet by 36. It stands on a lot 50 feet by 100.

Fayette-Street Church.—This church arose out of a division of the Bethel in 1791, both parties claimed the name of *Second* until 1802, when their differences were adjusted, and they by mutual consent gave up their claims to priority, and took the names they now bear.

The first pastor of the church under consideration was Mr. Benjamin Montanye, now of Deer Park in this State. Successor to him was Mr. John Williams, under whose ministry they have been built up to a large and flourishing body, and to his conciliatory maxims, must, in a good measure, be attributed the adjustment of the former difficulties in which they were involved. Their first house of worship was small, their present, erected about 1800, is 60 feet by 43, situated on the street from which the church was named.

Mr. Williams was born in Carnarvon county, South-Wales, in 1768, and landed in New-York, 1795.

Mulberry-Street Church.—The origin of this church was marked with some peculiarities, which were briefly as follow : In 1805, Mr. Archibald Maclay, its founder and present pastor, arrived in this city from Scotland. He was then an Independent, under the patronage of the churches of that order in his native land. He, no more than Mr. Williams, had fixed upon this metropolis as a place of settlement. Mr. Williams had designed to have gone to Pennsylvania ; Mr. Maclay's place of destination was Boston ; but finding here a few brethren of his own persuasion, he, in compliance with their solicitation, agreed to tarry a few weeks with them. They rented at first, and afterwards purchased the house in Rose-Street, formerly occupied by the Bethel Church. Here Mr. Maclay began his labours, a respectable congregation soon collected, and in the course of a few months a small church of the

Independent persuasion was formed, which, in three years, increased to forty members. This little church arose under many discouragements, had enjoyed many tokens of Divine favour, and was united to an uncommon degree in the tender ties of christian affection. But their pastor, after a thorough investigation of the subject, was constrained to become a Baptist, and had the ordinance administered to him, December, 1808, by Mr. Williams above named, and four days after seventeen of his church were baptized by the same administrator, a number more soon after followed their example, and in February, 1809, they were formed into a Baptist church. They hold and practise weekly communion, but are not disposed to break fellowship with their brethren, who differ from them on this point. Their number has increased to about 200.

Their house of worship stands on the Street, from which the church is named, is 60 feet by 40, and cost, together with their lot, about 8000 dollars. The lot is 48 feet by 104.

Mr. Maclay is a native of Scotland, studied in Mr. Haldane's Academy at Edinburgh, and is probably about 35 years of age.

The North Baptist church was formed of members from the Gold-Street in 1809. Their pastor, Mr. Cornelius P. Wyckoff, was formerly a member of the North Dutch church in this city.

The Abyssinian or African Church was also formed from the Gold-Street, in 1809. They have purchased a very commodious house of worship in Anthony-Street, for which it is feared they will not be able to pay. Their present minister is Jacob Bishop from Baltimore.

A church called *Ebenezer*, was gathered a few years since under the ministry of the late Mr. John Inglesby, which is now small, and has never been large.

In 1811, a church was formed in Mulberry-Street, called *Union*, from a schism in the Bethel Church respecting discipline. Their number is 24. They were at first under the care of Mr. Thomas Stevens, who has since removed from them. They have still a preacher by the name of Sylvian Bijotat, a native of Paris, France, whose ancestors were Seventh-Day Baptists in that city.

A church once existed in Fair-Street ; under the ministry of Mr. John Stanford, which has many years been dissolved.

In 1806, a church was gathered mostly of natives from Wales, called the *Welch Church.* Their pastor, Mr. John Stephens, from Newport, Pembrokeshire, in the Principality, was for a few years its pastor. But he has removed to Utica, and the church has become extinct.

A church called *Zoar,* because it was a *little one,* was formed a few years since from the Gold-Street, which has also disbanded.

Besides these there is a small church in this city of Weekly Communion Baptists, and another of Free-Will Baptists, and how many other kinds I know not.

At Oyster Bay, on Long-Island, a church arose in early times, but the exact date of its origin cannot be ascertained. As early as 1700, the gospel was preached here by one William Roads, an unordained minister of the Baptist persuasion, who fled hither to avoid persecution, from what place does not appear. By his ministry a number were brought to an acquaintance with the truth, among whom was one Robert Feeks, who was ordained pastor of the church in 1724, by Elders from Rhode-Island. In 1741, Elder Feeks wrote to his brethren in Newport as follows : " God has begun a good work among us, which I hope he will carry on. There have been seventeen added to our little band in about three months. When Mr. Feeks was far advanced in years, this church obtained for its pastor one Thomas Davis, who laboured with them several years, and then removed to other parts. After him a young man by the name of Caleb Wright, one of their members, engaged in the ministry ; his gifts appeared promising to an uncommon degree, a day was appointed for his ordination, which proved to be the day of his burial ! After this melancholy event the church was supplied by visiting ministers, until Mr. Benjamin Coles, one of their number, began to labour among them. Mr. Coles was born in the township, April 6, 1737, began to preach when young, spent six years with the church at Stratfield in Connecticut, seven with the one at Hopewell, and two at the Scotch Plains, both in New-Jersey ; the rest of his ministry was spent in Oyster Bay, where he died in a good old age, August,

1810. A few years before his death, the infirmities of age and a burdensome corpulency disqualified him for stated ministerial services, and as Mr. Marmaduke Earle had removed to take charge of an Academy in the place, the church invited him to succeed in the pastoral office. Under his ministry in 1805 a revival commenced, in which about a hundred members were added by baptism. Mr. Earle is a native of New-York, and was educated in the college in that city.

Besides this church, there are, on the Island, those of Coram, Southhold, and Newtown, all destitute of pastors. Newtown is frequently supplied by ministers from New-York, but the others, on account of their remote situations, are seldom visited.

At Mount Pleasant, on the Hudson River, thirty-six miles from New-York, a church was founded in 1790; it is now under the care of Mr. Stephen S. Nelson, a native of Middlebury, Massachusetts, formerly pastor of the church in Hartford, Connecticut. In this place the New-York Association attempted to found an Academy, for the purpose of assisting young preachers in their studies. A convenient edifice was erected, and some measures were taken to carry the design into effect, which, however, soon fell through for the want of patronage. When Mr. Nelson settled in the place, he purchased the building and premises, and under his superintendance, a seminary of a respectable character has been conducted to the present time.

NEW-YORK ASSOCIATION.

This association was begun in 1791. Most of the churches, of which it was formed, had previously belonged to the ancient Association of Philadelphia. A number of them are situated in New-Jersey, where they will be noticed under the next head. This body has uniformly held its anniversaries in the city where it was formed; nothing special occurred in its progress until 1812, when, on account of the affair of Mr. Parkinson, a number of its churches withdrew, and now remain out of any associate connexion.

WARWICK ASSOCIATION.

This body was also formed in 1791, and its oldest churches had before stood connected in the same Association with those of the one last mentioned. They are situated some distance up the country on both sides of the Hudson River.

The Warwick church, from which this Association received its name, was planted in 1766, by Mr. James Benedict, from Ridgefield, Connecticut, who became its pastor, and continued in that office till his death. This church at first was exceeding small, but the year after it was formed, it increased to about 70, and soon amounted to 200, when it began to branch out in different directions, and from it were set off in the early stage of its existence, Wantage, Deer Park, Middleton, &c. In 1769, it joined the Philadelphia Association, under the name of Goshen. After Mr. Benedict was Mr. Thomas Jones, and then Mr. Thomas Montanye, who was ordained its pastor in 1788, at which time the war had so scattered its members, that but about thirty were to be found, and these were spread over a circumference of almost as many miles. Soon a revival commenced, and in less than a year and a half 140 were added by baptism. Many of these soon dispersed to the western country and other parts, and by them a number of other churches were founded. Mr. Montanye, after labouring here a few years, removed to his present situation at Southampton, Pennsylvania, and was succeeded by Mr. Thomas Stephens, who tarried with them but a short time. Successor to him was Lebeus Lathrop, their present pastor. They have lately built a commodious house for worship, and have an estate supposed to be worth about 1500 dollars. From this church originated James Finn, Amos and Moses Parks, Dr. John Munro, late of Galway in this State, Jehiel Wisner, and Ephraim Sanford.

Mr. John Gano resided a number of years within the bounds of this church, while exiled from his station at New-York.

UNION ASSOCIATION

Was organized in 1809. Some of its churches had belonged to the one last mentioned, a few came off from the Danbury, the others had not been in any associate connexion. The centre of this body is about sixty miles above the city of New-York, on the east side of Hudson River; four of the churches are in Connecticut.

In the town of Fishkill are two churches belonging to this Association, but no historical accounts of them have come to hand. It appears there was a church in this town as early as 1745, of which Mr. Holstead was pastor.

On north of this Association are a number of churches, which arose in early times; they are situated in Dutchess county, about 70 or 80 miles north of the metropolis of the State, at no great distance from the western line of Connecticut. Here seems to have been a distinguished resort for Baptists, when there were but few in any other part of the State.

In this region a considerable number of preachers have laboured at different times for about sixty years past, and a still greater number have emigrated from it to other parts. Elders Dakin, Waldo, and Bullock, appear to have been the most distinguished of the company, and of them we shall give some brief accounts in speaking of the churches which arose under their labours.

Northeast Town.—The church, which at present bears this name, was, according to the best information, begun about the time of the remarkable revival under Whitefield, Tennant, and others, to which we have so frequently referred in the history of the New-England States. While that work was going on, a number of the members of a Presbyterian church, in a place then called South-Precinct, now Franklin, withdrew and joined one in the neighbourhood of the Congregational order, which held to open communion. Among these dissenters was Mr. Simon Dakin and many others, who soon fell in with Baptist principles, and founded a church in 1751, of which Mr. Dakin was ordained pastor about three years after. Respecting the early movements of this church no historical accounts can be obtained, as the Herveys, its principal promoters, some years after it began, removed beyond the Hudson River, and carried the records with them. But we are informed, that Mr. Dakin's ministry was greatly blessed, and that a numerous church arose, which branched out to different places. Some removed to what is now called Northeast Town, where a church was gathered under the ministry of Mr. James Philips, who, after serving it some years, went to Fishkill. To this place Mr. Dakin repaired in 1773 ; many of his church in Franklin it seems came with him; what were left behind fell in with a southern branch, which arose under the ministry of Mr. Nathan Cole, one of Mr. Dakin's members.

In Northeast Town Mr. Dakin spent the most of his long and pious ministry. He was born in Concord, Massachusetts, 1721, came with his father to this region at the age of sixteen, and died in 1803, in the 83d year of his age, and the 50th of his ministry, leaving behind him a character fair, amiable, and unspotted. The church is now under the care of Mr. Isaac Allerton ; from it originated Mr. James M. Winchell, now preaching with the first church in Boston.

In Dover, below Northeast Town, are two churches, which arose from one founded by Elder William Marsh from New-Jersey, in 1755. Mr. Marsh was succeeded in the pastoral office by the late Samuel Waldo, in 1758, who ministered here with much reputation and success, upwards of thirty-five years. This church was at first called Beekman's Precinct, and under that name belonged to the Philadelphia Association as early as 1772, and probably much earlier. It afterwards took the name of Pauling's Precinct, then of Pauling's town, and finally it assumed the name it now bears. In 1762, a church was set off from this in a place called the Oblong. In 1794, another was formed from it, which took the name of the Second in Dover ; and besides these branches multitudes of its members have emigrated at different times to many places in Vermont and other parts.

Mr. Waldo was born in the eastern part of Connecticut in 1739, but was brought up in Mansfield in that State. At the age of eighteen he professed religion in the Baptist connexion, and soon after was ordained to the pastoral office in the church under consideration. His parents belonged to a Presbyterian church, but became Baptists after this son united with the denomination. Mr. Waldo's ministry was distinguished for nothing so much as piety and success. Those, who were long acquainted with him, speak of him in the highest terms of approbation, as a man of an unspotted life, of a sound mind, unusually edifying as a preacher, affable and engaging in every circle, skillful in the discipline of his church, remarkable and inimitable in the government of his family; in a word, in him was united every qualification, necessary for a plain, profitable, and successful minister of the cross. Soon after he settled with this church, a revival commenced in which over sixty were added in a short time.

In 1775, another refreshing season was granted, in which over fifty were added to his flock in about ten months. Besides seasons of special revival, he had many seals of his ministry during the whole of its continuance. Having served this church over thirty-five years, he was called away to receive his reward, 1792, in the 62d year of his age. His widow is yet living, aged 82. Seven children out of nine he had the happiness of receiving into his church before his death. One of his sons is now resident in Georgetown, South-Carolina.

Since the death of this venerable pastor, the church has had various supplies, but have lately settled among them a pastor by the name of Elisha Booth.

In the Great Nine Partners a church was formed under the ministry of the late Elder Comer Bullock, about 1779; it has, at times, flourished much, and embraced a multitude of members in many of the surrounding parts of the country. In 1790, according to Asplund's Register, it contained 370 members, and its preachers, besides Elder Bullock, were Christopher Newcum, Christopher Newcum, jr. Nicholas Hare, James Purdy, and Abraham Adams. Mr. Bullock was born in Rehoboth, Massachusetts, probably about 1736; was named after John Comer, once pastor of a church in that town, to which he belonged before his removal to this place, where he was ordained about 1780, by Elders Charles Thompson, then of Warren, and Samuel Hicks of the place of his nativity. Mr. Bullock finished his pious course in 1811.

In the neighbourhood of Mr. Bullock's church, another arose in 1788, to which Dr. Gano, now of Providence, ministered a few years before his removal to his present station.

In Poughkeepsie a church was founded in 1807, partly out of the ruins of one, which had existed in the place a few years before, under the ministry of a boisterous preacher by the name of Palmer. They had for their pastor a short time after their re-organization, Mr. Francis Wayland, now of Troy, above Albany. Their present pastor is a young man by the name of Lewis Leonard, from Bridgewater, Massachusetts. They have a new commodious house of worship, and appear in a promising condition.

As we go north from this region, we find sixteen churches, belonging to the Shaftsbury Association, containing about half of the members of that body.

In New-Canaan a church was planted over forty years ago by Elder Jacob Drake, from which many others originated. Mr. Drake removed from Windsor, Connecticut, and settled in this town in 1769. He was then a Pedobaptist minister of the Separate connexion, and finding a number of his own persuasion in the neighbourhood, he formed them into a church and was ordained their pastor, 1770. After travelling on the Pedobaptist plan about eight or nine years, he, with many of his flock, embraced the Baptist principles, and formed a church of baptized believers only. One article of their covenant was, "A church consists of a Pastor and Teacher, Ruling Elders and Deacons." Mr. Drake travelled and preached abundantly with great success, insomuch that his church in ten years from its beginning amounted to between five and six hundred members. They were spread over a great extent of country, not only in the neighbouring towns, but branches were scattered at many miles distant, on both sides of the Hudson River, for wherever Mr. Drake baptized any disciples, he gave them fellowship as members of his flock. When this wide-spread church contained the number just mentioned, there were in it, besides its pastor, eleven Teachers and Ruling Elders. Their names were David Skeels, Bariah Kelly, jun. David Mudge, Jeduthan Gray, Reuben Mudge, John Mudge, Nathaniel Kellogg, Hezekiah Baldwin, Aaron

Drake, jun. Nathaniel Culver and Asahel Drake. The four last were Ruling Elders, but had a right to administer ordinances. Dr. Gano of Providence was about this time preaching at Hillsdale, not far distant, where he founded a church, which he served a number of years ; he laboured with Mr. Drake's people to show them the impropriety of their proceedings, and mostly by his influence they set off from their great unwieldly body, five distinct churches in 1789, viz. Great Barrington and Egremont, Warren's Bush, Coeyman's Patent, Duane's Bush, and Rensellaerville. The church in West-Stockbridge had been formed from it in 1781, and the one at New-Concord was set off in 1791. Thus, from the labours of this itinerating pastor and his spiritual sons, arose eight churches in the course of about twelve years. " Some," observes Mr. John Leland, who furnished this account, " say that Mr. Drake contended for an Apostolical gift ; be that as it may, he has been a successful preacher, and he is the best *fisherman*, who catches the most *fish*," &c.

In 1792, Mr. Drake removed to Wyoming in Pennsylvania, where he founded a church, which has spread extensively, along the Susquehannah River. In this country he died at an advanced age, having been some time blind ; the date of his death I have not learnt. The Church at Canaan, after having adopted some different maxims, was received into the Shaftsbury Association. It is now in a feeble State without a pastor. A second church was formed in this town in 1793, which is also destitute.

In Berlin a church arose in 1785, under the ministry of Mr. Justus Hull, which has been distinguished for unusual prosperity, and now contains over 600 members. It was at first called Little Hoosick, from the name of a river on which it is situated. Afterwards it was named Stephentown, then Stephentown and Petersburgh ; these frequent changes of name would puzzle the searcher of registers to identify this body, were it not that Justus Hull has, from first to last, been its pastor. Some of its original members removed from Exeter, Rhode-Island. Mr. Hull was born in Reading, Connecticut, in 1755, where, and in different parts near, he, not long after his commencement in the ministry, laboured with good effect.

A revival of an uncommon nature was experienced in Berlin in 1811 ; over 200 joined the church under consideration. Fifty-seven were baptized in one day, in the space of thirty-two minutes. Over 100 joined the Sabbatarians, and about thirty were added to the open communion church in the town.*

By this church were sent into the ministry Robert Niles, Eber Moffit, Alderman Baker, and probably many others.

In Albany, Troy, and Lansingburgh, all within nine miles of each other, on the Hudson River, are churches, which do not appear to have been marked with any peculiar events. The church in Troy was formed in 1795, under the ministry of Mr. Elias Lee, now at the Ballstown Springs. It has a commodious house for worship, and is under the care of Mr. Francis Wayland, a native of England, who was sent into the ministry by the Fayette Street church in the city of New-York.

The church in Lansingburgh is three miles north of it. Its late pastor, Mr. Nathaniel Kendrick, is now at Middlebury, Vermont.

In the city of Albany a small Baptist church was gathered in 1811, which has since increased to upwards of seventy members. Soon after they were embodied, a revival commenced under the ministry of Elder Joseph Utley, belonging to the second church in Groton, Connecticut. This work progressed under the labours of Mr. Francis Wayland of Troy. The church is now under the care of Mr. Isaac Webb, from Ireland.

In Cambridge a church was planted in 1772, by Elder William Wait from Rhode-Island. It was at first called White's Creek, is situated near the line of Vermont, and within half a mile of Elder Wait's house the Bennington Battle terminated. The night before the battle, some of his church went over to the enemy, where they were obliged to fight, and during the bloody conflict the heavens and the earth witnessed the shocking spectacle of brethren, who, but a few days before had set together at the table of the Lord, arranged in direful hostility against each other, amidst the clangor of arms and the rage of battle. Brother fighting against brother! Such are the horrors and unnatural effects of war! O, tell it not in Gath, publish it not in the streets of Ashkelon. This melancholy affair threw the church into confusion, and entirely broke

* M. B. M. Magazine, Vol. iii. p. 172—3.

it up. The next year Mr. Wait collected three members besides himself, and began anew, a revival soon commenced, so that, in 1780, the number amounted to 140. It is now something smaller, and has for its pastor Elder Obed Warren, a native of Dudley, Massachusetts, who has long been with the Salem church, still above this. Mr. Warren has been a successful minister in these parts, and has at different times travelled and laboured much in regions remote and destitute.

In Granville, not far from the place last mentioned, a church was gathered in 1788 by Elder Richard Sill from Connecticut, whose ministerial course was short but highly respectable and useful. The church has had since his death various supplies, but since 1806 has been under the care of Mr. Samuel Rowley, a native of Rutland in Vermont. Under his labour they have enjoyed a season of revival, and have been built up to a large and flourishing community.

RENSELLAERVILLE ASSOCIATION.

This Association is on the west side of the Hudson River, and many of the churches composing it are at no great distance from it. The town from which it took its name is about twenty miles south-west of Albany. It began in 1796, with only three churches, viz. two in Rensellaerville and one in Broome. It has since increased to over twenty churches, and nearly two thousand members, but has been much reduced lately by dismissing churches to associate elsewhere. Many of the members of this community removed hither from New-England. Elder Philip Jenkins, late pastor of the church in Bern, died in 1811, in the 85th year of his age. He was born in one of the Kingstons, Rhode-Island, in 1727; was first a member, then a deacon of the church in Exeter, in that State. After he began to preach he planted a church in North-Kingston, which he continued to serve until about 1795, when he removed to this part of the vineyard. For more than half a century Mr. Jenkins was zealously engaged in the work of the ministry, and according to Mr. Andrew Brown, one of his members, was a man of eminent piety and usefulness, during the whole of his long and unspotted life.

SARATOGA ASSOCIATION.

This Association was formed by a division of the Shaftsbury in 1805. The churches of which it is composed are mostly on the east side of the Hudson River, between that and the Mohawk, and are scattered in every direction around the famous Saratoga Springs. The ground occupied by this body was, for the most part, in a wilderness state at the close of the American war, and very few of the churches were constituted previous to 1790. A number of them are large, but as no accounts of their origin and progress have been communicated, but little can be said respecting them. At the Ballstown Springs is a church under the care of Elder Elias Lee, a native of Connecticut, whose name is known throughout an extensive circle, on account of his publishing a number of well-written pieces on different points of theological controversy. In this church a very extraordinary case of healing took place in the person of Martha Howel, a few years since, who, from a state of helpless decrepitude, was suddenly restored to perfect soundness, without the application of any external means. Those, who may wish to gain more particular information of this uncommon occurrence, may find it in a pamphlet published by Elder Lee.

The late eminent Lemuel Covel was sent into the ministry by the church of Providence, belonging to this Association, now under the care of Elder Jonathan Finch.

At Stillwater, within the bounds of this community, and near the place where General Burgoyne was taken, a church was formed over forty years ago, which was broken up and scattered by the devastations of the war. About 1780, Elders Beriah Kelly, one of Mr. Drake's connexion, and Lemuel Powers from Northbridge, Massachusetts, began to labour in the place, and raised two distinct churches, which in about ten years were incorporated into one under the care of Elder Powers. This church increased abundantly and spread its branches into all the surrounding country, insomuch that in 1793, after between forty and fifty had been set off from it, to found the church at Fish Creek, it contained upwards of four hundred members. But in ten years from that time it was reduced to a little more than twenty, and is now small, though beginning again to revive. The cause of this dispersion was owing partly to the spirit of emigration, which possessed the members, but mostly to some misconduct in their pastor, or at least to some reports unfavourable to his chastity. He confessed he had been imprudent, but at the time, and in his dying moments, denied having been actually guilty. But so it was, that his usefulness was ruined, his church scattered, and he went mourning down to his grave, which he entered in peace in 1800, in the 45th year of his age.

The dispersion of this great body might well be compared to a shipwreck : and on that account, Mr. Leland, being called to preach among them in the time of their troubles, took for his text, Acts xxvii. 44, *And some on boards, and some on broken pieces of the ship—and so it came to pass, that they all escaped safe to land.* The members though scattered were not lost, but united with the other surrounding churches. Elder David Irish, once a member of this church, and an assistant to Mr. Powers, is now in Aurelius, in the western part of this State.

The church in Clifton Park, but eight or ten miles westward of Half Moon Point, did not see fit to take a dismission with the rest of the Saratoga churches, but still belongs to the Shaftsbury Association. It is a large and flourishing community, under the pastoral care of Elder Abijah Peek.

LAKE GEORGE ASSOCIATION

Is still north of the one last described. It is a small body, formed about the year 1809. Its name suggests its local situation. Elder Jehiel Fox, formerly of St. Coyt, appears to have been the first Baptist minister in these parts. He settled in Chester in 1797, and in this then destitute region, in the course of about twelve years, travelled about as many thousand miles, to sound the gospel to the scattered inhabitants. Elder Daniel M'Bride, a few years since, was sent into the ministry by the church in Chester, founded by Mr. Fox, and is now labouring with good effect in those parts. Mr. James Whitehead, the third minister in the Association, has lately removed to the State of Vermont.

THE ESSEX ASSOCIATION

Is in the north-east corner of this State, on the western shore of Lake Champlain. It was formed in 1802. The first and almost only minister in these parts for many years was Elder Solomon Brown, by whom most of the first churches in this body were planted.

ST. LAWRENCE ASSOCIATION

Was begun in 1812, of a few small churches mostly the fruits of missionary labours. It took its name from the country in which the churches are situated, which was called after a well known river, which proceeds from Lake Ontario.

BLACK RIVER ASSOCIATION.

This Association takes its name from that of a newly settled region, near the east end of Lake Ontario. It was formed in 1808. One of their principal ministers is Elder Emery Osgood, from Massachusetts, who settled here in 1803, at which time there was no ordained minister of the Baptist order within sixty miles of him. At Turin, within the bounds of this Association, now resides Elder Stephen Parsons, formerly of Middletown, Connecticut.

In what is usually called the western part of New-York, that is, in that vast range of territory west of the old settlements on the Hudson and Mohawk Rivers, between the northern Lakes and the State of Pennsylvania, is a very large assemblage of churches, which have mostly been planted within less than twenty years past. They are, with a very few exceptions, included in the Otsego, Madison, Franklin, Cayuga, and Holland Purchase Associations, which we shall briefly describe in the order here stated.

OTSEGO.

This Association was organized in 1795; but was begun under the name of a Conference the year before. At the time of its organization, Elders Werden, Cornell, and Craw, from the Shaftsbury Association, were present to counsel and assist them. The churches, of which it was composed, had arisen very suddenly in the infant settlements around, and at no great distance from the Otsego Lake, about sixty or seventy miles west of Albany. This Association began under very encouraging prospects, and increased with great rapidity, so that by the year 1807, twelve years from its commencement, its churches amounted to fifty-five, its preachers to thirty, and its communicants to upwards of 3000. It had then become so extensive, that a division was thought proper; accordingly in 1808, a number of the western churches were dismissed and united with others in forming an Association, to which they gave the name of

MADISON.

It consisted at first of eighteen churches and fourteen ministers, among whom were some of the principal ones in the country. Its total number of members amounted to a little more than a thousand.

FRANKLIN.

This Association was formed in the southern bounds of the Otsego, and of churches mostly from that body in 1811. It received its name from the town of Franklin, in the county of Delaware, where there is a church of more than two hundred and fifty members, by far the largest in this body.

CAYUGA.

This Association lies at a considerable distance to the westward of those just mentioned, around the lake from which it received its name.

In 1799, a number of churches in this quarter united together, under the name of the Scipio General Conference, which arose to an Association in 1801. It had, in 1811, increased to 38 churches, 24 ministers, and over 3000 members.

From these brief sketches of the rise of these four Associations, we shall proceed to some general observations on their boundaries, ministers, &c.

Boundaries and general Account of four Associations. 557

The Otsego Association, in 1799, extended from east to west about 140 miles, and from north to south not far from 60. It probably became much more extensive before it was divided in 1808. But after fitting out two Associations, it is reduced to narrower limits, which I am not able precisely to state; it is, however, sufficient to say, that its churches are on both sides of the Mohawk River, on the head waters of the Unadilla River, the Butternut Creek, and about the Otsego Lake.

The churches of the Madison Association are on the east, west, and middle branches of the Chenango River, and the east range of townships in the Military Tract, so called, extending about fifty miles north and south, and forty east and west.

The Franklin Association lies mostly between the Delaware and Chenango Rivers, and extends from the southern bounds of the Otsego Association, on south towards the State of Pennsylvania.

The Cayuga Association occupies an extent of country of about a hundred miles from east to west, and not far from forty north and south. Its churches are situated on the east, west, and north sides of the Cayuga and Seneca Lakes, and are scattered along westward as far as the Genessee River. This extensive body will probably be soon divided. In its bounds are at least five churches of respectable standing, which have not yet associated, besides many collections of brethren, called conferences, which are maturing for churches.

In these four Associations are now a hundred and thirty odd churches, about seventy ministers, and not far from nine thousand members. These churches, with a very few exceptions, have been raised up in the space of about twenty years. Most of the ministers by whom they have been planted are still alive, and actively engaged in this part of the Lord's vineyard. Many of them, especially of the older class, began their labours in this wilderness region, under many trials and disadvantages, being generally low in their worldly circumstances, and often too much neglected by the churches. But we are happy to state, that they now enjoy a competence of worldly things, and some have arisen to a considerable degree of opulence, not by the munificence of their brethren, but by the smiles of Providence on their own exertions.

Among the large body of elders in these Associations, William Furman, Joel Butler, Ashbel Hosmer, and David Irish, are represented by their brethren as having been the most successful in their labours. Mr. Irish removed to Scipio in the early settlement of the place, and planted a church in 1795, which now contains about 250 members. He has sometime been pastor of a church in Aurelius, whose members amount to over four hundred. When he settled at Scipio, there was no Baptist minister in regular standing, (impostors were plenty) within more than a hundred miles of him, and most of the way was through a wilderness. In this western region he has baptized about a thousand persons.

Elder Hosmer was born in West-Hartford, Connecticut, 1758. At the age of sixteen he entered the service of his country, in which he received a severe wound. When about thirty years of age, he was baptized and became a member of the church in Canaan, in his native State, where he began to preach soon after. From that place he removed to Wallingford, where he was ordained in 1792, and three years after settled in Burlington, New-York. In that place he resided a number of years, and travelled and preached abundantly in all the surrounding country, being poor and often much straitened in his worldly circumstances. From Burlington he removed to Hamilton, where he resided till his death. There he found himself among a people, who knew how to explain aright the Apostle's meaning, when he says, *They, that preach the gospel, shall live of the gospel.*—By them he was placed in circumstances easy and comfortable. But in the midst of a course of distinguished usefulness, this eminent servant of God and the churches was suddenly arrested with a violent fever, of which he died April, 1812, in the 55th year of his age.

Elder William Furman removed from St. Coyt, not far from Albany, and settled in Springfield at the head of the Otsego Lake in 1789. After labouring many years in that quarter, he removed to Avon, within the bounds of the Cayuga Association, where he died in 1812.

Elder Joel Butler, from what place I do not find, settled between the two Canada Creeks, north of the Mohawk River, in 1793. He lately had the misfortune to fall into the fire in a fit, which afflictive event has mostly laid him by from his ministerial labours.

By the three last mentioned ministers, most of the first churches in the Otsego Association were set in order; by them also most of the baptisms in early times were administered, and very few ministers were ordained without their assistance.

Elder Peter P. Roots, and a great number of others might be mentioned, as having been distinguished for usefulness, in the new settlements in this western region, to which multitudes have emigrated from all the New-England States. By these emigrants many of the churches have been enlarged, but they are mostly indebted, for their prosperity and numbers, to those many and extensive revivals, which the gracious Lord has granted to this highly favoured country. It is asserted by brethren, capable of giving correct information on the subject, that since 1794, scarce a month has passed without some special outpourings of the Divine Spirit, within the bounds of these four Associations.

HOLLAND PURCHASE CONFERENCE.

This name was given to a small collection of churches, which convened for the purpose of beginning an Association at a place called Willink, in the county of Niagara, in 1811. The number at first was seven, all of which were small, and amongst them were but three ministers. The Holland Purchase is an extensive tract of country, in the western part of New-York. A Baptist church was formed in it in 1808, at a place called township No. 10. This was the first church of any denomination founded in this Purchase, and is the fruit of missionary labours. Mr. Roots and other missionaries have laboured much and with good effect in this remote region, in which there is now an encouraging prospect of an extensive spread of the Redeemer's cause.

From these brief sketches we see that Baptist principles and Baptist churches have, within a few years past, spread into every corner, and been established in almost every part of this extensive State.*

To the History of this State we shall subjoin a brief account of the Baptists in

UPPER CANADA.

WHAT few churches are found in this Province were built up mostly by missionaries from NewYork, Vermont, and some other States. An Association, called Thurlow, was formed in the place from which it took its name, in 1804, of only three small churches, whose ministers were Asa Turner, Joseph Winn, and Reuben Crandal. These churches were scattered over an extensive country, along the Bay of Canta, in the districts of Midland and New-Castle. About the time they were organized into an Association, they were visited by Elders Joseph Cornell and Peter P. Roots, by whose labours they were much refreshed and encouraged. The late Lemuel Covel and many other missionaries have travelled in this remote part of his Britannic Majesty's dominions, whose labours have been crowned with success, insomuch that the Thurlow Association in 1811, had increased to eleven churches, eight or nine ministers, five only ordained, and about a thousand members. What is their state since this Canadian war commenced, I have not learnt. Elder Turner who communicated this information, is now settled at Scipio, New-York. A few churches in this Province belong to the Shaftsbury Association. The one at Niagara, under the care of Elder Elkanah Holmes, has a seat in the New-York Association.

* For a part of the information respecting this western region, the author is indebted to a work published in 1794, by Elders Hosmer and Lawton, entitled, A View, &c. of the Otsego Association All the late information was furnished by the same Elder Lawton and Elder John Peck, who travelled extensively and took much pains to collect it.

CHAPTER XVI.

NEW-JERSEY.

"SOMETIME after the year 1608, the Hollanders made a settlement on the spot where New-York now stands; and in 1614 obtained a patent from their countrymen. In consequence of which, and a pretended purchase from Capt. Hudson, they claimed a right to all the country from the river Connecticut to the river Delaware, and, therefore, that part now called Jersey. But neither patent nor purchase availed them; for Charles II. put in a prior claim, and supported it with armed forces, which the Hollanders were not able to resist; nevertheless, they kept possession to the treaty of Breda, in 1667. About four years before said treaty, the king gave the country to his brother the Duke of York; and the Duke, the same year, sold the western part, Jersey, to Lord Berkeley and Sir George Carteret. Those two gentlemen immediately formed a constitution, or bill of rights, for such as should be settlers; the sixth and seventh articles of which promise a "full liberty of conscience to all religious sects that should behave well." This, and the terms of obtaining land, being known abroad, British subjects began to resort hither from New-York, New-England, Long Island, &c. these settled in the parts next to them, afterwards called East-Jersey; some of whom were Baptists. In the year 1675, and afterwards, emigrants arrived in the Delaware from England, and settled in the parts adjoining the river, since distinguished by the name of West-Jersey; some of them, also, were Baptists. About 1683, a company of Baptists, from the county of Tiperary, in Ireland, arrived at Amboy; they proceeded towards the interior parts. In the fall of 1729, about 30 families of the Tunker Baptists from Holland, but originally from Schwartzeneau in Germany, arrived at Philadelphia; some of whom, in 1733, crossed the river Delaware, and settled at Amwell in Hunterdon county. In 1734, the Rogerene Baptists arrived from Connecticut, and settled near Schooly Mountain, in the county of Morris. Thus it appears, that among the first Jersey settlers, some were of the Baptist denomination. The present Baptists are, partly, the offspring of those adventurous Baptists; and, partly, such as have been proselyted to their sentiments."

This State has been famous with the Baptists, for containing a number of old and very respectable churches, which have been supplied with preachers of peculiar eminence; some emigrated from Wales and England, but most of them were born in the country, and nurtured in the churches.

New-Jersey has given birth to a number of very eminent ministers, who removed and spent their days in other parts; among the most distinguished of these, we may reckon John Gano, James Manning, and Hezekiah Smith.

MIDDLETON.—" This is the oldest church in the State; it is thus distinguished from the village where the meeting house stands, in a township of the same name, and county of Monmouth, about 79 miles E. N. E. from Philadelphia. The meeting house is 42 feet by 32, erected in 1734, on the lot where the old place of worship stood.

"For the origin of this church we must look back to the year 1667; for that was the year when Middleton, containing a part of Monmouth, and a part of Sussex counties, was purchased from the Indians by twelve men and twenty-four associates; their names are in the town book. Of them the following were Baptists, viz. Richard Stout, John Stout, James Grover, Jonathan Bown, Obadiah Holmes, John Buckman, John Wilson, Walter Hall, John Cox, Jonathan Holmes, George Mount, William Cheeseman, William Layton, William Compton, James Ashton, John Bown, Thomas Whitlock, and James Grover, jun. It is probable, that some of the above had wives and children of their own way of thinking; however, the forenamed eighteen men appear to have been the constituents of the church of Middleton, and the winter of 1688, the time.

" How matters went on among these people for a period of 24 years, viz. from the constitution to 1712, cannot be known. But in the year 1711, a variance arose in the church, insomuch that one party excommunicated the other; and imposed silence on two gifted brothers that preached to them, viz. John Bray and John Okison. Wearied with their situation, they agreed to refer matters to a council, congregated from neighbouring churches.

The council met, May 25, 1712; it consisted of Rev. Messrs. Timothy Brooks, of Cohansey; Abel Morgan and Joseph Wood, of Pennepek; and Elisha Thomas, of Welch Tract, with six Elders, viz. Nicholas Johnson, James James, Griffith Miles, Edward Church, William Bettridge and John Manners. Their advice was, "To bury their proceedings in oblivion, and erase the records of them;" accordingly four leaves are torn out of the church book. "To continue the silence imposed on John Bray and John Okison the preceding year." One would think by this, that those two brethren were the cause of the disturbance. "To sign a covenant relative to their future conduct;" accordingly 42 did sign, and 26 refused; nevertheless most of the non-signers came in afterwards; but the first 42 were declared to be the church that should be owned by sister churches. "That Messrs. Abel Morgan, sen. and John Barrows should supply the pulpit till the next yearly meeting; that the members should keep their places and not wander to other societies;" for at this time there was a Presbyterian congregation in Middleton, and mixed communion in vogue.

"The first who preached at Middleton, was Mr. John Bown, of whom we can learn no more than that he was not ordained; and that it was he who gave the lot on which the first meeting house was built. Cotemporary with him was Mr. Ashton, of whom more will be said soon; and after him rose the forementioned Bray and Okison; neither of whom was ordained, and the latter was disowned. Mr. George Eaglesfield was another unordained preacher; but the first that may be styled pastor of the church, was,

"James Ashton. He probably was ordained by Thomas Killingsworth, at the time the church was constituted in 1688; for Mr. Killingsworth assisted at the constitution, which gave rise to the tradition " that he was the first minister." Mr. Ashton's successor was

"Rev. John Barrows. He was born at Taunton, Somersetshire, England, and there ordained: arrived at Philadelphia in the month of November, 1711, and from thence came to Middleton in 1713, where he died in a good old age. Mr. Barrows is said to have been a happy compound of gravity and facetiousness; the one made the people stand in awe of him, while the other produced familiarity. As he was travelling one day, a young man passed by him in full speed ; and in passing, Mr. Barrows said, " if you considered whither you are going, you would slacken your pace." He went on, but presently turned back to inquire into the meaning of that passing salute ? Mr. Barrows reasoned with him on the folly and danger of horse-racing : (to which the youth was hastening,) he gave attention to the reproof. This encouraged Mr. Barrows to proceed to more serious matters. The issue was a sound conversion. Here was a bow drawn at a venture ; and a sinner shot flying !—

Mr. Barrows was succeeded by Rev. Abel Morgan, A.M. He was born in Welsh Tract, April 18. 1713 : had his learning at an academy kept by Rev. Thomas Evans, in Pencader ; ordained at Welsh Tract in the year 1734 ; became pastor of Middleton in 1738 ; died there November 24, 1785. He was never married ; the reason, it is supposed, was, that none of his attention and attendance might be taken off of his mother, who lived with him, and whom he honoured to an uncommon degree. Mr. Morgan was a man of sound learning and solid judgment ; he has given specimens of both in his publick disputes and publications ; for it appears that he held two publick disputes on the subject of baptism. The first was at Kingwood ; to which he was challenged by Rev. Samuel Harker, a Presbyterian minister. The other was held at Capemay, in 1743, with the Rev. afterwards, Dr. Samuel Finley, President of Princeton College.

" Mr. Morgan's successor was his nephew, Rev. Samuel Morgan. He was born in Welsh Tract, August 23, 1750 ; called to the ministry in Virginia ; ordained at Middleton, November 29, 1785 ; at which time he took on him the care of the church."

No account of Mr. Morgan's death has been obtained. This ancient church has for its present pastor, Mr. Benjamin Bennet. It was once well endowed, but a considerable part of its temporalities were sunk by that sacrilegious thing, (as Edwards calls it) *Congress Money*. What are its present possessions I have not learnt.

Account of Piscataway Church.

PISCATAWAY.—"The history of this church, which is the next to Middleton in point of seniority, from the beginning to the present time, is not easy of acquisition. The reason is, their records were destroyed in the revolutionary war. The following historical sketches have been gleaned partly from publick records; partly from the town book; partly from the records of the Sabbatarian church, which sprang from this church; and partly from current tradition, and the information of ancient persons. The publick records tell us, "That the large tract, on the east side of Rariton river, which comprises the towns of Piscataway, Elizabeth, &c. was purchased from the Indians in 1663. The purchasers were John Baily, Daniel Denton, Luke Watson, &c. These persons and their associates obtained a patent the following year, from Governor Nicholas, who acted under the Duke of York; but the Duke having, the same year, sold Jersey to Lord Berkeley and Sir George Carteret, the validity of Nicholas's patent has been called in question." However, the inhabitants keep possession to this day. The said tract does not, by the town records, appear to have been settled at once, but in the following successions. "In 1677, the Blackshaws, Drakes, Hands, and Hendricks, were inhabitants of Piscataway; in 1678, the Dottys and the Wolfs; in 1679, the Smalleys, Hulls, and Trotters; in 1680, the Hansworths, Martins, and Higgins; in 1681, the Dunhams, Laflowers, and Fitzrandolphs; in 1682, the Suttons, Brindleys, Bounds, and Fords; in 1683, the Davises and Slaughters; in 1684, the Pregmores; in 1685, the Grubs and Adams; in 1687, the Chandlers and Smiths; in 1689, the Mortons, Molesons and M'Daniels; the Gilmans were settlers in 1663, which is one year before the patent." Were we to judge of the religion of these settlers by the lists of members in the two Baptist churches of Piscataway, we should conclude they were of that denomination, for most of the names are to be found in those lists. Nevertheless, tradition will allow of no more than six to have been professed Baptists, viz. Hugh Dunn, who was an exhorter; John Drake, afterwards their pastor; Nicholas Bonham, John Smalley, Edmond Dunham, afterwards minister of the Seventh-Day Baptists; and John Randolph; the above persons were constituted a Gospel church, in the spring of 1689, by the help of Rev. Thomas Killingsworth, at which time it is probable Mr. Drake was ordained their pastor. It is not to be doubted, but the said men had wives, or sisters, or daughters of the same way of thinking : however, none but the male members are mentioned, either here or at Middleton, or Cohansey. It is a current tradition, that some of the above Baptists emigrated hither from Piscataqua, in the District of Maine, and gave the name to this part of Jersey. This is a probable supposition, for there were a number of Baptists in that place at this time, and it appears, that this part of Jersey was written *New-Piscataqua* in their town book, and in the printed folio, which contains the original Jersey papers.

"The first who preached at Piscataway, from the beginning of the settlement to 1689, were the following unordained ministers, viz. Messrs. Hugh Dunn, John Drake, and Edmond Dunham. About 1689, Rev. Thomas Killingsworth visited them, and settled them into a church, and ordained Mr. Drake to be their minister; this gave rise to the tradition, "that Mr. Killingsworth was the first minister of Piscataway, Middletown, and Cohansey." The last is true ; but the first minister of Piscataway was Rev. John Drake, who was one of the first settlers, and bore an excellent character; he laboured among them from the beginning to 1689, when he was ordained their pastor, and continued in the pastorship to his death, in 1739, which was a period of about 50 years. Mr. Drake's descendants are very numerous, and respectable among the Baptists in this region; they claim kindred to the famous Sir Francis Drake.

Cotemporary with Mr. Drake, was the unworthy Henry Loveall. He was ordained in this church to assist old Mr. Drake, but never administered ordinances ; for the vileness of his character was soon discovered. From Piscataway he went to Maryland, where see an account of him.

"Mr. Drake's successor was Benjamin Stelle who held the office of a magistrate. He was of French original, though born in New-York ; ordained in this church, and continued in the pastorship to the month of January, in 1759, when he died in the 76th year of his age. He is said to have been a popular preacher, and a very upright magistrate.

"He was succeeded by his own son, Isaac Stelle, who became minister of Piscataway in 1752, as an assistant to his father, who was old and infirm, and continued in the ministry here to October 9, 1781, when he died in the 63d year of his age. Mr. Stelle was remarkable for his travels among the American churches, in company with his other self, Rev. Benjamin Miller."

Rev. Reune Runyon, the late pastor of this church, succeeded Mr. Stelle. He also was of French extraction, and son of Reune Runyon, Esq.; born March 29, 1741; called to the ministry in this church, March, 1771; ordained at Morristown, March, 1772, where he continued to April, 1780, and then returned hither. He took on him the oversight of the church in 1783, and continued therein with credit and success till his death in Nov. 1811.

Mr. James M'Laughlin succeeded him, October, 1812. He preaches half of the time at New-Brunswick, two and a half miles distant, where there is a branch of the church and a commodious house of worship lately built of brick, 60 feet by 40, on a lot of near an acre. The lot and house cost about 6000 dollars.

The Piscataway church is the mother of the Scotch-Plains, Morristown, and the Sabbatarian church, in the same neighbourhood.

COHANSEY—"Cohansey is the name of a river, which meanders in the neighbourhood, and from which this church takes its distinction; the meeting house stands in the township of Hopewell, and county of Cumberland, 47 miles south by west from Philadelphia.

"The rise and progress of Cohansey church cannot be easily investigated, because their records have been destroyed; nevertheless, the following historical sketches will, in part, supply the loss: "About the year 1683* some Baptists from the county of Tiperary in Ireland settled in the neighbourhood of Cohansey; particularly

---

* "In Cohansey grave-yard is a stone with this inscription upon it: "Here lies Deborah Swinney, who died April 4, 1760, aged 77 years. She was the first white female child born at Cohansey." If we take her age out of 1760, it will appear she was born in 1683, the time fixed, by Mr. Kelsay, for the settling of the place by *Irish* Baptists; and Swinney was an *Irish* man."

David Sheppard, Thomas Abbot, William Button, &c. In 1685, arrived hither from Rhode-Island government, Obadiah Holmes and John Cornelius: In 1688, Kinner Vanhyst, John Child and Thomas Lamstone were baptized by the Rev. Elias Keach, of Pennepek. About this time Rev. Thomas Killingsworth settled not far off, which increased the number of Baptists to nine souls; and probably to near as many more, including the sisters; however, the above nine persons were formed into a church, by the assistance of said Killingsworth, whom they chose to be their minister; this was done in the spring of 1690. Soon after the few Baptists who lived about Gloucester, Salem, Pennsneck, &c. united with them; so that the cords of this Zion were at first very lengthy, and continued so for 66 years; viz. till distant members began to form themselves into distinct churches, in the several neighbourhoods." The churches which were thus formed were those of Salem, Dividing Creek, and Pittsgrove.

Most of the Baptist churches in America originated from England and Wales; but Cohansey from Ireland. The Baptist church whence it sprang, is still extant in Tiperary, and distinguished by the name of Cloughketin.

"In 1710, Rev. Timothy Brooks and his company united with this church. They had emigrated hither from Swanzey, in Massachusetts, about the year 1687; and had kept a separate society for 23 years, on account of difference in opinion relative to predestination, singing psalms, laying-on-of-hands, &c. Rev. Valentine Wightman of Groton, Connecticut, formed the union, on the terms of *bearance and forbearance.*

" In 1711, they built their first meeting house, which was taken down to erect the present in its place; for from the beginning till then, they held worship in private houses, though a period of about 28 years.

" It does not appear that this people had any stated preacher, before the constitution, except Obadiah Holmes, the son of the famous Obadiah Holmes, who endured such cruel scourgings at Boston, in 1651, for the Word of God, and the testimony of Jesus. He was not ordained. His settling at Cohansey is placed under the year 1685, which was four years prior to the constitution; he continued an occasional preacher while he lived, though a Judge of the Common Pleas in Salem Court.

"The first pastor of Cohansey was Thomas Killingsworth, Esq. He took the oversight of the church at the constitution in 1690, and continued therein to his death, in the year 1708. This honourable gentleman, (for he was Judge of Salem court) was probably a native of Norwich, in England. He must have arrived in America in early times; and must have been an ordained minister before he arrived; for we find him exercising the ministerial functions, at Middleton in 1688; at Piscataway in 1689; and at Philadelphia in 1697. He had a wife, but no issue. It seems that the troubles, which came on dissenters, in Queen Ann's reign, reached the Jersey; for Mr. Killingsworth put himself under the protection of the toleration act, at a court held in Salem, December 24, 1706, and took out a license for a preaching place at Penn's-Neck, then the dwelling-house of one Jeremiah Nickson.

"His successor was Rev. Timothy Brooks. It has already been observed that Mr. Brooks' company and the church at Cohansey, coalesced into one body in the year 1710. It was at that time that he took the care of the Cohansey church; he continued in the care thereof to 1716, when he died in the 55th year of his age, and had upwards of 80 of his own offspring to follow him to his grave. Though Mr. Brooks was not eminent for either parts or learning, yet was a very useful preacher, meek in his carriage, and of a sweet and loving temper, and always open to conviction, which gained him universal esteem, and made the Welch ministers labour to instruct him in the ways of the Lord more perfectly.

"Mr. Brooks was succeeded by Rev. William Butcher. He became the minister of this church in 1721, and continued therein to December 12, 1724, when he died in the 27th year of his age. Mr. Butcher was a very popular preacher, and, withal, very tall and of a majestic appearance, which procured him the name of the *High Priest.*

"Rev. Nathaniel Jenkins took the oversight of this church, at an advanced age, in 1730; and continued therein to his death, January 2, 1754.

"He was succeeded by Rev. Robert Kelsey, who was a native of Ireland, born near Drummore in 1711; arrived in Maryland in 1734; came to Cohansey, in 1738; embraced the sentiments of the Baptists in 1741; was ordained in 1750, and became pastor of this church in 1756, in which office he continued to his death, which came to pass, May 30, 1789. The publick print which announced his death, adds, "as a man and companion, he was amusing and instructive; as a christian, he was animated and exemplary; as a preacher, fervent and truly orthodox; warmly engaged was he in the service of th sanctuary, to which he repaired without interruption, till a few Lord's days previous to his decease."

The present pastor of this church is Mr. Henry Smalley, who was sent into the ministry by the church in Piscataway, and ordained here September, 1790.

This church was well endowed in early times, but what their present income is, I have not ascertained.

CAPE-MAY.—The foundation for this church was laid in the year 1675, when a company of emigrants from England arrived in the Delaware, some of whom settled at the Cape. Among these were two Baptists, whose names were George Taylor and Philip Hill. Taylor kept a meeting at his house till his death in 1701. Mr. Hill kept up the meeting till 1704, when he also died. After this the few brethren, who had been collected here, were visited by George Eaglesfield, Elias Keach, Thomas Griffiths, and Nathaniel Jenkins, the last of whom became the pastor of the church, which was constituted in 1712. Mr. Jenkins was a Welchman, born in Caerdicanshire, 1678, arrived in America in 1710, and two years after settled at the Cape. "He was a man of good parts and tolerable education; and quitted himself with honour in the loan office, whereof he was a trustee, and, also, in the Assembly, particularly in 1721, when a bill was brought in "to punish such as denied the doctrine of the Trinity, the Divinity of Christ, the Inspiration of the Holy Scriptures, &c." In opposition to which, Mr. Jenkins stood up, and with the warmth and accent of a Welshman, said, "I believe the doctrines in question, as firmly as the promoters of that ill-designed bill; but will never consent to oppose the opposers with law, or with any other weapon, save that of argument, &c."

Accordingly, the bill was suppressed, to the great mortification of them, who wanted to raise, in New-Jersey, the spirit which so raged in New-England."

The ministers, who have had the care of the church at the Cape, from this period, were Samuel Heaton, John Sutton, Peter P. Vanhorn, David Smith, Artis Seagrave, John Stancliff, Jonathan German and Jenkin David ; most of whom, except the last, appear to have been sojourners rather than stationed pastors.

HOPEWELL.—" This church is distinguished, as above, from the township where the meeting house stands, in Hunterdon county, bearing N. E. from Philadelphia, at the distance of 40 miles ; the dimensions of the house are 40 feet by 30 ; built, in 1747, on a lot of three quarters of an acre, the gift of John Hart, Esq.

" One of the three families, who first settled in the tract, now called Hopewell, was that of Jonathan Stout, who arrived here from Middleton, about 1706. The place then was a wilderness and full of Indians. Mr. Stout's wife was Ann Bullen, by whom he had nine children, viz. Joseph, Benjamin, Zebulon, Jonathan, David, Samuel, Sarah, Hannah, and Ann. Six of these children are said to have gone to Pennsylvania for baptism. Thus it appears, that Mr. Stout's family, including the father and mother, furnished eight members for the church. Seven other members are supposed to have been Thomas Curtis, Benjamin Drake, Ruth Stout, Alice Curtis, Sarah Fitzrandolph, Rachel Hide, and Mary Drake ; and these fifteen persons on the 23d of April, 1715, were organized into a church by the assistance of Abel Morgan and John Burrows, with their Elders Griffith Miles, Joseph Todd, and Samuel Ogden, and the same year they joined the Philadelphia Association.

" This church is remarkable for the number of ministers, who have been raised up in it. Thomas Curtis, John Alderson, John Gano, Joseph Powel, Hezekiah Smith, John Blackwell, Charles Thompson, and James Ewing, were all licensed or ordained at Hopewell.

" It is natural to think, that the first preaching of Believer's Baptism, at Hopewell, was owing to Jonathan Stout's settling in the parts ; and it is inferred from the church records, that from the settlement of Mr. Stout, to the constitution of the church, which was a period of nine years, that Messrs. Simmons, Eaglesfield, &c. from Middleton, were the men who preached here; neither of whom was ordained. Mr. Simmons afterwards went to Charleston, South-Carolina. From the constitution of the church to the coming of the Rev. Isaac Eaton, was another period of 33 years; during 15 of which, Joseph Eaton of Montgomery attended the place regularly once a month. After his desisting his visits, Thomas Davis, of the Great Valley, came to Hopewell, and preached statedly to the people for about four years, and then resigned to go to Oysterbay, on Long-Island. Mr. Davis was brother to Rev. John Davis of said Valley; he was born in the parish of L'lanfernach, and county of Pembroke, Wales, in 1707; he arrived in America, July 27, 1713; was ordained at Great Valley, and died at Yellow Springs, February 15, 1777, in the 70th year of his age. From his departure, the place was supplied for two years, by Messrs. Carman, Bonham, and Miller; and glorious years they were—55 souls were converted and added to the church; a meeting house was built, &c.

"The first minister who can be said to have been the settled pastor of this church, (for those before mentioned were but transiently among them) was Isaac Eaton, A. M. He was son of Joseph Eaton of Montgomery, joined Southampton church, and commenced preaching in early life. Mr. Eaton came to Hopewell in the month of April, 1748, and on the 29th of November following, was ordained pastor of the church by Messrs. Carman, Curtis, Miller, and Pots. He continued in the pastorship to July 4, 1772, when he died in the 47th year of his age; he was buried in the meeting house; and at the head of his grave, close to the base of the pulpit, is set up, by his congregation, a piece of fine marble, with this inscription upon it:

"In him, with grace and eminence did shine,
The man, the christian, scholar, and divine."

His funeral sermon was preached by Samuel Jones, D. D. of Pennepek; who thus briefly portrayed his character. "The natural endowments of his mind; the improvement of these by the accomplishments of literature; his early and genuine piety; his abilities as a divine and a preacher; his extensive knowledge of men and books; his catholicism, &c, would afford ample scope to flourish in a funeral oration, but it is needless." Mr. Eaton was the first man among the American Baptists, who set up a school for the education of youths for the ministry, which will be mentioned in its proper place."

About two years after Mr. Eaton's death, Rev. Benjamin Coles was elected to the pastoral office here, (October 15, 1774) without one dissenting voice; and continued with them to the spring of 1779. This church had enjoyed two very distinguished revivals of religion before one in 1747, when 55 were added; and another in 1764, when 123 were added; and soon after Mr. Coles became their pastor, there was a third, which added to their number, in about two years, 105 souls. But notwithstanding this success, Mr. Coles, in about seven years, found himself so uncomfortable among this people, that by the advice of his friends, he resigned his charge and settled at Scotch Plains about two years, when he returned to his native place at Oyster Bay.

Successor to him was Oliver Hart, A. M. who had fled hither from Charleston, South-Carolina, on account of the war. He took the oversight of this people, December, 1780, and continued with them till his death in 1795. A further account of this eminent minister will be given in his biography.

After him was Mr. James Ewing about nine years, and next to him was their present pastor, Mr. John Boggs, son of a minister of the same name, formerly of Welsh Tract.

This church has a farm with buildings for the accommodation of their pastor, valued at about 6000 dollars. From it originated the Second in Hopewell, and the one called Amwell.

HISTORY OF THE STOUTS.

" THE family of the Stouts are so remarkable for their number, origin, and character, in both church and state, that their history deserves to be conspicuously recorded; and no place can be so proper as that of Hopewell, where the bulk of the family resides. We have already seen that Jonathan Stout and family were the seed of the Hopewell church, and the beginning of Hopewell settlement; and that of the 15 which constituted the church, nine were Stouts. The church was constituted at the house of a Stout, and the meetings were held chiefly at the dwellings of the Stouts for 41 years, viz. from the beginning of the settlement to the building of the meeting-house, before described. Mr. Hart was of opinion (in 1790,) " that from first to last, half the members have been and were of that name ; for, in looking over the church book, (saith he) I find that near two hundred of the name have been added ; besides about as many more of the blood of the Stouts, who had lost the name by marriages. The present (1790) two deacons and four elders, are Stouts ; the late Zebulon and David Stout were two of its main pillars ; the last lived to see his offspring multiplied into an hundred and seventeen souls." The origin of this Baptist family is no less remarkable ; for they all sprang from one woman, and she as good as dead ; her history is in the mouths of most of her posterity, and is told as follows : " She was born at Amsterdam, about the year 1602 ; her father's name was Vanprincis ; she and her first husband, (whose name is not known) sailed for New-York, (then New-Amsterdam) about the year 1620 ; the vessel was stranded at Sandy-Hook ; the crew got ashore, and marched towards the said New-York ; but Penelope's (for that was her name) husband being hurt in the wreck, could not march with them ; therefore, he and the wife tarried in the woods ; they had not been long in the place, before the Indians killed them both, (as they thought) and stripped them to the skin ; however, Penelope came to, though her skull was fractured, and her left shoulder so hacked, that she could never use that arm like the other ; she was also cut across the abdomen, so that her bowels appeared ; these she kept in with her hand ; she continued in this situation for seven days, taking shelter in a hollow tree, and eating the excresence of it : the seventh day she saw a deer passing by with arrows sticking in it, and soon after two Indians appeared, whom she was glad to see, in hope they would put her out of her misery ; accordingly, one made towards her to knock her on the head ; but the other, who was an elderly man, prevented him ; and throwing his matchcoat about her, carried her to his wigwam, and cured her of her wounds and bruises ; after that he took her to New-York, and made a present of her to her countrymen, viz. an *Indian* present, expecting ten times the value in return.—It was in New-York, that one Richard Stout married her : he was a native of England, and of a good family ; she was now in her 22d year, and he in his 40th. She bore him seven sons and three daughters, viz. Jonathan, (founder of Hopewell) John, Richard, James, Peter, David, Benjamin, Mary, Sarah, and Alice ; the daughters married into the families of the Bounds, Pikes, Throckmortons, and Skeltons, and so lost the name of Stout ; the sons married into the families of Bullen, Crawford, Ashton, Traux, &c. and had many children. The mother lived to the age of 110, and saw her offspring multiplied into 502 in about 88 years."

KINGWOOD.—This church is the next in point of age. It was constituted in 1742, but I conclude has now either changed its name or become extinct. From it originated the following ministers, viz. William Lock, Elkanah Holmes, now at Niagara, Upper Canada, Thomas Runyon, William Tims, James Drake, and David Stout.

HIGHTSTOWN.—This church was formerly called Cranbury, because the first meeting-house stood in that township. Their present house of worship, built in 1785, 40 feet by 30, stands in a village from which the church takes its name, in the township of Windsor, and county of Middlesex, about 46 miles northeast of Philadelphia. The church was constituted in 1745 of 17 members. The first pastor was James Carman, who was almost as remarkable as Samuel Huntington for living by faith. He was born at Cape May in 1677, was baptized at Staten Island, near New-York, by Elias Keach, in the 15th year of his age, after this went first among the Quakers, then with the New-Light Presbyterians, whom he permitted to baptize one of his children. But in process of time, he came back to his first principles, united with the church in Middleton, began to preach in the branch of it at Cranbury, and was ordained its pastor at the time it was constituted. Here he died at the age of 79.

For many years after his death this church had only occasional supplies, and had nearly become extinct, when Mr. Peter Wilson, their present pastor, came amongst them in 1782. In nine years from his settlement, over 200 persons were added to the church by baptism; upwards of 800 have been baptized by this successful pastor, during the whole of his ministry here. The church is scattered over a wide extent of territory, and Mr. Wilson in his more active days, not unfrequently rode 15, sometimes 20 miles, and preached four times on a Lord's Day.

From this church originated the one at Trenton, now under the care of Mr. William Boswell. The church in Nottingham is also a branch of this body, and from it a great many other churches besides have received many of their members.

SCOTCH PLAINS.—This is a branch of the ancient church at Piscataway; it was constituted with fifteen members from that body in 1747; their meeting-house stands on the north border of the large and fertile tract of land, from which the church is named, in the township of Elizabeth, and county of Essex, between twenty and thirty miles from the city of New-York. This house is 50 feet by 30, built before, but enlarged to this size in 1759.

From this church have originated the First in New-York, Lyon's Farms, Mount Bethel and Samptown.

The first pastor at Scotch Plains was Mr. Benjamin Miller, a native of the place. He was ordained in 1748, and continued in office here till 1781, when he died in the 66th year of his age. "All that can be said of a good, laborious and successful minister will apply to him. His frequent companion in travels was Rev. Isaac Stelle; lovely and pleasant were they in their life, and in death they were not much divided, the one having survived the other but 35 days. He also travelled much with Mr. Peter P. Vanhorn and John Gano. Mr. Miller is said to have been a wild youth; but met with a sudden and surprising change under a sermon of Rev. Gilbert Tennent, a Presbyterian minister. Mr. Tennent, it is said, christened him, and encouraged him to study the languages, to qualify him for the ministry. However that may be, Mr. Miller did spend some time at learning, under the tuition of Rev. Mr. Biram. It was there he embraced the sentiments of the Baptists, owing to the discourse of Mr. Biram at the christening of a child, and a conversation that followed between him and his pupil."

Mr. Miller's funeral sermon was preached by his affectionate friend John Gano. Between these two ministers, there had long been a private agreement, that the funeral sermon of the first who died should be preached by the survivor, provided he had word of the death; and Providence so ordered matters that this promise was fulfilled. Mr. Gano was now a chaplain in the American army, and soon after Lord Cornwallis' surrender he was going to visit his family, when he heard of Mr. Miller's death. "Never, (said Mr. Gano) did I esteem a ministering brother so much as I did Mr. Miller, nor feel so sensibly a like bereavement, as that which I sustained by his death."

The next pastor of this church was William Vanhorn, A. M. He was a son of the evangelical Peter P. Vanhorn; was born in 1746, and ordained at Southampton, in Pennsylvania, where he continued 13 years; and in 1785, settled at the Scotch Plains, where he continued until 1807, when he resigned his pastoral care here, and set out with his family, on a journey into the State of Ohio, with a view of settling on a plantation, which he had purchased in that country, near the town of Lebanon, between the Miami rivers. Previous to the commencement of his journey, Mr. Vanhorn had been languishing for some time under a dropsical complaint, which, on his reaching Pittsburg, confined him to his bed; a mortification of the parts ensued, and he died on the 31st of October, 1807, in the 61st year of his age. This mournful event was peculiarly distressing, in a strange place, to his widow and only son, and six daughters, who were witnesses of his afflictions and exit. The attentions paid them by the inhabitants of the town were generally kind and sympathetic. The family, after a few days, pursued their journey and safely arrived at the place of destination, where they are now agreeably settled.

Mr. Vanhorn received his education at Dr. Samuel Jones's Academy at Pennepek, and afterwards received the honorary degree of Master of Arts, from the Rhode-Island College. During the revolutionary war he was chaplain to one of the brigades of the State of Massachusetts. He was also a member for Buck's county, Pennsylvania, of the convention which met in Philadelphia for the purpose of framing the first civil constitution of the State.

Successor to Mr. Vanhorn was Mr. Thomas Brown, a native of Newark, not far distant.

This church has a commodious parsonage house, with a small estate adjoining. It has lately received a legacy from the late James Brown, one of its deacons, of about 1400 dollars. From this body originated James Manning, D. D. the first President of Brown University.

At NEWARK, nine miles from the city of New-York, a church was formed in 1801, mostly of members from Lyon's Farms. They have a new house of worship 68 feet by 48. They have had to preach for them Messrs. Charles Lahatt, Peter Thurston, Daniel Sharp, and John Lamb, but are at present destitute, unless Dr. Rogers of Philadelphia has accepted their invitation to become their pastor, which has been some expected.

578 Infant Baptism condemned in a Court of Law.

In the northern part of this State are a number of other churches, whose dates, pastors, &c. will be exhibited in the General Table.

At a place called Dividing Creek, fifty six miles southwest of Philadelphia, a church arose in 1761, under the ministry of Mr. Samuel Heaton, whose history furnishes some interesting anecdotes, and is as follows : " He was born at Wrentham, Massachusetts, and was bred a Pedobaptist, he came to Jersey with three brothers about the year 1734, and settled near Black River, in the county of Morris, and there set up iron works ; while there he had a son born, whom he was anxious to have " christened" by Rev. Samuel Sweesy, a Presbyterian minister of the *Separate* order ; to which " christening" the wife stood averse, adding, *if you will shew me a text* that warrants christening a child, I will take him to Mr. Sweesy.* The husband offered several texts ; the wife would not allow that infant baptism was in either of them ; then the husband went to Mr. Sweesy, not doubting but a thing so old and so common as infant baptism, must be in the Bible ; Mr. Sweesy owned there was no text which directly proved the point ; but that it was provable by deductions from many texts ; this chagrined Mr. Heaton, as he had never doubted but that infant baptism was a gospel ordinance ; he went home with a resolution to act the part of the more noble Bereans, and soon met with convictions ; after that he went to Kingwood and was baptized by Mr. Bonham ; and so satisfied was he with what he had done, that he began to preach up the baptism of repentance in the mountains of Schooly ; he laboured not in vain ; for some of his proselytes went to Kingwood to receive believer's baptism. This was the beginning of the Baptist church at Schooly. In 1751, Mr. Heaton was ordained, and then went the next year to Millcreek in Virginia, where he

---

* " This transaction coming to the knowledge of Robert Calver, a *Rogerene* Baptist, induced him to publish an advertisement in the newspaper, offering *twenty* dollars reward to any that would produce a text to prove infant baptism. Rev. Samuel Harker took him up, and carried a text to the advertiser ; Calver would not allow that infant baptism was in it ; Harker sued him ; it seems the court were of Mr. Calver's mind, for Harker was cast and had court charges to pay. After that, Calver published another advertisement, offering a reward of *forty* dollars for such a text ; but none took him up, as Mr. Harker's attempts failed."

Infant baptism has been ten thousand times condemned by argument, but this is probably the first time it was ever condemned in a court of law.

continued a short time; and from thence to Konoloway, in Pennsylvania, where he founded another church; being driven from thence by the Indians, he settled next year at Capemay; from thence he came to Dividing Creek to settle a third church; in the care of which he died in the 66th year of his age, September 26, 1777."

In SALEM, 36 miles south-west of Philadelphia, a church was constituted of members from Cohansey in 1755. But Baptists, particularly the Killingsworths and Holmeses, had settled in the place before the year 1700.

The first pastor here was Job Shephard, a descendant of David Shephard from Ireland. His ministry was short, but respectable. Since him they have had, in succession, John Sutton, now in Kentucky, if alive, Abel Griffiths, Peter P. Vanhorn, and Isaac Skillman, D. D. It is now under the care of a young man, by the name of Joseph Shephard, who was educated in the University of Pennsylvania.

Most of the foregoing sketches are taken from Morgan Edwards' Materials, &c. for this State, published in 1792, at which time the number of churches was twenty-three; since then they have increased to over thirty. Of the temporalities of a number of churches, formerly in possession of good estates, no information has been obtained, and of course none can be given.

NEW-JERSEY ASSOCIATION.

FOR about a hundred years, most of the churches in this State belonged to the Philadelphia Association. Since the one at New-York was formed, the churches near the city have associated with that body. In 1811, a number of the Philadelphia churches were dismissed, and the same year were organized into a body by the name abovementioned. Nothing yet has occurred to furnish materials for an historical narrative. It was formed in perfect agreement with the mother body, from motives of convenience.

CHAPTER XVII.

PENNSYLVANIA.

MOST of the Baptists in this State, except the Tunkers and Mennonists, for a great number of years from their beginning, were either emigrants from Wales or their descendants; but the first church of the denomination in the country was formed at a place called the Coldspring, in Buck's county, between Bristol and Trenton, by Thomas Dungan,* who removed thither from Rhode-Island in 1684, only three years after William Penn obtained his patent of Charles II.

Pennepek, or Lower-Dublin Church.—This is now the oldest church in Pennsylvania, as the one gathered by Mr. Dungan was broken up in 1702.

"The history of this church will lead us back to the year 1686, when one John Eaton, George Eaton, and Jane his wife, Sarah Eaton, and Samuel Jones, members of a Baptist church residing in Llanddewi and Nautmel, in Radnorshire, whereof Rev. Henry Gregory was pastor; also, John Baker, member of a church in Kilkenny, in Ireland, under the pastoral care of Rev. Christopher Blackwell, and one Samuel Vaus, from England, arrived and settled on the banks of Pennepek, formerly written Pemmapeka. In the year 1687, Rev. Elias Keach, of London, came among them, and baptized one Joseph Ashton and Jane

---

* Respecting Mr. Dungan, Morgan Edwards has the following note in his history of the Baptists in Pennsylvania: "Of this venerable father, I can learn no more than that he came from Rhode-Island about the year 1684; that he and his family settled at Coldspring, where he gathered a church, of which nothing remains but a grave-yard and the names of the families which belonged to it, viz. the Dungans, Gardners, Woods, Doyles, &c. that he died in 1688, and was buried in said grave-yard; that his children were five sons and four daughters, viz. William, who married into the Wing family, of Rhode-Island, and had five children; Clement, who died childless; Thomas, who married into the Drake family, and had nine children; Jeremiah, who married into the same family, and had eight children; Elizabeth, who married into the West family, and had four children; Mary, who married into the Richards' family, and had three children; John, who died childless; Rebecca, who married into the Doyle family, and had three children; Sarah, who married into the family of the Kerrels, and had six children; in all 38. To mention the names, alliances, and offspring of these, would tend towards an endless genealogy. Sufficeth it, that the Rev. Thomas Dungan, the first Baptist minister in the province, now (1770) existeth in a progeny of between six and seven hundred.

his wife, William Fisher and John Watts, which increased their number to 12 souls, including the minister. These 12 did, by mutual consent, form themselves into a church in the month of January, 1688, choosing Mr. Keach to be their minister, and Samuel Vaus to be deacon. Soon after, the few emigrated Baptists in this province and West-Jersey joined them; also those, whom Mr. Keach baptized at the Falls, Coldspring, Burlington, Cohansey, Salem, Penn's-Neck, Chester, Philadelphia, &c. They were all one church, and Pennepek the centre of union, where, as many as could, met to celebrate the Lord's Supper; and for the sake of distant members, they administered the ordinance quarterly at Burlington, Cohansey, Chester, and Philadelphia; which quarterly meetings have since been transformed into three yearly meetings and an Association. Thus, for some time, continued their Zion with lengthened cords, till the brethren in remote parts set about forming themselves into distinct churches, which began in 1699. By these detachments it was reduced to narrow bounds, but continued among the churches, as a mother in the midst of many daughters. At their settlement, and during the administration of Mr. Keach, they were the same as they are now, with respect to faith and order; but when their number increased, and emigrants, from differing churches in Europe, incorporated with them, divisions began to take place about various things, such as absolute predestination, laying-on-of-hands, distributing the elements, singing psalms, seventh-day sabbath, &c. which threw the body ecclesiastic into a fever. In the year 1747, a tumult arose about the choice of a minister, which issued in a separation. But this, and the other maladies were healed, when the peccant humours had been purged off, and the design of Providence accomplished, which design is expressed in these notable words, *There must be divisions among you, that they who are approved may be made manifest.* 1 Cor. xi. 19.

" The first minister they had was the Rev. Elias Keach. He was son of the famous Benjamin Keach, of London; arrived in this country a very wild youth, about the year 1686. On his landing, he dressed in black, and wore a band, in order to pass for a minister. The project succeeded to his wishes, and many people resorted to hear the young London Divine. He performed well enough, till he had advanced pretty far in the sermon ; then stopping short, he looked like a man astonished. The audience concluded he had been seized with a sudden disorder; but on asking what the matter was, received from him a confession of the imposture, with tears in his eyes, and much trembling. Great was his distress, though it ended happily ; for from this time he dated his conversion. He heard of Mr. Dungan. To him he repaired to seek counsel and comfort, and by him he was baptized and ordained. From Coldspring, Mr. Keach came to Pennepek, and settled a church there as before related ; and thence travelled through Pennsylvania and the Jersies, preaching the Gospel in the wilderness with great success, insomuch that he may be considered as the chief apostle of the Baptists in these parts of America. He and his family embarked for England, early in the spring of the year 1692, and afterwards became a very famous and successful minister in London. Sometime before his embarkation, he had resigned the care of the church to

" Rev. John Watts, who was born November 3, 1661, at Lydd or Leed in the county of Kent ; came to this country about the year 1686 ; was baptized at Pennepek, November 21, 1687 ; called to the ministry in 1688 ; took on him the care of the church in 1690 ; continued in the care thereof to August 27, 1702, when he died of the small pox, and was buried at Pennepek, having had Mr. Samuel Jones to his assistant. Mr. Watts was a sound divine, and a man of some learning, as appears by a book he wrote, entitled, *Davis Disabled.* There was an order for printing this book, dated August 3, 1705, but it was not executed. He also composed a Catechism, or little system of divinity, which was published in 1700. Mr. Watts was succeeded by

" Rev. Evan Morgan, who came to this country very early, and was a man of piety and parts. He broke off from the Quakers along with many others of Mr. Keith's party in 1691 ; was baptized in 1697, by one Thomas Rutter, and the same year, renouncing the reliques of Quakerism, was received into the church. In 1702, he was called to the ministry, and ordained October 23, 1706, by Rev. Messrs. Thomas Griffith and Thomas Killingsworth. He died February 16, 1709, and was buried at Pennepek, after having had the joint care of the church for upwards of two years. Mr. Morgan's successor, who had also been his colleague, was the

"Rev. Samuel Jones, who was born, July 9, 1657, in the parish of Llanddewi, and the county of Radnor; came to this country about 1686; called to the ministry in 1697; ordained, October 23, 1706, at which time he took part of the ministry with Mr. Evan Morgan. He died February 3, 1722, and was buried at Pennepek. He had Mr. John Hart and others to his assistants. The ground on which the meeting-house stands was given by him. He also gave for the use of the church Pool's Annotations, 2 vols. Burkit's Annotations, 1 vol. Keach on the Parables, and Bishop's Body of Divinity, &c. His successor, who also had been his colleague, was

Rev. Joseph Wood, who was born in the year 1659, near Hull, in Yorkshire; came to this country about 1684; baptized by Mr. Keach, at Burlington, July 24, 1691; ordained September 25, 1708, at which time he took part of the ministry with Mr. Evan Morgan and Mr. Samuel Jones. He died, September 15, 1747, and was buried at Coldspring. Mr. Wood was succeeded by

"Rev. Abel Morgan. He was born in the year 1637, at a place called Alltgoch, in the parish of Llanwenog, and county of Carmarthen; entered on the ministry in the 19th year of his age; was ordained at Blaenegwent, in Monmouthshire. He arrived in this country, February 14, 1711; resided some time at Philadelphia, and then removed to Pennepek; took on him the care of the church as soon as he landed; and continued therein to his death, which came to pass, December 16, 1722. He was buried in the grave-yard of Philadelphia, where a stone is erected to his memory. Mr. Morgan was a man of considerable distinction. He compiled a folio Concordance to the Welch Bible printed at Philadelphia in 1730; he also translated the *Century Confession* to Welsh, and added thereto article the xxiii and xxxi. Several other pieces of his are yet extant in manuscripts. His successor was

"Rev. Jenkin Jones, who became minister of this church in the year 1725, which was near three years after Mr. Morgan's decease; and had Mr. William Kinnersley to his assistant. Mr. Wood was yet alive, but not very capable of serving the church. He continued in the care thereof for upwards of twenty years, and then resigned it, to become the minister of Philadelphia church, where we shall say more of him. The next in office here was

"Rev. Peter Peterson Vanhorn. He was born, August 24, 1719, at Middletown in Buck's county, and was bred a Lutheran; embraced the principles of the Baptists, September 6, 1741; ordained, June 18, 1747; continued in the oversight of the church to 1762, when he resigned, and settled at the Newmills, in the Jersey. His assistant was Mr. George Eaton. His wife is Margaret Marshall, by whom he has children, William, Gabriel, Peter, Aaron, Thomas, Elizabeth, Marshal, Charles. His successor is

"Rev. Samuel Jones, D. D. who yet continues the pastor of this ancient and respectable church, although he is almost 80 years old. He was born January 14, 1735, at a place called *Cefen y Gelli* in Bettus parish in Glamorganshire; came to America in 1737; was bred in the college of Philadelphia; was ordained, January 8, 1763, at which time he commenced minister of Pennepek and Southampton; but he resigned the care of the Southampton church in 1770, in favour of Erasmus Kelly."* This church is now called Lower Dublin, from the name of the township in which it is situated.

Their first meeting house was a neat stone building, 33 feet by 30, erected in 1707, on a lot of one acre, the gift of Rev. Samuel Jones. This house was taken down in 1805, to make room for the more spacious one, which was immediately erected on the spot, and was built of stone, 55 feet by 45.

This church has about 600 dollars at interest, which is accumulating yearly. In addition to this, Dr. Jones has given them a handsome sum in his Will, to be for their use when he is gone.

PHILADELPHIA.

First, or Second Street Church.—This church is in reality nearly as old as Pennepek, and its history will lead us almost to the founding of the city.

* Edwards' Materials for Pennsylvania, p. 6—17.

Origin of the First Church in Philadelphia. 585

"In the year 1686, one John Holmes, who was a Baptist, arrived and settled in the neighbourhood. He was a man of property and learning, and therefore we find him in the magistracy of the place in 1691, and was the same man who refused to act with the Quaker magistrates, against the Keithians. He died Judge of Salem Court. In 1696, John Farmer and his wife, members of a Baptist church in London, then under the pastoral care of the famous Hansard Knollis, arrived and settled in the place. In 1697, one Joseph Todd and Rebecca Woosoncroft came to the same neighbourhood, who belonged to a Baptist church at Limmington, in Hampshire, England, whereof Rev. John Rumsay was pastor. The same year one William Silverstone, William Elton and wife, and Mary Shepherd, were baptized by Thomas Killingworth. These nine persons, on the second Sunday in December, 1698, assembled at a house in Barbadoes lot, and coalesced into a church for the communion of saints, having Rev. John Watts to their assistance. From that time to the year 1746, they increased partly by emigrations from the old country, and partly by the occasional labours of Elias Keach, Thomas Killingworth, John Watts, Samuel Jones, Evan Morgan, John Hart, Joseph Wood, Nathaniel Jenkins, Thomas Griffiths, Elisha Thomas, Enoch Morgan, John Burrows, Thomas Selby, Abel Morgan, George Eglesfield, William Kinnersley, and others. From the beginning to the last mentioned time, (1746) they had no settled minister among them, though it was a period of 48 years. The first, that might be properly called their own, was Jenkin Jones; the rest belonging to other churches. They did, indeed, in 1723, choose George Eaglesfield to preach to them, contrary to the sense of the church at Pennepek; but in 1725, he left them and went to Middleton. About the year 1746, a question arose, whether Philadelphia was not a branch of Pennepek? and consequently, whether the latter had not a right to part of the legacies bestowed on the former? This, indeed, was a groundless question; but for fear the design of their benefactors should be perverted, the church, then consisting of 56 members, was formally constituted, May 15, 1746.

"The place where these people met, at first, was the corner of Second-street and Chesnut-street, known by the name of *Barbadoes lot.* The building was a store-house; but when the Barbadoes company left the place, the Baptists held their meetings there. So also did the Presbyterians, when either a Baptist or Presbyterian minister happened to be in town; for as yet neither had any settled among them. But when Jedidiah Andrews, from New-England, came to the latter, the Baptists, as has generally been their lot, were, in a manner, driven away. Several letters passed between the two societies on the occasion, which are yet extant. There was also a deputation of three Baptists appointed to remonstrate with the Presbyterians, for so unkind and rightless a conduct; but to no purpose. From that time forth, the Baptists held their worship at a place near the draw-bridge, known by the name of *Anthony Morris's brew-house*; here they continued to meet till March 15, 1707, when by invitation of the Keithians, they removed their worship to Second-street, where they hold it to this day. The Keithian meeting house was a small wooden building, erected in 1692. This the Baptists took down, in 1731, and raised on the same spot, a neat brick building, 42 feet by 30. This house was also taken down in 1762, and a more spacious one was erected on the spot, 61 feet by 42, which was also built with brick at the expense of £2200." This house was enlarged about 1808, so that their place of worship now is 61 feet by 75. The old lot was 43 feet front on Second-street, and 303 feet deep towards Third street.

The additional ground purchased for the recent enlargement of the house, extends 37½ feet from the old lot to a court called Fremberger's, on which it has a front of 130 feet. This, with the enlargement of the house, cost 18,000 dollars.

But to return: "An accident, in 1734, had like to have deprived the church, both of their house and lot; for then one Thomas Pearl died, after having made a conveyance of the premises to the church of England. The vestry demanded possession, but the Baptists refused, and a law-suit commenced, which brought the matter to a hearing before the Assembly. The Episcopalians being discouraged, offered to give up their claim for £.50. The offer was accepted, and contention ceased.

"This church experienced a painful division in 1711, occasioned by the turbulent spirit of an Irish preacher, who was among them, along with Mr. Burrows. His name was Thomas Selby. When he had formed a party, he shut Mr. Burrows and his friends out of the meeting-house, who thenceforth met at Mr. Burrows' house in Chesnut-Street. This was the situation of affairs when Mr. Abel Morgan arrived in 1711. But his presence soon healed the breach, and obliged Selby to quit the town, which he did in 1713, and went to Carolina, and there died the same year, but not before he had occasioned much disturbance. The ministers which this church have had from the beginning to the year 1746, are mentioned above, and some of them have been already characterized. The following are the ministers they have had since that time.

"Rev. Jenkin Jones. He was born about 1690 in the parish of Llanfernach, and county of Pembroke, and arrived in this country about 1710. He was called to the ministry in Welsh Tract in 1724; removed to Philadelphia in 1725, and became the minister of the church at that place, only, at the time of its reconstitution, May 15, 1746; for, theretofore, he had the care of Pennepek also. He died at Philadelphia, July 16, 1761, and was there buried, where a tomb is erected to his memory. Mr. Jones was a good man and did real services to this church, and to the Baptist interest. He secured to them the possession of their valuable lot, and place of worship before described. He was the moving cause of altering the direction of licenses, so as to enable dissenting ministers to perform marriages by them. He built a parsonage house, partly at his own charge. He gave a handsome legacy towards purchasing a silver cup for the Lord's Table, which is worth upwards of £60. His name is engraven upon it."*

"Rev. Ebenezer Kinnersly, A. M. was cotemporary with Mr. Jones. He was born, November 30, 1711, in the city of Gloucester, and arrived in this country, September 12, 1714; was ordained in 1743, and preached at Philadelphia and elsewhere to 1754, when he obtained a Professor's chair in the College of Philadelphia.

* Edwards' Materials, &c. p. 41—7

Mr. Kinnersley was a companion of Dr. Franklin in philosophical researches, and has immortalized his name on account of his improvements in electricity. He died in the vicinity of Philadelphia, and was buried in the Baptist cemetery at Lower Dublin.

It has been asserted that this eminent man "left the Baptist communion, laid aside his clerical character, and joined the Episcopal church."* That he declined preaching after he engaged in the duties of his professorship is not denied, but that he joined the Episcopalians, Dr. Rogers declares, is incorrect: "Mr. Kinnersley," says he, "continued a firm Baptist till his death, and was a constant attendant and communicant in the First Baptist church in Philadelphia till he removed to the country." His wife was an Episcopalian, and probably his sometimes waiting on her to church, gave rise to the groundless report above mentioned.

The next pastor to Mr. Jones was Morgan Edwards, A. M. for whose character the reader is referred to his biography.

Successor to Mr. Edwards was William Rogers, D. D. who served the church about three years. During his pastoral labours a revival took place in which between forty and fifty were added. Dr. Rogers was born in Newport, Rhode-Island, July 22, 1751, O. S. was educated in Rhode Island College, being the very first student that entered that institution, was baptized by the late Gardiner Thurston of Newport, who was his uncle, in 1770, was sent into the ministry by the church of which he was pastor in 1771, and the same year removed to Philadelphia, where he has since resided. During five years of the revolutionary war, he was a chaplain in the American army.

In 1789, he was appointed a Professor in the University of Pennsylvania, which office he held till 1812, when he resigned it. Dr. Rogers has long maintained an extensive correspondence, and is extensively known among the Baptists in America, Europe, and India.

This church remained destitute of a pastor, during the revolutionary war, but in 1782, Rev. Thomas Ustick, A. M. was inducted into the pastoral office. Mr. Ustick was born in the city of New-York, August 30, 1753.

* Retrospect of the 18th Century, note, vol. ii. p. 354.

city soon after, joined the church then under the care of Mr. Ustick, by which he was approbated to preach in 1802.

This church has erected a fine stone meeting-house 60 feet by 50, which was opened for publick worship February, 1811. It stands on South-second Street. Their lot has 63 feet front, is 200 feet deep, and 84 feet on the back side. This, with their house, cost about 16,000 dollars.

Sansom Street Church.—This also originated from the ancient community in Second Street. Its constituent members were 91, and received the fellowship of their brethren as a distinct church, January, 1811. Soon after they were organized, Dr. Staughton resigned his former charge, and became their pastor. He was born in January 4, 1770, at Coventry, Warwickshire, England. His parents are both members of Dr. Rippon's church in London, his father was many years deacon of the church in Coventry, of which the late Mr. Butterworth, the author of the Concordance, was pastor. Dr. Staughton had his education at the Bristol Academy, under Dr. Evans, came to America and landed at Charleston, South-Carolina, in 1793, spent some time in Georgetown in that State, where he planted the church now under the care of Mr. Botsford, came to the northward in 1795, spent a short time in New-York and its vicinity, was afterwards settled at Bordenton, then at Burlington, New-Jersey, and in the last place set in order the church, whose present pastor is Burgiss Allison, D. D. From Burlington he removed to Philadelphia, to succeed Mr. Ustick, as we have before related.

The church under consideration have erected a house of worship of an uncommon size and somewhat singular form. It is a circular building, 90 feet diameter, and with the lot on which it stands cost about 40,000 dollars. It is incumbered with a debt of no small amount, which however, individuals of the church have assumed in the form of a fund, until means shall be found for its liquidation. Their income from pew-rents and collections is said to be between four and five thousand dollars a year, and their prospect is fair soon to clear their great estate. None of their pews are sold or intended to be, and no society-men have any control of their house or affairs. As some readers may wish for a more particular description of the San-

feet by 18. The lower story is fitted up in the form of a vestry, with a pulpit and seats, in which the minister discourses previous to baptism. The upper story is divided into two rooms for the convenience of candidates. This lot and building cost 1600 dollars. The rent of their pews, as now rated, amounts to about 2000 dollars a year, which is appropriated to the minister and sexton.*

Second Church.—This church is situated in that part of the city called the Northern Liberties. It was constituted of twenty members from the First Church in 1803. They have a commodious brick meeting-house 66 feet by 46, built soon after they were constituted. It stands on a lot 220 feet by 200. The building and lot cost about 11,000 dollars. About nine months after this body was organized, Mr. William White became its pastor, which office he still sustains. He was born in New-York in 1768, began preaching in the church at Roxbury near this city in 1792, the year after was ordained at the same place, and for some years before he came to his present station, was pastor of the church at New-Britain.

From this church originated that at Frankfort, a few miles to the north of it, in 1807.

African Church.—This is the next in point of age, and was formed of twelve members from the First church, in June, 1809. They were supplied for a time by Mr. Henry Cunningham of Savannah, Georgia, but have now for their pastor Mr. John King, from Virginia. He joined the church before he began to preach, and was ordained to the pastoral office in 1812. This church has erected a small neat building 37 feet by 26, which they intend for a vestry, whenever they shall be able to build one of larger dimensions.

Third Church was constituted of 30 members, mostly from the first, in August, 1809. It is situated in Southwark, some distance from the other churches, and is under the care of Mr. John P. Peckworth, one of the constituent members. He was born in Chatham, Kent county, England, about 1770, came to Philadelphia at the age of thirteen, four years after was baptized in Wilmington, Delaware, by Mr. Thomas Fleeson, came back to this

* This, with much other information, was communicated by Dr. Rogers.

Successor to Mr. Ustick was William Staughton, D. D. He was invited to the pastoral care of this church early in 1805, and continued with them about six years, when he resigned his charge to become the pastor of the new church in Sansom-Street. Under his ministry the meeting-house was enlarged, and nearly 300 added to the church by baptism.

Next to him was their present pastor Henry Holcombe, D. D. He was born in Prince Edward county, Virginia, February 22, 1762; was carried when a child to South-Carolina; was a Captain in the latter part of the revolutionary war, and when the United States Constitution was adopted by South-Carolina, Mr. Holcombe was a member of the Convention.—Before this he had began to preach, and was settled in the pastoral care of the church on Pipe Creek, in that State. In 1791, he settled at Euhaw, afterwards was pastor of the church, which arose under his ministry at Beaufort, from which place he removed to Savannah in 1799, planted a church in that city soon after, which he served about eleven years, and then removed up the country to Mount Enon, where he intended to spend the remainder of his days in retirement. From this place he received two calls, one from the first church in Boston, the other from the one which he now serves, with the pastoral care of which he was invested in 1811.

This church has the most ample endowments of any of our connexion in America. Their property appropriated expressly for the support of their poor members is, 1st, Three small three story brick houses, the gift of Mrs. Sarah Branson, which now rent for 900 dollars a year. 2d, Three hundred pounds Pennsylvania currency, or 800 dollars, the gift of Mrs. Sarah Smith; the interest of two thirds of this legacy is designed for the poor, the other is for the minister. 3d, $ 13, 60, per annum, the gift of John Morgan, to be distributed by the pastor at his discretion, May 8, every year. The property for the general benefit of the church is two brick houses, which now rent for 720 dollars a year, one of them was formerly the parsonage. In addition to these possessions, they have a lot of large dimensions on the river Schuylkill, on which, a few years since, they erected a building for baptismal occasions. It is of brick, two stories high, 36

He was baptized by the Rev. John Gano, in that city, when he was but little more than 13 years of age. At his baptism, Mr. Gano gave out the 138th hymn, first book, Dr. Watts, and in the second verse he parodied thus:

" His honor is engag'd to save
The *youngest* of his sheep," &c.

" Why did you not give the words as they are?" said Mr. Ustick, " The *meanest* of his sheep," for truly I am so."

Mr. Ustick was educated at Rhode-Island College, where he graduated in 1771. About three years after he left college, he was called to the ministry by the church in the city of New-York, and on the 5th of August, 1777, was ordained at Providence, Rhode-Island, by President Manning, Rev. Job Seamans, of Attleborough, and Rev. William Williams, of Wrentham. Previous to his ordination, Mr. Ustick preached awhile at Stamford, in Connecticut, and soon after he was settled at Ashford, in the same State. From that place he removed to Grafton, in Massachusetts, and from Grafton he removed to Philadelphia, as above related. In this city he continued his ministry, with much reputation, for almost 21 years. But his work in the church militant being finished, he was, we trust, removed to the church triumphant, April, 1803, in the 50th year of his age.

During his confinement, the Gospel, which he had delivered to others, he assured a worthy friend, who visited him a day or two before his death, afforded him the greatest consolation. On Lord's day, being visited by several brethren, he proposed to them after prayer, to sing the 138th hymn, first book:

" Firm as the earth thy Gospel stands," &c.

the same that was sung at his baptism. The night which closed the scene of life, (his son sitting up with him) sensible, no doubt, of his approaching dissolution, he was heard distinctly to say, " The Lord is my shield and my buckler." It pleased God to grant him an easy passage into eternity; departing without a groan, *he fell asleep in Jesus.* A funeral sermon was delivered on the next Lord's-Day, by Dr. Rogers, who furnished this biography, from John xi. 11. *Our friend Lazarus sleepeth.*

Description of the Sansom-Street Meeting-house. 593

som-Street meeting-house, I shall for their gratification transcribe it in the note below.*

In the neighbourhood of Philadelphia, a number of churches arose in early times, of which we shall give some brief accounts. Of those which have been formed of late years, but little information has been obtained.

GREAT VALLEY.—This church was planted by people from Wales in 1711. Its seat is 18 miles westward

---

* " The plan of this house within is a rotundo, ninety feet diameter, surmounted by a dome, crowned with a lanthorn or cupola, upwards of twenty feet diameter. The walls, with the dome, are elevated upwards of fifty feet above the ground, built of brick, and the dome constructed of short pieces of plank, upon the principle adopted in that of the Halle de Bled, at Paris. From the top of the walls, three steps encircle the building before the swell of the dome appears, the rise of which is at an angle of forty-five degrees. In front and rear of the rotundo, square projections, of sixty feet extent, come forward; that in the rear to provide space for vestry rooms, rising only one story; that in the front, to accommodate the stair cases of the galleries, rising on a marble basement to the common height of the walls.

" The front projection comes to the line of the street, in form of wings, separated by a colonnade, and are crowned by two belfries or cupolas.

" The principal entrance into the house is by a flight of marble steps into an Ionic colonnade; on either hand are doors leading to the stair-cases of the galleries: from this colonnade you pass into the grand aisle, leading direct to the baptistery and pulpit; two other aisles run parallel with this, and one main aisle crosses the whole in the diameter of the house. At the termination of all these aisles, are doors of outlet from the building. The baptistery is situate in the centre of the circle, in view of every part of the gallery, and is surrounded by an open balustrade, and when not in use for the ordinance of baptism closed over by a floor to accommodate strangers.

" The galleries, which are described concentric with the great circle, circumscribe the nave of the building, except in that section occupied by the pulpit, and are supported by twelve columns. The pulpit, which is placed to front the grand aisle, is a continuation of the galleries, and comes forward supported by a screen of columns. The space under the pulpit is closed and thrown into the vestry rooms behind, but may at any time be opened, the screen being constituted of folding doors.

" The circumference of the building is lighted by large square windows below, and a ring of semi-circular windows above the galleries. The great lanthorn of the dome, immediately over the baptistery, lights the centre and ventilates the whole house, being encircled with sashes, which open and shut at pleasure. The height to the apex of this lanthorn, from the floor, is upwards of fifty feet.

" The foot of the dome is encompassed by a broad moulded band, above which two other bands run round. The lanthorn has its soffit enriched with mouldings.

" The pews below are so disposed as to run parallel with the transverse diameter of the room, the number of which, together with those in the galleries, exceed three hundred and twenty, and with the publick seats contain, with comfort, upwards of two thousand five hundred people.

" The design of this building was furnished by Mr. Mills, a pupil of Mr. Latrobe, and as the direction of the execution of his design has been wisely committed to him, the building does credit to his talents, and proves an ornament to the city.

" Mr. Mills is the first American architect, regularly educated to the profession in his own country."——*Picture of Philadelphia, p.* 326—8.

from Philadelphia. It was once handsomely endowed with lands and funds; what is the present state of its temporalities I have not been informed. The first pastor at the Valley was Mr. Hugh Davis, a native of Wales. After him was John Davis from the same country; their present pastor, Mr. David Jones, is also of Welsh extraction.

MONTGOMERY.—This church was also founded by Welsh Baptists, and was constituted in 1719. Two of its pastors, viz. Benjamin Griffiths and John Thomas were born in the Principality, the first in the county of Cardigan, 1688, the other in that of Radnor in 1703. Who have been pastors of this body since Mr. Thomas does not appear; it is now under the care of Dr. Silas Hough.

SOUTH-HAMPTON was the seventh church which arose in the Province of Pennsylvania, and was constituted in 1746. It was founded by some members of the church at Pennepek, and by the remains of a society of Keithians, who settled in the neighbourhood about 1700. The first pastor was Mr. Joshua Potts, who was ordained the same year the church was constituted, and continued in office till his death in 1761. Since Mr. Potts, this church has had in succession for its pastors or supplies, Thomas Davis, once at Oyster-Bay, New-York, Dr. Samuel Jones, now of Lower-Dublin, Erasmus Kelly, who died at Newport, Rhode-Island, the late William Vanhorn, David Jones, now at the Great-Valley, Thomas Memmenger, and Thomas B. Montanye, who is still with them, but talks of leaving his pleasant situation for the attracting, ultramontane regions of the west. Mr. Montanye was born in NewYork, 1769, was settled a number of years in Warwick in that State, and came to South-Hampton in 1801. This church has a valuable estate, the gift of John Morris, one of its ancient members.

It is pleasant to find that so many brethren and sisters in the old churches through New-Jersey, Pennsylvania, and Delaware, had the cause of Zion so much at heart, that they made provision for its support after they were gone. If more now would think of this matter, and if churches would see that all their members did their proportion, or else turn them out of fellowship, they would not have occasion so often to go down to Egypt for help.

From the South-Hampton church originated those eminent ministers, Isaac Eaton and Oliver Hart.

The church at NEW-BRITAIN arose out of a division of the Montgomery, and was formed in 1754. Their three first pastors were Joseph Eaton, William Davis, and Joshua Jones, all from Wales.

The HILLTOWN Church also sprang from the ancient community at Montgomery, of which it was formerly a branch. It was constituted a distinct body in 1781, had for its first pastor Mr. John Thomas, next to him Mr. James M'Laughlin, now pastor at Piscataway, and after his removal, Mr. Joseph Mathias, one of their number, began to preach, and was ordained their pastor in 1806.

PHILADELPHIA ASSOCIATION.

WHERE a particular account of churches is previously given, the less remains to be said of the Associations which they compose. We have already mentioned in Epoch Second, that this ancient Association was formed in 1707. It begun with five churches, but in process of time became a numerous body, and for many years extended from Ketockton in Virginia to Northeast-town in New-York, a distance of about 400 miles. From it originated the Ketockton, Baltimore, and Delaware Associations on the south; on the north, those of New-York, Warwick, and New-Jersey. Its ministers were sent for, and travelled to assist in regulating churches in trouble, in the lower parts of Virginia and even to the Carolinas. Its influence was exerted with good effect among the turbulent churchmen of Virginia, and also among the fleecing Pedobaptists of New-England. It being the oldest institution of the kind in America, was looked up to as a pattern of imitation by those which succeeded, and by it were given rules, and even doctrine, to many and indeed most of the first Associations in the southern and western States. This body has long maintained a correspondence with her sister communities in both extremes of the Union, with a number in England, and lately with the brethren in India.

In it originated the design for the Rhode-Island College, and by it have been projected many other plans, which had particularly in view the welfare of the Baptist interest in

America. It has now been in operation 106 years, and I do not find that it was ever complained of for infringing on the independency of any church in its connexion, a convincing proof that Associations, when skilfully conducted, are altogether harmless on this point.

About 200 miles west of Philadelphia, in and near to the Alleghany mountains, are the following churches belonging to the Baltimore Association, viz. Konoloway, Sideling-Hill, Huntington and Tuscarora-Valley.

In the county of Luzerne, near the line of New-York, on the Susquehannah River, a small Association was formed in 1807 by the name of

ABINGTON.

Its churches, in 1811, were only three in number; its ministers were William Purdy, Elijah Peck, John Miller, and Samuel Sturdivant, and its total number of members about 250.

CHEMUNG ASSOCIATION.

This body is situated in a region settled mostly since the last war in Pennsylvania and New-York. The churches in Pennsylvania are in the counties of Luzerne, Northumberland and Lycoming. Those in New-York are in the adjoining parts, the counties are not known. It was formed of five churches, viz. Chemung, Romulus, Fredericktown, New-Bedford, and Brantrim, in 1796. Its principal ministers appear to be Roswell Goff and Thomas Smiley. The oldest church, and the mother of a number of the rest, is the one called Chemung, which was founded in 1791, in the following manner. Soon after the war, Mr. Ebenezer Green and others from the Warwick church in New-York, settled on the west branch of the Susquehannah, at a place called the Black-hole. There they kept up a meeting till they were visited by James Finn, who baptized some among them. Being disappointed about their lands, they soon removed in a body to the Chemung Flats, then just beginning to be settled. Here they were soon joined by many others from different parts, among whom was Mr. Roswell Goff, who began to preach among them;

and under whose ministry they were gathered into a church at the time above mentioned. Mr. Goff was born in Spencertown, New-York, in 1763, and was baptized at Deer-Park, at the age of 25.

Mr. Smiley was born in Dauphin county, Pennsylvania, May 29, 1759, was brought up a Seceder, a rigid sect of Scotch-Presbyterians, was baptized by James Finn in 1792, at Wyoming. In the contentions about lands in this region, about the year 1800, Mr. Smiley, on account of having some governmental papers about him, was dragged out of his bed, in the dead of the night, by a band of what were called the Wild Yankees, with their faces blacked, and who, with pistols at his breast, compelled him first to burn his papers, and then tarred and feathered him. Besides this they threatened his life on account of his adhering to the Pennsylvania side, which led him to flee for safety to White Deer Valley, on the west branch of the Susquehannah, now in the county of Northumberland. Here he founded a church in 1808, over which he still presides, but travels much as a missionary in the surrounding parts under the patronage of the Philadelphia Association.

In the neighbourhood of this Association is a large church founded by Elder Jacob Drake, from Canaan, New-York, in 1796. They have become large and are scattered along the Susquehannah River to the distance of many miles. They have three Elders, whose names are David Dimock, Griffin Lewis, and Joel Rogers. They hold church meetings in eight different places every month. Their number of communicants is not stated, but it must probably amount to three hundred. They are said by their neighbours to be Arminians in every point of doctrine, except that of falling from grace. Their own account of their sentiments is as follows : " The Arminian principles we deny, believing salvation to be wholly and totally by grace ;—on the other hand, we deny particular election, and special vocation," &c. The reader must judge for himself how much these brethren have mended the matter.

THE RED STONE ASSOCIATION

Was organized in 1776. It is situated in the western part of this State, adjoining Ohio. Some few of its churches are in that State, and others are in Virginia. The centre of the Association is no great distance south of Pittsburg. One of its oldest churches was gathered in 1770, under the ministry of Elder John Sutton. It was at first called Great Bethel, now Uniontown, and is upwards of 50 miles south of Pittsburg, in the county of Fayette. This church was the mother of many others, which arose around it. Mr. Sutton was a native of New-Jersey, and was one of five brothers, who were Baptist preachers. He settled in the Red-stone country, when it was in a wilderness state, and was long a laborious and much respected preacher throughout an extensive circle of churches, which were planted either wholly or in part by his means. The time of his death is not known, but it is believed to have been not far from the year 1800.

Cotemporary with this evangelical servant of God, was the pious and successful John Corbly, who was made to drink deep of the cup of affliction. Mr. Corbly was a native of Ireland, and while young agreed to serve four years for his passage to Philadelphia. After the expiration of that term he settled in Virginia, in or near Culpepper county, where he was converted under the ministry of the renowned James Ireland. While persecution raged in that State, he was, among others, thrown into Culpepper gaol, where he remained a considerable time. This was, probably, previous to 1770, for about that date he settled in the region now under consideration, and in conjunction with Mr. Sutton, planted the first churches in it. Mr. Corbly was probably educated a Catholick, as his first wife was of that persuasion, and was a thorn in his side during her life. After her death he married an amiable woman of his own sentiments, by whom he had seven children, four of whom with their mother, were taken from him in a barbarous and most afflicting manner. The Indians, at that time, were extremely troublesome in this county, and often committed terrible ravages among the inhabitants.

Mr. Corbly and his family set out on a Lord's Day to walk to meeting, less than half a mile from his house. After going a short distance, it was found that his Bible, which had been given to his wife, had been forgotten, which obliged him to go back. On his return to overtake his family, he saw two Indians run, one of whom gave a direful yell. Suspecting evil he ran to a fort or blockhouse a short distance off, and obtained assistance. When he came to the place, he found his wife killed with a tomahawk; her infant, after having its brains dashed out against a tree, was thrown across her breast. Three other children lay dead on the spot, two more were terribly wounded, and scalped, and apparently dead, but afterwards recovered. Only one out of the seven children remained unhurt; she was a little girl, an Indian caught hold of her and was about to dispatch her, but being seized by a large dog, she escaped and hid herself in the bushes. It was afterwards ascertained that seven Indians were engaged in this barbarous transaction. The feelings of the bereaved husband and father may better be conceived than described. For a while he remained inconsolable; but reflecting on the signal act of Providence in preserving his own life, he recovered his spirits, recommenced his ministerial labours, which, from excess of grief, were for a time suspended, married a third time, and continued a zealous and successful minister till 1805, when he finished his course in peace. One of his sons is now a Baptist minister in the Indiana Territory.

Two other incidents befel this good man, which were peculiarly distressing: The first was the conduct of a base woman, who accused him of making frequent criminal propositions to her, which she offered to confirm on oath. When cited before a magistrate, she was taken with a fit of trembling, and for some time remained speechless. Some were for excusing the vile accuser, and letting the matter pass off; but Mr. Corbly insisted on her making oath—which she did, and expressly declared, that he was altogether innocent, adding, at the same time, that it was a plot laid by certain persons, whom she named.

In the Whiskey Insurrection, so called, Mr. Corbly was suspected of aiding and abetting the insurgents, and on that suspicion was suddenly arrested, carried to Philadelphia, conducted in disgrace through the streets, and lodged in gaol, where he remained some time in great affliction. While there, he was comforted and supplied by Dr. Rogers and other friends in the city. His case was never tried, and of course it was not legally determined whether he was accused falsely or not. In the opinion of his friends he by no means deserved the treatment he received.

At *Beulah*, in the county of Cambria, in the midst of the Alleghany mountains, a church was founded by emigrants from Wales in 1797, under the direction of the late Morgan J. Rees.

The original members of this body set sail from Milford Haven, South-Wales, March 8, 1796, and landed in New-York the May following. They soon went to Philadelphia, where they united in church fellowship with a number of their countrymen of the Independent and Calvinistic Methodist persuasions. Their minister was Mr. Simon James. After tarrying in Philadelphia a few months, a number of the members of this mixed communion church removed about 200 miles westward, and began a settlement, to which they gave the name of Beulah, hoping to experience the divine favour, which the term imports. This was in October, 1796. Others of their company followed them the ensuing spring, by which time the number of Baptists amounted to twenty-four, who, being dissatisfied with their plan of church building, in August, 1797, separated from their Pedobaptist brethren, and formed a community of baptized believers only. Since that time, they have been visited by a number of ministers from their native country, some preachers have also been raised up among them, but many both of preachers and members, have travelled on to the State of Ohio, where they have founded two or three churches. Thomas Powel settled in Licking county, Henry George at Owl Creek, David Kimpton has lately gone to a place in the New Purchase, and settled near Wooster, where he has gathered a church. Beulah appears to have been a stopping place for many Welsh brethren, who have removed to more distant regions. The present pastor here is Mr. Timothy Davis, and besides him they have two preachers, whose names are William Williams and John Jones. They sometimes preach in English, but mostly in their mother tongue.

Mr. Rees died among this people in December, 1804; he had travelled much, not only in his native country, but in England, France, and America. His widow now lives in Philadelphia.

Beulah is about 80 miles east of the Redstone country, some distance north of the main road from Philadelphia to Pittsburg. Of the remaining churches and ministers in this Association but a little information has been obtained.

Mr. David Philips, pastor of Peter's Creek church, is a native of Wales, came to America when a child, lived in Chester county in this State, till 36 years of age, when he removed to his present situation, and was one of the early settlers of the country.

Mr. Henry Spears, pastor of the Enon church, also settled in this quarter, when it was but a little more than a wilderness. He is a native of Dunmore county, Virginia, is of Dutch descent, and has a very large, luxuriant plantation on the Monongahela river, about 26 miles from Pittsburg.

The church at Connollsville on the Yohogany River was founded in 1796. Its principal promoters were two brothers by the name of Trevor, viz. Samuel and Caleb, natives of Leicestershire, England. Dr. James Estep was the pastor of this church in 1809; whether he still remains with them I have not ascertained. He, with others, proposed forwarding additional information, which has never been received.

The doctrine of the laying-on-of-hands became a subject of dispute among the Redstone churches a number of years ago, most of them had, from their beginning, practised the rite, but some were for making it a term of communion; it was, however, finally determined, that all should be left to act according to their respective opinions on the subject.

A church was formed in Pittsburg in 1812, which has probably united with the Association under consideration. In that year two Presbyterian ministers were baptized in Washington county, and another minister of the same denomination was to be baptized soon after at Chenango, in Ohio, not far distant.*

* Massachusetts Baptist Missionary Magazine, vol. iii. p. 205.

In the neighbourhood of this Association, a small collection of churches, some of whom were formerly members of it, have formed a Confederacy under the name of the Covenanted Independent Baptists. Their principal leader appears to be Dr. Thomas Hersey, a native of Massachusetts, who began preaching in the State of Ohio. These churches are, as they say, called by some Semi-Calvinists, by others, Semi-Arminians. From the best information it appears, that the principal difference between them and the Redstone Association turns upon the doctrine of the atonement as stated by Gill and Fuller.*

* Those who may wish for a further account of the sentiments of these Independent Baptists, may find them expressed in a work, published by Dr. Hersey in 1810, entitled, " Experimental Views," &c.

INDEX.

THE state of the world at the coming of Christ, p. 7.
First churches gathered—Temple of Janus, note—Extent of the Roman Empire—Ten persecutions—Christians falsely accused of burning Rome and other crimes, 8—10.
Pliny's letter to Trajan, 10—12.
Constantine the Great embraces christianity—the effects of this event—reflections on it, 13—14.
Beginning of the Church of Rome, 15. How the Pope obtained the title of Universal Bishop, 16.
Blasphemous pretensions of Gregory VII 19.
Origin of the Monkish orders, 21. Celibacy no friend to virtue, 22.
Councils, 23. Crusades, 25. Indulgencies, 27 Supererogation, 28. Persecutions of the Church of Rome, 29.
Greek Church, 31—34.
Protestants, Luther, Zuinglius, Calvin, Church of England established—Puritans, &c. 34—43.
Missions, Romish—Protestants of different sects, 43—45.
History of Baptism. John's baptismal stations—extravagant honours paid him by the Catholicks, 47.
Description of Jordan and Enon, 48, 49. A refutation of the criticisms on *polla udata*, 49. Dr. Guise's paraphrase, 50. John, not a Jewish priest, 51, 52. What Tertullian and Mosheim say of the ancient mode of baptism, 53.
Catechumen state, 55. How children were first admitted to baptism, 56. Tertullian against it, 57. Infant baptism not known in the Apostolic age, 58. First canon to enjoin it, 59.
Infant baptism introduced into Europe, 60. How it was hastened forward, 61.
Persons licensed to baptize dying infants, 63.
Pouring first allowed by Pope Stephen III, 65. Dr. Wall against sprinkling, 66.
Baptisteries began to be built, 67. Description of those at Constantinople—at Rome. Extract from Basil's discourses, &c. 68—70.
The Pope immerses three children, 71. Many evidences in favour of that mode, 73.
Concessions of Catholicks—Protestants—Gill's account of dipping places in Jerusalem—Calvin's concessions, and Campbell's, 74—78.
How doubtful words are to be determined—Dr. Gale's definition of baptizo, baptisma, &c. Note, 79.
The Greeks understand their own language best, they always have immersed, 79—82.
The Catholicks have 22 ceremonies in baptism—Bill of fare at a baptism—A hundred god-fathers, 82—84.
Different meanings of the word infant, 85, 86.
Proselyte baptism, 88. Different modes of defending infant baptism, 89.
Principal objections of the Baptists against it, 90. Infant baptism a perplexing study—believer's baptism plain, 91.
The terms Baptist and Anabaptist defined, 92.
Six sorts of Anabaptists, all reject the term, 93, 94.
The first christians Baptists—Council at Jerusalem, 95—100.

Dissenters from the Greek Church called Massalians and Cathari, 101, 2. Novatians, 104. Paterines, 105.

Waldenses. A general account of them, 107—123. Evidences of their denying infant baptism—their principal leaders---their peculiar sentiments--- persecutions, &c. 123---134.

Baptists in Germany, 135. Mosheim's string of hard names against them, 137. They are dissatisfied with Luther's plan of reformation, 139.

Luther defines baptism to mean dipping, 140. Infants immersed at Hamburg, note, 140.

Many drowned and beheaded for denying infant baptism, 143.

Menno Simon, his travels and character, 144---146. The progress of the Mennonites---they divide into different sects---are favoured by the Prince of Orange, 147. An account of the church at Dantzic, 148. Menno and the ancient Mennonites practise dipping---since fallen off to pouring, 150, 151.

Bohemia. John Huss and Jerome of Prague, both destroyed by the Council of Constance, 153. Ziska, curious anecdote of him, succeeded by Procopius, 154, 155. Their followers called Taborites---are visited by Æneas Sylvius, afterwards Pope Pius II, 156.

The *Unitus Fratrum*, arise out of the Taborites, 157. Waldenses or Picards settle in Bohemia, 158. What the Emperor Maximilian said of them, note, 159.

The Baptists increase in Bohemia---the Polish Baptists visit them, 160.

A general account of the number and banishment of the Moravian Baptists, 161---165. A letter from Bohemia to Erasmus, describing a people like the modern Baptists, 166.

Poland. The Waldenses settle in it, 167. The Pinckzovian society formed, 169. They were all Anti-pedobaptists, but not all Baptists, 170. They were dispersed, and the Racovian society formed, which prevailed much for a time, 172---174. Socinus received among them, some scholars stone a crucifix, which involves the whole community in calamity and ruin, 176. The Polish Baptists are dispersed in different parts of Europe---general observations on their sentiments, 177---180.

Transylvania. Davidis, Blandratta, Somer, Palæologus, settle in it, 181. Baptists prevail greatly, but are soon infected with Socinianism, and great men lead them into errors and snares, 182, 183.

Accounts of Bernard Ochin, Stanlius Lutomirski, Michael Servetus, and Andrew Dudith, 184---188.

England. Baptists divided into *General* and *Particular*, 189. Christianity planted in Britain, 60 years after Christ's ascension---an account of St. Austin's visiting England, 190. The first British christians Baptists, 191. Wickliff began to be famous in England---strong evidences that he became a Baptist, 192. William Sawtre, supposed to be a Baptist, the first English martyr--- The Lollards terribly persecuted, 193. George Van Pare and Joan of Kent, and many others burnt for heresy, 194, 195. Edward Wightman the last man put to death in England for heresy, 196. Baptist churches began to be founded in England, 197, 198.

The General Assembly publish a Confession of Faith, 200. Mr. Baxter's astonishing charges against the Baptists---Booth's reflections upon them--- Samuel Oates indicted for murder, 201---3. John Bunyan imprisoned--- Venner's insurrection, 204. Ministers ejected by the Act of Uniformity, 205. England visted with famine, plague, and fire---A piece published, entitled, *Baxter baptized in blood*, 206. Summary view of the persecutions of the Baptists in England, 207---11. Some of the most distinguished men among the English Baptists, William Kiffin, Gen. Harrison, Col. Hutchinson, Benjamin Keach, Dr. Gill, and others, 211---16. Jeremiah Ives disputes with a Romish Priest---an anecdote of an Irish minister, 217. Controversies about Laying-on-of-hands, and singing in publick, 218, 19. Bristol Academy--- Northern Education Society, and Stepney Green Academy, 220---23. Seven Associations of Particular Baptists, 224.

General Baptists, 224---27.

the young London Divine. He performed well enough, till he had advanced pretty far in the sermon ; then stopping short, he looked like a man astonished. The audience concluded he had been seized with a sudden disorder; but on asking what the matter was, received from him a confession of the imposture, with tears in his eyes, and much trembling. Great was his distress, though it ended happily ; for from this time he dated his conversion. He heard of Mr. Dungan. To him he repaired to seek counsel and comfort, and by him he was baptized and ordained. From Coldspring, Mr. Keach came to Pennepek, and settled a church there as before related ; and thence travelled through Pennsylvania and the Jersies, preaching the Gospel in the wilderness with great success, insomuch that he may be considered as the chief apostle of the Baptists in these parts of America. He and his family embarked for England, early in the spring of the year 1692, and afterwards became a very famous and successful minister in London. Sometime before his embarkation, he had resigned the care of the church to

" Rev. John Watts, who was born November 3, 1661, at Lydd or Leed in the county of Kent ; came to this country about the year 1686 ; was baptized at Pennepek, November 21, 1687 ; called to the ministry in 1688 ; took on him the care of the church in 1690 ; continued in the care thereof to August 27, 1702, when he died of the small pox, and was buried at Pennepek, having had Mr. Samuel Jones to his assistant. Mr. Watts was a sound divine, and a man of some learning, as appears by a book he wrote, entitled, *Davis Disabled*. There was an order for printing this book, dated August 3, 1705, but it was not executed. He also composed a Catechism, or little system of divinity, which was published in 1700. Mr. Watts was succeeded by

" Rev. Evan Morgan, who came to this country very early, and was a man of piety and parts. He broke off from the Quakers along with many others of Mr. Keith's party in 1691 ; was baptized in 1697, by one Thomas Rutter, and the same year, renouncing the reliques of Quakerism, was received into the church. In 1702, he was called to the ministry, and ordained October 23, 1706, by Rev. Messrs. Thomas Griffith and Thomas Killings-

his wife, William Fisher and John Watts, which increased their number to 12 souls, including the minister. These 12 did, by mutual consent, form themselves into a church in the month of January, 1688, choosing Mr. Keach to be their minister, and Samuel Vaus to be deacon. Soon after, the few emigrated Baptists in this province and West-Jersey joined them ; also those, whom Mr. Keach baptized at the Falls, Coldspring, Burlington, Cohansey, Salem, Penn's-Neck, Chester, Philadelphia, &c. They were all one church, and Pennepek the centre of union, where, as many as could, met to celebrate the Lord's Supper ; and for the sake of distant members, they administered the ordinance quarterly at Burlington, Cohansey, Chester, and Philadelphia ; which quarterly meetings have since been transformed into three yearly meetings and an Association. Thus, for some time, continued their Zion with lengthened cords, till the brethren in remote parts set about forming themselves into distinct churches, which began in 1699. By these detachments it was reduced to narrow bounds, but continued among the churches, as a mother in the midst of many daughters. At their settlement, and during the administration of Mr. Keach, they were the same as they are now, with respect to faith and order ; but when their number increased, and emigrants, from differing churches in Europe, incorporated with them, divisions began to take place about various things, such as absolute predestination, laying-on-of-hands, distributing the elements, singing psalms, seventh-day sabbath, &c. which threw the body ecclesiastic into a fever. In the year 1747, a tumult arose about the choice of a minister, which issued in a separation. But this, and the other maladies were healed, when the peccant humours had been purged off, and the design of Providence accomplished, which design is expressed in these notable words, *There must be divisions among you, that they who are approved may be made manifest.* 1 Cor. xi. 19.

"The first minister they had was the Rev. Elias Keach. He was son of the famous Benjamin Keach, of London ; arrived in this country a very wild youth, about the year 1686. On his landing, he dressed in black, and wore a band, in order to pass for a minister. The project succeeded to his wishes, and many people resorted to hear